POEMS IN ENGLISH
1530-1940

EDITED WITH CRITICAL AND HISTORICAL
NOTES AND ESSAYS

By

DAVID DAICHES
PROFESSOR OF ENGLISH, CORNELL UNIVERSITY

With the Assistance of

WILLIAM CHARVAT
PROFESSOR OF ENGLISH, OHIO STATE UNIVERSITY

THE RONALD PRESS COMPANY · NEW YORK

Copyright, 1950, by
THE RONALD PRESS COMPANY

All Rights Reserved

8

Library of Congress Catalog Card Number: 50-8060

PRINTED IN THE UNITED STATES OF AMERICA

FOREWORD

(*To the Teacher*)

The past ten years or so have witnessed something of a revolution in the methods of teaching poetry at the college level. This revolution has been bound up with the revolt against the "survey course," the disparagement of history and biography in favor of a close, analytic study of individual texts, and the insistence on the differentiating qualities of the poetic method of handling language. Few will deny that this movement was overdue and that it has done an immense amount of good. The discussion of a poem in terms of the author's life or of the qualities deemed to be characteristic of the period or school to which the poet was assigned leads to a blurring of the picture to the point where the poem is not read as a poem at all but as a document in the history of ideas or in the biography of the poet. Nobody who has followed the course of critical discussion in the last decade can now be unaware of these dangers, and no sensible teacher would be willing to train his students to memorize lists of adjectives applicable to authors and periods as a substitute for the careful reading of the poems themselves. Nevertheless, a recognition of the dangers inherent in the older method and of the achievements of the "new criticism" should not lead us to ignore the advantages of historical knowledge (even for an understanding of the actual meaning of the text) or prevent us from inquiring into the relation between historical and critical perceptions.

The fact is, of course, that even the most antihistorical critic of poetry is making full use of a historical tradition every time he analyzes a poem: he may make no overt use of this tradition, and he may not be aware at all that he is using it, but that is because he has absorbed it and takes it for granted. We may claim that we are discussing each poem as though it were anonymous and contemporary, but such an ideal is impossible even if it were desirable.

iii

Language itself is a phenomenon that manifests itself in history, and the ability to construe a poem properly therefore demands a knowledge of what the words meant for that poet at that time. Further, as we point out in the introduction which follows, we often have to turn to history to discover how a poem should be approached or even to learn what it is to be read as. This does not mean that there is no such thing as a self-existent poem, but it does mean that to recognize that poem for what it is—for what it is *as a poem,* and still more so for what it is as a document in the history of culture— we have often to seek aid from history. At the simplest level, that aid comes from the history of language, but sometimes we need to understand the social or other context which determined the occasion and use of the poem before we can begin to read it aright.

The enjoyment of a poem purely as a poem is, it need hardly be said, the primary objective of most readers of poetry, and we all recognize the aids to this enjoyment which some phases of modern criticism have provided. But there is nothing vicious about learning to appreciate a poem (or any work of art) also as a period piece, as the characteristic expression of a certain social and cultural atmosphere. What sensitive listener to a piece of Mozart's played on a harpsichord can deny that part of his pleasure comes from his projection into a specific area from an earlier period of our civilization? Is this a bad thing? Does it interfere with our enjoyment of the music as music? Does it interfere with our enjoyment of *Hamlet* if, when we watch the play being performed, we sense and relish the Elizabethan in Shakespeare at the same time as we appreciate the tragedy as both a unique and a universal art form? Much modern criticism would say that it does so interfere, or at any rate would deplore the confusion of kinds of appreciation. This seems to us both puritanical and unrealistic, for it peevishly restricts the area of our enjoyment for the most academic of reasons, and at the same time it ignores an undoubted *fact* about our appreciation of the arts—namely, that all appreciation of art, especially of the art of the past, is in a sense "impure," in that it includes a savoring of a quality in the civilization contemporary with the work of art which the work of art embodies. It is both civilized and enjoyable to include that savoring: it is a right that we should not deny to our students.

The search for a dependably pure approach to any art is bound to lead to the imposition of rules for the analysis of individual works which do violence to the facts of appreciation. That is why, in recent discussions of poems, intended to help the teacher, all the emphasis has been on the analysis, on "understanding" the poem in terms of its structure and organization, rather than distributing the emphasis to include all the reasons why a civilized and sensitive individual can enjoy reading a poem. The isolation of the purely poetic qualities of a poem may be useful in abstract aesthetic discussion, but it bears no relation to the way in which a poem is produced or in which it is read. A poem, perhaps more than any other kind of work of art, is a complex phenomenon, often an "impure" phenomenon, and its reality is much larger than any formal analysis of it could show. Those critics—and they include some of the most brilliant of our generation—who concentrate on the analysis of poems conceived as anonymous and contemporary works forget that they are denying to the young student of today all the rich aids to appreciation, all the pointers to interpretation and instructions for reading which are often provided by the historical situation—and of which the critics themselves, as we have remarked, take advantage without mentioning the fact.

Many of us have seen the results of this in practice. While in the hands of such a perceptive and well-informed critic as Mr. Cleanth Brooks the analysis of a poem without regard to historical perspective can yield brilliant results, in the hands of students with no historical background and no sense of the cultural climate of the age in which the poem was written, this method all too often yields only the most farfetched misinterpretations, in which the student loses touch altogether with the basic tone and quality of the poem and wanders amid absurd ingenuities. It is impossible to persuade such a student that he is wrong: after all, he claims, his analysis is as good as yours—indeed, if his is more ingenious the chances are that it is better. More and more, the ingenious analysis has come to be the objective of all study of poetry, so that students lose sight altogether of what the poem *is* in their search for *what it can be said to mean.*

It is time, we believe, to draw attention to what we have lost by abandoning history, while at the same time remembering what the

"new criticism" has taught us and avoiding at all costs the confusions and oversimplifications of the superficial survey course or
historico-biographical criticism. One of the things we have lost is
the ability to enjoy a poem as a period piece while also enjoying it
as a poem. Another is the sense of balance and perspective which
prevents us from thinking that the poem can be in some sense
identified with the analysis of it or from applying to that analysis
of it all kinds of irrelevant ingenuity. At any rate, in arranging
poems chronologically, as we have done, we can at least show the
student something of the development of the English and American
poetic tradition, give him some idea of the shifting cultural climates
and changing views of what poetry is and ought to be which lie
behind the production of the poems. Surely not even the most ardent
champion of a purely formal criticism would deny that it is useful
and helpful to know something of these matters, and if, by arranging the poems chronologically and including brief historical introductions to each section, we can kill two birds with one stone, why
should we not do so? If the student can get whatever benefits the
older type of survey course gave, while at the same time learning
to read the individual poems, it would be the worst kind of critical
puritanism that would deny him those benefits.

Critical puritanism is sometimes useful, and the devoted way in
which modern critics from F. R. Leavis to Cleanth Brooks have
championed a close and carefully worked out examination of individual poems to the exclusion of extraneous considerations commands wholehearted admiration: puritanism of their kind achieved
a most valuable reassessment of the methods of approaching and
discussing poetry. But in less able hands it can yield very unhappy
results. The equation of a poem with its analysis, the substitution
of argument about the sequence of ideas in a poem for an appreciation of the poem itself, have led us too often to forget the admirable advice given by Coleridge in a letter to Sotheby. "Be minute,"
he wrote, "and assign your reasons often, and your first impressions
always, and then, blame or praise, I care not which, I shall be satisfied." We have tried, in the critical notes on the individual poems,
to follow this wise advice and never let mere ingenuity supplant
first impressions. (Of course, the question of *whose* first impressions
is important: we hope it is not immodest to assume that we are

reasonably experienced and sensitive readers of poetry whose first impressions are significant.)

Further, we believe that it is thoroughly unwise (as well as unrealistic) to discard from the vocabulary of criticism any term which might indicate the kind of impact which the poem has on the reader. If a poem strikes one as charming, why should one not mention the fact? Poems are meant to be read and enjoyed, and the kind of enjoyment a poem gives is surely of the utmost relevance. No kind of discussion is illegitimate, in fact, if it helps the reader to see what the poem is, to capture its quality and atmosphere. All discourse about a poem is indirect and approximate, and it is often at least as helpful to discuss the poem's impact on oneself in terms which draw the reader's attention to the kind of effect the poem is meant to have as to avoid all such discussion in an attempt to be ruthlessly analytical. Careful analysis sometimes helps; sometimes it does not help. The most useful critic would seem to us to be the eclectic critic, who says what is most helpful in each case. The teacher's objective is to try to get the student to read the poem for what it is, to see what it has to offer, to appreciate and enjoy it. His methods will vary all the way from effective reading aloud to minute analysis, and the success or failure of any device should be judged by the event, not on *a priori* grounds.

We have tried, therefore, to restore to criticism some terms which correspond more closely to the ways in which poetry is read and appreciated than many of the terms to which modern critics restrict themselves. Recognizing that the teaching of poetry is always experimental, we have tried to draw on as large an experience as possible (both of ourselves and others) in order to make this anthology not only a worth-while collection of good poems but also an aid to both the teaching and the enjoyment of poetry which can be used by teachers and students of all shades of critical opinion. If in the process we have been able to lessen in any degree the gap which yawns today between the professional critic and the sensitive and appreciative reader of poetry, we shall be satisfied indeed.

In selecting these poems, we have found it necessary to lay down certain rules for ourselves. In the first place, we have included only complete poems. We have not, for example, included extracts from *Paradise Lost* or from any other epic. We have, however, included incidental lyrics from plays, which are complete poems in themselves, and other incidental lyrics which occur in longer works, provided always that they are complete and self-contained poems. We have included the first part of Crabbe's "Village" as being really a complete poem in itself. Many poets are best represented by works too long to include in such an anthology as this, so that we cannot pretend to have given adequate representation to Milton (although we have included a liberal selection from the minor poems) or even to Dryden and Pope. Dryden, in particular, we feel deserves much more representation than we have been able to give. His characteristic genius expressed itself in those long satirical and argumentative poems which, in virtue both of their length and of the multitude of contemporary references which they contain, are not easy either to find room for in this kind of collection or to annotate adequately for the modern nonspecialist reader. If, therefore, there seem to be too few poems from the late seventeenth and the eighteenth centuries, it is not because the editors are in any way prejudiced against the poetry of that period—far from it: it is simply that too many of the best poems of that period are too long for inclusion in their entirety, and we do not believe in presenting extracts.

Considerations both of space and of copyright have helped to determine our choice of more recent poems. Here again, our choice represents a compromise between what we should have liked to include in an ideal anthology and what was feasible under the circumstances. Many readers will miss some favorites, some will find here poems which they may consider inferior. But, all in all, we feel that what we have included in this collection does represent both a representative and an interesting collection of significant poems. We have deliberately tried to do justice to poets who have been unduly neglected in recent criticism and anthologies—the Victorians, for example; but in our endeavor to redress the balance we have tried not to be freakish or unbalanced in our turn, even though, of course, the choice does in the last analysis represent in some degree the personal taste of the editors.

Professor Daiches is responsible for all the English poems and for the selections from Pound, Eliot, Hart Crane, and E. E. Cummings.

for the notes to these poems, and for both the general introduction and the introductions to the individual sections. Professor Charvat has chosen and annotated the American poems (except for the few American poets noted above) and is also responsible for those paragraphs in the introductions to the individual sections which refer to American poetry of the period.

ACKNOWLEDGMENTS

Thanks are due the following poets, their copyright owners, and their publishers for permission to reprint certain poems in this anthology.

The Clarendon Press, for "London Snow" by Robert Bridges, from the *Shorter Poems of Robert Bridges* by permission of the Clarendon Press, Oxford.

Dodd, Mead & Company, for "Heaven," by Rupert Brooke, reprinted by permission of Dodd, Mead & Company from *The Collected Poems of Rupert Brooke*. Copyright 1915 by Dodd, Mead & Company, Inc.

Mr. T. S. Eliot and Charles Scribner's Sons, for the remarks on "Danny Deever" from Mr. T. S. Eliot's introduction to *A Choice of Kipling's Verse*.

Harcourt, Brace and Company, for the poems by T. S. Eliot, from *Collected Poems 1909–1935* by T. S. Eliot, copyright 1936 by Harcourt, Brace and Company, Inc.

Henry Holt and Company, for the selections by Robert Frost, from *Complete Poems of Robert Frost, 1949*. Copyright 1930, 1939, 1949, by Henry Holt and Company, Inc. Copyright 1936 by Robert Frost.

Henry Holt and Company, for the selections by A. E. Housman. "Loveliest of trees," "On Wenlock Edge," "With rue my heart is laden," from *A Shropshire Lad* by A. E. Housman, reproduced by permission of Henry Holt and Company, Inc. "Yonder see the morning blink," "Could man be drunk forever," from *Last Poems* by A. E. Housman, copyright 1922 by Henry Holt and Company, Inc.

Liveright Publishing Corporation, for "To Brooklyn Bridge" and "Praise for an Urn," from *The Collected Poems of Hart Crane* by Hart Crane, published by Liveright Publishing Corporation, New York, copyright 1933, Liveright, Inc.

New Directions, for permission to quote "Anthem for Doomed Youth," "Futility," and "Strange Meeting," by Wilfred Owen; "Ancient Music," "Exile's Letter," and "The Seafarer," by Ezra Pound; "The force that through the green fuse drives the flower," "In Memory of Ann Jones," and "The Marriage of a Virgin," by Dylan Thomas.

Oxford University Press, Inc., for permission to quote "Duns Scotus's Oxford" by Gerard Manley Hopkins.

Mrs. Helen Thomas and Faber & Faber, Ltd., for permission to quote "The Gallows" and "Tears" by Edward Thomas.

The Viking Press, for "Bavarian Gentians," from *Last Poems* by D. H

Lawrence, copyright 1933 by Frieda Lawrence; and for "Piano," from *Collected Poems* by D. H. Lawrence, copyright 1929 by Jonathan Cape & Harrison Smith, Inc. Both reprinted by permission of The Viking Press, Inc.

Certain other permissions are acknowledged in footnote form in the text, as required by individual contractual arrangements.

CONTENTS

II. THE SEVENTEENTH CENTURY

III. THE EIGHTEENTH CENTURY

IV. THE ROMANTIC MOVEMENT

V. THE VICTORIANS

VI. THE MODERN PERIOD

CONTENTS xxvii

GENERAL INTRODUCTION

Poetry is at once the most simple and the most complex form of literary expression. It is simple in the sense that it is primitive, that historically it precedes prose literature and represents a more direct and spontaneous method of rendering experience in language than prose. It is complex in that it utilizes the varied resources of language more richly and fully than prose, combining the appeal to the ear with the appeal to the mind more equally and using all kinds of overtone and suggestion to convey what might be called the feel and quality of a situation at the same time that it presents its overt meaning or superficial constituents. But any general definition of poetry is dangerous: the method of expression which we denote by that term includes such a great variety of different ways of using language that a definition derived from a study of the characteristics of any given selection of poems is almost bound to exclude many poems which are valuable and good of their kind. What poetry is can be discovered by reading as perceptively as possible as many poems as possible. Poetry, in fact, is what poets have written, and good poetry is what appeals most to experienced readers of poetry. If different kinds of poems appeal equally to experienced readers, then there must be different kinds of good poems—a fact which a premature definition of poetry tends to conceal.

Further, poetry exists to be read and enjoyed rather than to be discussed and analyzed. If discussion and analysis are necessary for full perception and full appreciation (and they frequently are), then of course they are valuable activities, but valuable as means rather than as ends. The student who feels that he has to "get up" poetry so that he can write impressive analyses of poems, or the teacher who considers that the end-product of the study of poetry consists of these analyses, is guilty of a barren academicism which is not calculated to increase either the prestige or the appreciation of poetry in our society. Criticism is helpful only when it increases the reader's awareness of what the poem really is, and does so without doing unnecessary violence to the reader's first impressions.

When, therefore, we present a collection of English and American poems complete with explanatory notes and critical remarks, we are presenting it in the first instance as a collection of poems that are worth reading, rather than as a piece of critical or historical apparatus. On the other hand, we know that a full appreciation of any work of art depends on the reader's (or listener's or observer's) sensitivity to what is going on in the work, on his ability to see it for what it really is, to realize the nature of the artist's achievement, to perceive fully how the artist has handled his materials and what results from this handling. Sensitivity of this kind is developed only by wide and deep reading, for even the most gifted reader of poetry will be unable to see the full potentialities of the art if he is exposed only to shoddy and imitative works. Appreciation involves discrimination, and discrimination comes from extensive and intensive literary experience. It is only because the general reader in our time has not the leisure for such an ambitious program of reading that short cuts to full appreciation become necessary. Such short cuts can never fully replace the less conscious training of taste which comes from much careful and cumulative reading, but they are better than nothing.

Criticism has at least two functions: the more purely philosophical function of inquiring into the nature and results of the "creative process" and estimating their place and value among human activities, and what might be called the more educational one of developing in the reader a heightened awareness, a keener perception, and a finer discrimination. These two branches of critical activity are not unrelated, but their immediate aims differ. The latter kind aims at increasing appreciation. The criterion of its success is quite simply whether the reader, after reading the criticism, comes back to the poem with a richer enjoyment. Poetry, to repeat what cannot be too often stated in an age of critical puritanism, is written to be read and enjoyed.

The obstacles to adequate reading and so to full enjoyment are more serious than the casual reader might imagine. There are, for example, historical obstacles, deriving from our lack of awareness of the associations a given word or reference may have in a particular age or in a more general sense of how a work is intended to be approached (as though we were to read Sophocles' *Oedipus the King* under the impression that it was a farce about sex designed to be staged realistically on a modern stage). There are obstacles posed by shifts in the meaning of words, even the most delicate of which may change the whole emotional pattern of a poem. There are obstacles posed by changes in convention—convention being that preliminary agreement about the way in which the medium is to be handled which makes art possible at all: the conventions of opera, for example, are different from those of drama, and if Hamlet suddenly began to sing his lines instead of to speak them, he would be breaking unexpectedly into another convention, thus ruining the effect. Conventions may differ almost as much within one art form as they do between opera and drama, and it is only wide experience of reading among works of different periods that can enable us to recognize these differences and to adjust our perspective as readers accordingly. Quite often the inexperienced reader judges a work written in an unfamiliar convention as bad, simply because he is assuming that it is employing the convention he is most familiar with, and judged this way it naturally appears unsuccessful. The inexperienced reader tends to imagine that the conventions with which he is most familiar are intrinsically good, while the unfamiliar ones are "artificial." But of course all conventions are artificial: it is just as artificial (if not more so) to produce plays on a stage which represents a room with one wall cut away but which is in all other respects a close replica of an actual room as it is to produce them on a bare platform with no scenery at all. All conventions are artificial, and few are intrinsically good or bad. And art, it must be remembered, is artificial. It is the expression of significance through a conventional (i.e., an artificial) medium, and is not to be confused with the real life experience which may have initially suggested the significance.

Yet if art is not life, its subject matter is often life, and with poetry, at least, its value often lies in the insights into experience which it affords. These insights are not, of course, abstract ideas to be applied to experience, but rather distillations of some quality in experience which the poet communicates in his verse by showing us something which is simultaneously recognizable as a significant experience and surprisingly, inconceivably new. "Poetry," wrote Keats in one of his letters, "should strike the reader as a wording of his own highest thoughts, and appear almost a remembrance." *Almost* a remembrance, for along with the "shock of recognition" is the shock of discovery.

There are any number of ways in which poetry can achieve its ends, every kind of direct presentation or oblique implication, innumerable ways of handling the resources of language poetically. Many of them are illustrated in this collection, and it is tempting to go no further but give up the attempt to discuss poetry in general terms and say simply: "Poetry is what is in this book." This procedure would not be as silly as it may appear, for poetry is in fact what poets have written, and there is no better way to find out what that is than by reading poems. But there is some point, nevertheless, in drawing the student's attention to some aspects of the poet's equipment.

We began by saying that poetry is at once the most simple and the most complex form of literary expression. It is free to utilize all the aspects of language—the sound and rhythm and associations of words, as well as their intellectual meaning or simple denotation, all the pointing up of significance and releasing of echoing overtones that can be achieved by their music and pattern, by the play of sounds and ideas against each other in order to develop hints or half-meanings or suggestions or states of mind which combine with the other aspects of the poem to produce a total richness of communication far beyond anything that can be indicated by a prose paraphrase or line-by-line explanation. The texture of a poem may be closely woven, with the totality of meaning developing cumulatively as the expression gets under way and the real significance held back until everything has been said and all the elements in the communication combine with one another, enriching, modifying, qualifying, clarifying, building the desired mood and tone and creating the proper emotional atmosphere to "explode" (the term is Gerard Manley Hopkins') into the final simultaneous complex of significance. Or the texture may be more open, with the meaning developing more episodically and with less intensity—like Tennyson's "Ulysses," for example, which is a much more openly worked poem than Keats's "Ode on a Grecian Urn."

Between the kind of expression which hews to the central line of simple meaning (denotation) and uses rhythm and balance simply in order to make the expression more agreeable, and the kind which exploits richly and simultaneously all the resources of language, there are any number of gradations. Good verse can consist of propositional statements neatly phrased, with an agreeable rhythm and pleasantly chiming rhymes serving more or less as pleasing decoration, and such we find, for example, in John Pomfret's "The Choice"; or, at the other end of the scale of poetic expression, it may be like a poem of Donne's or Dylan Thomas', a flaming organic unity in which every element in the expression contributes equally to the total communication. To place a poem in this scale is not necessarily to pass any value judgment on it, for there can be good poems at any place in the scale. We may with some justice hold, however, that the potentialities for really impressive poetic expression are less likely to exist at the lower end of the scale, and that the most effective poems are those which come in the middle or higher parts of the range. Such questions can only be resolved by reading poems and considering what each achieves. Is the best poetry the most poetical poetry, poetry which uses most of those aspects of language which differentiate the poet's use of language from the prose writer's? Many modern critics seem to think so, but the point is arguable.

To leave such a question unanswered is not to abandon standards, but only to keep the way open to recognizing different kinds of poetic merit. We can still recognize and condemn slovenliness and inadequacy at any point in the scale—though in fact the bad poet will, for obvious reasons, avoid, as a rule, attempting to operate at the higher or more characteristically "poetic" end. There are more bad poets at what might be called the prose end of the scale, not because it is more difficult to write well at that end, but for precisely the opposite reason: it is (or at least it seems) relatively easy to write well at that end, with the result that all sorts of inferior poetasters are tempted, with unhappy consequences. But it is not even possible to recognize that the poet is operating at the upper end of the scale unless he is reasonably successful.

Critics of poetry have gradually developed a vocabulary of technical terms which, while never altogether adequate, is helpful, and with which the student of poetry ought to be familiar. In discussing the rhythms of poetry, for example, the tradition which has descended to us from classical times is to isolate the individual "foot" and consider the line as made up of a number of more or less identical feet. This is easy enough to see in some simple and regular meters:

> The stág at éve had drúnk his fíll,
> Where dánced the móon on Mónan's ríll,
> And déep his mídnight láir had máde
> In lóne Glenártney's házel sháde.

The foot here consists of an unstressed, followed by a stressed syllable; such a foot is called an "iamb" and is conventionally indicated thus: ∪ —. The line consists of four such feet (such a line is technically called an "iambic tetrameter," a line with four iambic feet). When the stressed syllable comes before the unstressed (— ∪), the foot is called a "trochee," illustrated in the following lines.

> Yét were lífe a chárnel whére
> Hópe lay cóffined wíth Despáir
> Yét were trúth a sácred líe. . . .

Here again the pattern is — ∪/ — ∪/ — ∪/ —. The third of the three commonest feet in English poetry is the anapest (∪∪ —), illustrated in the following:

> In a coign of the cliff between lowland and highland,
>   At the sea-down's edge between windward and lee,
> Walled round with rocks as an inland island,
>   The ghost of a garden fronts the sea . . . .

It will be seen that the lilting rhythms of the anapestic line can be suggested without a consistent use of the anapest, which often gives way to an iamb (as in the second foot of the third line) or a spondee, two stresses together: —— ——, (as in the first foot of the third line). The names of other feet are given in the glossary.

The isolating of the rigidly defined foot is a very artificial procedure when applied to English poetry, which uses as a rule much more flexible rhythms than such classifications as "iambic pentameter" (a line with five iambic feet) would suggest. Even if we allow that extra syllables can be introduced at the beginning or the end of a line ("between lowland and highland" can be considered as two anapests with an unstressed syllable added) we still get no really adequate description of what goes on rhythmically in a line of poetry. Earlier critics tried to accommodate the use of feet in describing verse to the realities of the situation by laying down the law of equivalence. "The most important law of English prosody," wrote Saintsbury, "is that which permits and directs the interchange of certain of these feet with others, or, in technical language, the substitution of equivalent feet." Thus, in the four lines from Swinburne quoted above to illustrate anapestic meter, the third line begins with two examples of equivalence, a spondee for an anapest, and an iamb for an anapest. The theory is that there is a basic metrical pattern, which can be described in terms of specific feet, but that once this pattern has been set going all sorts of variations can be played on it, so long as it does not become wholly submerged or lost amid the variations. Though this is not, perhaps, the most adequate way of looking at English poetic rhythms, it is extremely useful, and in the notes at the end of the book such descriptions are occasionally employed.

Sometimes it is more helpful to think of the rhythms of a poem as one thinks of musical time—with each measure having a specific number of beats which can be made up in any way, provided that they take up the same amount of time. This is not far from Hopkins' theory, which counted the metrics of a line in terms of the number of beats rather than the number of syllables: in his view there could be any number of unstressed syllables between stresses. "Every foot has one principal stress or accent, and this or the syllable it falls on may be called the Stress of the foot and the other part, the one or two unaccented syllables, the Slack." He distinguished between "falling feet" and "falling rhythms," where the stress comes first, and rising feet and rhythms, where the slack comes first. (There are also "rocking rhythms" where the stress comes between two slacks.) Feet, he maintained, can be reversed (putting a trochee for an iamb, for example), to give reversed or counterpointed rhythm. His own practice, which he called "sprung rhythm," he described as "measured by feet of from one to four syllables, regularly, and for particular effects any number of weak or slack syllabies may be used": each foot would have only one stress, and the amount of slack would vary from foot to foot. This gives much more rhythmic flexibility than the traditional foot would give, even if varied by equivalence; and Hopkins' practice has been very influential on modern poetry.

In the poems in this collection the reader will note varying degrees of metrical freedom, from the regular beat of a strict iambic line to lines where a recurring standard foot can be traced only with difficulty. Metrical strictness is not in itself either good or bad: everything depends on the purpose to which it is put. The reader must consider the quality of the poetic expression as a whole before he can pass judgment on its metrical adequacy—its mood and tone and *tempo*. A verse epigram, for example, whose success depends entirely on neatness and point, on fitting the thought perfectly into a wholly formal expression, demands much greater metrical regularity than, say, an ode. (But again, that would depend in large measure on the particular ode.)

One must distinguish the metrical pattern from the *tempo* (to borrow that convenient expression from music). The latter refers to the speed at which the verse moves, and the same metrical pattern can be used with different speeds. Tempo is an element in poetic expression that has been too much ignored, and we have occasionally endeavored in the notes to draw attention to significant shifts in tempo within poems and to differences in tempo between poems of similar metrical pattern. Poets do not mark their compositions "allegro" or "andante," but it is not difficult for the experienced reader to judge the speed at which they should go. Compare, for example, the slow pace of "Tithonus" with the more rapid line of "The Rape of the Lock"—and both poems have the same metrical line, the iambic pentameter. Or consider Browning's "Andrea del Sarto," which, like "Tithonus," is unrhymed. All three poems have the five-foot iambic line, yet how they differ in tempo! The reader might consider how these differences are achieved.

One hears considerable talk these days of the "tone" of a poem, and we have used the term in the notes without necessarily subscribing to the critical doctrines which make most use of it, but in a rather general sense to indicate the intellectual and emotional atmosphere within which the poet handles his theme. The tone

may be dry and ironic, formal and ritualistic, social and sophisticated, personal and elegiac, to cite only a few possibilities; or it
may be combinations of these, or it may be—and very often is—
undescribable in that the tone is so bound up with the very expression of the poem that it cannot be separately defined. But even when
undescribable it remains an important element in the poem and one
which must be recognized and appreciated if the poem is to be read
properly.

Closely related to tone is the matter of "aesthetic distance" (a term,
incidentally, which does not originate, as is commonly supposed, in
contemporary criticism). The more formal and ritualistic a poem,
the greater the aesthetic distance, which diminishes as the diction
becomes more colloquial and the tone more urbane and sophisticated.
Milton requires a much greater aesthetic distance than Pope, and a
poem like MacNeice's "Bagpipe Music" requires much less than
anything by Pope. A love poem by Donne requires less aesthetic
distance than one by Sidney. It is a question of perspective. Certain
kinds of painting, to be seen for what aesthetically they really are,
must be looked at from a considerable distance, while others demand
a closer view. The actor in the Greek theater, with its ritualistic
associations and vast distances, had to speak a very different kind
of language and move in a very different way from anything that
would be suitable to the modern stage. The misjudging of a poem
through not properly estimating the aesthetic distance from which
it should be approached is one of the commonest faults in reading,
and one which only wide experience in reading poetry can correct.
One might add that a common fault in second-rate poets is to
use language appropriate to one degree of aesthetic distance and
employ other devices which suggest a very different degree. (This
can, of course, be done deliberately for purposes of irony: Eliot
does this frequently in his earlier poems.) It is the endeavor to
secure aesthetic distance that leads indifferent poets to use a stock
poetic diction, hoping thus to give formality and dignity to their
expression; but though a deliberately formal diction can indeed add
aesthetic distance, the language must be vital to the poem and not
represent simply an alternative, "fancy" phrasing of a simple notion.
It does not make a line poetical to substitute "feathered tribe" for
"birds." though a poet such as Gray can use a phrase of this kind

with success when he wants a note of deliberate artificiality or stylization in a poem (see the note to "Ode on a Distant Prospect of Eton College"). One might almost say that diction and tone together give the aesthetic distance, were it not equally true that any two terms in this equation might be considered as adding up to the remaining third (aesthetic distance and diction, for example, providing—or at least determining—tone, and tone and aesthetic distance determining diction).

But the reader will learn more about such matters from the notes to the individual poems than from any abstract discussion. We append a brief glossary to aid him in following the notes.

GLOSSARY

ALEXANDRINE
A line of twelve syllables or six iambic feet, sometimes introduced for variation among the iambic pentameters of the heroic couplet (see below), and used as a final longer line in certain stanza forms, notably the Spenserian stanza (see below). An example of the use of the Alexandrine in the midst of the heroic couplet is:

> A needless Alexandrine ends the song
> That, like a wounded snake, drags its slow
> length along.

ALLITERATION
The repetition of the same letter, generally at the beginning but sometimes in the middle of different words that are very close to each other. For example:

> The moan of doves in immemorial elms,
> And murmuring of innumerable bees.

ANAPEST
A metrical foot (see "General Introduction") of three syllables, two unstressed followed by one stressed ($\cup\cup-$).

ASSONANCE
An imperfect kind of rhyme where the vowels but not the consonants match; e.g., "seem" and "keen."

BLANK VERSE
Continuous unrhymed verse in iambic pentameters.

CAESURA
The pause in the middle of a line of verse.

CONCEIT
A witty turn of thought, unusual image or analogy, or effective metaphorical expression.

COUPLET
A pair of lines of verse of the same length and meter, generally rhymed.

DACTYL
A foot of three syllables, one stressed and two unstressed ($-\cup\cup$). For example:

> Once in the morning in early September.

DIDACTIC
Intended to suggest or teach some lesson or moral.

ELEGY
In modern English usage, generally a poem of lamentation for the dead. The adjective. "elegiac," means mournful or plaintive.

END-STOPPED
With the pause coming at the end of each line.

EPIC
A narrative poem dealing with heroic actions and conforming to certain conventions.

FEMININE RHYME
The rhyming of two syllables of each of the rhyme words; e.g., "shady" and "lady."

HEROIC COUPLET	Rhymed couplet in iambic pentameter.
IAMB	A foot of two syllables, the first unstressed and the second stressed. See "General Introduction."
LAPIDARY	Perfectly polished. (A lapidary is a polisher and engraver of precious stones, and normally the adjective "lapidary" refers to the art of cutting stones; hence, used of verse, the word means precise and polished.)
LYRIC	Used both as noun and adjective to denote a nonnarrative poem, generally in stanza form and not of very great length, which expresses the poet's reactions to a given situation.
METAPHOR	A figure of speech in which a word or phrase is used to refer to something to which it does not literally apply, the implied identity being illuminating, or in some way contributing to the total meaning desired. For example:

> Her smiles are lightning, though her pride despair,
> And her disdains are gall, her favours honey.

METAPHYSICAL POETRY	See introduction to Section II, "The Seventeenth Century."
OCTOSYLLABIC COUPLET	Rhymed couplet in iambic or trochaic tetrameter. For example:

> He loved—as many a lay can tell
> Preserved in Stanmore's lonely dell.

ODE	A term used rather loosely in English poetry. It generally denotes a poem constructed, at first sight, of irregular stanzas, but on closer examination showing a careful parallel between groups of stanzas; the ode is often freer in expression and stronger in its emotional tone than other lyric forms (though this is by no means always true) and is often addressed to some person or object. See the note on Dryden's "Alexander's Feast."
PASTORAL	See the note on poem No. 20.
PENTAMETER	A line of five feet. With reference to English poetry, the term generally means a five-foot iambic line. (It has a different meaning when used with reference to Greek and Latin poetry, where it denotes a line of dactyls or spondees divided into two groups of two and a half feet each.)
SIMILE	A figure of speech in which one object is compared to another. For example, "My love is like a red, red rose."
SONNET	See note to poem No. 1.
SPENSERIAN STANZA	A stanza of eight decasyllabic lines and a final Alexandrine with the rhyme scheme *a b a b b c b c c*. It is so called because it is the stanza used by Spenser in his "Faerie Queene." It is used by Tennyson in the first part of "The Lotos Eaters" (poem No. 255).

SPONDEE   A foot consisting of two stressed syllables. It is generally used in English poetry to vary an iambic line. Cf. the opening line of "Lycidas" (poem No. 114).

TETRAMETER   A line of four feet, generally applied, in English poetry, to the octosyllable.

TROCHEE   A foot of two syllables, the first stressed and the second unstressed. See "General Introduction."

I. TUDORS AND ELIZABETHANS

TUDORS AND ELIZABETHANS

We begin our anthology with the sixteenth century, one of the great germinating periods of English poetry. In this period we can see the deliberate cultivation of craftsmanship, the exercising of the English language in a variety of meters and verse forms, and the rapid flowering of a great poetic literature. Between the death of Chaucer in 1400 and the rise of the poets who wrote at the court of the Tudor monarchs in the sixteenth century, the English language had developed from the stage known as Middle English into substantially its modern form. This development brought with it changes in pronunciation and accentuation so that the metrical patterns so effectively handled by Chaucer had to be learned over again in later centuries by poets who had to use as their medium a very different kind of English. Between Chaucer and Sir Thomas Wyatt, the sixteenth-century poet with whom our anthology opens, there had gradually developed a drastic breakdown in the technique of English verse expression, and it might almost be said that modern English poetry begins with the attempt by Wyatt and his friends and followers to reconstruct English poetic idiom and technique.

Like Chaucer before him, Wyatt and his contemporaries learned a lot from the Italian poets and spent a great deal of effort trying, with patriotic zeal, to achieve in English what had already been achieved in Italian. George Puttenham, the Elizabethan critic whose *Arte of English Poesie* appeared in 1589, tells us in that work that at the end of the reign of Henry VIII (1509–1547) "there sprang up a new company of courtly makers [poets], of whom Sir Thomas Wyatt the elder and Henry Earl of Surrey were the two chieftains, who having travelled into Italy and there tasted the sweet and stately measures and style of the Italian poesie, as novices newly crept out of the schools of Dante, Ariosto, and Petrarch, they greatly polished our rude and homely manner of vulgar poesie from that it had been before, and for that cause may justly be said the first reformers of

3

our English metre and style." This was the view which the immediate successors of the "courtly makers" had of them, and though
modern readers are inclined to put Wyatt considerably above Surrey
both as a pioneer and as an original poet, the general picture which
Puttenham gives of their achievement has since been accepted as
part of the history of English poetry.

Some of the problems faced by the "courtly makers" in "reforming English metre and style" are indicated in the notes to the poems
in this section, which will be found at the back of the book, especially
in the note to poem No. 1. These poets were essentially craftsmen,
treating a conventional subject matter over and over again in their
attempts to hammer out a disciplined yet flexible poetic style. They
borrowed, imitated, and translated from Italian and French poets as
well as from one another, and had they not done so their ultimate
achievement would have been less. They circulated their work in
manuscript (publication during the poet's lifetime was not at this
time common) and engaged in mutual encouragement and criticism. In 1557 (after the death of both Wyatt and Surrey) the printer
Richard Tottel put out a collection of poetry by the "courtly makers"
with the title *Songs and Sonnets, written by the right honorable
Lord Henry Howard late Earl of Surrey and others,* generally
known as *Tottel's Miscellany,* which was a kind of belated manifesto
of the new poetry. Many more collections of songs and poems followed in Queen Elizabeth's reign (1558–1603), bearing such attractive titles as *The Paradise of Dainty Devices, A Gorgeous Gallery
of Gallant Inventions, A Handful of Pleasant Delights, A Banquet
of Dainty Conceits, The Arbor of Amorous Devices, England's
Helicon,* and *England's Parnassus.* Many of the poems in these
collections are little more than exercises; some are overingenious,
some crude and mechanical; but by and large they demonstrate
the immense success with which the earlier poets of the century
had flexed the poetic muscles of the English language, as it were,
to fit it for graceful poetic expression.

But it takes more than graceful expression to make great poetry,
and in addition to this purely technical achievement there were new
and exciting currents of ideas flowing in from many quarters which
helped to fertilize sensibility and, more generally, to produce that
mental and emotional stimulation out of which significant litera-

ture arises. In addition to the influence of the Italian poets from the thirteenth century on (Dante, Petrarch, the innumerable sonneteers who followed Petrarch, Ariosto, Tasso, and many others) and the French poets and critics of the Pléiade, who set themselves to recreate in French the achievements of classical Greek and Latin poetry, there was that whole complex of ideas and attitudes lumped together by historians under the general name of the Renaissance, whose impact on the English mind grew ever stronger throughout the century. And there was the Reformation, too, which shook up established religious notions and increased the receptivity of individual minds to new ideas. Humanism, that aspect of the Renaissance which dealt with the recovery of the purest ideals of Latin and Greek expression and the assimilation of the most civilized aspects of classical thought, held up before the minds of eager writers and thinkers models of thought and expression which they felt challenged to emulate in English. If we put beside these factors the new patriotism developed by the success of the Tudor monarchy in keeping the country united and respected after generations of disastrous civil war and by the struggle with Spain which culminated in the spectacular defeat of the great Spanish Armada in 1588; the effect on men's imaginations of geographical explorations and new discoveries both physical and mental; the shake-up of society which had produced a virtually new aristocracy drawn largely from the middle classes and much more adventurous and individualistic in temperament than their feudal predecessors who, however prone to private warfare and even rebellion, had been part of a static social order which, theoretically at least, embraced all Christendom; the special atmosphere of Queen Elizabeth's court, with its revival of extravagant knightly ideals of chivalry and service and its almost religious devotion to the Virgin Queen—if we put all these facts together, we can see at least part of the reason why the Elizabethan Age, after the preparatory experimentation of the "courtly makers," suddenly flowered into the greatest of all English literary periods.

The great nondramatic poet of this period was Edmund Spenser (1552?–1599), whose *Faerie Queene,* that immense, unfinished, allegorical romance, testifies to the extraordinary intellectual atmosphere of the time. Christianity, Platonism, classical humanism, medieval romance, all lived together in Spenser's mind in a context of English patriotism: he wrote the *Faerie Queene* partly in order to "overgo" Ariosto, to show that the English language could produce as monumental a poem as the Italian. Yet his Protestantism, his neo-Platonism, and his humanism were European rather than English qualities of thought. England was less provincial in the Elizabethan age than she has been at some periods since, and Spenser was a child of the Renaissance and the Reformation, a European poet, as well as a patriotic celebrator of Queen Elizabeth. Spenser in his poetry used just about every tradition and convention that European culture was then able to provide; in his sonnet sequence (*Amoretti*), he followed the by now established pattern of writing a series of poems to his beloved, a pattern deriving originally from Petrarch; in his *Shepherd's Calendar* (his first important work and the first real triumph, in a work of some length, of the "new" English poetry) he put the pastoral tradition through its paces; he wrote elegies, satires, marriage hymns, hymns in honor of beauty and of heavenly love deriving (as far as the thought goes) from Plato and the Italian neo-Platonists, prose and verse letters and literary criticism. In the *Faerie Queene* he tried to build a structure that would contain all his own intellectual, moral, and emotional experience. And always he was the perfect craftsman, master of a richly musical English poetic style unsurpassed before or since, a "poet's poet" with a cunning ear for the flow of a line and the balance of a stanza, an unerring feeling for the texture of verse, a continual joy in the potentialities of language. After Spenser there was no further road in that direction; the "reforming of our English metre and style" which Puttenham spoke of had been more than fully achieved; Spenser had wrought a series of English poetic styles and a kind of English poetic diction which no qualities of craftsmanship could develop further: English nondramatic poetry was now to take the simpler line of Jonson, with his skilful, firmly chiseled, epigrammatically turned lyrics, or of Donne, with his passionately personal idiom. Between Spenser and Milton there was no English nondramatic poet capable of sustaining a "grand style" in poetic expression throughout a really long poem. Milton, learning from Spenser yet far from being dominated by him, and coming after the Elizabethans had established the "art of English poesie" on a firm footing, had the opportunity and the genius to develop a new grand style of his own, emulating Spenser here as he did also in his ability to hold in his own mind (and reflect in his poetry) the synthesis of all that was most valuable in the Protestant Christian and the classical humanist tradition. Milton, like Spenser, was a Protestant humanist who developed a powerful poetic apparatus to express that remarkable cultural synthesis.

Tudor experimenters and pioneers, Elizabethan songsters, sonneteers, rhymers of every kind, the richly woven verse of "sage and serious Spenser," to say nothing of the immense dramatic activity which is outside the scope of this anthology—these are only some aspects of the crowded sixteenth-century poetic scene. We must remember, too, that the mixture of neo-Platonic philosophical idealism and the atmosphere of gallantry and chivalry which the poets were trying to create at Queen Elizabeth's court produced in such a figure as Sir Philip Sidney a type of soldier, courtier, statesman, philosopher and poet who was England's version of the "complete man" of the Renaissance. In Sidney all these aspects seem equally balanced, but in other Elizabethans one or the other tends to prevail: Fulke Greville, a close friend of Sidney's, was more purely the philosophic poet, George Chapman, the man of learning, Ben Jonson, the scholar and craftsman.

Jonson is generally thought of as the great antithesis to Shakespeare, for unlike Shakespeare's his plays are carefully constructed with classical models in view, and he was always more concerned with learning the tools of his trade by studying Latin and Greek models than with giving free rein to his own inspiration and imagination. In his lyric poems he also had his eye on classical models, and his achievement here was to develop a simple, cogent, compact, yet musical poetic style, unaffected in diction and restrained in imagery—a perfect "classical" poetry which can be opposed to the lusher poetry of Spenser, who ransacked earlier English as well as classical and Italian literature to develop a richly synthetic poetic style which offended Jonson by its extravagance. "Spenser," said Jonson of the *Faerie Queene,* "writ no language." His own was always "pure"; he chose his vocabulary from words neither quaintly old-fashioned nor strikingly new, trying always to attain a balance, a propriety, in diction as in other aspects of his poetry. The effect of ease and poise in his verse, of sureness of touch and perfectly controlled order, was the result of scholarship and self-discipline: a craftsmanlike poet who turned his learning to effective poetic uses, Jonson stands at the head of a whole poetic tradition in English.

After the death of Spenser in 1599 there were three general roads which an English poet could take. He could follow one of Spenser's paths (there was no poet in the early seventeenth century who had the genius to use together all the methods and unite all the traditions that Spenser was able to handle together), and write allegorical, pastoral, or patriotic poetry; or he could join one of the two different kinds of reaction against Spenser (and after a great poet has dominated his age there is always a reaction against him). That reaction was either in the direction of Ben Jonson, with his simpler yet very carefully wrought lyrical strain, or in that of John Donne, the "metaphysical" poet, whose highly individual mind produced harsh and passionate poems equally different from the conventional Petrarchan sonnet, the sweet Elizabethan lyric, the closely woven musical verse of Spenser, or the clear and forceful utterance of Ben Jonson. Of Donne and the "metaphysicals" we shall speak in the introduction to the next section.

SIR THOMAS WYATT (1503-1542)

1. THE LOVER COMPARETH HIS STATE TO A SHIP IN PERILOUS STORM TOSSED ON THE SEA

My galley chargèd with forgetfulness
Thorough sharp seas in winter nights doth pass
'Tween rock and rock; and eke mine enemy, alas,
That is my lord, steereth with cruelness;
And every oar a thought in readiness,
As though that death were light in such a case.
An endless wind doth tear the sail apace,
Of forcèd sights and trusty fearfulness;
A rain of tears, a cloud of dark disdain,
Have done the wearied cords great hinderance;   10
Wreathèd with error and with ignorance,
The stars be hid that led me to this pain;
Drownèd is reason, that should me comfórt,
And I remain despairing of the port.

2.   "FORGET NOT YET THE TRIED INTENT"

> Forget not yet the tried intent
> Of such a truth as I have meant,
> My great travail, so gladly spent,
>   Forget not yet.
>
> Forget not yet when first began
> The weary life ye know, since whan
> The suit, the service none tell can,
>   Forget not yet.
>
> Forget not yet the great assays,
> The cruel wrong, the scornful ways,
> The painful patience in denays,
>   Forget not yet.
>
> Forget not yet, forget not this,
> How long ago hath been, and is,
> The mind that never meant amiss,
>   Forget not yet.
>
> Forget not, then, thine own approved,
> The which so long hath thee so loved,
> Whose steadfast faith yet never moved,
>   Forget not this.

3.   THE LOVER SHOWETH HOW HE IS FORSAKEN
      OF SUCH AS HE SOMETIME ENJOYED

> They flee from me that sometime did me seek,
> With naked foot stalking within my chamber.
> Once have I seen them gentle, tame, and meek,
> That now are wild, and do not once remember
> That sometime they have put themselves in danger
> To take bread at my hand; and now they range,
> Busily seeking in continual change.
>
> Thankèd be fortune it hath been otherwise,
> Twenty times better; but once in special,
> In thin array, after a pleasant guise,
> When her loose gown did from her shoulders fall,
> And she me caught in her arms long and small,
> Therewith all sweetly did me kiss,
> And softly said, "Dear heart, how like you this?"

It was no dream; I lay broad waking:
But all is turned now, thorough my gentleness,
Into a strange fashion of forsaking;
And I have leave to go, of her goodness,
And she also to use newfangleness.
But since that I so kindely am served,   20
I would fain know what she hath deserved.

4.   "MARVEL NO MORE"

Marvel no more although
    The songs I sing do moan,
For other life than woe
    I never provèd none.
And in my heart also
    Is graven with letters deep
A thousand sighs and mo,
    A flood of tears to weep.

How may a man in smart
    Find matter to rejoice?   10
How may a mourning heart
    Set forth a pleasant voice?
Play who that can that part:
    Needs must in me appear
How fortune, overthwart,
    Doth cause my mourning cheer.

Perdie, there is no man
    If he never saw sight
That perfectly tell can
    The nature of the light.   20
Alas, how should I then,
    That never tasted but sour,
But do as I began,
    Continually to lour?

But yet perchance some chance
    May chance to change my tune,
And when such chance doth chance,
    Then shall I thank fortune.
And if I have chance,
    Perchance ere it be long   30
For such a pleasant chance
    To sing some pleasant song.

5. THE LOVER COMPLAINETH THE UNKINDNESS OF HIS LOVE

My lute, awake! perform the last
Labour that thou and I shall waste,
The end that I have now begun;
For when this song is sung and past,
My lute be still, for I have done.

As to be heard where ear is none,
As lead to grave in marble stone,
My song may pierce her heart as soon.
Should we then sigh, or sing, or moan?
No, no, my lute, for I have done.   10

The rocks do not so cruelly
Repulse the waves continually,
As she my suit and affection;
So that I am past remedy,
Whereby my lute and I have done.

Proud of the spoil that thou hast got
Of simple hearts, thorough love's shot;
By whom, unkind, thou hast them won,
Think not he hath his bow forgot,
Although my lute and I have done.   20

Vengeance shall fall on thy disdain,
That makest but game on earnest pain;
Think not alone under the sun
Unquit to cause thy lovers plain,
Although my lute and I have done.

Perchance thee lie withered and old,
The winter nights that are so cold,
Plaining in vain unto the moon;
Thy wishes then dare not be told.
Care then who list, for I have done.   30

And then may chance thee to repent
The time that thou hast lost and spent
To cause thy lovers sigh and swoon;
Then shalt thou know beauty but lent,
And wish and want as I have done.

Now cease, my lute; this is the last
Labour that thou and I shall waste,
And ended is that we begun.
Now is this song both sung and past:
My lute be still, for I have done.   40

HENRY HOWARD, EARL OF SURREY (1516–1547)

6.   PRISONED IN WINDSOR, HE RECOUNTETH HIS PLEASURE THERE PASSED

So cruel prison how could betide, alas,
As proud Windsor? Where I in lust and joy
With a king's son my childish years did pass
In greater feast than Priam's sons of Troy;
Where each sweet place returns a taste full sour:
The large green courts where we were wont to hove
With eyes cast up into the maidens' tower,
And easy sighs, such as folk draw in love;
The stately seats, the ladies bright of hue,
The dances short, long tales of great delight;   10
With words and looks that tigers could but rue,
Where each of us did plead the other's right;
The palm play where, despoilèd for the game,
With dazèd eyes oft we by gleams of love
Have missed the ball and got sight of our dame,
To bait her eyes, which kept the leads above;
The gravel ground, with sleeves tied on the helm,
On foaming horse, with swords and friendly hearts,
With cheer, as though one should another whelm,
Where we have fought, and chasèd oft with darts;   20
With silver drops the mead yet spread for ruth,
In active games of nimbleness and strength,
Where we did strain, trainèd with swarms of youth,
Our tender limbs that yet shot up in length;
The secret groves which oft we made resound
Of pleasant plaint and of our ladies' praise,
Recording oft what grace each one had found,
What hope of speed, what dread of long delays;
The wild forest, the clothèd holts with green,
With reins avaled, and swift ybreathèd horse,   30

With cry of hounds and merry blasts between,
Where we did chase the fearful hart of force;
The wide vales eke that harbored us each night,
Wherewith, alas, reviveth in my breast
The sweet accord; such sleeps as yet delight,
The pleasant dreams, the quiet bed of rest;
The secret thoughts imparted with such trust,
The wanton talk, the divers change of play,
The friendship sworn, each promise kept so just,
Wherewith we passed the winter night away.   40
And with this thought the blood forsakes the face,
The tears berain my cheeks of deadly hue,
The which as soon as sobbing sighs, alas,
Upsuppèd have, thus I my plaint renew:
O place of bliss, renewer of my woes,
Give me account. Where is my noble fere?
Whom in thy walls thou dost each night enclose,
To other lief, but unto me most dear!
Echo, alas, that doth my sorrow rue,
Returns thereto a hollow sound of plaint.   50
Thus I alone, where all my freedom grew,
In prison pine with bondage and restraint;
And with remembrance of the greater grief
To banish the less, I find my chief relief.

7. DESCRIPTION OF SPRING, WHEREIN EACH THING RENEWS SAVE ONLY THE LOVER

The soote season that bud and bloom forth brings
With green hath clad the hill and eke the vale,
The nightingale with feathers new she sings,
The turtle to her make hath told her tale.
Summer is come, for every spray now springs,
The hart hath hung his old head on the pale,
The buck in brake his winter coat he flings,
The fishes float with new repairèd scale,
The adder all her slough away she slings,
The swift swallow pursueth the flyès smale,   10
The busy bee her honey now she mings;
Winter is worn, that was the flowers' bale.
And thus I see, among these pleasant things
Each care decays, and yet my sorrow springs.

8. THE LOVER COMFORTETH HIMSELF WITH THE WORTHINESS OF HIS LOVE

When raging love with extreme pain
Most cruelly distrains my heart,
When that my tears, as floods of rain,
Bear witness of my woeful smart,
When sighs have wasted so my breath
That I lie at the point of death,
   I call to mind the navy great
That the Greeks brought to Troyè town,
And how the boysteous winds did beat
Their ships, and rent their sails adown,   10
Till Agamemnon's daughter's blood
Appeased the gods that them withstood.
   And how that in those ten years' war
Full many a bloody deed was done,
And many a lord that came full far
There caught his bane, alas, too soon;
And many a good knight overrun,
Before the Greeks had Helen won.
   Then think I thus: sith such repair,
So long time war of valiant men,   20
Was all to win a lady fair,
Shall I not learn to suffer then,
And think my life well spent to be,
Serving a worthier wight than she?
   Therefore I never will repent,
But pains contented still endure;
For like as when, rough winter spent,
The pleasant spring straight draweth in ure,
So, after raging storms of care,
Joyful at length may be my fare.   30

RICHARD EDWARDS (1523–1566)

9. AMANTIUM IRAE AMORIS REDINTEGRATIO EST

In going to my naked bed as one that would have slept,
I heard a wife sing to her child, that long before had wept.
She sighèd sore and sang full sweet to bring the babe to rest,
That would not rest, but crièd still, in sucking at her breast.

She was full weary of her watch and grievèd with her child,
She rockèd it and rated it until on her it smiled.
Then did she say, Now have I found the proverb true to prove,
The falling out of faithful friends is the renewing of love.

Then took I paper, pen, and ink, this proverb for to write,
In register for to remain of such a worthy wight.   10
As she proceeded thus in song unto her little brat,
Much matter uttered she of weight, in place whereas she sat;
And provèd plain there was no beast, nor creature bearing life,
Could well be known to live in love without discord and strife.
Then kissèd she her little babe and sware, by God above,
The falling out of faithful friends is the renewing of love.

She said that neither king, ne prince, ne lord could live aright
Until their puissance they did prove, their manhood, and their
          might;
When manhood shall be matchèd so that fear can take no place,
Then weary works make warriors each other to embrace,   20
And leave their force that failèd them, which did consume the rout,
That might before have lived their time and nature out.
Then did she sing as one that thought no man could her reprove,
The falling out of faithful friends is the renewing of love.

She said she saw ne fish, ne fowl, nor beast within her haunt
That met a stranger in their kind, but could give it a taunt.
Since flesh might not endure, but rest must wrath succeed,
And force the fight to fall to play in pasture where they feed,
So noble nature can well end the works she hath begun,
And bridle well that will not cease her tragedy in some.   30
Thus in her song she oft rehearsed, as did her well behove,
The falling out of faithful friends is the renewing of love.

I marvel much, perdy, (quoth she) for to behold the rout,
To see man, woman, boy, and beast, to toss the world about.
Some kneel, some crouch, some beck, some check, and some can
          smoothly smile,
And some embrace others in arms, and there think many a wile.
Some stand aloof at cap and knee, some humble and some stout,
Yet are they never friends indeed until they once fall out.
Thus ended she her song, and said, before she did remove,
The falling out of faithful friends is the renewing of love.   40

GEORGE GASCOIGNE (1542?–1577)

10.   GASCOIGNE'S LULLABY

Sing lullaby, as women do,
Wherewith they bring their babes to rest,
And lullaby can I sing too
As womanly as can the best.
With lullaby they still the child,
And if I be not much beguiled,
Full many wanton babes have I
Which must be stilled with lullaby.

First, lullaby my youthful years,
It is now time to go to bed,   10
For crooked age and hoary hairs
Have won the haven within my head;
With lullaby, then, youth be still,
With lullaby, content thy will,
Since courage quails and comes behind,
Go sleep, and so beguile thy mind.

Next, lullaby my gazing eyes,
Which wonted were to glance apace;
For every glass may now suffice
To show the furrows in my face.   20
With lullaby, then, wink awhile,
With lullaby, your looks beguile,
Let no fair face nor beauty bright
Entice you eft with vain delight.

And lullaby, my wanton will,
Let reason's rule now reign thy thought,
Since all too late I find by skill
How dear I have thy fancies bought;
With lullaby, now take thine ease,
With lullaby, thy doubts appease;   30
For trust to this, if thou be still,
My body shall obey thy will.

Eke, lullaby my loving boy,
My little Robin, take thy rest;
Since age is cold and nothing coy,

Keep close thy coin, for so is best;
With lullaby, be thou content,
With lullaby, thy lusts relent,
Let others pay which have mo pence,
Thou art too poor for such expense. 40

Thus lullaby, my youth, mine eyes,
My will, my ware, and all that was!
I can no mo delays devise,
But welcome pain, let pleasure pass;
With lullaby, now take your leave,
With lullaby, your dreams deceive,
And when you rise with waking eye,
Remember Gascoigne's lullaby.

EDWARD DE VERE, EARL OF OXFORD (1550–1604)

11. EPIGRAM

Were I a king, I could command content;
Were I obscure, hidden should be my cares;
Or were I dead, no cares should me torment,
No hopes, no hates, nor loves, nor griefs, nor fears.
A doubtful choice, of these three which to crave—
A kingdom, or a cottage, or a grave.

SIR PHILIP SIDNEY (1554–1586)

12. "MY TRUE LOVE HATH MY HEART"

My true love hath my heart and I have his,
By just exchange one for another given;
I hold his dear, and mine he cannot miss,
There never was a better bargain driven.
My true love hath my heart and I have his.

My heart in me keeps him and me in one,
My heart in him his thoughts and senses guides;
He loves my heart, for once it was his own,
I cherish his, because in me it bides.
My true love hath my heart and I have his.

13.   "WITH HOW SAD STEPS, O MOON, THOU
              CLIMB'ST THE SKIES!"

With how sad steps, O moon, thou climb'st the skies!
    How silently, and with how wan a face!
    What! may it be that even in heav'nly place
    That busy archer his sharp arrows tries?
Sure, if that long-with-love-acquainted eyes
    Can judge of love, thou feel'st a lover's case;
    I read it in thy looks; thy languished grace
    To me, that feel the like, thy state descries.
Then, ev'n of fellowship, O moon, tell me,
    Is constant love deemed there but want of wit?   10
    Are beauties there as proud as here they be?
Do they above love to be loved, and yet
    Those lovers scorn whom that love doth possess?
    Do they call virtue there ungratefulness?

14.   "COME SLEEP! O SLEEP, THE CERTAIN KNOT
                    OF PEACE"

Come sleep! O sleep, the certain knot of peace,
    The baiting place of wit, the balm of woe,
    The poor man's wealth, the prisoner's release,
    Th' indifferent judge between the high and low;
With shield of proof shield me from out the prease
    Of those fierce darts despair at me doth throw;
    O make in me those civil wars to cease;
    I will good tribute pay, if thou do so.
Take thou of me smooth pillows, sweetest bed,
    A chamber deaf to noise and blind to light,   10
    A rosy garland and a weary head;
And if these things, as being thine by right,
    Move not thy heavy grace, thou shalt in me,
    Livelier than elsewhere, Stella's image see.

15.   "STELLA OFT SEES THE VERY FACE OF WOE"

Stella oft sees the very face of woe
    Painted in my beclouded stormy face,
    But cannot skill to pity my disgrace,
    Not though thereof the cause herself she know;

Yet hearing late a fable, which did show
  Of lovers never known a grievous case,
  Pity thereof gat in her breast such place
  That, from the sea derived, tears' spring did flow.
Alas, if fancy, drawn by imaged things
  Though false, yet with free scope, more grace doth breed   10
  Than servant's wrack, where new doubts honor brings;
Then think, my dear, that you in me do read
  Of lovers' ruin some sad tragedy.
  I am not I; pity the tale of me.

16.   "LEAVE ME, O LOVE, WHICH REACHEST
            BUT TO DUST"

Leave me, O love, which reachest but to dust,
And thou, my mind, aspire to higher things;
Grow rich in that which never taketh rust,
Whatever fades but fading pleasure brings.
Draw in thy beams, and humble all thy might
To that sweet yoke where lasting freedoms be;
Which breaks the clouds and opens forth the light,
That doth both shine and give us sight to see.
O take fast hold; let that light be thy guide
In this small course which birth draws out to death,
And think how evil becometh him to slide,
Who seeketh heav'n, and comes of heav'nly breath.
  Then farewell, world; thy uttermost I see;
  Eternal Love, maintain thy life in me.

SIR EDWARD DYER (? –1607)

17.   "MY MIND TO ME A KINGDOM IS"

My mind to me a kingdom is;
Such perfect joy therein I find,
That it excels all other bliss
That world affords or grows by kind:
  Though much I want which most would have,
  Yet still my mind forbids to crave.

No princely pomp, no wealthy store,
No force to win the victory,
No wily wit to salve a sore,

No shape to feed a loving eye;   10
   To none of these I yield as thrall:
   For why my mind doth serve for all.

I see how plenty suffers oft,
And hasty climbers soon do fall:
I see that those which are aloft
Mishap doth threaten most of all:
   They get with toil, they keep with fear;
   Such cares my mind could never bear.

Content I live, this is my stay:
I seek no more than may suffice,   20
I press to bear no haughty sway;
Look, what I lack my mind supplies:
   Lo, thus I triumph like a king,
   Content with that my mind doth bring.

Some have too much, yet still do crave,
I little have, and seek no more:
They are but poor, though much they have,
And I am rich with little store:
   They poor, I rich; they beg, I give;
   They lack, I leave; they pine, I live.   30

I laugh not at another's loss,
I grudge not at another's gain:
No worldly waves my mind can toss,
My state at one doth still remain:
   I fear no foe, I fawn no friend,
   I loathe not life, nor dread my end.

Some weigh their pleasure by their lust,
Their wisdom by their rage of will;
Their treasure is their only trust,
A cloakèd craft their store of skill: 40
   But all the pleasure that I find
   Is to maintain a quiet mind.

My wealth is health and perfect ease,
My conscience clear my choice defence;
I neither seek by bribes to please,
Nor by deceit to breed offence.
   Thus do I live; thus will I die;
   Would all did so as well as I!

FULKE GREVILLE, LORD BROOKE (1544–1628)

18. "LOVE, THE DELIGHT OF ALL WELL-THINKING MINDS"

Love, the delight of all well-thinking minds;
Delight, the fruit of virtue dearly lov'd;
Virtue, the highest good that reason finds;
Reason, the fire wherein men's thoughts be prov'd;
    Are from the world by Nature's power bereft,
    And in one creature for her glory left.

Beauty her cover is, the eye's true pleasure;
In honour's fame she lives, the ear's sweet music;
Excess of wonder grows from her true measure;
Her worth is passion's wound, and passion's physic;   10
    From her true heart, clear springs of wisdom flow,
    Which, imag'd in her words and deeds, men know.

Time fain would stay, that she might never leave her,
Place doth rejoice, that she must needs contain her,
Death craves of Heaven, that she may not bereave her,
The Heavens know their own, and do maintain her;
    Delight, Love, Reason, Virtue, let it be
    To set all women light but only she.

19. "I WITH WHOSE COLORS MYRA DREST HER HEAD"

I with whose colors Myra drest her head,
I that ware posies of her own hand making,
I that mine own name in the chimneys read
By Myra finely wrought ere I was waking:
    Must I look on, in hope time coming may
    With change bring back my turn again to play?

I that on Sunday at the Church-stile found
A garland sweet, with true-love knots in flowers,
Which I to wear about mine arm was bound,
That each of us might know that all was ours: 10
    Must I now lead an idle life in wishes?
    And follow Cupid for his loaves and fishes?

I that did wear the ring her Mother left,
I for whose love she gloried to be blamed,
I with whose eyes her eyes committed theft,
I who did make her blush when I was named;
    Must I lose ring, flowers, blush, theft and go naked,
    Watching with sighs, till dead love be awakèd?

I that when drowsy Argus fell asleep,
Like jealousy o'erwatchèd with desire,   20
Was ever warnèd modesty to keep,
While her breath, speaking, kindled Nature's fire:
    Must I look on a-cold, while others warm them?
    Do Vulcan's brothers in such fine nets arm them?

Was it for this that I might Myra see
Washing the water with her beauties, white?
Yet would she never write her love to me;
Thinks wit of change while thoughts are in delight?
    Mad girls must safely love, as they may leave:
    No man can print a kiss: lines may deceive.   30

NICHOLAS BRETON (1545?–1626?)

20.   "WHO CAN LIVE IN HEART SO GLAD"

        Who can live in heart so glad
        As the merry country lad?
        Who upon a fair green balk
        May at pleasure sit and walk,
        And amid the azure skies
        See the morning sun arise;
        While he hears in every spring
        How the birds do chirp and sing;
        Or before the hounds in cry
        See the hare go stealing by;   10
        Or along the shallow brook
        Angling with a baited hook,
        See the fishes leap and play
        In a blessed sunny day;
        Or to hear the partridge call
        Till she shave her covey all;
        Or to see the subtle fox,

How the villain plies the box,
After feeding on his prey
How he closely sneaks away 20
Through the hedge and down the furrow,
Till he gets into his burrow;
Then the bee to gather honey,
And the little black-haired coney
On a bank for sunny place
With her forefeet wash her face:
Are not these, with thousands mo
Than the courts of kings do know,
The true pleasing-spirits sights
That may breed true love's delights? 30
But with all this happiness
To behold that shepherdess
To whose eyes all shepherds yield,
All the fairest of the field,
Fair Aglaia, in whose face
Lives the shepherds' highest grace,
In whose worthy-wonder praise
See what her true shepherd says:
She is neither proud nor fine,
But in spirit more divine; 40
She can neither lour nor leer,
But a sweeter smiling cheer;
She had never painted face,
But a sweeter smiling grace;
She can never love dissemble,
Truth doth so her thoughts assemble
That where wisdom guides her will
She is kind and constant still.
All in sum, she is that creature
Of that truest comfort's nature, 50
That doth show (but in exceedings)
How their praises had their breedings.
Let, then, poets feign their pleasure,
In their fictions of love's treasure,
Proud high spirits seek their graces
In their idol-painted faces;
My love's spirit's lowliness
In affection's humbleness

Under heav'n no happiness
Seeks but in this shepherdess.   60
For whose sake I say and swear
By the passions that I bear,
Had I got a kingly grace
I would leave my kingly place
And in heart be truly glad
To become a country lad,
Hard to lie, and go full bare,
And to feed on hungry fare,
So I might but live to be
Where I might but sit to see   70
Once a day, or all day long,
The sweet subject of my song;
In Aglaia's only eyes
All my worldly paradise.

CHRISTOPHER MARLOWE (1564?–1593)

21.   THE PASSIONATE SHEPHERD TO HIS LOVE

Come live with me and be my love,
And we will all the pleasures prove
That valleys, groves, hills, and fields,
Woods, or steepy mountains yields.

And we will sit upon the rocks,
Seeing the shepherds feed their flocks,
By shallow rivers to whose falls
Melodious birds sing madrigals.

And I will make thee beds of roses
And a thousand fragrant posies,   10
A cap of flowers, and a kirtle
Embroidered all with leaves of myrtle;

A gown made of the finest wool
Which from our pretty lambs we pull;
Fair linèd slippers for the cold,
With buckles of the purest gold;

A belt of straw and ivy buds,
With coral clasps and amber studs:
And if these pleasures may thee move,
Come live with me and be my love.   20

The shepherds' swains shall dance and sing
For thy delight each May morning.
If these delights thy mind may move,
Then live with me and be my love.

SIR WALTER RALEGH (1552–1618)

22.   THE NYMPH'S REPLY TO THE SHEPHERD

If all the world and love were young,
And truth in every shepherd's tongue,
These pretty pleasures might me move
To live with thee and be thy love.

Time drives the flocks from field to fold
When rivers rage and rocks grow cold,
And Philomel becometh dumb;
The rest complain of cares to come.

The flowers do fade, and wanton fields
To wayward winter reckoning yields;   10
A honey tongue, a heart of gall,
Is fancy's spring, but sorrow's fall.

Thy gowns, thy shoes, thy beds of roses,
Thy cap, thy kirtle, and thy posies
Soon break, soon wither, soon forgotten,
In folly ripe, in reason rotten.

Thy belt of straw and ivy buds,
Thy coral clasps and amber studs,
All these in me no means can move
To come to thee and be thy love.   20

But could youth last and love still breed,
Had joys no date nor age no need,
Then these delights my mind might move
To live with thee and be thy love.

23. "EVEN SUCH IS TIME, WHICH TAKES IN TRUST"

> Even such is Time, which takes in trust
>   Our youth, and joys, and all we have;
> And pays us but with age and dust,
>   Which, in the dark and silent grave,
> When we have wandered all our ways,
> Shuts up the story of our days:
>   And from which earth and grave and dust
>   The Lord shall raise me up, I trust.

24.   TO HIS SON

> Three things there be that prosper all apace
> And flourish, while they are asunder far;
> But on a day they meet all in a place,
> And when they meet, they one another mar.
> And they be these: the wood, the weed, the wag.
> The wood is that that makes the gallows tree;
> The weed is that that strings the hangman's bag;
> The wag, my pretty knave, betokens thee.
> Now mark, dear boy: while these assemble not,
> Green springs the tree, hemp grows, the wag is wild;   10
> But when they meet, it makes the timber rot,
> It frets the halter, and it chokes the child.
>   *God bless the child!*

25.   THE PASSIONATE MAN'S PILGRIMAGE,
        SUPPOSED TO BE WRITTEN BY ONE
            AT THE POINT OF DEATH

> Give me my scallop-shell of quiet,
> My staff of faith to walk upon,
> My scrip of joy, immortal diet,
> My bottle of salvatïon,
> My gown of glory, hope's true gage,
> And thus I'll take my pilgrimage.
>
> Blood must be my body's balmer,
> No other balm will there be given,
> Whilst my soul like a white palmer
> Travels to the land of heaven,   10

Over the silver mountains,
Where spring the nectar fountains;
And there I'll kiss
The bowl of bliss,
And drink my eternal fill
On every milken hill.
My soul will be a-dry before,
But after it will ne'er thirst more;
And by the happy blissful way
More peaceful pilgrims I shall see,   20
That have shook off their gowns of clay
And go apparelled fresh like me.
I'll bring them first
To slake their thirst,
And then to taste those nectar suckets,
At the clear wells
Where sweetness dwells,
Drawn up by saints in crystal buckets.

And when our bottles and all we
Are filled with immortality,   30
Then the holy paths we'll travel,
Strewed with rubies thick as gravel,
Ceilings of diamonds, sapphire floors,
High walls of coral, and pearl bowers.

From thence to heaven's bribeless hall
Where no corrupted voices brawl,
No conscience molten into gold,
Nor forged accusers bought and sold,
No cause deferred, nor vain-spent journey,
For there Christ is the king's attorney,   40
Who pleads for all without degrees,
And he hath angels, but no fees.
When the grand twelve million jury
Of our sins and sinful fury,
'Gainst our souls black verdicts give,
Christ pleads his death, and then we live.
Be thou my speaker, taintless pleader,
Unblotted lawyer, true proceeder;
Thou movest salvation even for alms,
Not with a bribèd lawyer's palms.   50

And this is my eternal plea
To him that made heaven, earth, and sea,
Seeing my flesh must die so soon,
And want a head to dine next noon:
Just at the stroke when my veins start and spread,
Set on my soul an everlasting head.
Then am I ready, like a palmer fit,
To tread those blest paths which before I writ.

EDMUND SPENSER (1552?–1599)

26.   "IT FELL UPON A HOLY EVE"

Perigot. It fell upon a holy eve,
Willie.   Hey, ho, holiday!
Per.   When holy fathers wont to shrieve;
Wil.   Now ginneth this roundelay.
Per.   Sitting upon a hill so high,
Wil.   Hey, ho, the high hill!
Per.   The while my flock did feed thereby;
Wil.   The while the shepherd self did spill;
Per.   I saw the bouncing Bellibone,
Wil.   Hey, ho, Bonibell!   10
Per.   Tripping over the dale alone,
Wil.   She can trip it very well!
Per.   Well deckèd in a frock of gray,
Wil.   Hey, ho, gray is greete!
Per.   And in a kirtle of green saye,
Wil.   The green is for maidens meet.
Per.   A chapelet on her head she wore,
Wil.   Hey, ho, chapelet!
Per.   Of sweet violets therein was store,
Wil.   She sweeter than the violet.   20
Per.   My sheep did leave their wonted food,
Wil.   Hey, ho, silly sheep!
Per.   And gazed on her as they were wood,
Wil.   Wood as he that did them keep!
Per.   As the bonilasse passèd by,
Wil.   Hey, ho, bonilasse!
Per.   She roved at me with glancing eye,
Wil.   As clear as the crystal glass:

Per.	All as the sunny beam so bright,
Wil.	Hey, ho, the sun beam!
Per.	Glanceth from Phoebus' face forthright,
Wil.	So love into thy heart did stream:
Per.	Or as the thunder cleaves the clouds.
Wil.	Hey, ho, the thunder!
Per.	Wherein the lightsome levin shrouds,
Wil.	So cleaves thy soul asunder:
Per.	Or as Dame Cynthia's silver ray,
Wil.	Hey, ho, the moonlight!
Per.	Upon the glittering wave doth play,
Wil.	Such play is a piteous plight.
Per.	The glance into my heart did glide;
Wil.	Hey, ho, the glider!
Per.	Therewith my soul was sharply gryde.
Wil.	Such wounds soon waxen wider.
Per.	Hasting to raunch the arrow out,
Wil.	Hey, ho, Perigot!
Per.	I left the head in my heart-root,
Wil.	It was a desperate shot.
Per.	There it rankleth, ay more and more,
Wil.	Hey, ho, the arrow!
Per.	Ne can I find salve for my sore:
Wil.	Love is a cureless sorrow.
Per.	And though my bale with death I bought,
Wil.	Hey, ho, heavy cheer!
Per.	Yet should thilk lass not from my thought,
Wil.	So you may buy gold too dear.
Per.	But whether in painful love I pine,
Wil.	Hey, ho, pinching pain!
Per.	Or thrive in wealth, she shall be mine,
Wil.	But if thou can her obtain.
Per.	And if for graceless grief I die,
Wil.	Hey, ho, graceless grief!
Per.	Witness she slew me with her eye,
Wil.	Let thy folly be the prief.
Per.	And you, that saw it, simple sheep,
Wil.	Hey, ho, the fair flock!
Per.	For prief thereof, my death shall weep,
Wil.	And moan with many a mock.
Per.	So learned I love on a holy eve.

30

40

50

60

Wil.   Hey, ho, holiday!
Per.   That ever since my heart did grieve.
Wil.   Now endeth our roundelay.

27.   "LONG WHILE I SOUGHT"

Long while I sought to what I might compare
    Those powerfull eyes, which lighten my dark spright,
    Yet find I nought on earth to which I dare
    Resemble th' image of their goodly light.
Not to the sun, for they do shine by night;
    Nor to the moon, for they are changèd never;
    Nor to the stars, for they have purer sight;
    Nor to the fire, for they consume not ever;
Nor to the lightning, for they still perséver;
    Nor to the diamond, for they are more tender;   10
    Nor unto crystal, for nought may them sever;
    Nor unto glass, such baseness might offend her;
Then to the Maker self they likest be,
    Whose light doth lighten all that here we see.

28.   "MOST GLORIOUS LORD OF LIFE"

Most glorious Lord of life that on this day,
    Didst make thy triumph over death and sin,
    And having harrowed hell didst bring away,
    Captivity thence captive us to win.
This joyous day, dear Lord, with joy begin,
    And grant that we for whom thou diddest die
    Being with thy dear blood clean washt from sin,
    May live for ever in felicity.
And that thy love we weighing worthily
    May likewise love thee for the same again: 10
    And for thy sake that all like dear didst buy,
    With love may one another entertain.
So let us love, dear love, like as we ought;
    Love is the lesson which the Lord us taught.

29.   "ONE DAY I WROTE HER NAME UPON
                    THE STRAND"

One day I wrote her name upon the strand,
    But came the waves and washèd it away:

Again I wrote it with a second hand,
But came the tide, and made my pains his prey.
Vain man, said she, that dost in vain assay
A mortal thing so to immortalize,
For I my self shall like to this decay,
And eke my name be wipèd out likewise.
Not so, (quoth I) let baser things devise,
To die in dust, but you shall live by fame;   10
My verse your virtues rare shall eternize,
And in the heavens write your glorious name.
Where whenas death shall all the world subdue,
Our love shall live, and later life renew.

30.   "FAIR IS MY LOVE"

Fair is my love, when her fair golden hairs
With the loose wind ye waving chance to mark;
Fair when the rose in her red cheeks appears,
Or in her eyes the fire of love does spark.
Fair when her breast like a rich laden bark,
With precious merchandise she forth doth lay,
Fair when that cloud of pride, which oft doth dark
Her goodly light with smiles she dries away.
But fairest she, when so she doth display
The gate with pearls and rubies richly dight   10
Through which her words so wise do make their way
To bear the message of her gentle spright.
The rest be works of nature's wonderment,
But this the work of heart's astonishment.

31.   PROTHALAMION

Calm was the day, and through the trembling air
Sweet breathing Zephyrus did softly play,
A gentle spirit, that lightly did delay
Hot Titan's beams, which then did glister fair;
When I whose sullen care,
Through discontent of my long fruitless stay
In prince's court, and expectation vain
Of idle hopes, which still do fly away
Like empty shadows, did afflict my brain,
Walked forth to ease my pain   10

Along the shore of silver streaming Thames,
Whose rutty bank, the which his river hems,
Was painted all with variable flowers,
And all the meads adorned with dainty gems,
Fit to deck maidens' bowers,
And crown their paramours,
Against the bridal day, which is not long:
   Sweet Thames, run softly, till I end my song.

There, in a meadow, by the river's side,
A flock of nymphs I chancèd to espy,   20
All lovely daughters of the flood thereby,
With goodly greenish locks all loose untied,
As each had been a bride;
And each one had a little wicker basket,
Made of fine twigs entrailèd curiously,
In which they gathered flowers to fill their flasket,
And with fine fingers cropped full feateously
The tender stalks on hye.
Of every sort, which in that meadow grew,
They gathered some; the violet pallid blue,   30
The little daisy, that at evening closes,
The virgin lily, and the primrose true,
With store of vermeil roses,
To deck their bridegrooms' posies,
Against the bridal day, which was not long:
   Sweet Thames, run softly, till I end my song.

With that, I saw two swans of goodly hue
Come softly swimming down along the Lee;
Two fairer birds I yet did never see.
The snow which doth the top of Pindus strew,   40
Did never whiter shew,
Nor Jove himself, when he a swan would be
For love of Leda, whiter did appear:
Yet Leda was they say as white as he,
Yet not so white as these, nor nothing near.
So purely white they were,
That even the gentle stream, the which them bare,
Seemed foul to them, and bade his billows spare
To wet their silken feathers, lest they might
Soil their fair plumes with water not so fair,   50

And mar their beauties bright,
That shone as heaven's light,
Against their bridal day, which was not long:
   Sweet Thames, run softly, till I end my song.

Eftsoons the nymphs, which now had flowers their fill,
Ran all in haste, to see that silver brood,
As they came floating on the crystal flood.
Whom when they saw, they stood amazèd still,
Their wondering eyes to fill.
Them seemed they never saw a sight so fair,   60
Of fowls so lovely, that they sure did deem
Them heavenly born, or to be that same pair
Which through the sky draw Venus' silver team;
For sure they did not seem
To be begot of any earthly seed,
But rather angels or of angels' breed:
Yet were they bred of Somers-heat they say,
In sweetest season, when each flower and weed
The earth did fresh array,
So fresh they seemed as day,   70
Even as their bridal day, which was not long:
   Sweet Thames, run softly, till I end my song.

Then forth they all out of their baskets drew
Great store of flowers, the honour of the field,
That to the sense did fragrant odours yield,
All which upon those goodly birds they threw,
And all the waves did strew,
That like old Peneus' waters they did seem,
When down along by pleasant Tempe's shore,
Scattered with flowers, through Thessaly they stream,   80
That they appear through lilies' plenteous store,
Like a bride's chamber floor.
Two of those nymphs, meanwhile, two garlands bound,
Of freshest flowers which in that mead they found,
The which presenting all in trim array,
Their snowy foreheads therewithal they crowned,
Whilst one did sing this lay,
Prepared against that day,
Against their bridal day, which was not long:
   Sweet Thames, run softly, till I end my song.   90

'Ye gentle birds, the world's fair ornament,
And heaven's glory, whom this happy hour
Doth lead unto your lovers' blissful bower,
Joy may you have and gentle heart's content
Of your love's couplement:
And let fair Venus, that is queen of love,
With her heart-quelling son upon you smile,
Whose smile, they say, hath virtue to remove
All love's dislike, and friendship's faulty guile
For ever to assoil.   100
Let endless peace your steadfast hearts accord,
And blessed plenty wait upon your board,
And let your bed with pleasures chaste abound,
That fruitful issue may to you afford,
Which may your foes confound,
And make your joys redound,
Upon your bridal day, which is not long:
    Sweet Thames, run softly, till I end my song.'

So ended she; and all the rest around
To her redoubled that her undersong,   110
Which said, their bridal day should not be long.
And gentle echo from the neighbour ground
Their accents did resound.
So forth those joyous birds did pass along,
Adown the Lee, that to them murmured low,
As he would speak, but that he lacked a tongue,
Yet did by signs his glad affection show,
Making his stream run slow.
And all the fowl which in his flood did dwell
'Gan flock about these twain, that did excel   120
The rest so far as Cynthia doth shend
The lesser stars. So they, enrangèd well,
Did on those two attend,
And their best service lend,
Against their wedding day, which was not long:
    Sweet Thames, run softly, till I end my song.

At length they all to merry London came,
To merry London, my most kindly nurse,
That to me gave this life's first native source;
Though from another place I take my name,   130

An house of ancient fame.
There when they came, whereas those bricky towers,
The which on Thames' broad agèd back do ride,
Where now the studious lawyers have their bowers
There whilom wont the Templar Knights to bide,
Till they decayed through pride:
Next whereunto there stands a stately place,
Where oft I gainèd gifts and goodly grace
Of that great lord, which therein wont to dwell,
Whose want too well now feels my friendless case.   140
But ah! here fits not well
Old woes but joys to tell
Against the bridal day, which is not long:
   Sweet Thames, run softly, till I end my song.

Yet therein now doth lodge a noble peer,
Great England's glory and the world's wide wonder,
Whose dreadful name late through all Spain did thunder,
And Hercules' two pillars standing near
Did make to quake and fear.
Fair branch of honor, flower of chivalry,   150
That fillest England with thy triumph's fame,
Joy have thou of thy noble victory,
And endless happiness of thine own name
That promiseth the same:
That through thy prowess and victorious arms,
Thy country may be freed from foreign harms;
And great Elisa's glorious name may ring
Through all the world, filled with thy wide alarms,
Which some brave muse may sing
To ages following,   160
Upon the bridal day, which is not long:
   Sweet Thames, run softly, till I end my song.

From those high towers this noble lord issuing,
Like radiant Hesper when his golden hair
In th' Ocean billows he hath bathèd fair,
Descended to the river's open viewing,
With a great train ensuing.
Above the rest were goodly to be seen
Two gentle knights of lovely face and feature
Beseeming well the bower of any queen,   170

With gifts of wit and ornaments of nature,
Fit for so goodly stature;
That like the twins of Jove they seemed in sight,
Which deck the baldric of the heavens bright.
They two forth pacing to the river's side,
Received those two fair birds, their love's delight,
Which at th' appointed tide
Each one did make his bride,
Against their bridal day, which is not long:
   Sweet Thames, run softly, till I end my song.   180

WILLIAM SHAKESPEARE (1564–1616)

32.   "SHALL I COMPARE THEE TO A SUMMER'S
DAY?"

Shall I compare thee to a summer's day?
Thou art more lovely and more temperate.
Rough winds do shake the darling buds of May,
And summer's lease hath all too short a date.
Sometime too hot the eye of heaven shines,
And often is his gold complexion dimm'd;
And every fair from fair sometime declines,
By chance or nature's changing course untrimm'd;
But thy eternal summer shall not fade
Nor lose possession of that fair thou ow'st;   10
Nor shall Death brag thou wand'rest in his shade
When in eternal lines to time thou grow'st.
   So long as men can breathe or eyes can see,
   So long lives this, and this gives life to thee.

33.   "WHEN, IN DISGRACE WITH FORTUNE AND
MEN'S EYES"

When, in disgrace with Fortune and men's eyes,
I all alone beweep my outcast state,
And trouble deaf heaven with my bootless cries,
And look upon myself and curse my fate,
Wishing me like to one more rich in hope,
Featur'd like him, like him with friends possess'd,
Desiring this man's art and that man's scope,
With what I most enjoy contented least;

Yet in these thoughts myself almost despising,
Haply I think on thee, and then my state,   10
Like to the lark at break of day arising
From sullen earth, sings hymns at heaven's gate;
   For thy sweet love remember'd such wealth brings
   That then I scorn to change my state with kings.

34.   "WHEN TO THE SESSIONS OF SWEET SILENT
THOUGHT"

When to the sessions of sweet silent thought
I summon up remembrance of things past,
I sigh the lack of many a thing I sought
And with old woes new wail my dear time's waste.
Then can I drown an eye, unus'd to flow,
For precious friends hid in death's dateless night,
And weep afresh love's long since cancell'd woe,
And moan the expense of many a vanish'd sight.
Then can I grieve at grievances foregone,
And heavily from woe to woe tell o'er   10
The sad account of fore-bemoanèd moan,
Which I new pay as if not paid before.
   But if the while I think on thee, dear friend,
   All losses are restor'd and sorrows end.

35.   "WHY DIDST THOU PROMISE SUCH A
BEAUTEOUS DAY"

Why didst thou promise such a beauteous day
And make me travel forth without my cloak,
To let base clouds o'ertake me in my way,
Hiding thy bravery in their rotten smoke?
'Tis not enough that through the cloud thou break
To dry the rain on my storm-beaten face,
For no man well of such a salve can speak
That heals the wound and cures not the disgrace.
Nor can thy shame give physic to my grief;
Though thou repent, yet I have still the loss.   10
The offender's sorrow lends but weak relief
To him that bears the strong offence's cross.
   Ah, but those tears are pearl which thy love sheds,
   And they are rich and ransom all ill deeds.

36.   "NOT MARBLE, NOR THE GILDED
                        MONUMENTS"

Not marble, nor the gilded monuments
Of princes, shall outlive this powerful rhyme;
But you shall shine more bright in these contents
Than unswept stone besmear'd with sluttish time.
When wasteful war shall statues overturn,
And broils root out the work of masonry,
Nor Mars his sword nor war's quick fire shall burn
The living record of your memory.
'Gainst death and all-oblivious enmity
Shall you pace forth; your praise shall still find room   10
Even in the eyes of all posterity
That wear this world out to the ending doom.
    So, till the Judgement that yourself arise,
    You live in this, and dwell in lovers' eyes.

37.   "NO LONGER MOURN FOR ME WHEN
                        I AM DEAD"

No longer mourn for me when I am dead
Than you shall hear the surly sullen bell
Give warning to the world that I am fled
From this vile world, with vilest worms to dwell.
Nay, if you read this line, remember not
The hand that writ it; for I love you so
That I in your sweet thoughts would be forgot
If thinking on me then should make you woe.
O, if, I say, you look upon this verse
When I perhaps compounded am with clay,   10
Do not so much as my poor name rehearse,
But let your love even with my life decay,
    Lest the wise world should look into your moan
    And mock you with me after I am gone.

38.   "THAT TIME OF YEAR THOU MAYST IN
                        ME BEHOLD"

That time of year thou mayst in me behold
When yellow leaves, or none, or few, do hang

Upon those boughs which shake against the cold,
Bare ruin'd choirs where late the sweet birds sang.
In me thou see'st the twilight of such day
As after sunset fadeth in the west,
Which by and by black night doth take away,
Death's second self, that seals up all in rest.
In me thou see'st the glowing of such fire
That on the ashes of his youth doth lie,   10
As the death-bed whereon it must expire,
Consum'd with that which it was nourish'd by.
   This thou perceiv'st, which makes thy love more strong,
   To love that well which thou must leave ere long.

39. "WHEN IN THE CHRONICLE OF WASTED TIME"

When in the chronicle of wasted time
I see descriptions of the fairest wights,
And beauty making beautiful old rhyme
In praise of ladies dead and lovely knights;
Then, in the blazon of sweet beauty's best,
Of hand, of foot, of lip, of eye, of brow,
I see their antique pen would have express'd
Even such a beauty as you master now.
So all their praises are but prophecies
Of this our time, all you prefiguring,   10
And, for they look'd but with divining eyes,
They had not skill enough your worth to sing;
   For we, which now behold these present days,
   Have eyes to wonder, but lack tongues to praise.

40.   "ALAS, 'TIS TRUE I HAVE GONE HERE AND THERE"

Alas, 'tis true I have gone here and there
And made myself a motley to the view,
Gor'd mine own thoughts, sold cheap what is most dear,
Made old offences of affections new.
Most true it is that I have look'd on truth
Askance and strangely; but, by all above,
These blenches gave my heart another youth,
And worse essays prov'd thee my best of love.

Now all is done, have what shall have no end!
Mine appetite I never more will grind   10
On newer proof, to try an older friend,
A god in love, to whom I am confin'd.
    Then give me welcome, next my heaven the best,
    Even to thy pure and most most loving breast.

41.   "LET ME NOT TO THE MARRIAGE OF TRUE MINDS"

Let me not to the marriage of true minds
Admit impediments. Love is not love
Which alters when it alteration finds,
Or bends with the remover to remove.
O no, it is an ever-fixèd mark
That looks on tempests and is never shaken;
It is the star to every wand'ring bark,
Whose worth's unknown, although his height be taken.
Love's not Time's fool, though rosy lips and cheeks
Within his bending sickle's compass come.   10
Love alters not with his brief hours and weeks,
But bears it out even to the edge of doom.
    If this be error, and upon me proved,
    I never writ, nor no man ever loved.

42.   "THE EXPENSE OF SPIRIT IN A WASTE OF SHAME"

The expense of spirit in a waste of shame
Is lust in action; and till action, lust
Is perjur'd, murd'rous, bloody, full of blame,
Savage, extreme, rude, cruel, not to trust;
Enjoy'd no sooner but despisèd straight,
Past reason hunted, and no sooner had
Past reason hated, as a swallowed bait
On purpose laid to make the taker mad;
Mad in pursuit and in possession so;
Had, having, and in quest to have, extreme;   10
A bliss in proof, and prov'd, a very woe;
Before, a joy propos'd; behind, a dream.
    All this the world well knows; yet none knows well
    To shun the heaven that leads men to this hell.

43. ## "MY MISTRESS' EYES ARE NOTHING LIKE THE SUN"

My mistress' eyes are nothing like the sun;
Coral is far more red than her lips' red;
If snow be white, why then her breasts are dun;
If hairs be wires, black wires grow on her head.
I have seen roses damask'd, red, and white,
But no such roses see I in her cheeks;
And in some perfumes is there more delight
Than in the breath that from my mistress reeks.
I love to hear her speak; yet well I know
That music hath a far more pleasing sound.   10
I grant I never saw a goddess go;
My mistress, when she walks, treads on the ground.
  And yet, by heaven, I think my love as rare
  As any she beli'd with false compare.

44. ## WINTER

When icicles hang by the wall,
  And Dick the shepherd blows his nail,
And Tom bears logs into the hall,
  And milk comes frozen home in pail,
When blood is nipped, and ways be foul,
Then nightly sings the staring owl,
    To-wit-to-who!
    A merry note,
While greasy Joan doth keel the pot.

When all around the wind doth blow,   10
  And coughing drowns the parson's saw,
And birds sit brooding in the snow,
  And Marian's nose looks red and raw,
When roasted crabs hiss in the bowl,
Then nightly sings the staring owl,
    To-wit-to-who!
    A merry note,
While greasy Joan doth keel the pot.

45.   "O MISTRESS MINE, WHERE ARE YOU
                        ROAMING?"

> O mistress mine, where are you roaming?
> Oh, stay and hear! your true Love's coming,
>   That can sing both high and low:
> Trip no further, pretty sweeting;
> Journeys end in lovers' meeting,
>   Every wise man's son doth know.
>
> What is love? 'tis not hereafter;
> Present mirth hath present laughter;
>   What's to come is still unsure:
> In delay there lies no plenty: 10
> Then come kiss me, sweet-and-twenty,
>   Youth's a stuff will not endure.

46.   "FEAR NO MORE THE HEAT O' THE SUN"

> Fear no more the heat o' the sun,
>   Nor the furious winter's rages;
> Thou thy worldly task hast done,
>   Home art gone, and ta'en thy wages:
> Golden lads and girls all must,
> As chimney-sweepers, come to dust.
>
> Fear no more the frown o' the great;
>   Thou art past the tyrant's stroke:
> Care no more to clothe and eat;
>   To thee the reed is as the oak: 10
> The sceptre, learning, physic, must
> All follow this, and come to dust.
>
> Fear no more the lightning-flash,
>   Nor the all-dreaded thunder-stone;
> Fear not slander, censure rash;
>   Thou hast finished joy and moan:
> All lovers young, all lovers must
> Consign to thee, and come to dust.
>
> No exorciser harm thee!
> Nor no witchcraft charm thee!   20
> Ghost unlaid forbear thee!

Nothing ill come near thee!
Quiet consummation have;
And renownèd be thy grave!

SAMUEL DANIEL (1562–1619)

47.   "WHEN MEN SHALL FIND THY FLOWER,
THY GLORY, PASS"

When men shall find thy flower, thy glory, pass,
And thou, with careful brow sitting alone,
Receivèd hast this message from thy glass,
That tells the truth and says that all is gone;
Fresh shalt thou see in me the wounds thou madest,
Though spent thy flame, in me the heat remaining:
I that have loved thee thus before thou fadest,
My faith shall wax, when thou art in thy waning.
The world shall find this miracle in me,
That fire can burn when all the matter's spent: 10
Then what my faith hath been thyself shalt see,
And that thou wast unkind thou may'st repent.
    Thou may'st repent that thou hast scorned my tears,
    When winter snows upon thy sable hairs.

MICHAEL DRAYTON (1563–1631)

48.   "SINCE THERE'S NO HELP, COME LET US
KISS AND PART"

Since there's no help, come let us kiss and part—
Nay, I have done: you get no more of me;
And I am glad, yea, glad with all my heart,
That thus so cleanly I myself can free.
Shake hands for ever, cancel all our vows,
And when we meet at any time again,
Be it not seen in either of our brows
That we one jot of former love retain.
Now at the last gasp of love's latest breath,
When, his pulse failing, Passion speechless lies,   10
When Faith is kneeling by his bed of death,

And Innocence is closing up his eyes,—
  Now, if thou wouldst, when all have given him over,
From death to life thou might'st him yet recover!

GEORGE CHAPMAN (1559?–1634)

49.   A CORONET FOR HIS MISTRESS PHILOSOPHY

Muses that sing love's sensual empery,
  And lovers kindling your enragèd fires
  At Cupid's bonfires burning in the eye,
  Blown with the empty breath of vain desires;
You that prefer the painted cabinet
  Before the wealthy jewels it doth store ye,
  That all your joys in dying figures set,
  And stain the living substance of your glory:
Abjure those joys, abhor their memory,
  And let my love the honored subject be   10
  Of love, and honor's cómplete history;
  Your eyes were never yet let in to see
The majesty and riches of the mind,
But dwell in darkness; for your god is blind.

GEORGE PEELE (1558?–1597?)

50.   "HIS GOLDEN LOCKS TIME HATH TO
            SILVER TURNED"

His golden locks time hath to silver turned;
  Oh, time too swift, oh, swiftness never ceasing!
His youth 'gainst time and age hath ever spurned,
  But spurned in vain; youth waneth by increasing.
Beauty, strength, youth, are flowers but fading seen;
Duty, faith, love, are roots, and ever green.

His helmet now shall make a hive for bees,
  And lovers' sonnets turned to holy psalms,
A man-at-arms must now serve on his knees,
  And feed on prayers, which are age his alms;   10
But though from court to cottage he depart,
His saint is sure of his unspotted heart.

And when he saddest sits in homely cell,
  He'll teach his swains this carol for a song:
Blest be the hearts that wish my sovereign well,
  Cursed be the souls that think her any wrong!
Goddess, allow this agèd man his right,
To be your beadsman now, that was your knight.

THOMAS NASHE (1567–1601)

51.   "ADIEU, FAREWELL EARTH'S BLISS"

Adieu, farewell earth's bliss,
This world uncertain is.
Fond are life's lustful joys,
Death proves them all but toys;
None from his darts can fly.
I am sick, I must die.
    Lord, have mercy on us!

Rich men, trust not in wealth,
Gold cannot buy you health.
Physic himself must fade,   10
All things to end are made;
The plague full swift goes by:
I am sick, I must die.
    Lord, have mercy on us!

Beauty is but a flower
Which wrinkles will devour:
Brightness falls from the air.
Queens have died young and fair,
Dust hath closed Helen's eye.
I am sick, I must die.   20
    Lord, have mercy on us!

Strength stoops unto the grave,
Worms feed on Hector brave,
Swords may not fight with fate.
Earth still holds ope her gate;
Come! come! the bells do cry.
I am sick, I must die.
    Lord, have mercy on us!

Wit with his wantonness
Tasteth death's bitterness;   30
Hell's executioner
Hath no ears for to hear
What vain art can reply.
I am sick, I must die.
    Lord, have mercy on us!

Haste, therefore, each degree,
To welcome destiny.
Heaven is our heritage,
Earth but a player's stage;
Mount we unto the sky.   40
I am sick, I must die.
    Lord, have mercy on us!

THOMAS DEKKER (1572?–1632?)

52.   "GOLDEN SLUMBERS KISS YOUR EYES"

Golden slumbers kiss your eyes,
Smiles awake you when you rise;
Sleep, pretty wantons, do not cry,
And I will sing a lullaby:
Rock them, rock them, lullaby.

Care is heavy, therefore sleep you,
You are care, and care must keep you;
Sleep, pretty wantons, do not cry,
And I will sing a lullaby:
Rock them, rock them, lullaby.

JOHN WEBSTER (1580?–1625?)

53.   "CALL FOR THE ROBIN REDBREAST AND
THE WREN"

Call for the robin redbreast and the wren,
Since o'er shady groves they hover,
And with leaves and flowers do cover
The friendless bodies of unburied men.

Call unto his funeral dole
The ant, the field-mouse, and the mole,
To rear him hillocks that shall keep him warm,
And, when gay tombs are robbed, sustain no harm;
But keep the wolf far thence, that's foe to men,
For with his nails he'll dig them up again.   10

THOMAS CAMPION (1567–1620?)

54.   "HARK, ALL YOU LADIES THAT DO SLEEP!"

Hark, all you ladies that do sleep!
    The fairy queen Proserpina
Bids you awake and pity them that weep.
You may do in the dark
    What the day doth forbid;
Fear not the dogs that bark,
    Night will have all hid.

But if you let your lovers moan,
    The fairy queen Proserpina
Will send abroad her fairies ev'ry one,   10
    That shall pinch black and blue
        Your white hands and fair arms
    That did not kindly rue
        Your paramours' harms.

In myrtle arbors on the downs
    The fairy queen Proserpina,
This night by moonshine leading merry rounds,
    Holds a watch with sweet love,
        Down the dale, up the hill;
    No plaints or groans may move   20
        Their holy vigil.

All you that will hold watch with love,
    The fairy queen Proserpina
Will make you fairer than Dione's dove;
    Roses red, lilies white,
        And the clear damask hue,
    Shall on your cheeks alight;
        Love will adorn you.

All you that love, or loved before,
　　The fairy queen Proserpina   30
Bids you increase that loving humor more;
　　They that yet have not fed
　　　　On delight amorous,
　　She vows that they shall lead
　　　　Apes in Avernus.

55.   "WHEN THOU MUST HOME TO SHADES
                  OF UNDERGROUND"

When thou must home to shades of underground,
　　And there arrived, a new admirèd guest,
The beauteous spirits do engirt thee round,
　　White Iope, blithe Helen, and the rest,
To hear the stories of thy finished love
From that smooth tongue whose music hell can move;

Then wilt thou speak of banqueting delights,
　　Of masks and revels which sweet youth did make,
Of tourneys and great challenges of knights,
　　And all these triumphs for thy beauty's sake;   10
When thou hast told these honors done to thee,
Then tell, O tell, how thou didst murder me.

56.   "ROSE-CHEEKED LAURA, COME"

　　　Rose-cheeked Laura, come,
　　　Sing thou smoothly with thy beauty's
　　　Silent music, either other
　　　　　Sweetly gracing.

　　　Lovely forms do flow
　　　From concent divinely framèd;
　　　Heav'n is music, and thy beauty's
　　　　　Birth is heavenly.

　　　These dull notes we sing
　　　Discords need for helps to grace them;   10
　　　Only beauty purely loving
　　　　　Knows no discord,

　　　But still moves delight,
　　　Like clear springs renewed by flowing,
　　　Ever perfect, ever in them-
　　　　　Selves eternal.

57.   FOLLOW YOUR SAINT

Follow your saint, follow with accents sweet!
Haste you, sad notes, fall at her flying feet!
There, wrapped in cloud of sorrow, pity move,
And tell the ravisher of my soul I perish for her love:
But, if she scorns my never-ceasing pain,
Then burst with sighing in her sight and ne'er return again.

All that I sung still to her praise did tend,
Still she was first, still she my songs did end;
Yet she my love and music both doth fly,
The music that her echo is and beauty's sympathy.
Then let my notes pursue her scornful flight:
It shall suffice that they were breathed and died for her delight.

II. THE SEVENTEENTH CENTURY

THE SEVENTEENTH CENTURY

Very roughly, we might say that the death of Spenser in 1599 left English poetry divided among two "schools," that of Ben Jonson (1572–1637) and that of John Donne (1573–1631), each of whom, as we have seen, represented in his own way a reaction against the Spenserian tradition. There were, in addition, those poets who continued to follow one or other of the paths which had been trodden at one time or another, or sometimes simultaneously, by Spenser—Giles and Phineas Fletcher, George Wither, William Browne, Michael Drayton, and other allegorists, pastoralists, and celebrators of the English countryside.

The "metaphysical" poetry of Donne and his followers is often a tortured, subtle, realistic poetry which repudiates the conventional Petrarchan properties and puts urgency before sweetness. The use of philosophical and scientific terms and ideas, combined with the starkest realistic images, helps to give many of Donne's poems a note both of complexity and of emotional authenticity that is not found in the same degree in, say, the characteristic Elizabethan sonnet. It has now become a commonplace that Donne possessed to a high degree that "unified sensibility" which combines thought and passion, deriving emotion from an idea and developing subtle ideas from an emotion. Thus the intellectual quality of his best poetry reinforces rather than weakens the emotional quality. His abrupt openings, violent images, and startling paradoxes give his poetry individuality and richness, while his sense of conflicting ideas and attitudes brought about by the new ideas in religion and science—

> The new philosophy calls all in doubt;
> The element of fire is quite put out—

makes his poetry a fascinating record of the impact of the thought of the period on one sensitive individual. Donne is thus interesting both historically and intrinsically, of equal importance to the lover of poetry and the historian of culture.

Classification of poets into schools is at best only a rough guide to any poetic scene, and the Spenserians, the metaphysicals, and the "sons of Ben" neither complete the picture nor represent accurately differences in technique and attitude among the various poets. If by the "sons of Ben" we mean the courtly and polished verse of Carew, Suckling, Lovelace, and other "Cavalier poets," we must recognize that though they learned a great deal from Ben Jonson's carefully modulated lyrics, these were also influenced, in varying degrees, by Donne's subtle and passionate thought, his bold and unconventional imagery, and his fierce psychological curiosity. Herrick, however, in many ways the most interesting of the followers of Jonson, shows little metaphysical influence: he kept to the simple classical lines of his master and went himself to the Latin and Greek lyrists—to Catullus, Anacreon, and the poets of the Greek Anthology. There is a simple pagan quality about many of Herrick's poems, a naïve but charming hedonism which represents one aspect of what the Renaissance brought to Europe. The other side, the passionate speculation about man and the universe let loose by the dissolution of the old order in philosophy, religion, and society, was not for him.

If the brilliance and wit of Donne's love poetry influenced in some degree the love poetry of those courtly poets generally considered more the followers of Jonson than of Donne, it was Donne's religious poetry, with its passionate personal questionings and outcries, which was at least as strong an influence on most of those later poets whom critics have agreed to call "metaphysical," especially on George Herbert, Richard Crashaw, and Henry Vaughan. Each of these poets has a clearly defined style and poetic personality of his own, and only in the most general sense can they be lumped together as "metaphysical" poets. In imagery and the handling of thought in imagery, however, they all owe something to or share something with Donne, even though their differences are more important than their similarities.

George Herbert was not faced with the struggle between the Catholic Church and the Church of England with which Donne, born and reared a Catholic, wrestled until his final not altogether happy acceptance of the Established Church. The conflict in Herbert was rather between the courtly, secular world and the spiritual life.

He eventually came to rest happily in the Church of England, seeing in its ritual a beautiful and satisfying symbolism and in its doctrines a clear and saving creed. Some of his poems are almost naïvely didactic, others are primarily devotional and show a remarkable ability to create a mood of utterly sincere worship which combines restraint in diction with an underlying note of self-surrender. He loved to meditate on the significance of various phases of Anglican worship and church architecture, and there is a "quaintness" about some of his poems, an individual and almost childlike charm, which is not easily paralleled in English poetry. The Church of England, that *via media* or middle road between Roman Catholicism on the one hand and individualistic Puritanism on the other, suited his temperament perfectly. His "metaphysical" qualities consist largely in the way in which he pushes his imagery to its logical conclusion, however far-fetched the "conceit" that might result, and in his ability to take images from everyday life and play with them intellectually until they became impressive symbols of spiritual reality.

Richard Crashaw, a convert to Catholicism, had a much more passionately devotional nature, and in his religious poetry expressed with a joyful violence his religious emotions and attitudes. He carried erotic imagery into his religious poems, in the manner of certain Italian religious poets, and this ardent mixture of erotic terminology and religious feeling—not unfamiliar in Catholic mystical writing—contrasts sharply with the quieter moods of Herbert and with the meditative mysticism of Vaughan and Traherne.

Vaughan shows something of Herbert's influence, but his own Welsh temperament led him into paths very different from Herbert's contented devotionalism. While Herbert was content to find God in the prescribed ritual and ceremonies of the Church, Vaughan's more imaginative and mystical temperament led him to seek identification with the ultimate spiritual reality and a recovery of the perfect vision through a contemplation of nature and of childhood—nature being nearer to God because it had not spoiled itself as man had, through exercising a corrupt will, and childhood being similarly nearer because of its innocence. There is a delicacy of perception and imagery in Vaughan which flowers in the very heart of his poetry, though he is often a less finished artist than Herbert. Traherne (whose poetry was not discovered until early in the present century) is a more consistent mystic than Vaughan, with a more carefully thought out philosophical base underlying his mysticism, but his poetry has something of the same quality.

Andrew Marvell, the last of the "metaphysical" poets here represented, can write love poetry with all the passionate subtlety of Donne, yet without Donne's violence: there is a fine calmness about his verse, but it is like the supposed calm at the center of a tornado—it is the calm of an intensely ordered passion. At his best he is perhaps the most perfect craftsman and accomplished poet of all the metaphysicals.

The age of Elizabeth had closed with the death of the old queen in 1603: by this time the currents sent by the Renaissance into England had become more complex and sometimes confused, and the cultural waters muddied. Humanism, Platonism, and Protestantism were not enough to put English civilization on a firm new basis: the "new philosophy" continued to "call all in doubt," political and religious controversies grew stronger, and men began to wonder whether the world was not perhaps running down steadily into an ever-steeper decline. The debate between those who believed in "the decline of the world" and those who believed that civilization was steadily improving was fundamental in seventeenth-century thought, and the century produced much evidence on either side. Politically, conflict between the Puritan middle classes and the aristocratic supporters of royal absolutism developed steadily until in 1639 it culminated in Civil War. Ten years later Charles I was executed and the country settled down to a decade of Puritan rule which turned out to be no more democratic than monarchy. The Civil War and the subsequent period of the Commonwealth were not happy periods for poets, who were inclined to feel that their fortunes lay with the aristocracy whose cultivated minds and love of the arts guaranteed the place of the poet in society. All revolutionary movements are, at least in their opening phases, suspicious of the artist to some degree, for they have sterner tasks than the leisured contemplation of beauty. In the seventeenth century the arts in general threw in their lot with aristocracy—with reaction, if that term be preferred—if only for the reason that the Puritans, who closed the theaters and frowned on dancing and merrymaking, had little use for that sort of thing:

Lament, lament, old abbeys,
   The fairies lost command;
They did but change priests' babies,
   But some have changed your land,
And all your children sprung from thence
   Are now grown Puritans,
Who live as changelings ever since,
   For love of your demains.

On the whole, both the "metaphysicals" and the "sons of Ben" were therefore on the Royalist side in the Civil War. Andrew Marvell, troubled as they all were troubled by having to take a stand on an issue which was not so clear-cut as it seemed, felt himself drawn both ways. Only Milton, who saw the conflict in his own terms and forced his own meaning on it, was throughout openly and actively on the Commonwealth side.

The Puritan movement was not entirely the work of humorless fundamentalists or middle-class despisers of the aesthetic side of life, who in fact represented a vulgarization of the Puritan tradition. An important and creative strain in the movement came from the high Platonic idealism of Spenser and Sidney, both of whom, as we have seen, combined humanist and Protestant thought. This Christian humanism is seen at its most splendid in Milton, classicist, idealist, Protestant, passionate lover of music and poetry, insatiable seeker after knowledge, individualist, champion of toleration, and flouter of all authority which was not confirmed by his own reason and experience. Soaked in the classics, in the Bible, in Italian and English literature, master of all his age had to teach him, Milton saw in the Civil War an opportunity to build in England a veritable heaven on earth, on the lofty principles of a humanism both Christian and Platonic. When the event proved his tremendous optimism wrong, he still fought to enlarge the scope of individual inspiration in public affairs, and when final disillusion came with the restoration of Charles II in 1660, he carried his sadder wisdom into a new poetic interpretation of man and his destiny. At all stages in his poetic career he aimed at synthesis, at the proper utilization of the Hebrew, classical, Christian, medieval and Renaissance traditions: he forged a poetic style capable of handling this comprehensive vision, and later poets who sought to imitate it with a less rich subject matter fell into a jargon for which some critics wrongheadedly see Milton responsible. The earlier and minor poems of Milton, which alone we have space to represent in this anthology, do not show the full scope of his achievement as a poet whose work is central to the Western tradition, but there is sufficient richness in such a poem as "Lycidas" to show the kind of poetic texture Milton was aiming at.

The Restoration produced a new settling of the cultural ground, and the "glorious Revolution" of 1689, when the people threw out the Stuarts and imported a new king and queen committed to a constitutional monarchy, represented the final achievement of the Commonwealth idea in the seventeenth century. As the atmosphere cleared and new certainties, based on compromise and moderation, developed as a basis for English life and thought, poetry lost much of the passionate complexity of the "metaphysicals" and all the rich comprehensiveness of Milton and became something more elegant and easy but much more restricted in scope.

BEN JONSON (1572–1637)

58. INVITING A FRIEND TO SUPPER

To-night, grave sir, both my poor house and I
    Do equally desire your company;
Not that we think us worthy such a guest,
    But that your worth will dignify our feast
With those that come, whose grace may make that seem
    Something, which else could hope for no esteem.
It is the fair acceptance, sir, creates
    The entertainment perfect, not the cates.
Yet shall you have, to rectify your palate,
    An olive, capers, or some better salad   10
Ush'ring the mutton; with a short-legged hen,
    If we can get her, full of eggs, and then
Lemons and wine for sauce; to these, a coney
    Is not to be despaired of for our money;
And though fowl now be scarce, yet there are clerks,
    The sky not falling, think we may have larks.
I'll tell you of more, and lie, so you will come;

Of partridge, pheasant, woodcock, of which some
May yet be there; and godwit, if we can,
   Gnat, rail, and ruff too. Howsoe'er, my man   20
Shall read a piece of Virgil, Tacitus,
   Livy, or of some better book to us,
Of which we'll speak our minds amidst our meat;
   And I'll profess no verses to repeat;
To this, if aught appear which I not know of,
   That will the pastry, not my paper, show of.
Digestive cheese, and fruit there sure will be;
   But that which most doth take my muse and me
Is a pure cup of rich Canary wine,
   Which is the Mermaid's now, but shall be mine;   30
Of which had Horace or Anacreon tasted,
   Their lives, as do their lines, till now had lasted.
Tobacco, nectar, or the Thespian springs
   Are all but Luther's beer to this I sing.
Of this we will sup free, but moderately,
   And we will have no polly, or parrot by;
Nor shall our cups make any guilty men,
   But at our parting we will be as when
We innocently met. No simple word
   That shall be uttered at our mirthful board   40
Shall make us sad next morning, or affright
   The liberty that we'll enjoy to-night.

59.   ON MY FIRST SON

Farewell, thou child of my right hand, and joy;
   My sin was too much hope of thee, loved boy.
Seven years thou wert lent to me, and I thee pay,
   Exacted by thy fate, on the just day.
Oh, could I lose all father now! For why
   Will man lament the state he should envý?
To have so soon 'scaped world's and flesh's rage,
   And if no other misery, yet age!
Rest in soft peace, and asked, say, Here doth lie
   Ben Jonson his best piece of poetry.   10
For whose sake henceforth all his vows be such
   As what he loves may never like too much.

60.   AN EPITAPH ON S. P., A CHILD OF QUEEN
                  ELIZABETH'S CHAPEL

Weep with me, all you that read
 This little story;
And know, for whom a tear you shed
 Death's self is sorry.
'Twas a child that so did thrive
 In grace and feature,
As heaven and nature seemed to strive
 Which owned the creature.
Years he numbered scarce thirteen
 When fates turned cruel,   10
Yet three filled zodiacs had he been
 The stage's jewel;
And did act, what now we moan,
 Old men so duly,
As, sooth, the Parcae thought him one,
 He played so truly.
So by error, to his fate
 They all consented;
But viewing him since, alas too late,
 They have repented,   20
And have sought, to give new birth,
 In baths to steep him;
But being so much too good for earth,
 Heaven vows to keep him.

61.   EPITAPH ON ELIZABETH, L. H.

Wouldst thou hear what man can say
 In a little? Reader, stay.
Underneath this stone doth lie
 As much beauty as could die;
Which in life did harbor give
 To more virtue than doth live.
If at all she had a fault,
 Leave it buried in this vault.
One name was Elizabeth,
 Th' other let it sleep with death;   10
Fitter, where it died to tell,
 Than that it lived at all. Farewell.

62.   SONG, TO CELIA

Drink to me only with thine eyes,
    And I will pledge with mine;
Or leave a kiss but in the cup,
    And I'll not look for wine.
The thirst that from the soul doth rise
    Doth ask a drink divine;
But might I of Jove's nectar sup,
    I would not change for thine.

I sent thee late a rosy wreath,
    Not so much honoring thee,   10
As giving it a hope that there
    It could not withered be.
But thou thereon didst only breathe,
    And sent'st it back to me,
Since when it grows and smells, I swear,
    Not of itself, but thee.

63.   "QUEEN AND HUNTRESS, CHASTE AND FAIR"

Queen and huntress, chaste and fair,
Now the sun is laid to sleep,
Seated in thy silver chair
State in wonted manner keep;
    Hesperus entreats thy light,
    Goddess excellently bright.

Earth, let not thy envious shade
Dare itself to interpose;
Cynthia's shining orb was made
Heaven to clear, when day did close;   10
    Bless us then with wishèd sight,
    Goddess excellently bright.

64.   "STILL TO BE NEAT, STILL TO BE DRESSED"

Still to be neat, still to be dressed
As you were going to a feast;
Still to be powdered, still perfumed:
Lady, it is to be presumed,
Though art's hid causes are not found,
All is not sweet, all is not sound.

Give me a look, give me a face
That makes simplicity a grace;
Robes loosely flowing, hair as free:
Such sweet neglect more taketh me   10
Than all th' adulteries of art;
They strike mine eyes, but not my heart.

RICHARD CORBET, BISHOP OF OXFORD AND NORWICH (1582–1635)

65.   A PROPER NEW BALLAD, INTITULED *THE FAIRIES' FAREWELL*, OR *GOD A MERCY WILL*

To be sung or whistled, to the tune of *Meadow Brow* by the
learned, by the unlearned to the tune of *Fortune*

Farewell, rewards and fairies,
    Good housewives now may say,
For now foul sluts in dairies
    Do fare as well as they.
And though they sweep their hearths no less
    Than maids were wont to do,
Yet who of late for cleanliness
    Finds six-pence in her shoe?

Lament, lament, old abbeys,
    The faires lost command;   10
They did but change priests' babies,
    But some have changed your land,
And all your children sprung from thence
    Are now grown Puritans,
Who live as changelings ever since,
    For love of your demains.

At morning and at evening both
    You merry were and glad,
So little care of sleep or sloth
    These pretty ladies had;   20
When Tom came home from labor,
    Or Ciss to milking rose,
Then merrily went their tabor,
    And nimbly went their toes.

Witness those rings and roundelays
  Of theirs, which yet remain,
Were footed in Queen Mary's days
  On many a grassy plain;
But since of late, Elizabeth,
  And later James came in,   30
They never danced on any heath
  As when the time hath been.

By which we note the fairies
  Were of the old profession;
Their songs were Ave Maries,
  Their dances were procession;
But now, alas, they all are dead
  Or gone beyond the seas,
Or further from religion fled,
  Or else they take their ease.   40

A tell-tale in their company
  They never could endure,
And whoso kept not secretly
  Their mirth was punished sure;
It was a just and Christian deed
  To pinch such black and blue—
Oh, how the commonwealth doth need
  Such justices as you!

Now they have left our quarters,
  A register they have,   50
Who can preserve their charters,
  A man both wise and grave;
A hundred of their merry pranks
  By one that I could name
Are kept in store; con twenty thanks
  To William for the same.

To William Chourne of Staffordshire
  Give laud and praises due,
Who every meal can mend your cheer
  With tales both old and true;   60
To William all give audience,
  And pray ye for his noddle,
For all the fairies' evidence
  Were lost, if that were addle.

JOHN DONNE (1572–1631)

66.

THE GOOD-MORROW

I wonder by my troth, what thou and I
Did, till we loved? Were we not weaned till then,
But sucked on country pleasures, childishly?
Or snorted we in the seven sleepers' den?
'Twas so; but this, all pleasures fancies be.
If ever any beauty I did see,
Which I desired, and got, 'twas but a dream of thee.

And now good morrow to our waking souls,
Which watch not one another out of fear;
For love all love of other sights controls,   10
And makes one little room an everywhere.
Let sea-discoverers to new worlds have gone,
Let maps to other, worlds on worlds have shown;
Let us possess one world; each hath one, and is one.

My face in thine eye, thine in mine appears,
And true plain hearts do in the faces rest;
Where can we find two better hemispheres
Without sharp north, without declining west?
Whatever dies was not mixed equally;
If our two loves be one, or thou and I   20
Love so alike that none do slacken, none can die.

67.

WOMAN'S CONSTANCY

Now thou hast loved me one whole day,
Tomorrow when thou leav'st, what wilt thou say?
Wilt thou then antedate some new made vow?
    Or say that now
We are not just those persons which we were?
Or, that oaths made in reverential fear
Of love, and his wrath, any may forswear?
Or, as true deaths true marriages untie,
So lovers' contracts, images of those,
Bind but till sleep, death's image, them unloose?   10
    Or, your own end to justify,
For having purposed change and falsehood, you
Can have no way but falsehood to be true?

Vain lunatic, against these 'scapes I could
      Dispute and conquer, if I would;
      Which I abstain to do,
For by tomorrow, I may think so too.

68.   THE SUN RISING

      Busy old fool, unruly sun,
      Why dost thou thus
Through windows and through curtains call on us?
Must to thy motions lovers' seasons run?
      Saucy pedantic wretch, go chide
      Late schoolboys and sour prentices,
    Go tell court-huntsmen that the King will ride,
    Call country ants to harvest offices;
Love, all alike, no season knows, nor clime,
Nor hours, days, months, which are the rags of time.   10

      Thy beams, so reverend and strong
      Why shouldst thou think?
I could eclipse and cloud them with a wink,
But that I could not lose her sight so long;
      If her eyes have not blinded thine,
      Look, and to-morrow late tell me
    Whether both the'Indias of spice and mine
    Be where thou left'st them, or lie here with me.
Ask for those kings whom thou saw'st yesterday,
And thou shalt hear, all here in one bed lay.   20

      She'is all states, and all princes I;
      Nothing else is.
Princes do but play us; compared to this,
All honor's mimic, all wealth alchemy.
      Thou, sun, art half as happy'as we,
      In that the world's contracted thus;
    Thine age asks ease, and since thy duties be
    To warm the world, that's done in warming us.
Shine here to us, and thou art everywhere;
This bed thy center is, these walls thy sphere.   30

69.   THE CANONIZATION

For God's sake hold your tongue, and let me love,
    Or chide my palsy, or my gout,

My five gray hairs, or ruined fortune flout;
　　With wealth your state, your mind with arts improve,
　　　Take you a course, get you a place,
　　　Observe his honor, or his grace;
Or the king's real, or his stampèd face
　　Contemplate; what you will, approve,
　　So you will let me love.

Alas, alas, who's injured by my love?　　　　　　10
　　What merchant's ships have my sighs drowned?
Who says my tears have overflowed his ground?
　　When did my colds a forward spring remove?
　　　When did the heats which my veins fill
　　　Add one more to the plaguy bill?
Soldiers find wars, and lawyers find out still
　　Litigious men, which quarrels move,
　　Though she and I do love.

Call us what you will, we are made such by love;
　　Call her one, me another fly,　　　　　　　　20
We're tapers too, and at our own cost die,
　　And we in us find the' eagle and the dove.
　　　The phoenix riddle hath more wit
　　　By us; we two being one, are it.
So to one neutral thing both sexes fit,
　　We die and rise the same, and prove
　　Mysterious by this love.

We can die by it, if not live by love,
　　And if unfit for tombs and hearse
Our legend be, it will be fit for verse;　　　　　30
　　And if no piece of chronicle we prove,
　　　We'll build in sonnets pretty rooms;
　　　As well a well-wrought urn becomes
The greatest ashes, as half-acre tombs,
　　And by these hymns, all shall approve
　　Us canonized for love,

And thus invoke us: You whom reverend love
　　Made one another's hermitage;
You, to whom love was peace, that now is rage;
　　Who did the whole world's soul contract, and drove　　40
　　　Into the glasses of your eyes—
　　　So made such mirrors and such spies

That they did all to you epitomize,—
  Countries, towns, courts; beg from above
  A pattern of your love!

70.   LOVERS' INFINITENESS

If yet I have not all thy love,
Dear, I shall never have it all;
I cannot breathe one other sigh, to move,
Nor can entreat one other tear to fall,
And all my treasure, which should purchase thee,
Sighs, tears, and oaths, and letters, I have spent.
Yet no more can be due to me,
Than at the bargain made was meant;
If then thy gift of love were partïal,
That some to me, some should to others fall,   10
  Dear, I shall never have thee all.

Or if then thou gavest me all,
All was but all, which thou hadst then;
But if in thy heart, since, there be or shall
New love created be, by other men
Which have their stocks entire, and can in tears,
In sighs, in oaths, and letters outbid me,
This new love may beget new fears,
For this love was not vowed by thee.
And yet it was; thy gift being general,   20
The ground, thy heart is mine; whatever shall
  Grow there, dear, I should have it all.

Yet I would not have all yet:
He that hath all can have no more,
And since my love doth every day admit
New growth, thou shouldst have new rewards in store;
Thou canst not every day give me thy heart;
If thou canst give it, then thou never gavest it:
Love's riddles are, that though thy heart depart,
It stays at home, and thou with losing savest it: 30
But we will have a way more liberal
Than changing hearts,—to join them; so we shall
  Be one, and one another's all.

71.   SONG

Sweetest love, I do not go
    For weariness of thee,
Nor in hope the world can show
    A fitter love for me;
        But since that I
Must die at last, 'tis best
To use myself in jest,
        Thus by feigned deaths to die.

Yesternight the sun went hence,
    And yet is here today;   10
He hath no desire nor sense,
    Nor half so short a way.
        Then fear not me,
But believe that I shall make
Speedier journeys, since I take
        More wings and spurs than he.

O how feeble is man's power,
    That, if good fortune fall,
Cannot add another hour,
    Nor a lost hour recall.   20
        But come bad chance,
And we join to it our strength,
And we teach it art and length,
        Itself o'er us to advance.

When thou sigh'st, thou sigh'st not wind,
    But sigh'st my soul away;
When thou weep'st, unkindly kind,
    My life's blood doth decay.
        It cannot be
That thou lov'st me as thou say'st,   30
If in thine my life thou waste,
        That art the best of me.

Let not thy divining heart
    Forethink me any ill.
Destiny may take thy part
    And may thy fears fulfill:
        But think that we
Are but turned aside to sleep:

They who one another keep
Alive, ne'er parted be.   40

72.   A NOCTURNAL UPON SAINT LUCY'S DAY,
         BEING THE SHORTEST DAY

'Tis the year's midnight, and it is the day's,
Lucy's, who scarce seven hours herself unmasks;
    The sun is spent, and now his flasks
    Send forth light squibs, no constant rays;
         The world's whole sap is sunk;
The general balm th' hydroptic earth hath drunk,
Whither, as to the bed's feet, life is shrunk,
Dead and interred; yet all these seem to laugh,
Compared with me, who am their epitaph.

Study me then, you who shall lovers be   10
At the next world, that is, at the next spring;
    For I am every dead thing,
    In whom Love wrought new alchemy.
         For his art did express
A quintessence even from nothingness,
From dull privations, and lean emptiness;
He ruined me, and I am re-begot
Of absence, darkness, death—things which are not.

All others from all things draw all that's good,
Life, soul, form, spirit, whence they being have;   20
    I, by Love's limbec, am the grave
    Of all that's nothing. Oft a flood
         Have we two wept, and so
Drowned the whole world, us two; oft did we grow
To be two chaoses, when we did show
Care to aught else; and often absences
Withdrew our souls, and made us carcasses.

But I am by her death (which word wrongs her)
Of the first nothing the elíxir grown;
    Were I a man, that I were one   30
    I needs must know; I should prefer,
         If I were any beast,
Some ends, some means; yea plants, yea stones detest
And love; all, all some properties invest;

If I an ordinary nothing were,
As shadow, a light and body must be here.

But I am none; nor will my sun renew.
You lovers, for whose sake the lesser sun
  At this time to the Goat is run
    To fetch new lust, and give it you,   40
      Enjoy your summer all;
Since she enjoys her long night's festival,
Let me prepare towards her, and let me call
This hour her vigil, and her eve, since this
Both the year's and the day's deep midnight is.

73.   LOVE'S DEITY

I long to talk with some old lover's ghost,
  Who died before the god of love was born;
I cannot think that he, who then loved most,
  Sunk so low as to love one which did scorn.
But since this god produced a destiny,
And that vice-nature, custom, lets it be,
I must love her that loves not me.

Sure, they which made him god meant not so much,
  Nor he in his young godhead practised it;
But when an even flame two hearts did touch,   10
  His office was indulgently to fit
Actives to passives; correspondency
Only, his subject was; it cannot be
Love, till I love her that loves me.

But every modern god will now extend
  His vast prerogative as far as Jove;
To rage, to lust, to write too, to commend,
  All is the purlieu of the god of love.
O were we wakened by this tyranny
To un-god this child again, it could not be   20
I should love her who loves not me.

Rebel and atheist, too, why murmur I,
  As though I felt the worst that Love could do?
Love might make me leave loving, or might try
  A deeper plague, to make her love me too,
Which, since she loves before, I am loath to see;

Falsehood is worse than hate; and that must be,
If she whom I love should love me.

74.   THE FUNERAL

Whoever comes to shroud me, do not harm
          Nor question much
That subtile wreath of hair which crowns my arm;
The mystery, the sign you must not touch,
          For 'tis my outward soul,
Viceroy to that, which then to heaven being gone,
          Will leave this to control
And keep these limbs, her provinces, from dissolutiòn.

For if the sinewy thread my brain lets fall
          Through every part   10
Can tie those parts, and make me one of all,
These hairs, which upward grew, and strength and art
          Have from a better brain,
Can better do it; except she meant that I
          By this should know my pain,
As prisoners then are manacled, when they are condemned to die.

Whate'er she meant by it, bury it with me,
          For since I am
Love's martyr, it might breed idolatry
If into others' hands these relics came;   20
          As 'twas humility
To afford to it all that a soul can do,
          So 'tis some bravery,
That since you would have none of me, I bury some of you.

75.   "DEATH, BE NOT PROUD"

Death, be not proud, though some have callèd thee
Mighty and dreadful, for thou art not so;
For those whom thou think'st thou dost overthrow
Die not, poor Death, nor yet canst thou kill me.
From rest and sleep, which but thy pictures be,
Much pleasure; then from thee much more must flow,
And soonest our best men with thee do go,
Rest of their bones, and soul's delivery.
Thou art slave to fate, chance, kings, and desperate men,
And dost with poison, war, and sickness dwell;   10

And poppy or charms can make us sleep as well
And better than thy stroke; why swell'st thou then?
One short sleep past, we wake eternally,
And death shall be no more: Death, thou shalt die.

76. "BATTER MY HEART, THREE-PERSONED GOD"

Batter my heart, three-personed God, for you
As yet but knock, breathe, whine, and seek to mend;
That I may rise and stand, o'erthrow me; 'and bend
Your force to break, blow, burn, and make me new.
I, like an usurped tower to'another due,
Labor to'admit you, but oh, to no end.
Reason, your viceroy in me, me should defend,
But is captived, and proves weak or untrue.
Yet dearly'I love you, 'and would be lovèd fain,
But am betrothed unto your enemy;   10
Divorce me, 'untie or break that knot again;
Take me to you, imprison me, for I,
Except you'enthrall me, never shall be free,
Nor ever chaste, except you ravish me.

77. A HYMN TO GOD THE FATHER

Wilt thou forgive that sin where I begun,
  Which was my sin, though it were done before?
Wilt thou forgive that sin through which I run,
  And do run still, though still I do deplore?
    When thou hast done, thou hast not done,
      For I have more.

Wilt thou forgive that sin which I have won
  Others to sin, and made my sin their door?
Wilt thou forgive that sin which I did shun
  A year or two, but wallowed in a score?   10
    When thou hast done, thou hast not done,
      For I have more.

I have a sin of fear, that when I have spun
  My last thread, I shall perish on the shore;
But swear by thyself, that at my death thy Son
  Shall shine as he shines now, and heretofore;
    And having done that, thou hast done:
      I fear no more.

GEORGE HERBERT (1593–1633)

78. ### THE BRITISH CHURCH

I joy, dear mother, when I view
Thy perfect lineaments, and hue
   Both sweet and bright.
Beauty in thee takes up her place,
And dates her letters from thy face,
   When she doth write.

A fine aspect in fit array,
Neither too mean nor yet too gay,
   Shows who is best.
Outlandish looks may not compare,   10
For all they either painted are,
   Or else undressed.

She on the hills which wantonly
Allureth all, in hope to be
   By her preferred,
Hath kissed so long her painted shrines,
That ev'n her face by kissing shines,
   For her reward.

She in the valley is so shy
Of dressing, that her hair doth lie   20
   About her ears;
While she avoids her neighbor's pride,
She wholly goes on th' other side,
   And nothing wears.

But, dearest mother, what those miss,
The mean, thy praise and glory is
   And long may be.
Blessed be God, whose love it was
To double-moat thee with his grace,
   And none but thee.   30

79. ### THE CHURCH FLOOR

Mark you the floor? That square and speckled stone,
   Which looks so firm and strong,
     Is Patience;

And th' other black and grave, wherewith each one
   Is checkered all along,
     Humility.

The gentle rising, which on either hand
   Leads to the choir above,
     Is Confidence.

But the sweet cement, which in one sure band   10
   Ties the whole frame, is Love
     And Charity.

   Hither sometimes sin steals, and stains
   The marble's neat and curious veins;
But all is cleansèd when the marble weeps.
   Sometimes death, puffing at the door,
   Blows all the dust about the floor;
But while he thinks to spoil the room, he sweeps.
   Blest be the architect whose art
   Could build so strong in a weak heart.   20

80.   REDEMPTION

Having been tenant long to a rich lord,
   Not thriving, I resolvèd to be bold,
   And made a suit unto him to afford
A new small-rented lease and cancel th' old.
In heaven at his manor I him sought.
   They told me there that he was lately gone
   About some land which he had dearly bought
Long since on earth, to take possession.
I straight returned, and knowing his great birth,
   Sought him accordingly in great resorts,   10
   In cities, theaters, gardens, parks, and courts.
At length I heard a ragged noise and mirth
   Of thieves and murderers; there I him espied,
   Who straight, Your suit is granted, said, and died.

81.   LOVE

Love bade me welcome, yet my soul drew back,
   Guilty of dust and sin.
But quick-eyed Love, observing me grow slack
   From my first entrance in,

Drew nearer to me, sweetly questioning
    If I lacked anything.

A guest, I answered, worthy to be here.
    Love said, You shall be he.
I, the unkind, the ungrateful? ah, my dear,
    I cannot look on thee.   10
Love took my hand and smiling did reply,
    Who made the eyes but I?

Truth, Lord, but I have marred them; let my shame
    Go where it doth deserve.
And know you not, says Love, who bore the blame?
    My dear, then I will serve.
You must sit down, says Love, and taste my meat.
    So I did sit and eat.

82.   THE COLLAR

    I struck the board and cried, No more!
            I will abroad.
    What? Shall I ever sigh and pine?
My lines and life are free, free as the road,
    Loose as the wind, as large as store.
            Shall I be still in suit?
    Have I no harvest but a thorn
    To let me blood, and not restore
What I have lost with cordial fruit?
            Sure there was wine   10
    Before my sighs did dry it; there was corn
        Before my tears did drown it.
    Is the year only lost to me?
        Have I no bays to crown it?
No flowers, no garlands gay? All blasted?
            All wasted?
    Not so, my heart! But there is fruit,
            And thou hast hands.
        Recover all thy sigh-blown age
On double pleasures. Leave thy cold dispute   20
Of what is fit and not. Forsake thy cage,
        Thy rope of sands,
Which petty thoughts have made, and made to thee
    Good cable, to enforce and draw,

And be thy law,
While thou didst wink and wouldst not see.
Away! Take heed!
I will abroad.
Call in thy death's head there. Tie up thy fears.
He that forbears   30
To suit and serve his need
Deserves his load.
But as I raved and grew more fierce and wild
At every word,
Me thought I heard one calling, Child!
And I replied, My Lord.

83   VIRTUE

Sweet day, so cool, so calm, so bright,
The bridal of the earth and sky;
The dew shall weep thy fall to-night,
            For thou must die.

Sweet rose, whose hue angry and brave
Bids the rash gazer wipe his eye;
Thy root is ever in its grave,
            And thou must die.

Sweet spring, full of sweet days and roses,
A box where sweets compacted lie;   10
My music shows ye have your closes,
            And all must die.

Only a sweet and virtuous soul,
Like seasoned timber, never gives;
But though the whole world turn to coal,
            Then chiefly lives.

RICHARD CRASHAW (1612–1649)

84.   A SONG

Lord, when the sense of thy sweet grace
Sends up my soul to seek thy face,
Thy blessed eyes breed such desire
I die in love's delicious fire.

O love, I am thy sacrifice.
Be still triumphant, blessed eyes;
Still shine on me, fair suns! that I
Still may behold, though still I die.

Though still I die, I live again,
Still longing so to be still slain;   10
So gainful is such loss of breath,
I die even in desire of death.
  Still live in me this loving strife
Of living death and dying life;
For while thou sweetly slayest me,
Dead to myself, I live in thee.

HENRY VAUGHAN (1622–1695)

85.   THE WATERFALL

With what deep murmurs through time's silent stealth
Doth thy transparent, cool, and wat'ry wealth
          Here flowing fall,
          And chide, and call,
As if his liquid, loose retínue stayed
Ling'ring, and were of this steep place afraid,
          The common pass
          Where, clear as glass,
          All must descend—
          Not to an end,   10
But quickened by this deep and rocky grave,
Rise to a longer course more bright and brave.

          Dear stream! dear bank, where often I
          Have sat and pleased my pensive eye,
          Why, since each drop of thy quick store
          Runs thither whence it flowed before,
          Should poor souls fear a shade or night,
          Who came, sure, from a sea of light?
          Or since those drops are all sent back
          So sure to thee, that none doth lack,   20
          Why should frail flesh doubt any more
          That what God takes he'll not restore?

O useful element and clear!
My sacred wash and cleanser here,
My first consigner unto those
Fountains of life where the Lamb goes!
What sublime truths and wholesome themes
Lodge in thy mystical deep streams!
Such as dull man can never find
Unless that spirit lead his mind   30
Which first upon thy face did move,
And hatched all with his quick'ning love.
As this loud brook's incessant fall
In streaming rings restagnates all,
Which reach by course the bank, and then
Are no more seen, just so pass men.
O my invisible estate,
My glorious liberty, still late!
Thou art the channel my soul seeks,
Not this with cataracts and creeks.   40

86.   THE WORLD

I saw eternity the other night
Like a great ring of pure and endless light,
        All calm as it was bright;
And round beneath it, time in hours, days, years,
        Driv'n by the spheres,
Like a vast shadow moved, in which the world
        And all her train were hurled.
The doting lover in his quaintest strain
        Did there complain;
Near him his lute, his fancy, and his flights,   10
        Wit's sour delights,
With gloves and knots, the silly snares of pleasure,
        Yet his dear treasure,
All scattered lay, while he his eyes did pore
        Upon a flower.

The darksome statesman, hung with weights and woe,
Like a thick midnight fog moved there so slow
        He did not stay, nor go;
Condemning thoughts, like sad eclipses, scowl
        Upon his soul,   20

And clouds of crying witnesses without
  Pursued him with one shout;
Yet digged the mole, and lest his ways be found
  Worked underground,
Where he did clutch his prey, but One did see
  That policy;
Churches and altars fed him; perjuries
  Were gnats and flies;
It rained about him blood and tears, but he
  Drank them as free.   30

The fearful miser on a heap of rust
Sat pining all his life there, did scarce trust
  His own hands with the dust,
Yet would not place one piece above, but lives
  In fear of thieves.
Thousands there were as frantic as himself,
  And hugged each one his pelf.
The downright epicure placed heav'n in sense,
  And scorned pretense;
While others, slipped into a wide excess, 40
  Said little less;
The weaker sort slight trivial wares enslave,
  Who think them brave;
And poor despisèd truth sat counting by
  Their victory.

Yet some, who all this while did weep and sing,
And sing and weep, soared up into the ring;
  But most would use no wing.
O fools, said I, thus to prefer dark night
  Before true light,   50
To live in grots and caves, and hate the day
  Because it shows the way,
The way which from this dead and dark abode
  Leads up to God,
A way where you might tread the sun, and be
  More bright than he.
But as I did their madness so discuss,
  One whispered thus:
This ring the bridegroom did for none provide
  But for his bride.   60

87.   "THEY ARE ALL GONE INTO THE WORLD
                    OF LIGHT"

They are all gone into the world of light!
   And I alone sit lingering here;
Their very memory is fair and bright,
   And my sad thoughts doth clear.

It glows and glitters in my cloudy breast
   Like stars upon some gloomy grove,
Or those faint beams in which this hill is dressed
   After the sun's remove.

I see them walking in an air of glory,
   Whose light doth trample on my days,   10
My days, which are at best but dull and hoary,
   Mere glimmering and decays.

O holy hope and high humility,
   High as the heavens above!
These are your walks, and you have showed them me
   To kindle my cold love.

Dear, beauteous death! the jewel of the just!
   Shining no where but in the dark;
What mysteries do lie beyond thy dust,
   Could man outlook that mark!   20

He that hath found some fledged bird's nest may know
   At first sight if the bird be flown;
But what fair well or grove he sings in now,
   That is to him unknown.

And yet, as angels in some brighter dreams
   Call to the soul when man doth sleep,
So some strange thoughts transcend our wonted themes,
   And into glory peep.

If a star were confined into a tomb,
   Her captive flames must needs burn there;   30
But when the hand that locked her up gives room,
   She'll shine through all the sphere.

O Father of eternal life, and all
   Created glories under thee,

Resume thy spirit from this world of thrall
   Into true liberty!

Either disperse these mists which blot and fill
   My pérspective, still, as they pass,
Or else remove me hence unto that hill
   Where I shall need no glass.   40

THOMAS TRAHERNE (1636?–1674)

88.   WONDER

How like an angel came I down!
   How bright are all things here!
When first among his works I did appear,
   Oh, how their glory did me crown!
The world resembled his eternity,
      In which my soul did walk;
   And ev'rything that I did see
      Did with me talk.

The skies in their magnificence,
   The lovely lively air,   10
Oh, how divine, how soft, how sweet, how fair!
   The stars did entertain my sense,
And all the works of God so bright and pure,
      So rich and great, did seem,
   As if they ever must endure
      In my esteem.

A native health and innocence
   Within my bones did grow,
And while my God did all his glories show,
   I felt a vigor in my sense   20
That was all spirit; I within did flow
      With seas of life like wine;
   I nothing in the world did know,
      But 'twas divine.

Harsh rugged objects were concealed;
   Oppressions, tears, and cries,
Sins, griefs, complaints, dissensions, weeping eyes,

Were hid, and only things revealed
Which heavenly spirits and the angels prize:
    The state of innocence   30
And bliss, not trades and poverties,
    Did fill my sense.

The streets seemed paved with golden stones,
    The boys and girls all mine—
To me how did their lovely faces shine!
    The sons of men all holy ones,
In joy and beauty then appeared to me;
    And ev'rything I found,
    While like an angel I did see,
    Adorned the ground.   40

Rich diamonds, and pearl, and gold
    Might ev'rywhere be seen;
Rare colors, yellow, blue, red, white, and green,
    Mine eyes on ev'ry side behold;
All that I saw a wonder did appear,
    Amazement was my bliss,
    That and my wealth met ev'rywhere;
    No joy to this!

Cursed, ill-devised proprieties,
    With envy, avarice,   50
And fraud, those fiends that spoil ev'n paradise,
    Were not the object of mine eyes;
Nor hedges, ditches, limits, narrow bounds,
    I dreamt not aught of those,
    But in surveying all men's grounds
    I found repose.

For property itself was mine,
    And hedges, ornaments,
Walls, houses, coffers, and their rich contents,
    To make me rich combine.   60
Clothes, costly jewels, laces, I esteemed
    My wealth, by others worn,
    For me they all to wear them seemed,
    When I was born.

ANDREW MARVELL (1621–1678)

89.   THE GARDEN

How vainly men themselves amaze
To win the palm, the oak, or bays,
And their uncessant labors see
Crowned from some single herb or tree,
Whose short and narrow vergèd shade
Does prudently their toils upbraid;
While all flowers and all trees do close
To weave the garlands of repose.

Fair quiet, have I found thee here,
And innocence, thy sister dear!   10
Mistaken long, I sought you then
In busy companies of men;
Your sacred plants, if here below,
Only among the plants will grow.
Society is all but rude,
To this delicious solitude.

No white nor red was ever seen
So am'rous as this lovely green.
Fond lovers, cruel as their flame,
Cut in these trees their mistress' name;   20
Little, alas, they know or heed
How far these beauties hers exceed!
Fair trees! wheres'e'er your barks I wound,
No name shall but your own be found.

When we have run our passion's heat,
Love hither makes his best retreat.
The gods that mortal beauty chase,
Still in a tree did end their race:
Apollo hunted Daphne so,
Only that she might laurel grow;   30
And Pan did after Syrinx speed,
Not as a nymph, but for a reed.

What wond'rous life in this I lead!
Ripe apples drop about my head;

The luscious clusters of the vine
Upon my mouth do crush their wine;
The nectarine and curious peach
Into my hands themselves do reach;
Stumbling on melons as I pass,
Ensnared with flowers, I fall on grass.   40

Meanwhile, the mind, from pleasure less,
Withdraws into its happiness;
The mind, that ocean where each kind
Does straight its own resemblance find,
Yet it creates, transcending these,
Far other worlds and other seas,
Annihilating all that's made
To a green thought in a green shade.

Here at the fountain's sliding foot,
Or at some fruit tree's mossy root,   50
Casting the body's vest aside,
My soul into the boughs does glide:
There like a bird it sits and sings,
Then whets, then combs its silver wings;
And till prepared for longer flight,
Waves in its plumes the various light.

Such was that happy garden-state,
While man there walked without a mate;
After a place so pure and sweet,
What other help could yet be meet!   60
But 'twas beyond a mortal's share
To wander solitary there:
Two paradises 'twere, in one,
To live in paradise alone.

How well the skillful gard'ner drew
Of flowers and herbs this dial new,
Where, from above, the milder sun
Does through a fragrant zodiac run;
And as it works, th' industrious bee
Computes its time as well as we.   70
How could such sweet and wholesome hours
Be reckoned but with herbs and flowers?

90.   BERMUDAS

    Where the remote Bermudas ride
In th' ocean's bosom unespied,
From a small boat that rowed along,
The list'ning winds received this song:
    What should we do but sing his praise
That led us through the wat'ry maze
Unto an isle so long unknown,
And yet far kinder than our own?
Where he the huge sea-monsters wracks,
That lift the deep upon their backs,   10
He lands us on a grassy stage,
Safe from the storms and prelates' rage.
He gave us this eternal spring
Which here enamels everything,
And sends the fowls to us in care,
On daily visits through the air.
He hangs in shades the orange bright,
Like golden lamps in a green night;
And does in the pomegranates close
Jewels more rich than Ormus shows.   20
He makes the figs our mouths to meet
And throws the melons at our feet,
But apples plants of such a price,
No tree could ever bear them twice.
With cedars, chosen by his hand,
From Lebanon, he stores the land,
And makes the hollow seas that roar
Proclaim the ambergris on shore.
He cast, of which we rather boast,
The Gospel's pearl upon our coast,   30
And in these rocks for us did frame
A temple, where to sound his name.
Oh, let our voice his praise exalt,
Till it arrive at heaven's vault;
Which thence, perhaps, rebounding, may
Echo beyond the Mexic Bay.
    Thus sung they in the English boat
An holy and a cheerful note,
And all the way, to guide their chime,
With falling oars they kept the time.   40

91.   THE PICTURE OF LITTLE T. C. IN A
              PROSPECT OF FLOWERS

See with what simplicity
This nymph begins her golden days!
In the green grass she loves to lie,
And there with her fair aspect tames
The wilder flowers, and gives them names;
But only with the roses plays,
     And them does tell
What color best becomes them, and what smell.

Who can foretell for what high cause
This darling of the gods was born?   10
Yet this is she whose chaster laws
The wanton Love shall one day fear,
And under her command severe
See his bow broke and ensigns torn.
     Happy, who can
Appease this virtuous enemy of man!

O then let me in time compound,
And parley with those conquering eyes,
Ere they have tried their force to wound,
Ere with their glancing wheels they drive   20
In triumph over hearts that strive,
And them that yield but more despise.
     Let me be laid
Where I may see thy glories from some shade.

Meantime, whilst every verdant thing
Itself does at thy beauty charm,
Reform the errors of the spring:
Make that the tulips may have share
Of sweetness, seeing they are fair;
And roses of their thorns disarm;   30
     But most procure
That violets may a longer age endure.

But, O young beauty of the woods,
Whom nature courts with fruits and flowers,
Gather the flowers, but spare the buds,
Lest Flora, angry at thy crime.

To kill her infants in their prime,
Do quickly make th' example yours;
    And ere we see,
Nip in the blossom all our hopes and thee.   40

92.   THE DEFINITION OF LOVE

My love is of a birth as rare
As 'tis for object strange and high:
It was begotten by despair
Upon impossibility.

Magnanimous despair alone
Could show me so divine a thing,
Where feeble hope could ne'er have flown,
But vainly flapped its tinsel wing.

And yet I quickly might arrive
Where my extended soul is fixed,   10
But fate does iron wedges drive,
And always crowds itself betwixt.

For fate with jealous eye does see
Two perfect loves, nor lets them close;
Their union would her ruin be,
And her tyrannic power depose.

And therefore her decrees of steel
Us as the distant poles have placed,
(Though love's whole world on us doth wheel)
Not by themselves to be embraced;   20

Unless the giddy heaven fall,
And earth some new convulsion tear,
And, us to join, the world should all
Be cramped into a planisphere.

As lines, so loves oblique may well
Themselves in every angle greet;
But ours so truly parallel,
Though infinite, can never meet.

Therefore the love which us doth bind,
But fate so enviously debars,   30
Is the conjunction of the mind,
And opposition of the stars.

93.   TO HIS COY MISTRESS

Had we but world enough, and time,
This coyness, lady, were no crime.
We would sit down and think which way
To walk, and pass our long love's day;
Thou by the Indian Ganges' side
Shouldst rubies find; I by the tide
Of Humber would complain. I would
Love you ten years before the Flood;
And you should, if you please, refuse
Till the conversion of the Jews.   10
My vegetable love should grow
Vaster than empires, and more slow.
An hundred years should go to praise
Thine eyes, and on thy forehead gaze;
Two hundred to adore each breast,
But thirty thousand to the rest;
An age at least to every part,
And the last age should show your heart.
For, lady, you deserve this state,
Nor would I love at lower rate.   20
    But at my back I always hear
Time's wingèd chariot hurrying near;
And yonder all before us lie
Deserts of vast eternity.
Thy beauty shall no more be found,
Nor in thy marble vault shall sound
My echoing song; then worms shall try
That long preserved virginity,
And your quaint honor turn to dust,
And into ashes all my lust.   30
The grave's a fine and private place,
But none, I think, do there embrace.
    Now therefore, while the youthful hue
Sits on thy skin like morning dew,
And while thy willing soul transpires
At every pore with instant fires,
Now let us sport us while we may;
And now, like am'rous birds of prey,
Rather at once our time devour,
Than languish in his slow-chapped power.   4c

Let us roll all our strength, and all
Our sweetness, up into one ball;
And tear our pleasures with rough strife
Thorough the iron gates of life.
Thus, though we cannot make our sun
Stand still, yet we will make him run.

ROBERT HERRICK (1591–1674)

94.   THE ARGUMENT OF HIS BOOK

I sing of brooks, of blossoms, birds, and bowers,
Of April, May, of June, and July flowers;
I sing of may-poles, hock-carts, wassails, wakes,
Of bridegrooms, brides, and of their bridal cakes;
I write of youth, of love, and have access
By these to sing of cleanly wantonness;
I sing of dews, of rains, and piece by piece
Of balm, of oil, of spice, and ambergris;
I sing of times trans-shifting, and I write
How roses first came red, and lilies white;   10
I write of groves, of twilights, and I sing
The court of Mab, and of the Fairy King;
I write of hell; I sing, and ever shall,
Of heaven, and hope to have it after all.

95.   CHERRY-RIPE

Cherry-ripe, ripe, ripe, I cry,
Full and fair ones; come and buy.
If so be you ask me where
They do grow, I answer: There,

Where my Julia's lips do smile;
There's the land, or cherry-isle,
Whose plantations fully show
All the year where cherries grow.

96.   DELIGHT IN DISORDER

A sweet disorder in the dress
Kindles in clothes a wantonness;
A lawn about the shoulders thrown
Into a fine distraction,

An erring lace, which here and there
Enthralls the crimson stomacher,
A cuff neglectful, and thereby
Ribands to flow confusedly,
A winning wave, deserving note,
In the tempestuous petticoat,   10
A careless shoe-string, in whose tie
I see a wild civility,
Do more bewitch me than when art
Is too precise in every part.

97.   TO THE VIRGINS, TO MAKE MUCH OF TIME

Gather ye rosebuds while ye may,
    Old time is still a-flying,
And this same flower that smiles to-day,
    Tomorrow will be dying.

The glorious lamp of heaven, the sun,
    The higher he's a-getting,
The sooner will his race be run,
    And nearer he's to setting.

That age is best which is the first,
    When youth and blood are warmer;   10
But being spent, the worse, and worst
    Times still succeed the former.

Then be not coy, but use your time,
    And while ye may, go marry;
For having lost but once your prime,
    You may for ever tarry.

98.   TO DAFFODILS

Fair daffodils, we weep to see
    You haste away so soon;
As yet the early-rising sun
    Has not attained his noon.
       Stay, stay,
    Until the hasting day
       Has run
     But to the even-song;
And, having prayed together, we
    Will go with you along.   10

We have short time to stay, as you;
  We have as short a spring,
As quick a growth to meet decay,
  As you, or anything.
     We die
  As your hours do, and dry
     Away
Like to the summer's rain,
Or as the pearls of morning's dew,
  Ne'er to be found again.   20

99. THE HOCK-CART, OR HARVEST HOME; TO THE RIGHT HONORABLE MILDMAY, EARL OF WESTMORLAND

Come, sons of summer, by whose toil
We are the lords of wine and oil;
By whose tough labors and rough hands,
We rip up first, then reap our lands.
Crowned with the ears of corn, now come,
And to the pipe sing harvest home.
Come forth, my lord, and see the cart
Dressed up with all the country art.
See here a maukin, there a sheet
As spotless pure as it is sweet;   10
The horses, mares, and frisking fillies,
Clad all in linen, white as lilies;
The harvest swains and wenches bound
For joy to see the hock-cart crowned.
About the cart hear how the rout
Of rural younglings raise the shout,
Pressing before, some coming after:
Those with a shout, and these with laughter.
Some bless the cart; some kiss the sheaves;
Some prank them up with oaken leaves;   20
Some cross the fill-horse; some with great
Devotion stroke the home-borne wheat;
While other rustics, less attent
To prayers than to merriment,
Run after with their breeches rent.
Well on, brave boys, to your lord's hearth,

Glitt'ring with fire, where for your mirth
Ye shall see first the large and chief
Foundation of your feast, fat beef,
With upper stories, mutton, veal,   30
And bacon, which makes full the meal;
With sev'ral dishes standing by,
As here a custard, there a pie,
And here all-tempting frumenty.
And for to make the merry cheer,
If smirking wine be wanting here,
There's that which drowns all care, stout beer,
Which freely drink to your lord's health;
Then to the plow, the commonwealth,
Next to your flails, your fans, your fats;   40
Then to the maids with wheaten hats;
To the rough sickle and crook'd scythe,
Drink, frolic boys, till all be blithe.
Feed and grow fat, and as ye eat
Be mindful that the lab'ring neat,
As you, may have their fill of meat.
And know, besides, ye must revoke
The patient ox unto his yoke,
And all go back unto the plow
And harrow, though they're hanged up now.   50
And, you must know, your lord's word's true:
Feed him you must, whose food fills you,
And that this pleasure is like rain,
Not sent ye for to drown your pain
But for to make it spring again.

100.   AN ODE FOR BEN JONSON

Ah Ben!
Say how, or when
Shall we thy guests
Meet at those lyric feasts
Made at the Sun,
The Dog, the Triple Tun,
Where we such clusters had
As made us nobly wild, not mad;
And yet each verse of thine
Outdid the meat, outdid the frolic wine.   10

        My Ben!
     Or come again,
     Or send to us
   Thy wit's great overplus;
     But teach us yet
    Wisely to husband it.
   Lest we that talent spend,
  And having once brought to an end
   That precious stock, the store
Of such a wit the world should have no more.   20

101.   HIS LITANY TO THE HOLY SPIRIT

In the hour of my distress,
When temptations me oppress,
And when I my sins confess,
    Sweet Spirit, comfort me!

When I lie within my bed,
Sick in heart and sick in head,
And with doubts discomforted,
    Sweet Spirit, comfort me!

When the house doth sigh and weep,
And the world is drowned in sleep,   10
Yet mine eyes the watch do keep,
    Sweet Spirit, comfort me!

When the artless doctor sees
No one hope, but of his fees,
And his skill runs on the lees,
    Sweet Spirit, comfort me!

When his potion and his pill
Has or none or little skill,
Meet for nothing but to kill,
    Sweet Spirit, comfort me!   20

When the passing bell doth toll,
And the furies in a shoal
Come to fright a parting soul,
    Sweet Spirit, comfort me!

When the tapers now burn blue,
And the comforters are few,

And that number more than true,
    Sweet Spirit, comfort me!

When the priest his last hath prayed,
And I nod to what is said,   30
'Cause my speech is now decayed,
    Sweet Spirit, comfort me!

When, God knows, I'm tossed about,
Either with despair, or doubt,
Yet before the glass be out,
    Sweet Spirit, comfort me!

When the tempter me pursu'th
With the sins of all my youth,
And half damns me with untruth,
    Sweet Spirit, comfort me!   40

When the flames and hellish cries
Fright mine ears, and fright mine eyes,
And all terrors me surprise,
    Sweet Spirit, comfort me!

When the judgment is revealed,
And that opened which was sealed,
When to thee i have appealed,
    Sweet Spirit, comfort me!

102.   A THANKSGIVING TO GOD FOR HIS HOUSE

Lord, thou hast given me a cell
    Wherein to dwell,
A little house, whose humble roof
    Is weather-proof;
Under the spars of which I lie
    Both soft and dry,
Where thou my chamber for to ward
    Hast set a guard
Of harmless thoughts, to watch and keep
    Me while I sleep.   10
Low is my porch, as is my fate,
    Both void of state;
And yet the threshold of my door
    Is worn by'th' poor,

Who thither come and freely get
    Good words or meat;
Like as my parlor, so my hall
    And kitchen's small;
A little buttery, and therein
    A little bin   20
Which keeps my little loaf of bread
    Unchipped, unflead.

Some brittle sticks of thorn or briar
    Make me a fire,
Close by whose living coal I sit,
    And glow like it.

Lord, I confess, too, when I dine,
    The pulse is thine,
And all those other bits that be
    There placed by thee: 30
The worts, the purslain, and the mess
    Of water-cress,
Which of thy kindness thou hast sent;
    And my content
Makes those, and my beloved beet,
    To be more sweet.

'Tis thou that crown'st my glittering hearth
    With guiltless mirth;
And giv'st me wassail bowls to drink,
    Spiced to the brink.   40

Lord, 'tis thy plenty-dropping hand
    That soils my land,
And giv'st me for my bushel sown
    Twice ten for one.

Thou mak'st my teeming hen to lay
    Her egg each day;
Besides my healthful ewes to bear
    Me twins each year,
The while the conduits of my kine
    Run cream for wine.   50

All these, and better, thou dost send
    Me to this end:
That I should render, for my part,
    A thankful heart,

> Which, fired with incense, I resign
>   As wholly thine;
> But the acceptance, that must be,
>   My Christ, by thee.

THOMAS CAREW (1594?–1639?)

103.   THE SPRING

Now that the winter's gone, the earth hath lost
Her snow-white robes, and now no more the frost
Candies the grass, or casts an icy cream
Upon the silver lake or crystal stream;
But the warm sun thaws the benumbèd earth,
And makes it tender; gives a sacred birth
To the dead swallow; wakes in hollow tree
The drowsy cuckoo and the humble-bee.
Now do a choir of chirping minstrels bring
In triumph to the world the youthful spring.   10
The valleys, hills, and woods in rich array
Welcome the coming of the longed-for May.
Now all things smile, only my love doth lour;
Nor hath the scalding noonday sun the power
To melt that marble ice, which still doth hold
Her heart congealed, and makes her pity cold.
The ox, which lately did for shelter fly
Into the stall, doth now securely lie
In open fields; and love no more is made
By the fireside, but in the cooler shade   20
Amyntas now doth with his Chloris sleep
Under a sycamore, and all things keep
Time with the season; only she doth carry
June in her eyes, in her heart January.

104.   A SONG

> Ask me no more where Jove bestows,
> When June is past, the fading rose;
> For in your beauty's orient deep
> These flowers, as in their causes, sleep.
>
> Ask me no more whither doth stray
> The golden atoms of the day;

For in pure love heaven did prepare
Those powders to enrich your hair.

Ask me no more whither doth haste
The nightingale when May is past;   10
For in your sweet dividing throat
She winters, and keeps warm her note.

Ask me no more where those stars light
That downwards fall in dead of night;
For in your eyes they sit, and there
Fixèd become as in their sphere.

Ask me no more if east or west
The phoenix builds her spicy nest;
For unto you at last she flies,
And in your fragrant bosom dies.   20

SIR JOHN SUCKLING (1609–1642)

105.   SONG

Why so pale and wan, fond lover?
    Prithee, why so pale?
Will, when looking well can't move her,
    Looking ill prevail?
    Prithee, why so pale?

Why so dull and mute, young sinner?
    Prithee, why so mute?
Will, when speaking well can't win her,
    Saying nothing do't?
    Prithee, why so mute?   10

Quit, quit, for shame, this will not move,
    This cannot take her.
If of herself she will not love,
    Nothing can make her.
    The devil take her!

106.   "OUT UPON IT! I HAVE LOVED"

Out upon it! I have loved
    Three whole days together;

And am like to love three more,
 If it prove fair weather.

Time shalt moult away his wings,
 Ere he shall discover
In the whole wide world again
 Such a constant lover.

But the spite on 't is, no praise
 Is due at all to me;   10
Love with me had made no stays,
 Had it any been but she.

Had it any been but she,
 And that very face,
There had been at least ere this
 A dozen dozen in her place.

RICHARD LOVELACE (1618–1657?)

107.   TO ALTHEA, FROM PRISON

When Love with unconfinèd wings
 Hovers within my gates,
And my divine Althea brings
 To whisper at the grates;
When I lie tangled in her hair,
 And fettered to her eye,
The gods that wanton in the air
 Know no such liberty.

When flowing cups run swiftly round
 With no allaying Thames,   10
Our careless heads with roses bound,
 Our hearts with loyal flames;
When thirsty grief in wine we steep,
 When healths and draughts go free,
Fishes that tipple in the deep
 Know no such liberty.

When, like committed linnets, I
 With shriller throat shall sing
The sweetness, mercy, majesty,
 And glories of my king;   20

When I shall voice aloud, how good
  He is, how great should be,
Enlargèd winds that curl the flood
  Know no such liberty.

Stone walls do not a prison make
  Nor iron bars a cage;
Minds innocent and quiet take
  That for an hermitage;
If I have freedom in my love,
  And in my soul am free,   30
Angels alone that soar above
  Enjoy such liberty.

JOHN MILTON (1608–1674)

108.   ON THE MORNING OF CHRIST'S
NATIVITY

I

This is the month, and this the happy morn,
Wherein the Son of Heaven's eternal King,
Of wedded Maid and Virgin Mother born,
Our great redemption from above did bring;
For so the holy sages once did sing,
  That he our deadly forfeit should release,
And with his Father work us a perpetual peace.

II

That glorious form, that light unsufferable,
And that far-beaming blaze of majesty,
Wherewith he wont at Heaven's high council-table   10
To sit the midst of Trinal Unity,
He laid aside; and here with us to be,
  Forsook the courts of everlasting day,
And chose with us a darksome house of mortal clay.

III

Say, Heavenly Muse, shall not thy sacred vein
Afford a present to the infant God?
Hast thou no verse, no hymn, or solemn strain,
To welcome him to this his new abode,

Now while the Heaven, by the sun's team untrod,
  Hath took no print of the approaching light,   20
And all the spangled host keep watch in squadrons bright?

IV

See how from far upon the eastern road
The star-led wizards haste with odors sweet!
O run, prevent them with thy humble ode,
And lay it lowly at his blessed feet;
Have thou the honor first thy Lord to greet,
  And join thy voice unto the angel choir,
From out his secret altar touched with hallowed fire.

THE HYMN

I

It was the winter wild
While the Heaven-born child   30
  All meanly wrapped in the rude manger lies;
Nature in awe to him
Had doffed her gaudy trim,
  With her great Master so to sympathize:
It was no season then for her
To wanton with the sun, her lusty paramour.

II

Only with speeches fair
She woos the gentle air
  To hide her guilty front with innocent snow,
And on her naked shame,   40
Pollute with sinful blame,
  The saintly veil of maiden white to throw,
Confounded, that her Maker's eyes
Should look so near upon her foul deformities.

III

But he her fears to cease,
Sent down the meek-eyed Peace;
  She, crowned with olive green, came softly sliding
Down through the turning sphere,
His ready harbinger,
  With turtle wing the amorous clouds dividing,   50
And waving wide her myrtle wand,
She strikes a universal peace through sea and land.

IV

No war or battle's sound
Was heard the world around:
 The idle spear and shield were high uphung;
The hookèd chariot stood
Unstained with hostile blood;
 The trumpet spake not to the armèd throng;
And kings sat still with awful eye,
As if they surely knew their sovran Lord was by. 60

V

But peaceful was the night
Wherein the Prince of Light
 His reign of peace upon the earth began:
The winds, with wonder whist,
Smoothly the waters kissed,
 Whispering new joys to the mild ocëan,
Who now hath quite forgot to rave,
While birds of calm sit brooding on the charmèd wave.

VI

The stars with deep amaze
Stand fixed in steadfast gaze, 70
 Bending one way their precious influence,
And will not take their flight
For all the morning light,
 Or Lucifer that often warned them thence;
But in their glimmering orbs did glow,
Until their Lord himself bespake, and bid them go.

VII

And though the shady gloom
Had given day her room,
 The sun himself withheld his wonted speed,
And hid his head for shame, 80
As his inferior flame
 The new-enlightened world no more should need;
He saw a greater sun appear
Than his bright throne or burning axletree could bear.

VIII

The shepherds on the lawn,
Or ere the point of dawn,

Sat simply chatting in a rustic row;
Full little thought they than
That the mighty Pan
    Was kindly come to live with them below;   90
Perhaps their loves, or else their sheep,
Was all that did their silly thoughts so busy keep.

IX

When such music sweet
Their hearts and ears did greet
    As never was by mortal finger strook,
Divinely warbled voice
Answering the stringèd noise,
    As all their souls in blissful rapture took;
The air, such pleasure loth to lose,
With thousand echoes still prolongs each heavenly close.   100

X

Nature that heard such sound
Beneath the hollow round
    Of Cynthia's seat, the airy region thrilling,
Now was almost won
To think her part was done,
    And that her reign had here its last fulfilling;
She knew such harmony alone
Could hold all Heaven and Earth in happier union.

XI

At last surrounds their sight
A globe of circular light,   110
    That with long beams the shame-faced night arrayed;
The helmed Cherubim
And sworded Seraphim
    Are seen in glittering ranks with wings displayed,
Harping in loud and solemn choir,
With unexpressive notes to Heaven's new-born Heir.

XII

Such music (as 'tis said)
Before was never made,
    But when of old the sons of morning sung,
While the Creator great   120
His constellations set,

And the well-balanced world on hinges hung,
And cast the dark foundations deep,
And bid the weltering waves their oozy channel keep.

XIII

Ring out, ye crystal spheres,
Once bless our human ears
  (If ye have power to touch our senses so),
And let your silver chime
Move in melodious time,
  And let the bass of Heaven's deep organ blow;   130
And with your ninefold harmony
Make up full consort to the angelic symphony.

XIV

For if such holy song
Enwrap our fancy long,
  Time will run back and fetch the age of gold,
And speckled vanity
Will sicken soon and die,
  And leprous sin will melt from earthly mold,
And Hell itself will pass away,
And leave her dolorous mansions to the peering day.   140

XV

Yea, Truth and Justice then
Will down return to men,
  Orbed in a rainbow; and, like glories wearing,
Mercy will sit between,
Throned in celestial sheen,
  With radiant feet the tissued clouds down steering;
And Heaven, as at some festival,
Will open wide the gates of her high palace hall.

XVI

But wisest Fate says no,
This must not yet be so;   150
  The Babe lies yet in smiling infancy,
That on the bitter cross
Must redeem our loss,
  So both himself and us to glorify;
Yet first to those ychained in sleep,
The wakeful trump of doom must thunder through the deep,

XVII

With such a horrid clang
As on Mount Sinai rang
   While the red fire and smoldering clouds outbrake:
The aged Earth aghast   160
With terror of that blast,
   Shall from the surface to the center shake,
When at the world's last sessïon
The dreadful Judge in middle air shall spread his throne.

XVIII

And then at last our bliss
Full and perfect is,
   But now begins; for from this happy day
The old Dragon under ground,
In straiter limits bound,
   Not half so far casts his usurpèd sway,   170
And, wroth to see his kingdom fail,
Swinges the scaly horror of his folded tail.

XIX

The oracles are dumb,
No voice or hideous hum
   Runs through the archèd roof in words deceiving.
Apollo from his shrine
Can no more divine,
   With hollow shriek the steep of Delphos leaving.
No nightly trance or breathèd spell
Inspires the pale-eyed priest from the prophetic cell.   180

XX

The lonely mountains o'er,
And the resounding shore,
   A voice of weeping heard, and loud lament;
From haunted spring and dale,
Edged with poplar pale,
   The parting Genius is with sighing sent;
With flower-inwoven tresses torn
The nymphs in twilight shade of tangled thickets mourn.

XXI

In consecrated earth,
And on the holy hearth,   190

The Lars and Lemures moan with midnight plaint;
In urns and altars round,
A drear and dying sound
  Affrights the flamens at their service quaint;
And the chill marble seems to sweat,
While each peculiar power forgoes his wonted seat.

XXII

Peor and Baalim
Forsake their temples dim,
  With that twice-battered god of Palestine;
And moonèd Ashtaroth,   200
Heaven's queen and mother both,
  Now sits not girt with tapers' holy shine;
The Libyc Hammon shrinks his horn,
In vain the Tyrian maids their wounded Thammuz mourn.

XXIII

And sullen Moloch, fled,
Hath left in shadows dread
  His burning idol all of blackest hue;
In vain with cymbals' ring
They call the grisly king,
  In dismal dance about the furnace blue;   210
The brutish gods of Nile as fast,
Isis and Orus, and the dog Anubis, haste.

XXIV

Nor is Osiris seen
In Memphian grove or green,
  Trampling the unshowered grass with lowings loud;
Nor can he be at rest
Within his sacred chest,
  Nought but profoundest Hell can be his shroud;
In vain with timbreled anthems dark
The sable-stoled sorcerers bear his worshiped ark.   220

XXV

He feels from Juda's land
The dreaded Infant's hand,
  The rays of Bethlehem blind his dusky eyn;
Nor all the gods beside
Longer dare abide,

Not Typhon huge ending in snaky twine:
Our Babe, to show his Godhead true,
Can in his swaddling bands control the damnèd crew.

XXVI

So when the sun in bed,
Curtained with cloudy red,   230
 Pillows his chin upon an orient wave,
The flocking shadows pale
Troop to th' infernal jail;
 Each fettered ghost slips to his several grave,
And the yellow-skirted fays
Fly after the night-steeds, leaving their moon-loved maze.

XXVII

But see, the Virgin blest
Hath laid her Babe to rest.
 Time is our tedious song should here have ending;
Heaven's youngest-teemèd star   240
Hath fixed her polished car,
 Her sleeping Lord with handmaid lamp attending;
And all about the courtly stable
Bright-harnessed angels sit in order serviceable.

109.   L'ALLEGRO

Hence, loathèd Melancholy,
 Of Cerberus and blackest Midnight born,
In Stygian cave forlorn
 'Mongst horrid shapes, and shrieks, and sights unholy,
Find out some uncouth cell,
 Where brooding darkness spreads his jealous wings,
And the night-raven sings;
 There under ebon shades and low-browed rocks,
As ragged as thy locks,
 In dark Cimmerian desert ever dwell.   10
But come, thou Goddess fair and free,
In heaven yclept Euphrosyne,
And by men, heart-easing Mirth,
Whom lovely Venus, at a birth,
With two sister Graces more,
To ivy-crownèd Bacchus bore;

Or whether (as some sager sing)
The frolic wind that breathes the spring,
Zephyr, with Aurora playing,
As he met her once a-Maying, 20
There on beds of violets blue,
And fresh-blown roses washed in dew,
Filled her with thee, a daughter fair,
So buxom, blithe, and debonair.
Haste thee, Nymph, and bring with thee
Jest and youthful Jollity,
Quips and Cranks and wanton Wiles,
Nods, and Becks, and wreathèd Smiles,
Such as hang on Hebe's cheek,
And love to live in dimple sleek; 30
Sport that wrinkled Care derides,
And Laughter holding both his sides.
Come, and trip it as ye go
On the light fantastic toe,
And in thy right hand lead with thee
The mountain nymph, sweet Liberty;
And if I give thee honor due,
Mirth, admit me of thy crew,
To live with her, and live with thee,
In unreprovèd pleasures free; 40
To hear the lark begin his flight,
And singing startle the dull night,
From his watch-tower in the skies,
Till the dappled dawn doth rise;
Then to come, in spite of sorrow,
And at my window bid good-morrow,
Through the sweet-briar, or the vine,
Or the twisted eglantine;
While the cock, with lively din,
Scatters the rear of darkness thin, 50
And to the stack or the barn door
Stoutly struts his dames before;
Oft listening how the hounds and horn
Cheerly rouse the slumbering morn,
From the side of some hoar hill,
Through the high wood echoing shrill:
Sometime walking, not unseen,

By hedgerow elms, on hillocks green,
Right against the eastern gate,
Where the great sun begins his state,   60
Robed in flames and amber light,
The clouds in thousand liveries dight;
While the ploughman, near at hand,
Whistles o'er the furrowed land,
And the milkmaid singeth blithe,
And the mower whets his scythe,
And every shepherd tells his tale
Under the hawthorn in the dale.
Straight mine eye hath caught new pleasures,
Whilst the landscape round it measures: 70
Russet lawns and fallows gray,
Where the nibbling flocks do stray,
Mountains on whose barren breast
The laboring clouds do often rest,
Meadows trim with daisies pied,
Shallow brooks and rivers wide;
Towers and battlements it sees
Bosomed high in tufted trees,
Where perhaps some beauty lies,
The cynosure of neighboring eyes.   80
Hard by, a cottage chimney smokes
From betwixt two agèd oaks,
Where Corydon and Thyrsis met
Are at their savory dinner set
Of herbs and other country messes,
Which the neat-handed Phillis dresses;
And then in haste her bower she leaves,
With Thestylis to bind the sheaves;
Or if the earlier season lead,
To the tanned haycock in the mead.   90
Sometimes with secure delight
The upland hamlets will invite,
When the merry bells ring round,
And the jocund rebecks sound
To many a youth and many a maid
Dancing in the chequered shade;
And young and old come forth to play
On a sunshine holiday,

Till the livelong daylight fail:
Then to the spicy nut-brown ale,   100
With stories told of many a feat,
How fairy Mab the junkets eat;
She was pinched and pulled, she said,
And he, by friar's lantern led,
Tells how the drudging goblin sweat
To earn his cream-bowl duly set,
When in one night, ere glimpse of morn,
His shadowy flail hath threshed the corn
That ten day-laborers could not end;
Then lies him down the lubber fiend,   110
And, stretched out all the chimney's length,
Basks at the fire his hairy strength;
And crop-full out of doors he flings,
Ere the first cock his matin rings.
Thus done the tales, to bed they creep,
By whispering winds soon lulled asleep.
Towered cities please us then,
And the busy hum of men,
Where throngs of knights and barons bold
In weeds of peace high triumphs hold,   120
With store of ladies, whose bright eyes
Rain influence, and judge the prize
Of wit or arms, while both contend
To win her grace whom all commend.
There let Hymen oft appear
In saffron robe, with taper clear,
And pomp, and feast, and revelry,
With masque and antique pageantry;
Such sights as youthful poets dream
On summer eves by haunted stream.   130
Then to the well-trod stage anon,
If Jonson's learnèd sock be on,
Or sweetest Shakespeare, Fancy's child,
Warble his native wood-notes wild.
And ever against eating cares,
Lap me in soft Lydian airs,
Married to immortal verse,
Such as the meeting soul may pierce
In notes with many a winding bout

Of linkèd sweetness long drawn out,   140
With wanton heed and giddy cunning,
The melting voice through mazes running,
Untwisting all the chains that tie
The hidden soul of harmony;
That Orpheus' self may heave his head
From golden slumber on a bed
Of heaped Elysian flowers, and hear
Such strains as would have won the ear
Of Pluto, to have quite set free
His half-regainèd Eurydice.   150
These delights if thou canst give,
Mirth, with thee I mean to live.

110.   IL PENSEROSO

Hence, vain deluding Joys,
    The brood of Folly without father bred,
How little you bestead,
    Or fill the fixèd mind with all your toys;
Dwell in some idle brain,
    And fancies fond with gaudy shapes possess,
As thick and numberless
    As the gay motes that people the sunbeams,
Or likest hovering dreams,
    The fickle pensioners of Morpheus' train.   10
But hail, thou Goddess sage and holy,
Hail, divinest Melancholy,
Whose saintly visage is too bright
To hit the sense of human sight,
And therefore to our weaker view
O'erlaid with black, staid Wisdom's hue;
Black, but such as in esteem
Prince Memnon's sister might beseem,
Or that starred Ethiop queen that strove
To set her beauty's praise above   20
The sea nymphs, and their powers offended.
Yet thou art higher far descended:
Thee bright-haired Vesta long of yore
To solitary Saturn bore;
His daughter she (in Saturn's reign
Such mixture was not held a stain).

Oft in glimmering bowers and glades
He met her, and in secret shades
Of woody Ida's inmost grove,
While yet there was no fear of Jove.   30
Come, pensive Nun, devout and pure,
Sober, steadfast, and demure,
All in a robe of darkest grain,
Flowing with majestic train,
And sable stole of cypress lawn
Over thy decent shoulders drawn.
Come, but keep thy wonted state,
With even step and musing gait,
And looks commercing with the skies,
Thy rapt soul sitting in thine eyes;   40
There held in holy passion still,
Forget thyself to marble, till
With a sad leaden downward cast
Thou fix them on the earth as fast.
And join with thee calm Peace and Quiet,
Spare Fast, that oft with gods doth diet,
And hears the Muses in a ring
Aye round about Jove's altar sing;
And add to these retirèd Leisure,
That in trim gardens takes his pleasure;   50
But first, and chiefest, with thee bring
Him that yon soars on golden wing,
Guiding the fiery-wheelèd throne,
The Cherub Contemplatïon;
And the mute Silence hist along,
'Less Philomel will deign a song,
In her sweetest, saddest plight,
Smoothing the rugged brow of Night,
While Cynthia checks her dragon yoke
Gently o'er the accustomed oak.   60
Sweet bird, that shunn'st the noise of folly,
Most musical, most melancholy!
Thee, chantress, oft the woods among
I woo to hear thy even-song;
And missing thee, I walk unseen
On the dry smooth-shaven green,
To behold the wandering moon,

Riding near her highest noon,
Like one that had been led astray
Through the Heaven's wide pathless way;   70
And oft, as if her head she bowed,
Stooping through a fleecy cloud.
Oft on a plat of rising ground
I hear the far-off curfew sound
Over some wide-watered shore,
Swinging slow with sullen roar;
Or if the air will not permit,
Some still removèd place will fit,
Where glowing embers through the room
Teach light to counterfeit a gloom,   80
Far from all resort of mirth,
Save the cricket on the hearth,
Or the bellman's drowsy charm,
To bless the doors from nightly harm.
Or let my lamp at midnight hour
Be seen in some high lonely tower,
Where I may oft outwatch the Bear,
With thrice great Hermes, or unsphere
The spirit of Plato to unfold
What worlds or what vast regions hold   90
The immortal mind that hath forsook
Her mansion in this fleshly nook;
And of those daemons that are found
In fire, air, flood, or under ground,
Whose power hath a true consent
With planet or with element.
Sometime let gorgeous Tragedy
In sceptred pall come sweeping by,
Presenting Thebes, or Pelops' line,
Or the tale of Troy divine,   100
Or what (though rare) of later age
Ennobled hath the buskined stage.
But, O sad Virgin, that thy power
Might raise Musaeus from his bower,
Or bid the soul of Orpheus sing
Such notes as, warbled to the string,
Drew iron tears down Pluto's cheek,
And made Hell grant what love did seek;

Or call up him that left half told
The story of Cambuscan bold,   110
Of Camball, and of Algarsife,
And who had Canace to wife,
That owned the virtuous ring and glass,
And of the wondrous horse of brass,
On which the Tartar king did ride;
And if aught else great bards beside
In sage and solemn tunes have sung,
Of tourneys and of trophies hung,
Of forests and enchantments drear,
Where more is meant than meets the ear.   120
Thus, Night, oft see me in thy pale career,
Till civil-suited Morn appear,
Not tricked and frounced as she was wont
With the Attic boy to hunt,
But kerchieft in a comely cloud,
While rocking winds are piping loud,
Or ushered with a shower still,
When the gust hath blown his fill,
Ending on the rustling leaves,
With minute drops from off the eaves.   130
And when the sun begins to fling
His flaring beams, me, Goddess, bring
To archèd walks of twilight groves,
And shadows brown that Sylvan loves,
Of pine or monumental oak,
Where the rude axe with heavèd stroke
Was never heard the nymphs to daunt,
Or fright them from their hallowed haunt.
There in close covert by some brook,
Where no profaner eye may look,   140
Hide me from Day's garish eye,
While the bee with honied thigh,
That at her flowery work doth sing,
And the waters murmuring
With such consort as they keep,
Entice the dewy-feathered Sleep;
And let some strange mysterious dream
Wave at his wings in airy stream
Of lively portraiture displayed,

Softly on my eyelids laid. 150
And as I wake, sweet music breathe
Above, about, or underneath,
Sent by some spirit to mortals good,
Or the unseen Genius of the wood.
But let my due feet never fail
To walk the studious cloister's pale,
And love the high embowèd roof,
With antique pillars massy proof,
And storied windows richly dight,
Casting a dim religious light. 160
There let the pealing organ blow
To the full-voiced choir below,
In service high and anthems clear,
As may with sweetness, through mine ear,
Dissolve me into ecstasies,
And bring all Heaven before mine eyes.
And may at last my weary age
Find out the peaceful hermitage,
The hairy gown and mossy cell,
Where I may sit and rightly spell 170
Of every star that Heaven doth shew,
And every herb that sips the dew,
Till old experience do attain
To something like prophetic strain.
These pleasures, Melancholy, give,
And I with thee will choose to live.

111.   ON TIME

Fly, envious Time, till thou run out thy race;
Call on the lazy leaden-stepping hours,
Whose speed is but the heavy plummet's pace;
And glut thyself with what thy womb devours,
Which is no more than what is false and vain,
And merely mortal dross;
So little is our loss,
So little is thy gain.
For whenas each thing bad thou hast entombed,
And last of all thy greedy self consumed, 10
Then long Eternity shall greet our bliss
With an individual kiss;

And joy shall overtake us as a flood,
When everything that is sincerely good
And perfectly divine,
With Truth, and Peace, and Love shall ever shine
About the súpreme throne
Of him t' whose happy-making sight alone,
When once our heavenly-guided soul shall climb,
Then all this earthly grossness quit,   20
Attired with stars, we shall forever set,
   Triumphing over Death, and Chance, and thee O Time.

112.   AT A SOLEMN MUSIC

Blest pair of sirens, pledges of heaven's joy,
Sphere-born harmonious sisters, voice, and verse,
Wed your divine sounds, and mixed power employ,
Dead things with inbreathed sense able to pierce,
And to our high-raised phantasy present,
That undisturbèd song of pure concent,
Aye sung before the sapphire-colored throne
To him that sits thereon
With saintly shout, and solemn jubilee,
Where the bright seraphim in burning row   10
Their loud uplifted angel trumpets blow,
And the cherubic host in thousand choirs
Touch their immortal harps of golden wires,
With those just spirits that wear victorious palms,
Hymns devout and holy psalms
Singing everlastingly;
That we on earth with undiscording voice
May rightly answer that melodious noise;
As once we did, till disproportioned sin
Jarred against nature's chime, and with harsh din   20
Broke the fair music that all creatures made
To their great Lord, whose love their motion swayed
In perfect diapason, whilst they stood
In first obedience, and their state of good.
O may we soon again renew that song,
And keep in tune with heaven, till God ere long
To his celestial consort us unite,
To live with him, and sing in endless morn of light.

113.   "LAWRENCE OF VIRTUOUS FATHER
                    VIRTUOUS SON"

Lawrence, of virtuous father virtuous son,
        Now that the fields are dank and ways are mire,
        Where shall we sometimes meet, and by the fire
        Help waste a sullen day, what may be won
From the hard season gaining? Time will run
        On smoother, till Favonius reinspire
        The frozen earth, and clothe in fresh attire
        The lily and rose, that neither sowed nor spun.
What neat repast shall feast us, light and choice,
        Of Attic taste, with wine, whence we may rise   10
        To hear the lute well touched, or artful voice
Warble immortal notes and Tuscan air?
        He who of those delights can judge, and spare
        To interpose them oft, is not unwise.

114.   LYCIDAS

Yet once more, O ye laurels, and once more,
Ye myrtles brown, with ivy never sere,
I come to pluck your berries harsh and crude,
And with forced fingers rude
Shatter your leaves before the mellowing year.
Bitter constraint, and sad occasion dear,
Compels me to disturb your season due;
For Lycidas is dead, dead ere his prime,
Young Lycidas, and hath not left his peer.
Who would not sing for Lycidas? he knew   10
Himself to sing, and build the lofty rhyme.
He must not float upon his watery bier
Unwept, and welter to the parching wind,
Without the meed of some melodious tear.
    Begin then, sisters of the sacred well
That from beneath the seat of Jove doth spring,
Begin, and somewhat loudly sweep the string.
Hence with denial vain, and coy excuse;
So may some gentle Muse
With lucky words favor my destined urn,   20
And as he passes turn,
And bid fair peace be to my sable shroud.

For we were nursed upon the self-same hill,
Fed the same flock, by fountain, shade, and rill.
   Together both, ere the high lawns appeared
Under the opening eyelids of the morn,
We drove afield, and both together heard
What time the gray-fly winds her sultry horn,
Battening our flocks with the fresh dews of night,
Oft till the star that rose, at evening, bright   30
Toward Heaven's descent had sloped his westering wheel.
Meanwhile the rural ditties were not mute,
Tempered to the oaten flute;
Rough satyrs danced, and fauns with cloven heel
From the glad sound would not be absent long,
And old Damoetas loved to hear our song.
   But O the heavy change, now thou art gone,
Now thou art gone, and never must return!
Thee, shepherd, thee the woods and desert caves,
With wild thyme and the gadding vine o'ergrown,   40
And all their echoes mourn.
The willows and the hazel copses green
Shall now no more be seen
Fanning their joyous leaves to thy soft lays.
As killing as the canker to the rose,
Or taint-worm to the weanling herds that graze,
Or frost to flowers, that their gay wardrobe wear,
When first the white-thorn blows;
Such, Lycidas, thy loss to shepherd's ear.
   Where were ye, nymphs, when the remorseless deep   50
Closed o'er the head of your loved Lycidas?
For neither were ye playing on the steep
Where your old bards, the famous Druids, lie,
Nor on the shaggy top of Mona high,
Nor yet where Deva spreads her wizard stream.
Ay me, I fondly dream!
Had ye been there—for what could that have done?
What could the Muse herself that Orpheus bore,
The Muse herself, for her enchanting son,
Whom universal nature did lament,   60
When by the rout that made the hideous roar
His gory visage down the stream was sent,
Down the swift Hebrus to the Lesbian shore?

Alas! what boots it with uncessant care
To tend the homely slighted shepherd's trade,
And strictly meditate the thankless Muse?
Were it not better done as others use,
To sport with Amaryllis in the shade,
Or with the tangles of Neaera's hair?
Fame is the spur that the clear spirit doth raise   70
(That last infirmity of noble mind)
To scorn delights, and live laborious days;
But the fair guerdon when we hope to find,
And think to burst out into sudden blaze,
Comes the blind Fury with the abhorrèd shears,
And slits the thin-spun life. "But not the praise,"
Phoebus replied, and touched my trembling ears:
"Fame is no plant that grows on mortal soil,
Nor in the glistering foil
Set off to the world, nor in broad rumor lies,   80
But lives and spreads aloft by those pure eyes
And perfect witness of all-judging Jove;
As he pronounces lastly on each deed,
Of so much fame in Heaven expect thy meed."
O fountain Arethuse, and thou honored flood,
Smooth-sliding Mincius, crowned with vocal reeds,
That strain I heard was of a higher mood.
But now my oat proceeds,
And listens to the herald of the sea,
That came in Neptune's plea.   90
He asked the waves, and asked the felon winds,
What hard mishap hath doomed this gentle swain?
And questioned every gust of rugged wings
That blows from off each beakèd promontory;
They knew not of his story,
And sage Hippotades their answer brings,
That not a blast was from his dungeon strayed;
The air was calm, and on the level brine
Sleek Panope with all her sisters played.
It was that fatal and perfidious bark,   100
Built in the eclipse, and rigged with curses dark,
That sunk so low that sacred head of thine.
Next Camus, reverend sire, went footing slow,
His mantle hairy, and his bonnet sedge,

Inwrought with figures dim, and on the edge
Like to that sanguine flower inscribed with woe.
"Ah, who hath reft," quoth he, "my dearest pledge?"
Last came, and last did go,
The pilot of the Galilean Lake;
Two massy keys he bore of metals twain   110
(The golden opes, the iron shuts amain).
He shook his mitred locks, and stern bespake:
"How well could I have spared for thee, young swain,
Enow of such as for their bellies' sake
Creep and intrude and climb into the fold!
Of other care they little reckoning make
Than how to scramble at the shearers' feast,
And shove away the worthy bidden guest.
Blind mouths! that scarce themselves know how to hold
A sheep-hook, or have learned aught else the least   120
That to the faithful herdman's art belongs!
What recks it them? What need they? They are sped;
And when they list, their lean and flashy songs
Grate on their scrannel pipes of wretched straw.
The hungry sheep look up, and are not fed,
But swoln with wind and the rank mist they draw,
Rot inwardly, and foul contagion spread;
Besides what the grim wolf with privy paw
Daily devours apace, and nothing said;
But that two-handed engine at the door   130
Stands ready to smite once, and smite no more."
    Return, Alpheus, the dread voice is past
That shrunk thy streams; return, Sicilian Muse,
And call the vales, and bid them hither cast
Their bells and flowrets of a thousand hues.
Ye valleys low where the mild whispers use
Of shades and wanton winds and gushing brooks,
On whose fresh lap the swart star sparely looks,
Throw hither all your quaint enameled eyes,
That on the green turf suck the honied showers,   140
And purple all the ground with vernal flowers.
Bring the rathe primrose that forsaken dies,
The tufted crow-toe, and pale jessamine,
The white pink, and the pansy freaked with jet,
The glowing violet,

The musk-rose, and the well-attired woodbine,
With cowslips wan that hang the pensive head,
And every flower that sad embroidery wears.
Bid amaranthus all his beauty shed,
And daffadillies fill their cups with tears,   150
To strew the laureate hearse where Lycid lies.
For so to interpose a little ease,
Let our frail thoughts dally with false surmise.
Ay me! whilst thee the shores and sounding seas
Wash far away, where'er thy bones are hurled,
Whether beyond the stormy Hebrides,
Where thou perhaps under the whelming tide
Visit'st the bottom of the monstrous world;
Or whether thou, to our moist vows denied,
Sleep'st by the fable of Bellerus old,   160
Where the great vision of the guarded mount
Looks toward Namancos and Bayona's hold;
Look homeward, Angel, now, and melt with ruth;
And, O ye dolphins, waft the hapless youth.
  Weep no more, woeful shepherds, weep no more,
For Lycidas, your sorrow, is not dead,
Sunk though he be beneath the watery floor;
So sinks the day-star in the ocean bed,
And yet anon repairs his drooping head,
And tricks his beams, and with new-spangled ore   170
Flames in the forehead of the morning sky:
So Lycidas, sunk low, but mounted high,
Through the dear might of him that walked the waves,
Where, other groves and other streams along,
With nectar pure his oozy locks he laves,
And hears the unexpressive nuptial song,
In the blest kingdoms meek of joy and love.
There entertain him all the saints above,
In solemn troops and sweet societies
That sing, and singing in their glory move,   180
And wipe the tears for ever from his eyes.
Now, Lycidas. the shepherds weep no more;
Henceforth thou art the Genius of the shore,
In thy large recompense, and shalt be good
To all that wander in that perilous flood.
  Thus sang the uncouth swain to the oaks and rills,

While the still morn went out with sandals gray;
He touched the tender stops of various quills,
With eager thought warbling his Doric lay.
And now the sun had stretched out all the hills,   190
And now was dropped into the western bay;
At last he rose, and twitched his mantle blue:
To-morrow to fresh woods, and pastures new.

III. THE EIGHTEENTH CENTURY

THE EIGHTEENTH CENTURY

"The eighteenth century" is a convenient chronological label to apply to a phase of English culture, but of course shifts in cultural climate do not coincide with the end of a century, and the period we are now reviewing really begins with the Restoration in 1660 and has no easily defined end point. Changes in attitude, movements in the history of ideas, have no fixed beginning and end, and to divide literature into periods is always an artificial procedure. But the procedure, if artificial, is none the less necessary, for the intellectual atmosphere of a civilization *does* change, and the difference in outlook between an Englishman of 1600 and one of 1700 is immense, even if it is impossible to lay one's finger on the precise moment of change.

What one thinks of as the typical eighteenth-century attitude is an urban gentility which combines a suspicion of "enthusiasm" in religious and other matters with a calm assurance that the forms and fashions of contemporary society and the diction and conventions of contemporary poetry represent that reasonable compromise between ritual and common sense which makes civilized living possible. Like all stereotyped notions of an age, this view is easy to quarrel with, for of course it represents an oversimplification. But there is enough truth in it to make it worth repeating as a rough index to the tone and temper of English civilization at least in the early part of the eighteenth century. The compromise between Puritan and Cavalier was achieved by the end of the seventeenth century in terms of an optimistic gentility and an acceptance of the vital distinction between "gentlemen" (who could, in virtue of their education, recognize classical allusions in poetry and appreciate wit, polish, and smoothness in versification) and "low" people whose language and sentiments never entered into poetry except for comic effect and who were cut off by their lack of education from an appreciation of the elegancies of literary discourse.

It was the tradition of Ben Jonson and the Cavalier poets that triumphed at the Restoration. Ease, elegance, and polish became more and more the sought-after qualities of a true poetic style, and late seventeenth-century poets congratulated each other on the "refinement of our numbers" by such men as Sir John Denham (1615–1669) and Edmund Waller (1606–1687)—poets whose style was characterized by smoothness. The vocabulary of poetry now became restricted to that found in "the conversation of gentlemen," and it was widely supposed that there had been a happy progress in poetic style since the days of the Elizabethans and the Jacobeans which guaranteed a greater sweetness and polish than was possible to those rough geniuses. In Dryden's *Essay of Dramatic Poesy,* published in 1668, in which persons representing several different points of view are introduced, it is emphasized that all were agreed that "the sweetness of English verse was never understood or practised by our fathers." As Eugenius, one of the speakers in the *Essay,* put it, earlier literature "can produce nothing so courtly writ, or which expresses so much the conversation of a gentleman, as Sir John Suckling; nothing so even, sweet, and flowing as Mr. Waller; nothing so majestic, so correct, as Sir John Denham. . . ."

The movement in poetry is related to a parallel movement in prose, for which the Royal Society (established in 1662) was in part responsible. Instead of the highly individual, imaginative, prose style that we find in Sir Thomas Browne and in so many earlier seventeenth-century sermons, we now begin to get a prose style whose ideal is the prose of Dryden in the *Essay of Dramatic Poesy*—conversational, yet forceful and carefully modulated. The Royal Society, whose function was the promotion of science, demanded that its members employ "a close, naked, natural way of speaking; positive expressions; clear senses; a native easiness"; and as the Society's members were not professional scientists (a class which at that time barely existed) but poets, clergymen, and gentlemen of leisure, this policy influenced, as it reflected, the contemporary view of good style. Dryden, Edmund Waller, and the diarist Evelyn were all members of the Royal Society.

As the seventeenth century drew to a close, London became more and more the center of the literary and intellectual life of the country and poets came to look upon "polite" London society as their chief if not their sole audience. It must be remembered that there

was a correlation between social class and education, between elegance and learning, that has not always existed in subsequent
periods, and if poets were to use a fairly standardized body of references to the Latin and Greek classics as well as to events in the
contemporary world of learning, they had to consider themselves
addressing a very limited audience. Men were very much aware at
this time of what man had made of himself by submitting his raw
impulses to conventions and polishing his speech in accordance with
the demands of those conventions. It was that sort of thing that
made life livable, and that made personal and social relationships
contribute to the agreeableness of existence. Civilization was very
precious; it was the product of the refinement of primitive impulses
by a series of conventions which were transmitted and improved
upon by education. "We are refined," wrote Lord Chesterfield to
his son; "and plain manners, plain dress, and plain diction, would
as little do in life, as acorns, herbage, and the water of the neighbouring spring, would do at table."

The period has been called the "Age of Reason," but it might just
as well be described as an age which carefully refrained from employing reason to follow arguments to their ultimate conclusion.
It was an age of compromise, convention, and refusal to go to extremes. Christianity tended to be interpreted in a vague and general way as meaning that a First Cause had originally set the world
going and had arranged the machinery in such a way as to make
sure that things turned out for the best; Newtonian physics was
accepted as the final "explanation" of the physical universe, and the
ideas of John Locke as the most sensible account of the relation
between man's mind and the external world. But this pose of intellectual and emotional suavity bred its own reaction, and an age
which frowned on religious "enthusiasm" (a word defined by Dr.
Johnson in his *Dictionary* as "a vain confidence of divine favour or
communication") saw the rise of the Methodist movement under the
guidance of the brothers Wesley and many other much stranger
escapes from oppressive moderation and good sense.

Poetry in such a period worked within relatively narrow limits.
Poetry was a civilized activity, and civilization demanded a certain
kind of perspective in looking at things, a certain polish and elegance and consciousness of good society, wit, restraint, good taste,

and the subordination of personal idiosyncrasy to a social norm. The heroic couplet becomes the standard—at times there seems to be a feeling that it is virtually the only—verse technique, partly because it is the best form for conveying that combination of elegance and wit, of ease and polish, which the age demanded, but also because it lent itself to the utterance of "what oft was thought but ne'er so well expressed" and encouraged a nice balance between individual cleverness and the rhetoric of social belief.

In Dryden's poetry the poet is not yet the civilized Londoner speaking to other civilized Londoners: the tone is freer and the techniques more flexible. Dryden developed a rich, trumpet-like utterance—less rich and musical than Milton's, but bearing to Milton's verse something of the relation which a first-rate brass band bears to a complete orchestra—which has a splendid vitality about it, and we feel that though he, too, speaks in the language of gentlemen he is not simply addressing the genteel of his generation. But with Pope, a more delicate artist whose perfectly modulated verse bears no analogy to an orchestra at all, but can perhaps be compared to the tones of the clarinet, the field is definitely restricted, and we can see him turn this restriction to his advantage by using more delicate instruments and working the subtlest variations within the end-stopped couplet.

The atmosphere of the reign of Queen Anne (who reigned from 1702 to 1714) was congenial to Pope's genius: it encouraged him to write for a civilized urban group whose education he could take for granted, whose attitudes he understood, and whose standards of wit and elegance coincided with his own. This limitation of audience, of diction, and of subject matter (the period often discussed what was "proper" and what improper material for poetry) did not, however, necessarily mean that a kind of poetry inferior to that of the previous century would be produced. Limitations of this kind are a challenge to art, and art thrives on such challenges. The delicate satire and oblique wisdom developed by Pope in "The Rape of the Lock" (see the notes to that poem, page 677) show what perfect poetic achievements were possible in—were in fact encouraged by— a social atmosphere of this kind.

Such an atmosphere also produced the kind of *vers de société* or society verse so happily exemplified by the poems of Matthew Prior.

Prior's playful elegance is to be distinguished from the more formal performances of Pope; Prior is familiar, relaxed, smiling, and his verse often has the air of social chat or even a dig in the ribs. He sometimes has a graceful vulgarity which indicates that he is writing at a lower temperature than Pope, that he represents the poet at play rather than at work. This "occasional" poetry is just as important in this period as more deliberately formal works such as Pope's "Essay on Man." Elegant trifles—the Romans had a word for them, *nugae*—represent the poet at play in a society which understands him and which knows perfectly the rules of the game.

Another aspect of early eighteenth-century civilization is caught perfectly by Pomfret's poem, "The Choice" (1700), which is a verse essay describing the gentleman's ideal way of life. We are reminded, as so often in this period, of the mood and tone of many of the poems of the Roman poet Horace, who was understandably enough one of the favorite poets of the age. It was from this balanced viewpoint that the early eighteenth century tended to observe life and to judge human affairs. Closely related to this attitude is the insistence that poetry should concern itself with *general* human nature, that it should take as the norm the highest common factor of civilized man; such a view had its effect on tone and diction as well as on choice of subject matter and underlying philosophy. George Saintsbury called the age "a place of rest and refreshment" and there is in many of its aspects a feeling of ease and relief after the turbulence, both intellectual and political, of the preceding century.

The verse essay is a quite different use of the medium of poetry from the more closely organized expression that we find in "Lycidas" or an ode of Keats. Whereas in the latter kind of poetry, form and content develop together and the totality of meaning can only be conveyed by repeating the poem itself, in much eighteenth-century verse there is a deliberate attempt to express a preconceived content as neatly and elegantly as possible, and the regular metrical beat and the recurring pairs of rhymes serve to emphasize each point as it is made rather than to give it the subtle shade of meaning it would not otherwise possess. Yet the heroic couplet is not limited to serving as the graceful medium of detachable thought, and in "The Rape of the Lock" we see the antithetical structure of couplet verse

being employed to achieve a subtle and effective distillation of meaning far richer than anything which could be achieved by a prose
paraphrase of the poem.

As the century progressed, more meditative and more melancholy
voices began to challenge the optimistic and civilized surface polish
characteristic of much Queen Anne verse. Dr. Johnson, whose
sonorous rhetorical poetry (see the note on his "Vanity of Human
Wishes," page 684) is so much graver in tone than Pope's, is much
less of the social urban poet writing for a contemporary genteel
audience than most earlier writers of the century, although he
shares their view of the language of poetry and the importance of
concerning himself with general civilized human nature. But for
some time yet eccentricities of personal feeling remained on the
whole outside the recognized scope of poetry. (Poetry, remarked
Addison in the *Spectator,* could at best hope "to represent the common sense of mankind in more strong, more beautiful, or more uncommon lights.") This was a social world, and man was made what
he was by sharing in social beliefs and conventions.

But new voices kept breaking in. The eighteenth century regarded the Pindaric ode (so-called because it was deemed to follow
the general kind of structure and emotional tone of the odes of the
Greek poet, Pindar) as a specially licensed kind of verse in which
the decorum of tone and feeling demanded of other forms might be
abandoned in favor of a deliberate wildness. Dryden had produced
something of the sort in his "Alexander's Feast," and most of the
important poets of this period tried their hands at it. But in the
hands of a poet like Gray, the ode, while retaining a highly formal
poetic diction, sometimes moved beyond licensed exuberance into a
realm of passion and imagination that startled such critics as Dr.
Johnson.

The middle of the eighteenth century was a period of transition
and experiment in poetic styles and subjects (perhaps this remark
is true in some degree of every period), and it is interesting to see
how the view of poetry as the refined and pleasing communication
to educated ears of an aspect of civilized and generalized humanity
seems to be abandoned in practice long before it was officially dis-
carded by critics. It would be a mistake, however, to diagnose all
poets who show a stronger personal feeling or a passionate interest

in the old and the odd and the unique as "pre-Romantics" who point forward to a liberation of poetry which takes place in a violent poetic revolution at the end of the century. Shifts in the view of poetry's nature and function proceed gradually and continuously, and in fact the attitude of the self-styled "Augustan" age of Queen Anne was scarcely established as an attitude before it began to be modified under the impact of a great variety of forces. The stability which English thought and society regained at the end of the seventeenth century could not in the nature of things be long maintained, and the unstable equilibrium of Queen Anne's period gave way to more complex and contradictory attitudes. Melancholy, interest in the uncivilized and the odd, a sense of change and of the impossibility of keeping civilization static—some or all of these attitudes are seen quite early in the century; and by the time we get to Gray and Goldsmith and Cowper the first and third of them are almost standard. The enclosing of village ground in the interest of big landowners and relatively large-scale farmers produced a change and unrest in the countryside (as Goldsmith's "Deserted Village" records), and the beginnings of the Industrial Revolution toward the end of the century produced a very different view of the value of life in urban society. Blake's "London" is written in another world altogether. Further, the strain of thought most clearly represented by the French thinker Rousseau encouraged the notion that the conventions of civilization, far from being all that made a decent life possible, far from representing the refinement of crude humanity into a gracious pattern of worth-while living, represented intolerable restrictions on the individual personality and produced every kind of corruption and evil. This is in some degree the theme of Blake's *Songs of Experience,* and Blake thus represents as complete an antithesis to the view which prevailed earlier in the century as can be found. In this respect the poets of the full-fledged "Romantic Movement" early in the nineteenth century represented no advance on Blake, who had gone as far in that direction as it was possible to go.

Blake voiced the protest of individual insight against social norms and accepted patterns of order, and his attitude would have seemed equally absurd to Pope and to Dr. Johnson—and perhaps to all earlier English poets. It is this urgent note of personal vision

challenging the claims of conventional morality that gives Blake's
poetry that almost trancelike quality, that sense of a new world seen
through fresh eyes. No lover of poetry would wish to have to
choose between Dr. Johnson (or Pope) on the one hand and Blake
on the other—but the fact remains that Johnson and Blake were
doing quite different things with language, and in addition possessed quite different attitudes to man and society, so that we have
to make a drastic adjustment in our own approach if we come from
one to the other.

Burns's position is quite different from that of any other poet of
the century we have discussed. He is not an English but a Scottish
poet, working in a revived Scottish literary tradition. Any similarity
in approach or attitude between his poetry and the so-called Romantic movement in England is purely coincidental. His work in fact
represents the end rather than the beginning of a movement—the
end of a long tradition in Scottish literature. We have not included
other representatives of Scottish poetry in this collection (Thomson
was a Scots poet, but he wrote as an English one) because there
are linguistic and other difficulties for the ordinary American reader;
but Burns is so well known and so often thought of as having a
place in English as well as Scottish literature that it seems appropriate to include him, even though his best work develops from a
tradition to which most of the preceding remarks are irrelevant.

EDMUND WALLER (1606–1687)

115.   "GO, LOVELY ROSE!"

Go, lovely rose!
Tell her that wastes her time and me
That now she knows,
When I resemble her to thee,
How sweet and fair she seems to be.

Tell her that's young
And shuns to have her graces spied,
That hadst thou sprung
In deserts where no men abide,
Thou must have uncommended died.   10

Small is the worth
Of beauty from the light retired;
Bid her come forth,
Suffer herself to be desired,
And not blush so to be admired.

Then die, that she
The common fate of all things rare
May read in thee;
How small a part of time they share
That are so wondrous sweet and fair! 20

116. OF THE LAST VERSES IN THE BOOK

When we for age could neither read nor write,
The subject made us able to indite;
The soul, with nobler resolutions decked,
The body stooping, does herself erect.
No mortal parts are requisite to raise
Her that, unbodied, can her Maker praise.

The seas are quiet when the winds give o'er;
So, calm are we when passions are no more.
For then we know how vain it was to boast
Of fleeting things, so certain to be lost. 10
Clouds of affection from our younger eyes
Conceal that emptiness which age descries.

The soul's dark cottage, battered and decayed,
Lets in new light through chinks that time has made;
Stronger by weakness, wiser, men become
As they draw near to their eternal home;
Leaving the old, both worlds at once they view,
That stand upon the threshold of the new.

JOHN DRYDEN (1631–1700)

117. PROLOGUE TO THE TEMPEST

As when a tree's cut down, tne secret root
Lives under ground, and thence new branches shoot,
So from old Shakespeare's honoured dust this day
Springs up and buds a new reviving play:

Shakespeare, who (taught by none) did first impart
To Fletcher wit, to labouring Jonson art;
He monarch-like, gave those his subjects law,
And is that Nature which they paint and draw.
Fletcher reach'd that which on his heights did grow,
Whilst Jonson crept and gather'd all below.   10
This did his love, and this his mirth digest:
One imitates him most, the other best.
If they have since out-writ all other men,
'Tis with the drops which fell from Shakespeare's pen.
The storm which vanish'd on the neighb'ring shore
Was taught by Shakespeare's *Tempest* first to roar.
That innocence and beauty, which did smile
In Fletcher, grew on this *Enchanted Isle*.
But Shakespeare's magic could not copy'd be;
Within that circle none durst walk but he.   20
I must confess 'twas bold, nor would you now
That liberty to vulgar wits allow,
Which works by magic supernatural things;
But Shakespeare's pow'r is sacred as a king's.
Those legends from old priest-hood were receiv'd,
And he then writ, as people then believ'd.
But if for Shakespeare we your grace implore,
We for our theatre shall want it more;
Who by our dearth of youths are forc'd t' employ
One of our women to present a boy,   30
And that's a transformation you will say
Exceeding all the magic in the play.
Let none expect in the last act to find
Her sex transform'd from man to womankind.
Whate'er she was before the play began,
All you shall see of her is perfect man.
Or, if your fancy will be farther led
To find her woman, it must be abed.

118.   MAC FLECKNOE

OR, A SATIRE UPON THE TRUE-BLUE-PROTESTANT POET

T. S.

All human things are subject to decay,
And when Fate summons, monarchs must obey.

This Flecknoe found, who, like Augustus, young
Was call'd to empire, and had govern'd long:
In prose and verse, was own'd, without dispute,
Thro' all the realms of Nonsense, absolute.
This aged prince, now flourishing in peace,
And blest with issue of a large increase,
Worn out with business, did at length debate
To settle the succession of the state;   10
And, pondr'ing which of all his sons was fit
To reign, and wage immortal war with wit,
Cried: " 'Tis resolv'd; for Nature pleads, that he
Should only rule, who most resembles me.
Sh—— alone my perfect image bears,
Mature in dullness from his tender years:
Sh—— alone of all my sons is he
Who stands confirm'd in full stupidity.
The rest to some faint meaning make pretense,
But Sh—— never deviates into sense.   20
Some beams of wit on other souls may fall,
Strike thro', and make a lucid interval;
But Sh——'s genuine night admits no ray,
His rising fogs prevail upon the day.
Besides, his goodly fabric fills the eye,
And seems design'd for thoughtless majesty:
Thoughtless as monarch oaks that shade the plain,
And, spread in solemn state, supinely reign.
Heywood and Shirley were but types of thee,
Thou last great prophet of tautology.   30
Even I, a dunce of more renown than they,
Was sent before but to prepare thy way:
And coarsely clad in Norwich drugget came
To teach the nations in thy greater name.
My warbling lute, the lute I whilom strung,
When to King John of Portugal I sung,
Was but the prelude to that glorious day,
When thou on silver Thames didst cut thy way,
With well-tim'd oars before the royal barge,
Swell'd with the pride of thy celestial charge;   40
And, big with hymn, commander of a host,
The like was ne'er in Epsom blankets toss'd.
Methinks I see the new Arion sail,

The lute still trembling underneath thy nail.
At thy well-sharpen'd thumb from shore to shore
The treble squeaks for fear, the basses roar;
Echoes from Pissing Alley Sh—— call,
And Sh—— they resound from Aston Hall.
About thy boat the little fishes throng,
As at the morning toast that floats along.   50
Sometimes, as prince of thy harmonious band,
Thou wield'st thy papers in thy threshing hand.
St. André's feet ne'er kept more equal time,
Not ev'n the feet of thy own *Psyche's* rhyme:
Tho' they in number as in sense excel,
So just, so like tautology, they fell,
That, pale with envy, Singleton forswore
The lute and sword, which he in triumph bore,
And vow'd he ne'er would act Villerius more."
Here stopp'd the good old sire, and wept for joy   60
In silent raptures of the hopeful boy.
All arguments, but most his plays, persuade,
That for anointed dullness he was made.

   Close to the walls which fair Augusta bind,
(The fair Augusta much to fears inclin'd)
An ancient fabric rais'd t' inform the sight,
There stood of yore, and Barbican it hight:
A watchtower once; but now, so fate ordains,
Of all the pile an empty name remains.
From its old ruins brothel-houses rise,   70
Scenes of lewd loves, and of polluted joys,
Where their vast courts the mother-strumpets keep,
And, undisturb'd by watch, in silence sleep.
Near these a Nursery erects its head,
Where queens are form'd, and future heroes bred;
Where unfledg'd actors learn to laugh and cry,
Where infant punks their tender voices try,
And little Maximins the gods defy.
Great Fletcher never treads in buskins here,
Nor greater Jonson dares in socks appear;   80
But gentle Simkin just reception finds
Amidst this monument of vanish'd minds:
Pure clinches the suburbian Muse affords,
And Panton waging harmless war with words.

Here Flecknoe, as a place to fame well known,
Ambitiously design'd his Sh——'s throne;
For ancient Dekker prophesied long since,
That in this pile should reign a mighty prince,
Born for a scourge of wit, and flail of sense,
To whom true dullness should some *Psyches* owe,   90
But worlds of *Misers* from his pen should flow;
Humorists and hypocrites it should produce,
Whole Raymond families, and tribes of Bruce.
   Now Empress Fame had publish'd the renown
Of Sh——'s coronation thro' the town.
Rous'd by report of Fame, the nations meet,
From near Bunhill, and distant Watling Street.
No Persian carpets spread th' imperial way,
But scatter'd limbs of mangled poets lay;
From dusty shops neglected authors come,   100
Martyrs of pies, and relics of the bum.
Much Heywood, Shirley, Ogleby there lay,
But loads of Sh—— almost chok'd the way.
Bilk'd stationers for yeomen stood prepar'd
And Herringman was captain of the guard.
The hoary prince in majesty appear'd,
High on a throne of his own labours rear'd.
At his right hand our young Ascanius sat,
Rome's other hope, and pillar of the State.
His brows thick fogs, instead of glories, grace,   110
And lambent dullness play'd around his face.
As Hannibal did to the altars come,
Sworn by his sire a mortal foe to Rome;
So Sh—— swore, nor should his vow be vain,
That he till death true dullness would maintain;
And, in his father's right, and realm's defense,
Ne'er to have peace with wit, nor truce with sense.
The king himself the sacred unction made,
As king by office, and as priest by trade.
In his sinister hand, instead of ball,   120
He plac'd a mighty mug of potent ale;
Love's Kingdom to his right he did convey.
At once his scepter, and his rule of sway;
Whose righteous lore the prince had practis'd young
And from whose loins recorded *Psyche* sprung.

His temples, last, with poppies were o'erspread,
That nodding seem'd to consecrate his head:
Just at that point of time, if fame not lie,
On his left hand twelve reverend owls did fly.
So Romulus, 't is sung, by Tiber's brook,   130
Presage of sway from twice six vultures took.
Th' admiring throng loud acclamations make,
And omens of his future empire take.
The sire then shook the honours of his head,
And from his brows damps of oblivion shed
Full on the filial dullness: long he stood,
Repelling from his breast the raging god;
At length burst out in this prophetic mood:
   "Heavens bless my son, from Ireland let him reign
To far Barbadoes on the western main;   140
Of his dominion may no end be known,
And greater than his father's be his throne;
Beyond *Love's Kingdom* let him stretch his pen!"
He paus'd, and all the people cried, "Amen."
Then thus continued he: "My son, advance
Still in new impudence, new ignorance.
Success let others teach, learn thou from me
Pangs without birth, and fruitless industry.
Let *Virtuosos* in five years be writ;
Yet not one thought accuse thy toil of wit.   150
Let gentle George in triumph tread the stage,
Make Dorimant betray, and Loveit rage;
Let Cully, Cockwood, Fopling, charm the pit,
And in their folly shew the writer's wit.
Yet still thy fools shall stand in thy defense
And justify their author's want of sense.
Let 'em be all by thy own model made
Of dullness, and desire no foreign aid,
That they to future ages may be known,
Not copies drawn, but issue of thy own.   160
Nay, let thy men of wit too be the same,
All full of thee, and differing but in name.
But let no alien S—dl—y interpose,
To lard with wit thy hungry *Epsom* prose.
And when false flowers of rhetoric thou wouldst cull,
Trust nature, do not labor to be dull;

But write thy best, and top; and, in each line,
Sir Formal's oratory will be thine:
Sir Formal, tho' unsought, attends thy quill,
And does thy northern dedications fill.   170
Nor let false friends seduce thy mind to fame,
By arrogating Jonson's hostile name.
Let father Flecknoe fire thy mind with praise,
And uncle Ogleby thy envy raise.
Thou art my blood, where Jonson has no part:
What share have we in nature, or in art?
Where did his wit on learning fix a brand,
And rail at arts he did not understand?
Where made he love in Prince Nicander's vein,
Or swept the dust in *Psyche's* humble strain?   180
Where sold he bargains, 'whip-stitch, kiss my arse,'
Promis'd a play and dwindled to a farce?
When did his Muse from Fletcher scenes purloin,
As thou whole Eth'rege dost transfuse to thine?
But so transfus'd, as oil on water's flow,
His always floats above, thine sinks below.
This is thy province, this thy wondrous way,
New humours to invent for each new play:
This is that boasted bias of thy mind,
By which one way, to dullness, 't is inclin'd,   190
Which makes thy writings lean on one side still,
And, in all changes, that way bends thy will.
Nor let thy mountain-belly make pretense
Of likeness; thine 's a tympany of sense.
A tun of man in thy large bulk is writ,
But sure thou 'rt but a kilderkin of wit.
Like mine, thy gentle numbers feebly creep;
Thy tragic Muse gives smiles, thy comic sleep.
With whate'er gall thou sett'st thyself to write,
Thy inoffensive satires never bite.   200
In thy felonious heart tho' venom lies,
It does but touch thy Irish pen, and dies.
Thy genius calls thee not to purchase fame
In keen iambics, but mild anagram.
Leave writing plays, and choose for thy command
Some peaceful province in acrostic land.
There thou may'st wings display and altars raise.

And torture one poor word ten thousand ways;
Or, if thou wouldst thy diff'rent talents suit,
Set thy own songs, and sing them to thy lute."   210
   He said: but his last words were scarcely heard,
For Bruce and Longvil had a trap prepar'd,
And down they sent the yet declaiming bard.
Sinking he left his drugget robe behind,
Borne upwards by a subterranean wind.
The mantle fell to the young prophet's part,
With double portion of his father's art.

119.   TO MY DEAR FRIEND MR. CONGREVE

Well then, the promis'd hour is come at last;
The present age of wit obscures the past:
Strong were our sires, and as they fought they writ,
Conqu'ring with force of arms, and dint of wit;
Theirs was the giant race, before the flood;
And thus, when Charles return'd our empire stood.
Like Janus he the stubborn soil manur'd,
With rules of husbandry the rankness cur'd:
Tam'd us to manners, when the stage was rude,
And boist'rous English wit with art indued.   10
Our age was cultivated thus at length,
But what we gain'd in skill we lost in strength.
Our builders were with want of genius cursed;
The second temple was not like the first:
Till you, the best Vitruvius, come at length,
Our beauties equal, but excel our strength.
Firm Doric pillars found your solid base,
The fair Corinthian crowns the higher space:
Thus all below is strength, and all above is grace.
In easy dialogue is Fletcher's praise;   20
He mov'd the mind, but had not power to raise.
Great Jonson did by strength of judgment please,
Yet, doubling Fletcher's force, he wants his ease.
In diff'ring talents both adorn'd their age;
One for the study, t'other for the stage:
But both to Congreve justly shall submit,
One match'd in judgment, both o'ermatch'd in wit.
In him all beauties of this age we see,

Etherege his courtship, Southerne's purity,
The satire, wit, and strength of manly Wycherley.   30
All this in blooming youth you have achiev'd,
Nor are your foil'd contemporaries griev'd.
So much the sweetness of your manners move,
We cannot envy you, because we love.
Fabius might joy in Scipio, when he saw
A beardless consul made against the law,
And join his suffrage to the votes of Rome,
Tho' he with Hannibal was overcome.
Thus old Romano bow'd to Raphael's fame,
And scholar to the youth he taught became.   40
  O that your brows my laurel had sustain'd;
Well had I been depos'd, if you had reign'd!
The father had descended for the son;
For only you are lineal to the throne.
Thus, when the state one Edward did depose,
A greater Edward in his room arose.
But now, not I, but poetry is curst;
For Tom the Second reigns like Tom the First.
But let 'em not mistake my patron's part
Nor call his charity their own desert.   50
Yet this I prophesy: thou shalt be seen,
(Tho' with some short parenthesis between)
High on the throne of wit; and, seated there,
Not mine (that's little) but thy laurel wear.
Thy first attempt an early promise made;
That early promise this has more than paid.
So bold, yet so judiciously you dare,
That your least praise, is to be regular.
Time, place, and action may with pains be wrought,
But Genius must be born, and never can be taught.   60
This is your portion, this your native store:
Heav'n, that but once was prodigal before,
To *Shakespeare* gave as much; she cou'd not give
   him more.
  Maintain your post: that 's all the fame you need;
For 'tis impossible you should proceed.
Already I am worn with cares and age,
And just abandoning th' ungrateful stage:
Unprofitably kept at heav'n's expense,

I live a rent-charge on his providence:
But you, whom ev'ry Muse and Grace adorn,   70
Whom I foresee to better fortune born,
Be kind to my remains; and oh defend,
Against your judgment, your departed friend!
Let not th' insulting foe my fame pursue,
But shade those laurels which descend to you;
And take for tribute what these lines express:
You merit more; nor could my love do less.

120.   ALEXANDER'S FEAST

I

'T was at the royal feast, for Persia won
          By Philip's warlike son:
      Aloft in awful state
      The godlike hero sate
          On his imperial throne;
      His valiant peers were plac'd around;
Their brows with roses and with myrtles bound:
      (So should desert in arms be crown'd.)
The lovely Thais, by his side,
Sate like a blooming Eastern bride   10
In flow'r of youth and beauty's pride.
      Happy, happy, happy pair!
      None but the brave,
      None but the brave,
      None but the brave deserves the fair.

CHORUS

      Happy, happy, happy pair!
      None but the brave,
      None but the brave,
      None but the brave deserves the fair.

II

Timotheus, plac'd on high   20
      Amid the tuneful choir,
      With flying fingers touch'd the lyre:
      The trembling notes ascend the sky,
          And heav'nly joys inspire.

The song began from Jove,
Who left his blissful seats above,
(Such is the pow'r of mighty love.)
A dragon's fiery form belied the god:
Sublime on radiant spires he rode,
  When he to fair Olympia press'd;   30
  And while he sought her snowy breast:
Then, round her slender waist he curl'd,
And stamp'd an image of himself, a sov'reign of the world.
The list'ning crowd admire the lofty sound,
"A present deity," they shout around:
"A present deity," the vaulted roofs rebound.
   With ravish'd ears
   The monarch hears,
   Assumes the god,
   Affects to nod,   40
 And seems to shake the spheres.

CHORUS

   With ravish'd ears
   The monarch hears,
   Assumes the god,
   Affects to nod,
 And seems to shake the spheres.

III

The praise of Bacchus then the sweet musician sung,
 Of Bacchus ever fair and ever young:
  The jolly god in triumph comes;
  Sound the trumpets; beat the drums;   50
   Flush'd with a purple grace
   He shews his honest face:
Now give the hautboys breath; he comes, he comes.
  Bacchus, ever fair and young
   Drinking joys did first ordain;
  Bacchus' blessings are a treasure,
  Drinking is a soldier's pleasure;
   Rich the treasure,
   Sweet the pleasure,
  Sweet is pleasure after pain.   60

CHORUS

Bacchus' blessings are a treasure,
Drinking is the soldier's pleasure;
Rich the treasure,
Sweet the pleasure,
Sweet is pleasure after pain.

IV

Sooth'd with the sound, the king grew vain;
Fought all his battles o'er again;
And thrice he routed all his foes; and thrice he slew the slain.
The master saw the madness rise,
His glowing cheeks, his ardent eyes;   70
And, while he heav'n and earth defied,
Chang'd his hand, and check'd his pride.
He chose a mournful Muse,
Soft pity to infuse;
He sung Darius great and good,
By too severe a fate,
Fallen, fallen, fallen, fallen,
Fallen from his high estate,
And welt'ring in his blood;
Deserted, at his utmost need   80
By those his former bounty fed;
On the bare earth expos'd he lies,
With not a friend to close his eyes.
With downcast looks the joyless victor sate,
Revolving in his alter'd soul
The various turns of chance below;
And, now and then, a sigh he stole,
And tears began to flow.

CHORUS

Revolving in his alter'd soul
The various turns of chance below;   90
And, now and then, a sigh he stole,
And tears began to flow.

V

The mighty master smil'd to see
That love was in the next degree;

'Twas but a kindred sound to move,
For pity melts the mind to love.
   Softly sweet, in Lydian measures,
   Soon he sooth'd his soul to pleasures.
   "War," he sung, "is toil and trouble;
   Honor, but an empty bubble.
    Never ending, still beginning,
   Fighting still, and still destroying:
    If the world be worth thy winning,
   Think, O think it worth enjoying.
    Lovely Thais sits beside thee,
    Take the good the gods provide thee."
The many rend the skies with loud applause;
So Love was crown'd, but Music won the cause.
   The prince, unable to conceal his pain,
     Gaz'd on the fair
     Who caus'd his care,
   And sigh'd and look'd, sigh'd and look'd,
  Sigh'd and look'd, and sigh'd again:
At length, with love and wine at once oppress'd,
The vanquish'd victor sunk upon her breast.

CHORUS

   The prince, unable to conceal his pain,
     Gaz'd on the fair
     Who caus'd his care,
   And sigh'd and look'd, sigh'd and look'd,
  Sigh'd and look'd, and sigh'd again:
At length, with love and wine at once oppress'd,
The vanquish'd victor sunk upon her breast.

VI

Now strike the golden lyre again:
A louder yet, and yet a louder strain.
Break his bands of sleep asunder,
And rouse him, like a rattling peal of thunder.
    Hark, hark, the horrid sound
     Has rais'd up his head:
     As wak'd from the dead,
    And amaz'd, he stares around.
"Revenge, revenge!" Timotheus cries,

"See the Furies arise!
See the snakes that they rear,
How they hiss in their hair,
And the sparkles that flash from their eyes!
Behold a ghastly band,
Each a torch in his hand!
Those are Grecian ghosts, that in battle were slain,
And unburied remain
Inglorious on the plain: 140
Give the vengeance due
To the valiant crew.
Behold how they toss their torches on high,
How they point to the Persian abodes,
And glitt'ring temples of their hostile gods!"
The princes applaud, with a furious joy;
And the king seiz'd a flambeau with zeal to destroy;
Thais led the way,
To light him to his prey,
And, like another Helen, fir'd another Troy.   150

CHORUS

And the king seiz'd a flambeau with zeal to destroy;
Thais led the way,
To light him to his prey,
And, like another Helen, fir'd another Troy.

VII

Thus long ago,
Ere heaving bellows learn'd to blow,
While organs yet were mute;
Timotheus, to his breathing flute,
And sounding lyre,
Could swell the soul to rage, or kindle soft desire.   160
At last, divine Cecilia came,
Inventress of the vocal frame;
The sweet enthusiast, from her sacred store,
Enlarg'd the former narrow bounds,
And added length to solemn sounds,
With nature's mother wit, and arts unknown before.
Let old Timotheus yield the prize,
Or both divide the crown:

He rais'd a mortal to the skies;
  She drew an angel down. 170

GRAND CHORUS

  At last, divine Cecilia came,
  Inventress of the vocal frame;
The sweet enthusiast, from her sacred store,
  Enlarg'd the former narrow bounds,
  And added length to solemn sounds,
With nature's mother wit, and arts unknown before.
  Let old Timotheus yield the prize,
    Or both divide the crown:
  He rais'd a mortal to the skies;
    She drew an angel down. 180

JOHN POMFRET (1667–1702)

121. ## THE CHOICE

If Heaven the grateful liberty would give
That I might choose my method how to live,
And all those hours propitious fate should lend,
In blissful ease and satisfaction spend:
  Near some fair town I'd have a private seat,
Built uniform, not little, nor too great:
Better if on a rising ground it stood;
Fields on this side, on that a neighbouring wood;
It should within no other things contain
But what were useful, necessary, plain: 10
Methinks 'tis nauseous, and I'd ne'er endure
The needless pomp of gaudy furniture.
A little garden, grateful to the eye,
And a cool rivulet run murmuring by,
On whose delicious banks a stately row
Of shady limes or sycamores should grow;
At th' end of which a silent study placed
Should be with all the noblest authors graced:
Horace and Virgil, in whose mighty lines
Immortal wit and solid learning shines; 20
Sharp Juvenal, and amorous Ovid too,
Who all the turns of love's soft passion knew;

He that with judgment reads his charming lines,
In which strong art with stronger nature joins,
Must grant his fancy does the best excel,
His thoughts so tender and expressed so well;
With all those moderns, men of steady sense,
Esteemed for learning and for eloquence.
In some of these, as fancy should advise,
I'd always take my morning exercise: 30
For sure no minutes bring us more content
Than those in pleasing, useful studies spent.
    I'd have a clear and competent estate,
That I might live genteelly, but not great;
As much as I could moderately spend,
A little more, sometimes t' oblige a friend.
Nor should the sons of poverty repine
Too much at fortune, they should taste of mine;
And all that objects of true pity were
Should be relieved with what my wants could spare.   40
For that our Maker has too largely given
Should be returned, in gratitude to heaven.
A frugal plenty should my table spread,
With healthy, not luxurious, dishes fed:
Enough to satisfy, and something more,
To feed the stranger and the neighbouring poor.
Strong meat indulges vice, and pampering food
Creates diseases and inflames the blood.
But what's sufficient to make nature strong
And the bright lamp of life continue long   50
I'd freely take, and as I did possess,
The bounteous Author of my plenty bless.
    I'd have a little vault, but always stored
With the best wines each vintage could afford.
Wine whets the wit, improves its native force,
And gives a pleasant flavour to discourse:
By making all our spirits debonair,
Throws off the lees, the sediment of care.
But as the greatest blessing heaven lends
May be debauched and serve ignoble ends,   60
So, but too oft, the grape's refreshing juice
Does many mischievous effects produce.
My house should no such rude disorders know

As from high drinking consequently flow.
Nor would I use what was so kindly given
To the dishonour of indulgent heaven.
If any neighbour came, he should be free,
Used with respect, and not uneasy be
In my retreat, or to himself or me.
What freedom, prudence, and right reason give   70
All men may with impunity receive:
But the least swerving from their rule's too much,
For what's forbidden us, 'tis death to touch.
   That life may be more comfortable yet,
And all my joys refined, sincere and great,
I'd choose two friends, whose company would be
A great advance to my felicity:
Well-born, of humours suited to my own;
Discreet, and men, as well as books, have known.
Brave, generous, witty, and exactly free   80
From loose behaviour or formality;
Airy and prudent, merry, but not light;
Quick in discerning, and in judging right.
Secret they should be, faithful to their trust;
In reasoning cool, strong, temperate and just;
Obliging, open, without huffing, brave,
Brisk in gay talking, and in sober, grave;
Close in dispute, but not tenacious, tried
By solid reason, and let that decide;
Not prone to lust, revenge, or envious hate,   90
Nor busy meddlers with intrigues of state;
Strangers to slander, and sworn foes to spite;
Not quarrelsome, but stout enough to fight;
Loyal and pious, friends to Cæsar, true
As dying martyrs to their Maker too.
In their society, I could not miss
A permanent, sincere, substantial bliss.
   Would bounteous heaven once more indulge, I'd choose
(For who would so much satisfaction lose
As witty nymphs in conversation give?)   100
Near some obliging, modest fair to live;
For there's that sweetness in a female mind
Which in a man's we cannot hope to find,
That by a secret but a powerful art

Winds up the springs of life, and does impart
Fresh vital heat to the transported heart.
   I'd have her reason all her passions sway;
Easy in company, in private gay:
Coy to a fop, to the deserving free,
Still constant to herself, and just to me.   110
A soul she should have for great actions fit;
Prudence and wisdom to direct her wit:
Courage to look bold danger in the face,
No fear, but only to be proud or base:
Quick to advise, by an emergence pressed,
To give good counsel, or to take the best.
I'd have th' expression of her thoughts be such
She might not seem reserved nor talk too much;
That shows a want of judgment and of sense:
More than enough is but impertinence.   120
Her conduct regular, her mirth refined,
Civil to strangers, to her neighbours kind;
Averse to vanity, revenge, and pride,
In all the methods of deceit untried;
So faithful to her friend, and good to all,
No censure might upon her actions fall;
Then would e'en envy be compelled to say
She goes the least of womankind astray.
   To this fair creature I'd sometimes retire;
Her conversation would new joys inspire;   130
Give life an edge so keen, no surly care
Would venture to assault my soul, or dare
Near my retreat to hide one secret snare.
But so divine, so noble a repast
I'd seldom and with moderation taste;
For highest cordials all their virtue lose
By a too frequent and too bold a use:
And what would cheer the spirits in distress
Ruins our health, when taken to excess.
   I'd be concerned in no litigious jar,   140
Beloved by all, not vainly popular;
Whate'er assistance I had power to bring
T' oblige my country, or to serve my king,
Whene'er they called, I'd readily afford
My tongue, my pen, my counsel, or my sword.

Lawsuits I'd shun, with as much studious care
As I would dens where hungry lions are,
And rather put up injuries than be
A plague to him who'd be a plague to me.
I value quiet at a price too great   150
To give for my revenge so dear a rate;
For what do we by all our bustle gain
But counterfeit delight, for real pain?
   If Heaven a date of many years would give,
Thus I'd in pleasure, ease, and plenty live;
And as I near approached the verge of life,
Some kind relation (for I'd have no wife)
Should take upon him all my worldly care
While I did for a better state prepare.
Then I'd not be with any trouble vexed,   160
Nor have the evening of my days perplexed;
But by a silent and a peaceful death,
Without a sigh, resign my aged breath:
And when committed to the dust, I'd have
Few tears, but friendly, dropped into my grave.
Then would my exit so propitious be,
All men would wish to live and die like me.

THOMAS PARNELL (1679–1718)

122.   ON A LADY WITH FOUL BREATH

Art thou alive? It cannot be,
There's so much rottenness in thee.
Corruption only is in death,
And what's more putrid than thy breath?
Think not you live because you speak,
For graves such hollow sounds can make;
And respiration can't suffice,
For vapours do from caverns rise:
From thee such noisome stenches come,
Thy mouth betrays thy breast a tomb.   10
Thy body is a corpse that goes,
By magic rais'd from its repose:
A pestilence, that walks by day,
But falls at night to worms and clay.

But I will to my Chloris run,
Who will not let me be undone:
The sweets her virgin-breath contains
Are fitted to remove my pains;
There will I healing nectar sip,
And, to be sav'd, approach her lip,   20
Though, if I touch the matchless dame,
I'm sure to burn with inward flame,
Thus, when I would one danger shun,
I'm straight upon another thrown:
I seek a cure, one sore to ease,
Yet in that cure's a new disease.
But Love, though fatal, still can bless,
And greater dangers hide the less;
I'll go where passion bids me fly,
And choose my death, since I must die;   30
As doves, pursued by birds of prey,
Venture with milder man to stay.

MATTHEW PRIOR (1664–1721)

123.   AN ODE

The merchant, to secure his treasure,
    Conveys it in a borrow'd name:
Euphelia serves to grace my measure;
    But Cloe is my real flame.

My softest verse, my darling lyre,
    Upon Euphelia's toilet lay;
When Cloe noted her desire,
    That I should sing, that I should play.

My lyre I tune, my voice I raise;
    But with my numbers mix my sighs: 10
And whilst I sing Euphelia's praise,
    I fix my soul on Cloe's eyes.

Fair Cloe blush'd: Euphelia frown'd:
    I sung and gaz'd: I play'd and trembled:
And Venus to the Loves around
    Remark'd, how ill we all dissembled.

124. A BETTER ANSWER TO CLOE JEALOUS

Dear Cloe, how blubber'd is that pretty face;
 Thy cheek all on fire, and thy hair all uncurl'd:
Pr'ythee quit this caprice; and (as old Falstaff says)
 Let us e'en talk a little like folks of this world.

How canst thou presume, thou has leave to destroy
 The beauties which Venus but lent to thy keeping?
Those looks were design'd to inspire love and joy:
 More ord'nary eyes may serve people for weeping.

To be vext at a trifle or two that I writ,
 Your judgment at once, and my passion you wrong: 10
You take that for fact, which will scarce be found wit:
 Odds life! must one swear to the truth of a song?

What I speak, my fair Cloe, and what I write, shows
 The difference there is betwixt nature and art:
I court others in verse; but I love thee in prose:
 And they have my whimsies, but thou hast my heart.

The god of us verse-men (you know, child), the sun,
 How after his journeys he sets up his rest:
If at morning o'er earth 'tis his fancy to run,
 At night he declines on his Thetis's breast. 20

So when I am wearied with wandering all day,
 To thee, my delight, in the evening I come:
No matter what beauties I saw in my way;
 They were but my visits, but thou art my home.

Then finish, dear Cloe, this pastoral war;
 And let us, like Horace and Lydia, agree:
For thou art a girl as much brighter than her,
 As he was a poet sublimer than me.

125. WRITTEN IN THE BEGINNING OF MEZERAY'S
HISTORY OF FRANCE

Whate'er thy countrymen have done
By law and wit, by sword and gun,
 In thee is faithfully recited:
And all the living world, that view
Thy work, give thee the praises due,
 At once instructed and delighted.

Yet for the fame of all these deeds,
What beggar in the Invalides,
   With lameness broke, with blindness smitten,
Wished ever decently to die,   10
To have been either Mezeray,
   Or any monarch he has written?

It strange, dear author, yet it true is,
That, down from Pharamond to Louis,
   All covet life, yet call it pain:
All feel the ill, yet shun the cure:
Can sense this paradox endure?
   Resolve me, Cambray, or Fontaine.

The man in graver tragic known
(Though his best part long since was done)   20
   Still on the stage desires to tarry:
And he who played the Harlequin,
After the jest still loads the scene
   Unwilling to retire, though weary.

126.   THE SECRETARY

While with labour assiduous due pleasures I mix,
And in one day atone for the business of six,
In a little Dutch chaise on a Saturday night,
On my left hand my Horace, a nymph on my right:
No memoire to compose, and no postboy to move,
That on Sunday may hinder the softness of love;
For her, neither visits, nor parties at tea,
Nor the long-winded cant of a dull refugee.
This night, and the next shall be hers, shall be mine,
To good or ill fortune the third we resign: 10
Thus scorning the world, and superior to fate,
I drive on my car in processional state.
So with Phia through Athens Pisistratus rode:
Men thought her Minerva, and him a new god.
But why should I stories of Athens rehearse,
Where people knew love, and were partial to verse;
Since none can with justice my pleasures oppose,
In Holland half drowned in interest and prose?
By Greece and past ages what need I be tried,
When the Hague and the present are both on my side? 20

And is it enough for the joys of the day,
To think what Anacreon or Sappho would say?
When good Vandergoes and his provident Vrow,
As they gaze on my triumph, do freely allow,
That, search all the province, you'll find no man there is
So blest as the Englishen Heer Secretaris.

127.   AN EPITAPH

Interred beneath this marble stone,
Lie sauntering Jack and idle Joan.
While rolling threescore years and one
Did round this globe their courses run,
If human things went ill or well,
If changing empires rose or fell,
The morning passed, the evening came,
And found this couple still the same.
They walked and eat, good folks—what then?
Why then they walked and eat again.   10
They soundly slept the night away;
They did just nothing all the day;
And having buried children four,
Would not take pains to try for more.
Nor sister either had, nor brother;
They seemed just tallied for each other.
   Their moral and economy
Most perfectly they made agree;
Each virtue kept its proper bound,
Nor trespassed on the other's ground.   20
Nor fame nor censure they regarded;
They neither punished nor rewarded.
He cared not what the footmen did;
Her maids she neither praised, nor chid;
So every servant took his course,
And bad at first, they all grew worse.
Slothful disorder filled his stable,
And sluttish plenty decked her table.
Their beer was strong; their wine was port;
Their meal was large; their grace was short.   30
They gave the poor the remnant-meat,
Just when it grew not fit to eat.
   They paid the church and parish rate,

And took, but read not the receipt;
For which they claimed their Sunday's due,
Of slumbering in an upper pew.
    No man's defects sought they to know;
So never made themselves a foe.
No man's good deeds did they commend;
So never raised themselves a friend.   40
Nor cherished they relations poor,
That might decrease their present store;
Nor barn nor house did they repair,
That might oblige their future heir.
    They neither added nor confounded;
They neither wanted nor abounded.
Each Christmas they accompts did clear,
And wound their bottom round the year.
Nor tear nor smile did they employ
At news of public grief or joy.   50
When bells were rung, and bonfires made,
If asked, they ne'er denied their aid:
Their jug was to the ringers carried,
Whoever either died or married.
Their billet at the fire was found,
Whoever was deposed, or crowned.
    Nor good, nor bad, nor fools, nor wise;
They would not learn, nor could advise:
Without love, hatred, joy or fear,
They led—a kind of—as it were: 60
Nor wished, nor cared, nor laughed, nor cried:
And so they lived; and so they died.

JOHN GAY (1685–1732)

128.   ### TO A LADY ON HER PASSION
FOR OLD CHINA

What ecstasies her bosom fire!
How her eyes languish with desire!
How blessed, how happy should I be,
Were that fond glance bestowed on me!
New doubts and fears within me war:
What rival's near? A China jar.

China's the passion of her soul;
A cup, a plate, a dish, a bowl
Can kindle wishes in her breast,
Inflame with joy, or break her rest.   10
   Some gems collect; some medals prize,
And view the rust with lovers' eyes;
Some court the stars at midnight hours;
Some dote on Nature's charms in flowers!
But every beauty I can trace
In Laura's mind, in Laura's face;
My stars are in this brighter sphere,
My lily and my rose is here.
   Philosophers more grave than wise
Hunt science down in butterflies;   20
Or fondly poring on a spider,
Stretch human contemplation wider;
Fossils give joy to Galen's soul;
He digs for knowledge like a mole;
In shells so learned, that all agree
No fish that swims knows more than he!
In such pursuits if wisdom lies,
Who, Laura, shall thy taste despise?
   When I some antique jar behold,
Or white, or blue, or specked with gold,   30
Vessels so pure and so refined
Appear the types of womankind:
Are they not valued for their beauty,
Too fair, too fine for household duty,
With flowers and gold and azure dyed,
Of every house the grace and pride?
How white, how polished is their skin,
And valued most when only seen!
She who before was highest prized,
Is for a crack or flaw despised;   40
I grant they're frail, yet they're so rare,
The treasure cannot cost too dear!
But man is made of coarser stuff,
And serves convenience well enough;
He's a strong earthern vessel, made
For drudging, labour, toil, and trade;
And when wives lose their other self,

With ease they bear the loss of Delf.
  Husbands more covetous than sage
Condemn this China-buying rage;   50
They count that woman's prudence little,
Who sets her heart on things so brittle.
But are those wise men's inclinations
Fixed on more strong, more sure foundations?
If all that's frail we must despise,
No human view or scheme is wise.
Are not Ambition's hopes as weak?
They swell like bubbles, shine, and break.
A courtier's promise is so slight,
'Tis made at noon, and broke at night.   60
What pleasure's sure? The miss you keep
Breaks both your fortune and your sleep.
The man who loves a country life
Breaks all the comforts of his wife;
And if he quit his farm and plough,
His wife in town may break her vow.
Love, Laura, love, while youth is warm,
For each new winter breaks a charm;
And woman's not like China sold,
But cheaper grows in growing old;   70
Then quickly choose the prudent part,
Or else you break a faithful heart.

129.   AN ELEGY ON A LAP DOG

Shock's fate I mourn; poor Shock is now no more,
Ye Muses mourn, ye chamber-maids deplore.
Unhappy Shock! yet more unhappy Fair,
Doomed to survive thy joy and only care!
Thy wretched fingers now no more shall deck,
And tie the fav'rite ribband round his neck;
No more thy hand shall smooth his glossy hair,
And comb the wavings of his pendent ear.
Yet cease thy flowing grief, forsaken maid;
All mortal pleasures in a moment fade: 10
Our surest hope is in an hour destroyed,
And love, best gift of heaven, not long enjoyed.

  Methinks I see her frantic with despair,
Her streaming eyes, wrung hands, and flowing hair;

Her Mechlen pinners rent the floor bestrow,
And her torn fan gives real signs of woe.
Hence Superstition, that tormenting guest,
That haunts with fancied fears the coward breast;
No dread events upon this fate attend,
Stream eyes no more, no more thy tresses rend.   20
Tho' certain omens oft forewarn a state,
And dying lions show the monarch's fate;
Why should such fears bid Celia's sorrow rise
For when a Lap-dog falls no lover dies.

    Cease, Celia, cease; restrain thy flowing tears,
Some warmer passion will dispel thy cares.
In man you'll find a more substantial bliss,
More grateful toying and a sweeter kiss.

    He's dead. Oh lay him gently in the ground!
And may his tomb be by this verse renowned: 30
Here Shock, the pride of all his kind, is laid,
Who fawned like man, but ne'er like man betrayed.

JONATHAN SWIFT (1667–1745)

130.   A DESCRIPTION OF A CITY SHOWER

Careful observers may foretell the hour
(By sure prognostics) when to dread a shower.
While rain depends, the pensive cat gives o'er
Her frolics, and pursues her tail no more.
Returning home at night, you'll find the sink
Strike your offended sense with double stink.
If you be wise, then go not far to dine;
You'll spend in coach-hire more than save in wine.
A coming shower your shooting corns presage,
Old aches throb, your hollow tooth will rage: 10
Sauntering in coffee-house is Dulman seen;
He damns the climate and complains of spleen.
  Meanwhile the South, rising with dabbled wings,
A sable cloud athwart the welkin flings,
That swilled more liquor than it could contain,
And, like a drunkard, gives it up again.
Brisk Susan whips her linen from the rope,

While the first drizzling shower is borne aslope:
Such is that sprinkling which some careless quean
Flirts on you from her mop, but not so clean: 20
You fly, invoke the gods; then turning, stop
To rail; she singing, still whirls on her mop.
Nor yet the dust had shunned the unequal strife,
But, aided by the wind, fought still for life,
And wafted with its foe by violent gust,
'Twas doubtful which was rain and which was dust.
Ah! where must needy poet seek for aid,
When dust and rain at once his coat invade?
Sole coat, where dust cemented by the rain
Erects the nap, and leaves a cloudy stain.   30
　　Now in contiguous drops the flood comes down,
Threatening with deluge this devoted town.
To shops in crowds the daggled females fly,
Pretend to cheapen goods, but nothing buy.
The Templar spruce, while every spout's abroach,
Stays till 'tis fair, yet seems to call a coach.
The tucked-up sempstress walks with hasty strides,
While streams run down her oiled umbrella's sides.
Here various kinds, by various fortunes led,
Commence acquaintance underneath a shed.   40
Triumphant Tories and desponding Whigs
Forget their feuds, and join to save their wigs.
Boxed in a chair the beau impatient sits,
While spouts run clattering o'er the roof by fits;
And ever and anon with frightful din
The leather sounds; he trembles from within.
So when Troy chairmen bore the wooden steed,
Pregnant with Greeks impatient to be freed
(Those bully Greeks, who, as the moderns do,
Instead of paying chairmen, run them through),   50
Laocoön struck the outside with his spear,
And each imprisoned hero quaked for fear.
　　Now from all parts the swelling kennels flow,
And bear their trophies with them as they go:
Filth of all hues and odours seem to tell
What street they sailed from, by their sight and smell.
They, as each torrent drives with rapid force,
From Smithfield or St. Pulchre's shape their course,

And in huge confluence joined at Snow Hill ridge,
Fall from the conduit prone to Holborn Bridge.　　　60
Sweepings from butchers' stalls, dung, guts, and blood,
Drowned puppies, stinking sprats, all drenched in mud,
Dead cats, and turnip-tops, come tumbling down the flood.

ALEXANDER POPE (1688–1744)

131.　　　　　ODE ON SOLITUDE

Happy the man whose wish and care
　　A few paternal acres bound,
Content to breathe his native air,
　　　　In his own ground.

Whose herds with milk, whose fields with bread,
　　Whose flocks supply him with attire,
Whose trees in summer yield him shade,
　　　　In winter fire.

Blest, who can unconcern'dly find
　　Hours, days, and years slide soft away,　　　10
In health of body, peace of mind,
　　　　Quiet by day,

Sound sleep by night; study and ease,
　　Together mixt; sweet recreation;
And Innocence, which most does please
　　　　With meditation.

Thus let me live, unseen, unknown,
　　Thus unlamented let me die,
Steal from the world, and not a stone
　　　　Tell where I lie.　　　　　　20

132.　　　　THE RAPE OF THE LOCK

CANTO I

What dire offence from amorous causes springs,
What mighty contests rise from trivial things,
I sing—This verse to Caryll, Muse! is due:
This, even Belinda may vouchsafe to view:
Slight is the subject, but not so the praise,

If she inspire, and he approve my lays.
    Say what strange motive, Goddess! could compel
A well-bred lord to assault a gentle belle?
O say what stranger cause, yet unexplored,
Could make a gentle belle reject a lord?   10
In tasks so bold, can little men engage,
And in soft bosoms dwells such mighty rage?
    Sol through white curtains shot a timorous ray,
And oped those eyes that must eclipse the day:
Now lap-dogs give themselves the rousing shake,
And sleepless lovers, just at twelve, awake:
Thrice rung the bell, the slipper knocked the ground,
And the pressed watch returned a silver sound.
Belinda still her downy pillow pressed,
Her guardian sylph prolonged the balmy rest: 20
'Twas he had summoned to her silent bed
The morning-dream that hovered o'er her head;
A youth more glittering than a birth-night beau,
(That even in slumber caused her cheek to glow)
Seemed to her ear his winning lips to lay,
And thus in whispers said, or seemed to say:
    "Fairest of mortals, thou distinguished care
Of thousand bright inhabitants of air!
If e'er one vision touched thy infant thought,
Of all the nurse and all the priest have taught;   30
Of airy elves by moonlight shadows seen,
The silver token, and the circled green,
Or virgins visited by angel-powers,
With golden crowns and wreaths of heavenly flowers;
Hear and believe! thy own importance know,
Nor bound thy narrow views to things below.
Some secret truths, from learnèd pride concealed,
To maids alone and children are revealed:
What though no credit doubting wits may give?
The fair and innocent shall still believe.   40
Know, then, unnumbered spirits round thee fly,
The light militia of the lower sky:
These, though unseen, are ever on the wing,
Hang o'er the box, and hover round the Ring.
Think what an equipage thou hast in air,
And view with scorn two pages and a chair.

As now your own, our beings were of old,
And once inclosed in woman's beauteous mould;
Thence, by a soft transition, we repair
From earthly vehicles to these of air. 50
Think not, when woman's transient breath is fled,
That all her vanities at once are dead;
Succeeding vanities she still regards,
And though she plays no more, o'erlooks the cards.
Her joy in gilded chariots, when alive,
And love of ombre, after death survive.
For when the fair in all their pride expire,
To their first elements their souls retire:
The sprites of fiery termagants in flame
Mount up, and take a salamander's name. 60
Soft yielding minds to water glide away,
And sip, with nymphs, their elemental tea.
The graver prude sinks downward to a gnome,
In search of mischief still on earth to roam.
The light coquettes in sylphs aloft repair,
And sport and flutter in the fields of air.
"Know further yet: whoever fair and chaste
Rejects mankind, is by some sylph embraced;
For spirits, freed from mortal laws, with ease
Assume what sexes and what shapes they please. 70
What guards the purity of melting maids,
In courtly balls, and midnight masquerades,
Safe from the treacherous friend, the daring spark,
The glance by day, the whisper in the dark,
When kind occasion prompts their warm desires,
When music softens, and when dancing fires?
'Tis but their sylph, the wise celestials know,
Though honour is the word with men below.
"Some nymphs there are, too conscious of their face,
For life predestined to the gnomes' embrace. 80
These swell their prospects and exalt their pride,
When offers are disdained, and love denied:
Then gay ideas crowd the vacant brain,
While peers, and dukes, and all their sweeping train,
And garters, stars, and coronets appear,
And in soft sounds, 'Your Grace' salutes their ear.
'Tis these that early taint the female soul,

Instruct the eyes of young coquettes to roll,
Teach infant cheeks a bidden blush to know,
And little hearts to flutter at a beau.   90
"Oft, when the world imagine women stray,
The sylphs through mystic mazes guide their way;
Through all the giddy circle they pursue,
And old impertinence expel by new.
What tender maid but must a victim fall
To one man's treat, but for another's ball?
When Florio speaks what virgin could withstand,
If gentle Damon did not squeeze her hand?
With varying vanities, from every part,
They shift the moving toyshop of their heart;   100
Where wigs with wigs, with sword-knots sword-knots strive,
Beaux banish beaux, and coaches coaches drive.
This erring mortals levity may call;
Oh blind to truth! the sylphs contrive it all.
"Of these am I, who thy protection claim,
A watchful sprite, and Ariel is my name.
Late, as I ranged the crystal wilds of air,
In the clear mirror of thy ruling star
I saw, alas! some dread event impend,
Ere to the main this morning sun descend,   110
But Heaven reveals not what, or how, or where:
Warned by the sylph, O pious maid, beware!
This to disclose is all thy guardian can:
Beware of all, but most beware of man!"
He said; when Shock, who thought she slept too long,
Leaped up, and waked his mistress with his tongue.
'Twas then, Belinda, if report say true,
Thy eyes first opened on a billet-doux;
Wounds, charms, and ardors were no sooner read,
But all the vision vanished from thy head.   120
And now, unveiled, the toilet stands displayed,
Each silver vase in mystic order laid.
First, robed in white, the nymph intent adores,
With head uncovered, the cosmetic powers.
A heavenly image in the glass appears,
To that she bends, to that her eyes she rears;
Th' inferior priestess, at her altar's side,
Trembling begins the sacred rites of pride.

Unnumbered treasures ope at once, and here
The various offerings of the world appear;   130
From each she nicely culls with curious toil,
And decks the Goddess with the glittering spoil.
This casket India's glowing gems unlocks,
And all Arabia breathes from yonder box.
The tortoise here and elephant unite,
Transformed to combs, the speckled, and the white.
Here files of pins extend their shining rows,
Puffs, powders, patches, Bibles, billet-doux.
Now awful beauty puts on all its arms;
The fair each moment rises in her charms,   140
Repairs her smiles, awakens every grace,
And calls forth all the wonders of her face;
Sees by degrees a purer blush arise,
And keener lightnings quicken in her eyes.
The busy sylphs surround their darling care,
These set the head, and those divide the hair,
Some fold the sleeve, whilst others plait the gown;
And Betty's praised for labours not her own.

CANTO II

Not with more glories, in the ethereal plain,
The sun first rises o'er the purpled main,
Than, issuing forth, the rival of his beams
Launched on the bosom of the silver Thames.
Fair nymphs and well-dressed youths around her shone,
But every eye was fixed on her alone.
On her white breast a sparkling cross she wore,
Which Jews might kiss, and infidels adore.
Her lively looks a sprightly mind disclose,
Quick as her eyes, and as unfixed as those: 10
Favours to none, to all she smiles extends;
Oft she rejects, but never once offends.
Bright as the sun, her eyes the gazers strike,
And, like the sun, they shine on all alike.
Yet graceful ease, and sweetness void of pride,
Might hide her faults, if belles had faults to hide:
If to her share some female errors fall,
Look on her face, and you'll forget 'em all.
    This nymph, to the destruction of mankind.

Nourished two locks, which graceful hung behind   20
In equal curls, and well conspired to deck
With shining ringlets the smooth ivory neck.
Love in these labyrinths his slaves detains,
And mighty hearts are held in slender chains.
With hairy springes we the birds betray,
Slight lines of hair surprise the finny prey,
Fair tresses man's imperial race ensnare,
And beauty draws us with a single hair.

The adventurous Baron the bright locks admired;
He saw, he wished, and to the prize aspired.   30
Resolved to win, he meditates the way,
By force to ravish, or by fraud betray;
For when success a lover's toil attends,
Few ask, if fraud or force attained his ends.

For this, ere Phœbus rose, he had implored
Propitious heaven, and every power adored,
But chiefly Love—to Love an altar built,
Of twelve vast French romances, neatly gilt.
There lay three garters, half a pair of gloves;
And all the trophies of his former loves;   40
With tender billet-doux he lights the pyre,
And breathes three amorous sighs to raise the fire.
Then prostrate falls, and begs with ardent eyes
Soon to obtain, and long possess the prize;
The powers gave ear, and granted half his prayer,
The rest, the winds dispersed in empty air.

But now secure the painted vessel glides,
The sunbeams trembling on the floating tides:
While melting music steals upon the sky,
And softened sounds along the waters die;   50
Smooth flow the waves, the zephyrs gently play,
Belinda smiled, and all the world was gay.
All but the sylph—with careful thoughts oppressed,
The impending woe sat heavy on his breast.
He summons straight his denizens of air;
The lucid squadrons round the sails repair;
Soft o'er the shrouds aërial whispers breathe,
That seemed but zephyrs to the train beneath.
Some to the sun their insect-wings unfold,
Waft on the breeze, or sink in clouds of gold;   60

Transparent forms, too fine for mortal sight,
Their fluid bodies half dissolved in light,
Loose to the wind their airy garments flew,
Thin glittering textures of the filmy dew,
Dipped in the richest tincture of the skies,
Where light disports in ever-mingling dyes,
While every beam new transient colours flings,
Colours that change whene'er they wave their wings.
Amid the circle, on the gilded mast,
Superior by the head, was Ariel placed;   70
His purple pinions opening to the sun,
He raised his azure wand, and thus begun:
   "Ye sylphs and sylphids, to your chief give ear!
Fays, fairies, genii, elves, and dæmons, hear!
Ye know the spheres and various tasks assigned
By laws eternal to the aërial kind.
Some in the fields of purest ether play,
And bask and whiten in the blaze of day.
Some guide the course of wandering orbs on high,
Or roll the planets through the boundless sky.   80
Some less refined, beneath the moon's pale light
Pursue the stars that shoot athwart the night,
Or suck the mists in grosser air below,
Or dip their pinions in the painted bow,
Or brew fierce tempests on the wintry main,
Or o'er the glebe distil the kindly rain.
Others on earth o'er human race preside.
Watch all their ways, and all their actions guide:
Of these the chief the care of nations own,
And guard with arms divine the British throne.   90
   "Our humbler province is to tend the fair,
Not a less pleasing, though less glorious care;
To save the powder from too rude a gale,
Nor let the imprisoned essences exhale;
To draw fresh colours from the vernal flowers;
To steal from rainbows e'er they drop in showers
A brighter wash; to curl their waving hairs,
Assist their blushes, and inspire their airs;
Nay oft, in dreams, invention we bestow,
To change a flounce, or add a furbelow.   100
   "This day, black omens threat the brightest fair

That e'er deserved a watchful spirit's care;
Some dire disaster, or by force, or slight;
But what, or where, the fates have wrapped in night.
Whether the nymph shall break Diana's law,
Or some frail china jar receive a flaw;
Or stain her honour or her new brocade;
Forget her prayers, or miss a masquerade;
Or lose her heart, or necklace, at a ball;
Or whether Heaven has doomed that Shock must fall.   110
Haste, then, ye spirits! to your charge repair:
The fluttering fan be Zephyretta's care;
The drops to thee, Brillante, we consign;
And, Momentilla, let the watch be thine;
Do thou, Crispissa, tend her favorite lock;
Ariel himself shall be the guard of Shock.
     "To fifty chosen sylphs, of special note,
We trust the important charge, the petticoat:
Oft have we known that seven-fold fence to fail,
Though stiff with hoops, and armed with ribs of whale;   120
Form a strong line about the silver bound,
And guard the wide circumference around.
     "Whatever spirit, careless of his charge,
His post neglects, or leaves the fair at large,
Shall feel sharp vengeance soon o'ertake his sins,
Be stopped in vials, or transfixed with pins;
Or plunged in lakes of bitter washes lie,
Or wedged whole ages in a bodkin's eye:
Gums and pomatums shall his flight restrain,
While clogged he beats his silken wings in vain;   130
Or alum styptics with contracting power
Shrink his thin essence like a rivelled flower:
Or, as Ixion fixed, the wretch shall feel
The giddy motion of the whirling mill,
In fumes of burning chocolate shall glow,
And tremble at the sea that froths below!"
     He spoke; the spirits from the sails descend;
Some, orb in orb, around the nymph extend;
Some thrid the mazy ringlets of her hair;
Some hang upon the pendants of her ear;   140
With beating hearts the dire event they wait,
Anxious, and trembling for the birth of Fate.

CANTO III

Close by those meads, forever crowned with flowers,
Where Thames with pride surveys his rising towers,
There stands a structure of majestic frame,
Which from the neighboring Hampton takes its name.
Here Britain's statesmen oft the fall foredoom
Of foreign tyrants and of nymphs at home;
Here thou, great Anna! whom three realms obey,
Dost sometimes counsel take—and sometimes tea.
  Hither the heroes and the nymphs resort,
To taste awhile the pleasures of a court; 10
In various talk the instructive hours they passed,
Who gave the ball, or paid the visit last;
One speaks the glory of the British Queen,
And one describes a charming Indian screen;
A third interprets motions, looks, and eyes;
At every word a reputation dies.
Snuff, or the fan, supply each pause of chat,
With singing, laughing, ogling, *and all that.*
  Meanwhile, declining from the noon of day,
The sun obliquely shoots his burning ray; 20
The hungry judges soon the sentence sign,
And wretches hang that jurymen may dine;
The merchant from the Exchange returns in peace,
And the long labours of the toilet cease.
Belinda now, whom thirst of fame invites,
Burns to encounter two adventurous knights,
At ombre singly to decide their doom;
And swells her breast with conquests yet to come.
Straight the three bands prepare in arms to join,
Each band the number of the sacred nine. 30
Soon as she spreads her hand, the aërial guard
Descend, and sit on each important card:
First Ariel perched upon a Matadore,
Then each, according to the rank they bore;
For sylphs, yet mindful of their ancient race,
Are, as when women, wondrous fond of place.
  Behold, four kings in majesty revered,
With hoary whiskers and a forky beard;
And four fair queens whose hands sustain a flower,

The expressive emblem of their softer power;   40
Four knaves in garbs succinct, a trusty band,
Caps on their heads, and halberts in their hand;
And particolored troops, a shining train,
Draw forth to combat on the velvet plain.
    The skilful nymph reviews her force with care:
"Let spades be trumps!" she said, and trumps they were.
    Now move to war her sable Matadores,
In show like leaders of the swarthy Moors.
Spadillio first, unconquerable lord!
Led off two captive trumps, and swept the board.   50
As many more Manillio forced to yield,
And marched a victor from the verdant field.
Him Basto followed, but his fate more hard
Gained but one trump and one plebeian card.
With his broad sabre next, a chief in years,
The hoary majesty of spades appears,
Puts forth one manly leg, to sight revealed,
The rest, his many-colored robe concealed.
The rebel knave, who dares his prince engage,
Proves the just victim of his royal rage.   60
Even mighty Pam, that kings and queens o'erthrew
And mowed down armies in the fights of loo,
Sad chance of war! now destitute of aid,
Falls undistinguished by the victor spade!
    Thus far both armies to Belinda yield;
Now to the Baron fate inclines the field.
His warlike Amazon her host invades,
The imperial consort of the crown of spades.
The club's black tyrant first her victim died,
Spite of his haughty mien, and barbarous pride: 70
What boots the regal circle on his head,
His giant limbs, in state unwieldy spread;
That long behind he trails his pompous robe,
And, of all monarchs, only grasps the globe?
    The Baron now his diamonds pours apace;
The embroidered king who shows but half his face,
And his refulgent queen, with powers combined
Of broken troops an easy conquest find.
Clubs, diamonds, hearts, in wild disorder seen,
With throngs promiscuous strow the level green.   80

Thus when dispersed a routed army runs,
Of Asia's troops, and Afric's sable sons,
With like confusion different nations fly,
Of various habit, and of various dye;
The pierced battalions disunited fall,
In heaps on heaps; one fate o'erwhelms them all.
   The knave of diamonds tries his wily arts,
And wins (oh shameful chance!) the queen of hearts.
At this, the blood the virgin's cheek forsook,
A livid paleness spreads o'er all her look;   90
She sees, and trembles at the approaching ill,
Just in the jaws of ruin, and codille.
And now (as oft in some distempered state)
On one nice trick depends the general fate.
An ace of hearts steps forth: the king unseen
Lurked in her hand, and mourned his captive queen:
He springs to vengeance with an eager pace,
And falls like thunder on the prostrate ace.
The nymph exulting fills with shouts the sky;
The walls, the woods, and long canals reply.   100
   Oh thoughtless mortals! ever blind to fate,
Too soon dejected, and too soon elate.
Sudden, these honours shall be snatched away,
And cursed forever this victorious day.
   For lo! the board with cups and spoons is crowned,
The berries crackle, and the mill turns round;
On shining altars of Japan they raise
The silver lamp; the fiery spirits blaze:
From silver spouts the grateful liquors glide,
While China's earth receives the smoking tide: 110
At once they gratify their scent and taste,
And frequent cups prolong the rich repast.
Straight hover round the fair her airy band;
Some, as she sipped, the fuming liquor fanned,
Some o'er her lap their careful plumes displayed,
Trembling, and conscious of the rich brocade.
Coffee, (which makes the politician wise,
And see through all things with his half-shut eyes)
Sent up in vapours to the Baron's brain
New stratagems, the radiant lock to gain.   120
Ah cease, rash youth! desist ere 'tis too late,

Fear the just gods, and think of Scylla's fate!
Changed to a bird, and sent to flit in air,
She dearly pays for Nisus' injured hair!
  But when to mischief mortals bend their will,
How soon they find fit instruments of ill!
Just then, Clarissa drew with tempting grace
A two-edged weapon from her shining case:
So ladies in romance assist their knight,
Present the spear, and arm him for the fight.   130
He takes the gift with reverence, and extends
The little engine on his fingers' ends;
This just behind Belinda's neck he spread,
As o'er the fragrant steams she bends her head.
Swift to the lock a thousand sprites repair,
A thousand wings, by turns, blow back the hair;
And thrice they twitched the diamond in her ear;
Thrice she looked back, and thrice the foe drew near.
Just in that instant, anxious Ariel sought
The close recesses of the virgin's thought;   140
As on the nosegay in her breast reclined,
He watched the ideas rising in her mind,
Sudden he viewed, in spite of all her art,
An earthly lover lurking at her heart.
Amazed, confused, he found his power expired,
Resigned to fate, and with a sigh retired.
  The Peer now spreads the glittering forfex wide,
To inclose the lock; now joins it, to divide.
Even then, before the fatal engine closed,
A wretched sylph too fondly interposed;   150
Fate urged the shears, and cut the sylph in twain,
(But airy substance soon unites again)
The meeting points the sacred hair dissever
From the fair head, forever, and forever!
  Then flashed the living lightning from her eyes,
And screams of horror rend the affrighted skies.
Not louder shrieks to pitying Heaven are cast,
When husbands, or when lap-dogs breathe their last;
Or when rich China vessels fall'n from high,
In glittering dust and painted fragments lie!   160
  "Let wreaths of triumph now my temples twine,"
The victor cried; "the glorious prize is mine!

While fish in streams, or birds delight in air,
Or in a coach and six the British fair,
As long as *Atalantis* shall be read,
Or the small pillow grace a lady's bed,
While visits shall be paid on solemn days,
When numerous wax-lights in bright order blaze,
While nymphs take treats, or assignations give,
So long my honour, name, and praise shall live!   170
What time would spare, from steel receives its date,
And monuments, like men, submit to fate!
Steel could the labour of the gods destroy,
And strike to dust the imperial towers of Troy;
Steel could the works of mortal pride confound,
And hew triumphal arches to the ground.
What wonder then, fair nymph! thy hairs should feel
The conquering force of unresisted steel?"

CANTO IV

But anxious cares the pensive nymph oppressed,
And secret passions laboured in her breast.
Not youthful kings in battle seized alive,
Not scornful virgins who their charms survive,
Not ardent lovers robbed of all their bliss,
Not ancient ladies when refused a kiss,
Not tyrants fierce that unrepenting die,
Not Cynthia when her manteau's pinned awry,
E'er felt such rage, resentment, and despair,
As thou, sad virgin! for thy ravished hair.   10
    For, that sad moment, when the sylphs withdrew,
And Ariel weeping from Belinda flew,
Umbriel, a dusky, melancholy sprite,
As ever sullied the fair face of light,
Down to the central earth, his proper scene,
Repaired to search the gloomy Cave of Spleen.
    Swift on his sooty pinions flits the gnome,
And in a vapour reached the dismal dome.
No cheerful breeze this sullen region knows,
The dreaded east is all the wind that blows.   20
Here in a grotto, sheltered close from air,
And screened in shades from day's detested glare,
She sighs forever on her pensive bed,

Pain at her side, and Megrim at her head.
  Two handmaids wait the throne: alike in place,
But differing far in figure and in face.
Here stood Ill-nature like an ancient maid,
Her wrinkled form in black and white arrayed;
With store of prayers, for mornings, nights, and noons,
Her hand is filled; her bosom with lampoons.   30
  There Affectation, with a sickly mien,
Shows in her cheek the roses of eighteen,
Practised to lisp, and hang the head aside,
Faints into airs, and languishes with pride,
On the rich quilt sinks with becoming woe,
Wrapped in a gown, for sickness, and for show.
The fair ones feel such maladies as these,
When each new night-dress gives a new disease.
  A constant vapour o'er the palace flies,
Strange phantoms rising as the mists arise;   40
Dreadful, as hermit's dreams in haunted shades,
Or bright as visions of expiring maids.
Now glaring fiends, and snakes on rolling spires,
Pale spectres, gaping tombs, and purple fires:
Now lakes of liquid gold, Elysian scenes,
And crystal domes, and angels in machines.
  Unnumbered throngs on every side are seen,
Of bodies changed to various forms by Spleen.
Here living teapots stand, one arm held out,
One bent; the handle this, and that the spout: 50
A pipkin there, like Homer's tripod walks;
Here sighs a jar, and there a goose-pie talks;
Men prove with child, as powerful fancy works,
And maids turned bottles, call aloud for corks.
  Safe passed the gnome through this fantastic band,
A branch of healing spleenwort in his hand.
Then thus addressed the power: "Hail, wayward Queen!
Who rule the sex to fifty from fifteen:
Parent of vapours and of female wit,
Who give the hysteric or poetic fit,   60
On various tempers act by various ways,
Make some take physic, others scribble plays;
Who cause the proud their visits to delay,
And send the godly in a pet to pray.

A nymph there is, that all thy power disdains,
And thousands more in equal mirth maintains.
But oh! if e'er thy gnome could spoil a grace,
Or raise a pimple on a beauteous face,
Like citron-waters matrons' cheeks inflame,
Or change complexions at a losing game;   70
If e'er with airy horns I planted heads,
Or rumpled petticoats, or tumbled beds,
Or caused suspicion when no soul was rude,
Or discomposed the head-dress of a prude,
Or e'er to costive lap-dog gave disease,
Which not the tears of brightest eyes could ease:
Hear me, and touch Belinda with chagrin,
That single act gives half the world the spleen."
   The goddess with a discontented air
Seems to reject him, though she grants his prayer.   80
A wondrous bag with both her hands she binds,
Like that where once Ulysses held the winds;
There she collects the force of female lungs,
Sighs, sobs, and passions, and the war of tongues.
A vial next she fills with fainting fears,
Soft sorrows, melting griefs, and flowing tears.
The gnome rejoicing bears her gifts away,
Spreads his black wings, and slowly mounts to day.
   Sunk in Thalestris' arms the nymph he found,
Her eyes dejected and her hair unbound.   90
Full o'er their heads the swelling bag he rent,
And all the Furies issued at the vent.
Belinda burns with more than mortal ire,
And fierce Thalestris fans the rising fire.
"Oh wretched maid!" she spread her hands, and cried,
(While Hampton's echoes, "Wretched maid!" replied)
"Was it for this you took such constant care
The bodkin, comb, and essence to prepare?
For this your locks in paper durance bound,
For this with torturing irons wreathed around?   100
For this with fillets strained your tender head,
And bravely bore the double loads of lead?
Gods! shall the ravisher display your hair,
While the fops envy, and the ladies stare!
Honour forbid! at whose unrivalled shrine

Ease, pleasure, virtue, all our sex resign.
Methinks already I your tears survey,
Already hear the horrid things they say,
Already see you a degraded toast,
And all your honour in a whisper lost!   110
How shall I, then, your helpless fame defend?
'Twill then be infamy to seem your friend!
And shall this prize, the inestimable prize,
Exposed through crystal to the gazing eyes,
And heightened by the diamond's circling rays,
On that rapacious hand forever blaze?
Sooner shall grass in Hyde Park Circus grow,
And wits take lodgings in the sound of Bow;
Sooner let earth, air, sea, to chaos fall,
Men, monkeys, lap-dogs, parrots, perish all!"   120
   She said; then raging to Sir Plume repairs,
And bids her beau demand the precious hairs
(Sir Plume of amber snuff-box justly vain,
And the nice conduct of a clouded cane);
With earnest eyes, and round unthinking face,
He first the snuff-box opened, then the case,
And thus broke out—"My lord, why, what the devil?
Z—ds! damn the lock! 'fore Gad, you must be civil!
Plague on't! 'tis past a jest—nay prithee, pox!
Give her the hair"—he spoke, and rapped his box.   130
   "It grieves me much," replied the Peer again,
"Who speaks so well should ever speak in vain.
But by this lock, this sacred lock, I swear,
(Which never more shall join its parted hair;
Which never more its honours shall renew,
Clipped from the lovely head where late it grew)
That while my nostrils draw the vital air,
This hand, which won it, shall forever wear."
He spoke, and speaking, in proud triumph spread
The long-contended honours of her head.   140
   But Umbriel, hateful gnome! forbears not so;
He breaks the vial whence the sorrows flow.
Then see! the nymph in beauteous grief appears,
Her eyes half-languishing, half-drowned in tears;
On her heaved bosom hung her drooping head,
Which, with a sigh, she raised; and thus she said:

"Forever cursed be this detested day,
Which snatched my best, my favorite curl away!
Happy! ah ten times happy had I been,
If Hampton Court these eyes had never seen!   150
Yet am not I the first mistaken maid,
By love of courts to numerous ills betrayed.
Oh had I rather unadmired remained
In some lone isle, or distant northern land;
Where the gilt chariot never marks the way,
Where none learn ombre, none e'er taste bohea!
There kept my charms concealed from mortal eye,
Like roses that in deserts bloom and die.
What moved my mind with youthful lords to roam?
Oh had I stayed, and said my prayers at home!   160
'Twas this, the morning omens seemed to tell,
Thrice from my trembling hand the patch-box fell;
The tottering china shook without a wind,
Nay, Poll sat mute, and Shock was most unkind!
A sylph too warned me of the threats of fate,
In mystic visions, now believed too late!
See the poor remnants of these slighted hairs!
My hands shall rend what even thy rapine spares:
These in two sable ringlets taught to break,
Once gave new beauties to the snowy neck;   170
The sister-lock now sits uncouth, alone,
And in its fellow's fate foresees its own;
Uncurled it hangs, the fatal shears demands,
And tempts once more thy sacrilegious hands.
Oh hadst thou, cruel! been content to seize
Hairs less in sight, or any hairs but these!"

CANTO V

She said: the pitying audience melt in tears;
But Fate and Jove had stopped the Baron's ears.
In vain Thalestris with reproach assails,
For who can move when fair Belinda fails?
Not half so fixed the Trojan could remain,
While Anna begged and Dido raged in vain.
Then grave Clarissa graceful waved her fan;
Silence ensued, and thus the nymph began:
"Say why are beauties praised and honoured most,

The wise man's passion, and the vain man's toast?   10
Why decked with all that land and sea afford,
Why angels called, and angel-like adored?
Why round our coaches crowd the white-gloved beaux,
Why bows the side-box from its inmost rows?
How vain are all these glories, all our pains,
Unless good sense preserve what beauty gains:
That men may say, when we the front-box grace:
'Behold the first in virtue as in face!'
Oh! if to dance all night, and dress all day,
Charmed the smallpox, or chased old age away;   20
Who would not scorn what housewife's cares produce,
Or who would learn one earthly thing of use?
To patch, nay ogle, might become a saint,
Nor could it sure be such a sin to paint.
But since, alas! frail beauty must decay,
Curled or uncurled, since locks will turn to grey;
Since painted, or not painted, all shall fade,
And she who scorns a man, must die a maid;
What then remains but well our power to use,
And keep good humour still whate'er we lose?   30
And trust me, dear! good humour can prevail,
When airs, and flights, and screams, and scolding fail.
Beauties in vain their pretty eyes may roll;
Charms strike the sight, but merit wins the soul."

So spoke the dame, but no applause ensued;
Belinda frowned, Thalestris called her prude.
"To arms, to arms!" the fierce virago cries,
And swift as lightning to the combat flies.
All side in parties, and begin the attack;
Fans clap, silks rustle, and tough whalebones crack;   40
Heroes' and heroines' shouts confus'dly rise,
And bass and treble voices strike the skies.
No common weapons in their hands are found,
Like gods they fight, nor dread a mortal wound.

So when bold Homer makes the gods engage,
And heavenly breasts with human passions rage;
'Gainst Pallas, Mars; Latona, Hermes arms;
And all Olympus rings with loud alarms:
Jove's thunder roars, heaven trembles all around,
Blue Neptune storms, the bellowing deeps resound: 50

Earth shakes her nodding towers, the ground gives way,
And the pale ghosts start at the flash of day!
    Triumphant Umbriel on a sconce's height
Clapped his glad wings, and sate to view the fight:
Propped on their bodkin spears, the sprites survey
The growing combat, or assist the fray.
    While through the press enraged Thalestris flies,
And scatters death around from both her eyes,
A beau and witling perished in the throng,
One died in metaphor, and one in song.   60
"O cruel nymph! a living death I bear,"
Cried Dapperwit, and sunk beside his chair.
A mournful glance Sir Fopling upwards cast,
"Those eyes are made so killing"—was his last.
Thus on Mæander's flowery margin lies
The expiring swan, and as he sings he dies.
    When bold Sir Plume had drawn Clarissa down,
Chloe stepped in, and killed him with a frown;
She smiled to see the doughty hero slain,
But, at her smile, the beau revived again.   70
    Now Jove suspends his golden scales in air,
Weighs the men's wits against the lady's hair;
The doubtful beam long nods from side to side;
At length the wits mount up, the hairs subside.
    See, fierce Belinda on the Baron flies,
With more than usual lightning in her eyes:
Nor feared the chief the unequal fight to try,
Who sought no more than on his foe to die.
But this bold lord with manly strength endued,
She with one finger and a thumb subdued;   80
Just where the breath of life his nostrils drew,
A charge of snuff the wily virgin threw;
The gnomes direct, to every atom just,
The pungent grains of titillating dust.
Sudden, with starting tears each eye o'erflows,
And the high dome re-echoes to his nose.
    "Now meet thy fate," incensed Belinda cried,
And drew a deadly bodkin from her side.
(The same, his ancient personage to deck,
Her great great grandsire wore about his neck,   90
In three seal-rings; which after, melted down,

Formed a vast buckle for his widow's gown:
Her infant grandame's whistle next it grew,
The bells she jingled, and the whistle blew;
Then in a bodkin graced her mother's hairs,
Which long she wore, and now Belinda wears.)
  "Boast not my fall," he cried, "insulting foe!
Thou by some other shalt be laid as low;
Nor think, to die dejects my lofty mind:
All that I dread is leaving you behind!   100
Rather than so, ah let me still survive,
And burn in Cupid's flames—but burn alive."
  "Restore the lock!" she cries; and all around
"Restore the lock!" the vaulted roofs rebound.
Not fierce Othello in so loud a strain
Roared for the handkerchief that caused his pain.
But see how oft ambitious aims are crossed,
And chiefs contend 'till all the prize is lost!
The lock, obtained with guilt, and kept with pain,
In every place is sought, but sought in vain: 110
With such a prize no mortal must be blessed,
So Heaven decrees! with Heaven who can contest?
  Some thought it mounted to the lunar sphere,
Since all things lost on earth are treasured there.
There heroes' wits are kept in ponderous vases,
And beaux' in snuff-boxes and tweezer-cases.
There broken vows and death-bed alms are found,
And lovers' hearts with ends of riband bound,
The courtier's promises, and sick man's prayers,
The smiles of harlots, and the tears of heirs,   120
Cages for gnats, and chains to yoke a flea,
Dried butterflies, and tomes of casuistry.
  But trust the Muse—she saw it upward rise,
Though marked by none but quick, poetic eyes:
(So Rome's great founder to the heavens withdrew,
To Proculus alone confessed in view)
A sudden star, it shot through liquid air,
And drew behind a radiant trail of hair.
Not Berenice's locks first rose so bright,
The heavens bespangling with dishevelled light.   130
The sylphs behold it kindling as it flies,
And pleased pursue its progress through the skies.

This the beau monde shall from the Mall survey,
And hail with music its propitious ray.
This the blest lover shall for Venus take,
And send up vows from Rosamonda's lake.
This Partridge soon shall view in cloudless skies,
When next he looks through Galileo's eyes;
And hence the egregious wizard shall foredoom
The fate of Louis, and the fall of Rome.   140
   Then cease, bright nymph! to mourn thy ravished hair,
Which adds new glory to the shining sphere!
Not all the tresses that fair head can boast,
Shall draw such envy as the lock you lost.
For, after all the murders of your eye,
When, after millions slain, yourself shall die:
When those fair suns shall set, as set they must,
And all those tresses shall be laid in dust,
This lock, the Muse shall consecrate to fame,
And 'midst the stars inscribe Belinda's name.   150

133

ELEGY TO THE MEMORY OF AN
UNFORTUNATE LADY

What beckoning ghost, along the moonlight shade
Invites my steps, and points to yonder glade?
'Tis she!—but why that bleeding bosom gored?
Why dimly gleams the visionary sword?
O ever beauteous, ever friendly! tell,
Is it in heaven a crime to love too well?
To bear too tender or too firm a heart,
To act a lover's or a Roman's part?
Is there no bright reversion in the sky,
For those who greatly think, or bravely die?   10
   Why bade ye else, ye powers! her soul aspire
Above the vulgar flight of low desire?
Ambition first sprung from your blest abodes,
The glorious fault of angels and of gods;
Thence to their images on earth it flows,
And in the breasts of kings and heroes glows.
Most souls, 'tis true, but peep out once an age,
Dull sullen prisoners in the body's cage:
Dim lights of life, that burn a length of years
Useless, unseen, as lamps in sepulchres;   20

Like Eastern Kings a lazy state they keep,
And close confined to their own palace, sleep.
  From these perhaps (ere nature bade her die)
Fate snatched her early to the pitying sky.
As into air the purer spirits flow,
And separate from their kindred dregs below;
So flew the soul to its congenial place,
Nor left one virtue to redeem her race.
  But thou, false guardian of a charge too good,
Thou, mean deserter of thy brother's blood!   30
See on these ruby lips the trembling breath,
These cheeks now fading at the blast of death:
Cold is that breast which warmed the world before,
And those love-darting eyes must roll no more.
Thus, if eternal justice rules the ball,
Thus shall your wives, and thus your children fall;
On all the line a sudden vengeance waits,
And frequent hearses shall besiege your gates.
There passengers shall stand, and pointing say,
(While the long funerals blacken all the way)   40
"Lo these were they whose souls the Furies steeled,
And cursed with hearts unknowing how to yield.
Thus unlamented pass the proud away,
The gaze of fools, and pageant of a day!
So perish all, whose breast ne'er learned to glow
For others' good, or melt at others' woe."
  What can atone (O ever-injured shade!)
Thy fate unpitied, and thy rites unpaid?
No friend's complaint, no kind domestic tear
Pleased thy pale ghost, or graced thy mournful bier.   50
By foreign hands thy dying eyes were closed,
By foreign hands thy decent limbs composed,
By foreign hands thy humble grave adorned,
By strangers honoured, and by strangers mourned!
What though no friends in sable weeds appear,
Grieve for an hour, perhaps, then mourn a year,
And bear about the mockery of woe
To midnight dances, and the public show?
What though no weeping loves thy ashes grace,
Nor polished marble emulate thy face?   60
What though no sacred earth allow thee room,

Nor hallowed dirge be muttered o'er thy tomb?
Yet shall thy grave with rising flowers be dressed,
And the green turf lie lightly on thy breast:
There shall the morn her earliest tears bestow,
There the first roses of the year shall blow;
While angels with their silver wings o'ershade
The ground, now sacred by thy reliques made.
  So peaceful rests, without a stone, a name,
What once had beauty, titles, wealth, and fame.   70
How loved, how honoured once, avails thee not,
To whom related, or by whom begot;
A heap of dust alone remains of thee;
'Tis all thou art, and all the proud shall be!
  Poets themselves must fall, like those they sung,
Deaf the praised ear, and mute the tuneful tongue.
Even he, whose soul now melts in mournful lays,
Shall shortly want the generous tear he pays;
Then from his closing eyes thy form shall part,
And the last pang shall tear thee from his heart,   80
Life's idle business at one gasp be o'er,
The muse forgot, and thou beloved no more!

134.   EPISTLE TO DR. ARBUTHNOT

P. Shut, shut the door, good John! fatigued, I said;
Tie up the knocker, say I'm sick, I'm dead.
The Dog Star rages! nay 'tis past a doubt,
All Bedlam, or Parnassus, is let out:
Fire in each eye, and papers in each hand,
They rave, recite, and madden round the land.
  What walls can guard me, or what shades can hide?
They pierce my thickets, through my grot they glide;
By land, by water, they renew the charge;
They stop the chariot, and they board the barge.   10
No place is sacred, not the church is free;
Even Sunday shines no sabbath-day to me;
Then from the Mint walks forth the man of rhyme,
Happy to catch me just at dinner time.
  Is there a parson much bemused in beer,
A maudlin poetess, a rhyming peer,
A clerk, foredoomed his father's soul to cross,
Who pens a stanza, when he should engross?

Is there who, locked from ink and paper, scrawls
With desperate charcoal round his darkened walls?   20
All fly to Twit'nam, and in humble strain
Apply to me, to keep them mad or vain.
Arthur, whose giddy son neglects the laws,
Imputes to me and my damned works the cause;
Poor Cornus sees his frantic wife elope,
And curses wit, and poetry, and Pope.

   Friend to my life! (which did not you prolong,
The world had wanted many an idle song)
What drop or nostrum can this plague remove?
Or which must end me, a fool's wrath or love?   30
A dire dilemma! either way I'm sped;
If foes, they write, if friends, they read me dead.
Seized and tied down to judge, how wretched I!
Who can't be silent, and who will not lie.
To laugh, were want of goodness and of grace,
And to be grave, exceeds all power of face.
I sit with sad civility, I read
With honest anguish and an aching head;
And drop at last, but in unwilling ears,
This saving counsel, "Keep your piece nine years."   40

   "Nine years!" cries he, who high in Drury Lane,
Lulled by soft zephyrs through the broken pane,
Rhymes ere he wakes, and prints before term ends,
Obliged by hunger, and request of friends:
"The piece, you think, is incorrect? why, take it;
I'm all submission, what you'd have it, make it."

   Three things another's modest wishes bound,
My friendship, and a prologue, and ten pound.

   Pitholeon sends to me: "You know his Grace,
I want a patron; ask him for a place."   50
"Pitholeon libelled me,"—"But here's a letter
Informs you, sir, 'twas when he knew no better.
Dare you refuse him? Curll invites to dine;
He'll write a journal, or he'll turn divine."

   Bless me! a packet.—"'Tis a stranger sues,
A virgin tragedy, an orphan muse."
If I dislike it, "Furies, death and rage!"
If I approve, "Commend it to the stage."
There (thank my stars) my whole commission ends:

The players and I are, luckily, no friends.   60
Fired that the house reject him, " 'Sdeath I'll print it,
And shame the fools——Your interest, sir, with Lintot!"
"Lintot, dull rogue! will think your price too much."
"Not, sir, if you revise it, and retouch."
All my demurs but double his attacks;
At last he whispers, "Do, and we go snacks."
Glad of a quarrel, straight I clap the door;
"Sir, let me see your works and you no more."
    'Tis sung, when Midas' ears began to spring,
(Midas, a sacred person and a king)   70
His very minister who spied them first,
(Some say his queen) was forced to speak, or burst.
And is not mine, my friend, a sorer case,
When every coxcomb perks them in my face?
A.   Good friend, forbear! you deal in dangerous things.
I'd never name queens, ministers or kings;
Keep close to ears, and those let asses prick;
'Tis nothing— P.   Nothing? If they bite and kick?
Out with it, Dunciad! let the secret pass,
That secret to each fool, that he's an ass: 80
The truth once told (and wherefore should we lie?)
The queen of Midas slept, and so may I.
    You think this cruel? take it for a rule,
No creature smarts so little as a fool.
Let peals of laughter, Codrus! round thee break,
Thou unconcerned canst hear the mighty crack:
Pit, box, and gallery in convulsions hurled,
Thou standest unshook amidst a bursting world.
Who shames a scribbler? break one cobweb through,
He spins the slight, self-pleasing thread anew: 90
Destroy his fib or sophistry, in vain,
The creature's at his dirty work again,
Throned in the centre of his thin designs,
Proud of a vast extent of flimsy lines!
Whom have I hurt? has poet yet, or peer,
Lost the arched eye-brow, or Parnassian sneer?
And has not Colley still his lord, and whore?
His butchers, Henley? his free-masons, Moore?
Does not one table Bavius still admit?
Still to one bishop Philips seem a wit?   100

Still Sappho— A.   Hold! for God's sake—you'll offend;
No names—be calm—learn prudence of a friend!
I too could write, and I am twice as tall;
But foes like these— P.   One flatterer's worse than all.
Of all mad creatures, if the learned are right,
It is the slaver kills, and not the bite.
A fool quite angry is quite innocent;
Alas! 'tis ten times worse when they *repent*.

One dedicates in high heroic prose,
And ridicules beyond a hundred foes: 110
One from all Grub Street will my fame defend,
And, more abusive, calls himself my friend.
This prints my *Letters*, that expects a bribe,
And others roar aloud, "Subscribe, subscribe."

There are who to my person pay their court:
I cough like Horace, and, though lean, am short;
Ammon's great son one shoulder had too high,
Such Ovid's nose, and "Sir! you have an eye"—
Go on, obliging creatures, make me see
All that disgraced my betters, met in me.   120
Say for my comfort, languishing in bed,
"Just so immortal Maro held his head":
And when I die, be sure you let me know
Great Homer died three thousand years ago.

Why did I write? what sin to me unknown
Dipped me in ink, my parents', or my own?
As yet a child, nor yet a fool to fame,
I lisped in numbers, for the numbers came.
I left no calling for this idle trade,
No duty broke, no father disobeyed.   130
The muse but served to ease some friend, not wife,
To help me through this long disease, my life,
To second, Arbuthnot! thy art and care,
And teach the being you preserved, to bear.

But why then publish? Granville the polite,
And knowing Walsh, would tell me I could write;
Well-natured Garth inflamed with early praise;
And Congreve loved, and Swift endured my lays;
The courtly Talbot, Somers, Sheffield read;
Even mitred Rochester would nod the head,   140
And St. John's self (great Dryden's friends before)

With open arms received one poet more.
Happy my studies, when by these approved!
Happier their author, when by these beloved!
From these the world will judge of men and books,
Not from the Burnets, Oldmixons, and Cookes.
　　Soft were my numbers; who could take offence,
While pure description held the place of sense?
Like gentle Fanny's was my flowery theme,
A painted mistress, or a purling stream.   150
Yet then did Gildon draw his venal quill;—
I wished the man a dinner, and sat still.
Yet then did Dennis rave in furious fret;
I never answered,—I was not in debt.
If want provoked, or madness made them print,
I waged no war with Bedlam or the Mint.
　　Did some more sober critic come abroad;
If wrong, I smiled; if right, I kissed the rod.
Pains, reading, study, are their just pretence,
And all they want is spirit, taste, and sense.   160
Commas and points they set exactly right,
And 'twere a sin to rob them of their mite.
Yet ne'er one sprig of laurel graced these ribalds,
From slashing Bentley down to pidling Tibbalds:
Each wight, who reads not, and but scans and spells,
Each word-catcher, that lives on syllables,
Even such small critics some regard may claim,
Preserved in Milton's or in Shakespeare's name.
Pretty! in amber to observe the forms
Of hairs, or straws, or dirt, or grubs, or worms!   170
The things, we know, are neither rich nor rare,
But wonder how the devil they got there.
　　Were others angry, I excused them too;
Well might they rage, I gave them but their due.
A man's true merit 'tis not hard to find;
But each man's secret standard in his mind,
That casting-weight pride adds to emptiness,
This, who can gratify? for who can guess?
The bard whom pilfered pastorals renown,
Who turns a Persian tale for half a crown,   180
Just writes to make his barrenness appear,
And strains, from hard-bound brains, eight lines a year:

He who still wanting, though he lives on theft,
Steals much, spends little, yet has nothing left;
And he who now to sense, now nonsense leaning,
Means not, but blunders round about a meaning;
And he whose fustian 's so sublimely bad,
It is not poetry, but prose run mad:
All these, my modest satire bade translate,
And owned that nine such poets made a Tate.   190
How did they fume, and stamp, and roar, and chafe!
And swear, not Addison himself was safe.

   Peace to all such! but were there one whose fires
True genius kindles, and fair fame inspires;
Blessed with each talent and each art to please,
And born to write, converse, and live with ease:
Should such a man, too fond to rule alone,
Bear, like the Turk, no brother near the throne;
View him with scornful, yet with jealous eyes,
And hate for arts that caused himself to rise;   200
Damn with faint praise, assent with civil leer,
And without sneering, teach the rest to sneer;
Willing to wound, and yet afraid to strike,
Just hint a fault, and hesitate dislike;
Alike reserved to blame, or to commend,
A timorous foe, and a suspicious friend;
Dreading even fools, by flatterers besieged,
And so obliging, that he ne'er obliged;
Like Cato, give his little senate laws,
And sit attentive to his own applause;   210
While wits and templars every sentence raise,
And wonder with a foolish face of praise—
Who but must laugh, if such a man there be?
Who would not weep, if Atticus were he?

   What though my name stood rubric on the walls,
Or plastered posts, with claps, in capitals?
Or smoking forth, a hundred hawkers' load
On wings of winds came flying all abroad?
I sought no homage from the race that write;
I kept, like Asian monarchs, from their sight: 220
Poems I heeded (now be-rhymed so long)
No more than thou, great George! a birthday song.
I ne'er with wits or witlings passed my days,

To spread about the itch of verse and praise;
Nor like a puppy, daggled through the town,
To fetch and carry sing-song up and down;
Nor at rehearsals sweat, and mouthed, and cried,
With handkerchief and orange at my side;
But sick of fops, and poetry, and prate,
To Bufo left the whole Castalian state.   230
　　Proud as Apollo on his forkèd hill,
Sat full-blown Bufo, puffed by every quill;
Fed with soft dedication all day long,
Horace and he went hand in hand in song.
His library (where busts of poets dead
And a true Pindar stood without a head,)
Received of wits an undistinguished race,
Who first his judgment asked, and then a place:
Much they extolled his pictures, much his seat,
And flattered every day, and some days eat: 240
Till grown more frugal in his riper days,
He paid some bards with port, and some with praise;
To some a dry rehearsal was assigned,
And others (harder still) he paid in kind.
Dryden alone (what wonder?) came not nigh;
Dryden alone escaped this judging eye:
But still the great have kindness in reserve;
He helped to bury whom he helped to starve.
　　May some choice patron bless each grey goose quill!
May every Bavius have his Bufo still!   250
So, when a statesman wants a day's defence,
Or envy holds a whole week's war with sense
Or simple pride for flattery makes demands,
May dunce by dunce be whistled off my hands!
Blessed be the great! for those they take away,
And those they left me—for they left me Gay;
Left me to see neglected genius bloom,
Neglected die, and tell it on his tomb:
Of all thy blameless life the sole return
My verse, and Queensbury weeping o'er thy urn!   260
　　Oh let me live my own, and die so too!
(To live and die is all I have to do:)
Maintain a poet's dignity and ease,
And see what friends, and read what books I please;

Above a patron, though I condescend
Sometimes to call a minister my friend.
I was not born for courts or great affairs;
I pay my debts, believe, and say my prayers;
Can sleep without a poem in my head,
Nor know if Dennis be alive or dead.   270
   Why am I asked what next shall see the light?
Heavens! was I born for nothing but to write?
Has life no joys for me? or, (to be grave)
Have I no friend to serve, no soul to save?
"I found him close with Swift"—"Indeed? no doubt,"
Cries prating Balbus, "something will come out."
'Tis all in vain, deny it as I will.
"No, such a genius never can lie still;"
And then for mine obligingly mistakes
The first lampoon Sir Will or Bubo makes.   280
Poor guiltless I! and can I choose but smile,
When every coxcomb knows me by my style?
   Cursed be the verse, how well soe'er it flow,
That tends to make one worthy man my foe,
Give virtue scandal, innocence a fear,
Or from the soft-eyed virgin steal a tear!
But he who hurts a harmless neighbour's peace,
Insults fallen worth, or beauty in distress,
Who loves a lie, lame slander helps about,
Who writes a libel, or who copies out: 290
That fop, whose pride affects a patron's name,
Yet absent, wounds an author's honest fame:
Who can your merit selfishly approve,
And show the sense of it without the love;
Who has the vanity to call you friend,
Yet wants the honour, injured, to defend;
Who tells whate'er you think, whate'er you say,
And, if he lie not, must at least betray;
Who to the dean, and silver bell can swear,
And sees at Canons what was never there;   300
Who reads, but with a lust to misapply,
Make satire a lampoon, and fiction, lie.
A lash like mine no honest man shall dread,
But all such babbling blockheads in his stead.
   Let Sporus tremble— A. What? that thing of silk,

Sporus, that mere white curd of ass's milk?
Satire or sense, alas! can Sporus feel?
Who breaks a butterfly upon a wheel?
P. Yet let me flap this bug with gilded wings,
This painted child of dirt, that stinks and stings;   310
Whose buzz the witty and the fair annoys,
Yet wit ne'er tastes, and beauty ne'er enjoys:
So well-bred spaniels civilly delight
In mumbling of the game they dare not bite.
Eternal smiles his emptiness betray,
As shallow streams run dimpling all the way,
Whether in florid impotence he speaks,
And, as the prompter breathes, the puppet squeaks;
Or at the ear of Eve, familiar toad,
Half froth, half venom, spits himself abroad,   320
In puns, or politics, or tales, or lies,
Or spite, or smut, or rhymes, or blasphemies,
His wit all see-saw, between that and this,
Now high, now low, now master up, now miss,
And he himself one vile antithesis.
Amphibious thing! that acting either part,
The trifling head or the corrupted heart,
Fop at the toilet, flatterer at the board,
Now trips a lady, and now struts a lord.
Eve's tempter thus the rabbins have expressed,   330
A cherub's face, a reptile all the rest;
Beauty that shocks you, parts that none will trust,
Wit that can creep, and pride that licks the dust.
    Not fortune's worshipper, nor fashion's fool,
Not lucre's madman, nor ambition's tool,
Not proud, nor servile;—be one poet's praise,
That, if he pleased, he pleased by manly ways:
That flattery, even to kings, he held a shame,
And thought a lie in verse or prose the same;
That not in fancy's maze he wandered long,   340
But stooped to truth, and moralized his song;
That not for fame, but virtue's better end,
He stood the furious foe, the timid friend,
The damning critic, half approving wit,
The coxcomb hit, or fearing to be hit;
Laughed at the loss of friends he never had.

The dull, the proud, the wicked, and the mad;
The distant threats of vengeance on his head
The blow unfelt, the tear he never shed;
The tale revived, the lie so oft o'erthrown,   350
The imputed trash and dulness not his own;
The morals blackened when the writings 'scape,
The libelled person, and the pictured shape;
Abuse, on all he loved, or loved him, spread,
A friend in exile, or a father dead;
The whisper that, to greatness still too near,
Perhaps yet vibrates on his Sovereign's ear:—
Welcome for thee, fair virtue! all the past;
For thee, fair virtue! welcome even the last!
    A. But why insult the poor, affront the great?   360
P. A knave 's a knave, to me, in every state:
Alike my scorn, if he succeed or fail,
Sporus at court, or Japhet in a jail,
A hireling scribbler, or a hireling peer,
Knight of the post corrupt, or of the shire;
If on a pillory, or near a throne,
He gain his prince's ear, or lose his own.
    Yet soft by nature, more a dupe than wit,
Sappho can tell you how this man was bit;
This dreaded satirist Dennis will confess   370
Foe to his pride, but friend to his distress:
So humble, he has knocked at Tibbald's door,
Has drunk with Cibber, nay, has rhymed for Moore.
Full ten years slandered, did he once reply?
Three thousand suns went down on Welsted's lie.
To please a mistress one aspersed his life;
He lashed him not, but let her be his wife.
Let Budgel charge low Grub Street on his quill,
And write whate'er he pleased, except his will;
Let the two Curlls of town and court, abuse   380
His father, mother, body, soul, and muse.
Yet why? that father held it for a rule
It was a sin to call our neighbour fool:
That harmless mother thought no wife a whore:
Hear this, and spare his family, James Moore!
Unspotted names, and memorable long!
If there be force in virtue, or in song.

   Of gentle blood (part shed in honour's cause,
While yet in Britain honour had applause)
Each parent sprung— A. What fortune, pray?— P. Their
      own,   390
And better got, than Bestia's from the throne.
Born to no pride, inheriting no strife,
Nor marrying discord in a noble wife,
Stranger to civil and religious rage,
The good man walked innoxious through his age.
No courts he saw, no suits would ever try,
Nor dared an oath, nor hazarded a lie.
Unlearned, he knew no schoolman's subtle art,
No language but the language of the heart.
By nature honest, by experience wise,   400
Healthy by temperance and by exercise;
His life, though long, to sickness passed unknown,
His death was instant, and without a groan.
Oh grant me thus to live, and thus to die!
Who sprung from kings shall know less joy than I.
   O friend! may each domestic bliss be thine!
Be no unpleasing melancholy mine:
Me, let the tender office long engage,
To rock the cradle of reposing age,
With lenient arts extend a mother's breath,   410
Make languor smile, and smooth the bed of death,
Explore the thought, explain the asking eye,
And keep a while one parent from the sky!
On cares like these if length of days attend,
May Heaven, to bless those days, preserve my friend,
Preserve him social, cheerful, and serene,
And just as rich as when he served a Queen.
A. Whether that blessing be denied or given,
Thus far was right, the rest belongs to Heaven.

GEORGE BERKELEY (1685–1753)

135.   VERSES ON THE PROSPECT OF PLANTING
         ARTS AND LEARNING IN AMERICA

        The Muse, disgusted at an age and clime
          Barren of every glorious theme,

In distant lands now waits a better time,
  Producing subjects worthy fame:

In happy climes where from the genial sun
  And virgin earth such scenes ensue,
The force of art by nature seems outdone,
  And fancied beauties by the true:

In happy climes, the seat of innocence,
  Where nature guides and virtue rules,   10
Where men shall not impose for truth and sense
  The pedantry of courts and schools:

There shall be sung another golden age,
  The rise of empire and of arts,
The good and great inspiring epic rage,
  The wisest heads and noblest hearts.

Not such as Europe breeds in her decay;
  Such as she bred when fresh and young,
When heavenly flame did animate her clay,
  By future poets shall be sung.   20

Westward the course of empire takes its way;
  The four first acts already past,
A fifth shall close the drama with the day;
  Time's noblest offspring is the last.

HENRY CAREY (1687?–1743)

136.   THE BALLAD OF SALLY IN OUR ALLEY

Of all the girls that are so smart,
  There's none like pretty Sally;
She is the darling of my heart,
  And she lives in our alley.
There is no lady in the land
  Is half so sweet as Sally;
She is the darling of my heart,
  And she lives in our alley.

Her father he makes cabbage-nets,
  And through the streets does cry 'em;   10

Her mother she sells laces long,
    To such as please to buy 'em;
But sure such folks could ne'er beget
    So sweet a girl as Sally!
She is the darling of my heart,
    And she lives in our alley.

When she is by, I leave my work
    (I love her so sincerely);
My master comes, like any Turk,
    And bangs me most severely;   20
But let him bang his bellyful,
    I'll bear it all for Sally;
She is the darling of my heart,
    And she lives in our alley.

Of all the days that's in the week,
    I dearly love but one day,
And that's the day that comes betwixt
    A Saturday and Monday;
For then I'm dressed, all in my best,
    To walk abroad with Sally;   30
She is the darling of my heart,
    And she lives in our alley.

My master carries me to church,
    And often am I blamed,
Because I leave him in the lurch,
    As soon as text is named:
I leave the church in sermon time,
    And slink away to Sally;
She is the darling of my heart,
    And she lives in our alley.   40

When Christmas comes about again,
    O then I shall have money;
I'll hoard it up, and box and all
    I'll give it to my honey:
And would it were ten thousand pounds,
    I'd give it all to Sally;
She is the darling of my heart,
    And she lives in our alley.

My master and the neighbours all
   Make game of me and Sally;   50
And (but for her) I'd better be
   A slave, and row a galley:
But when my seven long years are out,
   O then I'll marry Sally!
O then we'll wed, and then we'll bed;
   But not in our alley!

MATTHEW GREEN (1696–1737)

137.   AN EPIGRAM

ON THE REVEREND MR. LAURENCE ECHARD'S, AND BISHOP GILBERT BURNET'S
HISTORIES

Gil's history appears to me
Political anatomy,
A case of skeletons well done,
And malefactors every one.
His sharp and strong incision pen
Historically cuts up men,
And does with lucid skill impart
Their inward ails of head and heart.
Laurence proceeds another way,
And well-dressed figures doth display: 10
His characters are all in flesh,
Their hands are fair, their faces fresh;
And from his sweetening art derive
A better scent than when alive.
He wax-work made to please the sons,
Whose fathers were Gil's skeletons.

JOHN DYER (1700?–1758)

138.   GRONGAR HILL

Silent nymph, with curious eye!
Who, the purple evening, lie
On the mountain's lonely van,
Beyond the noise of busy man,
Painting fair the form of things,
While the yellow linnet sings;

Or the tuneful nightingale
Charms the forest with her tale;
Come with all thy various hues,
Come, and aid thy sister Muse;   10
Now while Phoebus riding high
Gives lustre to the land and sky!
Grongar Hill invites my song,
Draw the landscape bright and strong;
Grongar, in whose mossy cells
Sweetly musing Quiet dwells;
Grongar, in whose silent shade,
For the modest Muses made,
So oft I have, the evening still,
At the fountain of a rill,   20
Sate upon a flowery bed,
With my hand beneath my head;
While strayed my eyes o'er Towy's flood,
Over mead and over wood,
From house to house, from hill to hill,
Till Contemplation had her fill.
 About his checkered sides I wind,
And leave his brooks and meads behind,
And groves, and grottoes where I lay,
And vistas shooting beams of day;   30
Wide and wider spreads the vale,
As circles on a smooth canal;
The mountains round—unhappy fate,
Sooner or later, of all height—
Withdraw their summits from the skies,
And lessen as the others rise;
Still the prospect wider spreads,
Adds a thousand woods and meads,
Still it widens, widens still,
And sinks the newly-risen hill.   40
 Now I gain the mountain's brow,
What a landscape lies below!
No clouds, no vapours intervene,
But the gay, the open scene
Does the face of nature show
In all the hues of heaven's bow,
And, swelling to embrace the light,

Spreads around beneath the sight.
　Old castles on the cliffs arise,
Proudly towering in the skies!   50
Rushing from the woods, the spires
Seem from hence ascending fires!
Half his beams Apollo sheds
On the yellow mountain-heads,
Gilds the fleeces of the flocks,
And glitters on the broken rocks!
　Below me trees unnumbered rise,
Beautiful in various dyes:
The gloomy pine, the poplar blue,
The yellow beech, the sable yew,   60
The slender fir that taper grows,
The sturdy oak with broad-spread boughs.
And beyond the purple grove,
Haunt of Phyllis, queen of love!
Gaudy as the opening dawn,
Lies a long and level lawn,
On which a dark hill, steep and high,
Holds and charms the wandering eye!
Deep are his feet in Towy's flood,
His sides are clothed with waving wood,   70
And ancient towers crown his brow,
That cast an awful look below;
Whose ragged walls the ivy creeps,
And with he arms from falling keeps;
So both a safety from the wind
On mutual dependence find.
　'Tis now the raven's bleak abode;
'Tis now th' apartment of the toad;
And there the fox securely feeds;
And there the poisonous adder breeds,   80
Concealed in ruins, moss, and weeds,
While, ever and anon, there falls
Huge heaps of hoary mouldered walls.
Yet Time has seen, that lifts the low,
And level lays the lofty brow,
Has seen this broken pile complete,
Big with the vanity of state;
But transient is the smile of fate!

A little rule, a little sway,
A sunbeam in a winter's day, 90
Is all the proud and mighty have
Between the cradle and the grave.
    And see the rivers, how they run
Through woods and meads, in shade and sun;
Sometimes swift, sometimes slow,
Wave succeeding wave, they go
A various journey to the deep,
Like human life to endless sleep!
Thus is nature's vesture wrought,
To instruct our wandering thought; 100
Thus she dresses green and gay,
To disperse our cares away.
    Ever charming, ever new,
When will the landscape tire the view!
The fountain's fall, the river's flow,
The woody valleys warm and low;
The windy summit, wild and high,
Roughly rushing on the sky!
The pleasant seat, the ruined tower,
The naked rock, the shady bower, 110
The town and village, dome and farm,
Each give each a double charm,
As pearls upon an Ethiop's arm.
    See on the mountain's southern side,
Where the prospect opens wide,
Where the evening gilds the tide,
How close and small the hedges lie!
What streaks of meadows cross the eye!
A step methinks may pass the stream,
So little distant dangers seem; 120
So we mistake the future's face,
Eyed through hope's deluding glass;
As yon summits soft and fair,
Clad in colours of the air,
Which to those who journey near,
Barren, brown, and rough appear;
Still we tread the same coarse way,
The present's still a cloudy day.
    Oh, may I with myself agree,

And never covet what I see: 130
Content me with an humble shade,
My passions tamed, my wishes laid;
For while our wishes wildly roll,
We banish quiet from the soul;
'Tis thus the busy beat the air,
And misers gather wealth and care.
   Now, even now, my joys run high,
As on the mountain turf I lie;
While the wanton Zephyr sings,
And in the vale perfumes his wings; 140
While the waters murmur deep,
While the shepherd charms his sheep,
While the birds unbounded fly,
And with music fill the sky;
Now, even now, my joys run high.
   Be full, ye courts, be great who will;
Search for Peace with all your skill;
Open wide the lofty door;
Seek her on the marble floor;
In vain you search, she is not there; 150
In vain ye search the domes of care!
Grass and flowers Quiet treads,
On the meads and mountain-heads,
Along with Pleasure, close allied,
Ever by each other's side:
And often, by the murmuring rill,
Hears the thrush, while all is still,
Within the groves of Grongar Hill.

JAMES THOMSON (1700–1748)

139.   A HYMN ON THE SEASONS

These, as they change, Almighty Father! these
Are but the varied God. The rolling year
Is full of Thee. Forth in the pleasing Spring
Thy beauty walks, Thy tenderness and love.
Wide flush the fields; the softening air is balm;
Echo the mountains round; the forest smiles;
And every sense, and every heart, is joy.

Then comes Thy glory in the Summer-months,
With light and heat refulgent. Then Thy sun
Shoots full perfection through the swelling year: 10
And oft Thy voice in dreadful thunder speaks,
And oft, at dawn, deep noon, or falling eve,
By brooks and groves, in hollow-whispering gales.
Thy bounty shines in Autumn unconfined,
And spreads a common feast for all that lives.
In Winter awful Thou! with clouds and storms
Around Thee thrown, tempest o'er tempest rolled,
Majestic darkness! On the whirlwind's wing
Riding sublime, Thou bidst the world adore,
And humblest nature with Thy northern blast.   20
    Mysterious round! what skill, what force divine,
Deep-felt in these appear! a simple train,
Yet so delightful mixed, with such kind art,
Such beauty and beneficence combined,
Shade unperceived so softening into shade,
And all so forming an harmonious whole
That, as they still succeed, they ravish still.
But, wandering oft with brute unconscious gaze,
Man marks not Thee, marks not the mighty hand
That ever busy wheels the silent spheres,   30
Works in the secret deep, shoots steaming thence
The fair profusion that o'erspreads the Spring,
Flings from the sun direct the flaming day,
Feeds every creature, hurls the tempest forth,
And, as on earth this grateful change revolves,
With transport touches all the springs of life.
    Nature, attend! join every living soul
Beneath the spacious temple of the sky,
In adoration join; and ardent raise
One general song! To Him, ye vocal gales,   40
Breathe soft, whose spirit in your freshness breathes:
Oh! talk of Him in solitary glooms,
Where, o'er the rock, the scarcely-waving pine
Fills the brown shade with a religious awe.
And ye, whose bolder note is heard afar,
Who shake the astonished world, lift high to Heaven
The impetuous song, and say from whom you rage.
His praise, ye brooks, attune, ye trembling rills;

And let me catch it as I muse along.
Ye headlong torrents, rapid and profound;   50
Ye softer floods, that lead the humid maze
Along the vale; and thou, majestic main,
A secret world of wonders in thyself,
Sound His stupendous praise, whose greater voice
Or bids you roar or bids your roarings fall.
Soft roll your incense, herbs, and fruits, and flowers,
In mingled clouds to Him, whose sun exalts,
Whose breath perfumes you, and whose pencil paints.
Ye forests, bend; ye harvests, wave to Him—
Breathe your still song into the reaper's heart   60
As home he goes beneath the joyous moon.
Ye that keep watch in heaven, as earth asleep
Unconscious lies, effuse your mildest beams,
Ye constellations! while your angels strike
Amid the spangled sky the silver lyre.
Great source of day! best image here below
Of thy Creator, ever pouring wide
From world to world the vital ocean round,
On nature write with every beam His praise.
The thunder rolls: be hushed the prostrate world,   70
While cloud to cloud returns the solemn hymn.
Bleat out afresh, ye hills; ye mossy rocks,
Retain the sound; the broad responsive low,
Ye valleys, raise; for the Great Shepherd reigns,
And His unsuffering kingdom yet will come.
Ye woodlands all, awake: a boundless song
Burst from the groves; and, when the restless day,
Expiring, lays the warbling world asleep,
Sweetest of birds, sweet Philomela! charm
The listening shades, and teach the night His praise.   80
Ye, chief, for whom the whole creation smiles,
At once the head, the heart, the tongue of all,
Crown the great hymn! In swarming cities vast,
Assembled men, to the deep organ join
The long-resounding voice, oft breaking clear
At solemn pauses through the swelling bass;
And, as each mingling flame increases each,
In one united ardor rise to Heaven.
Or, if you rather choose the rural shade,

And find a fane in every sacred grove, 90
There let the shepherd's flute, the virgin's lay,
The prompting seraph, and the poet's lyre
Still sing the God of Seasons, as they roll.
For me, when I forget the darling theme,
Whether the blossom blows, the summer-ray
Russets the plain, inspiring Autumn gleams,
Or Winter rises in the blackening east,
Be my tongue mute, may fancy paint no more,
And, dead to joy, forget my heart to beat!

Should fate command me to the farthest verge 100
Of the green earth, to distant barbarous climes,
Rivers unknown to song, where first the sun
Gilds Indian mountains, or his setting beam
Flames on the Atlantic isles, 'tis naught to me;
Since God is ever present, ever felt,
In the void waste as in the city full,
And where He vital spreads there must be joy.
When even at last the solemn hour shall come,
And wing my mystic flight to future worlds,
I cheerful will obey; there, with new powers, 110
Will rising wonders sing: I cannot go
Where Universal Love not smiles around,
Sustaining all yon orbs and all their sons;
From seeming evil still educing good,
And better thence again, and better still,
In infinite progression.—But I lose
Myself in Him, in light ineffable!
Come then, expressive Silence, muse His praise.

ISAAC WATTS (1674–1748)

140.   MAN FRAIL AND GOD ETERNAL

Our God, our help in ages past,
    Our hope for years to come,
Our shelter from the stormy blast,
    And our eternal home:

Under the shadow of thy throne
    Thy saints have dwelt secure;

Sufficient is thine arm alone,
　And our defence is sure.

Before the hills in order stood,
　Or earth received her frame,   10
From everlasting thou art God,
　To endless years the same.

Thy word commands our flesh to dust,
　"Return, ye sons of men:"
All nations rose from earth at first,
　And turn to earth again.

A thousand ages in thy sight
　Are like an evening gone;
Short as the watch that ends the night
　Before the rising sun.   20

The busy tribes of flesh and blood
　With all their lives and cares
Are carried downwards by thy flood,
　And lost in following years.

Time like an ever-rolling stream
　Bears all its sons away;
They fly forgotten as a dream
　Dies at the opening day.

Like flowery fields the nations stand
　Pleased with the morning light;   30
The flowers beneath the mower's hand
　Lie withering e'er 'tis night.

Our God, our help in ages past,
　Our hope for years to come,
Our shelter from the stormy blast,
　And our eternal home.

CHARLES WESLEY (1707–1788)

141.   IN TEMPTATION

Jesu, Lover of my soul,
　Let me to Thy bosom fly,

While the nearer waters roll,
　While the tempest still is high!
Hide me, O my Saviour, hide,
　Till the storm of life is past;
Safe into the haven guide;
　O receive my soul at last!

Other refuge have I none;
　Hangs my helpless soul on Thee; 10
Leave, ah! leave me not alone,
　Still support and comfort me!
All my trust on Thee is stayed,
　All my help from Thee I bring:
Cover my defenceless head
　With the shadow of Thy wing!

Wilt Thou not regard my call?
　Wilt Thou not accept my prayer?
Lo! I sink, I faint, I fall!
　Lo! on Thee I cast my care! 20
Reach me out Thy gracious hand!
　While I of Thy strength receive,
Hoping against hope I stand,
　Dying, and behold I live!

Thou, O Christ, art all I want;
　More than all in Thee I find:
Raise the fallen, cheer the faint,
　Heal the sick, and lead the blind!
Just and holy is Thy Name;
　I am all unrighteousness; 30
False and full of sin I am,
　Thou art full of truth and grace.

Plenteous grace with Thee is found,
　Grace to cover all my sin;
Let the healing streams abound;
　Make and keep me pure within!
Thou of Life the Fountain art,
　Freely let me take of Thee;
Spring Thou up within my heart!
　Rise to all eternity! 40

WILLIAM SHENSTONE (1714–1763)

142.   WRITTEN AT AN INN AT HENLEY

> To thee, fair Freedom! I retire
>   From flattery, cards, and dice, and din;
> Nor art thou found in mansions higher
>   Than the low cot or humble inn.
>
> 'Tis here with boundless power I reign;
>   And every health which I begin,
> Converts dull port to bright champagne;
>   Such freedom crowns it, at an inn.
>
> I fly from pomp, I fly from plate,
>   I fly from Falsehood's specious grin!   10
> Freedom I love and form I hate,
>   And choose my lodgings at an inn.
>
> Here, waiter! take my sordid ore,
>   Which lackeys else might hope to win;
> It buys what courts have not in store;
>   It buys me freedom at an inn.
>
> Whoe'er has travelled life's dull round,
>   Where'er his stages may have been,
> May sigh to think he still has found
>   The warmest welcome at an inn.   20

WILLIAM COLLINS (1721–1759)

143.   ODE WRITTEN IN THE BEGINNING OF
THE YEAR 1746

> How sleep the brave, who sink to rest,
> By all their country's wishes blest!
> When Spring, with dewy fingers cold,
> Returns to deck their hallowed mold,
> She there shall dress a sweeter sod
> Than Fancy's feet have ever trod.
>
> By fairy hands their knell is rung;
> By forms unseen their dirge is sung;
> There Honor comes, a pilgrim gray,

To bless the turf that wraps their clay,   10
And Freedom shall awhile repair,
To dwell a weeping hermit there!

144.   ODE TO EVENING

If aught of oaten stop or pastoral song
May hope, chaste Eve, to soothe thy modest ear,
   Like thy own solemn springs,
   Thy springs and dying gales,

O nymph reserved, while now the bright-haired sun
Sits in yon western tent, whose cloudy skirts,
   With brede ethereal wove,
   O'erhang his wavy bed—

Now air is hushed, save where the weak-eyed bat,
With short shrill shriek, flits by on leathern wing;   10
   Or where the beetle winds
   His small but sullen horn,

As oft he rises 'midst the twilight path,
Against the pilgrim borne in heedless hum—
   Now teach me, maid composed,
   To breathe some softened strain,

Whose numbers, stealing through thy darkening vale,
May not unseemly with its stillness suit,
   As musing slow I hail
   Thy genial loved return!   20

For when thy folding-star arising shows
His paly circlet, at his warning lamp
   The fragrant Hours, and Elves
   Who slept in flowers the day,

And many a nymph who wreathes her brows with sedge,
And sheds the freshening dew, and, lovelier still,
   The pensive Pleasures sweet
   Prepare thy shadowy car.

Then lead, calm vot'ress, where some sheety lake
Cheers the lone heath, or some time-hallowed pile   30
   Or upland fallows gray
   Reflect its last cool gleam.

But when chill blustering winds or driving rain
Forbid my willing feet, be mine the hut
   That from the mountain's side
   Views wilds, and swelling floods,

And hamlets brown, and dim-discovered spires,
And hears their simple bell, and marks o'er all
   Thy dewy fingers draw
   The gradual dusky veil.   40

While Spring shall pour his showers, as oft he wont,
And bathe thy breathing tresses, meekest Eve;
   While Summer loves to sport
   Beneath thy lingering light;

While sallow Autumn fills thy lap with leaves;
Or Winter, yelling through the troublous air,
   Affrights thy shrinking train,
   And rudely rends thy robes;

So long, sure-found beneath the sylvan shed,
Shall Fancy, Friendship, Science, rose-lipped Health,   50
   Thy gentlest influence own,
   And hymn thy favorite name!

THOMAS GRAY (1716–1771)

145.   ODE ON A DISTANT PROSPECT OF
ETON COLLEGE

   Ye distant spires, ye antique towers,
That crown the watery glade,
Where grateful Science still adores
Her Henry's holy Shade;
And ye, that from the stately brow
Of Windsor's heights th' expanse below
Of grove, of lawn, of mead survey,
Whose turf, whose shade, whose flowers among
Wanders the hoary Thames along
His silver-winding way: 10

   Ah, happy hills! ah, pleasing shade!
Ah, fields beloved in vain!
Where once my careless childhood strayed,

A stranger yet to pain!
I feel the gales that from ye blow
A momentary bliss bestow,
As, waving fresh their gladsome wing,
My weary soul they seem to soothe,
And, redolent of joy and youth,
To breathe a second spring.   20

 Say, Father Thames, for thou hast seen
Full many a sprightly race
Disporting on thy margent green
The paths of pleasure trace;
Who foremost now delight to cleave
With pliant arm thy glassy wave?
The captive linnet which enthrall?
What idle progeny succeed
To chase the rolling circle's speed,
Or urge the flying ball?   30

 While some on earnest business bent
Their murmuring labors ply
'Gainst graver hours, that bring constraint
To sweeten liberty;
Some bold adventurers disdain
The limits of their little reign,
And unknown regions dare descry;
Still as they run they look behind;
They hear a voice in every wind,
And snatch a fearful joy.   40

 Gay hope is theirs, by fancy fed,
Less pleasing when possessed;
The tear forgot as soon as shed,
The sunshine of the breast;
Theirs buxom health of rosy hue,
Wild wit, invention ever new,
And lively cheer of vigor born;
The thoughtless day, the easy night,
The spirits pure, the slumbers light,
That fly th' approach of morn.   50

 Alas, regardless of their doom,
The little victims play!

No sense have they of ills to come,
Nor care beyond to-day!
Yet see how all around 'em wait
The ministers of human fate,
And black Misfortune's baleful train!
Ah, show them where in ambush stand
To seize their prey the murderous band!
Ah, tell them they are men!   60

These shall the fury Passions tear,
The vultures of the mind,
Disdainful Anger, pallid Fear,
And Shame that skulks behind;
Or pining Love shall waste their youth,
Or Jealousy with rankling tooth,
That inly gnaws the secret heart,
And Envy wan, and faded Care,
Grim-visaged comfortless Despair,
And Sorrow's piercing dart.   70

Ambition this shall tempt to rise,
Then whirl the wretch from high,
To bitter Scorn a sacrifice,
And grinning Infamy.
The stings of Falsehood those shall try,
And hard Unkindness' altered eye,
That mocks the tear it forced to flow;
And keen Remorse with blood defiled,
And moody Madness laughing wild
Amid severest woe.   80

Lo, in the vale of years beneath
A grisly troop are seen,
The painful family of Death,
More hideous than their queen:
This racks the joints, this fires the veins,
That every laboring sinew strains,
Those in the deeper vitals rage;
Lo, Poverty, to fill the band,
That numbs the soul with icy hand,
And slow-consuming Age.   90

To each his sufferings; all are men,
Condemned alike to groan—

The tender for another's pain,
Th' unfeeling for his own.
Yet, ah! why should they know their fate,
Since sorrow never comes too late,
And happiness too swiftly flies?
Thought would destroy their paradise.
No more; where ignorance is bliss,
'Tis folly to be wise.   100

146.   SONNET ON THE DEATH OF MR.
                      RICHARD WEST

In vain to me the smiling mornings shine,
    And reddening Phœbus lifts his golden fire;
The birds in vain their amorous descant join,
    Or cheerful fields resume their green attire;
These ears, alas! for other notes repine,
    A different object do these eyes require;
My lonely anguish melts no heart but mine,
    And in my breast the imperfect joys expire.
Yet morning smiles the busy race to cheer,
    And new-born pleasure brings to happier men;   10
The fields to all their wonted tribute bear;
    To warm their little loves the birds complain:
I fruitless mourn to him that cannot hear,
    And weep the more, because I weep in vain.

147.   ELEGY WRITTEN IN A COUNTRY
                          CHURCHYARD

The curfew tolls the knell of parting day,
    The lowing herd wind slowly o'er the lea,
The ploughman homeward plods his weary way,
    And leaves the world to darkness and to me.

Now fades the glimmering landscape on the sight,
    And all the air a solemn stillness holds,
Save where the beetle wheels his droning flight,
    And drowsy tinklings lull the distant folds;

Save that from yonder ivy-mantled tower
    The moping owl does to the moon complain   10
Of such as, wandering near her secret bower,
    Molest her ancient solitary reign.

Beneath those rugged elms, that yew-tree's shade,
  Where heaves the turf in many a moldering heap,
Each in his narrow cell forever laid,
  The rude forefathers of the hamlet sleep.

The breezy call of incense-breathing morn,
  The swallow twittering from the straw-built shed,
The cock's shrill clarion, or the echoing horn,
  No more shall rouse them from their lowly bed.   20

For them no more the blazing hearth shall burn,
  Or busy housewife ply her evening care:
No children run to lisp their sire's return,
  Or climb his knees the envied kiss to share.

Oft did the harvest to their sickle yield;
  Their furrow oft the stubborn glebe has broke;
How jocund did they drive their team afield!
  How bowed the woods beneath their sturdy stroke!

Let not Ambition mock their useful toil,
  Their homely joys, and destiny obscure;   30
Nor Grandeur hear with a disdainful smile
  The short and simple annals of the poor.

The boast of heraldry, the pomp of power,
  And all that beauty, all that wealth e'er gave,
Awaits alike the inevitable hour:
  The paths of glory lead but to the grave.

Nor you, ye proud, impute to these the fault,
  If Memory o'er their tomb no trophies raise,
Where through the long-drawn aisle and fretted vault
  The pealing anthem swells the note of praise.   40

Can storied urn or animated bust
  Back to its mansion call the fleeting breath?
Can Honor's voice provoke the silent dust,
  Or Flattery soothe the dull, cold ear of Death?

Perhaps in this neglected spot is laid
  Some heart once pregnant with celestial fire;
Hands that the rod of empire might have swayed,
  Or waked to ecstasy the living lyre.

But Knowledge to their eyes her ample page,
  Rich with the spoils of time, did ne'er unroll;   50
Chill Penury repressed their noble rage,
  And froze the genial current of the soul.

Full many a gem of purest ray serene,
  The dark unfathomed caves of ocean bear:
Full many a flower is born to blush unseen,
  And waste its sweetness on the desert air.

Some village Hampden, that with dauntless breast
  The little tyrant of his fields withstood;
Some mute, inglorious Milton here may rest,
  Some Cromwell, guiltless of his country's blood.   60

The applause of listening senates to command,
  The threats of pain and ruin to despise,
To scatter plenty o'er a smiling land,
  And read their history in a nation's eyes,

Their lot forbade: nor circumscribed alone
  Their growing virtues, but their crimes confined;
Forbade to wade through slaughter to a throne,
  And shut the gates of mercy on mankind;

The struggling pangs of conscious truth to hide,
  To quench the blushes of ingenuous shame,   70
Or heap the shrine of Luxury and Pride
  With incense kindled at the Muse's flame.

Far from the madding crowd's ignoble strife
  Their sober wishes never learned to stray;
Along the cool, sequestered vale of life
  They kept the noiseless tenor of their way.

Yet even these bones from insult to protect,
  Some frail memorial still erected nigh,
With uncouth rhymes and shapeless sculpture decked,
  Implores the passing tribute of a sigh.   80

Their name, their years, spelt by th' unlettered Muse,
  The place of fame and elegy supply;
And many a holy text around she strews,
  That teach the rustic moralist to die.

For who, to dumb forgetfulness a prey,
  This pleasing anxious being e'er resigned,
Left the warm precincts of the cheerful day,
  Nor cast one longing lingering look behind?

On some fond breast the parting soul relies,
  Some pious drops the closing eye requires;   90
E'en from the tomb the voice of Nature cries,
  E'en in our ashes live their wonted fires.

For thee who, mindful of the unhonored dead,
  Dost in these lines their artless tale relate;
If chance, by lonely contemplation led,
  Some kindred spirit shall inquire thy fate,

Haply some hoary-headed swain may say,
  "Oft have we seen him at the peep of dawn
Brushing with hasty steps the dews away,
  To meet the sun upon the upland lawn.   100

"There at the foot of yonder nodding beech
  That wreathes its old fantastic roots so high,
His listless length at noontide would he stretch,
  And pore upon the brook that babbles by.

"Hard by yon wood, now smiling as in scorn,
  Muttering his wayward fancies he would rove;
Now drooping, woeful-wan, like one forlorn,
  Or crazed with care, or crossed in hopeless love.

"One morn I missed him on the customed hill,
  Along the heath, and near his favorite tree;   110
Another came; nor yet beside the rill,
  Nor up the lawn, nor at the wood was he;

"The next, with dirges due, in sad array,
  Slow through the church-way path we saw him borne.
Approach and read (for thou canst read) the lay,
  Graved on the stone beneath yon aged thorn."

THE EPITAPH

Here rests his head upon the lap of earth,
  A youth to Fortune and to Fame unknown;

Fair Science frowned not on his humble birth,
  And Melancholy marked him for her own. 120

Large was his bounty, and his soul sincere;
  Heaven did a recompense as largely send:
He gave to Misery (all he had) a tear;
  He gained from Heaven ('twas all he wished) a friend.

No farther seek his merits to disclose,
  Or draw his frailties from their dread abode,
(There they alike in trembling hope repose,)
  The bosom of his Father and his God.

148. ODE ON THE DEATH OF A FAVOURITE CAT

'Twas on a lofty vase's side,
Where China's gayest art had dyed
  The azure flow'rs, that blow;
Demurest of the tabby kind,
The pensive Selima reclined,
  Gazed on the lake below.

Her conscious tail her joy declared;
The fair round face, the snowy beard,
  The velvet of her paws,
Her coat, that with the tortoise vies, 10
Her ears of jet, and emerald eyes,
  She saw; and purred applause.

Still had she gazed; but 'midst the tide
Two angel forms were seen to glide,
  The genii of the stream:
Their scaly armour's Tyrian hue
Thro' richest purple to the view
  Betrayed a golden gleam.

The hapless nymph with wonder saw:
A whisker first and then a claw, 20
  With many an ardent wish,
She stretched in vain to reach the prize.
What female heart can gold despise?
  What cat's averse to fish?

Presumptuous maid! with looks intent
Again she stretched, again she bent,

Nor knew the gulf between.
(Malignant Fate sat by, and smiled)
The slippery verge her feet beguiled,
   She tumbled headlong in.   30

Eight times emerging from the flood,
She mewed to every watery god,
   Some speedy aid to send.
No Dolphin came, no Nereid stirred:
Nor cruel Tom, nor Susan heard.
   A favorite has no friend!

From hence, ye beauties, undeceived,
Know, one false step is ne'er retrieved,
   And be with caution bold.
Not all that tempts your wandering eyes   40
And heedless hearts, is lawful prize;
   Nor all that glisters, gold.

SAMUEL JOHNSON (1709–1784)

149.   ## THE VANITY OF HUMAN WISHES

IN IMITATION OF THE TENTH SATIRE OF JUVENAL

Let Observation, with extensive view,
Survey mankind from China to Peru;
Remark each anxious toil, each eager strife,
And watch the busy scenes of crowded life;
Then say how hope and fear, desire and hate,
O'erspread with snares the clouded maze of fate,
Where wavering man, betrayed by venturous pride
To tread the dreary paths without a guide,
As treacherous phantoms in the mist delude,
Shuns fancied ills, or chases airy good.   10
How rarely reason guides the stubborn choice,
Rules the bold hand, or prompts the suppliant voice;
How nations sink, by darling schemes oppressed,
When vengeance listens to the fool's request.
Fate wings with every wish the afflictive dart,
Each gift of nature, and each grace of art;
With fatal heat impetuous courage glows,

With fatal sweetness elocution flows;
Impeachment stops the speaker's powerful breath,
And restless fire precipitates on death.   20
  But scarce observed, the knowing and the bold
Fall in the general massacre of gold;
Wide-wasting pest! that rages unconfined,
And crowds with crimes the records of mankind:
For gold his sword the hireling ruffian draws;
For gold the hireling judge distorts the laws;
Wealth heaped on wealth, nor truth nor safety buys,
The dangers gather as the treasures rise.
  Let history tell, where rival kings command,
And dubious title shakes the madded land,   30
When statutes glean the refuse of the sword,
How much more safe the vassal than the lord;
Low skulks the hind beneath the rage of power,
And leaves the wealthy traitor in the Tower;
Untouched his cottage, and his slumbers sound,
Though confiscation's vultures hover round.
  The needy traveller, serene and gay,
Walks the wild heath, and sings his toil away.
Does envy seize thee? crush the upbraiding joy,
Increase his riches, and his peace destroy;   40
New fears in dire vicissitude invade,
The rustling brake alarms, and quivering shade;
Nor light nor darkness bring his pain relief,
One shows the plunder, and one hides the thief.
  Yet still one general cry the skies assails,
And gain and grandeur load the tainted gales;
Few know the toiling statesman's fear or care,
The insidious rival and the gaping heir.
  Once more, Democritus, arise on earth,
With cheerful wisdom and instructive mirth,   50
See motley life in modern trappings dressed,
And feed with varied fools the eternal jest:
Thou who couldst laugh where want enchained caprice,
Toil crushed conceit, and man was of a piece;
Where wealth unloved without a mourner died,
And scarce a sycophant was fed by pride;
Where ne'er was known the form of mock debate,
Or seen a new-made mayor's unwieldy state;

Where change of favorites made no change of laws,
And senates heard before they judged a cause;   60
How wouldst thou shake at Britain's modish tribe,
Dart the quick taunt, and edge the piercing gibe,
Attentive truth and nature to descry,
And pierce each scene with philosophic eye!
To thee were solemn toys or empty show
The robes of pleasure and the veils of woe;
All aid the farce, and all thy mirth maintain,
Whose joys are causeless, or whose griefs are vain.
    Such was the scorn that filled the sage's mind,
Renewed at every glance on human kind;   70
How just that scorn ere yet thy voice declare,
Search every state, and canvass every prayer.
    Unnumbered suppliants crowd Preferment's gate,
Athirst for wealth, and burning to be great;
Delusive Fortune hears the incessant call,
They mount, they shine, evaporate, and fall.
On every stage the foes of peace attend;
Hate dogs their flight, and insult mocks their end.
Love ends with hope; the sinking statesman's door
Pours in the morning worshipper no more;   80
For growing names the weekly scribbler lies,
To growing wealth the dedicator flies;
From every room descends the painted face,
That hung the bright Palladium of the place,
And, smoked in kitchens or in auctions sold,
To better features yields the frame of gold;
For now no more we trace in every line
Heroic worth, benevolence divine:
The form distorted justifies the fall,
And detestation rids the indignant wall.   90
    But will not Britain hear the last appeal,
Sign her foes' doom, or guard her favorites' zeal?
Through Freedom's sons no more remonstrance rings,
Degrading nobles and controlling kings;
Our supple tribes repress their patriot throats,
And ask no questions but the price of votes;
With weekly libels and septennial ale,
Their wish is full to riot and to rail.
    In full-blown dignity see Wolsey stand,

Law in his voice, and fortune in his hand: 100
To him the church, the realm, their powers consign,
Through him the rays of regal bounty shine,
Still to new heights his restless wishes tower,
Claim leads to claim, and power advances power;
Till conquest unresisted ceased to please,
And rights submitted, left him none to seize.
At length his sovereign frowns—the train of state
Mark the keen glance, and watch the sign to hate.
Where'er he turns he meets a stranger's eye,
His suppliants scorn him, and his followers fly;   110
At once is lost the pride of awful state,
The golden canopy, the glittering plate,
The regal palace, the luxurious board,
The liveried army, and the menial lord.
With age, with cares, with maladies oppressed,
He seeks the refuge of monastic rest.
Grief aids disease, remembered folly stings,
And his last sighs reproach the faith of kings.
 Speak thou, whose thoughts at humble peace repine,
Shall Wolsey's wealth, with Wolsey's end, be thine? 120
Or liv'st thou now, with safer pride content,
The wisest justice on the banks of Trent?
For why did Wolsey near the steeps of fate
On weak foundations raise the enormous weight?
Why but to sink beneath misfortune's blow,
With louder ruin to the gulfs below?
 What gave great Villiers to the assassin's knife,
And fixed disease on Harley's closing life?
What murdered Wentworth, and what exiled Hyde,
By kings protected and to kings allied?   130
What but their wish indulged in courts to shine,
And power too great to keep or to resign?
 When first the college rolls receive his name,
The young enthusiast quits his ease for fame;
Through all his veins the fever of renown
Spreads from the strong contagion of the gown;
O'er Bodley's dome his future labors spread,
And Bacon's mansion trembles o'er his head.
Are these thy views? Proceed, illustrious youth,
And Virtue guard thee to the throne of Truth!   140

Yet should thy soul indulge the generous heat,
Till captive Science yields her last retreat;
Should Reason guide thee with her brightest ray,
And pour on misty Doubt resistless day;
Should no false Kindness lure to loose delight,
Nor Praise relax, nor Difficulty fright;
Should tempting Novelty thy cell refrain,
And Sloth effuse her opiate fumes in vain;
Should Beauty blunt on fops her fatal dart,
Nor claim the triumph of a lettered heart;   150
Should no disease thy torpid veins invade,
Nor Melancholy's phantoms haunt thy shade;
Yet hope not life from grief or danger free,
Nor think the doom of man reversed for thee:
Deign on the passing world to turn thine eyes,
And pause awhile from letters, to be wise;
There mark what ills the scholar's life assail,
Toil, envy, want, the patron, and the jail.
See nations slowly wise, and meanly just,
To buried merit raise the tardy bust.   160
If dreams yet flatter, once again attend,
Hear Lydiat's life, and Galileo's end.
　　Nor deem, when Learning her last prize bestows,
The glittering eminence exempt from woes;
See, when the vulgar 'scape, despised or awed,
Rebellion's vengeful talons seize on Laud.
From meaner minds, though smaller fines content,
The plundered palace or sequestered rent;
Marked out by dangerous parts he meets the shock,
And fatal Learning leads him to the block: 170
Around his tomb let Art and Genius weep,
But hear his death, ye blockheads, hear and sleep.
　　The festal blazes, the triumphal show,
The ravished standard, and the captive foe,
The senate's thanks, the gazette's pompous tale,
With force resistless o'er the brave prevail.
Such bribes the rapid Greek o'er Asia whirled;
For such the steady Romans shook the world;
For such in distant lands the Britons shine,
And stain with blood the Danube or the Rhine;   180
This power has praise that virtue scarce can warm,

Till fame supplies the universal charm.
Yet Reason frowns on War's unequal game,
Where wasted nations raise a single name,
And mortgaged states their grandsires' wreaths regret,
From age to age in everlasting debt;
Wreaths which at last the dear-bought right convey
To rust on medals, or on stones decay.
　　On what foundation stands the warrior's pride,
How just his hopes, let Swedish Charles decide;　　190
A frame of adamant, a soul of fire,
No dangers fright him and no labors tire;
O'er love, o'er fear, extends his wide domain,
Unconquered lord of pleasure and of pain;
No joys to him pacific sceptres yield;
War sounds the trump, he rushes to the field;
Behold surrounding kings their powers combine,
And one capitulate, and one resign;
Peace courts his hand, but spreads her charms in vain;
"Think nothing gained," he cries, "till naught remain,　200
On Moscow's walls till Gothic standards fly,
And all be mine beneath the polar sky."
The march begins in military state,
And nations on his eye suspended wait;
Stern Famine guards the solitary coast,
And Winter barricades the realms of Frost;
He comes, nor want nor cold his course delay;—
Hide, blushing Glory, hide Pultowa's day!
The vanquished hero leaves his broken bands,
And shows his miseries in distant lands;　　　　210
Condemned a needy suppliant to wait,
While ladies interpose and slaves debate.
But did not Chance at length her error mend?
Did no subverted empire mark his end?
Did rival monarchs give the fatal wound?
Or hostile millions press him to the ground?
His fall was destined to a barren strand,
A petty fortress, and a dubious hand;
He left the name at which the world grew pale,
To point a moral or adorn a tale.　　　　　　　220
　　All times their scenes of pompous woes afford,
From Persia's tyrant to Bavaria's lord.

In gay hostility and barbarous pride,
With half mankind embattled at his side,
Great Xerxes comes to seize the certain prey,
And starves exhausted regions in his way;
Attendant Flattery counts his myriads o'er,
Till counted myriads soothe his pride no more;
Fresh praise is tried till madness fires his mind;
The waves he lashes, and enchains the wind;   230
New powers are claimed, new powers are still bestowed,
Till rude resistance lops the spreading god;
The daring Greeks deride the martial show,
And heap their valleys with the gaudy foe;
The insulted sea with humbler thoughts he gains;
A single skiff to speed his flight remains;
The encumbered oar scarce leaves the dreaded coast
Through purple billows and a floating host.
    The bold Bavarian, in a luckless hour,
Tries the dread summits of Caesarean power,   240
With unexpected legions bursts away,
And sees defenceless realms receive his sway;
Short sway! fair Austria spreads her mournful charms;
The queen, the beauty, sets the world in arms;
From hill to hill the beacon's rousing blaze
Spreads wide the hope of plunder and of praise;
The fierce Croatian, and the wild Hussar,
And all the sons of ravage crowd the war;
The baffled prince in honor's flattering bloom
Of hasty greatness finds the fatal doom,   250
His foes' derision, and his subjects' blame,
And steals to death from anguish and from shame.
    "Enlarge my life with multitude of days!"
In health, in sickness, thus the suppliant prays;
Hides from himself his state, and shuns to know
That life protracted is protracted woe.
Time hovers o'er, impatient to destroy,
And shuts up all the passages of joy:
In vain their gifts the bounteous seasons pour,
The fruit autumnal and the vernal flower;   260
With listless eyes the dotard views the store,
He views, and wonders that they please no more;
Now pall the tasteless meats and joyless wines,

And Luxury with sighs her slave resigns.
Approach, ye minstrels, try the soothing strain,
And yield the tuneful lenitives of pain:
No sounds, alas, would touch the impervious ear,
Though dancing mountains witnessed Orpheus near;
Nor lute nor lyre his feeble powers attend,
Nor sweeter music of a virtuous friend,   270
But everlasting dictates crowd his tongue,
Perversely grave or positively wrong.
The still returning tale and lingering jest
Perplex the fawning niece and pampered guest,
While growing hopes scarce awe the gathering sneer,
And scarce a legacy can bribe to hear;
The watchful guests still hint the last offence,
The daughter's petulance, the son's expense,
Improve his heady rage with treacherous skill,
And mould his passions till they make his will.   280
    Unnumbered maladies his joints invade,
Lay siege to life, and press the dire blockade;
But unextinguished avarice still remains,
And dreaded losses aggravate his pains;
He turns, with anxious heart and crippled hands,
His bonds of debt and mortgages of lands;
Or views his coffers with suspicious eyes,
Unlocks his gold, and counts it till he dies.
    But grant, the virtues of a temperate prime
Bless with an age exempt from scorn or crime;   290
An age that melts in unperceived decay,
And glides in modest innocence away;
Whose peaceful day Benevolence endears,
Whose night congratulating Conscience cheers;
The general favorite as the general friend:
Such age there is, and who could wish its end?
    Yet even on this her load Misfortune flings,
To press the weary minutes' flagging wings:
New sorrow rises as the day returns;
A sister sickens, or a daughter mourns.   300
Now kindred Merit fills the sable bier,
Now lacerated Friendship claims a tear.
Year chases year, decay pursues decay,
Still drops some joy from withering life away;

New forms arise, and different views engage,
Superfluous lags the veteran on the stage,
Till pitying Nature signs the last release,
And bids afflicted worth retire to peace.
　　But few there are whom hours like these await,
Who set unclouded in the gulfs of fate. 310
From Lydia's monarch should the search descend,
By Solon cautioned to regard his end,
In life's last scene what prodigies surprise,
Fears of the brave, and follies of the wise!
From Marlborough's eyes the streams of dotage flow,
And Swift expires a driveller and a show.
　　The teeming mother, anxious for her race,
Begs for each birth the fortune of a face;
Yet Vane could tell what ills from beauty spring,
And Sedley cursed the form that pleased a king. 320
Ye nymphs of rosy lips and radiant eyes,
Whom Pleasure keeps too busy to be wise,
Whom joys with soft varieties invite,
By day the frolic, and the dance by night,
Who frown with vanity, who smile with art,
And ask the latest fashion of the heart,
What care, what rules your heedless charms shall save,
Each nymph your rival, and each youth your slave?
Against your fame with fondness hate combines,
The rival batters, and the lover mines. 330
With distant voice neglected Virtue calls,
Less heard and less, the faint remonstrance falls;
Tired with contempt, she quits the slippery reign,
And Pride and Prudence take her seat in vain.
In crowd at once, where none the pass defend,
The harmless freedom, and the private friend.
The guardians yield, by force superior plied;
By Interest, Prudence; and by Flattery, Pride.
Now Beauty falls betrayed, despised, distressed,
And hissing Infamy proclaims the rest. 340
　　Where then shall Hope and Fear their objects find?
Must dull Suspense corrupt the stagnant mind?
Must helpless man, in ignorance sedate,
Roll darkling down the torrent of his fate?
Must no dislike alarm, no wishes rise,

No cries attempt the mercies of the skies?
Inquirer, cease; petitions yet remain
Which Heaven may hear, nor deem religion vain.
Still raise for good the supplicating voice,
But leave to Heaven the measure and the choice.   350
Safe in his power, whose eyes discern afar
The secret ambush of a specious prayer;
Implore his aid, in his decisions rest,
Secure whate'er he gives, he gives the best.
Yet, when the sense of sacred presence fires,
And strong devotion to the skies aspires,
Pour forth thy fervors for a healthful mind,
Obedient passions, and a will resigned;
For love, which scarce collective man can fill;
For patience, sovereign o'er transmuted ill;   360
For faith, that, panting for a happier seat,
Counts death kind Nature's signal of retreat:
These goods for man the laws of Heaven ordain,
These goods he grants, who grants the power to gain;
With these celestial Wisdom calms the mind,
And makes the happiness she does not find.

150.   ON THE DEATH OF MR. ROBERT LEVET

Condemned to hope's delusive mine,
  As on we toil from day to day,
By sudden blasts, or slow decline,
  Our social comforts drop away.

Well tried through many a varying year,
  See Levet to the grave descend,
Officious, innocent, sincere,
  Of every friendless name the friend.

Yet still he fills affection's eye,
  Obscurely wise and coarsely kind;   10
Nor, lettered arrogance, deny
  Thy praise to merit unrefined.

When fainting nature called for aid.
  And hovering death prepared the blow,
His vigorous remedy displayed
  The power of art without the show.

In misery's darkest caverns known,
　　His useful care was ever nigh,
Where hopeless anguish poured his groan,
　　And lonely want retired to die.　　　　　　　　20

No summons mocked by chill delay,
　　No petty gain disdained by pride;
The modest wants of every day
　　The toil of every day supplied.

His virtues walked their narrow round,
　　Nor made a pause, nor left a void;
And sure the Eternal Master found
　　The single talent well employed.

The busy day, the peaceful night,
　　Unfelt, uncounted, glided by;　　　　　　　　30
His frame was firm, his powers were bright,
　　Though now his eightieth year was nigh.

Then with no throbbing, fiery pain,
　　No cold gradations of decay,
Death broke at once the vital chain,
　　And freed his soul the nearest way.

OLIVER GOLDSMITH (1730?–1774)

151.　　　　　　THE DESERTED VILLAGE

Sweet Auburn! loveliest village of the plain,
Where health and plenty cheered the laboring swain,
Where smiling spring its earliest visit paid,
And parting summer's lingering blooms delayed;
Dear lovely bowers of innocence and ease,
Seats of my youth, when every sport could please,
How often have I loitered o'er thy green,
Where humble happiness endeared each scene!
How often have I paused on every charm,
The sheltered cot, the cultivated farm,　　　　　　10
The never-failing brook, the busy mill,
The decent church that topped the neighboring hill,

The hawthorn bush, with seats beneath the shade,
For talking age and whispering lovers made!
How often have I blessed the coming day,
When toil remitting lent its turn to play,
And all the village train, from labor free,
Led up their sports beneath the spreading tree;
While many a pastime circled in the shade,
The young contending as the old surveyed;   20
And many a gambol frolicked o'er the ground,
And slights of art and feats of strength went round;
And still, as each repeated pleasure tired,
Succeeding sports and mirthful hand inspired;
The dancing pair that simply sought renown,
By holding out to tire each other down;
The swain mistrustless of his smutted face,
While secret laughter tittered round the place;
The bashful virgin's sidelong looks of love,
The matron's glance that would those looks reprove: 30
These were thy charms, sweet village! sports like these,
With sweet succession taught even toil to please;
These round thy bowers their cheerful influence shed;
These were thy charms—but all these charms are fled.
    Sweet smiling village, loveliest of the lawn,
Thy sports are fled and all thy charms withdrawn;
Amidst thy bowers the tyrant's hand is seen,
And desolation saddens all thy green;
One only master grasps the whole domain,
And half a tillage stints thy smiling plain;   40
No more thy glassy brook reflects the day,
But choked with sedges works its weedy way;
Along thy glades, a solitary guest,
The hollow-sounding bittern guards its nest;
Amidst thy desert walks the lapwing flies,
And tires their echoes with unvaried cries.
Sunk are thy bowers in shapeless ruin all,
And the long grass o'ertops the moldering wall;
And, trembling, shrinking from the spoiler's hand,
Far, far away, thy children leave the land.   50
    Ill fares the land, to hastening ills a prey,
Where wealth accumulates and men decay;
Princes and lords may flourish or may fade;

A breath can make them as a breath has made:
But a bold peasantry, their country's pride,
When once destroyed, can never be supplied.
A time there was, ere England's griefs began,
When every rood of ground maintained its man;
For him light labor spread her wholesome store,
Just gave what life required, but gave no more: 60
His best companions, innocence and health;
And his best riches, ignorance of wealth.
But times are altered; trade's unfeeling train
Usurp the land, and dispossess the swain;
Along the lawn, where scattered hamlets rose,
Unwieldy wealth and cumbrous pomp repose;
And every want to opulence allied,
And every pang that folly pays to pride.
Those gentle hours that plenty bade to bloom,
Those calm desires that asked but little room,   70
Those healthful sports that graced the peaceful scene,
Lived in each look, and brightened all the green—
These, far departing, seek a kinder shore,
And rural mirth and manners are no more.
Sweet Auburn! parent of the blissful hour,
Thy glades forlorn confess the tyrant's power.
Here, as I take my solitary rounds
Amidst thy tangling walks and ruined grounds,
And, many a year elapsed, return to view
Where once the cottage stood, the hawthorn grew,   80
Remembrance wakes with all her busy train,
Swells at my breast, and turns the past to pain.
In all my wanderings round this world of care,
In all my griefs—and God has given my share—
I still had hopes, my latest hours to crown,
Amidst these humble bowers to lay me down;
To husband out life's taper at the close,
And keep the flame from wasting by repose.
I still had hopes, for pride attends us still,
Amidst the swains to show my book-learned skill,   90
Around my fire an evening group to draw,
And tell of all I felt, and all I saw;
And, as a hare whom hounds and horns pursue,
Pants to the place from whence at first she flew,

I still had hopes, my long vexations past,
Here to return—and die at home at last.
  O blessed retirement, friend to life's decline,
Retreats from care, that never must be mine,
How happy he who crowns in shades like these
A youth of labor with an age of ease;   100
Who quits a world where strong temptations try,
And, since 'tis hard to combat, learns to fly!
For him no wretches, born to work and weep,
Explore the mine, or tempt the dangerous deep;
No surly porter stands in guilty state,
To spurn imploring famine from the gate;
But on he moves to meet his latter end,
Angels around befriending virtue's friend;
Bends to the grave with unperceived decay,
While resignation gently slopes the way;   110
And, all his prospects brightening to the last,
His heaven commences ere the world be past.
  Sweet was the sound, when oft at evening's close
Up yonder hill the village murmur rose;
There, as I passed with careless steps and slow,
The mingling notes came softened from below;
The swain responsive as the milkmaid sung,
The sober herd that lowed to meet their young,
The noisy geese that gabbled o'er the pool,
The playful children just let loose from school,   120
The watch-dog's voice that bayed the whispering wind,
And the loud laugh that spoke the vacant mind:
These all in sweet confusion sought the shade,
And filled each pause the nightingale had made.
But now the sounds of population fail,
No cheerful murmurs fluctuate in the gale,
No busy steps the grass-grown footway tread,
For all the bloomy flush of life is fled;
All but yon widowed, solitary thing,
That feebly bends beside the plashy spring;   130
She, wretched matron, forced in age, for bread,
To strip the brook with mantling cresses spread,
To pick her wintry fagot from the thorn,
To seek her nightly shed, and weep till morn—
She only left of all the harmless train,

The sad historian of the pensive plain.
   Near yonder copse, where once the garden smiled,
And still where many a garden flower grows wild,
There, where a few torn shrubs the place disclose,
The village preacher's modest mansion rose.   140
A man he was to all the country dear,
And passing rich with forty pounds a year;
Remote from towns he ran his godly race,
Nor e'er had changed, nor wished to change his place;
Unpractised he to fawn, or seek for power,
By doctrines fashioned to the varying hour;
Far other aims his heart had learned to prize,
More skilled to raise the wretched than to rise.
His house was known to all the vagrant train;
He chid their wanderings, but relieved their pain;   150
The long-remembered beggar was his guest,
Whose beard descending swept his aged breast;
The ruined spendthrift, now no longer proud,
Claimed kindred there, and had his claims allowed;
The broken soldier, kindly bade to stay,
Sat by his fire and talked the night away;
Wept o'er his wounds, or, tales of sorrow done,
Shouldered his crutch and showed how fields were won.
Pleased with his guests, the good man learned to glow,
And quite forgot their vices in their woe;   160
Careless their merits or their faults to scan,
His pity gave ere charity began.
   Thus to relieve the wretched was his pride,
And e'en his failings leaned to virtue's side;
But in his duty prompt at every call,
He watched and wept, he prayed and felt for all:
And, as a bird each fond endearment tries
To tempt its new-fledged offspring to the skies,
He tried each art, reproved each dull delay,
Allured to brighter worlds, and led the way.   170
   Beside the bed where parting life was laid,
And sorrow, guilt, and pain by turns dismayed,
The reverend champion stood. At his control
Despair and anguish fled the struggling soul;
Comfort came down the trembling wretch to raise,
And his last faltering accents whispered praise.

At church, with meek and unaffected grace,
His looks adorned the venerable place;
Truth from his lips prevailed with double sway,
And fools who came to scoff remained to pray.   180
The service past, around the pious man,
With steady zeal, each honest rustic ran;
Even children followed, with endearing wile,
And plucked his gown, to share the good man's smile.
His ready smile a parent's warmth expressed,
Their welfare pleased him and their cares distressed;
To them his heart, his love, his griefs were given,
But all his serious thoughts had rest in Heaven.
As some tall cliff, that lifts its awful form,
Swells from the vale, and midway leaves the storm,   190
Though round its breast the rolling clouds are spread,
Eternal sunshine settles on its head.
    Beside yon straggling fence that skirts the way,
With blossomed furze unprofitably gay,
There, in his noisy mansion, skilled to rule,
The village master taught his little school.
A man severe he was, and stern to view;
I knew him well, and every truant knew;
Well had the boding tremblers learned to trace
The day's disasters in his morning face;   200
Full well they laughed with counterfeited glee
At all his jokes, for many a joke had he;
Full well the busy whisper, circling round,
Conveyed the dismal tidings when he frowned;
Yet he was kind, or, if severe in aught,
The love he bore to learning was in fault;
The village all declared how much he knew;
'Twas certain he could write, and cipher too;
Lands he could measure, terms and tides presage,
And even the story ran that he could gauge: 210
In arguing, too, the parson owned his skill,
For even though vanquished, he could argue still;
While words of learned length and thundering sound
Amazed the gazing rustics ranged around;
And still they gazed, and still the wonder grew
That one small head could carry all he knew.
    But past is all his fame. The very spot

Where many a time he triumphed is forgot.
Near yonder thorn that lifts its head on high,
Where once the sign-post caught the passing eye,   220
Low lies that house where nut-brown draughts inspired,
Where graybeard mirth and smiling toil retired,
Where village statesmen talked with looks profound,
And news much older than their ale went round.
Imagination fondly stoops to trace
The parlor splendors of that festive place;
The whitewashed wall, the nicely sanded floor,
The varnished clock that clicked behind the door;
The chest contrived a double debt to pay,
A bed by night, a chest of drawers by day;   230
The pictures placed for ornament and use,
The twelve good rules, the royal game of goose;
The hearth, except when winter chilled the day,
With aspen boughs and flowers and fennel gay;
While broken teacups, wisely kept for show,
Ranged o'er the chimney, glistened in a row.
    Vain transitory splendors! Could not all
Reprieve the tottering mansion from its fall?
Obscure it sinks, nor shall it more impart
An hour's importance to the poor man's heart;   240
Thither no more the peasant shall repair
To sweet oblivion of his daily care;
No more the farmer's news, the barber's tale,
No more the woodman's ballad shall prevail;
No more the smith his dusky brow shall clear,
Relax his ponderous strength, and lean to hear;
The host himself no longer shall be found
Careful to see the mantling bliss go round;
Nor the coy maid, half willing to be pressed,
Shall kiss the cup to pass it to the rest.   250
    Yes! let the rich deride, the proud disdain,
These simple blessings of the lowly train;
To me more dear, congenial to my heart,
One native charm, than all the gloss of art;
Spontaneous joys, where nature has its play,
The soul adopts, and owns their first-born sway;
Lightly they frolic o'er the vacant mind,
Unenvied, unmolested, unconfined.

But the long pomp, the midnight masquerade,
With all the freaks of wanton wealth arrayed,— 260
In these, ere triflers half their wish obtain,
The toiling pleasure sickens into pain;
And e'en while fashion's brightest arts decoy,
The heart distrusting asks if this be joy.
    Ye friends to truth, ye statesmen, who survey
The rich man's joys increase, the poor's decay,
'Tis yours to judge how wide the limits stand
Between a splendid and an happy land.
Proud swells the tide with loads of freighted ore,
And shouting Folly hails them from her shore; 270
Hoards even beyond the miser's wish abound,
And rich men flock from all the world around.
Yet count our gains: this wealth is but a name
That leaves our useful products still the same.
Not so the loss: the man of wealth and pride
Takes up a space that many poor supplied;
Space for his lake, his park's extended bounds,
Space for his horses, equipage, and hounds;
The robe that wraps his limbs in silken sloth
Has robbed the neighboring fields of half their growth; 280
His seat, where solitary sports are seen,
Indignant spurns the cottage from the green;
Around the world each needful product flies,
For all the luxuries the world supplies;
While thus the land, adorned for pleasure all,
In barren splendor feebly waits the fall.
    As some fair female, unadorned and plain,
Secure to please while youth confirms her reign,
Slights every borrowed charm that dress supplies,
Nor shares with art the triumph of her eyes; 290
But when those charms are past, for charms are frail,
When time advances and when lovers fail,
She then shines forth, solicitous to bless,
In all the glaring impotence of dress:
Thus fares the land, by luxury betrayed,
In nature's simplest charms at first arrayed;
But verging to decline, its splendors rise,
Its vistas strike, its palaces surprise;
While, scourged by famine from the smiling land,

The mournful peasant leads his humble band;   300
And while he sinks, without one arm to save,
The country blooms—a garden and a grave.
    Where then, ah where, shall poverty reside,
To 'scape the pressure of contiguous pride?
If to some common's fenceless limits strayed,
He drives his flock to pick the scanty blade,
Those fenceless fields the sons of wealth divide,
And even the bare-worn common is denied.
    If to the city sped—what waits him there?
To see profusion that he must not share;   310
To see ten thousand baneful arts combined
To pamper luxury, and thin mankind;
To see those joys the sons of pleasure know
Extorted from his fellow-creature's woe.
Here while the courtier glitters in brocade,
There the pale artist plies the sickly trade;
Here while the proud their long-drawn pomps display,
There the black gibbet glooms beside the way;
The dome where Pleasure holds her midnight reign,
Here, richly decked, admits the gorgeous train;   320
Tumultuous grandeur crowds the blazing square,
The rattling chariots clash, the torches glare.
Sure scenes like these no troubles e'er annoy!
Sure these denote one universal joy!
Are these thy serious thoughts?—Ah, turn thine eyes
Where the poor houseless shivering female lies.
She once, perhaps, in village plenty blessed,
Has wept at tales of innocence distressed;
Her modest looks the cottage might adorn,
Sweet as the primrose peeps beneath the thorn;   330
Now lost to all—her friends, her virtue fled—
Near her betrayer's door she lays her head,
And, pinched with cold, and shrinking from the shower,
With heavy heart deplores that luckless hour,
When idly first, ambitious of the town,
She left her wheel and robes of country brown.
    Do thine, sweet Auburn, thine, the loveliest train—
Do thy fair tribes participate her pain?
E'en now, perhaps, by cold and hunger led,
At proud men's doors they ask a little bread.   340

Ah, no! To distant climes, a dreary scene,
Where half the convex world intrudes between,
Through torrid tracts with fainting steps they go,
Where wild Altama murmurs to their woe.
Far different there from all that charmed before,
The various terrors of that horrid shore;
Those blazing suns that dart a downward ray,
And fiercely shed intolerable day;
Those matted woods where birds forget to sing,
But silent bats in drowsy clusters cling;   350
Those poisonous fields with rank luxuriance crowned,
Where the dark scorpion gathers death around;
Where at each step the stranger fears to wake
The rattling terrors of the vengeful snake;
Where crouching tigers wait their hapless prey,
And savage men more murderous still than they;
While oft in whirls the mad tornado flies,
Mingling the ravaged landscape with the skies.
Far different these from every former scene,
The cooling brook, the grassy-vested green,   360
The breezy covert of the warbling grove,
That only sheltered thefts of harmless love.
   Good Heaven! what sorrows gloomed that parting day
That called them from their native walks away;
When the poor exiles, every pleasure past,
Hung round their bowers, and fondly looked their last,
And took a long farewell, and wished in vain
For seats like these beyond the western main;
And, shuddering still to face the distant deep,
Returned and wept, and still returned to weep.   370
The good old sire the first prepared to go
To new-found worlds, and wept for others' woe;
But for himself, in conscious virtue brave,
He only wished for worlds beyond the grave.
His lovely daughter, lovelier in her tears,
The fond companion of his helpless years,
Silent went next, neglectful of her charms,
And left a lover's for a father's arms.
With louder plaints the mother spoke her woes,
And blessed the cot where every pleasure rose,   380
And kissed her thoughtless babes with many a tear,

And clasped them close, in sorrow doubly dear;
Whilst her fond husband strove to lend relief
In all the silent manliness of grief.
    O Luxury! thou cursed by Heaven's decree,
How ill exchanged are things like these for thee!
How do thy potions, with insidious joy,
Diffuse their pleasures only to destroy!
Kingdoms by thee, to sickly greatness grown,
Boast of a florid vigor not their own: 390
At every draught more large and large they grow,
A bloated mass of rank, unwieldly woe;
Till, sapped their strength, and every part unsound,
Down, down they sink, and spread a ruin round.
    E'en now the devastation is begun,
And half the business of destruction done;
E'en now, methinks, as pondering here I stand,
I see the rural virtues leave the land:
Down where yon anchoring vessel spreads the sail,
That idly waiting flaps with every gale,   400
Downward they move, a melancholy band,
Pass from the shore, and darken all the strand.
Contented Toil, and hospitable Care,
And kind connubial Tenderness are there;
And Piety with wishes placed above,
And steady Loyalty, and faithful Love.
And thou, sweet Poetry, thou loveliest maid,
Still first to fly where sensual joys invade,
Unfit, in these degenerate times of shame,
To catch the heart, or strike for honest fame;   410
Dear charming nymph, neglected and decried,
My shame in crowds, my solitary pride;
Thou source of all my bliss and all my woe,
That found'st me poor at first, and keep'st me so;
Thou guide by which the nobler arts excel,
Thou nurse of every virtue, fare thee well!
Farewell, and O! where'er thy voice be tried,
On Torno's cliffs, or Pambamarca's side,
Whether where equinoctial fervors glow,
Or winter wraps the polar world in snow,   420
Still let thy voice, prevailing over time,
Redress the rigors of the inclement clime;

Aid slighted truth with thy persuasive train;
Teach erring man to spurn the rage of gain;
Teach him, that states of native strength possessed,
Though very poor, may still be very blessed;
That trade's proud empire hastes to swift decay,
As ocean sweeps the labored mole away;
While self-dependent power can time defy,
As rocks resist the billows and the sky.   430

WILLIAM COWPER (1731–1800)

152.   LIGHT SHINING OUT OF DARKNESS

God moves in a mysterious way,
    His wonders to perform;
He plants his footsteps in the sea,
    And rides upon the storm.

Deep in unfathomable mines
    Of never failing skill,
He treasures up his bright designs,
    And works his sovereign will.

Ye fearful saints fresh courage take;
    The clouds ye so much dread   10
Are big with mercy, and shall break
    In blessings on your head.

Judge not the Lord by feeble sense,
    But trust him for his grace;
Behind a frowning providence,
    He hides a smiling face.

His purposes will ripen fast,
    Unfolding every hour:
The bud may have a bitter taste,
    But sweet will be the flower.   20

Blind unbelief is sure to err,
    And scan his work in vain;
God is his own interpreter,
    And he will make it plain.

153.   ON THE RECEIPT OF MY MOTHER'S
PICTURE OUT OF NORFOLK

THE GIFT OF MY COUSIN ANN BODHAM

Oh that those lips had language! Life has passed
With me but roughly since I heard thee last.
Those lips are thine—thy own sweet smiles I see,
The same that oft in childhood solaced me;
Voice only fails, else, how distinct they say,
"Grieve not, my child, chase all thy fears away!"
The meek intelligence of those dear eyes
(Blessed be the art that can immortalize,
The art that baffles time's tyrannic claim
To quench it) here shines on me still the same.   10
    Faithful remembrancer of one so dear,
O welcome guest, though unexpected, here!
Who biddest me honor with an artless song,
Affectionate, a mother lost so long,
I will obey, not willingly alone,
But gladly, as the precept were her own;
And, while that face renews my filial grief,
Fancy shall weave a charm for my relief—
Shall steep me in Elysian reverie,
A momentary dream, that thou art she.   20
    My mother! when I learned that thou wast dead,
Say, wast thou conscious of the tears I shed?
Hovered thy spirit o'er thy sorrowing son,
Wretch even then, life's journey just begun?
Perhaps thou gav'st me, though unseen, a kiss;
Perhaps a tear, if souls can weep in bliss—
Ah that maternal smile! it answers—Yes.
I heard the bell tolled on thy burial day,
I saw the hearse that bore thee slow away,
And, turning from my nursery window, drew   30
A long, long sigh, and wept a last adieu!
But was it such?—It was.—Where thou art gone
Adieus and farewells are a sound unknown.
May I but meet thee on that peaceful shore,
The parting sound shall pass my lips no more!
Thy maidens grieved themselves at my concern,
Oft gave me promise of a quick return.

What ardently I wished, I long believed,
And, disappointed still, was still deceived;
By disappointment every day beguiled,   40
Dupe of to-morrow even from a child.
Thus many a sad to-morrow came and went,
Till, all my stock of infant sorrow spent,
I learned at last submission to my lot;
But, though I less deplored thee, ne'er forgot.
   Where once we dwelt our name is heard no more,
Children not thine have trod my nursery floor;
And where the gardener Robin, day by day,
Drew me to school along the public way
Delighted with my bauble coach, and wrapped   50
In scarlet mantle warm, and velvet capped,
'Tis now become a history little known,
That once we called the pastoral house our own.
Short-lived possession! but the record fair
That memory keeps of all thy kindness there,
Still outlives many a storm that has effaced
A thousand other themes less deeply traced.
Thy nightly visits to my chamber made,
That thou might'st know me safe and warmly laid;
Thy morning bounties ere I left my home,   60
The biscuit, or confectionary plum;
The fragrant waters on my cheeks bestowed
By thy own hand, till fresh they shone and glowed;
All this, and more endearing still than all,
Thy constant flow of love, that knew no fall,
Ne'er roughened by those cataracts and brakes
That humour interposed too often makes;
All this still legible in memory's page,
And still to be so, to my latest age,
Adds joy to duty, makes me glad to pay   70
Such honors to thee as my numbers may;
Perhaps a frail memorial, but sincere,
Not scorned in heaven, though little noticed here.
  Could time, his flight reversed, restore the hours,
When, playing with thy vesture's tissued flowers,
The violet, the pink, and jessamine,
I pricked them into paper with a pin,
(And thou wast happier than myself the while,

Would'st softly speak, and stroke my head and smile)
Could those few pleasant hours again appear,					80
Might one wish bring them, would I wish them here?
I would not trust my heart—the dear delight
Seems so to be desired, perhaps I might.—
But no—what here we call our life is such,
So little to be loved, and thou so much,
That I should ill requite thee to constrain
Thy unbound spirit into bonds again.
    Thou, as a gallant bark from Albion's coast
(The storms all weathered and the ocean crossed)
Shoots into port at some well-havened isle,					90
Where spices breathe and brighter seasons smile,
There sits quiescent on the floods that show
Her beauteous form reflected clear below,
While airs impregnated with incense play
Around her, fanning light her streamers gay;
So thou, with sails how swift! hast reached the shore
"Where tempests never beat nor billows roar,"
And thy loved consort on the dangerous tide
Of life, long since, has anchored at thy side.
But me, scarce hoping to attain that rest,					100
Always from port withheld, always distressed—
Me howling winds drive devious, tempest-tossed,
Sails ripped, seams opening wide, and compass lost,
And day by day some current's thwarting force
Sets me more distant from a prosperous course.
But oh, the thought that thou art safe, and he!
That thought is joy, arrive what may to me.
My boast is not that I deduce my birth
From loins enthroned, and rulers of the earth;
But higher far my proud pretensions rise—					110
The son of parents passed into the skies.
And now, farewell—time, unrevoked, has run
His wonted course, yet what I wished is done.
By contemplation's help, not sought in vain,
I seem to have lived my childhood o'er again;
To have renewed the joys that once were mine,
Without the sin of violating thine:
And, while the wings of fancy still are free,
And I can view this mimic show of thee,

Time has but half succeeded in his theft— 120
Thyself removed, thy power to soothe me left.

154.   THE CASTAWAY

Obscurest night involved the sky,
    Th' Atlantic billows roared,
When such a destined wretch as I,
    Washed headlong from on board,
Of friends, of hope, of all bereft,
His floating home forever left.

No braver chief could Albion boast
    Than he with whom he went,
Nor ever ship left Albion's coast,
    With warmer wishes sent. 10
He loved them both, but both in vain,
Nor him beheld, nor her again.

Not long beneath the whelming brine,
    Expert to swim, he lay;
Nor soon he felt his strength decline,
    Or courage die away;
But waged with death a lasting strife,
Supported by despair of life.

He shouted: nor his friends had failed
    To check the vessel's course,
But so the furious blast prevailed, 20
    That, pitiless perforce,
They left their outcast mate behind,
And scudded still before the wind.

Some succor yet they could afford;
    And, such as storms allow,
The cask, the coop, the floated cord,
    Delayed not to bestow.
But he (they knew) nor ship, nor shore,
Whate'er they gave, should visit more. 30

Nor, cruel as it seemed, could he
    Their haste himself condemn,
Aware that flight, in such a sea,
    Alone could rescue them;

Yet bitter felt it still to die
Deserted, and his friends so nigh.

He long survives, who lives an hour
   In ocean, self-upheld;
And so long he, with unspent power,
   His destiny repelled;   40
And ever, as the minutes flew,
Entreated help, or cried "Adieu!"

At length, his transient respite past,
   His comrades, who before
Had heard his voice in every blast,
   Could catch the sound no more.
For then, by toil subdued, he drank
The stifling wave, and then he sank.

No poet wept him; but the page
   Of narrative sincere,   50
That tells his name, his worth, his age,
   Is wet with Anson's tear.
And tears by bards or heroes shed
Alike immortalize the dead.

I therefore purpose not, or dream,
   Descanting on his fate,
To give the melancholy theme
   A more enduring date;
But misery still delights to trace
Its semblance in another's case.   60

No voice divine the storm allayed,
   No light propitious shone,
When, snatched from all effectual aid,
   We perished, each alone;
But I beneath a rougher sea,
And whelmed in deeper gulfs than he.

ROBERT BURNS (1759–1796)

HOLY WILLIE'S PRAYER

155.

O Thou, wha in the Heavens dost dwell,
Wha, as it pleases best thysel',

Sends ane to heaven and ten to hell,
   A' for thy glory,
And no for ony guid or ill
    They've done afore thee!

I bless and praise thy matchless might,
Whan thousands thou hast left in night,
That I am here afore thy sight,
    For gifts an' grace   10
A burnin an' a shinin light,
    To a' this place.

What was I, or my generation,
That I should get sic exaltation?
I, wha deserve most just damnation,
    For broken laws,
Sax thousand years 'fore my creation,
    Thro' Adam's cause.

When frae my mither's womb I fell,
Thou might hae plungèd me in hell,   20
To gnash my gums, to weep and wail,
    In burnin lakes,
Where damnèd devils roar and yell,
    Chain'd to their stakes;

Yet I am here a chosen sample,
To show thy grace is great and ample;
I'm here a pillar in thy temple,
    Strong as a rock,
A guide, a buckler, an example
    To a' thy flock.   30

O Lord, thou kens what zeal I bear,
When drinkers drink, and swearers swear,
And singin there and dancin here,
    Wi' great an' sma':
For I am keepit by thy fear
    Free frae them a'.

But yet, O Lord! confess I must
At times I'm fash'd wi' fleshy lust;
An' sometimes too, wi' warldly trust,
    Vile self gets in;   40

But thou remembers we are dust,
      Defil'd in sin.

O Lord! yestreen, thou kens, wi' Meg—
Thy pardon I sincerely beg;
O! may't ne'er be a livin' plague
      To my dishonour,
An' I'll ne'er lift a lawless leg
      Again upon her.

Besides I farther maun allow,
Wi' Lizzie's lass, three times I trow—   50
But, Lord, that Friday I was fou,
      When I cam near her,
Or else thou kens thy servant true
      Wad never steer her.

May be thou lets this fleshly thorn
Beset thy servant e'en and morn
Lest he owre high and proud should turn,
      That he's sae gifted;
If sae, thy hand maun e'en be borne,
      Until thou lift it.   60

Lord, bless thy chosen in this place,
For here thou hast a chosen race;
But God confound their stubborn face,
      And blast their name,
Wha bring thy elders to disgrace
      An' public shame.

Lord, mind Gawn Hamilton's deserts,
He drinks, an' swears, an' plays at cartes,
Yet has sae mony takin arts
      Wi' grit an' sma',   70
Frae God's ain priest the people's hearts
      He steals awa'.

An' when we chasten'd him therefor,
Thou kens how he bred sic a splore
As set the warld in a roar
      O' laughin' at us;
Curse thou his basket and his store,
      Kail and potatoes.

Lord, hear my earnest cry an' pray'r,
Against that Presbytry o' Ayr;   80
Thy strong right hand, Lord, make it bare
      Upo' their heads;
Lord, weigh it down, and dinna spare,
      For their misdeeds.

O Lord my God, that glib-tongu'd Aiken,
My very heart and soul are quakin',
To think how we stood sweatin, shakin,
      An' piss'd wi' dread,
While he, wi' hingin lips and snakin,
      Held up his head.   90

Lord in the day of vengeance try him;
Lord, visit them wha did employ him,
And pass not in thy mercy by them,
      Nor hear their pray'r:
But, for thy people's sake, destroy them,
      And dinna spare.

But, Lord, remember me and mine
Wi' mercies temp'ral and divine,
That I for gear and grace may shine
      Excell'd by nane,   100
And a' the glory shall be thine,
      Amen, Amen!

156.   ADDRESS TO THE DEIL

> O Prince, O chief of many throned pow'rs,
> That led th' embattl'd Seraphim to war.
>   *Milton.*

O thou! whatever title suit thee,
Auld Hornie, Satan, Nick, or Clootie,
Wha in yon cavern grim an' sootie,
      Clos'd under hatches,
Spairges about the brunstane cootie,
      To scaud poor wretches!

Hear me, auld Hangie, for a wee,
An' let poor damnèd bodies be;

I'm sure sma' pleasure it can gie,
   Ev'n to a deil,   10
To skelp an' scaud poor dogs like me,
   An' hear us squeel!

Great is thy pow'r, an' great thy fame;
Far kenn'd an' noted is thy name;
An' tho' yon lowin heugh's thy hame,
   Thou travels far;
An' faith! thou's neither lag nor lame,
   Nor blate nor scaur.

Whyles, ranging like a roarin lion
For prey, a' holes an' corners tryin;   20
Whyles on the strong-wing'd tempest flyin,
   Tirling the kirks;
Whyles, in the human bosom pryin,
   Unseen thou lurks.

I've heard my reverend graunie say,
In lanely glens ye like to stray;
Or where auld ruin'd castles gray
   Nod to the moon,
Ye fright the nightly wand'rer's way,
   Wi' eldritch croon.   30

When twilight did my graunie summon,
To say her pray'rs, douce, honest woman!
Aft yont the dyke she's heard you bummin,
   Wi' eerie drone;
Or, rustlin, thro' the boortries comin,
   Wi' heavy groan.

Ae dreary, windy, winter night,
The stars shot down wi' sklentin light,
Wi' you mysel I gat a fright
   Ayont the lough;   40
Ye, like a rash-buss stood in sight
   Wi' waving sough.

The cudgel in my nieve did shake,
Each bristl'd hair stood like a stake,
When, wi' an eldritch, stoor quaick, quaick,
   Amang the springs,

Awa ye squatter'd, like a drake,
          On whistlin' wings.

Let warlocks grim, an' wither'd hags,
Tell how wi' you on ragweed nags,   50
They skim the muirs, an' dizzy crags,
          Wi' wicked speed;
And in kirk-yards renew their leagues,
          Owre howkit dead.

Thence countra wives, wi' toil an' pain,
May plunge an' plunge the kirn in vain;
For, oh! the yellow treasure's taen
          By witching skill;
An' dawtit, twal-pint Hawkie's gaen
          As yell's the bill.   60

Thence mystic knots mak great abuse
On young guidmen, fond, keen, an' crouse;
When the best wark-lume i' the house,
          By cantrip wit,
Is instant made no worth a louse,
          Just at the bit.

When thowes dissolve the snawy hoord,
An' float the jinglin icy-boord,
Then water-kelpies haunt the foord,
          By your direction,   70
An' 'nighted trav'llers are allur'd
          To their destruction.

An' aft your moss-traversing spunkies
Decoy the wight that late an' drunk is:
The bleezin, curst, mischievous monkies
          Delude his eyes,
Till in some miry slough he sunk is,
          Ne'er mair to rise.

When masons' mystic word an' grip
In storms an' tempests raise you up,   80
Some cock or cat your rage maun stop,
          Or, strange to tell!
The youngest brother ye wad whip
          Aff straught to hell.

Lang syne, in Eden's bonie yard,
When youthfu' lovers first were pair'd,
And all the soul of love they shar'd,
    The raptur'd hour,
Sweet on the fragrant flow'ry swaird,
    In shady bow'r: 90

Then you, ye auld, snick-drawing dog!
Ye cam to Paradise incog,
An' play'd on man a cursed brogue,
    (Black be you fa!)
An' gied the infant warld a shog,
    'Maist ruin'd a'.

Dy'e mind that day, when in a bizz,
Wi' reekit duds, an' reestit gizz,
Ye did present your smoutie phiz
    'Mang better folk,   100
An' sklented on the man of Uz
    Your spitefu' joke?

An' how ye gat him i' your thrall,
An' brak him out o' house an' hal',
While scabs an' blotches did him gall
    Wi' bitter claw,
An' lows'd his ill-tongu'd, wicked scawl,
    Was warst ava?

But a' your doings to rehearse,
Your wily snares an' fechtin fierce,   110
Sin' that day Michael did you pierce,
    Down to this time,
Wad ding a' Lallan tongue, or Erse,
    In prose or rhyme.

An' now, auld Cloots, I ken ye're thinkin,
A certain Bardie's rantin, drinkin,
Some luckless hour will send him linkin,
    To your black pit;
But faith! he'll turn a corner jinkin,
    An' cheat you yet.   120

But fare you weel, auld Nickie-ben!
O wad ye tak a thought an' men'!

Ye aiblins might—I dinna ken—
        Still hae a stake:
I'm wae to think upo' yon den,
        Ev'n for your sake!

157.   TO A LOUSE

Ha! whare ye gaun, ye crowlin ferlie?
Your impudence protects you sairly:
I canna say but ye strunt rarely
        Owre gauze and lace;
Tho', faith! I fear ye dine but sparely
        On sic a place.

Ye ugly, creepin, blastet wonner,
Detested, shunn'd by saunt an' sinner,
How daur ye set your fit upon her—
        Sae fine a lady!   10
Gae somewhere else, and seek your dinner
        On some poor body.

Swith! in some beggar's hauffet squattle;
There ye may creep, and sprawl, and sprattle,
Wi' ither kindred, jumping cattle,
        In shoals and nations;
Whare horn nor bane ne'er daur unsettle
        Your thick plantations.

Now haud you there! ye're out o' sight,
Below the fatt'rels, snug an' tight;   20
Na, faith ye yet! ye'll no be right
        Till ye've got on it—
The vera tapmost, tow'rin height
        O' Miss's bonnet.

My sooth! right bauld ye set your nose out,
As plump an' gray as onie grozet:
O for some rank, mercurial rozet,
        Or fell, red smeddum,
I'd gie you sic a hearty dose o't,
        Wad dress your droddum.   30

I wad na been surpris'd to spy
You on an auld wife's flainen toy;

Or aiblins some bit duddie boy,
  On's wyliecoat;
But Miss's fine Lunardi! fye!
  How daur ye do't?

O Jenny, dinna toss your head,
An' set your beauties a' abread!
Ye little ken what cursèd speed
  The blastie's makin!   40
Thae winks an' finger-ends, I dread,
  Are notice takin!

O wad some Power the giftie gie us
To see oursels as ithers see us!
It wad frae monie a blunder free us,
  An' foolish notion:
What airs in dress an' gait wad lea'e us,
  An' ev'n devotion!

158.   TAM O' SHANTER

When chapman billies leave the street,
And drouthy neebors neebors meet,
As market-days are wearing late,
An' folk begin to tak the gate;
While we sit bousing at the nappy,
An' getting fou and unco happy,
We think na on the lang Scots miles,
The mosses, waters, slaps, and styles,
That lie between us and our hame,
Where sits our sulky sullen dame,   10
Gathering her brows like gathering storm,
Nursing her wrath to keep it warm.
 This truth fand honest Tam o' Shanter,
As he frae Ayr ae night did canter,
(Auld Ayr, wham ne'er a town surpasses
For honest men and bonnie lasses).
 O Tam! hadst thou but been sae wise,
As ta'en thy ain wife Kate's advice!
She tauld thee weel thou was a skellum,

A blethering, blustering, drunken blellum;   20
That frae November till October,
Ae market-day thou was na sober;
That ilka melder, wi' the miller
Thou sat as lang as thou had siller;
That every naig was ca'd a shoe on,
The smith and thee gat roarin' fou on;
That at the Lord's house, even on Sunday,
Thou drank wi' Kirkton Jean till Monday.
She prophesied that, late or soon,
Thou would be found deep drowned in Doon;   30
Or catched wi' warlocks in the mirk,
By Alloway's auld haunted kirk.
   Ah, gentle dames! it gars me greet
To think how mony counsels sweet,
How mony lengthened sage advices,
The husband frae the wife despises!
   But to our tale: Ae market night,
Tam had got planted unco right;
Fast by an ingle, bleezing finely,
Wi' reaming swats, that drank divinely;   40
And at his elbow, Souter Johnny,
His ancient, trusty, drouthy crony;
Tam lo'ed him like a vera brither;
They had been fou for weeks thegither.
The night drave on wi' sangs and clatter;
And aye the ale was growing better:
The landlady and Tam grew gracious,
Wi' favours secret, sweet, and precious:
The souter tauld his queerest stories;
The landlord's laugh was ready chorus: 50
The storm without might rair and rustle,
Tam did na mind the storm a whistle.
   Care, mad to see a man sae happy,
E'en drowned himself amang the nappy.
As bees flee hame wi' lades o' treasure,
The minutes winged their way wi' pleasure;
Kings may be blest, but Tam was glorious,
O'er a' the ills o' life victorious!
   But pleasures are like poppies spread,
You seize the flow'r, its bloom is shed;   60

Or like the snow falls in the river,
A moment white—then melts for ever;
Or like the borealis race,
That flit ere you can point their place;
Or like the rainbow's lovely form
Evanishing amid the storm.
Nae man can tether time nor tide;
The hour approaches Tam maun ride;
That hour, o' night's black arch the key-stane,
That dreary hour, he mounts his beast in;   70
And sic a night he taks the road in,
As ne'er poor sinner was abroad in.

   The wind blew as 'twad blawn its last;
The rattling show'rs rose on the blast;
The speedy gleams the darkness swallowed;
Loud, deep, and lang, the thunder bellowed:
That night, a child might understand,
The Deil had business on his hand.

   Weel mounted on his grey mare, Meg,
A better never lifted leg,   80
Tam skelpit on thro' dub and mire,
Despising wind, and rain, and fire;
Whiles holding fast his guid blue bonnet;
Whiles crooning o'er some auld Scots sonnet;
Whiles glow'ring round wi' prudent cares,
Lest bogles catch him unawares.
Kirk-Alloway was drawing nigh,
Whare ghaists and houlets nightly cry.

   By this time he was cross the ford,
Where in the snaw the chapman smoored;   90
And past the birks and meikle stane,
Where drunken Charlie brak's neck-bane;
And thro' the whins, and by the cairn,
Where hunters fand the murder'd bairn;
And near the thorn, aboon the well,
Where Mungo's mither hang'd hersel.
Before him Doon pours all his floods;
The doubling storm roars thro' the woods;
The lightnings flash from pole to pole;
Near and more near the thunders roll: 100
When, glimmering thro' the groaning trees,

Kirk-Alloway seem'd in a bleeze;
Thro' ilka bore the beams were glancing;
And loud resounded mirth and dancing.
  Inspiring bold John Barleycorn!
What dangers thou canst make us scorn!
Wi' tippenny, we fear nae evil;
Wi' usquebae we'll face the devil!
The swats sae ream'd in Tammie's noddle,
Fair play, he cared na deils a boddle.   110
But Maggie stood right sair astonished,
Till, by the heel and hand admonished,
She ventured forward on the light;
And, vow! Tam saw an unco sight!
Warlocks and witches in a dance!
Nae cotillon brent new frae France,
But hornpipes, jigs, strathspeys, and reels,
Put life and mettle in their heels.
A winnock-bunker in the east,
There sat auld Nick, in shape o' beast;   120
A touzie tyke, black, grim, and large!
To gie them music was his charge:
He screwed the pipes and gart them skirl,
Till roof and rafters a' did dirl.
Coffins stood round like open presses,
That shaw'd the dead in their last dresses;
And by some devilish cantraip slight
Each in its cauld hand held a light,
By which heroic Tam was able
To note upon the haly table   130
A murderer's banes in gibbet-airns;
Twa span-lang, wee, unchristen'd bairns;
A thief new-cutted frae a rape—
Wi' his last gasp his gab did gape;
Five tomahawks, wi' blude red-rusted;
Five scymitars, wi' murder crusted;
A garter, which a babe had strangled;
A knife, a father's throat had mangled,
Whom his ain son o' life bereft—
The gray hairs yet stack to the heft;   140
Wi' mair of horrible and awfu',
Which even to name wad be unlawfu'.

As Tammie glowr'd, amaz'd, and curious,
The mirth and fun grew fast and furious:
The piper loud and louder blew;
The dancers quick and quicker flew;
They reeled, they set, they crossed, they cleekit,
Till ilka carlin swat and reekit,
And coost her duddies to the wark,
And linkit at it in her sark! 150

Now Tam, O Tam! had thae been queans,
A' plump and strapping in their teens;
Their sarks, instead o' creeshie flannen,
Been snaw-white seventeen hunder linen!
Thir breeks o' mine, my only pair,
That ance were plush, o' gude blue hair,
I wad hae gi'en them off my hurdies,
For ae blink o' the bonie burdies!

But wither'd beldams, auld and droll,
Rigwoodie hags wad spean a foal, 160
Louping and flinging on a crummock,
I wonder didna turn thy stomach.

But Tam kend what was what fu' brawlie;
There was ae winsome wench and wawlie
That night enlisted in the core,
Lang after kent on Carrick shore!
(For mony a beast to dead she shot,
And perished mony a bonie boat,
And shook baith meikle corn and bear,
And kept the country-side in fear) 170
Her cutty sark, o' Paisley harn,
That while a lassie she had worn,
In longitude tho' sorely scanty,
It was her best, and she was vauntie.—
Ah! little kend thy reverend grannie
That sark she coft for her wee Nannie
Wi' twa pund Scots ('twas a' her riches)
Wad ever graced a dance of witches!

But here my Muse her wing maun cour;
Sic flights are far beyond her pow'r-- 180
To sing how Nannie lap and flang,
(A souple jade she was, and strang),
And how Tam stood, like ane bewitched,

And thought his very een enriched;
Even Satan glowr'd, and fidg'd fu' fain,
And hotched and blew wi' might and main:
Till first ae caper, syne anither,
Tam tint his reason a' thegither,
And roars out "Weel done, Cutty-sark!"
And in an instant all was dark!   190
And scarcely had he Maggie rallied,
When out the hellish legion sallied.
   As bees bizz out wi' angry fyke,
When plundering herds assail their byke;
As open pussie's mortal foes,
When pop! she starts before their nose;
As eager runs the market-crowd,
When "Catch the thief!" resounds aloud;
So Maggie runs; the witches follow,
Wi' mony an eldritch skriech and hollow.   200
   Ah, Tam! ah, Tam! thou'll get thy fairin!
In hell they'll roast thee like a herrin!
In vain thy Kate awaits thy comin!
Kate soon will be a woefu' woman!
Now do thy speedy utmost, Meg,
And win the key-stane o' the brig;
There at them thou thy tail may toss,
A running stream they darena cross.
But ere the key-stane she could make,
The fient a tail she had to shake!   210
For Nannie, far before the rest,
Hard upon noble Maggie prest,
And flew at Tam wi' furious ettle;
But little wist she Maggie's mettle.—
Ae spring brought off her master hale,
But left behind her ain gray tail:
The carlin claught her by the rump,
And left poor Maggie scarce a stump.
   Now, wha this tale o' truth shall read,
Each man and mother's son, take heed: 220
Whene'er to drink you are inclined,
Or cutty-sarks run in your mind,
Think! ye may buy the joys o'er dear;
Remember Tam o' Shanter's mare.

159.   GREEN GROW THE RASHES

Green grow the rashes, O,
  Green grow the rashes, O;
The sweetest hours that e'er I spend,
  Are spent amang the lasses, O!

There's nought but care on ev'ry han',
  In ev'ry hour that passes, O;
What signifies the life o' man,
  An' 'twere na for the lasses, O.

The warly race may riches chase,
  An' riches still may fly them, O;
An' tho' at last they catch them fast,
  Their hearts can ne'er enjoy them, O.

But gie me a canny hour at e'en,
  My arms about my dearie, O;
An' warly cares, an' warly men,
  May a' gae tapsalteerie, O!

For you sae douce, ye sneer at this,
  Ye're nought but senseless asses, O:
The wisest man the warl' saw,
  He dearly lov'd the lasses, O.   20

Auld Nature swears, the lovely dears
  Her noblest work she classes, O;
Her prentice han' she tried on man,
  An' then she made the lasses, O.

160.   JOHN ANDERSON MY JO

John Anderson my jo, John,
  When we were first acquent,
Your locks were like the raven,
  Your bonie brow was brent;
But now your brow is beld, John,
  Your locks are like the snow;
But blessings on your frosty pow,
  John Anderson, my jo.

John Anderson my jo, John,
  We clamb the hill thegither;   10

And mony a canty day, John,
  We've had wi' ane anither:
Now we maun totter down, John,
  And hand in hand we'll go,
And sleep thegither at the foot,
  John Anderson, my jo.

161.   CA' THE YOWES

Ca' the yowes to the knowes,
Ca' them where the heather grows,
Ca' them where the burnie rows,
    My bonie dearie.

Hark! the mavis' evening sang
Sounding Clouden's woods amang;
Then a-faulding let us gang,
    My bonie dearie.

We'll gae down by Clouden side,
Thro' the hazels spreading wide   10
O'er the waves that sweetly glide
    To the moon sae clearly.

Yonder's Clouden's silent towers,
Where at moonshine midnight hours,
O'er the dewy-bending flowers,
    Fairies dance sae cheery.

Ghaist nor bogle shalt thou fear;
Thou'rt to love and Heaven sae dear,
Nocht of ill may come thee near,
    My bonie dearie.   20

Fair and lovely as thou art,
Thou hast stown my very heart;
I can die—but canna part,
    My bonie dearie.

162.   GO FETCH TO ME A PINT O' WINE

Go fetch to me a pint o' wine,
  An' fill it in a silver tassie;
That I may drink, before I go,
  A service to my bonie lassie.

The boat rocks at the pier o' Leith,
  Fu' loud the wind blaws frae the Ferry,
The ship rides by the Berwick-law,
  And I maun leave my bonie Mary.

The trumpets sound, the banners fly,
  The glittering spears are rankèd ready;   10
The shouts o' war are heard afar,
  The battle closes thick and bloody;
But it's no the roar o' sea or shore
  Wad mak me langer wish to tarry;
Nor shout o' war that's heard afar,
  It's leaving thee, my bonie Mary.

163.   A RED, RED ROSE

O my luve's like a red, red rose,
  That's newly sprung in June:
O my luve's like the melodie
  That's sweetly play'd in tune.

As fair art thou, my bonie lass,
  So deep in luve am I;
And I will luve thee still, my dear,
  Till a' the seas gang dry.

Till a' the seas gang dry, my dear,
  And the rocks melt wi' the sun: 10
And I will luve thee still, my dear,
  While the sands o' life shall run.

And fare thee weel, my only luve!
  And fare thee weel awhile!
And I will come again, my luve,
  Tho' it were ten thousand mile!

164.   AULD LANG SYNE

Should auld acquaintance be forgot,
  And never brought to mind?
Should auld acquaintance be forgot,
  And auld lang syne!

    For auld lang syne, my dear,
      For auld lang syne,

We'll tak a cup o' kindness yet
  For auld lang syne.

And surely ye'll be your pint-stowp!
  And surely I'll be mine!   10
And we'll tak a cup o' kindness yet
  For auld lang syne.

We twa hae run about the braes,
  And pu'd the gowans fine;
But we've wander'd mony a weary fitt
  Sin auld lang syne.

We twa hae' paidl'd i' the burn,
  From morning sun till dine;
But seas between us braid hae roar'd,
  Sin auld lang syne.   20

And there's a hand, my trusty fiere!
  And gie's a hand o' thine!
And we'll tak a right guid-willie waught,
  For auld lang syne.

GEORGE CRABBE (1754–1832)

165. ## THE VILLAGE

The village life, and every care that reigns
O'er youthful peasants and declining swains;
What labour yields, and what, that labour past,
Age, in its hour of languor, finds at last;
What form the real picture of the poor,
Demand a song—the Muse can give no more.
  Fled are those times when, in harmonious strains,
The rustic poet praised his native plains:
No shepherds now, in smooth alternate verse,
Their country's beauty or their nymphs' rehearse;   10
Yet still for these we frame the tender strain,
Still in our lays fond Corydons complain,
And shepherds' boys their amorous pains reveal,
The only pains, alas! they never feel.

On Mincio's banks, in Caesar's bounteous reign,
If Tityrus found the Golden Age again,
Must sleepy bards the flattering dream prolong,
Mechanic echoes of the Mantuan song?
From Truth and Nature shall we widely stray,
Where Virgil, not where Fancy, leads the way?   20
  Yes, thus the Muses sing of happy swains,
Because the Muses never knew their pains:
They boast their peasants' pipes; but peasants now
Resign their pipes and plod behind the plough;
And few, amid the rural tribe, have time
To number syllables and play with rhyme;
Save honest Duck, what son of verse could share
The poet's rapture, and the peasant's care?
Or the great labours of the field degrade,
With the new peril of a poorer trade?   30
  From this chief cause these idle praises spring,
That themes so easy few forbear to sing.
For no deep thought the trifling subjects ask;
To sing of shepherds is an easy task.
The happy youth assumes the common strain,
A nymph his mistress, and himself a swain;
With no sad scenes he clouds his tuneful prayer,
But all, to look like her, is painted fair.
  I grant indeed that fields and flocks have charms
For him that grazes or for him that farms;   40
But when amid such pleasing scenes I trace
The poor laborious natives of the place,
And see the midday sun, with fervid ray,
On their bare heads and dewy temples play;
While some, with feebler heads and fainter hearts,
Deplore their fortune, yet sustain their parts,
Then shall I dare these real ills to hide
In tinsel trappings of poetic pride?
  No; cast by Fortune on a frowning coast,
Which neither groves nor happy valleys boast;   50
Where other cares than those the Muse relates,
And other shepherds dwell with other mates;
By such examples taught, I paint the cot,
As Truth will paint it, and as bards will not:
Nor you, ye poor, of lettered scorn complain,

To you the smoothest song is smooth in vain;
O'ercome by labour, and bowed down by time,
Feel you the barren flattery of a rhyme?
Can poets soothe you, when you pine for bread,
By winding myrtles round your ruined shed?   60
Can their light tales your weighty griefs o'erpower,
Or glad with airy mirth the toilsome hour?
   Lo! where the heath, with withering brake grown o'er,
Lends the light turf that warms the neighbouring poor;
From thence a length of burning sand appears,
Where the thin harvest waves its withered ears;
Rank weeds, that every art and care defy,
Reign o'er the land, and rob the blighted rye:
There thistles stretch their prickly arms afar,
And to the ragged infant threaten war;   70
There poppies, nodding, mock the hope of toil;
There the blue bugloss paints the sterile soil;
Hardy and high, above the slender sheaf,
The slimy mallow waves her silky leaf;
O'er the young shoot the charlock throws a shade,
And clasping tares cling round the sickly blade;
With mingled tints the rocky coasts abound,
And a sad splendour vainly shines around.
So looks the nymph whom wretched arts adorn,
Betrayed by man, then left for man to scorn;   80
Whose cheek in vain assumes the mimic rose,
While her sad eyes the troubled breast disclose;
Whose outward splendour is but folly's dress,
Exposing most, when most it gilds distress.
   Here joyless roam a wild amphibious race,
With sullen woe displayed in every face;
Who, far from civil arts and social fly,
And scowl at strangers with suspicious eye.
   Here too the lawless merchant of the main
Draws from his plough th' intoxicated swain;   90
Want only claimed the labour of the day,
But vice now steals his nightly rest away.
   Where are the swains, who, daily labour done,
With rural games played down the setting sun;
Who struck with matchless force the bounding ball,
Or made the ponderous quoit obliquely fall:

While some huge Ajax, terrible and strong,
Engaged some artful stripling of the throng,
And fell beneath him, foiled, while far around
Hoarse triumph rose, and rocks returned the sound?   100
Where now are these?—Beneath yon cliff they stand,
To show the freighted pinnace where to land;
To load the ready steed with guilty haste,
To fly in terror o'er the pathless waste,
Or, when detected in their straggling course,
To foil their foes by cunning or by force;
Or, yielding part (which equal knaves demand),
To gain a lawless passport through the land.
   Here, wandering long, amid these frowning fields,
I sought the simple life that Nature yields;   110
Rapine and Wrong and Fear usurped her place,
And a bold, artful, surly, savage race;
Who, only skilled to take the finny tribe,
The yearly dinner or septennial bribe,
Wait on the shore, and, as the waves run high,
On the tossed vessel bend their eager eye,
Which to their coast directs its venturous way;
Theirs, or the ocean's, miserable prey.
   As on their neighbouring beach yon swallows stand,
And wait for favouring winds to leave the land;   120
While still for flight the ready wing is spread:
So waited I the favouring hour, and fled—
Fled from these shores where guilt and famine reign,
And cried, "Ah! hapless they who still remain;
Who still remain to hear the ocean roar,
Whose greedy waves devour the lessening shore;
Till some fierce tide, with more imperious sway,
Sweeps the low hut and all it holds away;
When the sad tenant weeps from door to door,
And begs a poor protection from the poor!"   130
   But these are scenes where Nature's niggard hand
Gave a spare portion to the famished land;
Hers is the fault, if here mankind complain
Of fruitless toil and labour spent in vain;
But yet in other scenes more fair in view,
Where Plenty smiles—alas! she smiles for few—
And those who taste not, yet behold her store,

Are as the slaves that dig the golden ore,—
The wealth around them makes them doubly poor.
   Or will you deem them amply paid in health,   140
Labour's fair child, that languishes with wealth?
Go then! and see them rising with the sun,
Through a long course of daily toil to run;
See them beneath the dog-star's raging heat,
When the knees tremble and the temples beat;
Behold them, leaning on their scythes, look o'er
The labour past, and toils to come explore;
See them alternate suns and showers engage,
And hoard up aches and anguish for their age;
Through fens and marshy moors their steps pursue,   150
When their warm pores imbibe the evening dew;
Then own that labour may as fatal be
To these thy slaves, as thine excess to thee.
   Amid this tribe too oft a manly pride
Strives in strong toil the fainting heart to hide;
There may you see the youth of slender frame
Contend with weakness, weariness, and shame;
Yet, urged along, and proudly loth to yield,
He strives to join his fellows of the field.
Till long-contending nature droops at last,   160
Declining health rejects his poor repast,
His cheerless spouse the coming danger sees,
And mutual murmurs urge the slow disease.
   Yet grant them health, 'tis not for us to tell,
Though the head droops not, that the heart is well;
Or will you praise that homely, healthy fare,
Plenteous and plain, that happy peasants share?
Oh! trifle not with wants you cannot feel,
Nor mock the misery of a stinted meal;
Homely, not wholesome, plain, not plenteous, such   170
As you who praise would never deign to touch.
   Ye gentle souls, who dream of rural ease,
Whom the smooth stream and smoother sonnet please;
Go! if the peaceful cot your praises share,
Go look within, and ask if peace be there;
If peace be his—that drooping weary sire,
Or theirs, that offspring round their feeble fire;
Or hers, that matron pale, whose trembling hand

Turns on the wretched hearth th' expiring brand!
Nor yet can time itself obtain for these   180
Life's latest comforts, due respect and ease;
For yonder see that hoary swain, whose age
Can with no cares except his own engage;
Who, propped on that rude staff, looks up to see
The bare arms broken from the withering tree,
On which, a boy, he climbed the loftiest bough,
Then his first joy, but his sad emblem now.

He once was chief in all the rustic trade;
His steady hand the straightest furrow made;
Full many a prize he won, and still is proud   190
To find the triumphs of his youth allowed;
A transient pleasure sparkles in his eyes,
He hears and smiles, then thinks again and sighs
For now he journeys to his grave in pain;
The rich disdain him; nay, the poor disdain:
Alternate masters now their slave command,
Urge the weak efforts of his feeble hand,
And, when his age attempts its task in vain,
With ruthless taunts, of lazy poor complain.

Oft may you see him, when he tends the sheep,   200
His winter charge, beneath the hillock weep;
Oft hear him murmur to the winds that blow
O'er his white locks and bury them in snow,
When, roused by rage and muttering in the morn,
He mends the broken hedge with icy thorn:—

"Why do I live, when I desire to be
At once from life and life's long labour free?
Like leaves in spring, the young are blown away,
Without the sorrows of a slow decay;
I, like yon withered leaf, remain behind,   210
Nipped by the frost and shivering in the wind;
There it abides till younger buds come on,
As I, now all my fellow-swains are gone;
Then, from the rising generation thrust,
It falls, like me, unnoticed to the dust.

"These fruitful fields, these numerous flocks I see,
Are others' gain, but killing cares to me;
To me the children of my youth are lords,
Cool in their looks, but hasty in their words:

Wants of their own demand their care; and who   220
Feels his own want and succours others too?
A lonely, wretched man, in pain I go,
None need my help, and none relieve my woe;
Then let my bones beneath the turf be laid,
And men forget the wretch they would not aid."
    Thus groan the old, till, by disease oppressed,
They taste a final woe and then they rest.
    Theirs is yon house that holds the parish-poor,
Whose walls of mud scarce bear the broken door;
There, where the putrid vapours, flagging, play,   230
And the dull wheel hums doleful through the day—
There children dwell, who know no parents' care;
Parents who know no children's love, dwell there!
Heartbroken matrons on their joyless bed,
Forsaken wives, and mothers never wed;
Dejected widows with unheeded tears,
And crippled age with more than childhood fears;
The lame, the blind, and, far the happiest they!
The moping idiot and the madman gay.
Here too the sick their final doom receive,   240
Here brought, amid the scenes of grief, to grieve,
Where the loud groans from some sad chamber flow,
Mixed with the clamours of the crowd below;
Here, sorrowing, they each kindred sorrow scan,
And the cold charities of man to man:
Whose laws indeed for ruined age provide,
And strong compulsion plucks the scrap from pride;
But still that scrap is bought with many a sigh,
And pride embitters what it can deny.
    Say ye, oppressed by some fantastic woes,   250
Some jarring nerve that baffles your repose;
Who press the downy couch, while slaves advance
With timid eye, to read the distant glance;
Who with sad prayers the weary doctor tease,
To name the nameless ever-new disease;
Who with mock patience dire complaints endure,
Which real pain and that alone can cure;
How would ye bear in real pain to lie,
Despised, neglected, left alone to die?
How would ye bear to draw your latest breath,   260

Where all that's wretched paves the way for death?
  Such is that room which one rude beam divides,
And naked rafters form the sloping sides;
Where the vile bands that bind the thatch are seen,
And lath and mud are all that lie between;
Save one dull pane, that, coarsely patched, gives way
To the rude tempest, yet excludes the day:
Here, on a matted flock, with dust o'erspread,
The drooping wretch reclines his languid head;
For him no hand the cordial cup applies,   270
Or wipes the tear that stagnates in his eyes;
No friends with soft discourse his pain beguile,
Or promise hope till sickness wears a smile.
  But soon a loud and hasty summons calls,
Shakes the thin roof, and echoes round the walls;
Anon, a figure enters, quaintly neat,
All pride and business, bustle and conceit;
With looks unaltered by these scenes of woe,
With speed that, entering, speaks his haste to go,
He bids the gazing throng around him fly,   280
And carries fate and physic in his eye:
A potent quack, long versed in human ills,
Who first insults the victim whom he kills;
Whose murderous hand a drowsy Bench protect,
And whose most tender mercy is neglect.
  Paid by the parish for attendance here,
He wears contempt upon his sapient sneer;
In haste he seeks the bed where Misery lies,
Impatience marked in his averted eyes;
And, some habitual queries hurried o'er,   290
Without reply, he rushes on the door:
His drooping patient, long inured to pain,
And long unheeded, knows remonstrance vain;
He ceases now the feeble help to crave
Of man, and silent sinks into the grave.
  But ere his death some pious doubts arise,
Some simple fears, which "bold bad" men despise;
Fain would he ask the parish-priest to prove
His title certain to the joys above:
For this he sends the murmuring nurse, who calls   300
The holy stranger to these dismal walls.

And doth not he, the pious man, appear,
He, "passing rich with forty pounds a year?"
Ah! no; a shepherd of a different stock,
And far unlike him, feeds this little flock:
A jovial youth, who thinks his Sunday's task
As much as God or man can fairly ask;
The rest he gives to loves, and labours light,
To fields the morning, and to feasts the night;
None better skilled the noisy pack to guide,   310
To urge their chase, to cheer them or to chide;
A sportsman keen, he shoots through half the day,
And, skilled at whist, devotes the night to play:
Then, while such honours bloom around his head,
Shall he sit sadly by the sick man's bed,
To raise the hope he feels not, or with zeal
To combat fears that e'en the pious feel?
    Now once again the gloomy scene explore,
Less gloomy now; the bitter hour is o'er,
The man of many sorrows sighs no more.—   320
Up yonder hill, behold how sadly slow
The bier moves winding from the vale below;
There lie the happy dead, from trouble free,
And the glad parish pays the frugal fee.
No more, O Death! thy victim starts to hear
Churchwarden stern, or kingly overseer;
No more the farmer claims his humble bow,
Thou art his lord, the best of tyrants thou!
    Now to the church behold the mourners come,
Sedately torpid and devoutly dumb;   330
The village children now their games suspend,
To see the bier that bears their ancient friend:
For he was one in all their idle sport,
And like a monarch ruled their little court;
The pliant bow he formed, the flying ball,
The bat, the wicket, were his labours all;
Him now they follow to his grave, and stand
Silent and sad and gazing, hand in hand;
While bending low, their eager eyes explore
The mingled relics of the parish poor.   340
The bell tolls late, the moping owl flies round,
Fear marks the flight and magnifies the sound;

The busy priest, detained by weightier care,
Defers his duty till the day of prayer;
And, waiting long, the crowd retire distressed,
To think a poor man's bones should lie unblessed.

WILLIAM BLAKE (1757–1827)

166. SONG

How sweet I roamed from field to field,
 And tasted all the summer's pride,
Till I the Prince of Love beheld,
 Who in the sunny beams did glide!

He showed me lilies for my hair,
 And blushing roses for my brow;
He led me through his gardens fair,
 Where all his golden pleasures grow.

With sweet May dews my wings were wet,
 And Phoebus fired my vocal rage;   10
He caught me in his silken net,
 And shut me in his golden cage.

He loves to sit and hear me sing,
 Then, laughing, sports and plays with me;
Then stretches out my golden wing,
 And mocks my loss of liberty.

167. SONG

My silks and fine array,
 My smiles and languished air,
By love are driven away;
 And mournful lean Despair
Brings me yew to deck my grave:
Such end true lovers have.

His face is fair as heaven,
 When springing buds unfold;
O why to him was 't given
 Whose heart is wintry cold?   10
His breast is love's all-worshipped tomb,
Where all love's pilgrims come.

Bring me an axe and spade,
  Bring me a winding sheet;
When I my grave have made,
  Let winds and tempests beat:
Then down I'll lie, as cold as clay.
True love doth pass away!

168.   MAD SONG

    The wild winds weep,
      And the night is a-cold;
    Come hither, Sleep,
      And my griefs unfold:
    But lo! the morning peeps
      Over the eastern steeps,
    And the rustling birds of dawn
    The earth do scorn.

    Lo! to the vault
      Of pavèd heaven,   10
    With sorrow fraught
      My notes are driven:
    They strike the ear of night,
      Make weep the eyes of day;
    They make mad the roaring winds,
      And with tempests play.

    Like a fiend in a cloud,
      With howling woe,
    After night I do crowd,
      And with night will go;   20
    I turn my back to the east
    From whence comforts have increased;
    For light doth seize my brain
    With frantic pain.

            From SONGS OF INNOCENCE

169.   INTRODUCTION

    Piping down the valleys wild,
    Piping songs of pleasant glee,
    On a cloud I saw a child,
    And he laughing said to me:

"Pipe a song about a Lamb!"
So I piped with merry cheer.
"Piper, pipe that song again;"
So I piped: he wept to hear.

"Drop thy pipe, thy happy pipe;
Sing thy songs of happy cheer:"   10
So I sang the same again,
While he wept with joy to hear.

"Piper, sit thee down and write
In a book, that all may read."
So he vanished from my sight,
And I plucked a hollow reed,

And I made a rural pen,
And I stained the water clear,
And I wrote my happy songs
Every child may joy to hear.   20

170.   HOLY THURSDAY

'Twas on a Holy Thursday, their innocent faces clean,
The children walking two and two, in red and blue and green,
Grey-headed beadles walked before, with wands as white as snow,
Till into the high dome of Paul's they like Thames' waters flow.

O what a multitude they seemed, these flowers of London town!
Seated in companies they sit with radiance all their own.
The hum of multitudes was there, but multitudes of lambs,
Thousands of little boys and girls raising their innocent hands.

Now like a mighty wind they raise to Heaven the voice of song,
Or like harmonious thunderings the seats of Heaven among.   10
Beneath them sit the aged men, wise guardians of the poor;
Then cherish pity, lest you drive an angel from your door.

171.   NIGHT

The sun descending in the west,
The evening star does shine;
The birds are silent in their nest,
And I must seek for mine.
The moon, like a flower,
In heaven's high bower,

With silent delight
Sits and smiles on the night.

Farewell, green fields and happy groves,
Where flocks have took delight.   10
Where lambs have nibbled, silent moves
The feet of angels bright;
Unseen they pour blessing,
And joy without ceasing,
On each bud and blossom,
And each sleeping bosom.

They look in every thoughtless nest,
Where birds are cover'd warm;
They visit caves of every beast,
To keep them all from harm.   20
If they see any weeping
That should have been sleeping,
They pour sleep on their head,
And sit down by their bed.

When wolves and tigers howl for prey,
They pitying stand and weep;
Seeking to drive their thirst away,
And keep them from the sheep.
But if they rush dreadful,
The angels, most heedful,   30
Receive each mild spirit,
New worlds to inherit.

And there the lion's ruddy eyes
Shall flow with tears of gold,
And pitying the tender cries,
And walking round the fold,
Saying 'Wrath, by his meekness,
And, by his health, sickness
Is driven away
From our immortal day.   40

"And now beside thee, bleating lamb,
I can lie down and sleep;
Or think on him who bore thy name,
Graze after thee and weep.
For, wash'd in life's river.

My bright mane for ever
Shall shine like the gold
As I guard o'er the fold."

From SONGS OF EXPERIENCE

172.   HOLY THURSDAY

Is this a holy thing to see
In a rich and fruitful land,
Babes reduced to misery,
Fed with cold and usurous hand?

Is that trembling cry a song?
Can it be a song of joy?
And so many children poor?
It is a land of poverty!

And their sun does never shine,
And their fields are bleak and bare,   10
And their ways are filled with thorns:
It is eternal winter there.

For where'er the sun does shine,
And where'er the rain does fall,
Babe can never hunger there,
Nor poverty the mind appal.

173.   THE TYGER

Tyger! Tyger! burning bright
In the forests of the night,
What immortal hand or eye
Could frame thy fearful symmetry?

In what distant deeps or skies
Burned the fire of thine eyes?
On what wings dare he aspire?
What the hand dare seize the fire?

And what shoulder, and what art,
Could twist the sinews of thy heart?   10
And when thy heart began to beat,
What dread hand? and what dread feet?

What the hammer? what the chain?
In what furnace was thy brain?
What the anvil? what dread grasp
Dare its deadly terrors clasp?

When the stars threw down their spears,
And watered heaven with their tears,
Did he smile his work to see?
Did he who made the Lamb make thee?   20

Tyger! Tyger! burning bright
In the forests of the night,
What immortal hand or eye,
Dare frame thy fearful symmetry?

174.   AH! SUNFLOWER

Ah, Sunflower! weary of time,
Who countest the steps of the sun;
Seeking after that sweet golden clime
Where the traveller's journey is done:

Where the Youth pined away with desire,
And the pale Virgin shrouded in snow
Arise from their graves, and aspire
Where my Sunflower wishes to go.

175.   THE GARDEN OF LOVE

I went to the Garden of Love
And saw what I never had seen:
A Chapel was built in the midst,
Where I used to play on the green.

And the gates of this Chapel were shut,
And "Thou shalt not" writ over the door;
So I turn'd to the Garden of Love
That so many sweet flowers bore;

And I saw it was filled with graves,
And tomb-stones where flowers should be;   10
And priests in black gowns were walking their rounds,
And binding with briars my joys and desires.

176.   LONDON

I wander through each chartered street,
Near where the chartered Thames does flow,
And mark in every face I meet
Marks of weakness, marks of woe.

In every cry of every Man,
In every Infant's cry of fear,
In every voice, in every ban,
The mind-forged manacles I hear.

How the chimney-sweeper's cry
Every blackening church appalls;   10
And the hapless soldier's sigh
Runs in blood down palace walls.

But most through midnight streets I hear
How the youthful harlot's curse
Blasts the new-born infant's tear,
And blights with plagues the marriage hearse.

177.   NEVER SEEK TO TELL THY LOVE

Never seek to tell thy love,
Love that never told can be;
For the gentle wind does move
Silently, invisibly.

I told my love, I told my love,
I told her all my heart;
Trembling, cold, in ghastly fears,
Ah! she doth depart.

Soon as she was gone from me,
A traveller came by,   10
Silently, invisibly:
He took her with a sigh.

From MILTON

178. "AND DID THOSE FEET IN ANCIENT TIME"

And did those feet in ancient time
Walk upon England's mountains green?

And was the holy Lamb of God
On England's pleasant pastures seen?

And did the Countenance Divine
Shine forth upon our clouded hills?
And was Jerusalem builded here
Among these dark Satanic Mills?

Bring me my bow of burning gold:
Bring me my arrows of desire: 10
Bring me my spear: O clouds unfold!
Bring me my chariot of fire.

I will not cease from mental fight,
Nor shall my sword sleep in my hand
Till we have built Jerusalem
In England's green and pleasant land.

IV. THE ROMANTIC MOVEMENT

THE ROMANTIC MOVEMENT

The changes in taste and attitude which brought about those various literary activities which are conventionally lumped together under the title, the "Romantic Movement," are neither easily described nor readily explained. We have already noted the unstable equilibrium of English literary culture in the age of Queen Anne, and pointed out the shifts in sensibility which were taking place quite early in the eighteenth century. In many respects Blake is much further away from Dr. Johnson than is Coleridge, and Gray is in many senses of the word more "romantic" than Wordsworth. It does not help to label poets like Gray or Blake "pre-Romantic," for that suggests that there was a single movement developing in a straight line and those who came later were more thoroughly in the movement than those who preceded them. In his view that poetry should use the real language of men, Wordsworth was closer to Dryden and Pope than to Gray—or to Coleridge. Wordsworth's "Tintern Abbey" has been called by a distinguished historian of English poetry "the fine flower of eighteenth-century meditative poetry" in the tradition of the eighteenth-century poets Akenside and Thomson.

But having recognized all these difficulties in the way of describing honestly and accurately the special qualities of the "romantic" poets, we have nevertheless to agree that the term "romantic" has some justification in the light of actual poetic production, to recognize that there *was* a significant shift in taste and attitude taking place throughout Europe in the latter part of the eighteenth century (however far back we might ultimately trace it), and that this shift is reflected in poetry. It is perhaps no great oversimplification to say that people of the earlier eighteenth century, in their gratitude for what civilization had achieved by way not only of making life agreeable but also of making men more amenable to regular observation, tended to think of the arts as a product of conventional urban society and of the function of literature as the representation of general aspects of human nature expressed in the language of that society and with all the resources of that society's traditional culture. One of the shifts in attitude which produced the romantic movement (we can at this stage allow ourselves to omit the quotation marks) was the questioning of this very point. A generation that had survived the religious and civil disputes of the seventeenth century might well have accepted with relief and gratitude a norm of urbane moderation operating within strictly defined conventional limits, but a later generation, which had no memory of those disputes, and no feeling of relief at having escaped from the perpetual conflicts between single-minded religious or political enthusiasts, came to feel a sense of constraint rather than a sense of freedom in the demands of urban gentility. They lifted their eyes from the gentlemanly limitations imposed on their horizon to contemplate with a certain fascination the world of "gothic" superstition (by which they meant the Middle Ages) or heroic violence or primitive behavior of one sort or another. And of course the great paradox was that at the very core of eighteenth-century genteel culture lay two venerated works dealing with life in a very ungenteel society—the Bible and Homer. Sooner or later neoclassic culture would have had to come to terms with primitivism.

Perhaps, therefore, we can allow ourselves to say that the romantic movement resulted in part from the growing feeling that civilization was as much restrictive and inhibiting as it was freedom-giving. "Man was born free and is everywhere in chains," wrote Rousseau, and it was civilization that forged the chains. In England, Bishop Hurd, after examining with fascinated interest the earlier world of "chivalry and romance," summed up the balance sheet of eighteenth-century civilization by explaining: "What we have gotten by this revolution, you will say, is a great deal of good sense. What we have lost, is a world of fine fabling, the illusion of which is so grateful to the charmed Spirit."

The extension of the horizon was social as well as chronological. Primitive and heroic societies became more and more objects of poetic interest, and at the same time the life of men living outside the pale of urban gentility was coming to be regarded as legitimate— nay, as the most proper—subject matter for poets. "Since it often happens that the most obvious phrases, and those which are used in ordinary conversation, become too familiar to the ear and contract a kind of meanness by passing through the mouths of the vulgar, a poet should take particular care to guard himself against idiomatic ways of speaking." So wrote Addison in 1712. By 1800 Wordsworth was writing: "Humble and rustic life was generally chosen, [as the subject of his poems] because, in that condition, the essential passions of the heart find a better soil in which they can attain their maturity, are less under restraint, and speak a plainer and more emphatic language; because in that condition of life our elementary feelings coexist in a state of greater simplicity, and, consequently, may be more accurately contemplated, and more forcibly communicated." Dryden and Pope had insisted that the language of poetry should be based on the conversation of gentlemen; Wordsworth held that it should be based on the conversation of peasants. The real difference lay in differing views as to whether the civilizing conventions of society were more liberating or restrictive. One might almost say that it was a matter of emphasis: convention has both its liberating and its restrictive aspects, and which aspect you most insist on will depend very much on which of the two you take for granted. The earlier eighteenth century took the restrictive aspects for granted, and emphasized the liberating aspects, for these they most needed—liberation from freakishness, superstition, and even civil war. The Queen Anne wits did their job well, so that later generations felt free to concentrate on those elements in social convention which limited their imaginative and moral horizons.

To look beyond the polished life of educated men in cities to wilder and cruder ways of living, to explore kinds of emotion and sensibility which someone like Lord Chesterfield would have carefully shunned as simply inviting trouble, to include as proper subject matter for poetry aspects of life which Dr. Johnson would have considered "low" or "mean" ("men who do not wear fine clothes can feel deeply," said Wordsworth—a proposition Johnson would not have denied, but which he would have considered irrelevant to the production of poetry), and in general to hold that the conventions of contemporary civilization did not represent the only guarantee of valuable human behavior—we can at least say that these were attitudes which became increasingly common as the eighteenth century advanced. In some directions these attitudes had been developed as far as they could go before the poets generally known as romantic appeared on the scene—witness Blake's *Songs of Experience.*

The *Lyrical Ballads* of Wordsworth and Coleridge, which appeared in 1798, showed two of these attitudes working in two different directions. Many years later Coleridge, looking back on the earlier plans that he and Wordsworth had made together, explained what each of them had considered himself to be doing: "It was agreed, that my endeavors should be directed to persons and characters supernatural, or at least romantic; yet so as to transfer from our inward nature a human interest and a semblance of truth sufficient to procure for these shadows of imagination that willing suspension of disbelief for the moment, which constitutes poetic faith. Mr. Wordsworth, on the other hand, was to propose to himself as his object, to give the charm of novelty to things of every day, and to excite a feeling analogous to the supernatural, by awakening the mind's attention to the lethargy of custom, and directing it to the loveliness and the wonders of the world before us." Here we see the poet's glance directed away from the world of social politeness in two different directions—to the imaginative world of the supernatural, and to the everyday world of ordinary people outside "society." Both poets were seeking a deeper reality than they considered any account of the urbane, conventional world of men and manners could yield.

This may perhaps help to explain why the term "romantic movement" has been used to cover such different literary phenomena as the studied rustic realism of Wordsworth's "Michael"—whose most often quoted line is the impressively matter-of-fact

And never lifted up a single stone—

and the deliberate indulgence of an exotic imagination that we get in Coleridge and Keats and which reaches its sometimes fantastic culmination in such a poet as Beddoes.

New political and social ideas helped to complicate the picture. The French Revolution, the developing Industrial Revolution in England which changed the physical appearance and the social structure of the country, and new notions in psychology and metaphysics, all played their part. Wordsworth, enthusiastic about the

French Revolution when it first broke out, suspicious of "the increasing accumulation of men in cities" and eager to find the fundamental truths about man and the universe through a contemplation of external nature, interested in the way in which "we associate ideas in a state of excitement," showed the effect of these new ideas no less than Shelley, who moved from the atheistic rationalism of William Godwin to a passionate Platonic idealism. Byron, who combined an antisocial irony with an equally antisocial self-pity, and Keats, who understood what the individual life of the imagination could do for a poet more clearly, perhaps, than any other English creative writer, developed their own characteristic poetic themes, modes, and techniques—but they, too, like the early Wordsworth and like Shelley, were in some sense alienated from polite society; they rejected the earlier eighteenth-century view that polite society was what made man capable of civilized achievements, and explored areas of the imagination and the sensibility to which their readers had access *only* by reading and surrendering to their poems. Keats's "Eve of St. Agnes" distils the purest essence of passionate living in a society that is symbolically violent and magical, and his "La Belle Dame sans Merci" broods with strange beauty over the fact that we can love to despair what is nevertheless horrible: society as Pope or Prior saw it is wholly ignored in these poems. The poet is on his own, drawing nourishment from his solitary reading and imaginings. This means that each poem must create its own world and present it persuasively to the reader. In Keats's odes, as in Wordsworth's "Tintern Abbey," the mood and ideas of the poet are generated from a sensitive brooding over—sometimes even a surrender to—natural objects, and the poem becomes an organic unity wholly different in meaning and effect from any paraphrase or summary of its content.

It is thus to be expected that poets begin to consider a poem as an organic whole to be explained in terms of analogies from biology rather than as a craftsmanlike rendering of a previously discerned content to be discussed in mechanistic terms. Coleridge was the first important English critic to emphasize and bring home the organic nature of form in art. Poetry which does not rest on a basis of social agreement, and one might almost add of social exclusiveness, becomes more and more concerned with the unique universe, as it were, created by the individual poem, and discussions of "propriety" or "rules" become wholly irrelevant. What is "proper" is determined by the life generated by the specific poem, not by the attitudes of any social group to which it may be addressed. This view could not, of course, long survive, for after a period of unrest and poetic individualism new norms arise and a new relation between the poet and his public develops: Tennyson was as much concerned with propriety as Pope, but it was a very different sort of propriety.

Whether the romantic poet moves out into the country with Wordsworth, or into a symbolic Middle Ages, as Keats sometimes did, or proceeds to have a passionate Platonic love affair with the universe such as we find in Shelley, he is illustrating in one way or another his isolation, his inability to draw poetic nourishment from the conventional behavior and culture patterns of a select society, his desire to escape from his loneliness not by normal human companionship but by discovering man in general through external nature:

> For I have learned
> To look on nature, not as in the hour
> Of thoughtless youth; but hearing often-times
> The still, sad music of humanity.

The poet escapes from his fellows to find man—and it is "man" in the abstract—through nature, or to find himself:

> There is a pleasure in the pathless woods,
> There is a rapture on the lonely shore,
> There is society, where none intrudes,
> By the deep Sea, and music in its roar:
> I love not man the less but nature more,
> From these our interviews, in which I steal
> From all I may be, or have been before,
> To mingle with the Universe, and feel
> What I can ne'er express, yet cannot all conceal.

The voice of Byron here, for all its individuality, is also the voice of the romantic poet in his alienation from society.

The dangers in this kind of poetry are an excessively self-indulged emotion, a mawkish self-pity, which we are liable to find in the less successful poems of the period. There is also the danger of a false picturesqueness, of imagining that the less well-known and the less clearly envisaged are simply for that reason interesting and significant. There are also minor successes in this kind of poetry, made possible by a utilization of attitudes and material developed by the romantic poets in their endeavors to create a poetic universe independent of society. Sir Walter Scott in his narrative verse uses what are essentially eighteenth-century poetic techniques, but he has learned from his generation the interestingness of heroic action and from the ballads he has acquired a sense of the elemental in human behavior; and the combination of the elemental and the heroic produces some of his best verse. (Incidentally, it might be noted that conflict between the heroic and the elemental on the one hand and the civilized and refined on the other is the theme of most of Scott's best novels: the "world of fine fabling" which Bishop Hurd sighed after, and the "great deal of good sense" which Hurd at the same time did not want to lose, face each other in Scott's novels as equally valuable but incompatible aspects of life, and in the incompatibility of these equally necessary elements lies the tragic force at the heart of much of his fiction.)

A poet too aware of the social norms that bound his imagination may be led into the dreariest kind of conventional utterance, and this happened often enough in the eighteenth century; and a poet too anxious to escape from those norms at any cost may be led into all sorts of sensationalism and emotional exhibitionism, and this was a not uncommon fault of the romantic period. Every age has its characteristic excess, and it is only the naïve critic who will condemn the age for those excesses. The shift in perspective which we see in the romantic poets brought new potentialities (for both good and ill) to poetry, and enlarged as well as endangered the field of poetic activity. The same can be said of every fruitful new movement in the history of art and of thought. By the end of the first quarter of the nineteenth century the romantic poets had pretty much said their say and familiarized the audience for poetry with new techniques, attitudes, and poetic materials which later poets were to use in their own way.

Romantic moods and modes produced no memorable poetry in America until the British movement had almost run its course. We do not know why the creative energy of a society is channelized into great poetry in some periods and not in others. One might ask why, if American culture during the first two centuries was simply an extension of Old World culture, we did not have poets who wrote like their British contemporaries. To a certain extent we did, as the seventeenth-century verse of Edward Taylor and Anne Bradstreet attests. But the truth is that our culture was not "simply" anything. Ideas, traditions, and ways of life cannot be transported to a new environment without being transformed. Those that were implicit in the poetry of Shakespeare, Donne, Milton, Pope, and Gray arrived in America on every boat, but these gentlemen themselves stayed home. We must fall back on the old pat explanation that for the first two hundred years our best energies went into the creation of a new country. The quality of that energy is apparent in the great political and social writings of Franklin, Jefferson, Paine, and the Adamses, but one realizes the problem of poetry in their time by reading the work of Philip Freneau. This "father" of American verse was both native in outlook and responsive to the best European thought and literature of his day. But no one as sensitive to society's needs and pressures as he could keep out of the ideological war that had to be fought before America could even know what it was or where it wanted to go. Most of Freneau's verse was an instrument of propaganda in that war. Read as cultural history it is rich and illuminating, but it would lose little interest if it were paraphrased in prose.

Romanticism was an international phenomenon, and during the decades of its ascendancy almost all of its characteristics were reflected in American literature. Before 1830 most of our "bards," as they were hopefully called, wore the clothing of some British poet they admired, but it fitted badly. One exception was William Cullen Bryant, who steeped himself so thoroughly in British poetic tradition that he cannot be dismissed as an imitator of anyone in particular. American culture was still, after all, more British than American, and Bryant, after he reached maturity, escaped the mediocrity of his versifying contemporaries by staying within the scope of such British thought and idiom as had become naturalized in America. He experimented with traditional blank verse, couplets, and quatrains as freely as poets in England, but he avoided ideas and attitudes that had no reference to his time and place. Experience with nature was of course as available to him in the Berkshires as it was to Wordsworth at the English Lakes; but, as he wrote to his brother, "the skylark is an English bird, and an American who has never visited Europe has no right to be in raptures about it." Bryant's verse is the high point of British poetic tradition as modified by the facts and ideals of American life.

The only other American poet who achieved a form and idiom of his own before 1837 was Edgar Allan Poe. Unlike Bryant, whose verse implies an acceptance of or adjustment to the ideals of his time and country, Poe was moved to poetic utterance chiefly by his rejection of or conflict with those ideals. In the midst of a materially prosperous and vigorous society, Poe was poor, unpopular, and chronically insecure. Finding no solid values in contemporary social aspirations, little comfort or inspiration in past or present philosophy or religion, no beauty in natural objects except to the extent that he could idealize them, he declared his allegiance to "supernal beauty." Much of his verse consists simply of yearning after this undescribed objective. Occasionally, however, his imagination carried him into unexplored regions of supernatural gloom or madness or loneliness; in such poems he powerfully effects a willing suspension of disbelief, and we are spared the "I-me-my" self-centeredness that pervades so much romantic verse. In his worst as well as in his best poetry, there are isolated phrases that are unforgettable—and unequaled in his time; and much of his work has a fine musical quality which is, however, too often achieved at the expense of meaning.

WILLIAM WORDSWORTH (1770–1850)

179.   LINES WRITTEN IN EARLY SPRING

I heard a thousand blended notes,
While in a grove I sate reclined,
In that sweet mood when pleasant thoughts
Bring sad thoughts to the mind.

To her fair works did Nature link
The human soul that through me ran;

And much it grieved my heart to think
What man has made of man.

Through primrose tufts, in that green bower,
The periwinkle trailed its wreaths;   10
And 'tis my faith that every flower
Enjoys the air it breathes.

The birds around me hopped and played,
Their thoughts I cannot measure:—
But the least motion which they made,
It seemed a thrill of pleasure.

The budding twigs spread out their fan,
To catch the breezy air;
And I must think, do all I can,
That there was pleasure there.   20

If this belief from heaven be sent,
If such be Nature's holy plan,
Have I not reason to lament
What man has made of man?

180.   EXPOSTULATION AND REPLY

"Why, William, on that old grey stone,
Thus for the length of half a day,
Why, William, sit you thus alone,
And dream your time away?

"Where are your books?—that light bequeathed
To Beings else forlorn and blind!
Up! up! and drink the spirit breathed
From dead men to their kind.

"You look round on your Mother Earth,
As if she for no purpose bore you;   10
As if you were her first-born birth,
And none had lived before you!"

One morning thus, by Esthwaite lake,
When life was sweet, I knew not why,
To me my good friend Matthew spake,
And thus I made reply:

"The eye—it cannot choose but see;
We cannot bid the ear be still;
Our bodies feel, where'er they be,
Against or with our will.   20

"Nor less I deem that there are Powers
Which of themselves our minds impress;
That we can feed this mind of ours
In a wise passiveness.

"Think you, 'mid all this mighty sum
Of things for ever speaking,
That nothing of itself will come,
But we must still be seeking?

"—Then ask not wherefore, here, alone,
Conversing as I may,   30
I sit upon this old grey stone,
And dream my time away."

181.   TO MY SISTER

It is the first mild day of March.
Each minute, sweeter than before,
The redbreast sings from the tall larch
That stands beside our door.

There is a blessing in the air,
Which seems a sense of joy to yield
To the bare trees, and mountains bare,
And grass in the green field.

My sister! ('tis a wish of mine)
Now that our morning meal is done,   10
Make haste, your morning task resign;
Come forth and feel the sun.

Edward will come with you; and, pray,
Put on with speed your woodland dress;
And bring no book; for this one day
We'll give to idleness.

No joyless forms shall regulate
Our living calendar;
We from today, my friend, will date
The opening of the year.   20

Love, now a universal birth,
From heart to heart is stealing,
From earth to man, from man to earth—
It is the hour of feeling.

One moment now may give us more
Than years of toiling reason;
Our minds shall drink at every pore
The spirit of the season.

Some silent laws our hearts will make,
Which they shall long obey;   30
We for the year to come may take
Our temper from today.

And from the blessed power that rolls
About, below, above,
We'll frame the measure of our souls;
They shall be tuned to love.

Then come, my sister! come, I pray,
With speed put on your woodland dress;
And bring no book; for this one day
We'll give to idleness.   40

182.   TINTERN ABBEY

Five years have past; five summers, with the length
Of five long winters! and again I hear
These waters, rolling from their mountain-springs
With a soft inland murmur.—Once again
Do I behold these steep and lofty cliffs,
That on a wild secluded scene impress
Thoughts of more deep seclusion; and connect
The landscape with the quiet of the sky.
The day is come when I again repose
Here, under this dark sycamore, and view   10
These plots of cottage-ground, these orchard-tufts,
Which at this season, with their unripe fruits,
Are clad in one green hue, and lose themselves
'Mid groves and copses. Once again I see
These hedge-rows, hardly hedge-rows, little lines
Of sportive wood run wild: these pastoral farms,
Green to the very door; and wreaths of smoke

Sent up, in silence from among the trees!
With some uncertain notice, as might seem
Of vagrant dwellers in the houseless woods,   20
Or of some Hermit's cave, where by his fire
The Hermit sits alone.
                        These beauteous forms
Through a long absence, have not been to me
As is a landscape to a blind man's eye:
But oft, in lonely rooms, and 'mid the din
Of towns and cities, I have owed to them
In hours of weariness, sensations sweet,
Felt in the blood, and felt along the heart;
And passing even into my purer mind,
With tranquil restoration:—feelings too   30
Of unremembered pleasure: such, perhaps,
As have no slight or trivial influence
On that best portion of a good man's life.
His little, nameless, unremembered acts
Of kindness and of love. Nor less, I trust,
To them I may have owed another gift,
Of aspect more sublime; that blessed mood,
In which the burthen of the mystery,
In which the heavy and the weary weight
Of all this unintelligible world,   40
Is lightened:—that serene and blessed mood,
In which the affections gently lead us on,—
Until, the breath of this corporeal frame
And even the motion of our human blood
Almost suspended, we are laid asleep
In body, and become a living soul:
While with an eye made quiet by the power
Of harmony, and the deep power of joy,
We see into the life of things.
                              If this
Be but a vain belief, yet, oh! how oft—   50
In darkness and amid the many shapes
Of joyless daylight; when the fretful stir
Unprofitable, and the fever of the world,
Have hung upon the beatings of my heart—
How oft, in spirit, have I turned to thee,
O sylvan Wye! thou wanderer thro' the woods,
How often has my spirit turned to thee!

And now, with gleams of half-extinguished thought,
With many recognitions dim and faint,
And somewhat of a sad perplexity,   60
The picture of the mind revives again:
While here I stand, not only with the sense
Of present pleasure, but with pleasing thoughts
That in this moment there is life and food
For future years. And so I dare to hope,
Though changed, no doubt, from what I was when first
I came among these hills; when like a roe
I bounded o'er the mountains, by the sides
Of the deep rivers, and the lonely streams,
Wherever nature led: more like a man   70
Flying from something that he dreads, than one
Who sought the thing he loved. For nature then
(The coarser pleasures of my boyish days,
And their glad animal movements all gone by)
To me was all in all.—I cannot paint
What then I was. The sounding cataract
Haunted me like a passion: the tall rock,
The mountain, and the deep and gloomy wood,
Their colors and their forms, were then to me
An appetite; a feeling and a love,   80
That had no need of a remoter charm,
By thought supplied, nor any interest
Unborrowed from the eye.—That time is past,
And all its aching joys are now no more,
And all its dizzy raptures. Not for this
Faint I, nor mourn nor murmur; other gifts
Have followed; for such loss, I would believe,
Abundant recompense. For I have learned
To look on nature, not as in the hour
Of thoughtless youth; but hearing oftentimes   90
The still, sad music of humanity,
Nor harsh nor grating, though of ample power
To chasten and subdue. And I have felt
A presence that disturbs me with the joy
Of elevated thoughts; a sense sublime
Of something far more deeply interfused,
Whose dwelling is the light of setting suns,
And the round ocean and the living air,
And the blue sky, and in the mind of man;

A motion and a spirit, that impels   100
All thinking things, all objects of all thought,
And rolls through all things. Therefore am I still
A lover of the meadows and the woods,
And mountains; and of all that we behold
From this green earth; of all the mighty world
Of eye, and ear,—both what they half create,
And what perceive; well pleased to recognise
In nature and the language of the sense,
The anchor of my purest thoughts, the nurse,
The guide, the guardian of my heart, and soul   110
Of all my moral being.
                          Nor perchance,
If I were not thus taught, should I the more
Suffer my genial spirits to decay:
For thou art with me here upon the banks
Of this fair river; thou my dearest Friend,
My dear, dear Friend; and in thy voice I catch
The language of my former heart, and read
My former pleasures in the shooting lights
Of thy wild eyes. Oh! yet a little while
May I behold in thee what I was once,   120
My dear, dear Sister! and this prayer I make
Knowing that Nature never did betray
The heart that loved her; 'tis her privilege,
Through all the years of this our life, to lead
From joy to joy: for she can so inform
The mind that is within us, so impress
With quietness and beauty, and so feed
With lofty thoughts, that neither evil tongues,
Rash judgments, nor the sneers of selfish men,
Nor greetings where no kindness is, nor all   130
The dreary intercourse of daily life,
Shall e'er prevail against us, or disturb
Our cheerful faith, that all which we behold
Is full of blessings. Therefore let the moon
Shine on thee in thy solitary walk;
And let the misty mountain-winds be free
To blow against thee: and, in after years,
When these wild ecstasies shall be matured
Into a sober pleasure; when thy mind
Shall be a mansion for all lovely forms,   140

Thy memory be as a dwelling-place
For all sweet sounds and harmonies; oh! then,
If solitude, or fear, or pain, or grief,
Should be thy portion, with what healing thoughts
Of tender joy wilt thou remember me,
And these my exhortations! Nor, perchance—
If I should be where I no more can hear
Thy voice, nor catch from thy wild eyes these gleams
Of past existence—wilt thou then forget
That on the banks of this delightful stream   150
We stood together, and that I, so long
A worshipper of Nature, hither came
Unwearied in that service: rather say
With warmer love—oh! with far deeper zeal
Of holier love. Nor wilt thou then forget,
That after many wanderings, many years
Of absence, these steep woods and lofty cliffs,
And this green pastoral landscape, were to me
More dear, both for themselves and for thy sake!

183.   WE ARE SEVEN

    ——A simple Child,
That lightly draws its breath,
And feels its life in every limb,
What should it know of death?

I met a little cottage Girl:
She was eight years old, she said;
Her hair was thick with many a curl
That clustered round her head.

She had a rustic, woodland air,
And she was wildly clad: 10
Her eyes were fair, and very fair:
—Her beauty made me glad.

"Sisters and brothers, little Maid,
How many may you be?"
"How many? Seven in all," she said,
And wondering looked at me.

"And where are they? I pray you tell."
She answered, "Seven are we:

And two of us at Conway dwell,
And two are gone to sea.   20

"Two of us in the church-yard lie,
My sister and my brother;
And, in the church-yard cottage, I
Dwell near them with my mother."

"You say that two at Conway dwell,
And two are gone to sea,
Yet ye are seven!—I pray you tell,
Sweet Maid, how this may be."

Then did the little Maid reply,
"Seven boys and girls are we;   30
Two of us in the church-yard lie,
Beneath the church-yard tree."

"You run about, my little Maid,
Your limbs they are alive;
If two are in the church-yard laid,
Then ye are only five."

"Their graves are green, they may be seen,"
The little Maid replied,
"Twelve steps or more from my mother's door,
And they are side by side.   40

"My stockings there I often knit,
My kerchief there I hem;
And there upon the ground I sit,
And sing a song to them.

"And often after sunset, Sir,
When it is light and fair,
I take my little porringer,
And eat my supper there.

"The first that died was sister Jane;
In bed she moaning lay,   50
Till God released her of her pain;
And then she went away.

"So in the church-yard she was laid;
And, when the grass was dry,

Together round her grave we played,
My brother John and I.

"And when the ground was white with snow,
And I could run and slide,
My brother John was forced to go,
And he lies by her side."   60

"How many are you, then," said I,
"If they two are in heaven?"
Quick was the little Maid's reply,
"O Master! we are seven."

"But they are dead; those two are dead!
Their spirits are in heaven!"
'Twas throwing words away; for still
The little Maid would have her will,
And said, "Nay, we are seven!"

184.   THE OLD CUMBERLAND BEGGAR

I saw an aged beggar in my walk;
And he was seated, by the highway side,
On a low structure of rude masonry
Built at the foot of a huge hill, that they
Who lead their horses down the steep rough road
May thence remount at ease. The aged man
Had placed his staff across the broad smooth stone
That overlays the pile; and, from a bag
All white with flour, the dole of village dames,
He drew his scraps and fragments, one by one;   10
And scanned them with a fixed and serious look
Of idle computation. In the sun,
Upon the second step of that small pile,
Surrounded by those wild unpeopled hills,
He sat, and ate his food in solitude:
And ever, scattered from his palsied hand,
That, still attempting to prevent the waste,
Was baffled still, the crumbs in little showers
Fell on the ground; and the small mountain birds,
Not venturing yet to peck their destined meal,   20
Approached within the length of half his staff.

Him from my childhood have I known; and then
He was so old, he seems not older now;

He travels on, a solitary man,
So helpless in appearance, that for him
The sauntering horseman throws not with a slack
And careless hand his alms upon the ground,
But stops,—that he may safely lodge the coin
Within the old man's hat; nor quits him so,
But still, when he has given his horse the rein,   30
Watches the aged beggar with a look
Sidelong, and half-reverted. She who tends
The toll-gate, when in summer at her door
She turns her wheel, if on the road she sees
The aged beggar coming, quits her work,
And lifts the latch for him that he may pass.
The post-boy, when his rattling wheels o'ertake
The aged beggar in the woody lane,
Shouts to him from behind; and, if thus warned
The old man does not change his course, the boy   40
Turns with less noisy wheels to the roadside,
And passes gently by, without a curse
Upon his lips or anger at his heart.

　　He travels on, a solitary man;
His age has no companion. On the ground
His eyes are turned, and, as he moves along,
They move along the ground; and, evermore,
Instead of common and habitual sight
Of fields with rural works, of hill and dale,
And the blue sky, one little span of earth   50
Is all his prospect. Thus, from day to day,
Bow-bent, his eyes forever on the ground,
He plies his weary journey; seeing still,
And seldom knowing that he sees, some straw,
Some scattered leaf, or marks which, in one track,
The nails of cart or chariot-wheel have left
Impressed on the white road,—in the same line,
At distance still the same. Poor traveller!
His staff trails with him; scarcely do his feet
Disturb the summer dust; he is so still   60
In look and motion, that the cottage curs,
Ere he has passed the door, will turn away,
Weary of barking at him. Boys and girls,
The vacant and the busy, maids and youths.

And urchins newly breeched—all pass him by:
Him even the slow-paced wagon leaves behind.

　　But deem not this man useless.—Statesmen! ye
Who are so restless in your wisdom, ye
Who have a broom still ready in your hands
To rid the world of nuisances; ye proud,　　　　　　　70
Heart-swoln, while in your pride ye contemplate
Your talents, power, or wisdom, deem him not
A burthen of the earth! 'Tis Nature's law
That none, the meanest of created things,
Of forms created the most vile and brute,
The dullest or most noxious, should exist
Divorced from good—a spirit and pulse of good,
A life and soul, to every mode of being
Inseparably linked. Then be assured
That least of all can aught—that ever owned　　　　80
The heaven-regarding eye and front sublime
Which man is born to—sink, howe'er depressed,
So low as to be scorned without a sin;
Without offence to God cast out of view;
Like the dry remnant of a garden-flower
Whose seeds are shed, or as an implement
Worn out and worthless. While from door to door,
This old man creeps, the villagers in him
Behold a record which together binds
Past deeds and offices of charity,　　　　　　　　　90
Else unremembered, and so keeps alive
The kindly mood in hearts which lapse of years,
And that half-wisdom half-experience gives,
Make slow to feel, and by sure steps resign
To selfishness and cold oblivious cares.
Among the farms and solitary huts,
Hamlets and thinly-scattered villages,
Where'er the aged beggar takes his rounds,
The mild necessity of use compels
To acts of love; and habit does the work　　　　　100
Of reason; yet prepares that after-joy
Which reason cherishes. And thus the soul,
By that sweet taste of pleasure unpursued,
Doth find herself insensibly disposed
To virtue and true goodness.

Some there are,
By their good works exalted, lofty minds,
And meditative, authors of delight
And happiness, which to the end of time
Will live, and spread, and kindle: even such minds
In childhood, from this solitary being,   110
Or from like wanderer, haply have received
(A thing more precious far than all that books
Or the solicitudes of love can do!)
That first mild touch of sympathy and thought,
In which they found their kindred with a world
Where want and sorrow were. The easy man
Who sits at his own door,—and, like the pear
That overhangs his head from the green wall,
Feeds in the sunshine; the robust and young,
The prosperous and unthinking, they who live   120
Sheltered, and flourish in a little grove
Of their own kindred;—all behold in him
A silent monitor, which on their minds
Must needs impress a transitory thought
Of self-congratulation, to the heart
Of each recalling his peculiar boons,
His charters and exemptions; and, perchance,
Though he to no one give the fortitude
And circumspection needful to preserve
His present blessings, and to husband up   130
The respite of the season, he, at least,
And 'tis no vulgar service, makes them felt.

Yet further.——Many, I believe, there are
Who live a life of virtuous decency,
Men who can hear the Decalogue and feel
No self-reproach; who of the moral law
Established in the land where they abide
Are strict observers; and not negligent
In acts of love to those with whom they dwell,
Their kindred, and the children of their blood.   140
Praise be to such, and to their slumbers peace!
—But of the poor man ask, the abject poor;
Go, and demand of him, if there be here
In this cold abstinence from evil deeds,
And these inevitable charities,

Wherewith to satisfy the human soul?
No—man is dear to man; the poorest poor
Long for some moments in a weary life
When they can know and feel that they have been,
Themselves, the fathers and the dealers-out   150
Of some small blessings; have been kind to such
As needed kindness, for this single cause,
That we have all of us one human heart.
—Such pleasure is to one kind being known,
My neighbor, when with punctual care, each week,
Duly as Friday comes, though pressed herself
By her own wants, she from her store of meal
Takes one unsparing handful for the scrip
Of this old mendicant, and, from her door
Returning with exhilarated heart,   160
Sits by her fire, and builds her hope in heaven.

Then let him pass, a blessing on his head!
And while in that vast solitude to which
The tide of things has borne him, he appears
To breathe and live but for himself alone,
Unblamed, uninjured, let him bear about
The good which the benignant law of heaven
Has hung around him: and, while life is his,
Still let him prompt the unlettered villagers
To tender offices and pensive thoughts.   170
—Then let him pass, a blessing on his head!
And, long as he can wander, let him breathe
The freshness of the valleys; let his blood
Struggle with frosty air and winter snows;
And let the chartered wind that sweeps the heath
Beat his gray locks against his withered face.
Reverence the hope whose vital anxiousness
Gives the last human interest to his heart.
May never House, misnamed of Industry,
Make him a captive!—for that pent-up din,   180
Those life-consuming sounds that clog the air,
Be his the natural silence of old age!
Let him be free of mountain solitudes;
And have around him, whether heard or not,
The pleasant melody of woodland birds.
Few are his pleasures: if his eyes have now

Been doomed so long to settle upon earth
That not without some effort they behold
The countenance of the horizontal sun,
Rising or setting, let the light at least   190
Find a free entrance to their languid orbs,
And let him, *where* and *when* he will, sit down
Beneath the trees, or on a grassy bank
Of highway side, and with the little birds
Share his chance-gathered meal; and, finally,
As in the eye of Nature he has lived,
So in the eye of Nature let him die!

185.   "STRANGE FITS OF PASSION HAVE
                          I KNOWN"

Strange fits of passion have I known:
And I will dare to tell,
But in the lover's ear alone,
What once to me befell.

When she I loved looked every day
Fresh as a rose in June,
I to her cottage bent my way,
Beneath an evening moon.

Upon the moon I fixed my eye,
All over the wide lea;   10
With quickening pace my horse drew nigh
Those paths so dear to me.

And now we reached the orchard-plot;
And, as we climbed the hill,
The sinking moon to Lucy's cot
Came near, and nearer still.

In one of those sweet dreams I slept,
Kind nature's gentlest boon!
And all the while my eyes I kept
On the descending moon.   20

My horse moved on; hoof after hoof
He raised, and never stopped:
When down behind the cottage roof,
At once, the bright moon dropped.

What fond and wayward thoughts will slide
Into a lover's head!
"O mercy!" to myself I cried,
"If Lucy should be dead!"

186.   "SHE DWELT AMONG THE UNTRODDEN
WAYS"

She dwelt among the untrodden ways
    Beside the springs of Dove,
A Maid whom there were none to praise
    And very few to love:

A violet by a mossy stone
    Half hidden from the eye!
—Fair as a star, when only one
    Is shining in the sky.

She lived unknown, and few could know
    When Lucy ceased to be;   10
But she is in her grave, and, oh,
    The difference to me!

187.   "THREE YEARS SHE GREW IN
SUN AND SHOWER"

Three years she grew in sun and shower,
Then Nature said, "A lovelier flower
On earth was never sown;
This Child I to myself will take;
She shall be mine, and I will make
A Lady of my own.

"Myself will to my darling be
Both law and impulse: and with me
The Girl, in rock and plain,
In earth and heaven, in glade and bower,   10
Shall feel an overseeing power
To kindle or restrain.

"She shall be sportive as the fawn
That wild with glee across the lawn,
Or up the mountain springs;

And hers shall be the breathing balm,
And hers the silence and the calm
Of mute insensate things.

"The floating clouds their state shall lend
To her; for her the willow bend;   20
Nor shall she fail to see
Even in the motions of the Storm
Grace that shall mold the Maiden's form
By silent sympathy.

"The stars of midnight shall be dear
To her; and she shall lean her ear
In many a secret place
Where rivulets dance their wayward round,
And beauty born of murmuring sound
Shall pass into her face.   30

"And vital feelings of delight
Shall rear her form to stately height,
Her virgin bosom swell;
Such thoughts to Lucy I will give
While she and I together live
Here in this happy dell."

Thus Nature spake—The work was done—
How soon my Lucy's race was run!
She died, and left to me
This heath, this calm, and quiet scene;   40
The memory of what has been,
And never more will be.

188.   "A SLUMBER DID MY SPIRIT SEAL"

A slumber did my spirit seal;
     I had no human fears:
She seemed a thing that could not feel
     The touch of earthly years.

No motion has she now, no force;
     She neither hears nor sees;
Rolled round in earth's diurnal course,
     With rocks, and stones, and trees.

MICHAEL

A PASTORAL POEM

If from the public way you turn your steps
Up the tumultuous brook of Greenhead Ghyll,
You will suppose that with an upright path
Your feet must struggle; in such bold ascent
The pastoral mountains front you, face to face.
But, courage! for around that boisterous brook
The mountains have all opened out themselves,
And made a hidden valley of their own.
No habitation can be seen; but they
Who journey thither find themselves alone   10
With a few sheep, with rocks and stones, and kites
That overhead are sailing in the sky.
It is in truth an utter solitude;
Nor should I have made mention of this Dell
But for one object which you might pass by,
Might see and notice not. Beside the brook
Appears a straggling heap of unhewn stones!
And to that simple object appertains
A story—unenriched with strange events,
Yet not unfit, I deem, for the fireside,   20
Or for the summer shade. It was the first
Of those domestic tales that spake to me
Of shepherds, dwellers in the valleys, men
Whom I already loved;—not verily
For their own sakes, but for the fields and hills
Where was their occupation and abode.
And hence this Tale, while I was yet a Boy
Careless of books, yet having felt the power
Of Nature, by the gentle agency
Of natural objects, led me on to feel   30
For passions that were not my own, and think
(At random and imperfectly indeed)
On man, the heart of man, and human life.
Therefore, although it be a history
Homely and rude, I will relate the same
For the delight of a few natural hearts;
And, with yet fonder feeling, for the sake
Of youthful Poets, who among these hills
Will be my second self when I am gone.

Upon the forest-side in Grasmere Vale 40
There dwelt a Shepherd, Michael was his name;
An old man, stout of heart, and strong of limb.
His bodily frame had been from youth to age
Of an unusual strength: his mind was keen,
Intense, and frugal, apt for all affairs,
And in his shepherd's calling he was prompt
And watchful more than ordinary men.
Hence had he learned the meaning of all winds,
Of blasts of every tone; and, oftentimes,
When others heeded not, He heard the South 50
Make subterraneous music, like the noise
Of bagpipers on distant Highland hills.
The Shepherd, at such warning, of his flock
Bethought him, and he to himself would say,
"The winds are now devising work for me!"
And, truly, at all times, the storm, that drives
The traveller to a shelter, summoned him
Up to the mountains: he had been alone
Amid the heart of many thousand mists,
That came to him, and left him, on the heights. 60
So lived he till his eightieth year was past.
And grossly that man errs, who should suppose
That the green valleys, and the streams and rocks,
Were things indifferent to the Shepherd's thoughts.
Fields, where with cheerful spirits he had breathed
The common air; hills, which with vigorous step
He had so often climbed; which had impressed
So many incidents upon his mind
Of hardship, skill or courage, joy or fear;
Which, like a book, preserved the memory 70
Of the dumb animals, whom he had saved,
Had fed or sheltered, linking to such acts
The certainty of honorable gain;
Those fields, those hills—what could they less?—had laid
Strong hold on his affections, were to him
A pleasurable feeling of blind love,
The pleasure which there is in life itself.

His days had not been passed in singleness.
His Helpmate was a comely matron, old—
Though younger than himself full twenty years. 80

She was a woman of a stirring life,
Whose heart was in her house: two wheels she had
Of antique form; this large, for spinning wool;
That small, for flax; and, if one wheel had rest,
It was because the other was at work.
The Pair had but one inmate in their house,
An only Child, who had been born to them
When Michael, telling o'er his years, began
To deem that he was old,—in shepherd's phrase,
With one foot in the grave. This only Son,   90
With two brave sheep-dogs tried in many a storm,
The one of an inestimable worth,
Made all their household. I may truly say,
That they were as a proverb in the vale
For endless industry. When day was gone,
And from their occupations out of doors
The Son and Father were come home, even then,
Their labor did not cease; unless when all
Turned to the cleanly supper-board, and there,
Each with a mess of pottage and skimmed milk,   100
Sat round the basket piled with oaten cakes,
And their plain home-made cheese. Yet when the meal
Was ended, Luke (for so the Son was named)
And his old Father both betook themselves
To such convenient work as might employ
Their hands by the fireside; perhaps to card
Wool for the Housewife's spindle, or repair
Some injury done to sickle, flail, or scythe,
Or other implement of house or field.

  Down from the ceiling, by the chimney's edge,   110
That in our ancient uncouth country style
With huge and black projection overbrowed
Large space beneath, as duly as the light
Of day grew dim the Housewife hung a lamp;
An aged utensil, which had performed
Service beyond all others of its kind.
Early at evening did it burn—and late,
Surviving comrade of uncounted hours,
Which, going by from year to year, had found,
And left, the couple neither gay perhaps   120
Nor cheerful, yet with objects and with hopes,

Living a life of eager industry.
And now, when Luke had reached his eighteenth year,
There by the light of this old lamp they sate,
Father and Son, while far into the night
The Housewife plied her own peculiar work,
Making the cottage through the silent hours
Murmur as with the sound of summer flies.
This light was famous in its neighborhood,
And was a public symbol of the life   130
That thrifty Pair had lived. For, as it chanced,
Their cottage on a plot of rising ground
Stood single, with large prospect, north and south,
High into Easedale, up to Dunmail-Raise,
And westward to the village near the lake;
And from this constant light, so regular
And so far seen, the House itself, by all
Who dwelt within the limits of the vale,
Both old and young, was named THE EVENING STAR.

    Thus living on through such a length of years,   140
The Shepherd, if he loved himself, must needs
Have loved his Helpmate; but to Michael's heart
This son of his old age was yet more dear—
Less from instinctive tenderness, the same
Fond spirit that blindly works in the blood of all—
Than that a child, more than all other gifts
That earth can offer to declining man,
Brings hope with it, and forward-looking thoughts,
And stirrings of inquietude, when they
By tendency of nature needs must fail.   150
Exceeding was the love he bare to him,
His heart and his heart's joy! For oftentimes
Old Michael, while he was a babe in arms,
Had done him female service, not alone
For pastime and delight, as is the use
Of fathers, but with patient mind enforced
To acts of tenderness; and he had rocked
His cradle, as with a woman's gentle hand.

    And, in a later time, ere yet the Boy
Had put on boy's attire, did Michael love,   160
Albeit of a stern unbending mind,

To have the Young-one in his sight, when he
Wrought in the field, or on his shepherd's stool
Sate with a fettered sheep before him stretched
Under the large old oak, that near his door
Stood single, and, from matchless depth of shade,
Chosen for the Shearer's covert from the sun,
Thence in our rustic dialect was called
The CLIPPING TREE, a name which yet it bears.
There, while they two were sitting in the shade,   170
With others round them, earnest all and blithe,
Would Michael exercise his heart with looks
Of fond correction and reproof bestowed
Upon the Child, if he disturbed the sheep
By catching at their legs, or with his shouts
Scared them, while they lay still beneath the shears.

   And when by Heaven's good grace the boy grew up
A healthy Lad, and carried in his cheek
Two steady roses that were five years old;
Then Michael from a winter coppice cut   180
With his own hand a sapling, which he hooped
With iron, making it throughout in all
Due requisites a perfect shepherd's staff,
And gave it to the Boy; wherewith equipped
He as a watchman oftentimes was placed
At gate or gap, to stem or turn the flock;
And, to his office prematurely called,
There stood the urchin, as you will divine,
Something between a hindrance and a help;
And for this cause not always, I believe,   190
Receiving from his Father hire of praise;
Though nought was left undone which staff, or voice,
Or looks, or threatening gestures, could perform.

   But soon as Luke, full ten years old, could stand
Against the mountain blasts; and to the heights,
Not fearing toil, nor length of weary ways,
He with his Father daily went, and they
Were as companions, why should I relate
That objects which the Shepherd loved before
Were dearer now? that from the Boy there came   200
Feelings and emanations—things which were

Light to the sun and music to the wind;
And that the old Man's heart seemed born again?

    Thus in his Father's sight the Boy grew up:
And now, when he had reached his eighteenth year,
He was his comfort and his daily hope.

    While in this sort the simple household lived
From day to day, to Michael's ear there came
Distressful tidings. Long before the time
Of which I speak, the Shepherd had been bound   210
In surety for his brother's son, a man
Of an industrious life, and ample means;
But unforeseen misfortunes suddenly
Had pressed upon him; and old Michael now
Was summoned to discharge the forfeiture,
A grievous penalty, but little less
Than half his substance. This unlooked-for claim,
At the first hearing, for a moment took
More hope out of his life than he supposed
That any old man ever could have lost.   220
As soon as he had armed himself with strength
To look his trouble in the face, it seemed
The Shepherd's sole resource to sell at once
A portion of his patrimonial fields.
Such was his first resolve; he thought again,
And his heart failed him. "Isabel," said he,
Two evenings after he had heard the news,
"I have been toiling more than seventy years,
And in the open sunshine of God's love
Have we all lived; yet if these fields of ours   230
Should pass into a stranger's hand, I think
That I could not lie quiet in my grave.
Our lot is a hard lot; the sun himself
Has scarcely been more diligent than I;
And I have lived to be a fool at last
To my own family. An evil man
That was, and made an evil choice, if he
Were false to us; and, if he were not false,
There are ten thousand to whom loss like this
Had been no sorrow. I forgive him;—but   240
'Twere better to be dumb than to talk thus.

When I began, my purpose was to speak
Of remedies and of a cheerful hope.
Our Luke shall leave us, Isabel; the land
Shall not go from us, and it shall be free;
He shall possess it, free as is the wind
That passes over it. We have, thou know'st,
Another kinsman—he will be our friend
In this distress. He is a prosperous man,
Thriving in trade—and Luke to him shall go,   250
And with his kinsman's help and his own thrift
He quickly will repair this loss, and then
He may return to us. If here he stay,
What can be done? Where every one is poor,
What can be gained?"

                    At this the old man paused,
And Isabel sat silent, for her mind
Was busy, looking back into past times.
There's Richard Bateman, thought she to herself,
He was a parish-boy—at the church-door   260
They made a gathering for him, shillings, pence,
And halfpennies, wherewith the neighbors bought
A basket, which they filled with pedlar's wares;
And, with this basket on his arm, the lad
Went up to London, found a master there,
Who, out of many, chose the trusty boy
To go and overlook his merchandise
Beyond the seas; where he grew wondrous rich,
And left estates and monies to the poor,
And, at his birth-place, built a chapel, floored   270
With marble, which he sent from foreign lands.
These thoughts, and many others of like sort,
Passed quickly through the mind of Isabel,
And her face brightened. The old Man was glad,
And thus resumed:—"Well, Isabel! this scheme,
These two days, has been meat and drink to me.
Far more than we have lost is left us yet.
    We have enough—I wish indeed that I
Were younger;—but this hope is a good hope.
Make ready Luke's best garments, of the best   280
Buy for him more, and let us send him forth

To-morrow, or the next day, or to-night:
If he *could* go, the Boy should go to-night."

   Here Michael ceased, and to the fields went forth
With a light heart. The Housewife for five days
Was restless morn and night, and all day long
Wrought on with her best fingers to prepare
Things needful for the journey of her son.
But Isabel was glad when Sunday came
To stop her in her work: for, when she lay   290
By Michael's side, she through the last two nights
Heard him, how he was troubled in his sleep;
And when they rose at morning she could see
That all his hopes were gone. That day at noon
She said to Luke, while they two by themselves
Were sitting at the door, "Thou must not go:
We have no other Child but thee to lose,
None to remember—do not go away,
For if thou leave thy Father he will die."
The Youth made answer with a jocund voice;   300
And Isabel, when she had told her fears,
Recovered heart. That evening her best fare
Did she bring forth, and all together sat
Like happy people round a Christmas fire.

   With daylight Isabel resumed her work;
And all the ensuing week the house appeared
As cheerful as a grove in Spring: at length
The expected letter from their kinsman came,
With kind assurances that he would do
His utmost for the welfare of the Boy;   310
To which, requests were added, that forthwith
He might be sent to him. Ten times or more
The letter was read over; Isabel
Went forth to show it to the neighbours round;
Nor was there at that time on English land
A prouder heart than Luke's. When Isabel
Had to her house returned, the old Man said,
"He shall depart to-morrow." To this word
The Housewife answered, talking much of things
Which, if at such short notice he should go,   320

Would surely be forgotten. But at length
She gave consent, and Michael was at ease.

  Near the tumultuous brook of Greenhead Ghyll,
In that deep valley, Michael had designed
To build a Sheepfold; and, before he heard
The tidings of his melancholy loss,
For this same purpose he had gathered up
A heap of stones, which by the streamlet's edge
Lay thrown together, ready for the work.
With Luke that evening thitherward he walked: 330
And soon as they had reached the place he stopped,
And thus the old Man spake to him:—"My Son,
To-morrow thou wilt leave me: with full heart
I look upon thee, for thou art the same
That wert a promise to me ere thy birth,
And all thy life hast been my daily joy.
I will relate to thee some little part
Of our two histories; 'twill do thee good
When thou art from me, even if I should touch
On things thou canst not know of.——After thou   340
First cam'st into the world—as oft befalls
To new-born infants—thou didst sleep away
Two days, and blessings from thy Father's tongue
Then fell upon thee. Day by day passed on,
And still I loved thee with increasing love.
Never to living ear came sweeter sounds
Than when I heard thee by our own fireside
First uttering, without words, a natural tune;
While thou, a feeding babe, didst in thy joy
Sing at thy Mother's breast. Month followed month,   350
And in the open fields my life was passed
And on the mountains; else I think that thou
Hadst been brought up upon thy Father's knees.
But we were playmates, Luke: among these hills,
As well thou knowest, in us the old and young
Have played together, nor with me didst thou
Lack any pleasure which a boy can know."
Luke had a manly heart; but at these words
He sobbed aloud. The old Man grasped his hand,
And said, "Nay, do not take it so—I see   360
That these are things of which I need not speak.

—Even to the utmost I have been to thee
A kind and a good Father: and herein
I but repay a gift which I myself
Received at others' hands; for, though now old
Beyond the common life of man, I still
Remember them who loved me in my youth.
Both of them sleep together: here they lived,
As all their Forefathers had done; and when
At length their time was come, they were not loth   370
To give their bodies to the family mould.
I wished that thou should'st live the life they lived:
But 'tis a long time to look back, my Son,
And see so little gain from threescore years.
These fields were burthened when they came to me;
Till I was forty years of age, not more
Than half of my inheritance was mine.
I toiled and toiled; God blessed me in my work,
And till these three weeks past the land was free.
—It looks as if it never could endure   380
Another Master. Heaven forgive me, Luke,
If I judge ill for thee, but it seems good
That thou shouldst go."

                At this the old Man paused;
Then, pointing to the stones near which they stood,
Thus, after a short silence, he resumed:
"This was a work for us; and now, my Son,
It is a work for me. But, lay one stone—
Here, lay it for me, Luke, with thine own hands.
Nay, Boy, be of good hope;—we both may live   390
To see a better day. At eighty-four
I still am strong and hale;—do thou thy part;
I will do mine.—I will begin again
With many tasks that were resigned to thee:
Up to the heights, and in among the storms,
Will I without thee go again, and do
All works which I was wont to do alone,
Before I knew thy face.—Heaven bless thee, Boy!
Thy heart these two weeks has been beating fast
With many hopes; it should be so—yes—yes—   400
I knew that thou couldst never have a wish
To leave me, Luke: thou hast been bound to me

Only by links of love: when thou art gone,
What will be left to us!—But I forget
My purposes. Lay now the corner-stone,
As I requested; and hereafter, Luke,
When thou art gone away, should evil men
Be thy companions, think of me, my Son,
And of this moment; hither turn thy thoughts,
And God will strengthen thee: amid all fear   410
And all temptation, Luke, I pray that thou
May'st bear in mind the life thy Fathers lived,
Who, being innocent, did for that cause
Bestir them in good deeds. Now, fare thee well—
When thou return'st, thou in this place wilt see
A work which is not here: a covenant
'Twill be between us; but, whatever fate
Befall thee, I shall love thee to the last,
And bear thy memory with me to the grave."

The Shepherd ended here; and Luke stooped down,   420
And, as his Father had requested, laid
The first stone of the Sheepfold. At the sight
The old Man's grief broke from him; to his heart
He pressed his Son, he kissèd him and wept;
And to the house together they returned.
—Hushed was that House in peace, or seeming peace,
Ere the night fell:—with morrow's dawn the Boy
Began his journey, and when he had reached
The public way, he put on a bold face;
And all the neighbors, as he passed their doors,   430
Came forth with wishes and with farewell prayers,
That followed him till he was out of sight.

A good report did from their Kinsman come,
Of Luke and his well-doing: and the Boy
Wrote loving letters, full of wondrous news,
Which, as the Housewife phrased it, were throughout
"The prettiest letters that were ever seen."
Both parents read them with rejoicing hearts.
So, many months passed on: and once again
The Shepherd went about his daily work   440
With confident and cheerful thoughts; and now
Sometimes when he could find a leisure hour
He to that valley took his way, and there

Wrought at the Sheepfold. Meantime Luke began
To slacken in his duty; and, at length,
He in the dissolute city gave himself
To evil courses: ignominy and shame
Fell on him, so that he was driven at last
To seek a hiding-place beyond the seas.

There is a comfort in the strength of love;   450
'Twill make a thing endurable, which else
Would overset the brain, or break the heart:
I have conversed with more than one who well
Remember the old Man, and what he was
Years after he had heard this heavy news.
His bodily frame had been from youth to age
Of an unusual strength. Among the rocks
He went, and still looked up to sun and cloud,
And listened to the wind; and, as before
Performed all kinds of labour for his sheep,   460
And for the land, his small inheritance.
And to that hollow dell from time to time
Did he repair to build the Fold of which
His flock had need. 'Tis not forgotten yet
The pity which was then in every heart
For the old Man—and 'tis believed by all
That many and many a day he thither went,
And never lifted up a single stone.

There, by the Sheepfold, sometimes was he seen
Sitting alone, or with his faithful Dog,   470
Then old, beside him, lying at his feet.
The length of full seven years, from time to time,
He at the building of this Sheepfold wrought,
And left the work unfinished when he died.
Three years, or little more, did Isabel
Survive her Husband: at her death the estate
Was sold, and went into a stranger's hand.
The Cottage which was named THE EVENING STAR
Is gone—the ploughshare has been through the ground
On which it stood; great changes have been wrought   480
In all the neighborhood:—yet the oak is left
That grew beside their door; and the remains
Of the unfinished Sheepfold may be seen
Beside the boisterous brook of Greenhead Ghyll.

190.   RESOLUTION AND INDEPENDENCE

There was a roaring in the wind all night;
The rain came heavily and fell in floods;
But now the sun is rising calm and bright;
The birds are singing in the distant woods;
Over his own sweet voice the stock-dove broods;
The jay makes answer as the magpie chatters;
And all the air is filled with pleasant noise of waters.

All things that love the sun are out of doors;
The sky rejoices in the morning's birth;
The grass is bright with rain-drops;—on the moors   10
The hare is running races in her mirth;
And with her feet she from the plashy earth
Raises a mist, that, glittering in the sun,
Runs with her all the way, wherever she doth run.

I was a traveller then upon the moor;
I saw the hare that raced about with joy;
I heard the woods and distant waters roar;
Or heard them not, as happy as a boy:
The pleasant season did my heart employ:
My old remembrances went from me wholly;   20
And all the ways of men, so vain and melancholy.

But, as it sometimes chanceth, from the might
Of joy in minds that can no further go,
As high as we have mounted in delight
In our dejection do we sink as low;
To me that morning did it happen so;
And fears and fancies thick upon me came;
Dim sadness—and blind thoughts, I knew not, nor could name.

I heard the skylark warbling in the sky;
And I bethought me of the playful hare: 30
Even such a happy child of earth am I;
Even as these blissful creatures do I fare;
Far from the world I walk, and from all care;
But there may come another day to me—
Solitude, pain of heart, distress, and poverty.

My whole life I have lived in pleasant thought,
As if life's business were a summer mood;

As if all needful things would come unsought
To genial faith, still rich in genial good;
But how can he expect that others should   40
Build for him, sow for him, and at his call
Love him, who for himself will take no heed at all?

I thought of Chatterton, the marvellous boy,
The sleepless soul that perished in his pride;
Of him who walked in glory and in joy
Following his plough, along the mountainside:
By our own spirits are we deified:
We poets in our youth begin in gladness;
But thereof come in the end despondency and madness.

Now, whether it were by peculiar grace,   50
A leading from above, a something given,
Yet it befell that, in this lonely place,
When I with these untoward thoughts had striven,
Beside a pool bare to the eye of heaven
I saw a man before me unawares:
The oldest man he seemed that ever wore gray hairs.

As a huge stone is sometimes seen to lie
Couched on the bald top of an eminence;
Wonder to all who do the same espy,
By what means it could thither come, and whence;   60
So that it seems a thing endued with sense:
Like a sea-beast crawled forth, that on a shelf
Of rock or sand reposeth, there to sun itself;

Such seemed this man, not all alive nor dead,
Nor all asleep—in his extreme old age:
His body was bent double, feet and head
Coming together in life's pilgrimage;
As if some dire constraint of pain, or rage
Of sickness felt by him in times long past,
A more than human weight upon his frame had cast.   70

Himself he propped, limbs, body, and pale face,
Upon a long gray staff of shaven wood:
And, still as I drew near with gentle pace,
Upon the margin of that moorish flood
Motionless as a cloud the old man stood,

That heareth not the loud winds when they call;
And moveth all together, if it move at all.

At length, himself unsettling, he the pond
Stirred with his staff, and fixedly did look
Upon the muddy water, which he conned,   80
As if he had been reading in a book:
And now a stranger's privilege I took;
And, drawing to his side, to him did say,
"This morning gives us promise of a glorious day."

A gentle answer did the old man make,
In courteous speech which forth he slowly drew:
And him with further words I thus bespake,
"What occupation do you there pursue?
This is a lonesome place for one like you."
Ere he replied, a flash of mild surprise   90
Broke from the sable orbs of his yet-vivid eyes.

His words came feebly, from a feeble chest,
But each in solemn order followed each,
With something of a lofty utterance drest—
Choice word and measured phrase, above the reach
Of ordinary men; a stately speech;
Such as grave livers do in Scotland use,
Religious men, who give to God and man their dues.

He told that to these waters he had come
To gather leeches, being old and poor: 100
Employment hazardous and wearisome!
And he had many hardships to endure:
From pond to pond he roamed, from moor to moor;
Housing, with God's good help, by choice or chance;
And in this way he gained an honest maintenance.

The old man still stood talking by my side;
But now his voice to me was like a stream
Scarce heard; nor word from word could I divide;
And the whole body of the man did seem
Like one whom I had met with in a dream;   110
Or like a man from some far region sent,
To give me human strength, by apt admonishment.

My former thoughts returned: the fear that kills;
And hope that is unwilling to be fed;
Cold, pain, and labour, and all fleshly ills;
And mighty poets in their misery dead.
—Perplexed, and longing to be comforted,
My question eagerly did I renew,
"How is it that you live, and what is it you do?"

He with a smile did then his words repeat;   120
And said that, gathering leeches, far and wide
He travelled, stirring thus about his feet
The waters of the pools where they abide.
"Once I could meet with them on every side;
But they have dwindled long by slow decay;
Yet still I persevere, and find them where I may."

While he was talking thus, the lonely place,
The old man's shape, and speech—all troubled me:
In my mind's eye I seemed to see him pace
About the weary moors continually,   130
Wandering about alone and silently.
While I these thoughts within myself pursued,
He, having made a pause, the same discourse renewed.

And soon with this he other matter blended,
Cheerfully uttered, with demeanor kind,
But stately in the main; and, when he ended,
I could have laughed myself to scorn to find
In that decrepit man so firm a mind.
"God," said I, "be my help and stay secure;
I'll think of the leech-gatherer on the lonely moor!"   140

191.   LONDON, 1802

Milton! thou shouldst be living at this hour:
England hath need of thee: she is a fen
Of stagnant waters: altar, sword, and pen,
Fireside, the heroic wealth of hall and bower,
Have forfeited their ancient English dower
Of inward happiness. We are selfish men;
Oh! raise us up, return to us again;
And give us manners, virtue, freedom, power.
Thy soul was like a Star, and dwelt apart;

Thou hadst a voice whose sound was like the sea: 10
Pure as the naked heavens, majestic, free
So didst thou travel on life's common way,
In cheerful godliness; and yet thy heart
The lowliest duties on herself did lay.

192.   COMPOSED BY THE SEASIDE, NEAR CALAIS

AUGUST, 1802

Fair star of evening, splendor of the west,
Star of my country!—on the horizon's brink
Thou hangest, stooping, as might seem, to sink
On England's bosom; yet well pleased to rest,
Meanwhile, and be to her a glorious crest
Conspicuous to the nations. Thou, I think,
Shouldst be my country's emblem, and shouldst wink,
Bright star! with laughter on her banners, dressed
In thy fresh beauty. There! that dusky spot
Beneath thee, that is England; there she lies.   10
Blessings be on you both! one hope, one lot,
One life, one glory!—I, with many a fear
For my dear country, many heartfelt sighs,
Among men who do not love her, linger here.

193.   COMPOSED UPON WESTMINSTER BRIDGE

SEPTEMBER 3, 1802

Earth has not anything to show more fair:
Dull would he be of soul who could pass by
A sight so touching in its majesty:
This City now doth, like a garment, wear
The beauty of the morning; silent, bare,
Ships, towers, domes, theatres, and temples lie
Open unto the fields, and to the sky;
All bright and glittering in the smokeless air.
Never did sun more beautifully steep
In his first splendour, valley, rock, or hill;   10
Ne'er saw I, never felt, a calm so deep!
The river glideth at his own sweet will:
Dear God! the very houses seem asleep;
And all that mighty heart is lying still!

194.

"IT IS A BEAUTEOUS EVENING,
CALM AND FREE"

It is a beauteous evening, calm and free,
The holy time is quiet as a Nun
Breathless with adoration; the broad sun
Is sinking down in its tranquillity;
The gentleness of heaven broods o'er the Sea:
Listen! the mighty Being is awake,
And doth with his eternal motion make
A sound like thunder—everlastingly.
Dear Child! dear Girl! that walkest with me here,
If thou appear untouched by solemn thought, 10
Thy nature is not therefore less divine:
Thou liest in Abraham's bosom all the year;
And worshipp'st at the Temple's inner shrine,
God being with thee when we know it not.

195.

"THE WORLD IS TOO MUCH WITH
US; LATE AND SOON"

The world is too much with us; late and soon,
Getting and spending, we lay waste our powers:
Little we see in Nature that is ours;
We have given our hearts away, a sordid boon!
This Sea that bares her bosom to the moon;
The winds that will be howling at all hours,
And are up-gathered now like sleeping flowers;
For this, for everything, we are out of tune;
It moves us not.—Great God! I'd rather be
A Pagan suckled in a creed outworn; 10
So might I, standing on this pleasant lea,
Have glimpses that would make me less forlorn;
Have sight of Proteus rising from the sea;
Or hear old Triton blow his wreathèd horn.

196.

THE SOLITARY REAPER

Behold her, single in the field,
Yon solitary Highland Lass!
Reaping and singing by herself;
Stop here, or gently pass!

Alone she cuts and binds the grain,
And sings a melancholy strain;
O listen! for the vale profound
Is overflowing with the sound.

No nightingale did ever chaunt
More welcome notes to weary bands   10
Of travellers in some shady haunt,
Among Arabian sands:
A voice so thrilling ne'er was heard
In springtime from the cuckoo bird,
Breaking the silence of the seas
Among the farthest Hebrides.

Will no one tell me what she sings?—
Perhaps the plaintive numbers flow
For old, unhappy, far-off things,
And battles long ago: 20
Or is it some more humble lay,
Familiar matter of to-day?
Some natural sorrow, loss, or pain,
That has been, and may be again?

Whate'er the theme, the maiden sang
As if her song could have no ending;
I saw her singing at her work,
And o'er the sickle bending;—
I listened, motionless and still;
And, as I mounted up the hill,   30
The music in my heart I bore,
Long after it was heard no more.

197.   "I WANDERED LONELY AS A CLOUD"

I wandered lonely as a cloud
That floats on high o'er vales and hills,
When all at once I saw a crowd,
A host, of golden daffodils;
Beside the lake, beneath the trees,
Fluttering and dancing in the breeze.

Continuous as the stars that shine
And twinkle on the milky way,

They stretched in never-ending line
Along the margin of a bay: 10
Ten thousand saw I at a glance,
Tossing their heads in sprightly dance.

The waves beside them danced; but they
Out-did the sparkling waves in glee:
A poet could not but be gay,
In such a jocund company:
I gazed—and gazed—but little thought
What wealth the show to me had brought:

For oft, when on my couch I lie
In vacant or in pensive mood, 20
They flash upon that inward eye
Which is the bliss of solitude;
And then my heart with pleasure fills,
And dances with the daffodils.

198.　　　COMPOSED UPON AN EVENING OF
EXTRAORDINARY SPLENDOR AND BEAUTY

Had this effulgence disappeared
With flying haste, I might have sent,
Among the speechless clouds, a look
Of blank astonishment;
But 'tis endued with power to stay,
And sanctify one closing day,
That frail mortality may see—
What is?—ah no, but what *can* be!
Time was when field and watery cove
With modulated echoes rang, 10
While choirs of fervent Angels sang
Their vespers in the grove;
Or, crowning, star-like, each some sovereign height,
Warbled, for heaven above and earth below,
Strains suitable to both.—Such holy rite,
Methinks, if audibly repeated now
From hill or valley, could not move
Sublimer transport, purer love,
Than doth this silent spectacle—the gleam—
The shadow—and the peace supreme! 20

No sound is uttered,—but a deep
And solemn harmony pervades
The hollow vale from steep to steep,
And penetrates the glades.
Far-distant images draw nigh,
Called forth by wondrous potency
Of beamy radiance, that imbues,
Whate'er it strikes, with gem-like hues!
In vision exquisitely clear,
Herds range along the mountain side;   30
And glistening antlers are descried;
And gilded flocks appear.
Thine is the tranquil hour, purpureal Eve!
But long as god-like wish, or hope divine,
Informs my spirit, ne'er can I believe
That this magnificence is wholly thine!
—From worlds not quickened by the sun
A portion of the gift is won;
An intermingling of Heaven's pomp is spread
On ground which British shepherds tread!   40

And, if there be whom broken ties
Afflict, or injuries assail,
Yon hazy ridges to their eyes
Present a glorious scale,
Climbing suffused with sunny air,
To stop—no record hath told where!
And tempting fancy to ascend,
And with immortal spirits blend!
—Wings at my shoulders seem to play;
But, rooted here, I stand and gaze   50
On those bright steps that heavenward raise
Their practicable way.
Come forth, ye drooping old men, look abroad,
And see to what fair countries ye are bound!
And if some traveller, weary of his road,
Hath slept since noontide on the grassy ground,
Ye Genii! to his covert speed;
And wake him with such gentle heed
As may attune his soul to meet the dower
Bestowed on this transcendent hour!   60

Such hues from their celestial urn
Were wont to stream before mine eye,
Where'er it wandered in the morn
Of blissful infancy.
This glimpse of glory, why renewed?
Nay, rather speak with gratitude;
For, if a vestige of those gleams
Survived, 'twas only in my dreams.
Dread Power! whom peace and calmness serve
No less than Nature's threatening voice,   70
If aught unworthy be my choice,
From THEE if I would swerve;
Oh, let Thy grace remind me of the light
Full early lost, and fruitlessly deplored;
Which, at this moment, on my waking sight
Appears to shine, by miracle restored;
My soul, though yet confined to earth,
Rejoices in a second birth!
—'Tis past, the visionary splendor fades;
And night approaches with her shades.   80

199.   MUTABILITY

From low to high doth dissolution climb,
And sink from high to low, along a scale
Of awful notes, whose concord shall not fail;
A musical but melancholy chime,
Which they can hear who meddle not with crime,
Nor avarice, nor over-anxious care.
Truth fails not; but her outward forms that bear
The longest date do melt like frosty rime,
That in the morning whitened hill and plain
And is no more; drop like the tower sublime   10
Of yesterday, which royally did wear
His crown of weeds, but could not even sustain
Some casual shout that broke the silent air,
Or the unimaginable touch of time.

SAMUEL TAYLOR COLERIDGE (1772–1834)

200.   THE RIME OF THE ANCIENT MARINER

IN SEVEN PARTS

PART THE FIRST

An ancient Mariner meet-
eth three Gallants, bidden to
a wedding-feast, and de-
taineth one.

It is an ancient Mariner
And he stoppeth one of three.
"By thy long grey beard and glittering eye,
Now wherefore stopp'st thou me?

The Bridegroom's doors are opened wide,
And I am next of kin;
The guests are met, the feast is set:
May'st hear the merry din."

He holds him with his skinny hand,
"There was a ship," quoth he.   10
"Hold off! unhand me, grey-beard loon!"
Eftsoons his hand dropt he.

The Wedding-Guest is
spell-bound by the eye of
the old seafaring man, and
constrained to hear his
tale.

He holds him with his glittering eye—
The Wedding-Guest stood still,
And listens like a three years' child:
The Mariner hath his will.

The Wedding-Guest sat on a stone:
He cannot choose but hear;
And thus spake on that ancient man,
The bright-eyed Mariner.   20

"The ship was cheered, the harbor cleared,
Merrily did we drop
Below the kirk, below the hill,
Below the lighthouse top.

The Mariner tells how the
ship sailed southward with
a good wind and fair
weather, till it reached the
Line.

The Sun came up upon the left,
Out of the sea came he!
And he shone bright, and on the right
Went down into the sea.

Higher and higher every day,
Till over the mast at noon—"   30
The Wedding-Guest here beat his breast.
For he heard the loud bassoon.

The Wedding-Guest hear-
eth the bridal music; but
the Mariner continueth his
tale.

The bride hath paced into the hall,
Red as a rose is she;
Nodding their heads before her goes
The merry minstrelsy.

The Wedding-Guest he beat his breast,
Yet he cannot choose but hear;
And thus spake on that ancient man,
The bright-eyed Mariner.   40

The ship driven by a storm
toward the south pole.

"And now the storm-blast came, and he
Was tyrannous and strong:
He struck with his o'ertaking wings,
And chased us south along.

With sloping masts and dipping prow,
As who pursued with yell and blow
Still treads the shadow of his foe
And forward bends his head,
The ship drove fast, loud roared the blast,
And southward aye we fled.   50

And now there came both mist and snow,
And it grew wondrous cold:
And ice, mast-high, came floating by,
As green as emerald.

The land of ice, and of
fearful sounds, where no
living thing was to be seen.

And through the drifts the snowy clifts
Did send a dismal sheen:
Nor shapes of men nor beasts we ken—
The ice was all between.

The ice was here, the ice was there,
The ice was all around: 60
It cracked and growled, and roared and howled,
Like noises in a swound!

Till a great sea-bird, called
the Albatross, came through
the snow-fog, and was re-
ceived with great joy and
hospitality.

At length did cross an Albatross:
Thorough the fog it came;
As if it had been a Christian soul,
We hailed it in God's name.

It ate the food it ne'er had eat,
And round and round it flew.
The ice did split with a thunder-fit;
The helmsman steered us through!   70

And lo! the Albatross proveth a Lird of good omen, and followeth the ship as it returned northward through fog and floating ice.

And a good south wind sprung up behind;
The Albatross did follow,
And every day, for food or play,
Came to the mariners' hollo!

In mist or cloud, on mast or shroud,
It perched for vespers nine;
Whiles all the night, through fog-smoke white,
Glimmered the white Moon-shine."

The ancient Mariner inhospitably killeth the pious bird of good omen.

"God save thee, ancient Mariner!
From the fiends, that plague thee thus!—   80
Why look'st thou so?"—"With my cross-bow
I shot the Albatross.

PART THE SECOND

The Sun now rose upon the right:
Out of the sea came he,
Still hid in mist, and on the left
Went down into the sea.

And the good south wind still blew behind,
But no sweet bird did follow,
Nor any day for food or play
Came to the mariners' hollo!   90

His shipmates cry out against the ancient Mariner, for killing the bird of good luck.

And I had done a hellish thing,
And it would work 'em woe:
For all averred, I had killed the bird
That made the breeze to blow.
'Ah, wretch!' said they, 'the bird to slay,
That made the breeze to blow!'

But when the fog cleared off, they justify the same, and thus make themselves accomplices in the crime.

Nor dim nor red, like God's own head,
The glorious Sun uprist:
Then all averred, I had killed the bird
That brought the fog and mist.   100
' 'Twas right,' said they, 'such birds to slay,
That bring the fog and mist.'

The fair breeze continues; the ship enters the Pacific Ocean, and sails northward, even till it reaches the Line.

The fair breeze blew, the white foam flew,
The furrow followed free;
We were the first that ever burst
Into that silent sea.

Down dropt the breeze, the sails dropt down,
'Twas sad as sad could be;

The ship hath been sud-
denly becalmed. And we did speak only to break
The silence of the sea!   110

All in a hot and copper sky,
The bloody Sun, at noon,
Right up above the mast did stand,
No bigger than the Moon.

Day after day, day after day,
We stuck, nor breath nor motion;
As idle as a painted ship
Upon a painted ocean.

And the Albatross begins
to be avenged. Water, water, every where,
And all the boards did shrink;   120
Water, water, every where,
Nor any drop to drink.

The very deep did rot: O Christ!
That ever this should be!
Yea, slimy things did crawl with legs
Upon the slimy sea.

About, about, in reel and rout
The death-fires danced at night;
The water, like a witch's oils,
Burnt green, and blue, and white.   130

A Spirit had followed
them; one of the invisible
inhabitants of this planet,
neither departed souls nor
angels; concerning whom
the learned Jew, Josephus,
and the Platonic Constan-
tinopolitan, Michael Psel-
lus, may be consulted.
They are very numerous,
and there is no climate or
element without one or
more. And some in dreams assurèd were
Of the Spirit that plagued us so;
Nine fathom deep he had followed us
From the land of mist and snow.

And every tongue, through utter drought,
Was withered at the root;
We could not speak, no more than if
We had been choked with soot.

Ah! well-a-day! what evil looks
Had I from old and young!   140
The shipmates, in their
sore distress, would fain
throw the whole guilt on
the ancient Mariner: in
sign whereof they hang the
dead sea-bird round his
neck. Instead of the cross, the Albatross
About my neck was hung.

PART THE THIRD

There passed a weary time. Each throat
Was parched, and glazed each eye.
A weary time! a weary time!

The ancient Mariner be-
holdeth a sign in the element afar off.

How glazed each weary eye,
When looking westward, I beheld
A something in the sky.

At first it seemed a little speck,
And then it seemed a mist;   150
It moved and moved, and took at last
A certain shape, I wist.

A speck, a mist, a shape, I wist!
And still it neared and neared:
As if it dodged a water-sprite,
It plunged and tacked and veered.

At its nearer approach, it
seemeth him to be a ship;
and at a dear ransom he
freeth his speech from the
bonds of thirst.

With throats unslaked, with black lips baked,
We could nor laugh nor wail;
Through utter drought all dumb we stood!
I bit my arm, I sucked the blood,   160
And cried, A sail! a sail!

With throats unslaked, with black lips baked,
Agape they heard me call:

A flash of joy,

Gramercy! they for joy did grin,
And all at once their breath drew in,
As they were drinking all.

And horror follows. For
can it be a ship that comes
onward without wind or
tide?

See! see! (I cried) she tacks no more!
Hither to work us weal;
Without a breeze, without a tide,
She steadies with upright keel!   170

The western wave was all a-flame.
The day was well-nigh done!
Almost upon the western wave
Rested the broad bright Sun;
When that strange shape drove suddenly
Betwixt us and the Sun.

It seemeth him but the
skeleton of a ship.

And straight the Sun was flecked with bars,
(Heaven's Mother send us grace!)
As if through a dungeon-grate he peered
With broad and burning face.   180

Alas! (thought I, and my heart beat loud)
How fast she nears and nears!
Are those her sails that glance in the Sun,
Like restless gossameres?

And its ribs are seen as bars on the face of the setting Sun. The Spectre-Woman and her Death-mate, and no other on board the skeleton-ship. Like vessel, like crew!

Are those her ribs through which the Sun
Did peer, as through a grate?
And is that Woman all her crew?
Is that a Death? and are there two?
Is Death that woman's mate?

Her lips were red, her looks were free,   190
Her locks were yellow as gold:
Her skin was as white as leprosy,
The Night-mare Life-in-Death was she,
Who thicks man's blood with cold.

Death and Life-in-Death have diced for the ship's crew, and she (the latter) winneth the ancient Mariner.

The naked hulk alongside came,
And the twain were casting dice;
'The game is done! I've won! I've won!'
Quoth she, and whistles thrice.

No twilight within the courts of the Sun.

The Sun's rim dips; the stars rush out:
At one stride comes the dark;   200
With far-heard whisper, o'er the sea,
Off shot the spectre-bark.

At the rising of the Moon,

We listened and looked sideways up!
Fear at my heart, as at a cup,
My life-blood seemed to sip!
The stars were dim, and thick the night,
The steersman's face by his lamp gleamed
From the sails the dew did drip—
Till clomb above the eastern bar
The hornèd Moon, with one bright star   210
Within the nether tip.

One after another,

One after one, by the star-dogged Moon,
Too quick for groan or sigh,
Each turned his face with a ghastly pang,
And cursed me with his eye.

His shipmates drop down dead.

Four times fifty living men,
(And I heard nor sigh nor groan)
With heavy thump, a lifeless lump,
They dropped down one by one.

But Life-in-Death begins
her work on the ancient
Mariner.

The souls did from their bodies fly,—   220
They fled to bliss or woe!
And every soul, it passed me by,
Like the whizz of my cross-bow!"

PART THE FOURTH

The Wedding-Guest feareth
that a Spirit is talking to
him;

"I fear thee, ancient Mariner!
I fear thy skinny hand!
And thou art long, and lank, and brown,
As is the ribbed sea-sand.

But the ancient Mariner
assureth him of his bodily
life, and proceedeth to relate his horrible penance.

I fear thee and thy glittering eye,
And thy skinny hand, so brown."—
"Fear not, fear not, thou Wedding-Guest!   230
This body dropt not down.

Alone, alone, all, all alone,
Alone on a wide wide sea!
And never a saint took pity on
My soul in agony.

He despiseth the creatures
of the calm.

The many men, so beautiful!
And they all dead did lie:
And a thousand thousand slimy things
Lived on; and so did I.

And envieth that they
should live, and so many
lie dead.

I looked upon the rotting sea,   240
And drew my eyes away;
I looked upon the rotting deck,
And there the dead men lay.

I looked to Heaven, and tried to pray;
But or ever a prayer had gusht,
A wicked whisper came, and made
My heart as dry as dust.

I closed my lids, and kept them close,
And the balls like pulses beat;
For the sky and the sea, and the sea and the sky
Lay like a load on my weary eye,   251
And the dead were at my feet.

But the curse liveth for him
in the eye of the dead men.

The cold sweat melted from their limbs,
Nor rot nor reek did they:
The look with which they looked on me
Had never passed away.

An orphan's curse would drag to hell
A spirit from on high;

But oh! more horrible than that
Is the curse in a dead man's eye!   260
Seven days, seven nights, I saw that curse,
And yet I could not die.

In his loneliness and fixed-
ness he yearneth towards
the journeying Moon, and
the stars that still sojourn,
yet still move onward; and
everywhere the blue sky
belongs to them, and is
their appointed rest, and
their native country and
their own natural homes,
which they enter unan-
nounced, as lords that are
certainly expected and yet
there is a silent joy at their
arrival.

The moving Moon went up the sky
And nowhere did abide:
Softly she was going up,
And a star or two beside—

Her beams bemocked the sultry main,
Like April hoar-frost spread;
But where the ship's huge shadow lay,
The charmèd water burnt alway   270
A still and awful red.

By the light of the Moon
he beholdeth God's crea-
tures of the great calm.

Beyond the shadow of the ship,
I watched the water-snakes:
They moved in tracks of shining white,
And when they reared, the elfish light
Fell off in hoary flakes.

Within the shadow of the ship
I watched their rich attire:
Blue, glossy green, and velvet black,
They coiled and swam; and every track   280
Was a flash of golden fire.

Their beauty and their
happiness.

O happy living things! no tongue
Their beauty might declare:
A spring of love gushed from my heart,

He blesseth them in his
heart.

And I blessed them unaware:
Sure my kind saint took pity on me,
And I blessed them unaware.

The spell begins to break.

The self-same moment I could pray;
And from my neck so free
The Albatross fell off, and sank   290
Like lead into the sea.

PART THE FIFTH

Oh sleep! it is a gentle thing,
Beloved from pole to pole!
To Mary Queen the praise be given!
She sent the gentle sleep from Heaven,
That slid into my soul.

The silly buckets on the deck,
That had so long remained,
I dreamt that they were filled with dew;
And when I awoke, it rained.   300

My lips were wet, my throat was cold,
My garments all were dank;
Sure I had drunken in my dreams,
And still my body drank.

I moved, and could not feel my limbs:
I was so light—almost
I thought that I had died in sleep,
And was a blessèd ghost.

And soon I heard a roaring wind:
It did not come anear;   310
But with its sound it shook the sails,
That were so thin and sere.

The upper air burst into life!
And a hundred fire-flags sheen,
To and fro they were hurried about!
And to and fro, and in and out,
The wan stars danced between.

And the coming wind did roar more loud,
And the sails did sigh like sedge;
And the rain poured down from one black cloud;
The Moon was at its edge.   321

The thick black cloud was cleft, and still
The Moon was at its side:
Like waters shot from some high crag,
The lightning fell with never a jag,
A river steep and wide.

The loud wind never reached the ship,
Yet now the ship moved on!
Beneath the lightning and the Moon
The dead men gave a groan.   330

They groaned, they stirred, they all uprose,
Nor spake, nor moved their eyes;
It had been strange, even in a dream,
To have seen those dead men rise.

The helmsman steered, the ship moved on;
Yet never a breeze up-blew;

The mariners all 'gan work the ropes,
Where they were wont to do;
They raised their limbs like lifeless tools—
We were a ghastly crew.   340

The body of my brother's son
Stood by me, knee to knee:
The body and I pulled at one rope,
But he said nought to me."

"I fear thee, ancient Mariner!"
"Be calm, thou Wedding-Guest!

But not by the souls of the men, nor by dæmons of earth or middle air, but by a blessed troop of angelic spirits, sent down by the invocation of the guardian saint.

'Twas not those souls that fled in pain,
Which to their corses came again,
But a troop of spirits blest:

For when it dawned—they dropped their arms,
And clustered round the mast;   351
Sweet sounds rose slowly through their mouths,
And from their bodies passed.

Around, around, flew each sweet sound,
Then darted to the Sun;
Slowly the sounds came back again,
Now mixed, now one by one.

Sometimes a-dropping from the sky
I heard the sky-lark sing;
Sometimes all little birds that are,   360
How they seemed to fill the sea and air
With their sweet jargoning!

And now 'twas like all instruments,
Now like a lonely flute;
And now it is an angel's song,
That makes the Heavens be mute.

It ceased; yet still the sails made on
A pleasant noise till noon,
A noise like of a hidden brook
In the leafy month of June,   370
That to the sleeping woods all night
Singeth a quiet tune.

Till noon we quietly sailed on,
Yet never a breeze did breathe:
Slowly and smoothly went the ship,
Moved onward from beneath.

The lonesome Spirit from the south pole carries on the ship as far as the Line, in obedience to the angelic troop, but still requireth vengeance.

Under the keel nine fathom deep,
From the land of mist and snow,
The spirit slid: and it was he
That made the ship to go.   380
The sails at noon left off their tune,
And the ship stood still also.

The Sun, right up above the mast,
Had fixed her to the ocean:
But in a minute she 'gan stir,
With a short uneasy motion—
Backwards and forwards half her length
With a short uneasy motion.

Then like a pawing horse let go,
She made a sudden bound: 390
It flung the blood into my head,
And I fell down in a swound.

The Polar Spirit's fellow-dæmons, the invisible inhabitants of the element, take part in his wrong; and two of them relate, one to the other, that penance long and heavy for the ancient Mariner hath been accorded to the Polar Spirit, who returneth southward.

How long in that same fit I lay,
I have not to declare;
But ere my living life returned,
I heard and in my soul discerned
Two voices in the air.

'Is it he?' quoth one, 'Is this the man?
By him who died on cross,
With his cruel bow he laid full low   400
The harmless Albatross.

The spirit who bideth by himself
In the land of mist and snow,
He loved the bird that loved the man
Who shot him with his bow.'

The other was a softer voice,
As soft as honey-dew:
Quoth he, 'The man hath penance done,
And penance more will do.'

PART THE SIXTH

FIRST VOICE

'But tell me, tell me! speak again,   410
Thy soft response renewing—
What makes that ship drive on so fast?
What is the ocean doing?'

SECOND VOICE

'Still as a slave before his lord,
The ocean hath no blast;
His great bright eye most silently
Up to the Moon is cast—

If he may know which way to go;
For she guides him smooth or grim.
See, brother, see! how graciously   420
She looketh down on him.'

FIRST VOICE

The Mariner hath been cast into a trance; for the angelic power causeth the vessel to drive northward faster than human life could endure.

'But why drives on that ship so fast,
Without or wave or wind?'

SECOND VOICE

'The air is cut away before,
And closes from behind.

Fly, brother, fly! more high, more high!
Or we shall be belated:
For slow and slow that ship will go,
When the Mariner's trance is abated.'

The supernatural motion is retarded; the Mariner awakes, and his penance begins anew.

I woke, and we were sailing on   430
As in a gentle weather:
'Twas night, calm night, the Moon was high;
The dead men stood together.

All stood together on the deck,
For a charnel-dungeon fitter:
All fixed on me their stony eyes,
That in the Moon did glitter.

The pang, the curse, with which they died,
Had never passed away:
I could not draw my eyes from theirs,   440
Nor turn them up to pray.

The curse is finally expiated.

And now this spell was snapt: once more
I viewed the ocean green,
And looked far forth, yet little saw
Of what had else been seen—

Like one, that on a lonesome road
Doth walk in fear and dread,

And having once turned round walks on
And turns no more his head;
Because he knows, a frightful fiend   450
Doth close behind him tread.

But soon there breathed a wind on me,
Nor sound nor motion made:
Its path was not upon the sea,
In ripple or in shade.

It raised my hair, it fanned my cheek
Like a meadow-gale of spring—
It mingled strangely with my fears,
Yet it felt like a welcoming.

Swiftly, swiftly flew the ship   460
Yet she sailed softly too:
Sweetly, sweetly blew the breeze—
On me alone it blew.

And the ancient Mariner beholdeth his native country. Oh! dream of joy! is this indeed
The light-house top I see?
Is this the hill? is this the kirk?
Is this mine own countree?

We drifted o'er the harbor-bar,
And I with sobs did pray—
O let me be awake, my God!   470
Or let me sleep alway.

The harbor-bay was clear as glass,
So smoothly it was strewn!
And on the bay the moonlight lay,
And the shadow of the Moon.

The rock shone bright, the kirk no less,
That stands above the rock:
The moonlight steeped in silentness
The steady weathercock.

The angelic spirits leave the dead bodies, And the bay was white with silent light   480
Till rising from the same,
Full many shapes, that shadows were,
In crimson colors came.

And appear in their own forms of light. A little distance from the prow
Those crimson shadows were:
I turned my eyes upon the deck—
Oh, Christ! what saw I there!

Each corse lay flat, lifeless and flat,
And, by the holy rood!
A man all light, a seraph-man,   490
On every corse there stood.

This seraph-band, each waved his hand:
It was a heavenly sight!
They stood as signals to the land,
Each one a lovely light;

This seraph-band, each waved his hand,
No voice did they impart—
No voice; but oh! the silence sank
Like music on my heart.

But soon I heard the dash of oars,   500
I heard the Pilot's cheer;
My head was turned perforce away,
And I saw a boat appear.

The Pilot, and the Pilot's boy,
I heard them coming fast:
Dear Lord in Heaven! it was a joy
The dead men could not blast.

I saw a third—I heard his voice:
It is the Hermit good!
He singeth loud his godly hymns   510
That he makes in the wood.
He'll shrieve my soul, he'll wash away
The Albatross's blood.

PART THE SEVENTH

The Hermit of the Wood   This Hermit good lives in that wood
Which slopes down to the sea.
How loudly his sweet voice he rears!
He loves to talk with marineers
That come from a far countree.

He kneels at morn, and noon, and eve—
He hath a cushion plump: 520
It is the moss that wholly hides
The rotted old oak-stump.

The skiff-boat neared: I heard them talk,
'Why this is strange, I trow!
Where are those lights so many and fair,
That signal made but now?'

'Strange, by my faith!' the Hermit said—
'And they answered not our cheer!
The planks looked warped! and see those sails
How thin they are and sere!   530
I never saw aught like to them,
Unless perchance it were

Brown skeletons of leaves that lag
My forest-brook along;
When the ivy-tod is heavy with snow,
And the owlet whoops to the wolf below,
That eats the she-wolf's young.'

'Dear Lord! it hath a fiendish look—
(The Pilot made reply)
I am a-feared'—'Push on, push on!'   540
Said the Hermit cheerily.

The boat came closer to the ship,
But I nor spake nor stirred;
The boat came close beneath the ship,
And straight a sound was heard.

Under the water it rumbled on,
Still louder and more dread:
It reached the ship, it split the bay;
The ship went down like lead.

Stunned by that loud and dreadful sound, 550
Which sky and ocean smote,
Like one that hath been seven days drowned
My body lay afloat;
But swift as dreams, myself I found
Within the Pilot's boat.

Upon the whirl, where sank the ship,
The boat spun round and round;
And all was still, save that the hill
Was telling of the sound.

I moved my lips—the Pilot shrieked   560
And fell down in a fit;
The holy Hermit raised his eyes,
And prayed where he did sit.

I took the oars: the Pilot's boy,
Who now doth crazy go,
Laughed loud and long, and all the while

His eyes went to and fro.
'Ha! ha!' quoth he, 'full plain I see,
The Devil knows how to row.'

And now, all in my own countree,   570
I stood on the firm land!
The Hermit stepped forth from the boat,
And scarcely he could stand.

The ancient Mariner earnestly entreateth the Hermit to shrieve him; and the penance of life falls on him.

'O shrieve me, shrieve me, holy man!'
The Hermit crossed his brow.
'Say quick,' quoth he, 'I bid thee say—
What manner of man art thou?'

Forthwith this frame of mine was wrenched
With a woeful agony,
Which forced me to begin my tale;   580
And then it left me free.

And ever and anon throughout his future life an agony constraineth him to travel from land to land;

Since then, at an uncertain hour,
That agony returns:
And till my ghastly tale is told,
This heart within me burns.

I pass, like night, from land to land;
I have strange power of speech;
That moment that his face I see,
I know the man that must hear me:
To him my tale I teach.   590

What loud uproar bursts from that door!
The wedding-guests are there:
But in the garden-bower the bride
And bride-maids singing are:
And hark the little vesper bell,
Which biddeth me to prayer!

O Wedding-Guest! this soul hath been
Alone on a wide wide sea:
So lonely 'twas, that God himself
Scarce seemèd there to be.   600

O sweeter than the marriage-feast,
'Tis sweeter far to me,
To walk together to the kirk
With a goodly company!—

To walk together to the kirk,
And all together pray,

While each to his great Father bends,
Old men, and babes, and loving friends,
And youths and maidens gay!

Farewell, farewell! but this I tell   610
To thee, thou Wedding-Guest!
He prayeth well, who loveth well
Both man and bird and beast.

And to teach, by his own example, love and reverence to all things that God made and loveth.

He prayeth best, who loveth best
All things both great and small;
For the dear God who loveth us,
He made and loveth all."

The Mariner, whose eye is bright,
Whose beard with age is hoar,
Is gone: and now the Wedding-Guest   620
Turned from the bridegroom's door.

He went like one that hath been stunned,
And is of sense forlorn:
A sadder and a wiser man,
He rose the morrow morn.

201.   FROST AT MIDNIGHT

The frost performs its secret ministry,
Unhelped by any wind. The owlet's cry
Came loud—and hark, again! loud as before.
The inmates of my cottage, all at rest,
Have left me to that solitude, which suits
Abstruser musings: save that at my side
My cradled infant slumbers peacefully.
'Tis calm indeed! so calm, that it disturbs
And vexes meditation with its strange
And extreme silentness. Sea, hill, and wood,   10
This populous village! Sea, and hill, and wood,
With all the numberless goings-on of life,
Inaudible as dreams! the thin blue flame
Lies on my low-burnt fire, and quivers not;
Only that film, which fluttered on the grate,
Still flutters there, the sole unquiet thing.
Methinks, its motion in this hush of nature
Gives it dim sympathies with me who live,
Making it a companionable form,

Whose puny flaps and freaks the idling spirit 20
By its own moods interprets, everywhere
Echo or mirror seeking of itself,
And makes a toy of thought.

                      But O! how oft,
How oft, at school, with most believing mind,
Presageful, have I gazed upon the bars,
To watch that fluttering *stranger!* and as oft
With unclosed lids, already had I dreamt
Of my sweet birth-place, and the old church-tower,
Whose bells, the poor man's only music, rang
From morn to evening, all the hot Fair-day, 30
So sweetly, that they stirred and haunted me
With a wild pleasure, falling on mine ear
Most like articulate sounds of things to come!
So gazed I, till the soothing things, I dreamt,
Lulled me to sleep, and sleep prolonged my dreams!
And so I brooded all the following morn,
Awed by the stern preceptor's face, mine eye
Fixed with mock study on my swimming book:
Save if the door half opened, and I snatched
A hasty glance, and still my heart leaped up, 40
For still I hoped to see the *stranger's* face,
Townsman, or aunt, or sister more beloved,
My playmate when we both were clothed alike!

  Dear babe, that sleepest cradled by my side,
Whose gentle breathings, heard in this deep calm,
Fill up the interspersèd vacancies
And momentary pauses of the thought!
My babe so beautiful! it thrills my heart
With tender gladness, thus to look at thee,
And think that thou shalt learn far other lore, 50
And in far other scenes! For I was reared
In the great city, pent 'mid cloisters dim,
And saw nought lovely but the sky and stars.
But *thou,* my babe! shalt wander like a breeze
By lakes and sandy shores, beneath the crags
Of ancient mountain, and beneath the clouds,
Which image in their bulk both lakes and shores
And mountain crags: so shalt thou see and hear

The lovely shapes and sounds intelligible
Of that eternal language, which thy God   60
Utters, who from eternity doth teach
Himself in all, and all things in himself.
Great universal Teacher! he shall mould
Thy spirit, and by giving make it ask.

    Therefore all seasons shall be sweet to thee,
Whether the summer clothe the general earth
With greenness, or the redbreast sit and sing
Betwixt the tufts of snow on the bare branch
Of mossy apple-tree, while the nigh thatch
Smokes in the sun-thaw; whether the eave-drops fall   70
Heard only in the trances of the blast,
Or if the secret ministry of frost
Shall hang them up in silent icicles,
Quietly shining to the quiet moon.

202.   KUBLA KHAN: OR, A VISION IN A DREAM

In Xanadu did Kubla Khan
A stately pleasure-dome decree:
Where Alph, the sacred river, ran
Through caverns measureless to man
   Down to a sunless sea.
So twice five miles of fertile ground
With walls and towers were girdled round:
And there were gardens bright with sinuous rills,
Where blossomed many an incense-bearing tree;
And here were forests ancient as the hills,   10
Enfolding sunny spots of greenery.

But oh! that deep romantic chasm which slanted
Down the green hill athwart a cedarn cover!
A savage place! as holy and enchanted
As e'er beneath a waning moon was haunted
By woman wailing for her demon-lover!
And from this chasm, with ceaseless turmoil seething,
As if this earth in fast thick pants were breathing,
A mighty fountain momently was forced:
Amid whose swift half-intermitted burst   20
Huge fragments vaulted like rebounding hail,
Or chaffy grain beneath the thresher's flail:

And 'mid these dancing rocks at once and ever
It flung up momently the sacred river.
Five miles meandering with a mazy motion
Through wood and dale the sacred river ran,
Then reached the caverns measureless to man,
And sank in tumult to a lifeless ocean:
And 'mid this tumult Kubla heard from far
Ancestral voices prophesying war!   30

    The shadow of the dome of pleasure
    Floated midway on the waves;
    Where was heard the mingled measure
    From the fountain and the caves.
It was a miracle of rare device,
A sunny pleasure-dome with caves of ice!

    A damsel with a dulcimer
    In a vision once I saw:
    It was an Abyssinian maid,
    And on her dulcimer she played,   40
    Singing of Mount Abora.
    Could I revive within me
    Her symphony and song,
    To such a deep delight 'twould win me,
That with music loud and long,
I would build that dome in air,
That sunny dome! those caves of ice!
And all who heard should see them there,
And all should cry, Beware! Beware!
His flashing eyes, his floating hair!   50
Weave a circle round him thrice,
And close your eyes with holy dread,
For he on honey-dew hath fed,
And drunk the milk of Paradise.

203.   DEJECTION: AN ODE

        Late, late yestreen I saw the new Moon,
        With the old Moon in her arms;
        And I fear, I fear, my Master dear!
        We shall have a deadly storm.
            Ballad of Sir Patrick Spence

Well! If the bard was weather-wise, who made
  The grand old ballad of *Sir Patrick Spence,*

This night, so tranquil now, will not go hence
Unroused by winds, that ply a busier trade
Than those which mould yon cloud in lazy flakes,
Or the dull sobbing draft, that moans and rakes
Upon the strings of this Æolian lute,
    Which better far were mute.
  For lo! the new-moon winter-bright!
  And overspread with phantom light,   10
  (With swimming phantom light o'erspread
  But rimmed and circled by a silver thread)
I see the old moon in her lap, foretelling
  The coming-on of rain and squally blast.
And oh! that even now the gust were swelling,
  And the slant night-shower driving loud and fast!
Those sounds which oft have raised me, whilst they awed,
    And sent my soul abroad,
Might now perhaps their wonted impulse give,
Might startle this dull pain, and make it move and live! 20

A grief without a pang, void, dark, and drear,
  A stifled, drowsy, unimpassioned grief,
  Which finds no natural outlet, no relief,
    In word, or sigh, or tear—
O Lady! in this wan and heartless mood,
To other thoughts by yonder throstle wooed,
  All this long eve, so balmy and serene,
Have I been gazing on the western sky,
  And its peculiar tint of yellow green:
And still I gaze—and with how blank an eye!   30
And those thin clouds above, in flakes and bars,
That give away their motion to the stars;
Those stars, that glide behind them or between,
Now sparkling, now bedimmed, but always seen:
Yon crescent moon, as fixed as if it grew
In its own cloudless, starless lake of blue;
I see them all so excellently fair,
I see, not feel, how beautiful they are!

    My genial spirits fail;
    And what can these avail   40
To lift the smothering weight from off my breast?
    It were a vain endeavour,

    Though I should gaze forever
On that green light that lingers in the west:
I may not hope from outward forms to win
The passion and the life, whose fountains are within.

O Lady! we receive but what we give,
And in our life alone does Nature live:
Ours is her wedding garment, ours her shroud!
    And would we aught behold, of higher worth,   50
Than that inanimate cold world allowed
To the poor loveless ever-anxious crowd,
    Ah! from the soul itself must issue forth
A light, a glory, a fair luminous cloud
    Enveloping the earth—
And from the soul itself must there be sent
    A sweet and potent voice, of its own birth,
Of all sweet sounds the life and element!

O pure of heart! thou need'st not ask of me
What this strong music in the soul may be!   60
What, and wherein it doth exist,
This light, this glory, this fair luminous mist,
This beautiful and beauty-making power.
    Joy, virtuous Lady! Joy that ne'er was given,
Save to the pure, and in their purest hour,
Life, and life's effluence, cloud at once and shower,
Joy, Lady! is the spirit and the power,
Which wedding Nature to us gives in dower
    A new earth and new heaven,
Undreamt of by the sensual and the proud—   70
Joy is the sweet voice, joy the luminous cloud—
    We in ourselves rejoice!
And thence flows all that charms or ear or sight,
    All melodies the echoes of that voice,
All colours a suffusion from that light.

There was a time when, though my path was rough,
    This joy within me dallied with distress,
And all misfortunes were but as the stuff
    Whence Fancy made me dreams of happiness:
For hope grew round me, like the twining vine,   80
And fruits, and foliage, not my own, seemed mine.
But now afflictions bow me down to earth:

Nor care I that they rob me of my mirth;
  But oh! each visitation
Suspends what nature gave me at my birth,
  My shaping spirit of Imagination.
For not to think of what I needs must feel,
  But to be still and patient, all I can;
And haply by abstruse research to steal
  From my own nature all the natural man—   90
  This was my sole resource, my only plan:
Till that which suits a part infects the whole,
And now is almost grown the habit of my soul.

Hence, viper thoughts, that coil around my mind,
    Reality's dark dream!
I turn from you, and listen to the wind,
  Which long has raved unnoticed. What a scream
Of agony by torture lengthened out
That lute sent forth! Thou Wind, that rav'st without,
Bare crag, or mountain-tairn, or blasted tree,   100
Or pine-grove whither woodman never clomb,
Or lonely house, long held the witches' home,
  Methinks were fitter instruments for thee,
Mad lutanist! who in this month of showers,
Of dark-brown gardens, and of peeping flowers,
Mak'st devils' yule, with worse than wintry song,
The blossoms, buds, and timorous leaves among.
  Thou Actor perfect in all tragic sounds!
Thou mighty Poet, e'en to frenzy bold!
    What tell'st thou now about?   110
    'Tis of the rushing of an host in rout,
With groans, of trampled men, with smarting wounds—
At once they groan with pain, and shudder with the cold!
But hush! there is a pause of deepest silence!
And all that noise, as of a rushing crowd,
With groans, and tremulous shudderings—all is over—
  It tells another tale, with sounds less deep and loud!
    A tale of less affright,
    And tempered with delight,
As Otway's self had framed the tender lay,—   120
    'Tis of a little child
    Upon a lonesome wild,
Not far from home, but she hath lost her way:

And now moans low in bitter grief and fear,
And now screams loud, and hopes to make her mother hear.

'Tis midnight, but small thoughts have I of sleep:
Full seldom may my friend such vigils keep!
Visit her, gentle Sleep! with wings of healing,
 And may this storm be but a mountain-birth,
May all the stars hang bright above her dwelling,   130
 Silent as though they watched the sleeping earth!
  With light heart may she rise,
  Gay fancy, cheerful eyes,
Joy lift her spirit, joy attune her voice;
To her may all things live, from pole to pole,
Their life the eddying of her living soul!
 O simple spirit, guided from above,
Dear Lady! friend devoutest of my choice,
Thus mayest thou ever, evermore rejoice.

CHARLES LAMB (1775–1834)

204.   HESTER

When maidens such as Hester die,
Their place ye may not well supply,
Though ye among a thousand try,
  With vain endeavour.

A month or more hath she been dead,
Yet cannot I by force be led
To think upon the wormy bed,
  And her together.

A springy motion in her gait,
A rising step, did indicate   10
Of pride and joy no common rate,
  That flushed her spirit.

I know not by what name beside
I shall it call:—if 'twas not pride,
It was a joy to that allied,
  She did inherit.

Her parents held the Quaker rule
Which doth the human feeling cool,

But she was trained in Nature's school,
　　Nature had blest her.　　　　　　　　　　20

A waking eye, a prying mind,
A heart that stirs, is hard to bind,
A hawk's keen sight ye cannot blind,
　　Ye could not Hester.

My sprightly neighbour, gone before
To that unknown and silent shore,
Shall we not meet, as heretofore,
　　Some summer morning,

When from thy cheerful eyes a ray
Hath struck a bliss upon the day,　　　　　30
A bliss that would not go away,
　　A sweet fore-warning?

SIR WALTER SCOTT (1771–1832)

205.　　　　　　　　LOCHINVAR

Oh! Young Lochinvar is come out of the west,
Through all the wide Border his steed was the best;
And save his good broadsword he weapons had none,
He rode all unarmed and he rode all alone.
So faithful in love and so dauntless in war,
There never was knight like the young Lochinvar.

He stayed not for brake and he stopped not for stone,
He swam the Eske river where ford there was none;
But ere he alighted at Netherby gate
The bride had consented, the gallant came late:　　　10
For a laggard in love and a dastard in war
Was to wed the fair Ellen of brave Lochinvar.

So boldly he entered the Netherby Hall,
Among bridesmen, and kinsmen, and brothers, and all:
Then spoke the bride's father, his hand on his sword,—
For the poor craven bridegroom said never a word,—
"Oh! come ye in peace here, or come ye in war,
Or to dance at our bridal, young Lord Lochinvar?"—

"I long wooed your daughter, my suit you denied;
Love swells like the Solway, but ebbs like its tide—　　　20
And now am I come, with this lost love of mine,

To lead but one measure, drink one cup of wine.
There are maidens in Scotland more lovely by far,
That would gladly be bride to the young Lochinvar."

The bride kissed the goblet; the knight took it up,
He quaffed off the wine, and he threw down the cup.
She looked down to blush, and she looked up to sigh,
With a smile on her lips and a tear in her eye.
He took her soft hand ere her mother could bar,—
"Now tread we a measure!" said young Lochinvar.   30

So stately his form, and so lovely her face,
That never a hall such a galliard did grace;
While her mother did fret, and her father did fume,
And the bridegroom stood dangling his bonnet and plume;
And the bride-maidens whispered, " 'T were better by far
To have matched our fair cousin with young Lochinvar."

One touch of her hand and one word in her ear,
When they reached the hall-door, and the charger stood near;
So light to the croupe the fair lady he swung,
So light to the saddle before her he sprung!   40
"She is won! we are gone, over bank, bush, and scaur;
They'll have fleet steeds that follow," quoth young Lochinvar.

There was mounting 'mong Græmes of the Netherby clan;
Forsters, Fenwicks, and Musgraves, they rode and they ran:
There was racing and chasing on Cannobie Lee,
But the lost bride of Netherby ne'er did they see.
So daring in love and so dauntless in war,
Have ye e'er heard of gallant like young Lochinvar?

206.   THE ROVER'S FAREWELL

"A weary lot is thine, fair maid,
    A weary lot is thine!
To pull the thorn thy brow to braid,
    And press the rue for wine!
A lightsome eye, a soldier's mien,
    A feather of the blue,
A doublet of the Lincoln green,—
    No more of me you knew,
                    My love!
No more of me you knew.   10

"This morn is merry June, I trow,
　　The rose is budding fain;
But she shall bloom in winter snow
　　Ere we two meet again."
He turned his charger as he spake
　　Upon the river shore,
He gave his bridle-reins a shake,
　　Said, "Adieu for evermore,
　　　　　　　　My love!
And adieu for evermore."   20

207.　　　　　　PROUD MAISIE

Proud Maisie is in the wood
　　Walking so early;
Sweet Robin sits on the bush,
　　Singing so rarely.

"Tell me, thou bonny bird,
　　When shall I marry me?"—
"When six braw gentlemen
　　Kirkward shall carry ye."

"Who makes the bridal bed,
　　Birdie, say truly?"—   10
"The gray-headed sexton
　　That delves the grave duly.

"The glow-worm o'er grave and stone
　　Shall light thee steady,
The owl from the steeple sing,
　　'Welcome, proud lady.'"

WALTER SAVAGE LANDOR (1775–1864)

208.　　　　　　ROSE AYLMER

Ah, what avails the sceptred race,
　　Ah, what the form divine!
What every virtue, every grace!
　　Rose Aylmer, all were thine.

Rose Aylmer, whom these wakeful eyes
　　May weep, but never see,

A night of memories and of sighs
I consecrate to thee.

209.   PAST RUINED ILION HELEN LIVES

Past ruined Ilion Helen lives,
  Alcestis rises from the shades;
Verse calls them forth; 'tis verse that gives
  Immortal youth to mortal maids.

Soon shall oblivion's deepening veil
  Hide all the peopled hills you see,
The gay, the proud, while lovers hail
  In distant ages you and me.

The tear for fading beauty check,
  For passing glory cease to sigh;   10
One form shall rise above the wreck,
  One name, Ianthe, shall not die.

210.   ON HIS SEVENTY-FIFTH BIRTHDAY

I strove with none; for none was worth my strife,
  Nature I loved, and next to Nature, Art;
I warmed both hands before the fire of life,
  It sinks, and I am ready to depart.

THOMAS MOORE (1779–1852)

211.   LET ERIN REMEMBER THE DAYS OF OLD

Let Erin remember the days of old,
  Ere her faithless sons betrayed her;
When Malachi wore the collar of gold,
  Which he won from her proud invader,
When her kings, with standard of green unfurled
  Led the Red-Branch Knights to danger;—
Ere the emerald gem of the western world
  Was set in the crown of a stranger.

On Lough Neagh's bank as the fisherman strays,
  When the clear cold eve's declining,   10
He sees the round towers of other days
  In the wave beneath him shining;

Thus shall memory often, in dreams sublime,
 Catch a glimpse of the days that are over;
Thus, sighing, look thro' the waves of time
 For the long-faded glories they cover.

212.   SCOTCH AIR

Oft, in the stilly night,
 Ere Slumber's chain has bound me,
Fond Memory brings the light
 Of other days around me;
  The smiles, the tears,
  Of boyhood's years,
 The words of love then spoken;
  The eyes that shone,
  Now dimmed and gone,
 The cheerful hearts now broken!   10
Thus, in the stilly night,
 Ere Slumber's chain has bound me,
Sad Memory brings the light
 Of other days around me.

When I remember all
 The friends, so linked together,
I've seen around me fall,
 Like leaves in wintry weather;
  I feel like one
  Who treads alone   20
 Some banquet hall deserted,
  Whose lights are fled,
  Whose garlands dead,
 And all but he departed!
Thus, in the stilly night,
 Ere Slumber's chain has bound me,
Sad Memory brings the light
 Of other days around me.

LORD BYRON (1788–1824)

213.   LINES TO MR. HODGSON

Huzza! Hodgson, we are going
 Our embargo's off at last;
Favourable breezes blowing
 Bend the canvass o'er the mast.

From aloft the signal's streaming,
  Hark! the farewell gun is fired;
Women screeching, tars blaspheming,
  Tell us that our time's expired.
      Here's a rascal
      Come to task all,
  Prying from the custom-house,
      Trunks unpacking,
      Cases cracking,
  Not a corner for a mouse
'Scapes unsearch'd amid the racket,
Ere we sail on board the Packet.

Now our boatmen quit their mooring,
  And all hands must ply the oar;
Baggage from the quay is lowering,
  We're impatient, push from shore.
"Have a care! that case holds liquor—
  Stop the boat—I'm sick—oh Lord!"
"Sick, ma'am, damme, you'll be sicker
Ere you've been an hour on board."
      Thus are screaming
      Men and women,
Gemmen, ladies, servants, Jacks;
      Here entangling,
      All are wrangling,
  Stuck together close as wax.—
Such the general noise and racket,
Ere we reach the Lisbon Packet.

Now we've reach'd her, lo! the captain,
  Gallant Kidd, commands the crew;
Passengers their berths are clapt in,
  Some to grumble, some to spew.
"Heyday! call you that a cabin?
  Why 'tis hardly three feet square:
Not enough to stow Queen Mab in—
  Who the deuce can harbour there?"
      "Who, sir? plenty—
      Nobles twenty
  Did at once my vessel fill."—
      Did they? Jesus,
      How you squeeze us!

10

20

30

40

Would to God they did so still:
Then I'd scape the heat and racket
Of the good ship, Lisbon Packet."

Fletcher! Murray! Bob! where are you?
    Stretch'd along the deck like logs—   50
Bear a hand, you jolly tar, you!
    Here's a rope's end for the dogs.
Hobhouse muttering fearful curses,
    As the hatchway down he rolls,
Now his breakfast, now his verses,
    Vomits forth—and damns our souls.
        "Here's a stanza
        On Braganza—
Help!"—"A couplet?"—"No, a cup
        Of warm water—"   60
        What's the matter?"
    "Zounds! my liver's coming up;
I shall not survive the racket
Of this brutal Lisbon Packet."

Now at length we're off for Turkey,
    Lord knows when we shall come back!
Breezes foul and tempests murky
    May unship us in a crack.
But, since life at most a jest is,
    As philosophers allow,   70
Still to laugh by far the best is,
    Then laugh on—as I do now.
        Laugh at all things,
        Great and small things,
    Sick or well, at sea or shore;
        While we're quaffing,
        Let's have laughing—
Who the devil cares for more?—
Some good wine! and who would lack it,
Ev'n on board the Lisbon Packet?   80

214.   WRITTEN AFTER SWIMMING FROM
                SESTOS TO ABYDOS

If, in the month of dark December,
    Leander, who was nightly wont

(What maid will not the tale remember?)
   To cross thy stream, broad Hellespont!

If, when the wintry tempest roar'd,
   He sped to Hero, nothing loth,
And thus of old thy current pour'd,
   Fair Venus! how I pity both!

For *me,* degenerate modern wretch,
   Though in the genial month of May,   10
My dripping limbs I faintly stretch,
   And think I've done a feat to-day.

But since he cross'd the rapid tide,
   According to the doubtful story,
To woo,—and—Lord knows what beside,
   And swam for Love, as I for Glory;

'Twere hard to say who fared the best:
   Sad mortals! thus the gods still plague you!
He lost his labour, I my jest;
   For he was drown'd, and I've the ague.   20

215.   THE DESTRUCTION OF SENNACHERIB

I

The Assyrian came down like the wolf on the fold,
And his cohorts were gleaming in purple and gold;
And the sheen of their spears was like stars on the sea,
When the blue wave rolls nightly on deep Galilee.

II

Like the leaves of the forest when Summer is green,
That host with their banners at sunset were seen:
Like the leaves of the forest when Autumn hath blown,
That host on the morrow lay wither'd and strown.

III

For the Angel of Death spread his wings on the blast,
And breathed in the face of the foe as he pass'd;   10
And the eyes of the sleepers wax'd deadly and chill,
And their hearts but once heaved, and for ever grew still!

IV

And there lay the steed with his nostril all wide,
But through it there roll'd not the breath of his pride;
And the foam of his gasping lay white on the turf,
And cold as the spray of the rock-beating surf.

V

And there lay the rider distorted and pale,
With the dew on his brow, and the rust on his mail:
And the tents were all silent, the banners alone,
The lances unlifted, the trumpet unblown.   20

VI

And the widows of Ashur are loud in their wail,
And the idols are broke in the temple of Baal;
And the might of the Gentile, unsmote by the sword,
Hath melted like snow in the glance of the Lord!

216.   STANZAS FOR MUSIC

There be none of Beauty's daughters
    With a magic like thee;
And like music on the waters
    Is thy sweet voice to me:
When, as if its sound were causing
The charmed ocean's pausing,
The waves lie still and gleaming,
And the lull'd winds seem dreaming:

And the midnight moon is weaving
    Her bright chain o'er the deep;   10
Whose breast is gently heaving,
    As an infant's asleep:
So the spirit bows before thee,
To listen and adore thee;
With a full but soft emotion,
Like the swell of Summer's ocean.

PERCY BYSSHE SHELLEY (1792–1822)

217.   HYMN TO INTELLECTUAL BEAUTY

I

The awful shadow of some unseen Power
  Floats though unseen amongst us,—visiting
  This various world with an inconstant wing
As summer winds that creep from flower to flower,—
Like moonbeams that behind some piny mountain shower.

    It visits with inconstant glance
    Each human heart and countenance;
Like hues and harmonies of evening,—
    Like clouds in starlight widely spread,—
    Like memory of music fled,—   10
    Like aught that for its grace may be
Dear, and yet dearer for its mystery.

II

Spirit of BEAUTY, that dost consecrate
  With thine own hues all thou dost shine upon
  Of human thought or form,—where art thou gone?
Why dost thou pass away and leave our state,
This dim vast vale of tears, vacant and desolate?
    Ask why the sunlight not for ever
    Weaves rainbows o'er yon mountain river,
Why aught should fail and fade that once is shown,   20
    Why fear and dream and death and birth
    Cast on the daylight of this earth
    Such gloom,—why man has such a scope
For love and hate, despondency and hope?

III

No voice from some sublimer world hath ever
  To sage or poet these responses given—
  Therefore the names of Demon, Ghost, and Heaven,
Remain the records of their vain endeavour,
Frail spells—whose uttered charm might not avail to sever,
    From all we hear and all we see,   30
    Doubt, chance, and mutability.

Thy light alone—like mist o'er mountains driven,
　　Or music by the night wind sent,
　　Through strings of some still instrument,
　　Or moonlight on a midnight stream,
Gives grace and truth to life's unquiet dream.

IV

Love, Hope, and Self-esteem, like clouds depart
　　And come, for some uncertain moments lent.
　　Man were immortal, and omnipotent,
Didst thou, unknown and awful as thou art,   40
Keep with thy glorious train firm state within his heart.
　　　Thou messenger of sympathies,
　　　That wax and wane in lovers' eyes—
Thou—that to human thought art nourishment,
　　　Like darkness to a dying flame!
　　　Depart not as thy shadow came,
　　　Depart not—lest the grave should be,
Like life and fear, a dark reality.

V

While yet a boy I sought for ghosts, and sped
　　Through many a listening chamber, cave and ruin,   50
　　And starlight wood, with fearful steps pursuing
Hopes of high talk with the departed dead,
I called on poisonous names with which our youth is fed;
　　　I was not heard—I saw them not—
　　　When musing deeply on the lot
Of life, at the sweet time when winds are wooing
　　　All vital things that wake to bring
　　　News of birds and blossoming,—
　　　Sudden, thy shadow fell on me;
I shrieked, and clasped my hands in ecstasy!   60

VI

I vowed that I would dedicate my powers
　　To thee and thine—have I not kept the vow?
　　With beating heart and streaming eyes, even now
I call the phantoms of a thousand hours
Each from his voiceless grave: they have in visioned bowers
　　　Of studious zeal or love's delight
　　　Outwatched with me the envious night—

They know that never joy illumined my brow
   Unlinked with hope that thou wouldst free
   This world from its dark slavery,   70
    That thou—O awful Loveliness,
Wouldst give whate'er these words cannot express.

VII

The day becomes more solemn and serene
   When noon is past—there is a harmony
   In autumn, and a luster in its sky,
Which through the summer is not heard or seen,
As if it could not be, as if it had not been!
    Thus let thy power, which like the truth
    Of nature on my passive youth
Descended, to my onward life supply   80
    Its calm—to one who worships thee,
    And every form containing thee,
    Whom, Spirit fair, thy spells did bind
To fear himself, and love all human kind.

218.   OZYMANDIAS

    I met a traveller from an antique land
    Who said: Two vast and trunkless legs of stone
    Stand in the desert. Near them, on the sand,
    Half sunk, a shattered visage lies, whose frown,
    And wrinkled lip, and sneer of cold command,
    Tell that its sculptor well those passions read
    Which yet survive, stamped on these lifeless things,
    The hand that mocked them, and the heart that fed:
    And on the pedestal these words appear:
    "My name is Ozymandias, king of kings: 10
    Look on my works, ye Mighty, and despair!'
    Nothing beside remains. Round the decay
    Of that colossal wreck, boundless and bare
    The lone and level sands stretch far away.

219.   ODE TO THE WEST WIND

I

O, wild West Wind, thou breath of Autumn's being,
Thou, from whose unseen presence the leaves dead
Are driven, like ghosts from an enchanter fleeing,

Yellow, and black, and pale, and hectic red,
Pestilence-stricken multitudes: O thou,
Who chariotest to their dark wintry bed

The wingèd seeds, where they lie cold and low,
Each like a corpse within its grave, until
Thine azure sister of the Spring shall blow

Her clarion o'er the dreaming earth, and fill   10
(Driving sweet buds like flocks to feed in air)
With living hues and odors plain and hill:

Wild Spirit, which art moving everywhere;
Destroyer and preserver; hear, O, hear!

II

Thou on whose stream, 'mid the steep sky's commotion,
Loose clouds like earth's decaying leaves are shed,
Shook from the tangled boughs of Heaven and Ocean,

Angels of rain and lightning: there are spread
On the blue surface of thine airy surge,
Like the bright hair uplifted from the head   20

Of some fierce Mænad, even from the dim verge
Of the horizon to the zenith's height
The locks of the approaching storm. Thou dirge

Of the dying year, to which this closing night
Will be the dome of a vast sepulchre,
Vaulted with all thy congregated might

Of vapours, from whose solid atmosphere
Black rain, and fire, and hail will burst: O, hear!

III

Thou who didst waken from his summer dreams
The blue Mediterranean, where he lay,   30
Lulled by the coil of his crystalline streams,

Beside a pumice isle in Baiæ's bay,
And saw in sleep old palaces aand towers
Quivering within the wave's intenser day,

All overgrown with azure moss and flowers
So sweet, the sense faints picturing them! Thou
For whose path the Atlantic's level powers

Cleave themselves into chasms, while far below
The sea-blooms and the oozy woods which wear
The sapless foliage of the ocean, know   40

Thy voice, and suddenly grow grey with fear,
And tremble and despoil themselves: O, hear!

IV

If I were a dead leaf thou mightest bear;
If I were a swift cloud to fly with thee;
A wave to pant beneath thy power, and share

The impulse of thy strength, only less free
Than thou, O uncontrollable! If even
I were as in my boyhood, and could be

The comrade of thy wanderings over Heaven,
As then, when to outstrip thy skiey speed   50
Scarce seemed a vision; I would ne'er have striven

As thus with thee in prayer in my sore need,
Oh, lift me as a wave, a leaf, a cloud!
I fall upon the thorns of life! I bleed!

A heavy weight of hours has chained and bowed
One too like thee: tameless, and swift, and proud.

V

Make me thy lyre, even as the forest is:
What if my leaves are falling like its own!
The tumult of thy mighty harmonies

Will take from both a deep, autumnal tone,   60
Sweet though in sadness. Be thou, Spirit fierce,
My spirit! Be thou me, impetuous one!

Drive my dead thoughts over the universe
Like withered leaves to quicken a new birth!
And, by the incantation of this verse,

Scatter, as from an unextinguished hearth
Ashes and sparks, my words among mankind!
Be through my lips to unawakened earth

The trumpet of a prophecy! O, wind,
If Winter comes, can Spring be far behind?   70

220.   THE CLOUD

I bring fresh showers for the thirsting flowers
    From the seas and the streams;
I bear light shade for the leaves when laid
    In their noonday dreams.
From my wings are shaken the dews that waken
    The sweet buds every one,
When rocked to rest on their mother's breast,
    As she dances about the sun.
I wield the flail of the lashing hail,
    And whiten the green plains under,   10
And then again I dissolve it in rain,
    And laugh as I pass in thunder.

I sift the snow on the mountains below,
    And their great pines groan aghast;
And all the night 'tis my pillow white,
    While I sleep in the arms of the blast.
Sublime on the towers of my skiey bowers,
    Lightning my pilot sits;
In a cavern under is fettered the thunder,—
    It struggles and howls at fits;   20
Over earth and ocean, with gentle motion,
    This pilot is guiding me,
Lured by the love of the genii that move
    In the depths of the purple sea;
Over the rills, and the crags, and the hills,
    Over the lakes and the plains,
Wherever he dream, under mountain or stream,
    The Spirit he loves remains;
And I all the while bask in heaven's blue smile,
    Whilst he is dissolving in rains.   30

The sanguine sunrise, with his meteor eyes,
    And his burning plumes outspread,

Leaps on the back of my sailing rack,
    When the morning star shines dead;
As on the jag of a mountain crag,
    Which an earthquake rocks and swings,
An eagle alit one moment may sit
    In the light of its golden wings.
And when sunset may breathe, from the lit sea beneath
    Its ardors of rest and of love   40
And the crimson pall of eve may fall
    From the depth of heaven above,
With wings folded I rest, on mine aëry nest,
    As still as a brooding dove.

That orbèd maiden with white fire laden,
    Whom mortals call the moon,
Glides glimmering o'er my fleece-like floor,
    By the midnight breezes strewn;
And wherever the beat of her unseen feet,
    Which only the angels hear,   50
May have broken the woof of my tent's thin roof,
    The stars peep behind her and peer;
And I laugh to see them whirl and flee,
    Like a swarm of golden bees,
When I widen the rent in my wind-built tent,
    Till the calm rivers, lakes, and seas,
Like strips of the sky fallen through me on high,
    Are each paved with the moon and these.

I bind the sun's throne with a burning zone,
    And the moon's with a girdle of pearl;   60
The volcanoes are dim and the stars reel and swim,
    When the whirlwinds my banner unfurl.
From cape to cape, with a bridge-like shape,
    Over a torrent sea,
Sunbeam-proof, I hang like a roof,—
    The mountains its columns be.
The triumphal arch through which I march
    With hurricane, fire, and snow,
When the powers of the air are chained to my chair,
    Is the million-colored bow;   70
The sphere-fire above its soft colors wove,
    While the moist earth was laughing below.

I am the daughter of earth and water,
    And the nursling of the sky;
I pass through the pores of the ocean and shores;
    I change, but I cannot die.
For after the rain when, with never a stain,
    The pavilion of heaven is bare,
And the winds and sunbeams with their convex gleams
    Build up the blue dome of air,   80
I silently laugh at my own cenotaph,
    And out of the caverns of rain,
Like a child from the womb, like a ghost from the tomb,
    I arise and unbuild it again.

221.   TO NIGHT

I

Swiftly walk o'er the western wave,
    Spirit of Night!
Out of the misty eastern cave,
Where all the long and lone daylight,
Thou wovest dreams of joy and fear,
Which make thee terrible and dear,—
    Swift be thy flight!

II

Wrap thy form in a mantle grey,
    Star-inwrought!
Blind with thine hair the eyes of Day;   10
Kiss her until she be wearied out,
Then wander o'er city, and sea, and land,
Touching all with thine opiate wand—
    Come, long sought!

III

When I arose and saw the dawn,
    I sighed for thee;
When light rode high, and the dew was gone,
And noon lay heavy on flower and tree,
And the weary Day turned to his rest,
Lingering like an unloved guest,   20
    I sighed for thee.

IV

Thy brother Death came, and cried,
     Wouldst thou me?
Thy sweet child Sleep, the filmy-eyed,
Murmured like a noontide bee,
Shall I nestle near thy side?
Wouldst thou me?—And I replied,
     No, not thee!

V

Death will come when thou art dead,
     Soon, too soon—   30
Sleep will come when thou art fled;
Of neither would I ask the boon
I ask of thee, belovèd Night—
Swift be thine approaching flight,
     Come soon, soon!

222.   TO ———

Music, when soft voices die,
Vibrates in the memory;
Odors, when sweet violets sicken,
Live within the sense they quicken.

Rose leaves, when the rose is dead,
Are heaped for the belovèd's bed;
And so thy thoughts, when thou art gone,
Love itself shall slumber on.

223.   TO ———

I

One word is too often profaned
     For me to profane it,
One feeling too falsely disdained
     For thee to disdain it.
One hope is too like despair
     For prudence to smother,
And pity from thee more dear
     Than that from another.

II

I can give not what men call love,
 But wilt thou accept not   10
The worship the heart lifts above
 And the Heavens reject not,—
The desire of the moth for the star,
 Of the night for the morrow,
The devotion to something afar
 From the sphere of our sorrow?

224.   ADONAIS

AN ELEGY ON THE DEATH OF JOHN KEATS

I

I weep for Adonais—he is dead!
O, weep for Adonais! though our tears
Thaw not the frost which binds so dear a head!
And thou, sad Hour, selected from all years
To mourn our loss, rouse thy obscure compeers,
And teach them thine own sorrow, say: "With me
Died Adonais; till the Future dares
Forget the Past, his fate and fame shall be
An echo and a light unto eternity."

II

Where wert thou, mighty Mother, when he lay, 10
When thy Son lay, pierced by the shaft which flies
In darkness? where was lorn Urania
When Adonais died? With veilèd eyes,
'Mid listening Echoes, in her Paradise
She sat, while one, with soft enamoured breath,
Rekindled all the fading melodies,
With which, like flowers that mock the corse beneath,
He had adorned and hid the coming bulk of Death.

III

O, weep for Adonais—he is dead!
Wake, melancholy Mother, wake and weep! 20
Yet wherefore? Quench within their burning bed
Thy fiery tears, and let thy loud heart keep,
Like his, a mute and uncomplaining sleep;

For he is gone, where all things wise and fair
Descend;—oh, dream not that the amorous Deep
Will yet restore him to the vital air;
Death feeds on his mute voice, and laughs at our despair.

IV

Most musical of mourners, weep again!
Lament anew, Urania!—He died,
Who was the Sire of an immortal strain,   30
Blind, old, and lonely, when his country's pride,
The priest, the slave, and the liberticide,
Trampled and mocked with many a loathèd rite
Of lust and blood; he went unterrified,
Into the gulf of death; but his clear Sprite
Yet reigns o'er earth; the third among the sons of light.

V

Most musical of mourners, weep anew!
Not all to that bright station dared to climb;
And happier they their happiness who knew,
Whose tapers yet burn through that night of time   40
In which suns perished; others more sublime,
Struck by the envious wrath of man or god,
Have sunk, extinct in their refulgent prime;
And some yet live, treading the thorny road,
Which leads, through toil and hate, to Fame's serene abode.

VI

But now, thy youngest, dearest one has perished,
The nursling of thy widowhood, who grew,
Like a pale flower by some sad maiden cherished,
And fed with true-love tears, instead of dew;
Most musical of mourners, weep anew!   50
Thy extreme hope, the loveliest and the last,
The bloom, whose petals, nipped before they blew,
Died on the promise of the fruit, is waste;
The broken lily lies—the storm is overpast.

VII

To that high Capital, where kingly Death
Keeps his pale court in beauty and decay,

He came; and bought, with price of purest breath,
A grave among the eternal.—Come away!
Haste, while the vault of blue Italian day
Is yet his fitting charnel-roof! while still   60
He lies, as if in dewy sleep he lay;
Awake him not! surely he takes his fill
Of deep and liquid rest, forgetful of all ill.

VIII

He will awake no more, oh, never more!—
Within the twilight chamber spreads apace,
The shadow of white Death, and at the door
Invisible Corruption waits to trace
His extreme way to her dim dwelling-place;
The eternal Hunger sits, but pity and awe
Soothe her pale rage, nor dares she to deface   70
So fair a prey, till darkness, and the law
Of change, shall o'er his sleep the mortal curtain draw.

IX

O, weep for Adonais!—The quick Dreams,
The passion-wingèd Ministers of thought,
Who were his flocks, whom near the living streams
Of his young spirit he fed, and whom he taught
The love which was its music, wander not,—
Wander no more, from kindling brain to brain,
But droop there, whence they sprung; and mourn their lot
Round the cold heart, where, after their sweet pain,   80
They ne'er will gather strength, or find a home again.

X

And one with trembling hands clasps his cold head,
And fans him with her moonlight wings, and cries;
"Our love, our hope, our sorrow, is not dead;
See, on the silken fringe of his faint eyes,
Like dew upon a sleeping flower, there lies
A tear some Dream has loosened from his brain."
Lost Angel of a ruined Paradise!
She knew not 'twas her own; as with no stain
She faded, like a cloud which had outwept its rain.   90

XI

One from a lucid urn of starry dew
Washed his light limbs as if embalming them;
Another clipped her profuse locks, and threw
The wreath upon him, like an anadem,
Which frozen tears instead of pearls begem;
Another in her wilful grief would break
Her bow and wingèd reeds, as if to stem
A greater loss with one which was more weak;
And dull the barbèd fire against his frozen cheek.

XII

Another Splendour on his mouth alit,   100
That mouth, whence it was wont to draw the breath
Which gave it strength to pierce the guarded wit,
And pass into the panting heart beneath
With lightning and with music: the damp death
Quenched its caress upon his icy lips;
And, as a dying meteor stains a wreath
Of moonlight vapour, which the cold night clips,
It flushed through his pale limbs, and passed to its eclipse.

XIII

And others came . . . Desires and Adorations,
Wingèd Persuasions and veiled Destinies,   110
Splendours, and Glooms, and glimmering Incarnations
Of hopes and fears, and twilight Phantasies;
And Sorrow, with her family of Sighs,
And Pleasure, blind with tears, led by the gleam
Of her own dying smile instead of eyes,
Came in slow pomp;—the moving pomp might seem
Like pageantry of mist on an autumnal stream.

XIV

All he had loved, and moulded into thought,
From shape, and hue, and odour, and sweet sound,
Lamented Adonais. Morning sought   120
Her eastern watch-tower, and her hair unbound,
Wet with the tears which should adorn the ground,
Dimmed the aërial eyes that kindle day;

Afar the melancholy thunder moaned,
Pale Ocean in unquiet slumber lay,
And the wild Winds flew round, sobbing in their dismay.

XV

Lost Echo sits amid the voiceless mountains,
And feeds her grief with his remembered lay,
And will no more reply to winds or fountains,
Or amorous birds perched on the young green spray,   130
Or herdsman's horn, or bell at closing day;
Since she can mimic not his lips, more dear
Than those for whose disdain she pined away
Into a shadow of all sounds:—a drear
Murmur, between their songs, is all the woodmen hear.

XVI

Grief made the young Spring wild, and she threw down
Her kindling buds, as if she Autumn were,
Or they dead leaves; since her delight is flown,
For whom should she have waked the sullen year?
To Phœbus was not Hyacinth so dear   140
Nor to himself Narcissus, as to both
Thou, Adonais: wan they stand and sere
Amid the faint companions of their youth,
With dew all turned to tears; odour, to sighing ruth.

XVII

Thy spirit's sister, the lorn nightingale,
Mourns not her mate with such melodious pain;
Not so the eagle, who like thee could scale
Heaven, and could nourish in the sun's domain
Her mighty youth with morning, doth complain,
Soaring and screaming round her empty nest,   150
As Albion wails for thee: the curse of Cain
Light on his head who pierced thy innocent breast,
And scared the angel soul that was its earthly guest!

XVIII

Ah woe is me! Winter is come and gone,
But grief returns with the revolving year;

The airs and streams renew their joyous tone;
The ants, the bees, the swallows reappear;
Fresh leaves and flowers deck the dead Seasons' bier;
The amorous birds now pair in every brake,
And build their mossy homes in fields and brere;   160
And the green lizard, and the golden snake,
Like unimprisoned flames, out of their trance awake.

XIX

Through wood and stream and field and hill and Ocean
A quickening life from the Earth's heart has burst
As it has ever done, with change and motion
From the great morning of the world when first
God dawned on Chaos; in its stream immersed
The lamps of Heaven flash with a softer light;
All baser things pant with life's sacred thirst;
Diffuse themselves; and spend in love's delight   170
The beauty and the joy of their renewèd might.

XX

The leprous corpse touched by this spirit tender
Exhales itself in flowers of gentle breath;
Like incarnations of the stars, when splendour
Is changed to fragrance, they illumine death
And mock the merry worm that wakes beneath;
Naught we know, dies. Shall that alone which knows
Be as a sword consumed beneath the sheath
By sightless lightning?—th' intense atom glows
A moment, then is quenched in a most cold repose.   180

XXI

Alas! that all we loved of him should be,
But for our grief, as if it had not been,
And grief itself be mortal! Woe is me!
Whence are we, and why are we? of what scene
The actors or spectators? Great and mean
Meet massed in death, who lends what life must borrow.
As long as skies are blue, and fields are green,
Evening must usher night, night urge the morrow,
Month follow month with woe, and year wake year to sorrow.

XXII

He will awake no more, oh, never more!   190
"Wake thou," cried Misery, "childless Mother, rise
Out of thy sleep, and slake, in thy heart's core,
A wound more fierce than his with tears and sighs."
And all the Dreams that watched Urania's eyes,
And all the Echoes whom their sister's song
Had held in holy silence, cried: "Arise!"
Swift as a Thought by the snake Memory stung,
From her ambrosial rest the fading Splendour sprung.

XXIII

She rose like an autumnal Night, that springs
Out of the East, and follows wild and drear
The golden Day, which, on eternal wings,
Even as a ghost abandoning a bier,
Had left the Earth a corpse. Sorrow and fear
So struck, so roused, so rapt Urania;
So saddened round her like an atmosphere
Of stormy mist; so swept her on her way
Even to the mournful place where Adonais lay.

XXIV

Out of her secret Paradise she sped,
Through camps and cities rough with stone, and steel,
And human hearts, which to her aëry tread   210
Yielding not, wounded the invisible
Palms of her tender feet where'er they fell:
And barbèd tongues, and thoughts more sharp than they,
Rent the soft Form they never could repel,
Whose sacred blood, like the young tears of May,
Paved with eternal flowers that undeserving way.

XXV

In the death-chamber for a moment Death,
Shamed by the presence of that living Might,
Blushed to annihilation, and the breath
Revisited those lips, and life's pale light   220
Flashed through those limbs, so late her dear delight.
"Leave me not wild and drear and comfortless,

As silent lightning leaves the starless night!
Leave me not!" cried Urania: her distress
Roused Death: Death rose and smiled, and met her vain caress.

XXVI

"Stay yet awhile! speak to me once again;
Kiss me, so long but as a kiss may live;
And in my heartless breast and burning brain
That word, that kiss shall all thoughts else survive,   230
With food of saddest memory kept alive,
Now thou art dead, as if it were a part
Of thee, my Adonais! I would give
All that I am to be as thou now art!
But I am chained to Time, and cannot thence depart!

XXVII

"Oh gentle child, beautiful as thou wert,
Why didst thou leave the trodden paths of men
Too soon, and with weak hands though mighty heart
Dare the unpastured dragon in his den?
Defenceless as thou wert, oh where was then
Wisdom the mirrored shield, or scorn the spear?   240
Or hadst thou waited the full cycle, when
Thy spirit should have filled its crescent sphere,
The monsters of life's waste had fled from thee like deer.

XXVIII

"The herded wolves, bold only to pursue;
The obscene ravens, clamorous o'er the dead;
The vultures to the conqueror's banner true,
Who feed where Desolation first has fed,
And whose wings rain contagion;—how they fled,
When like Apollo, from his golden bow,
The Pythian of the age one arrow sped   250
And smiled!—The spoilers tempt no second blow;
They fawn on the proud feet that spurn them lying low.

XXIX

"The sun comes forth, and many reptiles spawn;
He sets, and each ephemeral insect then

Is gathered into death without a dawn,
And the immortal stars awake again;
So is it in the world of living men:
A godlike mind soars forth, in its delight
Making earth bare and veiling heaven, and when
It sinks, the swarms that dimmed or shared its light   260
Leave to its kindred lamps the spirit's awful night."

XXX

Thus ceased she: and the mountain shepherds came,
Their garlands sere, their magic mantles rent;
The Pilgrim of Eternity, whose fame
Over his living head like Heaven is bent,
An early but enduring monument,
Came, veiling all the lightnings of his song
In sorrow; from her wilds Ierne sent
The sweetest lyrist of her saddest wrong,
And love taught grief to fall like music from his tongue.   270

XXXI

Midst others of less note, came one frail Form,
A phantom among men, companionless
As the last cloud of an expiring storm
Whose thunder is its knell; he, as I guess,
Had gazed on Nature's naked loveliness,
Actæon-like, and now he fled astray
With feeble steps o'er the world's wilderness,
And his own thoughts, along that rugged way,
Pursued, like raging hounds, their father and their prey.

XXXII

A pardlike Spirit beautiful and swift—   280
A Love in desolation masked;—a Power
Girt round with weakness;—it can scarce uplift
The weight of the superincumbent hour;
It is a dying lamp, a falling shower,
A breaking billow;—even whilst we speak
Is it not broken? On the withering flower
The killing sun smiles brightly; on a cheek
The life can burn in blood, even while the heart may break.

XXXIII

His head was bound with pansies overblown,
And faded violets, white, and pied, and blue;   290
And a light spear topped with a cypress cone,
Round whose crude shaft dark ivy tresses grew
Yet dripping with the forest's noonday dew,
Vibrated, as the ever-beating heart
Shook the weak hand that grasped it; of that crew
He came the last, neglected and apart;
A herd-abandoned deer struck by the hunter's dart.

XXXIV

All stood aloof, and at his partial moan
Smiled through their tears; well knew that gentle band
Who in another's fate now wept his own;   300
As, in the accents of an unknown land,
He sung new sorrow; sad Urania scanned
The Stranger's mien, and murmured: "Who art thou?"
He answered not, but with a sudden hand
Made bare his branded and ensanguined brow,
Which was like Cain's or Christ's—Oh! that it should be so!

XXXV

What softer voice is hushed over the dead?
Athwart what brow is that dark mantle thrown?
What form leans sadly o'er the white death-bed,
In mockery of monumental stone,   310
The heavy heart heaving without a moan?
If it be He, who, gentlest of the wise,
Taught, soothed, loved, honored the departed one,
Let me not vex with inharmonious sighs
The silence of that heart's accepted sacrifice.

XXXVI

Our Adonais has drunk poison—oh!
What deaf and viperous murderer could crown
Life's early cup with such a draught of woe?
The nameless worm would now itself disown:
It felt; yet could escape the magic tone   320
Whose prelude held all envy, hate, and wrong,

But what was howling in one breast alone,
  Silent with expectation of the song,
Whose master's hand is cold, whose silver lyre unstrung.

XXXVII

Live thou, whose infamy is not thy fame!
Live! fear no heavier chastisement from me,
Thou noteless blot on a remembered name!
But be thyself, and know thyself to be!
And ever at thy season be thou free
To spill the venom when thy fangs o'erflow: 330
Remorse and Self-contempt shall cling to thee;
Hot Shame shall burn upon thy secret brow,
And like a beaten hound, tremble thou shalt—as now.

XXXVIII

Nor let us weep that our delight is fled
Far from these carrion kites that scream below;
He wakes or sleeps with the enduring dead;
Thou canst not soar where he is sitting now.—
Dust to the dust! but the pure spirit shall flow
Back to the burning fountain whence it came,
A portion of the Eternal, which must glow   340
Through time and change, unquenchably the same,
Whilst thy cold embers choke the sordid hearth of shame.

XXXIX

Peace, peace! he is not dead, he doth not sleep—
He hath awakened from the dream of life—
'Tis we who, lost in stormy visions, keep
With phantoms an unprofitable strife,
And in mad trance strike with our spirit's knife
Invulnerable nothings.—*We* decay
Like corpses in a charnel; fear and grief
Convulse us and consume us day by day,   350
And cold hopes swarm like worms within our living clay.

XL

He has outsoared the shadow of our night;
Envy and calumny and hate and pain,

And that unrest which men miscall delight,
Can touch him not and torture not again;
From the contagion of the world's slow stain
He is secure, and now can never mourn
A heart grown cold, a head grown gray in vain;
Nor, when the spirit's self has ceased to burn,
With sparkless ashes load an unlamented urn.   360

XLI

He lives, he wakes—'tis Death is dead, not he;
Mourn not for Adonais.—Thou young Dawn
Turn all thy dew to splendour, nor from thee
The spirit thou lamentest is not gone;
Ye caverns and ye forests, cease to moan!
Cease ye faint flowers and fountains, and thou Air
Which like a mourning veil thy scarf hadst thrown
O'er the abandoned Earth, now leave it bare
Even to the joyous stars which smile on its despair!

XLII

He is made one with Nature: there is heard   370
His voice in all her music, from the moan
Of thunder, to the song of night's sweet bird;
He is a presence to be felt and known
In darkness and in light, from herb and stone,
Spreading itself where'er that Power may move
Which has withdrawn his being to its own;
Which wields the world with never-wearied love,
Sustains it from beneath, and kindles it above.

XLIII

He is a portion of the loveliness
Which once he made more lovely: he doth bear   380
His part, while the one Spirit's plastic stress
Sweeps through the dull dense world, compelling there
All new successions to the forms they wear;
Torturing th' unwilling dross that checks its flight
To its own likeness, as each mass may bear;
And bursting in its beauty and its might
From trees and beasts and men into the Heaven's light.

XLIV

The splendours of the firmament of time
May be eclipsed, but are extinguished not;
Like stars to their appointed height they climb,   390
And death is a low mist which cannot blot
The brightness it may veil. When lofty thought
Lifts a young heart above its mortal lair,
And love and life contend in it, for what
Shall be its earthly doom, the dead live there
And move like winds of light on dark and stormy air.

XLV

The inheritors of unfulfilled renown
Rose from their thrones, built beyond mortal thought,
Far in the Unapparent. Chatterton
Rose pale, his solemn agony had not   400
Yet faded from him; Sidney, as he fought
And as he fell and as he lived and loved
Sublimely mild, a Spirit without spot,
Arose; and Lucan, by his death approved:
Oblivion as they rose shrank like a thing reproved.

XLVI

And many more, whose names on Earth are dark
But whose transmitted effluence cannot die
So long as fire outlives the parent spark,
Rose, robed in dazzling immortality.
"Thou art become as one of us," they cry,   410
"It was for thee yon kingless sphere has long
Swung blind in unascended majesty,
Silent alone amid an Heaven of Song.
Assume thy wingèd throne, thou Vesper of our throng!"

XLVII

Who mourns for Adonais? oh come forth
Fond wretch! and know thyself and him aright.
Clasp with thy panting soul the pendulous Earth;
As from a center, dart thy spirit's light
Beyond all worlds, until its spacious might
Satiate the void circumference: then shrink   420
Even to a point within our day and night;

And keep thy heart light lest it make thee sink
When hope has kindled hope, and lured thee to the brink.

XLVIII

Or go to Rome, which is the sepulchre,
O, not of him, but of our joy: 'tis naught
That ages, empires, and religions there
Lie buried in the ravage they have wrought;
For such as he can lend,—they borrow not
Glory from those who made the world their prey;
And he is gathered to the kings of thought   430
Who waged contention with their time's decay,
And of the past are all that cannot pass away.

XLIX

Go thou to Rome,—at once the Paradise,
The grave, the city, and the wilderness;
And where its wrecks like shattered mountains rise,
And flowering weeds and fragrant copses dress
The bones of Desolation's nakedness
Pass, till the Spirit of the spot shall lead
Thy footsteps to a slope of green access
Where, like an infant's smile, over the dead,   440
A light of laughing flowers along the grass is spread.

L

And gray walls moulder round, on which dull Time
Feeds, like slow fire upon a hoary brand;
And one keen pyramid with wedge sublime,
Pavilioning the dust of him who planned
This refuge for his memory, doth stand
Like flames transformed to marble; and beneath,
A field is spread, on which a newer band
Have pitched in Heaven's smile their camp of death
Welcoming him we lose with scarce extinguished breath.   450

LI

Here pause: these graves are all too young as yet
To have outgrown the sorrow which consigned
Its charge to each; and if the seal is set,
Here, on one fountain of a mourning mind,
Break it not thou! too surely shalt thou find

Thine own well full, if thou returnest home,
Of tears and gall. From the world's bitter wind
Seek shelter in the shadow of the tomb.
What Adonais is, why fear we to become?

LII

The One remains, the many change and pass;   460
Heaven's light forever shines, Earth's shadows fly;
Life, like a dome of many-coloured glass,
Stains the white radiance of Eternity,
Until Death tramples it to fragments.—Die,
If thou wouldst be with that which thou dost seek!
Follow where all is fled!—Rome's azure sky,
Flowers, ruins, statues, music, words, are weak
The glory they transfuse with fitting truth to speak.

LIII

Why linger, why turn back, why shrink, my Heart?
Thy hopes are gone before: from all things here   470
They have departed; thou shouldst now depart!
A light is passed from the revolving year,
And man, and woman; and what still is dear
Attracts to crush, repels to make thee wither.
The soft sky smiles,—the low wind whispers near;
'Tis Adonais calls! oh, hasten thither,
No more let Life divide what Death can join together.

LIV

That Light whose smile kindles the Universe,
That Beauty in which all things work and move,
That Benediction which the eclipsing Curse   480
Of birth can quench not, that sustaining Love
Which, through the web of being blindly wove
By man and beast and earth and air and sea,
Burns bright or dim, as each are mirrors of
The fire for which all thirst, now beams on me,
Consuming the last clouds of cold mortality.

LV

The breath whose might I have invoked in song
Descends on me; my spirit's bark is driven,

Far from the shore, far from the trembling throng
Whose sails were never to the tempest given;   490
The massy earth and spherèd skies are riven!
I am borne darkly, fearfully, afar:
Whilst burning through the inmost veil of Heaven,
The soul of Adonais, like a star,
Beacons from the abode where the Eternal are.

225.   CHORUS FROM "HELLAS"

The world's great age begins anew,
    The golden years return,
The earth doth like a snake renew
    Her winter weeds outworn:
Heaven smiles, and faiths and empires gleam,
Like wrecks of a dissolving dream.

A brighter Hellas rears its mountains
    From waves serener far;
A new Peneus rolls his fountains
    Against the morning star.   10
Where fairer Tempes bloom, there sleep
Young Cyclads on a sunnier deep.

A loftier Argo cleaves the main,
    Fraught with a later prize;
Another Orpheus sings again,
    And loves, and weeps, and dies.
A new Ulysses leaves once more
Calypso for his native shore.

Oh, write no more the tale of Troy,
    If earth Death's scroll must be!   20
Nor mix with Laian rage the joy
    Which dawns upon the free:
Although a subtler Sphinx renew
Riddles of death Thebes never knew.

Another Athens shall arise,
    And to remoter time
Bequeath, like sunset to the skies,
    The splendour of its prime;
And leave, if nought so bright may live,
All earth can take or Heaven can give.   30

Saturn and Love their long repose
   Shall burst, more bright and good
Than all who fell, than One who rose,
   Than many unsubdued:
Not gold, not blood, their altar dowers,
But votive tears and symbol flowers.

Oh, cease! must hate and death return?
   Cease! must men kill and die?
Cease! drain not to its dregs the urn
   Of bitter prophecy.   40
The world is weary of the past,
Oh, might it die or rest at last!

226.   LINES

I

When the lamp is shattered
The light in the dust lies dead—
   When the cloud is scattered
The rainbow's glory is shed.
   When the lute is broken,
Sweet tones are remembered not;
   When the lips have spoken,
Loved accents are soon forgot.

II

As music and splendour
Survive not the lamp and the lute,   10
   The heart's echoes render
No song when the spirit is mute,—
   No song but sad dirges,
Like the wind through a ruined cell,
   Or the mournful surges
That ring the dead seaman's knell.

III

When hearts have once mingled
Love first leaves the well-built nest,—
   The weak one is singled
To endure what it once possessed.   20

O, Love! who bewailest
The frailty of all things here,
  Why choose you the frailest
For your cradle, your home and your bier?

IV

  Its passions will rock thee
As the storms rock the ravens on high:
  Bright reason will mock thee,
Like the sun from a wintry sky.
  From thy nest every rafter
Will rot, and thine eagle home   30
  Leave thee naked to laughter,
When leaves fall and cold winds come.

JOHN KEATS (1795–1821)

227.   "WHEN I HAVE FEARS THAT I MAY
CEASE TO BE"

When I have fears that I may cease to be
  Before my pen has gleaned my teeming brain,
Before high-pilèd books, in charactery,
  Hold like rich garners the full ripened grain;
When I behold, upon the night's starred face,
  Huge cloudy symbols of a high romance,
And think that I may never live to trace
  Their shadows, with the magic hand of chance;
And when I feel, fair creature of an hour,
  That I shall never look upon thee more,   10
Never have relish in the fairy power
  Of unreflecting love;—then on the shore
Of the wide world I stand alone, and think
Till love and fame to nothingness do sink.

228.   "IN A DREAR-NIGHTED DECEMBER"

  In a drear-nighted December,
    Too happy, happy tree,
  Thy branches ne'er remember
    Their green felicity:

The north cannot undo them,
With a sleety whistle through them;
Nor frozen thawings glue them
    From budding at the prime.

In a drear-nighted December,
    Too happy, happy brook,   10
Thy bubblings ne'er remember
    Apollo's summer look;
But with a sweet forgetting,
They stay their crystal fretting,
Never, never petting
    About the frozen time.

Ah! would 'twere so with many
    A gentle girl and boy!
But were there ever any
    Writhed not at passèd joy?   20
To know the change and feel it,
When there is none to heal it,
Nor numbèd sense to steel it,
    Was never said in rhyme.

229.   THE EVE OF ST. AGNES

St. Agnes' Eve—Ah, bitter chill it was!
The owl, for all his feathers, was a-cold;
The hare limped trembling through the frozen grass,
And silent was the flock in woolly fold:
Numb were the Beadsman's fingers, while he told
His rosary, and while his frosted breath,
Like pious incense from a censer old,
Seemed taking flight for heaven, without a death,
Past the sweet Virgin's picture, while his prayer he saith.

His prayer he saith, this patient, holy man;   10
Then takes his lamp, and riseth from his knees,
And back returneth, meagre, barefoot, wan,
Along the chapel aisle by slow degrees:
The sculptured dead, on each side, seem to freeze,
Emprisoned in black, purgatorial rails:
Knights, ladies, praying in dumb orat'ries,
He passeth by; and his weak spirit fails
To think how they may ache in icy hoods and mails.

Northward he turneth through a little door,
And scarce three steps, ere Music's golden tongue   20
Flattered to tears this agèd man and poor;
But no—already had his deathbell rung;
The joys of all his life were said and sung:
His was harsh penance on St. Agnes' Eve:
Another way he went, and soon among
Rough ashes sat he for his soul's reprieve,
And all night kept awake, for sinners' sake to grieve.

That ancient Beadsman heard the prelude soft;
And so it chanced, for many a door was wide,
From hurry to and fro. Soon, up aloft,   30
The silver, snarling trumpets 'gan to chide:
The level chambers, ready with their pride,
Were glowing to receive a thousand guests:
The carvèd angels, ever eager-eyed,
Stared, where upon their heads the cornice rests,
With hair blown back, and wings put cross-wise on their breasts.

At length burst in the argent revelry,
With plume, tiara, and all rich array,
Numerous as shadows, haunting fairily
The brain, new stuffed, in youth, with triumphs gay   40
Of old romance. These let us wish away,
And turn, sole-thoughted, to one Lady there,
Whose heart had brooded, all that wintry day,
On love, and winged St. Agnes' saintly care,
As she had heard old dames full many times declare.

They told her how, upon St. Agnes' Eve,
Young virgins might have visions of delight,
And soft adorings from their loves receive
Upon the honeyed middle of the night,
If ceremonies due they did aright;   50
As, supperless to bed they must retire,
And couch supine their beauties, lily white;
Nor look behind, nor sideways, but require
Of Heaven with upward eyes for all that they desire.

Full of this whim was thoughtful Madeline:
The music, yearning like a God in pain,
She scarcely heard: her maiden eyes divine,

Fixed on the floor, saw many a sweeping train
Pass by—she heeded not at all: in vain
Came many a tiptoe, amorous cavalier,   60
And back retired; not cooled by high disdain,
But she saw not: her heart was otherwhere:
She sighed for Agnes' dreams, the sweetest of the year.

She danced along with vague, regardless eyes,
Anxious her lips, her breathing quick and short:
The hallowed hour was near at hand: she sighs
Amid the timbrels, and the thronged resort
Of whisperers in anger, or in sport;
'Mid looks of love, defiance, hate, and scorn,
Hoodwinked with faery fancy; all amort,   70
Save to St. Agnes and her lambs unshorn,
And all the bliss to be before tomorrow morn.

So, purposing each moment to retire,
She lingered still. Meantime, across the moors,
Had come young Porphyro, with heart on fire
For Madeline. Beside the portal doors,
Buttressed from moonlight, stands he, and implores
All saints to give him sight of Madeline,
But for one moment in the tedious hours,
That he might gaze and worship all unseen;   80
Perchance speak, kneel, touch, kiss—in sooth such things have been.

He ventures in: let no buzzed whisper tell:
All eyes be muffled, or a hundred swords
Will storm his heart, Love's fev'rous citadel:
For him, those chambers held barbarian hordes,
Hyena foemen, and hot-blooded lords,
Whose very dogs with execrations howl
Against his lineage: not one breast affords
Him any mercy in that mansion foul,
Save one old beldame, weak in body and in soul.   90

Ah, happy chance! the agèd creature came,
Shuffling along with ivory-headed wand,
To where he stood, hid from the torch's flame,
Behind a broad hall-pillar, far beyond
The sound of merriment and chorus bland:
He startled her; but soon she knew his face,

And grasped his fingers in her palsied hand,
Saying, "Mercy, Porphyro! hie thee from this place;
"They are all here to-night the whole blood-thirsty race!

"Get hence! get hence! there's dwarfish Hildebrand;   100
"He had a fever late, and in the fit
"He cursèd thee and thine, both house and land:
"Then there's that old Lord Maurice, not a whit
"More tame for his grey hairs—Alas me! flit!
"Flit like a ghost away."—"Ah, Gossip dear,
"We're safe enough; here in this arm-chair sit,
"And tell me how"—"Good Saints! not here, not here;
"Follow, me, child, or else these stones will be thy bier."

He followed through a lowly archèd way,
Brushing the cobwebs with his lofty plume,   110
And as she muttered "Well-a—well-a-day!"
He found him in a little moonlight room,
Pale, latticed, chill, and silent as a tomb.
"Now tell me where is Madeline," said he,
"O tell me, Angela, by the holy loom
"Which none but secret sisterhood may see,
"When they St. Agnes' wool are weaving piously."

"St. Agnes! Ah! it is St. Agnes' Eve—
"Yet men will murder upon holy days:
"Thou must hold water in a witch's sieve,   120
"And be liege lord of all the Elves and Fays,
"To venture so: it fills me with amaze
"To see thee, Porphyro!—St. Agnes' Eve!
"God's help! my lady fair the conjuror plays
"This very night: good angels her deceive!
"But let me laugh awhile, I've mickle time to grieve."

Feebly she laugheth in the languid moon,
While Porphyro upon her face doth look,
Like puzzled urchin on an agèd crone
Who keepeth closed a wondrous riddle-book,   130
As spectacled she sits in chimney nook.
But soon his eyes grew brilliant, when she told
His lady's purpose; and he scarce could brook
Tears, at the thought of those enchantments cold,
And Madeline asleep in lap of legends old.

Sudden a thought came like a full-blown rose,
Flushing his brow, and in his painèd heart
Made purple riot: then doth he propose
A stratagem, that makes the beldame start:
"A cruel man and impious thou art: 140
"Sweet lady, let her pray, and sleep, and dream
"Alone with her good angels, far apart
"From wicked men like thee. Go, go!—I deem
"Thou canst not surely be the same that thou didst seem."

"I will not harm her, by all saints I swear,"
Quoth Porphyro: "O may I ne'er find grace
"When my weak voice shall whisper its last prayer,
"If one of her soft ringlets I displace,
"Or look with ruffian passion in her face:
"Good Angela, believe me by these tears;   150
"Or I will, even in a moment's space,
"Awake, with horrid shout, my foemen's ears,
"And beard them, though they be more fanged than wolves and
   bears."

"Ah! why wilt thou affright a feeble soul?
"A poor, weak, palsy-stricken, churchyard thing,
"Whose passing-bell may ere the midnight toll;
"Whose prayers for thee, each morn and evening,
"Were never missed."—Thus plaining, doth she bring
A gentler speech from burning Porphyro;
So woeful, and of such deep sorrowing,   160
That Angela gives promise she will do
Whatever he shall wish, betide her weal or woe.

Which was, to lead him, in close secrecy,
Even to Madeline's chamber, and there hide
Him in a closet, of such privacy
That he might see her beauty unespied,
And win perhaps that night a peerless bride,
While legioned faeries paced the coverlet,
And pale enchantment held her sleepy-eyed.
Never on such a night have lovers met,   170
Since Merlin paid his Demon all the monstrous debt.

"It shall be as thou wishest," said the Dame:
"All cates and dainties shall be storèd there

"Quickly on this feast night: by the tambour frame
"Her own lute thou wilt see: no time to spare,
"For I am slow and feeble, and scarce dare
"On such a catering trust my dizzy head.
"Wait here, my child, with patience; kneel in prayer
"The while: Ah! thou must needs the lady wed,
"Or may I never leave my grave among the dead."   180

So saying, she hobbled off with busy fear.
The lover's endless minutes slowly passed;
The Dame returned, and whispered in his ear
To follow her; with agèd eyes aghast
From fright of dim espial. Safe at last,
Through many a dusky gallery, they gain
The maiden's chamber, silken, hushed, and chaste;
Where Porphyro took covert, pleased amain.
His poor guide hurried back with agues in her brain.

Her falt'ring hand upon the balustrade,   190
Old Angela was feeling for the stair,
When Madeline, St. Agnes' charmèd maid,
Rose, like a missioned spirit, unaware:
With silver taper's light, and pious care,
She turned, and down the agèd gossip led
To a safe level matting. Now prepare,
Young Porphyro, for gazing on that bed;
She comes, she comes again, like ring-dove frayed and fled.

Out went the taper as she hurried in;
Its little smoke, in pallid moonshine, died: 200
She closed the door, she panted, all akin
To spirits of the air, and visions wide:
No uttered syllable, or, woe betide!
But to her heart, her heart was voluble,
Paining with eloquence her balmy side;
As though a tongueless nightingale should swell
Her throat in vain, and die, heart-stifled, in her dell.

A casement high and triple-arched there was,
All garlanded with carven imag'ries
Of fruits, and flowers, and bunches of knot-grass,   210
And diamonded with panes of quaint device,
Innumerable of stains and splendid dyes,

As are the tiger-moth's deep-damasked wings;
And in the midst, 'mong thousand heraldries,
And twilight saints, and dim emblazonings,
A shielded scutcheon blushed with blood of queens and kings.

Full on this casement shone the wintry moon,
And threw warm gules on Madeline's fair breast,
As down she knelt for heaven's grace and boon;
Rose-bloom fell on her hands, together pressed,   220
And on her silver cross soft amethyst,
And on her hair a glory, like a saint:
She seemed a splendid angel, newly dressed,
Save wings, for heaven:—Porphyro grew faint:
She knelt, so pure a thing, so free from mortal taint.

Anon his heart revives: her vespers done,
Of all its wreathèd pearls her hair she frees;
Unclasps her warmèd jewels one by one;
Loosens her fragrant bodice; by degrees
Her rich attire creeps rustling to her knees: 230
Half-hidden, like a mermaid in seaweed,
Pensive awhile she dreams awake, and sees,
In fancy, fair St. Agnes in her bed,
But dares not look behind, or all the charm is fled.

Soon, trembling in her soft and chilly nest,
In sort of wakeful swoon, perplexed she lay,
Until the poppied warmth of sleep oppressed
Her soothèd limbs, and soul fatigued away;
Flown, like a thought, until the morrow-day;
Blissfully havened both from joy and pain;   240
Clasped like a missal where swart Paynims pray;
Blinded alike from sunshine and from rain,
As though a rose should shut, and be a bud again.

Stolen to this paradise, and so entranced,
Porphyro gazed upon her empty dress,
And listened to her breathing, if it chanced
To wake into a slumberous tenderness:
Which when he heard, that minute did he bless,
And breathed himself: then from the closet crept,
Noiseless as fear in a wide wilderness,   250
And over the hushed carpet, silent, stepped,
And 'tween the curtains peeped, where, lo!—how fast she slept.

Then by the bedside, where the faded moon
Made a dim, silver twilight, soft he set
A table and, half anguished, threw thereon
A cloth of woven crimson, gold, and jet:—
O for some drowsy Morphean amulet!
The boisterous midnight, festive clarion,
The kettledrum, and far-heard clarinet,
Affray his ears, though but in dying tone:—   260
The hall door shuts again, and all the noise is gone.

And still she slept an azure-lidded sleep,
In blanchèd linen, smooth, and lavendered,
While he from forth the closet brought a heap
Of candied apple, quince, and plum, and gourd;
With jellies soother than the creamy curd,
And lucent syrops, tinct with cinnamon;
Manna and dates, in argosy transferred
From Fez; and spicèd dainties, every one,
From silken Samarcand to cedared Lebanon.   270

These delicates he heaped with glowing hand
On golden dishes and in baskets bright
Of wreathèd silver: sumptuous they stand
In the retirèd quiet of the night,
Filling the chilly room with perfume light.—
"And now, my love, my seraph fair, awake!
"Thou art my heaven, and I thine eremite:
"Open thine eyes, for meek St. Agnes' sake,
"Or I shall drowse beside thee, so my soul doth ache."

Thus whispering, his warm, unnervèd arm   280
Sank in her pillow. Shaded was her dream
By the dusk curtains:—'twas a midnight charm
Impossible to melt as icèd stream:
The lustrous salvers in the moonlight gleam;
Broad golden fringe upon the carpet lies:
It seemed he never, never could redeem
From such a steadfast spell his lady's eyes;
So mused awhile, entoiled in woofèd fantasies.

Awakening up, he took her hollow lute,—
Tumultuous,—and, in chords that tenderest be,   290
He played an ancient ditty, long since mute,

In Provence called, "La belle dame sans mercy:"
Close to her ear touching the melody;—
Wherewith disturbed, she uttered a soft moan:
He ceased—she panted quick—and suddenly
Her blue affrayèd eyes wide open shone:
Upon his knees he sank, pale as smooth-sculptured stone.

Her eyes were open, but she still beheld,
Now wide awake, the vision of her sleep:
There was a painful change, that nigh expelled   300
The blisses of her dream so pure and deep,
At which fair Madeline began to weep,
And moan forth witless words with many a sigh;
While still her gaze on Porphyro would keep;
Who knelt, with joinèd hands and piteous eye,
Fearing to move or speak, she looked so dreamingly.

"Ah, Porphyro!" said she, "but even now
"Thy voice was at sweet tremble in mine ear,
"Made tuneable with every sweetest vow;
"And those sad eyes were spiritual and clear: 310
"How changed thou art! how pallid, chill, and drear!
"Give me that voice again, my Porphyro,
"Those looks immortal, those complainings dear!
"Oh leave me not in this eternal woe,
"For if thou diest, my Love, I know not where to go."

Beyond a mortal man impassioned far
At these voluptuous accents, he arose,
Ethereal, flushed, and like a throbbing star
Seen mid the sapphire heaven's deep repose;
Into her dream he melted, as the rose   320
Blendeth its odor with the violet,—
Solution sweet: meantime the frost-wind blows
Like Love's alarum pattering the sharp sleet
Against the windowpanes; St. Agnes' moon hath set.

'Tis dark: quick pattereth the flaw-blown sleet.
"This is no dream, my bride, my Madeline!"
'Tis dark: the icèd gusts still rave and beat:
"No dream, alas! alas! and woe is mine!
"Porphyro will leave me here to fade and pine.—
"Cruel! what traitor could thee hither bring?   330

"I curse not, for my heart is lost in thine,
"Though thou forsakest a deceivèd thing;—
"A dove forlorn and lost with sick unprunèd wing."

"My Madeline! sweet dreamer! lovely bride!
"Say, may I be for aye thy vassal blest?
"Thy beauty's shield, heart-shaped and vermeil dyed?
"Ah, silver shrine, here will I take my rest
"After so many hours of toil and quest,
"A famished pilgrim,—saved by miracle.
"Though I have found, I will not rob thy nest   340
"Saving of thy sweet self; if thou think'st well
"To trust, fair Madeline, to no rude infidel.

"Hark! 'tis an elfin-storm from faery land
"Of haggard seeming, but a boon indeed:
"Arise—arise! the morning is at hand;—
"The bloated wassailers will never heed:—
"Let us away, my love, with happy speed;
"There are no ears to hear, or eyes to see,—
"Drowned all in Rhenish and the sleepy mead:
"Awake! arise! my love, and fearless be,   350
"For o'er the southern moors I have a home for thee."

She hurried at his words, beset with fears,
For there were sleeping dragons all around,
At glaring watch, perhaps, with ready spears—
Down the wide stairs a darkling way they found.—
In all the house was heard no human sound.
A chain-drooped lamp was flickering by each door;
The arras, rich with horseman, hawk, and hound,
Fluttered in the besieging wind's uproar;
And the long carpets rose along the gusty floor.   360

They glide, like phantoms, into the wide hall;
Like phantoms, to the iron porch, they glide;
Where lay the Porter, in uneasy sprawl,
With a huge empty flagon by his side:
The wakeful bloodhound rose, and shook his hide,
But his sagacious eye an inmate owns:
By one, and one, the bolts full easy slide:—
The chains lie silent on the footworn stones;—
The key turns, and the door upon its hinges groans.

And they are gone: aye, ages long ago   37⁰
These lovers fled away into the storm.
That night the Baron dreamt of many a woe,
And all his warrior-guests, with shade and form
Of witch, and demon, and large coffin-worm,
Were long be-nightmared. Angela the old
Died palsy-twitched, with meagre face deform;
The Beadsman, after thousand aves told,
For aye unsought-for slept among his ashes cold.

230.   TO SLEEP

O soft embalmer of the still midnight,
    Shutting, with careful fingers and benign,
Our gloom-pleased eyes, embowered from the light,
    Enshaded in forgetfulness divine:
O soothest Sleep! if so it please thee, close,
    In midst of this thine hymn, my willing eyes,
Or wait the "Amen," ere thy poppy throws
    Around my bed its lulling charities.
Then save me, or the passèd day will shine
Upon my pillow, breeding many woes,—   10
    Save me from curious Conscience, that still lords
Its strength for darkness, burrowing like a mole;
    Turn the key deftly in the oilèd wards,
And seal the hushèd casket of my soul.

231.   LA BELLE DAME SANS MERCI

'O what can ail thee, knight-at-arms,
    Alone and palely loitering?
The sedge has wither'd from the lake,
    And no birds sing.

'O what can ail thee, knight-at-arms,
    So haggard and so woe-begone?
The squirrel's granary is full,
    And the harvest's done.

'I see a lily on thy brow
With anguish moist and fever dew;   10
And on thy cheek a fading rose
    Fast withereth too.'

'I met a lady in the meads,
   Full beautiful—a faery's child,
Her hair was long, her foot was light,
   And her eyes were wild.

'I made a garland for her head,
   And bracelets too, and fragrant zone;
She look'd at me as she did love,
   And made sweet moan.   20

'I set her on my pacing steed
   And nothing else saw all day long,
For sidelong would she bend, and sing
   A faery's song.

'She found me roots of relish sweet,
   And honey wild, and manna dew,
And sure in language strange she said—
   "I love thee true."

'She took me to her elfin grot,
   And there she wept, and sigh'd full sore;   30
And there I shut her wild wild eyes
   With kisses four.

'And there she lullèd me asleep,
   And there I dream'd—Ah! woe betide!
The latest dream I ever dream'd
   On the cold hill's side.

'I saw pale kings and princes too,
   Pale warriors, death-pale were they all;
They cried—"La Belle Dame sans Merci
   Hath thee in thrall!"   40

'I saw their starv'd lips in the gloam,
   With horrid warning gapèd wide,
And I awoke and found me here,
   On the cold hill's side.

'And this is why I sojourn here,
   Alone and palely loitering,
Though the sedge is wither'd from the lake,
   And no birds sing.'

232.   "BRIGHT STAR, WOULD I WERE STEADFAST
AS THOU ART"

Bright star, would I were steadfast as thou art—
   Not in lone splendor hung aloft the night,
And watching, with eternal lids apart,
   Like nature's patient, sleepless Eremite,
The moving waters at their priest-like task
   Of pure ablution round earth's human shores,
Or gazing on the new soft-fallen mask
   Of snow upon the mountains and the moors—
No—yet still steadfast, still unchangeable,
   Pillowed upon my fair love's ripening breast,   10
To feel for ever its soft fall and swell,
   Awake for ever in a sweet unrest,
Still, still to hear her tender-taken breath,
And so live ever—or else swoon to death.

233.   ODE TO A NIGHTINGALE

My heart aches, and a drowsy numbness pains
   My sense, as though of hemlock I had drunk,
Or emptied some dull opiate to the drains
   One minute past, and Lethe-wards had sunk:
'Tis not through envy of thy happy lot,
   But being too happy in thy happiness,—
      That thou, light-wingèd Dryad of the trees,
      In some melodious plot
Of beechen green, and shadows numberless,
   Singest of summer in full-throated ease.   10

O for a draught of vintage! that hath been
   Cooled a long age in the deep-delvèd earth,
Tasting of Flora and the country green,
   Dance, and Provençal song, and sunburnt mirth!
O for a beaker full of the warm South,
   Full of the true, the blushful Hippocrene,
      With beaded bubbles winking at the brim,
      And purple-stainèd mouth;
That I might drink, and leave the world unseen,
   And with thee fade away into the forest dim: 20

Fade far away, dissolve, and quite forget
   What thou among the leaves hast never known,
The weariness, the fever, and the fret
   Here, where men sit and hear each other groan;
Where palsy shakes a few, sad, last grey hairs,
    Where youth grows pale, and spectre-thin, and dies;
      Where but to think is to be full of sorrow
        And leaden-eyed despairs,
    Where Beauty cannot keep her lustrous eyes,
      Or new Love pine at them beyond to-morrow.   30

Away! away! for I will fly to thee,
   Not charioted by Bacchus and his pards,
But on the viewless wings of Poesy,
   Though the dull brain perplexes and retards:
Already with thee! tender is the night,
    And haply the Queen-Moon is on her throne,
      Clustered around by all her starry Fays;
        But here there is no light,
   Save what from heaven is with the breezes blown
     Through verdurous glooms and winding mossy ways.   40

I cannot see what flowers are at my feet,
   Nor what soft incense hangs upon the boughs,
But, in embalmèd darkness, guess each sweet
   Wherewith the seasonable month endows
The grass, the thicket, and the fruit tree wild;
    White hawthorn, and the pastoral eglantine;
      Fast fading violets covered up in leaves;
        And mid-May's eldest child,
   The coming musk rose, full of dewy wine,
    The murmurous haunt of flies on summer eves.   50

Darkling I listen; and, for many a time
   I have been half in love with easeful Death,
Called him soft names in many a musèd rhyme,
   To take into the air my quiet breath;
Now more than ever seems it rich to die,
    To cease upon the midnight with no pain,
      While thou art pouring forth thy soul abroad
        In such an ecstasy!
   Still wouldst thou sing, and I have ears in vain—
    To thy high requiem become a sod.   60

Thou wast not born for death, immortal Bird!
  No hungry generations tread thee down;
The voice I hear this passing night was heard
  In ancient days by emperor and clown:
Perhaps the self-same song that found a path
    Through the sad heart of Ruth, when, sick for home,
    She stood in tears amid the alien corn;
        The same that oft-times hath
    Charmed magic casements, opening on the foam
    Of perilous seas, in faery lands forlorn.   70

Forlorn! the very word is like a bell
  To toll me back from thee to my sole self!
Adieu! the fancy cannot cheat so well
  As she is famed to do, deceiving elf.
Adieu! adieu! thy plaintive anthem fades
    Past the near meadows, over the still stream,
    Up the hillside; and now 'tis buried deep
        In the next valley glades:
    Was it a vision, or a waking dream?
    Fled is that music:—Do I wake or sleep?   80

234.   ODE ON A GRECIAN URN

Thou still unravished bride of quietness,
  Thou foster-child of silence and slow time,
Sylvan historian, who canst thus express
  A flowery tale more sweetly than our rhyme:
What leaf-fringed legend haunts about thy shape
  Of deities or mortals, or of both,
    In Tempe or the dales of Arcady?
  What men or gods are these? What maidens loth?
What mad pursuit? What struggle to escape?
    What pipes and timbrels? What wild ecstasy?   10

Heard melodies are sweet, but those unheard
  Are sweeter; therefore, ye soft pipes, play on;
Not to the sensual ear, but, more endeared,
  Pipe to the spirit ditties of no tone:
Fair youth, beneath the trees, thou canst not leave
  Thy song, nor ever can those trees be bare;
    Bold Lover, never, never canst thou kiss,

Though winning near the goal—yet, do not grieve;
  She cannot fade, though thou hast not thy bliss,
    For ever wilt thou love, and she be fair! 20

Ah, happy, happy boughs! that cannot shed
  Your leaves, nor ever bid the Spring adieu;
And, happy melodist, unwearièd,
  For ever piping songs for ever new;
More happy love! more happy, happy love!
  For ever warm and still to be enjoyed,
    For ever panting, and for ever young;
All breathing human passion far above,
  That leaves a heart high-sorrowful and cloyed,
    A burning forehead, and a parching tongue. 30

Who are these coming to the sacrifice?
  To what green altar, O mysterious priest,
Lead'st thou that heifer lowing at the skies,
  And all her silken flanks with garlands dressed?
What little town by river or sea-shore,
  Or mountain-built with peaceful citadel,
    Is emptied of its folk, this pious morn?
And, little town, thy streets for evermore
  Will silent be; and not a soul to tell
    Why thou art desolate, can e'er return. 40

O Attic shape! Fair attitude! with brede
  Of marble men and maidens overwrought,
With forest branches and the trodden weed;
  Thou, silent form, dost tease us out of thought
As doth eternity: Cold Pastoral!
  When old age shall this generation waste,
    Thou shalt remain, in midst of other woe
Than ours, a friend to man, to whom thou say'st,
  "Beauty is truth, truth beauty,"—that is all
    Ye know on earth, and all ye need to know. 50

235. ODE ON MELANCHOLY

No, no, go not to Lethe, neither twist
  Wolfsbane, tight-rooted, for its poisonous wine;
Nor suffer thy pale forehead to be kissed
  By nightshade, ruby grape of Proserpine;

Make not your rosary of yew-berries,
   Nor let the beetle, nor the death-moth be
      Your mournful Psyche, nor the downy owl
A partner in your sorrow's mysteries;
   For shade to shade will come too drowsily,
      And drown the wakeful anguish of the soul.   10

But when the melancholy fit shall fall
   Sudden from heaven like a weeping cloud,
That fosters the droop-headed flowers all,
   And hides the green hill in an April shroud;
Then glut thy sorrow on a morning rose,
   Or on the rainbow of the salt sand-wave,
      Or on the wealth of globèd peonies;
Or if thy mistress some rich anger shows,
   Emprison her soft hand, and let her rave,
      And feed deep, deep upon her peerless eyes.   20

She dwells with Beauty—Beauty that must die;
   And Joy, whose hand is ever at his lips
Bidding adieu; and aching Pleasure nigh,
   Turning to poison while the bee-mouth sips:
Aye, in the very temple of Delight
   Veiled Melancholy has her sovran shrine,
      Though seen of none save him whose strenuous tongue
   Can burst Joy's grape against his palate fine;
His soul shall taste the sadness of her might,
   And be among her cloudy trophies hung.   30

236.   TO AUTUMN

Season of mists and mellow fruitfulness,
   Close bosom-friend of the maturing sun;
Conspiring with him how to load and bless
   With fruit the vines that round the thatch-eves run;
To bend with apples the mossed cottage trees,
   And fill all fruit with ripeness to the core;
      To swell the gourd, and plump the hazel shells
   With a sweet kernel; to set budding more,
And still more, later flowers for the bees,
Until they think warm days will never cease,   10
      For Summer has o'er-brimmed their clammy cells.

Who hath not seen thee oft amid thy store?
  Sometimes whoever seeks abroad may find
Thee sitting careless on a granary floor,
  Thy hair soft-lifted by the winnowing wind;
Or on a half-reaped furrow sound asleep,
  Drowsed with the fume of poppies, while thy hook
    Spares the next swath and all its twinèd flowers:
And sometimes like a gleaner thou dost keep
  Steady thy laden head across a brook;   20
  Or by a cider-press, with patient look,
    Thou watchest the last oozings hours by hours.

Where are the songs of Spring? Aye, where are they?
  Think not of them, thou hast thy music too,—
While barrèd clouds bloom the soft-dying day,
  And touch the stubble plains with rosy hue;
Then in a wailful choir the small gnats mourn
  Among the river sallows, borne aloft
    Or sinking as the light wind lives or dies;
And full-grown lambs loud bleat from hilly bourn;   30
  Hedge-crickets sing; and now with treble soft
The red-breast whistles from a garden-croft;
  And gathering swallows twitter in the skies.

LEIGH HUNT (1784–1859)

237.   RONDEAU

Jenny kissed me when we met,
  Jumping from the chair she sat in;
Time, you thief, who love to get
  Sweets into your list, put that in:
Say I'm weary, say I'm sad,
  Say that health and wealth have missed me,
Say I'm growing old, but add,
  Jenny kissed me.

GEORGE DARLEY (1795–1846)

238.   IT IS NOT BEAUTY I DEMAND

It is not Beauty I demand,
  A crystal brow, the moon's despair,

Nor the snow's daughter, a white hand,
  Nor mermaid's yellow pride of hair.

Tell me not of your starry eyes,
  Your lips that seem on roses fed,
Your breasts where Cupid trembling lies,
  Nor sleeps for kissing of his bed.

A bloomy pair of vermeil cheeks,
  Like Hebe's in her ruddiest hours,   10
A breath that softer music speaks
  Than summer winds a-wooing flowers.

These are but gauds; nay, what are lips?
  Coral beneath the ocean-stream,
Whose brink when your adventurer sips
  Full oft he perisheth on them.

And what are cheeks but ensigns oft
  That wave hot youth to fields of blood?
Did Helen's breast though ne'er so soft,
  Do Greece or Ilium any good?   20

Eyes can with baleful ardour burn,
  Poison can breath that erst perfumed,
There's many a white hand holds an urn
  With lover's hearts to dust consumed.

For crystal brows—there's naught within,
  They are but empty cells for pride;
He who the Syren's hair would win
  Is mostly strangled in the tide.

Give me, instead of beauty's bust,
  A tender heart, a loyal mind,   30
Which with temptation I could trust,
  Yet never linked with error find.

One in whose gentle bosom I
  Could pour my secret heart of woes,
Like the care-burthened honey-fly
  That hides his murmurs in the rose.

My earthly comforter! whose love
  So indefeasible might be,
That when my spirit won above
  Hers could not stay for sympathy.   40

THOMAS LOVELL BEDDOES (1803–1849)

239. ISBRAND'S SONG

Squats on a toad-stool under a tree
  A bodiless childfull of life in the gloom
Crying with frog voice, 'What shall I be?
Poor unborn ghost, for my mother killed me
  Scarcely alive in her wicked womb.
What shall I be? shall I creep to the egg
  That's cracking asunder yonder by Nile,
    And with eighteen toes
    And a snuff-taking nose
  Make an Egyptian crocodile?   10
Sing, "Catch a mummy by the leg
    And crunch him with an upper jaw,
    Wagging tail and clenching claw;
    Take a bill-full from my craw,
    Neighbour raven, caw, O caw,
    Grunt, my crocky, pretty maw!
      And give a paw."

'Swine, shall I be you? Thou'rt a dear dog;
But for a smile and kiss and pout,
I must prefer *your* black-lipped snout,   20
  Little gruntless fairy hog,
  Godson of the hawthorn hedge.
For when Ringwood snuffs me out
  And 'gins my tender paunch to grapple,
  Sing, " 'Twixt your ancles visage wedge
    And roll up like an apple."

'Serpent Lucifer, how do you do?
Of your worms and your snakes I'd be one or two;
  For in this dear planet of wool and of leather
'Tis pleasant to need no shirt, breeches or shoe,   30
  And have arm, leg, and belly together.
  Then aches your head, or are you lazy?
    Sing, "Round your neck your belly wrap,
    Tail-a-top, and make your cap
      Any bee and daisy."

'I'll not be a fool like the nightingale
Who sits up all midnight without any ale,
    Making a noise with his nose;
Nor a camel, although 'tis a beautiful back;
Nor a duck, notwithstanding the music of quack,   40
    And the webby mud-patting toes.
I'll be a new bird with the head of an ass,
    Two pigs' feet, two men's feet. and two of a hen,
Devil-winged, dragon-bellied, grave-jawed, because grass
    Is a beard that's soon shaved and grows seldom again
      Before it is summer; so cow all the rest;
      The new Dodo is finished, O! come to my nest!'

240.   RESURRECTION SONG

    Thread the nerves through the right holes,
    Get out of my bones, you wormy souls.
    Shut up my stomach, the ribs are full:
    Muscles be steady and ready to pull.
    Heart and artery merrily shake
    And eyelid go up, for we're going to wake.—
    His eye must be brighter—one more rub!
    And pull up the nostrils! his nose was snub.

241.   SONG AT AMALA'S WEDDING

By female voices

    We have bathed, where none have seen us,
      In the lake and in the fountain,
        Underneath the charmed statue
    Of the timid, bending Venus,
      When the water-nymphs were counting
    In the waves the stars of night,
      And those maidens started at you,
    Your limbs shone through so soft and bright.
      But no secrets dare we tell,
        For thy slaves unlace thee,   10
        And he, who shall embrace thee,
    Waits to try thy beauty's spell.

By male voices

    We have crowned thee queen of women,
      Since love's love, the rose, hath kept her
      Court within thy lips and blushes,

And thine eye, in beauty swimming,
  Kissing, we rendered up the sceptre,
At whose touch the startled soul
  Like an ocean bounds and gushes,
And spirits bend at thy control.   20
    But no secrets dare we tell,
      For thy slaves unlace thee,
      And he, who shall embrace thee,
    Is at hand, and so farewell.

242.   DIRGE FOR WOLFRAM

If thou wilt ease thine heart
Of love and all its smart,
    Then sleep, dear, sleep;
And not a sorrow
  Hang any tear on your eyelashes;
    Lie still and deep,
  Sad soul, until the sea-wave washes
The rim o' th' sun to-morrow,
    In eastern sky.

But wilt thou cure thy heart   10
Of love and all its smart,
    Then die, dear, die;
'Tis deeper, sweeter,
  Than on a rose bank to lie dreaming
    With folded eye;
  And then alone, amid the beaming
Of love's stars, thou'lt meet her
    In eastern sky.

243.   SONG ON THE WATER

  As mad sexton's bell, tolling
    For earth's loveliest daughter
  Night's dumbness breaks rolling
    Ghostily:
  So our boat breaks the water
    Witchingly.

  As her look the dream troubles
  Of her tearful-eyed lover,

So our sails in the bubbles
  Ghostily   10
Are mirrored, and hover
  Moonily.

244.   SONG

Who tames the lion now?
Who smoothes Jove's wrinkles now?
Who is the reckless wight
 That in the horrid middle
Of the deserted night
Doth play upon man's brain,
 As on a wanton fiddle,
The mad and magic strain,
The reeling, tripping sound,
To which the world goes round?   10
 Sing heigh! ho! diddle!
  And then say—
Love, quotha, Love! Nay, nay!
It is a spirit fine
Of ale or ancient wine,
 Lord Alcohol, the drunken fay,
  Lord Alcohol alway!

Who maketh pipe-clay man
Think all that nature can?
Who dares the gods to flout,   20
 Lay fate beneath the table,
And maketh him stammer out
 A thousand monstrous things,
 For history a fable,
 Dish-clouts for kings?
And sends the world along
Singing a ribald song
 Of heighho! Babel?
  Who, I pray—
Love, quotha, Love? Nay, nay!   30
 It is a spirit fine
Of ale or ancient wine,
 Lord Alcohol, the drunken fay,
  Lord Alcohol alway!

JOHN CLARE (1793–1864)

245. ## SIGNS OF WINTER

The cat runs races with her tail. The dog
Leaps o'er the orchard hedge and knarls the grass.
The swine run round and grunt and play with straw,
Snatching out hasty mouthfuls from the stack.
Sudden upon the elmtree tops the crow
Unceremonious visit pays and croaks,
Then swops away. From mossy barn the owl
Bobs hasty out—wheels round and, scared as soon,
As hastily retires. The ducks grow wild
And from the muddy pond fly up and wheel   10
A circle round the village and soon, tired,
Plunge in the pond again. The maids in haste
Snatch from the orchard hedge the mizzled clothes
And laughing hurry in to keep them dry.

246. ## BADGER

When midnight comes a host of dogs and men
Go out and track the badger to his den,
And put a sack within the hole, and lie
Till the old grunting badger passes by.
He comes and hears—they let the strongest loose.
The old fox hears the noise and drops the goose.
The poacher shoots and hurries from the cry,
And the old hare half wounded buzzes bye.
They get a forked stick to bear him down
And clap the dogs and take him to the town,   10
And bait him all the day with many dogs,
And laugh and shout and fright the scampering hogs.
He runs along and bites at all he meets:
They shout and hollo down the noisy streets.

He turns about to face the loud uproar
And drives the rebels to their very door.
The frequent stone is hurled where eer they go;
When badgers fight, then every one's a foe.
The dogs are clapt and urged to join the fray;
The badger turns and drives them all away.   20

Though scarcely half as big, demure and small,
He fights with dogs for bones and beats them all.
The heavy mastiff, savage in the fray,
Lies down and licks his feet and turns away.
The bulldog knows his match and waxes cold,
The badger grins and never leaves his hold.
He drives the crowd and follows at their heels
And bites them through—the drunkard swears and reels.

The frighted women take the boys away,
The blackguard laughs and hurries on the fray.   30
He tries to reach the woods, an awkward race,
But sticks and cudgels quickly stop the chace.
He turns again and drives the noisy crowd
And beats the many dogs in noises loud.
He drives away and beats them every one,
And then they loose them all and set them on.
He falls as dead and kicked by boys and men,
Then starts and grins and drives the crowd again;
Till kicked and torn and beaten out he lies
And leaves his hold and cackles, groans, and dies.   40

247.   I AM

I AM: yet what I am none cares or knows,
    My friends forsake me like a memory lost;
I am the self-consumer of my woes,
    They rise and vanish in oblivious host,
Like shades in love and death's oblivion lost;
And yet I am, and live with shadows tost

Into the nothingness of scorn and noise,
    Into the living sea of waking dreams,
Where there is neither sense of life nor joys,
    But the vast shipwreck of my life's esteems;   10
And een the dearest—that I loved the best—
Are strange—nay, rather stranger than the rest.

I long for scenes where man has never trod;
    A place where woman never smiled or wept;
There to abide with my Creator, God,
    And sleep as I in childhood sweetly slept:
Untroubling and untroubled where I lie;
The grass below—above the vaulted sky.

WILLIAM CULLEN BRYANT (1796–1878)

248. TO A WATERFOWL

Whither, midst falling dew,
While glow the heavens with the last steps of day,
Far, through their rosy depths, dost thou pursue
    Thy solitary way?

Vainly the fowler's eye
Might mark thy distant flight to do thee wrong,
As, darkly seen against the crimson sky,
    Thy figure floats along.

Seek'st thou the plashy brink
Of weedy lake, or marge of river wide,   10
Or where the rocking billows rise and sink
    On the chafed ocean-side?

There is a Power whose care
Teaches thy way along that pathless coast—
The desert and illimitable air—
    Lone wandering, but not lost.

All day thy wings have fanned,
At that far height, the cold, thin atmosphere,
Yet stoop not, weary, to the welcome land,
    Though the dark night is near.   20

And soon that toil shall end;
Soon shalt thou find a summer home, and rest,
And scream among thy fellows; reeds shall bend,
    Soon, o'er thy sheltered nest.

Thou'rt gone, the abyss of heaven
Hath swallowed up thy form; yet, on my heart
Deeply has sunk the lesson thou hast given,
    And shall not soon depart.

He who, from zone to zone,
Guides through the boundless sky thy certain flight,   30
In the long way that I must tread alone,
    Will lead my steps aright.

249.   THE PRAIRIES

     These are the gardens of the Desert, these
The unshorn fields, boundless and beautiful,
For which the speech of England has no name—
The Prairies. I behold them for the first,
And my heart swells, while the dilated sight
Takes in the encircling vastness. Lo! they stretch
In airy undulations, far away,
As if the Ocean, in his gentlest swell,
Stood still, with all his rounded billows fixed,
And motionless forever. Motionless?—   10
No—they are all unchained again. The clouds
Sweep over with their shadows, and, beneath,
The surface rolls and fluctuates to the eye;
Dark hollows seem to glide along and chase
The sunny ridges. Breezes of the South!
Who toss the golden and the flame-like flowers,
And pass the prairie-hawk that, poised on high,
Flaps his broad wings, yet moves not—ye have played
Among the palms of Mexico and vines
Of Texas, and have crisped the limpid brooks   20
That from the fountains of Sonora glide
Into the calm Pacific—have ye fanned
A nobler or a lovelier scene than this?
Man hath no part in all this glorious work:
The hand that built the firmament hath heaved
And smoothed these verdant swells, and sown their slopes
With herbage, planted them with island-groves,
And hedged them round with forests. Fitting floor
For this magnificent temple of the sky—
With flowers whose glory and whose multitude   30
Rival the constellations! The great heavens
Seem to stoop down upon the scene in love,—
A nearer vault, and of a tenderer blue,
Than that which bends above our Eastern hills.

     As o'er the verdant waste I guide my steed,
Among the high rank grass that sweeps his sides
The hollow beating of his footstep seems
A sacrilegious sound. I think of those
Upon whose rest he tramples. Are they here—

The dead of other days?—and did the dust 40
Of these fair solitudes once stir with life
And burn with passion? Let the mighty mounds
That overlook the rivers, or that rise
In the dim forest crowded with old oaks,
Answer. A race, that long has passed away,
Built them; a disciplined and populous race
Heaped, with long toil, the earth, while yet the Greek
Was hewing the Pentelicus to forms
Of symmetry, and rearing on its rock
The glittering Parthenon. These ample fields 50
Nourished their harvests, here their herds were fed,
When haply by their stalls the bison lowed,
And bowed his manèd shoulder to the yoke.
All day this desert murmured with their toils,
Till twilight blushed, and lovers walked, and wooed
In a forgotten language, and old tunes,
From instruments of unremembered form,
Gave the soft winds a voice. The red-man came—
The roaming hunter-tribes, warlike and fierce,
And the mound-builders vanished from the earth. 60
The solitude of centuries untold
Has settled where they dwelt. The prairie-wolf
Hunts in their meadows, and his fresh-dug den
Yawns by my path. The gopher mines the ground
Where stood their swarming cities. All is gone;
All—save the piles of earth that hold their bones,
The platforms where they worshipped unknown gods,
The barriers which they builded from the soil
To keep the foe at bay—till o'er the walls
The wild beleaguerers broke, and, one by one, 70
The strongholds of the plain were forced, and heaped
With corpses. The brown vultures of the wood
Flocked to those vast uncovered sepulchres,
And sat, unscared and silent, at their feast.
Haply some solitary fugitive,
Lurking in marsh and forest, till the sense
Of desolation and of fear became
Bitterer than death, yielded himself to die.
Man's better nature triumphed then. Kind words
Welcomed and soothed him; the rude conquerors 80

Seated the captive with their chiefs; he chose
A bride among their maidens, and at length
Seemed to forget—yet ne'er forgot—the wife
Of his first love, and her sweet little ones,
Butchered, amid their shrieks, with all his race.

Thus change the forms of being. Thus arise
Races of living things, glorious in strength,
And perish, as the quickening breath of God
Fills them, or is withdrawn. The red-man, too,
Has left the blooming wilds he ranged so long,   90
And, nearer to the Rocky Mountains, sought
A wilder hunting-ground. The beaver builds
No longer by these streams, but far away,
On waters whose blue surface ne'er gave back
The white man's face—among Missouri's springs,
And pools whose issues swell the Oregon—
He rears his little Venice. In these plains
The bison feeds no more. Twice twenty leagues
Beyond remotest smoke of hunter's camp,
Roams the majestic brute, in herds that shake   100
The earth with thundering steps—yet here I meet
His ancient footprints stamped beside the pool.

Still this great solitude is quick with life.
Myriads of insects, gaudy as the flowers
They flutter over, gentle quadrupeds,
And birds, that scarce have learned the fear of man,
Are here, and sliding reptiles of the ground,
Startlingly beautiful. The graceful deer
Bounds to the wood at my approach. The bee,
A more adventurous colonist than man,   110
With whom he came across the eastern deep,
Fills the savannas with his murmurings,
And hides his sweets, as in the golden age,
Within the hollow oak. I listen long
To his domestic hum, and think I hear
The sound of that advancing multitude
Which soon shall fill these deserts. From the ground
Comes up the laugh of children, the soft voice
Of maidens, and the sweet and solemn hymn
Of Sabbath worshippers. The low of herds   120

Blends with the rustling of the heavy grain
Over the dark brown furrows. All at once
A fresher wind sweeps by, and breaks my dream,
And I am in the wilderness alone.

EDGAR ALLAN POE (1809–1849)

250. ROMANCE

Romance, who loves to nod and sing
With drowsy head and folded wing,
Among the green leaves as they shake
Far down within some shadowy lake,
To me a painted paroquet
Hath been—a most familiar bird—
Taught me my alphabet to say,
To lisp my very earliest word,
While in the wild wood I did lie,
A child—with a most knowing eye.   10

Of late, eternal Condor years
So shake the very Heaven on high
With tumult as they thunder by,
I have no time for idle cares
Through gazing on the unquiet sky.
And when an hour with calmer wings
Its down upon my spirit flings—
That little time with lyre and rhyme
To while away—forbidden things!
My heart would feel to be a crime   20
Unless it trembled with the strings.

251. THE CITY IN THE SEA

Lo! Death has reared himself a throne
In a strange city lying alone
Far down within the dim West,
Where the good and the bad and the worst and the best
Have gone to their eternal rest.
There shrines and palaces and towers
(Time-eaten towers that tremble not!)
Resemble nothing that is ours.

Around, by lifting winds forgot,
Resignedly beneath the sky   10
The melancholy waters lie.

No rays from the holy heaven come down
On the long night-time of that town;
But light from out the lurid sea
Streams up the turrets silently—
Gleams up the pinnacles far and free—
Up domes—up spires—up kingly halls—

Up fanes—up Babylon-like walls—
Up shadowy long-forgotten bowers
Of sculptured ivy and stone flowers—   20
Up many and many a marvellous shrine
Whose wreathèd friezes intertwine
The viol, the violet, and the vine.

Resignedly beneath the sky
The melancholy waters lie.
So blend the turrets and shadows there
That all seem pendulous in air,
While from a proud tower in the town
Death looks gigantically down.

There open fanes and gaping graves   30
Yawn level with the luminous waves;
But not the riches there that lie
In each idol's diamond eye—
Not the gaily-jewelled dead
Tempt the waters from their bed;
For no ripples curl, alas!
Along that wilderness of glass—
No swellings tell that winds may be
Upon some far-off happier sea—
No heavings hint that winds have been   40
On seas less hideously serene.

But lo, a stir is in the air!
The wave—there is a movement there!
As if the towers had thrust aside,
In slightly sinking, the dull tide—
As if their tops had feebly given
A void within the filmy Heaven.

The waves have now a redder glow—
The hours are breathing faint and low—
And when, amid no earthly moans,   50
Down, down that town shall settle hence,
Hell, rising from a thousand thrones,
Shall do it reverence.

252.   THE HAUNTED PALACE

In the greenest of our valleys
    By good angels tenanted,
Once a fair and stately palace—
    Radiant palace—reared its head.
In the monarch Thought's dominion,
    It stood there!
Never seraph spread a pinion
    Over fabric half so fair!

Banners yellow, glorious, golden,
    On its roof did float and flow   10
(This—all this—was in the olden
    Time long ago),
And every gentle air that dallied,
    In that sweet day,
Along the ramparts plumed and pallid,
    A wingèd odor went away.

Wanderers in that happy valley,
    Through two luminous windows, saw
Spirits moving musically,
    To a lute's well-tunèd law,   20
Round about a throne where, sitting,
    Porphyrogene!
In state his glory well befitting,
    The ruler of the realm was seen.

And all with pearl and ruby glowing
    Was the fair palace door,
Through which came flowing, flowing, flowing,
    And sparkling evermore,
A troop of Echoes, whose sweet duty
    Was but to sing,   30
In voices of surpassing beauty,
    The wit and wisdom of their king.

But evil things, in robes of sorrow,
  Assailed the monarch's high estate.
(Ah, let us mourn!—for never morrow
  Shall dawn upon him, desolate!)
And round about his home the glory
  That blushed and bloomed,
Is but a dim-remembered story
  Of the old time entombed.   40

And travellers, now, within that valley,
  Through the red-litten windows see
Vast forms that move fantastically
  To a discordant melody,
While, like a ghastly rapid river,
  Through the pale door
A hideous throng rush out forever,
  And laugh—but smile no more.

V. THE VICTORIANS

THE VICTORIANS

The poets of the middle and late nineteenth century inherited the techniques and imaginative resources of the romantics and used them in their own way. Though in terms of critical theory they had by now won the right to wander into any conceivable realm of human activity, history, or imagination in pursuit of a poetic subject, the demands of the rising middle-class audience for poetry imposed, though indirectly, their own restrictions on the poet's handling of his material. New ideas in science and religion also had their impact on the poet's imagination, as we can see in Tennyson's *In Memoriam* and in the troubled poems of Matthew Arnold's friend, Arthur Hugh Clough. The Victorians were, in fact, a troubled company, and the popular notion of them as enjoying a stability of belief and convention which our own century has lost is very wide of the mark. There is no more eloquent record of a sensitive mind confronting crumbling faith than Arnold's "Dover Beach"; and even Browning, who maintained a belligerent optimism based on a composite personal creed, did his best and most characteristic work by probing into the state of mind of such characters as Bishop Blougram and the Renaissance grammarian, avoiding looking his own age in the eye as much as possible.

One has the impression sometimes that the Victorian poets had more technical virtuosity than they knew what to do with. We know that Tennyson was continually in search of suitable subjects, while in Swinburne we find a virtuosity grown positively feverish for lack of an "objective correlative" (to use that useful term of T. S. Eliot's) to justify his verbal excitement. It has been suggested that with the growing claims of prose, poets in the nineteenth century counterattacked by insisting that the realm of poetry consisted of areas of magic and passion which prose was quite incapable of handling. What the Romantic poets had recovered as a legitimate subject for poetry was by the Victorians often regarded as the sole subject or at least as the *most poetic* subject. This is certainly true of many Victorian poets (and of Poe in America), and it perhaps explains why Tennyson and others avoided the graceful verse essay which the eighteenth century achieved with such success. But a poet who commanded a wide middle-class audience could not limit his themes to the musically elegiac or suggestively magical—and it is significant that Tennyson wrote *In Memoriam* as well as such poems as "The Lady of Shalott," and that he turned his *Idylls of the King* into a vehicle for moralizing rather than for the conveyance of simply the enchantment of Malory.

If Tennyson was the poetic craftsman in search of a subject, magnificently equipped to ring the changes on vowel sounds and develop delicately subtle rhythms but often unable to see these devices in organic relationship with some intellectual or other perception, Browning saw his subject first and battered at language until it captured the psychological reality he wanted to present to the reader. Browning's dramatic monologues, with their fresh diction, broken rhythms, and cunning (sometimes too cunning) rhymes, represent a wholly original contribution to English poetry. Yet if it is a poet's duty to put his art at the service of the sensibility of his age and give poetic expression to the patterns of significance as they strike him in the cultural *milieu* of which he is a part (and there is some reason for demanding that our greatest poets should, directly or indirectly, achieve this), then it must be admitted that Browning shirked this duty and found himself as a poet by a kind of intellectual and emotional exile. Only Matthew Arnold of the great Victorian poets stands as a man of both intellect and sensibility who looked his age in the face and expressed in a verse in which form and content condition each other his sense of its meaning and his response to its challenge. He has not the sheer virtuosity of Tennyson or Browning's tricky way with words, but his technique is proportioned to his insights and there are no leftover meanings wandering around his poems as there sometimes are in Tennyson.

The poet can be considered as craftsman or as prophet: Tennyson was the former who felt it his duty to play the part of the latter, but where he did not assume this latter role his success is often outstanding. There were many minor poets in this period who exercised craftsmanship in one way or another to produce an occasional poem of charm and even brilliance. While a major poet who devotes his life to the production of a series of what he hopes will be considered masterpieces must have a *position,* an intellectual power which governs his preference for one subject rather than another and a steady notion of what he is doing (which is not, of course, to say that he must have a specific and overt religious or political position), a minor poet who turns out an occasional poem of skill and charm may do so without such a central view of himself and his art. Matthew Arnold understood this, and in virtue of this understanding he is really the central literary figure of the Victorian age.

Of Rossetti and the pre-Raphaelite movement and the influence of ideals of painting on poetry in the latter half of the century, perhaps all that needs to be said here is that this is one of many attempts to limit the sphere and technique of poetry in the interests of a specific kind of skill. The widening of poetic horizons by the romantics and the amassing of a huge capital equipment of poetic techniques and subject matters by their successors bred their own reaction, not only in the view, already mentioned, that the most poetic poetry is magical and musical and passionate, but also in the desire to carve out some particular kind of magic or music or passion, some special use of imagery, some unique doctrine of the relation of the sensuous to the mystical, or whatever it may be. This tendency increased as the century progressed, and with the poetry of the nineties the search for the exotic emotion becomes mixed up with various kinds of exhibitionism and an anti-middle-class attitude which represents a very understandable turning away from all that industrial civilization stood for.

But classifications are always oversimplifications, and such an analysis does not properly account for William Morris, whose imagination was haunted by an ideal Middle Ages and whose technique moved between a decorative narrative verse and a violent lyricism. Nor does it account for such intensely personal religious poetry as Francis Thompson's "Hound of Heaven," and still less for the remarkable and original poetry of the Jesuit priest, Gerard Manley Hopkins. Hopkins, his sensibility divided between an intense yet highly intellectualized Catholic devotion on the one hand and a powerful awareness of the impact of the natural world on his senses and emotions on the other, developed a poetic technique which for flexibility of movement and ability to fit the exact pattern of the emotion at any given point is like nothing else in nineteenth-century poetry. Into Hopkins' discussions of his technique—such as his theory of "sprung rhythm"—we need not here enter, since the important thing is what he achieved in poetic practice. It will be seen from the poems of his included in our selection that Hopkins does not use the traditional English metrical foot, but thinks of the line in terms of the number of stresses, allowing varying numbers of unstressed syllables to fill the "troughs" between stresses. This helps him to achieve great immediacy and precision of effect. The discovery of Hopkins by twentieth-century poets and their adoption of many of his metrical and verbal devices had an effect on the course of both English and American poetry that is still being felt and which, therefore, at this stage is difficult to estimate. Hopkins broke right out of the bounds of Victorian poetry: he was a poet in a very special position who followed his own vision without regard for the demands of an audience, the chances of publication, or the cultural climate of his time.

There were other poets with highly individual sensibilities who nevertheless did not turn their attention to enlarging the technical resources of English poetry. Hardy, with his rugged pessimism, produced his flinty poems with an apparent technical carelessness, yet it is just this cragginess, this rough utterance, that gives them their peculiar note of authenticity and fits them to communicate his view of man's fate. A. E. Housman limited rather than expanded the technical horizon by confining himself on the whole to an almost epigrammatic style (though he has his moments of excessive rhetoric) which clearly owes something to Latin origins. And Kipling refined on the technique of the Methodist hymn and the street ballad to focus attention on areas of British life and activity that had not hitherto been handled poetically.

Apart from Hopkins, no major technical advances were made by the Victorian poets, who were on the whole living with great skill off inherited capital. They often refined and elaborated on what they inherited, and in some areas—notably the elgiac: both Tennyson and Arnold could handle magnificently, each in his own way, a studied plaintiveness—did as well as English poetry has ever done. But they were bothered by ideas (whereas the seventeenth-century poets were as a rule excited by ideas) and tended to take refuge in mere craftsmanship or, seizing the other horn of the dilemma, to accept the role of prophet without having a clearly defined social and intellectual base from which to prophesy. Such a situation did not make for great poetic inventiveness, and by the end of the century it began to appear that there were no more poems left to be written. The only way out of that dilemma was to enlarge the definition of poetry, as poets had done in the face of a similar situation a century before. The twentieth century turned to that task with an almost malicious enthusiasm.

By 1837 the great creative age of American literature had begun; it was to reach its peak between 1850 and 1855. On the whole, the imaginative strength of that age found its best outlet in prose. Prose was far more popular than verse, and Emerson, Thoreau, and Melville, who earnestly wished to communicate to their generation, recognized it as a more acceptable medium for their purposes. All three occasionally wrote poetry, but all found that the resources of rhythmed and imaged prose gave them scope for the expression of poetic insights.

There were other poets of lesser power who found, especially after 1845, that there was a growing demand for verse which expressed simply the ideals, interests, and tastes of the common reader. Such poetry was produced by Longfellow, Whittier, Bryant, Lowell, and Holmes. Poetry of this kind is condescendingly called "popular," but it needs to be distinguished from the merely commercial rhymes of an Edgar Guest. It may be defined as poetry which communicates *in its time* to readers who are more interested in content than in techniques, and which is technically acceptable because it grows out of respectable poetic traditions with which readers are familiar. Such poetry may not be accounted "deathless" by critics, but it keeps on living until the cultural conditions which it reflects disappear. After that it may have an additional span of life if it embodies values which the educational institutions of society wish to perpetuate.

By critical standards, popular poetry may be good, or bad, or neither. Ordinarily it is not conspicuously or radically experimental in form; it does not challenge the reader on grounds where he does not wish to be met; it is not intellectually daring or adventurous;

it is not pervadingly cynical or pessimistic. More positively, it is, or seems to be, clear and lucid; its rhythms and rhyme patterns are unmistakable; its imagery and symbolism are exposed rather than hidden,—functional, rather than ends in themselves. Its subject matter, not its method or its devices, is its reason for existing. It need not be moralistic in purpose, but it must not be immoral or amoral. Such poetry is often shallow, but it may be so good that it continues to appeal long after the culture that produced it has passed.

The poetry of Longfellow and Whittier performed an immense cultural service in its time, but inevitably much of it lacks relevance to modern readers who are not primarily concerned with historical values. Longfellow's verse on European themes widened the horizons of generations of Americans, but there is survival value in only those of his poems which rise above the sentimental and academic tone which the nineteenth century found unobjectionable. In such poems the modern reader discerns not only Longfellow's solid craftsmanship, but his ability to project himself into the culture of old civilizations. Whittier was primarily a propagandist for freedom, a folklorist, and a celebrant of the virtues and beauties of agrarian democracy. In a few poems on these subjects he was able to write so simply, so concretely, and with such moral intensity that his customary verbal and rhythmic triteness become inconspicuous.

Of the three great romantic writers, Emerson, Thoreau, and Melville, only Emerson did some things better in verse than he could have done them in prose. A writer whose idiom had been determined from the start by public speaking (in pulpit and lyceum) but whose message and point of view were so abstruse that mere exposition was an inadequate instrument, Emerson in his essays had to draw on many of the resources of poetry. But many of his poems are merely essays in rhyme, and as such they suffer the inadequacies of poetry as a medium of exposition without offering the advantages of poetic crystallization. Occasionally, however, his abstractions found their perfect expressions in images which did more to bring his thinking to life than scores of pages of his prose.

Whitman, who, as he himself said, had merely simmered until Emerson brought him to a boil, had quite a different problem. His drive was even more forensic than Emerson's, and he early contemplated the delivery of his message from the lyceum platform rather than in verse. But as a speaker he had none of the quiet magnetism of Emerson, and he finally embodied his message in (ironically enough) privately printed verse. Yet throughout his poetry the voice of the public speaker is audible; indeed, its best values emerge not when it is closely analyzed but when it is read aloud. It is like that kind of impressionistic painting which looks merely slovenly when one stands too close to it.

Broad, loose brushwork was appropriate to the purposes of a poet whose subject was nothing less than the whole universe— physical and spiritual, past, present, and future; who set out blithely to settle once and for all the ancient conflicting claims of matter and spirit, of the individual and the mass; who thought of himself as the official poet of democracy; and who saw in America the highest, though by no means the final, result of the train of events which was set in motion when life was first generated amidst primal chaos. To a poet of such vision the old and established forms of expression were simply irrelevant: he set out to invent a prosody which would give him the freedom he needed.

That prosody is now described as "organic." The form of organic art is determined solely by its content and purpose—by those natural laws of growth, as Whitman put it, that determine the shape of a leaf or a pear. There is a certain amount of cant in such a concept because a poem cannot "grow" any more than a house can grow; both are artifacts, products of human workmanship. But just as an architect can make a bank look like a bank instead of a Greek temple, a poet can refuse to work from borrowed or predetermined forms, or to force his words into iambic pentameter or fourteen-line packages. Whitman's lines are free of such restrictions; that is, they are not linked by end rhymes which might distort a meaning; their length is determined only by the cadence and content of the thought; and they cannot be scanned into a regular pattern of accents. Similarly, his "stanzas" are uneven packages made up of any number of lines, depending upon what he considers to be a unit of thought within a poem.

This does not mean that all of his poems are externally shapeless, though many of them are. Sometimes they contain discoverable stanza patterns. A poem may begin and end with three-line stanzas which have a comparable function, all the lines between being grouped in pairs. More common still is his "wave" or "pyramid" pattern—a gradual lengthening of lines, and then a shortening, with a corresponding expansion and contraction of rhetorical tone. Usually, however, one must be satisfied with such internal unity as the poem achieves through mood and image.

The warmth of Whitman's love for human beings—in fact, for all *being*; his response to the stimuli of science, technology, and industrialism whose symbols had generally been excluded from romantic poetry; his genuine but nonchauvinistic nationalism, which refused the restrictions of regional cultures while it opened the door to internationalism; his frank and joyous sensuality at a time when literature either sublimated animality or toyed with it pruriently— these were potential correctives for an age which badly needed them. Actually he had few readers in his time, and little influence, for though his outlook was basically social, he violated too many of the taboos of his day, and his free verse was an irritant. To the modern reader his urgency on many subjects seems either naïve or irrelevant. But his best poems reveal his vitality without exposing his limitations as a thinker and craftsman.

There is some significance in the fact that the two best and most original poets of the years 1855 to 1890 did not communicate to their contemporaries. The public rejected Whitman, and Emily Dickinson did not publish. In these decades the public arts of theater and architecture sank to their lowest level in American history; the semiprivate arts of fiction and painting (with some notable exceptions) suffered to the extent that they were addressed to a large public; and the private art of poetry flourished most when it exposed itself to readers least. It is as if the energies of the republic were once more being absorbed by the demands of material expansion as they had been during the great pioneering decades before 1820.

Almost unknown to the frantically energetic America in which she lived, Emily Dickinson humbly and correctly assumed that the tiny poems which she wrote in her New England village contained nothing which the verse readers of her time wished to hear. As she wryly reported of her efforts to make herself understood, "All men say 'What?' to me." When her verse was published in the nineties after her death, this was the question asked by many critics. Their hearing was poor, but to a certain extent the question was justified by the misreading of her poems by her editors, by the unfinished state of many of her poems, and by her almost eccentric passion for condensation.

She owed as little to poetic "schools" of the nineteenth century as Whitman: nothing in romantic or Victorian poetry (except possibly that of Emerson) could have prepared readers for either of them. She spun her perceptions out of the experiences of a life abnormally secluded once she reached maturity, and she exploited only those images and that idiom which inhered in the facts of her immediate environment. The experiences were with love (mostly one-sided on her part), nature, religion, and death. The images were derived from observation of life in her garden, home, and village. The idiom was a distillation of regional speech characteristics, and of the terminology of law (her family's profession) and of the Protestant church. All of this implies a restrictiveness of range and a concentration of effect which is in startling contrast to the expansiveness and diffuseness of her contemporary Whitman. If Whitman may be said to have tried to spread himself over the whole universe, Emily Dickinson tried to bore a hole into the middle of it from the town of Amherst.

When American poetry was ready for a renaissance about 1912, it was chiefly in these two that it found the basis for continuity in native poetic expression.

ALFRED TENNYSON (1809–1892)

253.   MARIANA

'Mariana in the moated grange.'
Measure for Measure

With blackest moss the flower-plots
    Were thickly crusted, one and all:
The rusted nails fell from the knots
    That held the pear to the gable-wall.

The broken sheds look'd sad and strange:
   Unlifted was the clinking latch;
   Weeded and worn the ancient thatch
Upon the lonely moated grange.
      She only said, 'My life is dreary,
         He cometh not,' she said;   10
      She said, 'I am aweary, aweary,
         I would that I were dead!'

Her tears fell with the dews at even;
   Her tears fell ere the dews were dried:
She could not look on the sweet heaven,
   Either at morn or eventide.
After the flitting of the bats,
   When thickest dark did trance the sky,
   She drew her casement-curtain by,
And glanced athwart the glooming flats.   20
      She only said, 'The night is dreary,
         He cometh not,' she said;
      She said, 'I am aweary, aweary,
         I would that I were dead!'

Upon the middle of the night,
   Waking she heard the night-fowl crow:
The cock sung out an hour ere light:
   From the dark fen the oxen's low
Came to her: without hope of change,
   In sleep she seem'd to walk forlorn,   30
   Till cold winds woke the gray-eyed morn
About the lonely moated grange.
      She only said, 'The day is dreary,
         He cometh not,' she said;
      She said, 'I am aweary, aweary,
         I would that I were dead!'

About a stone-cast from the wall
   A sluice with blacken'd waters slept,
And o'er it many, round and small,
   The cluster'd marish-mosses crept.   40
Hard by a poplar shook alway,
   All silver-green with gnarled bark:
   For leagues no other tree did mark
The level waste, the rounding gray.

She only said, 'My life is dreary,
  He cometh not,' she said;
She said, 'I am aweary, aweary,
  I would that I were dead!'

And ever when the moon was low,
  And the shrill winds were up and away,   50
In the white curtain, to and fro,
  She saw the gusty shadow sway.
But when the moon was very low,
  And wild winds bound within their cell,
The shadow of the poplar fell
Upon her bed, across her brow.
    She only said, 'The night is dreary,
      He cometh not,' she said;
    She said, 'I am aweary, aweary,
      I would that I were dead!'   60

All day within the dreamy house,
  The doors upon their hinges creak'd;
The blue fly sung in the pane; the mouse
  Behind the mouldering wainscot shriek'd,
Or from the crevice peer'd about.
  Old faces glimmer'd thro' the doors,
  Old footsteps trod the upper floors,
Old voices called her from without.
    She only said, 'My life is dreary,
      He cometh not,' she said;
    She said, 'I am aweary, aweary,   70
      I would that I were dead!'

The sparrow's chirrup on the roof,
  The slow clock ticking, and the sound
Which to the wooing wind aloof
  The poplar made, did all confound
Her sense; but most she loathed the hour
  When the thick-moted sunbeam lay
  Athwart the chambers, and the day
Was sloping toward his western bower.   80
    Then, said she, 'I am very dreary,
      He will not come,' she said;
    She wept, 'I am aweary, aweary,
      Oh God, that I were dead!'

254.   THE LADY OF SHALOTT

PART I

On either side the river lie
Long fields of barley and of rye,
That clothe the wold and meet the sky;
And thro' the field the road runs by
        To many-tower'd Camelot;
And up and down the people go,
Gazing where the lilies blow
Round an island there below,
        The island of Shalott.

Willows whiten, aspens quiver,   10
Little breezes dusk and shiver
Thro' the wave that runs for ever
By the island in the river
        Flowing down to Camelot.
Four gray walls, and four gray towers,
Overlook a space of flowers,
And the silent isle imbowers
        The Lady of Shalott.

By the margin, willow-veil'd,
Slide the heavy barges trail'd   20
By slow horses; and unhail'd
The shallop flitteth silken-sail'd
        Skimming down to Camelot:
But who hath seen her wave her hand?
Or at the casement seen her stand?
Or is she known in all the land,
        The Lady of Shalott?

Only reapers, reaping early
In among the bearded barley,
Hear a song that echoes cheerly   30
From the river winding clearly,
        Down to tower'd Camelot:
And by the moon the reaper weary,
Piling sheaves in uplands airy,
Listening, whispers ' 'Tis the fairy
        Lady of Shalott.'

PART II

There she weaves by night and day
A magic web with colours gay.
She has heard a whisper say,
A curse is on her if she stay   40
      To look down to Camelot.
She knows not what the curse may be,
And so she weaveth steadily,
And little other care hath she,
      The Lady of Shalott.

And moving thro' a mirror clear
That hangs before her all the year,
Shadows of the world appear.
There she sees the highway near
      Winding down to Camelot: 50
There the river eddy whirls,
And there the surly village-churls,
And the red cloaks of market girls,
      Pass onward from Shalott.

Sometimes a troop of damsels glad,
An abbot on an ambling pad,
Sometimes a curly shepherd-lad,
Or long-hair'd page in crimson clad,
      Goes by to tower'd Camelot;
And sometimes thro' the mirror blue   60
The knights come riding two and two:
She hath no loyal knight and true,
      The Lady of Shalott.

But in her web she still delights
To weave the mirror's magic sights,
For often thro' the silent nights
A funeral, with plumes and lights
      And music, went to Camelot:
Or when the moon was overhead,
Came two young lovers lately wed;   70
'I am half sick of shadows,' said
      The Lady of Shalott.

PART III

A bow-shot from her bower-eaves,
He rode between the barley-sheaves,

The sun came dazzling thro' the leaves,
And flamed upon the brazen greaves
    Of bold Sir Lancelot.
A red-cross knight for ever kneel'd
To a lady in his shield,
That sparkled on the yellow field,   80
    Beside remote Shalott.

The gemmy bridle glitter'd free,
Like to some branch of stars we see
Hung in the golden Galaxy.
The bridle bells rang merrily
    As he rode down to Camelot:
And from his blazon'd baldric slung
A mighty silver bugle hung,
And as he rode his armour rung,
    Beside remote Shalott.   90

All in the blue unclouded weather
Thick-jewell'd shone the saddle-leather,
The helmet and the helmet-feather
Burn'd like one burning flame together,
    As he rode down to Camelot.
As often thro' the purple night,
Below the starry clusters bright,
Some bearded meteor, trailing light,
    Moves over still Shalott.

His broad clear brow in sunlight glow'd;   100
On burnish'd hooves his war-horse trode;
From underneath his helmet flow'd
His coal-black curls as on he rode,
    As he rode down to Camelot.
From the bank and from the river
He flash'd into the crystal mirror,
'Tirra lirra,' by the river
    Sang Sir Lancelot.

She left the web, she left the loom,
She made three paces thro' the room,   110
She saw the water-lily bloom,
She saw the helmet and the plume,
    She look'd down to Camelot.

Out flew the web and floated wide;
The mirror crack'd from side to side;
'The curse is come upon me,' cried
        The Lady of Shalott.

PART IV

In the stormy east-wind straining,
The pale yellow woods were waning,
The broad stream in his banks complaining,   120
Heavily the low sky raining
        Over tower'd Camelot;
Down she came and found a boat
Beneath a willow left afloat,
And round about the prow she wrote
        The Lady of Shalott.

And down the river's dim expanse
Like some bold seër in a trance,
Seeing all his own mischance—
With a glassy countenance   130
        Did she look to Camelot.
And at the closing of the day
She loosed the chain, and down she lay;
The broad stream bore her far away,
        The Lady of Shalott.

Lying, robed in snowy white
That loosely flew to left and right—
The leaves upon her falling light—
Thro' the noises of the night
        She floated down to Camelot: 140
And as the boat-head wound along
The willowy hills and fields among,
They heard her singing her last song,
        The Lady of Shalott.

Heard a carol, mournful, holy,
Chanted loudly, chanted lowly,
Till her blood was frozen slowly,
And her eyes were darken'd wholly,
        Turn'd to tower'd Camelot.
For ere she reach'd upon the tide   150
The first house by the water-side,

Singing in her song she died,
        The Lady of Shalott.

Under tower and balcony,
By garden-wall and gallery,
A gleaming shape she floated by,
Dead-pale between the houses high,
        Silent into Camelot.
Out upon the wharfs they came,
Knight and burgher, lord and dame,   160
And round the prow they read her name,
        The Lady of Shalott.

Who is this? and what is here?
And in the lighted palace near
Died the sound of royal cheer;
And they cross'd themselves for fear,
        All the knights at Camelot:
But Lancelot mused a little space;
He said, 'She has a lovely face;
God in his mercy lend her grace,   170
        The Lady of Shalott.'

255.   THE LOTOS-EATERS

'Courage!' he said, and pointed toward the land,
'This mounting wave will roll us shoreward soon.'
In the afternoon they came unto a land
In which it seemed always afternoon.
All round the coast the languid air did swoon,
Breathing like one that hath a weary dream.
Full-faced above the valley stood the moon;
And like a downward smoke, the slender stream
Along the cliff to fall and pause and fall did seem.

A land of streams! some, like a downward smoke,   10
Slow-dropping veils of thinnest lawn, did go;
And some thro' wavering lights and shadows broke,
Rolling a slumbrous sheet of foam below.
They saw the gleaming river seaward flow
From the inner land: far off, three mountain-tops,
Three silent pinnacles of aged snow,
Stood sunset-flush'd: and, dew'd with showery drops,
Up-clomb the shadowy pine above the woven copse.

The charmed sunset linger'd low adown
In the red West: thro' mountain clefts the dale 20
Was seen far inland, and the yellow down
Border'd with palm, and many a winding vale
And meadow, set with slender galingale;
A land where all things always seem'd the same!
And round about the keel with faces pale,
Dark faces pale against that rosy flame,
The mild-eyed melancholy Lotos-eaters came.

Branches they bore of that enchanted stem,
Laden with flower and fruit, whereof they gave
To each, but whoso did receive of them, 30
And taste, to him the gushing of the wave
Far far away did seem to mourn and rave
On alien shores; and if his fellow spake,
His voice was thin, as voices from the grave;
And deep-asleep he seem'd, yet all awake,
And music in his ears his beating heart did make.

They sat them down upon the yellow sand,
Between the sun and moon upon the shore;
And sweet it was to dream of Fatherland,
Of child, and wife, and slave; but evermore 40
Most weary seem'd the sea, weary the oar,
Weary the wandering fields of barren foam.
Then some one said, 'We will return no more;'
And all at once they sang, 'Our island home
Is far beyond the wave; we will no longer roam.'

CHORIC SONG

I

There is sweet music here that softer falls
Than petals from blown roses on the grass,
Or night-dews on still waters between walls
Of shadowy granite, in a gleaming pass;
Music that gentlier on the spirit lies, 50
Than tir'd eyelids upon tir'd eyes;
Music that brings sweet sleep down from the blissful skies.
Here are cool mosses deep,
And thro' the moss the ivies creep,

And in the stream the long-leaved flowers weep,
And from the craggy ledge the poppy hangs in sleep.

II

Why are we weigh'd upon with heaviness,
And utterly consumed with sharp distress,
While all things else have rest from weariness?
All things have rest: why should we toil alone,   60
We only toil, who are the first of things,
And make perpetual moan,
Still from one sorrow to another thrown:
Nor ever fold our wings,
And cease from wanderings,
Nor steep our brows in slumber's holy balm;
Nor harken what the inner spirit sings,
'There is no joy but calm!'
Why should we only toil, the roof and crown of things?

III

Lo! in the middle of the wood,   70
The folded leaf is woo'd from out the bud
With winds upon the branch, and there
Grows green and broad, and takes no care,
Sun-steep'd at noon, and in the moon
Nightly dew-fed; and turning yellow
Falls, and floats adown the air.
Lo! sweeten'd with the summer light,
The full-juiced apple, waxing over-mellow,
Drops in a silent autumn night.
All its allotted length of days,   80
The flower ripens in its place,
Ripens and fades, and falls, and hath no toil,
Fast-rooted in the fruitful soil.

IV

Hateful is the dark-blue sky,
Vaulted o'er the dark-blue sea.
Death is the end of life; ah, why
Should life all labour be?
Let us alone. Time driveth onward fast,
And in a little while our lips are dumb.

Let us alone. What is it that will last?
All things are taken from us, and become
Portions and parcels of the dreadful Past.
Let us alone. What pleasure can we have
To war with evil? Is there any peace
In ever climbing up the climbing wave?
All things have rest, and ripen toward the grave
In silence; ripen, fall and cease:
Give us long rest or death, dark death, or dreamful ease.

V

How sweet it were, hearing the downward stream,
With half-shut eyes ever to seem
Falling asleep in a half-dream!
To dream and dream, like yonder amber light,
Which will not leave the myrrh-bush on the height;
To hear each other's whisper'd speech;
Eating the Lotos day by day,
To watch the crisping ripples on the beach,
And tender curving lines of creamy spray;
To lend our hearts and spirits wholly
To the influence of mild-minded melancholy;
To muse and brood and live again in memory,
With those old faces of our infancy
Heap'd over with a mound of grass,
Two handfuls of white dust, shut in an urn of brass!

VI

Dear is the memory of our wedded lives,
And dear the last embraces of our wives
And their warm tears: but all hath suffer'd change:
For surely now our household hearths are cold:
Our sons inherit us: our looks are strange:
And we should come like ghosts to trouble joy.
Or else the island princes over-bold
Have eat our substance, and the minstrel sings
Before them of the ten years' war in Troy,
And our great deeds, as half-forgotten things.
Is there confusion in the little isle?
Let what is broken so remain.
The Gods are hard to reconcile·

'Tis hard to settle order once again.
There *is* confusion worse than death,
Trouble on trouble, pain on pain,
Long labour unto aged breath,   130
Sore task to hearts worn out by many wars
And eyes grown dim with gazing on the pilot-stars.

VII

But, propt on beds of amaranth and moly,
How sweet (while warm airs lull us, blowing lowly)
With half-dropt eyelid still,
Beneath a heaven dark and holy,
To watch the long bright river drawing slowly
His waters from the purple hill—
To hear the dewy echoes calling
From cave to cave thro' the thick-twined vine—   140
To watch the emerald-colour'd water falling
Thro' many a wov'n acanthus-wreath divine!
Only to hear and see the far-off sparkling brine,
Only to hear were sweet, stretch'd out beneath the pine.

VIII

The Lotos blooms below the barren peak:
The Lotos blows by every winding creek:
All day the wind breathes low with mellower tone:
Thro' every hollow cave and alley lone
Round and round the spicy downs the yellow Lotos-dust is blown.
We have had enough of action, and of motion we,   150
Roll'd to starboard, roll'd to larboard, when the surge was seething
    free,
Where the wallowing monster spouted his foam-fountains in the
    sea.
Let us swear an oath, and keep it with an equal mind,
In the hollow Lotos-land to live and lie reclined
On the hills like Gods together, careless of mankind.
For they lie beside their nectar, and the bolts are hurl'd
Far below them in the valleys, and the clouds are lightly curl'd
Round their golden houses, girdled with the gleaming world:
Where they smile in secret, looking over wasted lands,
Blight and famine, plague and earthquake, roaring deeps and fiery
    sands,   160

Clanging fights, and flaming towns, and sinking ships, and praying
    hands.
But they smile, they find a music centred in a doleful song
Steaming up, a lamentation and an ancient tale of wrong,
Like a tale of little meaning tho' the words are strong;
Chanted from an ill-used race of men that cleave the soil,
Sow the seed, and reap the harvest with enduring toil,
Storing yearly little dues of wheat, and wine and oil;
Till they perish and they suffer—some, 'tis whisper'd—down in hell
Suffer endless anguish, others in Elysian valleys dwell,
Resting weary limbs at last on beds of asphodel.   170
Surely, surely, slumber is more sweet than toil, the shore
Than labour in the deep mid-ocean, wind and wave and oar;
Oh rest ye, brother mariners, we will not wander more.

256.   MORTE D'ARTHUR

    So all day long the noise of battle roll'd
    Among the mountains by the winter sea;
    Until King Arthur's table, man by man,
    Had fallen in Lyonnesse about their Lord,
    King Arthur: then, because his wound was deep,
    The bold Sir Bedivere uplifted him,
    Sir Bedivere, the last of all his knights,
    And bore him to a chapel nigh the field,
    A broken chancel with a broken cross,
    That stood on a dark strait of barren land.   10
    On one side lay the Ocean, and on one
    Lay a great water, and the moon was full.
       Then spake King Arthur to Sir Bedivere:
    'The sequel of to-day unsolders all
    The goodliest fellowship of famous knights
    Whereof this world holds record. Such a sleep
    They sleep—the men I loved. I think that we
    Shall never more, at any future time,
    Delight our souls with talk of knightly deeds,
    Walking about the gardens and the halls   20
    Of Camelot, as in the days that were.
    I perish by this people which I made,—
    Tho' Merlin sware that I should come again
    To rule once more—but let what will be, be,
    I am so deeply smitten thro' the helm
    That without help I cannot last till morn.

Thou therefore take my brand Excalibur,
Which was my pride: for thou rememberest how
In those old days, one summer noon, an arm
Rose up from out the bosom of the lake,   30
Clothed in white samite, mystic, wonderful,
Holding the sword—and how I row'd across
And took it, and have worn it, like a king.
And, wheresoever I am sung or told
In aftertime, this also shall be known:
But now delay not: take Excalibur,
And fling him far into the middle mere:
Watch what thou seëst, and lightly bring me word,'
  To him replied the bold Sir Bedivere:
'It is not meet, Sir King, to leave thee thus,   40
Aidless, alone, and smitten thro' the helm.
A little thing may harm a wounded man.
Yet I thy hest will all perform at full,
Watch what I see, and lightly bring thee word.'
  So saying, from the ruin'd shrine he stept
And in the moon athwart the place of tombs,
Where lay the mighty bones of ancient men,
Old knights, and over them the sea-wind sang
Shrill, chill, with flakes of foam. He, stepping down
By zig-zag paths, and juts of pointed rock,   50
Came on the shining levels of the lake.
  There drew he forth the brand Excalibur,
And o'er him, drawing it, the winter moon,
Brightening the skirts of a long cloud, ran forth
And sparkled keen with frost against the hilt:
For all the haft twinkled with diamond sparks
Myriads of topaz-lights, and jacinth-work
Of subtlest jewellery. He gazed so long
That both his eyes were dazzled, as he stood,
This way and that dividing the swift mind,   60
In act to throw: but at the last it seem'd
Better to leave Excalibur conceal'd
There in the many-knotted waterflags,
That whistled stiff and dry about the marge.
So strode he back slow to the wounded King.
  Then spake King Arthur to Sir Bedivere:
'Hast thou perform'd my mission which I gave?
What is it thou hast seen? or what hast heard?'

And answer made the bold Sir Bedivere:
'I heard the ripple washing in the reeds,   70
And the wild water lapping on the crag.'
    To whom replied King Arthur, faint and pale:
'Thou hast betray'd thy nature and thy name,
Not rendering true answer, as beseem'd
Thy fealty, nor like a noble knight:
For surer sign had follow'd, either hand,
Or voice, or else a motion of the mere.
This is a shameful thing for men to lie.
Yet now, I charge thee, quickly go again
As thou art lief and dear, and do the thing   80
I bad thee, watch, and lightly bring me word.'
    Then went Sir Bedivere the second time
Across the ridge, and paced beside the mere,
Counting the dewy pebbles, fix'd in thought;
But when he saw the wonder of the hilt,
How curiously and strangely chased, he smote
His palms together, and he cried aloud,
    'And if indeed I cast the brand away,
Surely a precious thing, one worthy note,
Should thus be lost for ever from the earth,   90
Which might have pleased the eyes of many men.
What good should follow this, if this were done?
What harm, undone? deep harm to disobey,
Seeing obedience is the bond of rule.
Were it well to obey then, if a king demand
An act unprofitable, against himself?
The King is sick, and knows not what he does.
What record, or what relic of my lord
Should be to aftertime, but empty breath
And rumours of a doubt? but were this kept,   100
Stored in some treasure-house of mighty kings,
Some one might show it at a joust of arms,
Saying, "King Arthur's sword, Excalibur,
Wrought by the lonely maiden of the Lake.
Nine years she wrought it, sitting in the deeps
Upon the hidden bases of the hills."
So might some old man speak in the aftertime
To all the people, winning reverence.
But now much honour and much fame were lost.'
    So spake he, clouded with his own conceit,   110

And hid Excalibur the second time,
And so strode back slow to the wounded King.
   Then spoke King Arthur, breathing heavily:
'What is it thou hast seen? or what hast heard?'
   And answer made the bold Sir Bedivere:
'I heard the water lapping on the crag,
And the long ripple washing in the reeds.'
   To whom replied King Arthur, much in wrath:
'Ah, miserable and unkind, untrue,
Unknightly, traitor-hearted! Woe is me!   120
Authority forgets a dying king,
Laid widow'd of the power in his eye
That bow'd the will. I see thee what thou art,
For thou, the latest-left of all my knights,
In whom should meet the offices of all,
Thou wouldst betray me for the precious hilt;
Either from lust of gold, or like a girl
Valuing the giddy pleasure of the eyes.
Yet, for a man may fail in duty twice,
And the third time may prosper, get thee hence: 130
But, if thou spare to fling Excalibur,
I will arise and slay thee with my hands.'
   Then quickly rose Sir Bedivere, and ran,
And, leaping down the ridges lightly, plunged
Among the bulrush-beds, and clutch'd the sword,
And strongly wheel'd and threw it. The great brand
Made lightnings in the splendour of the moon,
And flashing round and round, and whirl'd in an arch,
Shot like a streamer of the northern morn,
Seen where the moving isles of winter shock   140
By night, with noises of the northern sea.
So flash'd and fell the brand Excalibur:
But ere he dipt the surface, rose an arm
Clothed in white samite, mystic, wonderful,
And caught him by the hilt, and brandish'd him
Three times, and drew him under in the mere.
And lightly went the other to the King.
   Then spoke King Arthur, drawing thicker breath:
'Now see I by thine eyes that this is done.
Speak out: what is it thou hast heard, or seen?'   150
   And answer made the bold Sir Bedivere:
'Sir King, I closed mine eyelids, lest the gems

Should blind my purpose, for I never saw,
Nor shall see, here or elsewhere, till I die,
Not tho' I live three lives of mortal men,
So great a miracle as yonder hilt.
Then with both hands I flung him, wheeling him;
But when I look'd again, behold an arm,
Clothed in white samite, mystic, wonderful,
That caught him by the hilt, and brandish'd him   160
Three times, and drew him under in the mere.'
    And answer made King Arthur, breathing hard:
'My end draws nigh; 'tis time that I were gone.
Make broad thy shoulders to receive my weight,
And bear me to the margin; yet I fear
My wound hath taken cold, and I shall die.'
    So saying, from the pavement he half rose,
Slowly, with pain, reclining on his arm,
And looking wistfully with wide blue eyes
As in a picture. Him Sir Bedivere   170
Remorsefully regarded thro' his tears,
And would have spoken, but he found not words;
Then took with care, and kneeling on one knee,
O'er both his shoulders drew the languid hands,
And rising bore him thro' the place of tombs.
    But, as he walk'd, King Arthur panted hard,
Like one that feels a nightmare on his bed
When all the house is mute. So sigh'd the King,
Muttering and murmuring at his ear, 'Quick, quick!
I fear it is too late, and I shall die.'   180
But the other swiftly strode from ridge to ridge,
Clothed with his breath, and looking, as he walk'd,
Larger than human on the frozen hills.
He heard the deep behind him, and a cry
Before. His own thought drove him, like a goad.
Dry clash'd his harness in the icy caves
And barren chasms, and all to left and right
The bare black cliff clang'd round him, as he based
His feet on juts of slippery crag that rang
Sharp-smitten with the dint of armed heels—   190
And on a sudden, lo! the level lake,
And the long glories of the winter moon.
    Then saw they how there hove a dusky barge,
Dark as a funeral scarf from stem to stern,

Beneath them; and descending they were ware
That all the decks were dense with stately forms
Black-stoled, black-hooded, like a dream—by these
Three Queens with crowns of gold—and from them rose
A cry that shiver'd to the tingling stars,
And, as it were one voice, an agony   200
Of lamentation, like a wind, that shrills
All night in a waste land, where no one comes,
Or hath come, since the making of the world.
    Then murmur'd Arthur, 'Place me in the barge,'
And to the barge they came. There those three Queens
Put forth their hands, and took the King, and wept.
But she, that rose the tallest of them all
And fairest, laid his head upon her lap,
And loosed the shatter'd casque, and chafed his hands,
And call'd him by his name, complaining loud,   210
And dropping bitter tears against his brow
Striped with dark blood: for all his face was white
And colourless, and like the wither'd moon
Smote by the fresh beam of the springing east;
And all his greaves and cuisses dash'd with drops
Of onset; and the light and lustrous curls—
That made his forehead like a rising sun
High from the daïs-throne—were parch'd with dust;
Or, clotted into points and hanging loose,
Mix'd with the knightly growth that fringed his lips.   220
So like a shatter'd column lay the King;
Not like that Arthur who, with lance in rest,
From spur to plume a star of tournament,
Shot thro' the lists at Camelot, and charged
Before the eyes of ladies and of kings.
    Then loudly cried the bold Sir Bedivere,
'Ah! my Lord Arthur, whither shall I go?
Where shall I hide my forehead and my eyes?
For now I see the true old times are dead,
When every morning brought a noble chance,   230
And every chance brought out a noble knight.
Such times have been not since the light that led
The holy Elders with the gift of myrrh.
But now the whole ROUND TABLE is dissolved
Which was an image of the mighty world;
And I, the last, go forth companionless,

And the days darken round me, and the years,
Among new men, strange faces, other minds.'
   And slowly answered Arthur from the barge:
'The old order changeth, yielding place to new,   240
And God fulfils Himself in many ways,
Lest one good custom should corrupt the world.
Comfort thyself: what comfort is in me?
I have lived my life, and that which I have done
May He within Himself make pure! but thou,
If thou shouldst never see my face again,
Pray for my soul. More things are wrought by prayer
Than this world dreams of. Wherefore, let thy voice
Rise like a fountain for one night and day.
For what are men better than sheep or goats   250
That nourish a blind life within the brain,
If, knowing God, they lift not hands of prayer
Both for themselves and those who call them friend?
For so the whole round earth is every way
Bound by gold chains about the feet of God.
But now farewell. I am going a long way
With these thou seëst—if indeed I go—
(For all my mind is clouded with a doubt)
To the island-valley of Avilion;
Where falls not hail, or rain, or any snow,   260
Nor ever wind blows loudly; but it lies
Deep-meadow'd, happy, fair with orchard-lawns
And bowery hollows crown'd with summer sea,
Where I will heal me of my grievous wound.'
   So said he, and the barge with oar and sail
Moved from the brink, like some full-breasted swan
That, fluting a wild carol ere her death,
Ruffles her pure cold plume, and takes the flood
With swarthy webs. Long stood Sir Bedivere
Revolving many memories, till the hull   270
Look'd one black dot against the verge of dawn,
And on the mere the wailing died away.

257.   ULYSSES

It little profits that an idle king,
By this still hearth, among these barren crags,
Match'd with an aged wife, I mete and dole
Unequal laws unto a savage race,

That hoard, and sleep, and feed, and know not me.
I cannot rest from travel: I will drink
Life to the lees: all times I have enjoy'd
Greatly, have suffer'd greatly, both with those
That loved me, and alone; on shore, and when
Thro' scudding drifts the rainy Hyades   10
Vext the dim sea: I am become a name;
For always roaming with a hungry heart
Much have I seen and known; cities of men
And manners, climates, councils, governments,
Myself not least, but honour'd of them all;
And drunk delight of battle with my peers,
Far on the ringing plains of windy Troy.
I am a part of all that I have met;
Yet all experience is an arch wherethro'
Gleams that untravell'd world, whose margin fades   20
For ever and for ever when I move.
How dull it is to pause, to make an end,
To rust unburnish'd, not to shine in use!
As tho' to breathe were life. Life piled on life
Were all too little, and of one to me
Little remains: but every hour is saved
From that eternal silence, something more,
A bringer of new things; and vile it were
For some three suns to store and hoard myself,
And this gray spirit yearning in desire   30
To follow knowledge like a sinking star,
Beyond the utmost bound of human thought.

      This is my son, mine own Telemachus,
To whom I leave the sceptre and the isle—
Well-loved of me, discerning to fulfil
This labour, by slow prudence to make mild
A rugged people, and thro' soft degrees
Subdue them to the useful and the good.
Most blameless is he, centred in the sphere
Of common duties, decent not to fail   40
In offices of tenderness, and pay
Meet adoration to my household gods,
When I am gone. He works his work, I mine.

      There lies the port; the vessel puffs her sail:
There gloom the dark broad seas. My mariners,

Souls that have toil'd, and wrought, and thought with me—
That ever with a frolic welcome took
The thunder and the sunshine, and opposed
Free hearts, free foreheads—you and I are old;
Old age hath yet his honour and his toil;   50
Death closes all: but something ere the end,
Some work of noble note, may yet be done,
Not unbecoming men that strove with Gods.
The lights begin to twinkle from the rocks:
The long day wanes: the slow moon climbs: the deep
Moans round with many voices. Come, my friends,
'Tis not too late to seek a newer world.
Push off, and sitting well in order smite
The sounding furrows; for my purpose holds
To sail beyond the sunset, and the baths   60
Of all the western stars, until I die.
It may be that the gulfs will wash us down:
It may be we shall touch the Happy Isles,
And see the great Achilles, whom we knew.
Tho' much is taken, much abides; and tho'
We are not now that strength which in old days
Moved earth and heaven; that which we are, we are;
One equal temper of heroic hearts,
Made weak by time and fate, but strong in will
To strive, to seek, to find, and not to yield.   70

258.   TITHONUS

The woods decay, the woods decay and fall,
The vapours weep their burthen to the ground,
Man comes and tills the field and lies beneath,
And after many a summer dies the swan.
Me only cruel immortality
Consumes: I wither slowly in thine arms,
Here at the quiet limit of the world,
A white-hair'd shadow roaming like a dream
The ever-silent spaces of the East,
Far-folded mists, and gleaming halls of morn.   10

   Alas! for this gray shadow, once a man—
So glorious in his beauty and thy choice,
Who madest him thy chosen, that he seem'd

To his great heart none other than a God!
I ask'd thee, 'Give me immortality.'
Then didst thou grant mine asking with a smile,
Like wealthy men who care not how they give.
But thy strong Hours indignant work'd their wills,
And beat me down and marr'd and wasted me,
And tho' they could not end me, left me maim'd   20
To dwell in presence of immortal youth,
Immortal age beside immortal youth,
And all I was, in ashes. Can thy love,
Thy beauty, make amends, tho' even now,
Close over us, the silver star, thy guide
Shines in those tremulous eyes that fill with tears
To hear me? Let me go: take back thy gift:
Why should a man desire in any way
To vary from the kindly race of men,
Or pass beyond the goal of ordinance   30
Where all should pause, as is most meet for all?

    A soft air fans the cloud apart; there comes
A glimpse of that dark world where I was born.
Once more the old mysterious glimmer steals
From thy pure brows, and from thy shoulders pure,
And bosom beating with a heart renew'd.
Thy cheek begins to redden thro' the gloom,
Thy sweet eyes brighten slowly close to mine,
Ere yet they blind the stars, and the wild team
Which love thee, yearning for thy yoke, arise,   40
And shake the darkness from their loosen'd manes,
And beat the twilight into flakes of fire.

    Lo! ever thus thou growest beautiful
In silence, then before thine answer given
Departest, and thy tears are on my cheek.

    Why wilt thou ever scare me with thy tears,
And make me tremble lest a saying learnt,
In days far-off, on that dark earth, be true?
'The Gods themselves cannot recall their gifts.'

    Ay me! ay me! with what another heart   50
In days far-off, and with what other eyes
I used to watch—if I be he that watch'd—

The lucid outline forming round thee; saw
The dim curls kindle into sunny rings;
Changed with thy mystic change, and felt my blood
Glow with the glow that slowly crimson'd all
Thy presence and thy portals, while I lay,
Mouth, forehead, eyelids, growing dewy-warm
With kisses balmier than half-opening buds
Of April, and could hear the lips that kiss'd   60
Whispering I knew not what of wild and sweet,
Like that strange song I heard Apollo sing,
While Ilion like a mist rose into towers.

　　Yet hold me not for ever in thine East:
How can my nature longer mix with thine?
Coldly thy rosy shadows bathe me, cold
Are all thy lights, and cold my wrinkled feet
Upon thy glimmering thresholds, when the steam
Floats up from those dim fields about the homes
Of happy men that have the power to die,   70
And grassy barrows of the happier dead.
Release me, and restore me to the ground;
Thou seëst all things, thou wilt see my grave:
Thou wilt renew thy beauty morn by morn;
I earth in earth forget these empty courts,
And thee returning on thy silver wheels.

259.　　　　　"BREAK, BREAK, BREAK"

　　Break, break, break,
　　　On thy cold gray stones, O Sea!
　And I would that my tongue could utter
　　　The thoughts that arise in me.

　O well for the fisherman's boy,
　　　That he shouts with his sister at play!
　O well for the sailor lad,
　　　That he sings in his boat on the bay!

　And the stately ships go on
　　　To their haven under the hill;   10
　But O for the touch of a vanish'd hand,
　　　And the sound of a voice that is still!

Break, break, break,
   At the foot of thy crags, O Sea!
But the tender grace of a day that is dead
   Will never come back to me.

From THE PRINCESS

260.   "SWEET AND LOW"

Sweet and low, sweet and low,
   Wind of the western sea,
Low, low, breathe and blow,
   Wind of the western sea!
Over the rolling waters go,
Come from the dying moon, and blow,
   Blow him again to me;
While my little one, while my pretty one, sleeps.

Sleep and rest, sleep and rest,
   Father will come to thee soon;   10
Rest, rest, on mother's breast,
   Father will come to thee soon;
Father will come to his babe in the nest,
Silver sails all out of the west
   Under the silver moon:
Sleep, my little one, sleep, my pretty one, sleep.

261.   "THE SPLENDOUR FALLS ON
             CASTLE WALLS"

The splendour falls on castle walls
   And snowy summits old in story:
The long light shakes across the lakes,
   And the wild cataract leaps in glory.
Blow, bugle, blow, set the wild echoes flying,
Blow, bugle; answer, echoes, dying, dying, dying.

O hark, O hear! how thin and clear,
   And thinner, clearer, farther going!
O sweet and far from cliff and scar
   The horns of Elfland faintly blowing!   10
Blow, let us hear the purple glens reply:
Blow, bugle; answer, echoes, dying, dying, dying.

O love, they die in yon rich sky,
    They faint on hill or field or river:
Our echoes roll from soul to soul,
    And grow for ever and for ever.
Blow, bugle, blow, set the wild echoes flying,
And answer, echoes, answer, dying, dying, dying.

262.   "TEARS, IDLE TEARS"

Tears, idle tears, I know not what they mean,
Tears from the depth of some divine despair
Rise in the heart, and gather to the eyes,
In looking on the happy Autumn-fields,
And thinking of the days that are no more.

Fresh as the first beam glittering on a sail,
That brings our friends up from the underworld,
Sad as the last which reddens over one
That sinks with all we love below the verge;
So sad, so fresh, the days that are no more.   10

Ah, sad and strange as in dark summer dawns
The earliest pipe of half-awaken'd birds
To dying ears, when unto dying eyes
The casement slowly grows a glimmering square;
So sad, so strange, the days that are no more.

Dear as remember'd kisses after death,
And sweet as those by hopeless fancy feign'd
On lips that are for others; deep as love,
Deep as first love, and wild with all regret;
O Death in Life, the days that are no more.   20

263.   "NOW SLEEPS THE CRIMSON PETAL,
              NOW THE WHITE"

Now sleeps the crimson petal, now the white;
Nor waves the cypress in the palace walk;
Nor winks the gold fin in the porphyry font:
The fire-fly wakens; waken thou with me.

Now droops the milk-white peacock like a ghost,
And like a ghost she glimmers on to me.

Now lies the Earth all Danaë to the stars,
And all thy heart lies open unto me.

Now slides the silent meteor on, and leaves
A shining furrow, as thy thoughts in me.   10

Now folds the lily all her sweetness up,
And slips into the bosom of the lake.
So fold thyself, my dearest, thou, and slip
Into my bosom and be lost in me.

264.   "COME DOWN, O MAID, FROM YONDER
                    MOUNTAIN HEIGHT"

Come down, O maid, from yonder mountain height:
What pleasure lives in height (the shepherd sang),
In height and cold, the splendour of the hills?
But cease to move so near the heavens, and cease
To glide a sunbeam by the blasted pine,
To sit a star upon the sparkling spire;
And come, for Love is of the valley, come
For Love is of the valley, come thou down
And find him; by the happy threshold, he
Or hand in hand with Plenty in the maize,   10
Or red with spirited purple of the vats,
Or foxlike in the vine; nor cares to walk
With Death and Morning on the Silver Horns,
Nor wilt thou snare him in the white ravine,
Nor find him dropt upon the firths of ice,
That huddling slant in furrow-cloven falls
To roll the torrent out of dusky doors.
But follow; let the torrent dance thee down
To find him in the valley; let the wild
Lean-headed eagles yelp alone, and leave   20
The monstrous ledges there to slope, and spill
Their thousand wreaths of dangling water-smoke,
That like a broken purpose waste in air.
So waste not thou, but come; for all the vales
Await thee; azure pillars of the hearth
Arise to thee; the children call, and I
Thy shepherd pipe, and sweet is every sound,
Sweeter thy voice, but every sound is sweet;

Myriads of rivulets, hurrying through the lawn;
The moan of doves in immemorial elms, 30
And murmuring of innumerable bees.

265. *From* IN MEMORIAM

"DARK HOUSE, BY WHICH ONCE MORE I STAND"

Dark house, by which once more I stand
 Here in the long unlovely street,
  Doors, where my heart was used to beat
So quickly, waiting for a hand,

A hand that can be clasp'd no more—
 Behold me, for I cannot sleep,
  And like a guilty thing I creep
At earliest morning to the door.

He is not here; but far away
 The noise of life begins again, 10
  And ghastly thro' the drizzling rain
On the bald street breaks the blank day.

"CALM IS THE MORN"

Calm is the morn without a sound,
 Calm as to suit a calmer grief,
  And only thro' the faded leaf
The chestnut pattering to the ground:

Calm and deep peace on this high wold,
 And on these dews that drench the furze,
  And all the silvery gossamers
That twinkle into green and gold:

Calm and still light on yon great plain
 That sweeps with all its autumn bowers, 10
  And crowded farms and lessening towers,
To mingle with the bounding main:

Calm and deep peace in this wide air,
 These leaves that redden to the fall;
  And in my heart, if calm at all,
If any calm, a calm despair:

Calm on the seas, and silver sleep,
    And waves that sway themselves in rest,
    And dead calm in that noble breast
Which heaves but with the heaving deep.   20

"BE NEAR ME WHEN MY LIGHT IS LOW"

Be near me when my light is low,
    When the blood creeps, and the nerves prick
    And tingle; and the heart is sick,
And all the wheels of Being slow.

Be near me when the sensuous frame
    Is rack'd with pangs that conquer trust;
    And Time, a maniac scattering dust,
And Life, a Fury slinging flame.

Be near me when my faith is dry,
    And men the flies of latter spring,   10
    That lay their eggs, and sting and sing
And weave their petty cells and die.

Be near me when I fade away,
    To point the term of human strife,
    And on the low dark verge of life
The twilight of eternal day.

"OH YET WE TRUST THAT SOMEHOW GOOD"

Oh yet we trust that somehow good
    Will be the final goal of ill,
    To pangs of nature, sins of will,
Defects of doubt, and taints of blood;

That nothing walks with aimless feet;
    That not one life shall be destroy'd,
    Or cast as rubbish to the void,
When God hath made the pile complete;

That not a worm is cloven in vain;
    That not a moth with vain desire   10
    Is shrivell'd in a fruitless fire,
Or but subserves another's gain.

Behold, we know not anything;
    I can but trust that good shall fall
    At last—far off—at last, to all,
And every winter change to spring.

So runs my dream: but what am I?
    An infant crying in the night:
    An infant crying for the light:
And with no language but a cry.   20

"WHEN ON MY BED THE MOONLIGHT FALLS"

When on my bed the moonlight falls,
    I know that in thy place of rest
    By that broad water of the west,
There comes a glory on the walls:

Thy marble bright in dark appears,
    As slowly steals a silver flame
    Along the letters of thy name.
And o'er the number of thy years.

The mystic glory swims away;
    From off my bed the moonlight dies;   10
    And closing eaves of wearied eyes
I sleep till dusk is dipt in gray:

And then I know the mist is drawn
    A lucid veil from coast to coast,
    And in the dark church like a ghost
Thy tablet glimmers to the dawn.

"THE TIME DRAWS NEAR THE BIRTH
OF CHRIST"

The time draws near the birth of Christ;
    The moon is hid, the night is still;
    A single church below the hill
Is pealing, folded in the mist.

A single peal of bells below,
    That wakens at this hour of rest
    A single murmur in the breast,
That these are not the bells I know.

Like strangers' voices here they sound,
    In lands where not a memory strays,   10
    Nor landmark breathes of other days,
But all is new unhallow'd ground.

"RING OUT, WILD BELLS"

Ring out, wild bells, to the wild sky,
    The flying cloud, the frosty light:
    The year is dying in the night;
Ring out, wild bells, and let him die.

Ring out the old, ring in the new,
    Ring, happy bells, across the snow:
    The year is going let him go;
Ring out the false, ring in the true.

Ring out the grief that saps the mind,
    For those that here we see no more;   10
    Ring out the feud of rich and poor,
Ring in redress to all mankind.

Ring out a slowly dying cause,
    And ancient forms of party strife;
    Ring in the nobler modes of life,
With sweeter manners, purer laws.

Ring out the want, the care, the sin,
    The faithless coldness of the times;
    Ring out, ring out my mournful rhymes,
But ring the fuller minstrel in.   20

Ring out false pride in place and blood,
    The civic slander and the spite;
    Ring in the love of truth and right,
Ring in the common love of good.

Ring out old shapes of foul disease;
    Ring out the narrowing lust of gold;
    Ring out the thousand wars of old,
Ring in the thousand years of peace.

Ring in the valiant man and free,
    The larger heart, the kindlier hand;   30
    Ring out the darkness of the land,
Ring in the Christ that is to be.

"NOW FADES THE LAST LONG STREAK"

Now fades the last long streak of snow,
　　Now burgeons every maze of quick
　　About the flowering squares, and thick
By ashen roots the violets blow.

Now rings the woodland loud and long,
　　The distance takes a lovelier hue,
　　And drown'd in yonder living blue
The lark becomes a sightless song.

Now dance the lights on lawn and lea,
　　The flocks are whiter down the vale,　　　10
　　And milkier every milky sail
On winding stream or distant sea;

Where now the seamew pipes, or dives
　　In yonder greening gleam, and fly
　　The happy birds, that change their sky
To build and brood; that live their lives

From land to land; and in my breast
　　Spring wakens too; and my regret
　　Becomes an April violet,
And buds and blossoms like the rest.　　　20

266. CROSSING THE BAR

Sunset and evening star,
　　And one clear call for me!
And may there be no moaning of the bar
　　When I put out to sea,

But such a tide as moving seems asleep,
　　Too full for sound and foam,
When that which drew from out the boundless deep
　　Turns again home.

Twilight and evening bell,
　　And after that the dark!　　　10
And may there be no sadness of farewell,
　　When I embark;

For tho' from out our bourne of Time and Place
　　The flood may bear me far,
I hope to see my Pilot face to face
　　When I have crost the bar.

ROBERT BROWNING (1812–1889)

267.　　SOLILOQUY OF THE SPANISH CLOISTER

I

Gr-r-r—there go, my heart's abhorrence!
　　Water your damned flower-pots, do!
If hate killed men, Brother Lawrence,
　　God's blood, would not mine kill you!
What? your myrtle-bush wants trimming?
　　Oh, that rose has prior claims—
Needs its leaden vase filled brimming?
　　Hell dry you up with its flames!

II

At the meal we sit together:
　　Salve tibi! I must hear　　　　　　　10
Wise talk of the kind of weather,
　　Sort of season, time of year:
Not a plenteous cork-crop: scarcely
　　Dare we hope oak-galls, I doubt:
What's the Latin name for "parsley"?
　　What's the Greek name for Swine's Snout?

III

Whew! We'll have our platter burnished,
　　Laid with care on our own shelf!
With a fire-new spoon we're furnished,
　　And a goblet for ourself,　　　　　　20
Rinsed like something sacrificial
　　Ere 'tis fit to touch our chaps—
Marked with L. for our initial!
　　(He—he! There his lily snaps!)

IV

Saint, forsooth! While brown Dolores
　　Squats outside the Convent bank,

With Sanchicha, telling stories,
  Steeping tresses in the tank,
Blue-black, lustrous, thick like horsehairs,
  —Can't I see his dead eye glow,   30
Bright as 'twere a Barbary corsair's?
  (That is, if he'd let it show!)

V

When he finishes refection,
  Knife and fork he never lays
Cross-wise, to my recollection,
  As do I, in Jesu's praise.
I, the Trinity illustrate,
  Drinking watered orange-pulp—
In three sips the Arian frustrate;
  While he drains his at one gulp.   40

VI

Oh, those melons? If he's able
  We're to have a feast! so nice!
One goes to the Abbot's table,
  All of us get each a slice.
How go on your flowers? None double?
  Not one fruit-sort can you spy?
Strange!—And I, too, at such trouble,
  Keep them close-nipped on the sly!

VII

There's a great text in Galatians,
  Once you trip on it, entails   50
Twenty-nine distinct damnations,
  One sure, if another fails.
If I trip him just a-dying,
  Sure of heaven as sure can be,
Spin him round and send him flying
  Off to hell, a Manichee?

VIII

Or, my scrofulous French novel,
  On grey paper with blunt type!
Simply glance at it, you grovel
  Hand and foot in Belial's gripe: 60

If I double down its pages
    At the woeful sixteenth print,
When he gathers his greengages,
    Ope a sieve and slip it in't?

IX

Or, there's Satan!—one might venture
    Pledge one's soul to him, yet leave
Such a flaw in the indenture
    As he'd miss till, past retrieve,
Blasted lay that rose-acacia
    We're so proud of! *Hy, Zy, Hine* . . .   70
'St, there's Vespers! *Plena gratiâ*
    Ave, Virgo! Gr-r-r—you swine!

268.   MY LAST DUCHESS

FERRARA

That's my last Duchess painted on the wall,
Looking as if she were alive. I call
That piece a wonder, now: Frà Pandolf's hands
Worked busily a day, and there she stands.
Will't please you sit and look at her? I said
"Frà Pandolf" by design, for never read
Strangers like you that pictured countenance,
The depth and passion of its earnest glance,
But to myself they turned (since none puts by
The curtain I have drawn for you, but I)   10
And seemed as they would ask me, if they durst,
How such a glance came there; so, not the first
Are you to turn and ask thus. Sir, 'twas not
Her husband's presence only, called that spot
Of joy into the Duchess' cheek: perhaps
Frà Pandolf chanced to say "Her mantle laps
"Over my Lady's wrist too much," or "Paint
"Must never hope to reproduce the faint
"Half-flush that dies along her throat:" such stuff
Was courtesy, she thought, and cause enough   20
For calling up that spot of joy. She had
A heart—how shall I say?—too soon made glad,
Too easily impressed; she liked whate'er
She looked on, and her looks went everywhere.

Sir, 'twas all one! My favour at her breast,
The dropping of the daylight in the West,
The bough of cherries some officious fool
Broke in the orchard for her, the white mule
She rode with round the terrace—all and each
Would draw from her alike the approving speech,   30
Or blush, at least. She thanked men,—good! but thanked
Somehow—I know not how—as if she ranked
My gift of a nine hundred years old name
With anybody's gift. Who'd stoop to blame
This sort of trifling? Even had you skill
In speech—(which I have not)—to make your will
Quite clear to such an one, and say "Just this
"Or that in you disgusts me; here you miss,
"Or there exceed the mark"—and if she let
Herself be lessoned so, nor plainly set   40
Her wits to yours, forsooth, and made excuse,
—E'en then would be some stooping, and I choose
Never to stoop. Oh, Sir, she smiled, no doubt
Whene'er I passed her; but who passed without
Much the same smile? This grew; I gave commands;
Then all smiles stopped together. There she stands
As if alive. Will't please you rise? We'll meet
The company below, then. I repeat,
The Count your Master's known munificence
Is ample warrant that no just pretence   50
Of mine for dowry will be disallowed;
Though his fair daughter's self, as I avowed
At starting, is my object. Nay, we'll go
Together down, Sir! Notice Neptune, tho',
Taming a sea-horse, thought a rarity,
Which Claus of Innsbruck cast in bronze for me.

269.   THE PIED PIPER OF HAMELIN

                    A CHILD'S STORY

          (Written for, and inscribed to, W. M., The Younger)

                           I

Hamelin Town's in Brunswick,
    By famous Hanover city;

The river Weser, deep and wide,
Washes its wall on the southern side;
A pleasanter spot you never spied;
   But, when begins my ditty,
Almost five hundred years ago,
To see the townsfolk suffer so
   From vermin, was a pity.

II

Rats!   10
They fought the dogs and killed the cats,
   And bit the babies in the cradles,
And ate the cheeses out of the vats,
   And licked the soup from the cooks' own ladles,
Split open the kegs of salted sprats,
Made nests inside men's Sunday hats,
And even spoiled the women's chats
      By drowning their speaking
      With shrieking and squeaking
In fifty different sharps and flats.   20

III

At last the people in a body
   To the Town Hall came flocking:
" 'Tis clear," cried they, "our Mayor's a noddy;
   "And as for our Corporation—shocking
"To think we buy gowns lined with ermine
"For dolts that can't or won't determine
"What's best to rid us of our vermin!
"You hope, because you're old and obese,
"To find in the furry civic robe ease?
"Rouse up, sirs! Give your brains a racking   30
"To find the remedy we're lacking,
"Or, sure as fate, we'll send you packing!"
At this the Mayor and Corporation
Quaked with a mighty consternation.

IV

An hour they sat in council;
   At length the Mayor broke silence:

"For a guilder I'd my ermine gown sell,
  "I wish I were a mile hence!
"It's easy to bid one rack one's brain—
"I'm sure my poor head aches again,   40
"I've scratched it so, and all in vain.
"Oh for a trap, a trap, a trap!"
Just as he said this, what should hap
At the chamber door but a gentle tap?
"Bless us," cried the Mayor, "what's that?"
(With the Corporation as he sat,
Looking little though wondrous fat;
Nor brighter was his eye, nor moister
Than a too-long-opened oyster,
Save when at noon his paunch grew mutinous   50
For a plate of turtle green and glutinous)
"Only a scraping of shoes on the mat?
"Anything like the sound of a rat
"Makes my heart go pit-a-pat!"

v

"Come in!"—the Mayor cried, looking bigger:
And in did come the strangest figure!
His queer long coat from heel to head
Was half of yellow and half of red,
And he himself was tall and thin,
With sharp blue eyes, each like a pin,   60
And light loose hair, yet swarthy skin,
No tuft on cheek nor beard on chin,
But lips where smiles went out and in;
There was no guessing his kith and kin:
And nobody could enough admire
The tall man and his quaint attire.
Quoth one: "It's as my great-grandsire,
"Starting up at the Trump of Doom's tone,
"Had walked this way from his painted tombstone!"

vi

He advanced to the council-table: 70
And, "Please your honours," said he, "I'm able,
"By means of a secret charm, to draw
  "All creatures living beneath the sun,

"That creep or swim or fly or run,
"After me so as you never saw!
"And I chiefly use my charm
"On creatures that do people harm,
"The mole and toad and newt and viper;
"And people call me the Pied Piper."
(And here they noticed round his neck   80
   A scarf of red and yellow stripe,
To match with his coat of the self-same cheque;
   And at the scarf's end hung a pipe;
And his fingers, they noticed, were ever straying
As if impatient to be playing
Upon this pipe, as low it dangled
Over his vesture so old-fangled.)
"Yet," said he, "poor piper as I am,
"In Tartary I freed the Cham,
   "Last June, from his huge swarms of gnats;   90
"I eased in Asia the Nizam
   "Of a monstrous brood of vampyre-bats:
"And as for what your brain bewilders,
   "If I can rid your town of rats
"Will you give me a thousand guilders?"
"One? fifty thousand!"—was the exclamation
Of the astonished Mayor and Corporation.

VII

Into the street the Piper stept,
   Smiling first a little smile,
As if he knew what magic slept   100
   In his quiet pipe the while;
Then, like a musical adept,
To blow the pipe his lips he wrinkled,
And green and blue his sharp eyes twinkled,
Like a candle-flame where salt is sprinkled;
And ere three shrill notes the pipe uttered,
You heard as if an army muttered;
And the muttering grew to a grumbling;
And the grumbling grew to a mighty rumbling;
And out of the houses the rats came tumbling.   110
Great rats, small rats, lean rats, brawny rats,
Brown rats, black rats, grey rats, tawny rats,

Grave old plodders, gay young friskers,
  Fathers, mothers, uncles, cousins,
Cocking tails and pricking whiskers,
  Families by tens and dozens,
Brothers, sisters, husbands, wives—
Followed the Piper for their lives.
From street to street he piped advancing,
And step for step they followed dancing,   120
Until they came to the river Weser,
  Wherein all plunged and perished!
—Save one who, stout as Julius Caesar,
Swam across and lived to carry
  (As he, the manuscript he cherished)
To Rat-land home his commentary:
Which was, "At the first shrill notes of the pipe,
"I heard a sound as of scraping tripe,
"And putting apples, wondrous ripe,
"Into a cider-press's gripe: 130
"And a moving away of pickle-tub-boards,
"And a leaving ajar of conserve-cupboards,
"And a drawing the corks of train-oil-flasks,
"And a breaking the hoops of butter-casks:
"And it seemed as if a voice
  "(Sweeter far than by harp or by psaltery
"Is breathed) called out, 'Oh rats, rejoice!
  "'The world is grown to one vast drysaltery!
"'So munch on, crunch on, take your nuncheon,
"'Breakfast, supper, dinner, luncheon!'   140
"And just as a bulky sugar-puncheon,
"All ready staved, like a great sun shone
"Glorious scarce an inch before me,
"Just as methought it said, 'Come, bore me!'
"—I found the Weser rolling o'er me."

VIII

You should have heard the Hamelin people
Ringing the bells till they rocked the steeple.
"Go," cried the Mayor, "and get long poles,
"Poke out the nests and block up the holes!
"Consult with carpenters and builders,   150
"And leave in our town not even a trace

"Of the rats!"—when suddenly, up the face
Of the Piper perked in the market-place,
With a, "First, if you please, my thousand guilders!"

IX

A thousand guilders! The Mayor looked blue;
So did the Corporation too.
For council dinners made rare havoc
With Claret, Moselle, Vin-de-Grave, Hock;
And half the money would replenish
Their cellar's biggest butt with Rhenish.   160
To pay this sum to a wandering fellow
With a gipsy coat of red and yellow!
"Beside," quoth the Mayor with a knowing wink,
"Our business was done at the river's brink;
"We saw with our eyes the vermin sink,
"And what's dead can't come to life, I think.
"So, friend, we're not the folks to shrink
"From the duty of giving you something for drink,
"And a matter of money to put in your poke;
"But as for the guilders, what we spoke   170
"Of them, as you very well know, was in joke.
"Beside, our losses have made us thrifty.
"A thousand guilders! Come, take fifty!"

X

The Piper's face fell, and he cried,
"No trifling! I can't wait, beside!
"I've promised to visit by dinnertime
"Bagdat, and accept the prime
"Of the Head-Cook's pottage, all he's rich in,
"For having left, in the Caliph's kitchen,
"Of a nest of scorpions no survivor: 180
"With him I proved no bargain-driver,
"With you, don't think I'll bate a stiver!
"And folks who put me in a passion
"May find me pipe after another fashion."

XI

"How?" cried the Mayor, "d'ye think I brook
"Being worse treated than a Cook?

"Insulted by a lazy ribald
"With idle pipe and vesture piebald?
"You threaten us, fellow? Do your worst,
"Blow your pipe there till you burst!"   190

XII

Once more he stept into the street;
    And to his lips again
    Laid his long pipe of smooth straight cane;
And ere he blew three notes (such sweet
Soft notes as yet musician's cunning
    Never gave the enraptured air)
There was a rustling that seemed like a bustling
Of merry crowds justling at pitching and hustling,
Small feet were pattering, wooden shoes clattering,
Little hands clapping and little tongues chattering,   200
And, like fowls in a farm-yard when barley is scattering,
Out came the children running.
All the little boys and girls,
With rosy cheeks and flaxen curls
And sparkling eyes and teeth like pearls,
Tripping and skipping, ran merrily after
The wonderful music with shouting and laughter.

XIII

The Mayor was dumb, and the Council stood
As if they were changed into blocks of wood,
Unable to move a step, or cry   210
To the children merrily skipping by,
—Could only follow with the eye
That joyous crowd at the Piper's back.
But how the Mayor was on the rack,
And the wretched Council's bosoms beat,
As the Piper turned from the High Street
To where the Weser rolled its waters
Right in the way of their sons and daughters!
However he turned from South to West,
And to Koppelberg Hill his steps addressed,   220
And after him the children pressed;
Great was the joy in every breast.
"He never can cross that mighty top!

"He's forced to let the piping drop,
"And we shall see our children stop!"
When, lo, as they reached the mountain-side,
A wondrous portal opened wide,
As if a cavern was suddenly hollowed;
And the Piper advanced and the children followed,
And when all were in to the very last,   230
The door in the mountain-side shut fast.
Did I say, all? No! One was lame,
    And could not dance the whole of the way;
And in after years, if you would blame
    His sadness, he was used to say,—
"It's dull in our town since my playmates left!
"I can't forget that I'm bereft
"Of all the pleasant sights they see,
"Which the Piper also promised me.
"For he led us, he said, to a joyous land,   240
"Joining the town and just at hand,
"Where waters gushed and fruit-trees grew
"And flowers put forth a fairer hue,
"And everything was strange and new;
"The sparrows were brighter than peacocks here,
"And their dogs outran our fallow deer,
"And honey-bees had lost their stings,
"And horses were born with eagles' wings:
"And just as I became assured
"My lame foot would be speedily cured,   250
"The music stopped and I stood still,
"And found myself outside the hill,
"Left alone against my will,
"To go now limping as before,
"And never hear of the country more!"

XIV

Alas, alas for Hamelin!
    There came into many a burgher's pate
    A text which says that heaven's gate
    Opes to the rich at as easy rate
As the needle's eye takes a camel in!   260
The mayor sent East, West, North and South,
To offer the Piper, by word of mouth,
    Wherever it was men's lot to find him,

Silver and gold to his heart's content,
If he'd only return the way he went,
   And bring the children behind him.
But when they saw 't was a lost endeavour,
And Piper and dancers were gone for ever,
They made a decree that lawyers never
   Should think their records dated duly   270
If, after the day of the month and year,
These words did not as well appear,
"And so long after what happened here
   "On the Twenty-second of July,
"Thirteen hundred and seventy-six":
And the better in memory to fix
The place of the children's last retreat,
They called it, the Pied Piper's Street—
Where any one playing on pipe or tabor
Was sure for the future to lose his labour.   280
Nor suffered they hostelry or tavern
   To shock with mirth a street so solemn;
But opposite the place of the cavern
   They wrote the story on a column,
And on the great church-window painted
The same, to make the world acquainted
How their children were stolen away,
And there it stands to this very day.
And I must not omit to say
That in Transylvania there 's a tribe   290
Of alien people who ascribe
The outlandish ways and dress
On which their neighbours lay such stress,
To their fathers and mothers having risen
Out of some subterraneous prison
Into which they were trepanned
Long time ago in a mighty band
Out of Hamelin town in Brunswick land,
But how or why, they don't understand.

XV

So, Willy, let me and you be wipers   300
Of scores out with all men—especially pipers!
And, whether they pipe us free from rats or from mice,
If we've promised them aught, let us keep our promise!

270   THE BISHOP ORDERS HIS TOMB AT
                ST. PRAXED'S CHURCH

[ROME, 15—]

Vanity, saith the preacher, vanity!
Draw round my bed: is Anselm keeping back?
Nephews—sons mine . . . ah God, I know not! Well—
She, men would have to be your mother once,
Old Gandolf envied me, so fair she was!
What's done is done, and she is dead beside,
Dead long ago, and I am Bishop since,
And as she died so must we die ourselves,
And thence ye may perceive the world's a dream.
Life, how and what is it? As here I lie   10
In this state-chamber, dying by degrees,
Hours and long hours in the dead night, I ask
"Do I live, am I dead?" Peace, peace seems all.
Saint Praxed's ever was the church for peace;
And so, about this tomb of mine. I fought
With tooth and nail to save my niche, ye know:
—Old Gandolf cozened me, despite my care;
Shrewd was that snatch from out the corner South
He graced his carrion with, God curse the same!
Yet still my niche is not so cramped but thence   20
One sees the pulpit o' the epistle-side,
And somewhat of the choir, those silent seats,
And up into the aery dome where live
The angels, and a sunbeam's sure to lurk:
And I shall fill my slab of basalt there,
And 'neath my tabernacle take my rest,
With those nine columns round me, two and two,
The odd one at my feet where Anselm stands:
Peach-blossom marble all, the rare, the ripe
As fresh-poured red wine of a mighty pulse.   30
—Old Gandolf with his paltry onion-stone,
Put me where I may look at him! True peach,
Rosy and flawless: how I earned the prize!
Draw close: that conflagration of my church
—What then? So much was saved if aught were missed!
My sons, ye would not be my death? Go dig
The white-grape vineyard where the oil-press stood,

Drop water gently till the surface sinks,
And if ye find . . . Ah, God I know not, I! . . .
Bedded in store of rotten fig-leaves soft, 40
And corded up in a tight olive-frail,
Some lump, ah God, of *lapis lazuli,*
Big as a Jew's head cut off at the nape,
Blue as a vein o'er the Madonna's breast . . .
Sons, all have I bequeathed you, villas, all,
That brave Frascati villa with its bath,
So, let the blue lump poise between my knees,
Like God the Father's globe on both his hands
Ye worship in the Jesu Church so gay,
For Gandolf shall not choose but see and burst! 50
Swift as a weaver's shuttle fleet our years:
Man goeth to the grave, and where is he?
Did I say basalt for my slab, sons? Black—
'Twas ever antique-black I meant! How else
Shall ye contrast my frieze to come beneath?
The bas-relief in bronze ye promised me,
Those Pans and Nymphs ye wot of, and perchance
Some tripod, thyrsus, with a vase or so,
The Saviour at his sermon on the mount,
Saint Praxed in a glory, and one Pan 60
Ready to twitch the Nymph's last garment off,
And Moses with the tables . . . but I know
Ye mark me not! What do they whisper thee,
Child of my bowels, Anselm? Ah, ye hope
To revel down my villas while I gasp
Bricked o'er with beggar's mouldy travertine
Which Gandolf from his tomb-top chuckles at!
Nay, boys, ye love me—all of jasper, then!
'Tis jasper ye stand pledged to, lest I grieve
My bath must needs be left behind, alas! 70
One block, pure green as a pistachio nut,
There's plenty jasper somewhere in the world—
And have I not Saint Praxed's ear to pray
Horses for ye, and brown Greek manuscripts,
And mistresses with great smooth marbly limbs?
—That's if ye carve my epitaph aright,
Choice Latin, picked phrase, Tully's every word,
No gaudy ware like Gandolf's second line—
Tully, my masters? Ulpian serves his need!

And then how I shall lie through centuries,   80
And hear the blessed mutter of the mass,
And see God made and eaten all day long,
And feel the steady candle-flame, and taste
Good strong thick stupefying incense-smoke!
For as I lie here, hours of the dead night,
Dying in state and by such slow degrees,
I fold my arms as if they clasped a crook,
And stretch my feet forth straight as stone can point,
And let the bedclothes, for a mortcloth, drop
Into great laps and folds of sculptor's-work: 90
And as yon tapers dwindle, and strange thoughts
Grow, with a certain humming in my ears,
About the life before I lived this life,
And this life too, popes, cardinals and priests,
Saint Praxed at his sermon on the mount,
Your tall pale mother with her talking eyes,
And new-found agate urns as fresh as day,
And marble's language, Latin pure, discreet,
—Aha, ELUCESCEBAT quoth our friend?
No Tully, said I, Ulpian at the best!   100
Evil and brief hath been my pilgrimage.
All *lapis,* all, sons! Else I give the Pope
My villas! Will ye ever eat my heart?
Ever your eyes were as a lizard's quick,
They glitter like your mother's for my soul,
Or ye would heighten my impoverished frieze,
Piece out its starved design, and fill my vase
With grapes, and add a vizor and a term,
And to the tripod ye would tie a lynx
That in his struggle throws the thyrsus down,   110
To comfort me on my entablature
Whereon I am to lie till I must ask
"Do I live, am I dead?" There, leave me, there!
For ye have stabbed me with ingratitude
To death—ye wish it—God, ye wish it! Stone—
Gritstone, a-crumble! Clammy squares which sweat
As if the corpse they keep were oozing through—
And no more *lapis* to delight the world!
Well, go! I bless ye. Fewer tapers there,
But in a row: and, going, turn your backs   120
—Ay, like departing altar-ministrants,

Ana ,eave me in my church, the church for peace,
That I may watch at leisure if he leers—
Old Gandolf—at me, from his onion-stone,
As still he envied me, so fair she was!

271. A TOCCATA OF GALUPPI'S

I

Oh, Galuppi, Baldassaro, this is very sad to find!
I can hardly misconceive you; it would prove me deaf and blind;
But although I take your meaning, 'tis with such a heavy mind!

II

Here you come with your old music, and here's all the good it
  brings.
What, they lived once thus at Venice where the merchants were
  the kings,
Where St. Mark's is, where the Doges used to wed the sea with
  rings?

III

Ay, because the sea's the street there; and 'tis arched by . . . what
  you call
. . . Shylock's bridge with houses on it, where they kept the
  carnival:
I was never out of England—it's as if I saw it all!

IV

Did young people take their pleasure when the sea was warm in
  May?   10
Balls and masks begun at midnight, burning ever to mid-day,
When they made up fresh adventures for the morrow, do you say?

V

Was a lady such a lady, cheeks so round and lips so red,—
On her neck the small face buoyant, like a bell-flower on its bed,
O'er the breast's superb abundance where a man might base his
  head?

VI

Well, and it was graceful of them—they'd break talk off and afford
—She, to bite her mask's black velvet—he, to finger on his sword,
While you sat and played Toccatas, stately at the clavichord?

VII

What? Those lesser thirds so plaintive, sixths diminished, sigh on
    sigh,
Told them something? Those suspensions, those solutions—"Must
    we die?"   20
Those commiserating sevenths—"Life might last! we can but try!"

VIII

"Were you happy?"—"Yes."—"And are you still as happy?"—"Yes.
    And you?"
—"Then, more kisses!"—"Did I stop them, when a million seemed
    so few?"
Hark! the dominant's persistence, till it must be answered to!

IX

So an octave struck the answer. Oh, they praised you, I dare say!
"Brave Galuppi! that was music! good alike at grave and gay!
I can always leave off talking, when I hear a master play."

X

Then they left you for their pleasure: till in due time, one by one,
Some with lives that came to nothing, some with deeds as well
    undone,
Death came tacitly and took them where they never see the sun. 30

XI

But when I sit down to reason, think to take my stand nor swerve,
While I triumph o'er a secret wrung from nature's close reserve,
In you come with your cold music till I creep thro' every nerve.

XII

Yes, you, like a ghostly cricket, creaking where a house was burned:
"Dust and ashes, dead and done with, Venice spent what Venice
    earned.
The soul, doubtless, is immortal—where a soul can be discerned.

XIII

"Yours for instance, you know physics, something of geology,
"Mathematics are your pastime; souls shall rise in their degree;
"Butterflies may dread extinction,—you'll not die, it cannot be!

XIV

"As for Venice and her people, merely born to bloom and drop, 40
"Here on earth they bore their fruitage, mirth and folly were the
    crop:
"What of soul was left, I wonder, when the kissing had to stop?

XV

"Dust and ashes!" So you creak it, and I want the heart to scold.
Dear dead women, with such hair, too—what's become of all the
    gold
Used to hang and brush their bosoms? I feel chilly and grown old.

272.   A GRAMMARIAN'S FUNERAL

SHORTLY AFTER THE REVIVAL OF LEARNING IN EUROPE

Let us begin and carry up this corpse,
        Singing together.
Leave we the common crofts, the vulgar thorpes,
        Each in its tether
Sleeping safe in the bosom of the plain,
        Cared-for till cock-crow:
Look out if yonder be not day again
        Rimming the rock-row!
That's the appropriate country—there, man's thought,
        Rarer, intenser,   10
Self-gathered for an outbreak, as it ought,
        Chafes in the censer.
Leave we the unlettered plain its herd and crop;
        Seek we sepulture
On a tall mountain, cited to the top,
        Crowded with culture!
All the peaks soar, but one the rest excels;
        Clouds overcome it;
No! yonder sparkle is the citadel's
        Circling its summit.   20

Thither our path lies; wind we up the heights:
　　　Wait ye the warning?
Our low life was the level's and the night's;
　　　He's for the morning.
Step to a tune, square chests, erect each head,
　　　'Ware the beholders!
This is our master, famous calm and dead,
　　　Borne on our shoulders.

Sleep, crop and herd! sleep, darkling thorpe and croft,
　　　Safe from the weather!　　　　　　　　　　　　30
He, whom we convoy to his grave aloft,
　　　Singing together,
He was a man born with thy face and throat,
　　　Lyric Apollo!
Long he lived nameless: how should spring take note
　　　Winter would follow?
Till lo, the little touch, and youth was gone!
　　　Cramped and diminished,
Moaned he, "New measures, other feet anon!
　　　My dance is finished?"　　　　　　　　　　　　40
No, that's the world's way: (keep the mountain-side,
　　　Make for the city!)
He knew the signal, and stepped on with pride
　　　Over men's pity;
Left play for work, and grappled with the world
　　　Bent on escaping:
"What's in the scroll," quoth he, "thou keepest furled?
　　　"Show me their shaping,
"Theirs, who most studied man, the bard and sage,—
　　　"Give!"—So he gowned him,　　　　　　　　　　50
Straight got by heart that book to its last page:
　　　Learned, we found him!
Yea, but we found him bald too, eyes like lead,
　　　Accents uncertain:
"Time to taste life," another would have said,
　　　"Up with the curtain!"
This man said rather, "Actual life comes next?
　　　"Patience a moment!
"Grant I have mastered learning's crabbed text,
　　　"Still, there's the comment.　　　　　　　　　　60

"Let me know all! Prate not of most or least,
     "Painful or easy!
"Even to the crumbs I'd fain eat up the feast,
     "Ay, nor feel queasy."
Oh, such a life as he resolved to live,
     When he had learned it,
When he had gathered all books had to give!
     Sooner, he spurned it.
Image the whole, then execute the parts—
     Fancy the fabric   70
Quite, ere you build, ere steel strike fire from quartz,
     Ere mortar dab brick!

(Here's the town-gate reached: there's the market-place
     Gaping before us.)
Yea, this in him was the peculiar grace
     (Hearten our chorus!)
That before living he'd learn how to live—
     No end to learning:
Earn the means first—God surely will contrive
     Use for our earning.   80
Others mistrust and say "But time escapes,
     "Live now or never!"
He said, "What's Time? leave Now for dogs and apes!
     "Man has Forever."
Back to his book then: deeper drooped his head:
     Calculus racked him:
Leaden before, his eyes grew dross of lead:
     Tussis attacked him.
"Now, master, take a little rest!"—not he!
     (Caution redoubled,   90
Step two a-breast, the way winds narrowly!)
     Not a whit troubled,
Back to his studies, fresher than at first,
     Fierce as a dragon
He (soul-hydroptic with a sacred thirst)
     Sucked at the flagon.
Oh, if we draw a circle premature,
     Heedless of far gain,
Greedy for quick returns of profit, sure,
     Bad is our bargain!   100

Was it not great? did not he throw on God,
    (He loves the burthen)—
God's task to make the heavenly period
    Perfect the earthen?
Did not he magnify the mind, show clear
    Just what it all meant?
He would not discount life, as fools do here,
    Paid by instalment!
He ventured neck or nothing—heaven's success
    Found, or earth's failure: 110
"Wilt thou trust death or not?" He answered "Yes.
    "Hence with life's pale lure!"
That low man seeks a little thing to do,
    Sees it and does it:
This high man, with a great thing to pursue,
    Dies ere he knows it.
That low man goes on adding one to one,
    His hundred's soon hit:
This high man, aiming at a million,
    Misses an unit.   120
That, has the world here—should he need the next,
    Let the world mind him!
This, throws himself on God, and unperplexed
    Seeking shall find him.
So, with the throttling hands of death at strife,
    Ground he at grammar;
Still, thro' the rattle, parts of speech were rife:
    While he could stammer
He settled *Hoti's* business—let it be!—
    Properly based *Oun*—   130
Gave us the doctrine of the enclitic *De,*
    Dead from the waist down.
Well, here's the platform, here's the proper place:
    Hail to your purlieus
All ye highfliers of the feathered race,
    Swallows and curlews!
Here's the top-peak; the multitude below
    Live, for they can, there:
This man decided not to Live but Know—
    Bury this man there?   140
Here—here's his place, where meteors shoot, clouds form,
    Lightnings are loosened,

Stars come and go! Let joy break with the storm,
    Peace let the dew send!
Lofty designs must close in like effects:
    Loftily lying,
Leave him—still loftier than the world suspects,
    Living and dying.

273.   ANDREA DEL SARTO

(CALLED 'THE FAULTLESS PAINTER')

But do not let us quarrel any more,
No, my Lucrezia; bear with me for once:
Sit down and all shall happen as you wish.
You turn your face, but does it bring your heart?
I'll work then for your friend's friend, never fear,
Treat his own subject after his own way,
Fix his own time, accept too his own price,
And shut the money into this small hand
When next it takes mine. Will it? tenderly?
Oh, I'll content him,—but to-morrow, Love!   10
I often am much wearier than you think,
This evening more than usual, and it seems
As if—forgive now—should you let me sit
Here by the window with your hand in mine
And look a half-hour forth on Fiesole,
Both of one mind, as married people use,
Quietly, quietly, the evening through,
I might get up to-morrow to my work
Cheerful and fresh as ever. Let us try.
To-morrow how you shall be glad for this!   20
Your soft hand is a woman of itself,
And mine the man's bared breast she curls inside.
Don't count the time lost, either; you must serve
For each of the five pictures we require—
It saves a model. So! keep looking so—
My serpentining beauty, rounds on rounds!
—How could you ever prick those perfect ears,
Even to put the pearl there! oh, so sweet—
My face, my moon, my everybody's moon,
Which everybody looks on and calls his,   30
And, I suppose, is looked on by in turn,

While she looks—no one's: very dear, no less!
You smile? why, there's my picture ready made,
There's what we painters call our harmony!
A common greyness silvers everything,—
All in a twilight, you and I alike
—You, at the point of your first pride in me
(That's gone, you know),—but I, at every point;
My youth, my hope, my art, being all toned down
To yonder sober pleasant Fiesole.   40
There's the bell clinking from the chapel-top;
That length of convent-wall across the way
Holds the trees safer, huddled more inside;
The last monk leaves the garden; days decrease
And autumn grows, autumn in everything.
Eh? the whole seems to fall into a shape
As if I saw alike my work and self
And all that I was born to be and do,
A twilight-piece. Love, we are in God's hand.
How strange now, looks the life he makes us lead!   50
So free we seem, so fettered fast we are!
I feel He laid the fetter: let it lie!
This chamber for example—turn your head—
All that's behind us! you don't understand
Nor care to understand about my art,
But you can hear at least when people speak;
And that cartoon, the second from the door
—It is the thing, Love! so such things should be—
Behold Madonna, I am bold to say.
I can do with my pencil what I know,   60
What I see, what at bottom of my heart
I wish for, if I ever wish so deep—
Do easily, too—when I say, perfectly,
I do not boast, perhaps: yourself are judge
Who listened to the Legate's talk last week,
And just as much they used to say in France.
At any rate 'tis easy, all of it!
No sketches first, no studies, that's long past—
I do what many dream of all their lives
—Dream? strive to do, and agonize to do,   70
And fail in doing. I could count twenty such
On twice your fingers, and not leave this town,
Who strive—you don't know how the others strive

To paint a little thing like that you smeared
Carelessly passing with your robes afloat,—
Yet do much less, so much less, Someone says,
(I know his name, no matter) so much less!
Well, less is more, Lucrezia: I am judged.
There burns a truer light of God in them,
In their vexed, beating, stuffed and stopped-up brain, 80
Heart, or whate'er else, than goes on to prompt
This low-pulsed forthright craftsman's hand of mine.
Their works drop groundward, but themselves, I know,
Reach many a time a heaven that's shut to me,
Enter and take their place there sure enough,
Though they come back and cannot tell the world.
My works are nearer heaven, but I sit here.
The sudden blood of these men! at a word—
Praise them, it boils, or blame them, it boils too.
I, painting from myself and to myself, 90
Know what I do, am unmoved by men's blame
Or their praise either. Somebody remarks
Morello's outline there is wrongly traced,
His hue mistaken—what of that? or else,
Rightly traced and well ordered—what of that?
Speak as they please, what does the mountain care?
Ah, but a man's reach should exceed his grasp,
Or what's a heaven for? all is silver-grey
Placid and perfect with my art: the worse!
I know both what I want and what might gain, 100
And yet how profitless to know, to sigh
"Had I been two, another and myself.
"Our head would have o'erlooked the world!" No doubt.
Yonder's a work, now, of that famous youth,
The Urbinate who died five years ago.
('Tis copied, George Vasari sent it me.)
Well, I can fancy how he did it all,
Pouring his soul, with kings and popes to see,
Reaching, that Heaven might so replenish him,
Above and through his art—for it gives way; 110
That arm is wrongly put—and there again—
A fault to pardon in the drawing's lines,
Its body, so to speak: its soul is right,
He means right—that, a child may understand.
Still, what an arm! and I could alter it;

But all the play, the insight and the stretch
Out of me, out of me! And wherefore out?
Had you enjoined them on me, given me soul,
We might have risen to Rafael, I and you!
Nay, Love, you did give all I asked, I think—   120
More than I merit, yes, by many times.
But had you—oh, with the same perfect brow,
And perfect eyes, and more than perfect mouth,
And the low voice my soul hears, as a bird
The fowler's pipe, and follows to the snare—
Had you, with these the same, but brought a mind!
Some women do so. Had the mouth there urged
"God and the glory! never care for gain.
The present by the future, what is that?
Live for fame, side by side with Agnolo—   130
Rafael is waiting: up to God all three!"
I might have done it for you. So it seems:
Perhaps not. All is as God overrules.
Beside, incentives come from the soul's self;
The rest avail not. Why do I need you?
What wife had Rafael, or has Agnolo?
In this world, who can do a thing, will not;
And who would do it, cannot, I perceive:
Yet the will's somewhat—somewhat, too, the power—
And thus we half-men struggle. At the end,   140
God, I conclude, compensates, punishes.
'Tis safer for me, if the award be strict,
That I am something underrated here,
Poor this long while, despised, to speak the truth.
I dared not, do you know, leave home all day,
For fear of chancing on the Paris lords.
The best is when they pass and look aside;
But they speak sometimes; I must bear it all.
Well may they speak! That Francis, that first time,
And that long festal year at Fontainebleau!   150
I surely then could sometimes leave the ground,
Put on the glory, Rafael's daily wear,
In that humane great monarch's golden look,—
One finger in his beard or twisted curl
Over his mouth's good mark that made the smile,
One arm about my shoulder, round my neck,
The jingle of his gold chain in my ear,

I painting proudly with his breath on me,
All his court round him, seeing with his eyes,
Such frank French eyes, and such a fire of souls   160
Profuse, my hand kept plying by those hearts,—
And, best of all, this, this, this face beyond,
This in the background waiting on my work,
To crown the issue with a last reward!
A good time, was it not, my kingly days?
And had you not grown restless . . . but I know—
'Tis done and past; 'twas right, my instinct said;
Too live the life grew, golden and not grey,
And I'm the weak-eyed bat no sun should tempt
Out of the grange whose four walls make his world.   170
How could it end in any other way?
You called me, and I came home to your heart.
The triumph was—to reach and stay there; since
I reached it ere the triumph, what is lost?
Let my hands frame your face in your hair's gold,
You beautiful Lucrezia that are mine!
"Rafael did this, Andrea painted that—
The Roman's is the better when you pray,
But still the other's Virgin was his wife—"
Men will excuse me. I am glad to judge   180
Both pictures in your presence; clearer grows
My better fortune, I resolve to think.
For, do you know, Lucrezia, as God lives,
Said one day Agnolo, his very self,
To Rafael . . . I have known it all these years . . .
(When the young man was flaming out his thoughts
Upon a palace-wall for Rome to see,
Too lifted up in heart because of it)
"Friend, there's a certain sorry little scrub
Goes up and down our Florence, none cares how,   190
Who, were he set to plan and execute
As you are, pricked on by your popes and kings,
Would bring the sweat into that brow of yours!"
To Rafael's!—And indeed the arm is wrong.
I hardly dare . . . yet only you to see,
Give the chalk here—quick, thus the line should go!
Ay, but the soul! he's Rafael! rub it out!
Still, all I care for, if he spoke the truth,
(What he? why, who but Michel Agnolo?

Do you forget already words like those?)   200
If really there was such a chance, so lost,—
Is, whether you're—not grateful—but more pleased.
Well, let me think so. And you smile indeed!
This hour has been an hour! Another smile?
If you would sit thus by me every night
I should work better, do you comprehend?
I mean that I should earn more, give you more.
See, it is settled dusk now; there's a star;
Morello's gone, the watch-lights show the wall,
The cue-owls speak the name we call them by.   210
Come from the window, love,—come in, at last,
Inside the melancholy little house
We built to be so gay with. God is just.
King Francis may forgive me; oft at nights
When I look up from painting, eyes tired out,
The walls become illumined, brick from brick
Distinct, instead of mortar, fierce bright gold,
That gold of his I did cement them with!
Let us but love each other. Must you go?
That Cousin here again? he waits outside?   220
Must see you—you, and not with me? Those loans?
More gaming debts to pay? you smiled for that?
Well, let smiles buy me! have you more to spend?
While hand and eye and something of a heart
Are left me, work's my ware, and what's it worth?
I'll pay my fancy. Only let me sit
The grey remainder of the evening out,
Idle, you call it, and muse perfectly
How I could paint, were I but back in France,
One picture, just one more—the Virgin's face,   230
Not yours this time! I want you at my side
To hear them—that is, Michel Agnolo—
Judge all I do and tell you of its worth.
Will you? To-morrow satisfy your friend.
I take the subjects for his corridor,
Finish the portrait out of hand—there, there,
And throw him in another thing or two
If he demurs; the whole should prove enough
To pay for this same Cousin's freak. Beside,
What's better and what's all I care about,   240
Get you the thirteen scudi for the ruff.

Love, does that please you? Ah, but what does he,
The Cousin! what does he to please you more?

I am grown peaceful as old age to-night.
I regret little, I would change still less.
Since there my past life lies, why alter it?
The very wrong to Francis!—it is true
I took his coin, was tempted and complied,
And built this house and sinned, and all is said.
My father and my mother died of want.   250
Well, had I riches of my own? you see
How one gets rich! Let each one bear his lot.
They were born poor, lived poor, and poor they died:
And I have laboured somewhat in my time
And not been paid profusely. Some good son
Paint my two hundred pictures—let him try!
No doubt, there's something strikes a balance. Yes,
You loved me quite enough, it seems to-night.
This must suffice me here. What would one have?
In heaven, perhaps, new chances, one more chance—   260
Four great walls in the New Jerusalem
Meted on each side by the angel's reed,
For Leonard, Rafael, Agnolo and me
To cover—the three first without a wife,
While I have mine! So—still they overcome
Because there's still Lucrezia,—as I choose.

Again the Cousin's whistle! Go, my Love.

ELIZABETH BARRETT BROWNING (1806–1861)

274.   "I THOUGHT ONCE HOW THEOCRITUS
                        HAD SUNG"

From SONNETS FROM THE PORTUGUESE

I thought once how Theocritus had sung
Of the sweet years, the dear and wished-for years,
Who each one in a gracious hand appears
To bear a gift for mortals, old or young:
And, as I mused it in his antique tongue,
I saw, in gradual vision through my tears,
The sweet, sad years, the melancholy years,

Those of my own life, who by turns had flung
A shadow across me. Straightway I was 'ware,
So weeping, how a mystic Shape did move   10
Behind me, and drew me backward by the hair,
And a voice said in mastery, while I strove,—
'Guess now who holds thee?'—'Death,' I said. But, there,
The silver answer rang, . . 'Not Death, but Love.'

ARTHUR HUGH CLOUGH (1819–1861)

275.   THE LATEST DECALOGUE

Thou shalt have one God only; who
Would be at the expense of two?
No graven images may be
Worshipped, except the currency;
Swear not at all; for, for thy curse
Thine enemy is none the worse:
At church on Sunday to attend
Will serve to keep the world thy friend:
Honour thy parents; that is, all
From whom advancement may befall;   10
Thou shalt not kill; but need'st not strive
Officiously to keep alive:
Do not adultery commit;
Advantage rarely comes of it:
Thou shalt not steal; an empty feat,
When it's so lucrative to cheat:
Bear not false witness; let the lie
Have time on its own wings to fly:
Thou shalt not covet, but tradition
Approves all forms of competition.   20

HENRY WADSWORTH LONGFELLOW (1807–1882)

276.   THE JEWISH CEMETERY AT NEWPORT

How strange it seems! These Hebrews in their graves,
  Close by the street of this fair seaport town,
Silent beside the never-silent waves,
  At rest in all this moving up and down!

The trees are white with dust, that o'er their sleep
  Wave their broad curtains in the southwind's breath,
While underneath these leafy tents they keep
  The long, mysterious Exodus of Death.

And these sepulchral stones, so old and brown,
  That pave with level flags their burial-place,   10
Seem like the tablets of the Law, thrown down
  And broken by Moses at the mountain's base.

The very names recorded here are strange,
  Of foreign accent, and of different climes;
Alvares and Rivera interchange
  With Abraham and Jacob of old times.

"Blessed be God, for he created Death!"
  The mourners said, "and Death is rest and peace;"
Then added, in the certainty of faith,
  "And giveth Life that nevermore shall cease."   20

Closed are the portals of their Synagogue,
  No Psalms of David now the silence break,
No Rabbi reads the ancient Decalogue
  In the grand dialect the Prophets spake.

Gone are the living, but the dead remain,
  And not neglected; for a hand unseen,
Scattering its bounty, like a summer rain,
  Still keeps their graves and their remembrance green.

How came they here? What burst of Christian hate,
  What persecution, merciless and blind,   30
Drove o'er the sea—that desert desolate—
  These Ishmaels and Hagars of mankind?

They lived in narrow streets and lanes obscure,
  Ghetto and Judenstrass, in mirk and mire;
Taught in the school of patience to endure
  The life of anguish and the death of fire.

All their lives long, with the unleavened bread
  And bitter herbs of exile and its fears,
The wasting famine of the heart they fed,
  And slaked its thirst with marah of their tears.   40

Anathema maranatha! was the cry
   That rang from town to town, from street to street:
At every gate the accursed Mordecai
   Was mocked and jeered, and spurned by Christian feet.

Pride and humiliation hand in hand
   Walked with them through the world where'er they went;
Trampled and beaten were they as the sand,
   And yet unshaken as the continent.

For in the background figures vague and vast
   Of patriarchs and of prophets rose sublime,   50
And all the great traditions of the Past
   They saw reflected in the coming time.

And thus forever with reverted look
   The mystic volume of the world they read,
Spelling it backward, like a Hebrew book,
   Till life became a Legend of the Dead.

But ah! what once has been shall be no more!
   The groaning earth in travail and in pain
Brings forth its races, but does not restore,
   And the dead nations never rise again.   60

DIVINA COMMEDIA

277.   I

Oft have I seen at some cathedral door
   A laborer, pausing in the dust and heat,
   Lay down his burden, and with reverent feet
   Enter, and cross himself, and on the floor
Kneel to repeat his paternoster o'er;
   Far off the noises of the world retreat;
   The loud vociferations of the street
   Become an undistinguishable roar.
So, as I enter here from day to day,
   And leave my burden at this minster gate,   10
   Kneeling in prayer, and not ashamed to pray,
The tumult of the time disconsolate
   To inarticulate murmurs dies away,
   While the eternal ages watch and wait.

278.

II

How strange the sculptures that adorn these towers!
  This crowd of statues, in whose folded sleeves
  Birds build their nests; while canopied with leaves
  Parvis and portal bloom like trellised bowers,
And the vast minster seems a cross of flowers!
  But fiends and dragons on the gargoyled eaves
  Watch the dead Christ between the living thieves,
  And, underneath, the traitor Judas lowers!
Ah! from what agonies of heart and brain,
  What exaltations trampling on despair,   10
  What tenderness, what tears, what hate of wrong,
What passionate outcry of a soul in pain,
  Uprose this poem of the earth and air,
  This mediaeval miracle of song!

RALPH WALDO EMERSON (1803–1882)

279.   GIVE ALL TO LOVE

          Give all to love;
          Obey thy heart;
          Friends, kindred, days,
          Estate, good-fame,
          Plans, credit and the Muse,—
          Nothing refuse.

          'T is a brave master;
          Let it have scope:
          Follow it utterly,
          Hope beyond hope: 10
          High and more high
          It dives into noon,
          With wing unspent,
          Untold intent;
          But it is a god,
          Knows its own path
          And the outlets of the sky.

          It was never for the mean;
          It requireth courage stout.

Souls above doubt,　　　　　　　　　20
Valor unbending,
It will reward,—
They shall return
More than they were,
And ever ascending.

Leave all for love;
Yet, hear me, yet,
One word more thy heart behoved,
One pulse more of firm endeavor,—
Keep thee to-day,　　　　　　　　　30
To-morrow, forever,
Free as an Arab
Of thy beloved.

Cling with life to the maid;
But when the surprise,
First vague shadow of surmise
Flits across her bosom young,
Of a joy apart from thee,
Free be she, fancy-free;
Nor thou detain her vesture's hem,　　　40
Nor the palest rose she flung
From her summer diadem.

Though thou loved her as thyself,
As a self of purer clay,
Though her parting dims the day,
Stealing grace from all alive;
Heartily know,
When half-gods go,
The gods arrive.

280.　　　　　　　　　DAYS

Daughters of Time, the hypocritic Days,
Muffled and dumb like barefoot dervishes,
And marching single in an endless file,
Bring diadems and fagots in their hands.
To each they offer gifts after his will,
Bread, kingdoms, stars, and sky that holds them all.
I, in my pleached garden, watched the pomp,
Forgot my morning wishes, hastily

Took a few herbs and apples, and the Day
Turned and departed silent. I, too late,   10
Under her solemn fillet saw the scorn.

281.   THE SNOW-STORM

Announced by all the trumpets of the sky,
Arrives the snow, and, driving o'er the fields,
Seems nowhere to alight: the whited air
Hides hills and woods, the river, and the heaven,
And veils the farm-house at the garden's end.
The sled and traveller stopped, the courier's feet
Delayed, all friends shut out, the housemates sit
Around the radiant fireplace, enclosed
In a tumultuous privacy of storm.

     Come see the north wind's masonry.   10
Out of an unseen quarry evermore
Furnished with tile, the fierce artificer
Curves his white bastions with projected roof
Round every windward stake, or tree, or door.
Speeding, the myriad-handed, his wild work
So fanciful, so savage, nought cares he
For number or proportion. Mockingly,
On coop or kennel he hangs Parian wreaths;
A swan-like form invests the hidden thorn;
Fills up the farmer's lane from wall to wall,   20
Maugre the farmer's sighs; and at the gate
A tapering turret overtops the work.
And when his hours are numbered, and the world
Is all his own, retiring, as he were not,
Leaves, when the sun appears, astonished Art
To mimic in slow structures, stone by stone,
Built in an age, the mad wind's nightwork,
The frolic architecture of the snow.

282.   HAMATREYA

Bulkeley, Hunt, Willard, Hosmer, Meriam, Flint,
Possessed the land which rendered to their toil
Hay, corn, roots, hemp, flax, apples, wool and wood.

Each of these landlords walked amidst his farm,
Saying, " 'Tis mine, my children's and my name's.
How sweet the west wind sounds in my own trees!
How graceful climb those shadows on my hill!
I fancy these pure waters and the flags
Know me, as does my dog: we sympathize;
And, I affirm, my actions smack of the soil."   10

Where are these men? Asleep beneath their grounds:
And strangers, fond as they, their furrows plough.
Earth laughs in flowers, to see her boastful boys
Earth-proud, proud of the earth which is not theirs;
Who steer the plough, but cannot steer their feet
Clear of the grave.
They added ridge to valley, brook to pond,
And sighed for all that bounded their domain;
"This suits me for a pasture; that's my park;
We must have clay, lime, gravel, granite-ledge,   20
And misty lowland, where to go for peat.
The land is well,—lies fairly to the south.
'Tis good, when you have crossed the sea and back,
To find the sitfast acres where you left them."
Ah! the hot owner sees not Death, who adds
Him to his land, a lump of mould the more.
Hear what the Earth says:—

EARTH-SONG

"Mine and yours;
Mine, not yours.
Earth endures;   30
Stars abide—
Shine down in the old sea;
Old are the shores;
But where are old men?
I who have seen much,
Such have I never seen.

"The lawyer's deed
Ran sure,
In tail,
To them, and to their heirs   40

Who shall succeed,
Without fail,
Forevermore.

"Here is the land,
Shaggy with wood,
With its old valley,
Mound and flood.
But the heritors?—
Fled like the flood's foam.
The lawyer, and the laws,   50
And the kingdom,
Clean swept herefrom.

"They called me theirs,
Who so controlled me;
Yet every one
Wished to stay, and is gone.
How am I theirs,
If they cannot hold me,
But I hold them?"

When I heard the Earth-song,   60
I was no longer brave;
My avarice cooled
Like lust in the chill of the grave.

MATTHEW ARNOLD (1822–1888)

283.   THE SCHOLAR GIPSY

Go, for they call you, shepherd, from the hill;
  Go, shepherd, and untie the wattled cotes!
    No longer leave thy wistful flock unfed,
  Nor let thy bawling fellows rack their throats,
    Nor the cropp'd herbage shoot another head.
      But when the fields are still,
  And the tired men and dogs all gone to rest,
    And only the white sheep are sometimes seen
    Cross and recross the strips of moon-blanch'd green,
Come, shepherd, and again begin the quest.   10

Here, where the reaper was at work of late—
    In this high field's dark corner, where he leaves
        His coat, his basket, and his earthen cruse,
    And in the sun all morning binds the sheaves,
        Then here, at noon, comes back his stores to use—
            Here will I sit and wait,
    While to my ear from uplands far away
        The bleating of the folded flocks is borne,
        With distant cries of reapers in the corn—
All the live murmur of a summer's day.   20

Screen'd in this nook o'er the high, half-reap'd field,
    And here till sun-down, shepherd! will I be.
        Through the thick corn the scarlet poppies peep
    And round green roots and yellowing stalks I see
        Pale blue convolvulus in tendrils creep;
            And air-swept lindens yield
    Their scent, and rustle down their perfumed showers
        Of bloom on the bent grass where I am laid,
        And bower me from the August sun with shade;
And the eye travels down to Oxford's towers.   30

And near me on the grass lies Glanvil's book—
    Come, let me read the oft-read tale again!
        The story of that Oxford scholar poor
    Of pregnant parts and quick inventive brain,
        Who, tired of knocking at preferment's door,
            One summer morn forsook
    His friends, and went to learn the gipsy-lore,
        And roam'd the world with that wild brotherhood,
        And came, as most men deem'd to little good,
But came to Oxford and his friends no more.   40

But once, years after, in the country lanes,
    Two scholars whom at college erst he knew
        Met him, and of his way of life enquired.
    Whereat he answer'd, that the gipsy-crew,
        His mates, had arts to rule as they desired
            The workings of men's brains,
    And they can bind them to what thoughts they will.
        'And I,' he said, 'the secret of their art,
        When fully learn'd, will to the world impart;
But it needs heaven-sent moments for this skill.'   50

This said, he left them, and return'd no more.—
But rumours hung about the country-side
That the lost Scholar long was seen to stray,
Seen by rare glimpses, pensive and tongue-tied,
In hat of antique shape, and cloak of grey,
The same the Gipsies wore.
Shepherds had met him on the Hurst in spring;
At some lone alehouse in the Berkshire moors,
On the warm ingle-bench, the smock-frock'd boors
Had found him seated at their entering.   60

But, 'mid their drink and clatter, he would fly.
And I myself seem half to know thy looks,
And put the shepherds, wanderer, on thy trace;
And boys who in lone wheatfields scare the rooks
I ask if thou hast pass'd their quiet place;
Or in my boat I lie
Moor'd to the cool bank in the summer-heats,
Mid wide grass meadows which the sunshine fills,
And watch the warm green-muffled Cumner hills,
And wonder if thou haunt'st their shy retreats.   70

For most, I know, thou lov'st retired ground!
Thee, at the ferry, Oxford riders blithe,
Returning home on summer nights, have met
Crossing the stripling Thames at Bab-lock-hithe,
Trailing in the cool stream thy fingers wet,
As the punt's rope chops round;
And leaning backwards in a pensive dream,
And fostering in thy lap a heap of flowers
Pluck'd in shy fields and distant Wychwood bowers,
And thine eyes resting on the moonlit stream: 80

And then they land, and thou art seen no more!—
Maidens who from the distant hamlets come
To dance around the Fyfield elm in May,
Oft through the darkening fields have seen thee roam,
Or cross a stile into the public way.
Oft thou hast given them store
Of flowers—the frail-leaf'd, white anemony,
Dark bluebells drench'd with dews of summer eves,
And purple orchises with spotted leaves—
But none hath words she can report of thee.   90

And, above Godstow Bridge, when hay-time's here
   In June, and many a scythe in sunshine flames,
     Men who through those wide fields of breezy grass
   Where black-wing'd swallows haunt the glittering Thames,
     To bathe in the abandon'd lasher pass,
       Have often pass'd thee near
   Sitting upon the river bank o'ergrown;
     Mark'd thine outlandish garb, thy figure spare,
     Thy dark vague eyes, and soft abstracted air—
But, when they came from bathing, thou wast gone!   100

At some lone homestead in the Cumner hills,
   Where at her open door the housewife darns,
     Thou hast been seen, or hanging on a gate
   To watch the threshers in the mossy barns.
     Children, who early range these slopes and late
      For cresses from the rills,
   Have known thee eyeing, all an April day,
     The springing pastures and the feeding kine;
     And mark'd thee, when the stars come out and shine,
Through the long dewy grass move slow away.   110

In Autumn, on the skirts of Bagley Wood—
   Where most the Gipsies by the turf-edged way
     Pitch their smoked tents, and every bush you see
   With scarlet patches tagg'd and shreds of grey,
     Above the forest ground call'd Thessaly—
      The blackbird, picking food,
   Sees thee, nor stops his meal, nor fears at all;
     So often has he known thee past him stray,
     Rapt, twirling in thy hand a wither'd spray,
And waiting for the spark from heaven to fall.   120

And once, in winter, on the causeway chill
   Where home through flooded fields foot-travellers go,
     Have I not pass'd thee on the wooden bridge,
   Wrapt in thy cloak and battling with the snow,
     Thy face tow'rd Hinksey and its wintry ridge?
      And thou hast climb'd the hill
   And gain'd the white brow of the Cumner range;
     Turn'd once to watch, while thick the snowflakes fall,
     The line of festal light in Christ-Church hall—
Then sought thy straw in some sequester'd grange.   130

But what—I dream! Two hundred years are flown
  Since first thy story ran through Oxford halls,
    And the grave Glanvil did the tale inscribe
  That thou wert wander'd from the studious walls
    To learn strange arts, and join a gipsy-tribe:
      And thou from earth art gone
  Long since, and in some quiet churchyard laid—
    Some country nook, where o'er thy unknown grave
    Tall grasses and white flowering nettles wave,
Under a dark, red-fruited yew-tree's shade.   140

—No, no, thou hast not felt the lapse of hours!
  For what wears out the life of mortal men?
    'Tis that from change to change their being rolls;
  'Tis that repeated shocks, again, again
    Exhaust the energy of strongest souls,
      And numb the elastic powers.
  Till having used our nerves with bliss and teen,
    And tired upon a thousand schemes our wit,
    To the just-pausing Genius we remit
Our worn-out life, and are—what we have been.   150

Thou hast not lived, why should'st thou perish, so?
  Thou hadst *one* aim, *one* business, *one* desire;
    Else wert thou long since number'd with the dead!
  Else hadst thou spent, like other men, thy fire!
    The generations of thy peers are fled,
      And we ourselves shall go;
  But thou possessest an immortal lot,
    And we imagine thee exempt from age
    And living as thou liv'st on Glanvil's page,
Because thou hadst—what we, alas! have not.   160

For early didst thou leave the world, with powers
  Fresh, undiverted to the world without,
    Firm to their mark, not spent on other things;
  Free from the sick fatigue, the languid doubt,
    Which much to have tried, in much been baffled, brings.
      O life unlike to ours!
  Who fluctuate idly without term or scope,
    Of whom each strives, nor knows for what he strives,
    And each half lives a hundred different lives;
Who wait like thee, but not, like thee, in hope.   170

Thou waitest for the spark from heaven! and we,
   Light half-believers of our casual creeds,
     Who never deeply felt, nor clearly will'd,
   Whose insight never has borne fruit in deeds,
     Whose vague resolves never have been fulfill'd;
       For whom each year we see
   Breeds new beginnings, disappointments new;
     Who hesitate and falter life away,
     And lose to-morrow the ground won to-day—
Ah! do not we, wanderer! await it too?   180

Yes, we await it!—but it still delays,
   And then we suffer; and amongst us one,
     Who most has suffer'd, takes dejectedly
   His seat upon the intellectual throne;
     And all his store of sad experience he
       Lays bare of wretched days;
   Tells us his misery's birth and growth and signs,
     And how the dying spark of hope was fed,
     And how the breast was soothed, and how the head,
And all his hourly varied anodynes.   190

This for our wisest! and we others pine,
   And wish the long unhappy dream would end,
     And waive all claim to bliss, and try to bear;
   With close-lipp'd patience for our only friend,
     Sad patience, too near neighbour to despair—
       But none has hope like thine!
   Thou through the fields and through the woods dost stray,
     Roaming the country side, a truant boy,
     Nursing thy project in unclouded joy,
And every doubt long blown by time away.   200

O born in days when wits were fresh and clear,
   And life ran gaily as the sparkling Thames;
     Before this strange disease of modern life,
   With its sick hurry, its divided aims,
     Its heads o'ertax'd, its palsied hearts, was rife—
       Fly hence, our contact fear!
   Still fly, plunge deeper in the bowering wood!
     Averse, as Dido did with gesture stern
     From her false friend's approach in Hades turn,
Wave us away, and keep thy solitude.   210

Still nursing the unconquerable hope,
  Still clutching the inviolable shade,
    With a free, onward impulse brushing through,
  By night, the silver'd branches of the glade—
    Far on the forest skirts, where none pursue,
      On some mild pastoral slope
  Emerge, and resting on the moonlit pales,
    Freshen thy flowers, as in former years,
    With dew, or listen with enchanted ears,
From the dark dingles, to the nightingales.   220

But fly our paths, our feverish contact fly!
  For strong the infection of our mental strife,
    Which, though it gives no bliss, yet spoils for rest;
  And we should win thee from thy own fair life,
    Like us distracted, and like us unblest.
      Soon, soon thy cheer would die,
  Thy hopes grow timorous, and unfix'd thy powers,
    And thy clear aims be cross and shifting made:
    And then thy glad perennial youth would fade,
Fade, and grow old at last, and die like ours.   230

Then fly our greetings, fly our speech and smiles!
  —As some grave Tyrian trader, from the sea,
    Descried at sunrise an emerging prow
  Lifting the cool-hair'd creepers stealthily,
    The fringes of a southward-facing brow
      Among the Ægean isles;
  And saw the merry Grecian coaster come,
    Freighted with amber grapes, and Chian wine,
    Green bursting figs, and tunnies steep'd in brine—
And knew the intruders on his ancient home,   240

The young light-hearted masters of the waves—
  And snatch'd his rudder, and shook out more sail,
    And day and night held on indignantly
  O'er the blue Midland waters with the gale,
    Betwixt the Syrtes and soft Sicily,
      To where the Atlantic raves
  Outside the western straits; and unbent sails
    There, where down cloudy cliffs, through sheets of foam,
    Shy traffickers, the dark Iberians come;
And on the beach undid his corded bales.   250

284.   THYRSIS

A MONODY, TO COMMEMORATE THE AUTHOR'S FRIEND, ARTHUR HUGH
CLOUGH, WHO DIED AT FLORENCE, 1861

> Thus yesterday, to-day, to-morrow come,
> They hustle one another and they pass;
> But all our hustling morrows only make
> The smooth to-day of God.
>   From *Lucretius, an unpublished Tragedy*

How changed is here each spot man makes or fills!
  In the two Hinkseys nothing keeps the same;
    The village-street its haunted mansion lacks,
  And from the sign is gone Sibylla's name,
    And from the roofs the twisted chimney-stacks—
      Are ye too changed, ye hills?
  See, 'tis no foot of unfamiliar men
    To-night from Oxford up your pathway strays!
  Here came I often, often, in old days—
Thyrsis and I; we still had Thyrsis then.   10

Runs it not here, the track by Childsworth Farm,
  Past the high wood, to where the elm-tree crowns
    The hill behind whose ridge the sunset flames?
  The signal-elm, that looks on Ilsley Downs,
    The Vale, the three lone weirs, the youthful Thames?—
      This winter-eve is warm,
  Humid the air! leafless, yet soft as spring,
    The tender purple spray on copse and briers!
  And that sweet city with her dreaming spires,
She needs not June for beauty's heightening,   20

Lovely all times she lies, lovely to-night!—
  Only, methinks, some loss of habit's power
    Befalls me wandering through this upland dim.
  Once pass'd I blindfold here, at any hour;
    Now seldom come I, since I came with him.
      That single elm-tree bright
  Against the west—I miss it! is it gone?
    We prized it dearly; while it stood, we said,
  Our friend, the Gipsy Scholar, was not dead;
While the tree lived, he in these fields lived on.   30

Too rare, too rare, grow now my visits here,
    But once I knew each field, each flower, each stick;
      And with the country-folk acquaintance made
By barn in threshing-time, by new-built rick.
      Here, too, our shepherd-pipes we first assay'd.
        Ah me! this many a year
My pipe is lost, my shepherd's-holiday!
      Needs must I lose them, needs with heavy heart
      Into the world and wave of men depart;
But Thyrsis of his own will went away.   40

It irk'd him to be here, he could not rest.
    He loved each simple joy the country yields,
      He loved his mates; but yet he could not keep,
For that a shadow lour'd on the fields,
      Here with the shepherds and the silly sheep.
        Some life of men unblest
He knew, which made him droop, and fill'd his head.
      He went; his piping took a troubled sound
      Of storms that rage outside our happy ground;
He could not wait their passing, he is dead.   50

So, some tempestuous morn in early June,
    When the year's primal burst of bloom is o'er,
      Before the roses and the longest day—
When garden-walks and all the grassy floor,
      With blossoms red and white of fallen May,
        And chestnut-flowers are strewn—
So have I heard the cuckoo's parting cry,
      From the wet field, through the vext garden-trees,
      Come with the volleying rain and tossing breeze:
The bloom is gone, and with the bloom go I!   60

Too quick despairer, wherefore wilt thou go?
    Soon will the high Midsummer pomps come on,
      Soon will the musk carnations break and swell,
Soon shall we have gold-dusted snapdragon,
      Sweet-William with his homely cottage-smell,
        And stocks in fragrant blow;
Roses that down the alleys shine afar,
      And open, jasmine-muffled lattices,
      And groups under the dreaming garden-trees,
And the full moon, and the white evening-star.   70

He hearkens not! light comer, he is flown!
  What matters it? next year he will return,
    And we shall have him in the sweet spring-days,
  With whitening hedges, and uncrumpling fern,
    And blue-bells trembling by the forest-ways,
      And scent of hay new-mown.
  But Thyrsis never more we swains shall see;
    See him come back, and cut a smoother reed,
    And blow a strain the world at last shall heed—
  For Time, not Corydon, hath conquer'd thee.   80

Alack, for Corydon no rival now!—
  But when Sicilian shepherds lost a mate,
    Some good survivor with his flute would go,
  Piping a ditty sad for Bion's fate,
    And cross the unpermitted ferry's flow,
      And relax Pluto's brow,
  And make leap up with joy the beauteous head
    Of Proserpine, among whose crownèd hair
    Are flowers, first open'd on Sicilian air,
  And flute his friend, like Orpheus, from the dead.   90

O easy access to the hearer's grace,
  When Dorian shepherds sang to Proserpine!
    For she herself had trod Sicilian fields,
  She knew the Dorian water's gush divine,
    She knew each lily white which Enna yields,
      Each rose with blushing face;
  She loved the Dorian pipe, the Dorian strain.
    But ah, of our poor Thames she never heard!
    Her foot the Cumner cowslips never stirr'd;
  And we should tease her with our plaint in vain!   100

Well! wind-dispersed and vain the words will be,
  Yet, Thyrsis, let me give my grief its hour
    In the old haunt, and find our tree-topp'd hill!
  Who, if not I, for questing here hath power?
    I know the wood which hides the daffodil,
      I know the Fyfield tree,
  I know what white, what purple fritillaries
    The grassy harvest of the river-fields,
    Above by Ensham, down by Sandford, yields,
  And what sedged brooks are Thames's tributaries;   110

I know these slopes; who knows them if not I?—
   But many a dingle on the loved hill-side,
      With thorns once studded, old, white-blossom'd trees,
   Where thick the cowslips grew, and, far descried
      High tower'd the spikes of purple orchises,
         Hath since our day put by
   The coronals of that forgotten time;
      Down each green bank hath gone the ploughboy's team,
      And only in the hidden brookside gleam
Primroses, orphans of the flowery prime.   120

Where is the girl, who, by the boatman's door,
   Above the locks, above the boating throng,
      Unmoor'd our skiff, when, through the Wytham flats,
   Red loosestrife and blond meadow-sweet among,
      And darting swallows, and light water-gnats,
         We track'd the shy Thames shore?
   Where are the mowers, who, as the tiny swell
      Of our boat passing heaved the river-grass,
      Stood with suspended scythe to see us pass?—
They all are gone, and thou art gone as well.   130

Yes, thou art gone! and round me too the night
   In ever-nearing circle weaves her shade.
      I see her veil draw soft across the day,
   I feel her slowly chilling breath invade
      The cheek grown thin, the brown hair sprent with grey;
         I feel her finger light
   Laid pausefully upon life's headlong train;—
      The foot less prompt to meet the morning dew,
      The heart less bounding at emotion new,
And hope, once crush'd, less quick to spring again.   140

And long the way appears, which seem'd so short
   To the less practised eye of sanguine youth;
      And high the mountain-tops, in cloudy air,
   The mountain-tops where is the throne of Truth,
      Tops in life's morning-sun so bright and bare.
         Unbreachable the fort
   Of the long-batter'd world uplifts its wall;
      And strange and vain the earthly turmoil grows,
      And near and real the charm of thy repose,
And night as welcome as a friend would fall.   150

But hush! the upland hath a sudden loss
  Of quiet!—Look, adown the dusk hill-side,
    A troop of Oxford hunters going home,
As in old days, jovial and talking, ride!
    From hunting with the Berkshire hounds they come.
      Quick! let me fly, and cross
Into yon farther field!—'Tis done; and see,
    Back'd by the sunset, which doth glorify
    The orange and pale violet evening-sky,
Bare on its lonely ridge, the Tree! the Tree!   160

I take the omen! Eve lets down her veil,
  The white fog creeps from bush to bush about,
    The west unflushes, the high stars grow bright,
And in the scatter'd farms the lights come out.
    I cannot reach the signal-tree to-night,
      Yet, happy omen, hail!
Hear it from thy broad lucent Arno-vale
    (For there thine earth-forgetting eyelids keep
    The morningless and unawakening sleep
Under the flowery oleanders pale),   170

Hear it, O Thyrsis, still our tree is there!—
  Ah, vain! These English fields, this upland dim,
    These brambles pale with mist engarlanded,
That lone, sky-pointing tree, are not for him.
    To a boon southern country he is fled,
      And now in happier air,
Wandering with the great Mother's train divine
    (And purer or more subtle soul than thee,
    I trow, the mighty Mother doth not see!)
Within a folding of the Apennine,   180

Thou hearest the immortal chants of old!—
  Putting his sickle to the perilous grain,
    In the hot cornfield of the Phrygian king,
For thee the Lityerses song again
    Young Daphnis with his silver voice doth sing;
      Sings his Sicilian fold,
His sheep, his hapless love, his blinded eyes—
    And how a call celestial round him rang,
    And heavenward from the fountain-brink he sprang,
And all the marvel of the golden skies.   190

There thou art gone, and me thou leavest here
  Sole in these fields! yet will I not despair;
    Despair I will not, while I yet descry
  'Neath the mild canopy of English air
    That lonely tree against the western sky.
     Still, still these slopes, 'tis clear,
  Our Gipsy-Scholar haunts, outliving thee!
    Fields where soft sheep from cages pull the hay,
    Woods with anemonies in flower till May,
Know him a wanderer still; then why not me?   200

A fugitive and gracious light he seeks,
  Shy to illumine; and I seek it too.
    This does not come with houses or with gold,
  With place, with honour, and a flattering crew;
    'Tis not in the world's market bought and sold—
     But the smooth-slipping weeks
  Drop by, and leave its seeker still untired;
    Out of the heed of mortals he is gone,
    He wends unfollow'd, he must house alone;
Yet on he fares, by his own heart inspired.   210

Thou too, O Thyrsis, on like quest wast bound,
  Thou wanderedst with me for a little hour!
    Men gave thee nothing; but this happy quest,
  If men esteem'd thee feeble, gave thee power,
    If men procured thee trouble, gave thee rest.
     And this rude Cumner ground,
  Its fir-topped Hurst, its farms, its quiet fields,
    Here cam'st thou in thy jocund youthful time,
    Here was thine height of strength, thy golden prime!
And still the haunt beloved a virtue yields.   220

What though the music of thy rustic flute
  Kept not for long its happy, country tone;
    Lost it too soon, and learnt a stormy note
  Of men contention-tost, of men who groan,
    Which task'd thy pipe too sore, and tired thy throat—
     It fail'd, and thou wast mute!
  Yet hadst thou alway visions of our light,
    And long with men of care thou couldst not stay,
    And soon thy foot resumed its wandering way,
Left human haunt, and on alone till night.   230

Too rare, too rare, grow now my visits here!
  'Mid city-noise, not, as with thee of yore,
    Thyrsis! in reach of sheep-bells is my home.
  —Then through the great town's harsh, heart-wearying roar,
    Let in thy voice a whisper often come,
      To chase fatigue and fear:
Why faintest thou? I wander'd till I died.
  Roam on! the light we sought is shining still.
  Dost thou ask proof? Our tree yet crowns the hill,
Our Scholar travels yet the loved hill-side.   240

285.   DOVER BEACH

    The sea is calm to-night.
    The tide is full, the moon lies fair
    Upon the straits;—on the French coast, the light
    Gleams, and is gone; the cliffs of England stand,
    Glimmering and vast, out in the tranquil bay.
    Come to the window, sweet is the night air!
    Only, from the lone line of spray
    Where the sea meets the moon-blanch'd land,
    Listen! you hear the grating roar
    Of pebbles which the waves draw back, and fling,   10
    At their return, up the high strand,
    Begin, and cease, and then again begin,
    With tremulous cadence slow, and bring
    The eternal note of sadness in.

    Sophocles long ago
    Heard it on the Ægæan, and it brought
    Into his mind the turbid ebb and flow
    Of human misery; we
    Find also in the sound a thought,
    Hearing it by this distant northern sea.   20

    The Sea of Faith
    Was once, too, at the full, and round earth's shore
    Lay like the folds of a bright girdle furl'd.
    But now I only hear
    Its melancholy, long, withdrawing roar,
    Retreating, to the breath
    Of the night-wind down the vast edges drear
    And naked shingles of the world.

Ah, love, let us be true
To one another! for the world, which seems 30
To lie before us like a land of dreams,
So various, so beautiful, so new,
Hath really neither joy, nor love, nor light,
Nor certitude, nor peace, nor help for pain;
And we are here as on a darkling plain
Swept with confused alarms of struggle and flight,
Where ignorant armies clash by night.

286. RUGBY CHAPEL
NOVEMBER, 1857

Coldly, sadly descends
The autumn evening. The Field
Strewn with its dank yellow drifts
Of wither'd leaves, and the elms,
Fade into dimness apace,
Silent;—hardly a shout
From a few boys late at their play!
The lights come out in the street,
In the school-room windows;—but cold,
Solemn, unlighted, austere, 10
Through the gathering darkness, arise
The chapel-walls, in whose bound
Thou, my father! art laid.

There thou dost lie, in the gloom
Of the autumn evening. But ah!
That word, *gloom,* to my mind
Brings thee back in the light
Of thy radiant vigour again;
In the gloom of November we pass'd
Days not dark at thy side; 20
Seasons impair'd not the ray
Of thy buoyant cheerfulness clear.
Such thou wast! and I stand
In the autumn evening, and think
Of bygone autumns with thee.

Fifteen years have gone round
Since thou arosest to tread,
In the summer morning, the road

Of death, at a call unforeseen,
Sudden. For fifteen years,   30
We who till then in thy shade
Rested as under the boughs
Of a mighty oak, have endured
Sunshine and rain as we might,
Bare, unshaded, alone,
Lacking the shelter of thee.

O strong soul, by what shore
Tarriest thou now? For that force,
Surely, has not been left vain!
Somewhere, surely, afar,   40
In the sounding labour-house vast
Of being, is practised that strength,
Zealous, beneficent, firm!

Yes, in some far-shining sphere,
Conscious or not of the past,
Still thou performest the word
Of the Spirit in whom thou dost live—
Prompt, unwearied, as here!
Still thou upraisest with zeal
The humble good from the ground,   50
Sternly repressest the bad!
Still, like a trumpet, dost rouse
Those who with half-open eyes
Tread the border-land dim
'Twixt vice and virtue; reviv'st,
Succourest!—this was thy work,
This was thy life upon earth.

What is the course of the life
Of mortal men on the earth?—
Most men eddy about   60
Here and there—eat and drink,
Chatter and love and hate,
Gather and squander, are raised
Aloft, are hurl'd in the dust,
Striving blindly, achieving
Nothing, and then they die—
Perish;—and no one asks
Who or what they have been,

More than he asks what waves,
In the moonlit solitudes mild   70
Of the midmost Ocean, have swell'd,
Foam'd for a moment, and gone.

And there are some, whom a thirst
Ardent, unquenchable, fires,
Not with the crowd to be spent,
Not without aim to go round
In an eddy of purposeless dust,
Effort unmeaning and vain.
Ah yes! some of us strive
Not without action to die   80
Fruitless, but something to snatch
From dull oblivion, nor all
Glut the devouring grave!
We, we have chosen our path—
Path to a clear-purposed goal,
Path of advance!—but it leads
A long, steep journey, through sunk
Gorges, o'er mountains in snow.
Cheerful, with friends, we set forth—
Then, on the height, comes the storm.   90

Thunder crashes from rock
To rock, the cataracts reply,
Lightnings dazzle our eyes.
Roaring torrents have breach'd
The track, the stream-bed descends
In the place where the wayfarer once
Planted his footstep—the spray
Boils o'er its borders! aloft
The unseen snow-beds dislodge
Their hanging ruin; alas,   100
Havoc is made in our train!
Friends who set forth at our side
Falter, are lost in the storm.
We, we only, are left!
With frowning foreheads, with lips
Sternly compress'd, we strain on,
On—and at nightfall at last
Come to the end of our way,
To the lonely inn 'mid the rocks;

Where the gaunt and taciturn host   110
Stands on the threshold, the wind
Shaking his thin white hairs—
Holds his lantern to scan
Our storm-beat figures, and asks:
Whom in our party we bring?
Whom we have left in the snow?

Sadly we answer: We bring
Only ourselves! we lost
Sight of the rest in the storm.
Hardly ourselves we fought through,   120
Stripp'd, without friends, as we are.
Friends, companions, and train,
The avalanche swept from our side.

But thou would'st not *alone*
Be saved, my father! *alone*
Conquer and come to thy goal,
Leaving the rest in the wild.
We were weary, and we
Fearful, and we, in our march,
Fain to drop down and to die.   130
Still thou turnedst, and still
Beckonedst the trembler, and still
Gavest the weary thy hand.
If, in the paths of the world,
Stones might have wounded thy feet,
Toil or dejection have tried
Thy spirit, of that we saw
Nothing—to us thou wast still
Cheerful, and helpful, and firm!
Therefore to thee it was given   140
Many to save with thyself;
And, at the end of thy day,
O faithful shepherd! to come,
Bringing thy sheep in thy hand.

And through thee I believe
In the noble and great who are gone;
Pure souls honour'd and blest
By former ages, who else—
Such, so soulless, so poor,

Is the race of men whom I see— 150
Seem'd but a dream of the heart,
Seem'd but a cry of desire.
Yes! I believe that there lived
Others like thee in the past,
Not like the men of the crowd
Who all round me to-day
Bluster or cringe, and make life
Hideous, and arid, and vile;
But souls temper'd with fire,
Fervent, heroic, and good, 160
Helpers and friends of mankind.

Servants of God!—or sons
Shall I not call you? because
Not as servants ye knew
Your Father's innermost mind,
His, who unwillingly sees
One of his little ones lost—
Yours is the praise, if mankind
Hath not as yet in its march
Fainted, and fallen, and died! 170

See! in the rocks of the world
Marches the host of mankind,
A feeble, wavering line.
Where are they tending?—A God
Marshall'd them, gave them their goal.
Ah, but the way is so long!
Years they have been in the wild!
Sore thirst plagues them, the rocks,
Rising all round, overawe;
Factions divide them; their host 180
Threatens to break, to dissolve.
Ah, keep, keep them combined!
Else, of the myriads who fill
That army, not one shall arrive;
Sole they shall stray; in the rocks
Labour for ever in vain,
Die one by one in the waste.

Then, in such hour of need
Of your fainting, dispirited race,

Ye, like angels, appear,   190
Radiant with ardour divine!
Beacons of hope, ye appear!
Languor is not in your heart,
Weakness is not in your word,
Weariness not on your brow.
Ye alight in our van! at your voice,
Panic, despair, flee away.
Ye move through the ranks, recall
The stragglers, refresh the outworn,
Praise, re-inspire the brave!   200
Order, courage, return.
Eyes rekindling, and prayers,
Follow your steps as ye go.
Ye fill up the gaps in our files,
Strengthen the wavering line,
Stablish, continue our march,
On, to the bound of the waste,
On, to the City of God.

DANTE GABRIEL ROSSETTI (1828–1882)

287.   THE BLESSED DAMOZEL

The blessèd damozel leaned out
    From the gold bar of Heaven;
Her eyes were deeper than the depth
    Of waters stilled at even;
She had three lilies in her hand,
    And the stars in her hair were seven.

Her robe, ungirt from clasp to hem,
    No wrought flowers did adorn,
But a white rose of Mary's gift,
    For service meetly worn;   10
Her hair that lay along her back
    Was yellow like ripe corn.

Herseemed she scarce had been a day
    One of God's choristers;
The wonder was not yet quite gone
    From that still look of hers;

Albeit, to them she left, her day
    Had counted as ten years.

(To one, it is ten years of years.
    . . . Yet now, and in this place,   20
Surely she leaned o'er me—her hair
    Fell all about my face. . . .
Nothing: the autumn fall of leaves.
    The whole year sets apace.)

It was the rampart of God's house
    That she was standing on;
By God built over the sheer depth
    The which is Space begun;
So high, that looking downward thence
    She scarce could see the sun.   30

It lies in Heaven, across the flood
    Of ether, as a bridge.
Beneath, the tides of day and night
    With flame and darkness ridge
The void, as low as where this earth
    Spins like a fretful midge.

Around her, lovers, newly met
    'Mid deathless love's acclaims,
Spoke evermore among themselves
    Their heart-remembered names;   40
And the souls mounting up to God
    Went by her like thin flames.

And still she bowed herself and stooped
    Out of the circling charm;
Until her bosom must have made
    The bar she leaned on warm,
And the lilies lay as if asleep
    Along her bended arm.

From the fixed place of Heaven she saw
    Time like a pulse shake fierce   50
Through all the worlds. Her gaze still strove
    Within the gulf to pierce
Its path; and now she spoke as when
    The stars sang in their spheres.

The sun was gone now; the curled moon
   Was like a little feather
Fluttering far down the gulf; and now
   She spoke through the still weather.
Her voice was like the voice the stars
   Had when they sang together.   60

(Ah, sweet! Even now, in that bird's song,
   Strove not her accents there,
Fain to be hearkened? When those bells
   Possessed the mid-day air,
Strove not her steps to reach my side
   Down all the echoing stair?)

'I wish that he were come to me,
   For he will come,' she said.
'Have I not prayed in Heaven?—on earth;
   Lord, Lord, has he not pray'd?   70
Are not two prayers a perfect strength?
   And shall I feel afraid?

'When round his head the aureole clings,
   And he is clothed in white,
I'll take his hand and go with him
   To the deep wells of light;
We will step down as to a stream,
   And bathe there in God's sight.

'We two will stand beside that shrine,
   Occult, withheld, untrod,   80
Whose lamps are stirred continually
   With prayer sent up to God;
And see our old prayers, granted, melt
   Each like a little cloud.

'We two will lie i' the shadow of
   That living mystic tree
Within whose secret growth the Dove
   Is sometimes felt to be,
While every leaf that His plumes touch
   Saith His Name audibly.   90

'And I myself will teach to him,
   I myself, lying so,

The songs I sing here; which his voice
   Shall pause in, hushed and slow,
And find some knowledge at each pause,
   Or some new thing to know.'

(Alas! We two, we two, thou say'st!
   Yea, one wast thou with me
That once of old. But shall God lift
   To endless unity   100
The soul whose likeness with thy soul
   Was but its love for thee?)

'We two,' she said, 'will seek the groves
   Where the lady Mary is,
With her five handmaidens, whose names
   Are five sweet symphonies,
Cecily, Gertrude, Magdalen,
   Margaret and Rosalys.

'Circlewise sit they, with bound locks
   And foreheads garlanded;   110
Into the fine cloth white like flame
   Weaving the golden thread,
To fashion the birth-robes for them
   Who are just born, being dead.

'He shall fear, haply, and be dumb:
   Then will I lay my cheek
To his, and tell about our love,
   Not once abashed or weak:
And the dear Mother will approve
   My pride, and let me speak.   120

'Herself shall bring us, hand in hand,
   To Him round whom all souls
Kneel, the clear-ranged unnumbered heads
   Bowed with their aureoles:
And angels meeting us shall sing
   To their citherns and citoles.

'There will I ask of Christ the Lord
   Thus much for him and me:—
Only to live as once on earth
   With Love,—only to be,   130

As then awhile, for ever now
    Together, I and he.'

She gazed and listened and then said,
    Less sad of speech than mild,—
'All this is when he comes.' She ceased.
    The light thrilled towards her, fill'd
With angels in strong level flight.
    Her eyes prayed, and she smil'd.

(I saw her smile.) But soon their path   140
    Was vague in distant spheres;
And then she cast her arms along
    The golden barriers,
And laid her face between her hands,
    And wept. (I heard her tears.)

288.   SISTER HELEN

'Why did you melt your waxen man,
        Sister Helen?
To-day is the third since you began.'
'The time was long, yet the time ran,
        Little brother.'
      (O Mother, Mary Mother,
Three days to-day, between Hell and Heaven!)

'But if you have done your work aright,
        Sister Helen,
You'll let me play, for you said I might.'   10
'Be very still in your play to-night,
        Little brother.'
      (O Mother, Mary Mother,
Third night, to-night, between Hell and Heaven!)

'You said it must melt ere vesper-bell,
        Sister Helen;
If now it be molten, all is well.'
'Even so,—nay, peace! you cannot tell,
        Little brother.'
      (O Mother, Mary Mother,   20
What is this, between Hell and Heaven?)

'Oh the waxen knave was plump to-day,
    Sister Helen;
How like dead folk he has dropped away!'
'Nay now, of the dead what can you say,
    Little brother?'
   (O Mother, Mary Mother,
What of the dead, between Hell and Heaven?)

'See, see, the sunken pile of wood,
    Sister Helen,   30
Shines through the thinned wax red as blood!'
'Nay now, when looked you yet on blood,
    Little brother?'
   (O Mother, Mary Mother,
How pale she is, between Hell and Heaven!)

'Now close your eyes, for they're sick and sore,
    Sister Helen,
And I'll play without the gallery door.'
'Aye, let me rest,—I'll lie on the floor,
    Little brother.'   40
   (O Mother, Mary Mother,
What rest to-night between Hell and Heaven?)

'Here high up in the balcony,
    Sister Helen,
The moon flies face to face with me.'
'Aye, look and say whatever you see,
    Little brother.'
   (O Mother, Mary Mother,
What sight to-night, between Hell and Heaven?)

'Outside it's merry in the wind's wake,   50
    Sister Helen;
In the shaken trees the chill stars shake.'
'Hush, heard you a horse-tread as you spake,
    Little brother?'
   (O Mother, Mary Mother,
What sound to-night, between Hell and Heaven?)

'I hear a horse-tread, and I see,
    Sister Helen,
Three horsemen that ride terribly.'

'Little brother, whence come the three,   60
          Little brother?'
      (O Mother, Mary Mother,
Whence should they come, between Hell and Heaven?)

'They come by the hill-verge from Boyne Bar,
          Sister Helen,
And one draws nigh, but two are afar.'
'Look, look, do you know them who they are,
          Little brother?'
      (O Mother, Mary Mother,
Who should they be, between Hell and Heaven?)   70

'Oh, it's Keith of Eastholm rides so fast,
          Sister Helen,
For I know the white mane on the blast.'
'The hour has come, has come at last,
          Little brother!'
      (O Mother, Mary Mother,
Her hour at last, between Hell and Heaven!)

'He has made a sign and called Halloo!
          Sister Helen,
And he says that he would speak with you.'   80
'Oh tell him I fear the frozen dew,
          Little brother.'
      (O Mother, Mary Mother,
Why laughs she thus, between Hell and Heaven?)

'The wind is loud, but I hear him cry,
          Sister Helen,
That Keith of Ewern's like to die.'
'And he and thou, and thou and I,
          Little brother.'
      (O Mother, Mary Mother,   90
And they and we, between Hell and Heaven!)

'Three days ago, on his marriage-morn,
          Sister Helen,
He sickened, and lies since then forlorn.'
'For bridegroom's side is the bride a thorn,
          Little brother?'
      (O Mother, Mary Mother,
Cold bridal cheer, between Hell and Heaven!)

'Three days and nights he has lain abed,
                    Sister Helen,   100
And he prays in torment to be dead.'
'The thing may chance, if he have prayed,
                    Little brother!'
            (O Mother, Mary Mother,
If he have prayed, between Hell and Heaven!)

'But he has not ceased to cry to-day,
                    Sister Helen,
That you should take your curse away.'
'*My* prayer was heard,—he need but pray,
                    Little brother!'   110
            (O Mother, Mary Mother,
Shall God not hear, between Hell and Heaven?)

'But he says, till you take back your ban,
                    Sister Helen,
His soul would pass, yet never can.'
'Nay then, shall I slay a living man,
                    Little brother?'
            (O Mother, Mary Mother,
A living soul, between Hell and Heaven!)

'But he calls for ever on your name,   120
                    Sister Helen,
And says that he melts before a flame.'
'My heart for his pleasure fared the same,
                    Little brother.'
            (O Mother, Mary Mother,
Fire at the heart, between Hell and Heaven!)

'Here's Keith of Westholm riding fast,
                    Sister Helen,
For I know the white plume on the blast.'
'The hour, the sweet hour I forecast,   130
                    Little brother!'
            (O Mother, Mary Mother,
Is the hour sweet, between Hell and Heaven?)

'He stops to speak, and he stills his horse,
                    Sister Helen;
But his words are drowned in the wind's course.'

'Nay hear, nay hear, you must hear perforce,
                Little brother!'
        (O Mother, Mary Mother,
What word now heard, between Hell and Heaven?)   140

'Oh he says that Keith of Ewern's cry,
                Sister Helen,
Is ever to see you ere he die.'
'In all that his soul sees, there am I,
                Little brother!'
        (O Mother, Mary Mother,
The soul's one sight, between Hell and Heaven!)

'He sends a ring and a broken coin,
                Sister Helen,
And bids you mind the banks of Boyne.'   150
'What else he broke will he ever join,
                Little brother?'
        (O Mother, Mary Mother,
No, never joined, between Hell and Heaven!)

'He yields you these and craves full fain,
                Sister Helen,
You pardon him in his mortal pain.'
'What else he took will he give again,
                Little brother?'
        (O Mother, Mary Mother,   160
Not twice to give, between Hell and Heaven!)

'He calls your name in an agony,
                Sister Helen,
That even dead Love must weep to see.'
'Hate, born of Love, is blind as he,
                Little brother!'
        (O Mother, Mary Mother,
Love turned to hate, between Hell and Heaven!)

'Oh it's Keith of Keith now that rides fast,
                Sister Helen,   170
For I know the white hair on the blast.'
'The short, short hour will soon be past,
                Little brother!'
        (O Mother, Mary Mother,
Will soon be past, between Hell and Heaven!)

'He looks at me and he tries to speak,
    Sister Helen,
But oh! his voice is sad and weak!'
'What here should the mighty Baron seek,
    Little brother?'   180
  (O Mother, Mary Mother,
Is this the end, between Hell and Heaven?)

'Oh his son still cries, if you forgive,
    Sister Helen,
The body dies, but the soul shall live.'
'Fire shall forgive me as I forgive,
    Little brother!'
  (O Mother, Mary Mother,
As she forgives, between Hell and Heaven!)

'Oh he prays you, as his heart would rive, 190
    Sister Helen,
To save his dear son's soul alive.'
'Fire cannot slay it, it shall thrive,
    Little brother!'
  (O Mother, Mary Mother,
Alas, alas, between Hell and Heaven!)

'He cries to you, kneeling in the road,
    Sister Helen,
To go with him for the love of God!'
'The way is long to his son's abode,   200
    Little brother!'
  (O Mother, Mary Mother,
The way is long, between Hell and Heaven!)

'A lady's here, by a dark steed brought,
    Sister Helen,
So darkly clad, I saw her not.'
'See her now or never see aught,
    Little brother!'
  (O Mother, Mary Mother,
What more to see, between Hell and Heaven!) 210

'Her hood falls back, and the moon shines fair,
    Sister Helen,
On the lady of Ewern's golden hair.'

'Blest hour of my power and her despair,
        Little brother!'
      (*O Mother, Mary Mother,*
Hour blest and bann'd, between Hell and Heaven!)

'Pale, pale, her cheeks, that in pride did glow,
        Sister Helen,
'Neath the bridal-wreath three days ago.'   220
'One morn for pride and three days for woe,
        Little brother!'
      (*O Mother, Mary Mother,*
Three days, three nights, between Hell and Heaven!)

'Her clasped hands stretch from her bending head,
        Sister Helen;
With the loud wind's wail her sobs are wed.'
'What wedding-strains hath her bridal-bed,
        Little brother?'
      (*O Mother, Mary Mother,*   230
What strain but death's between Hell and Heaven?)

'She may not speak, she sinks in a swoon,
        Sister Helen,—
She lifts her lips and gasps on the moon.'
'Oh! might I but hear her soul's blithe tune,
        Little brother!'
      (*O Mother, Mary Mother,*
Her woe's dumb cry, between Hell and Heaven!)

'They've caught her to Westholm's saddle-bow,
        Sister Helen,   240
And her moonlit hair gleams white in its flow.'
'Let it turn whiter than winter snow,
        Little brother!'
      (*O Mother, Mary Mother,*
Woe-withered gold, between Hell and Heaven!)

'O Sister Helen, you heard the bell,
        Sister Helen!
More loud than the vesper-chime it fell.'
'No vesper-chime, but a dying knell,
        Little brother!'   250
      (*O Mother, Mary Mother,*
His dying knell, between Hell and Heaven!)

'Alas! but I fear the heavy sound,
            Sister Helen;
Is it in the sky or in the ground?'
'Say, have they turned their horses round,
            Little brother?'
        (O Mother, Mary Mother,
What would she more, between Hell and Heaven?)

'They have raised the old man from his knee,   260
            Sister Helen,
And they ride in silence hastily.'
'More fast the naked soul doth flee,
            Little brother!'
        (O Mother, Mary Mother,
The naked soul, between Hell and Heaven!)

'Flank to flank are the three steeds gone,
            Sister Helen,
But the lady's dark steed goes alone.'
'And lonely her bridegroom's soul hath flown,   270
            Little brother.'
        (O Mother, Mary Mother,
The lonely ghost, between Hell and Heaven!)

'Oh the wind is sad in the iron chill,
            Sister Helen,
And weary sad they look by the hill.'
'But he and I are sadder still,
            Little brother!'
        (O Mother, Mary Mother,
Most sad of all, between Hell and Heaven!)   280

'See, see, the wax has dropped from its place,
            Sister Helen,
And the flames are winning up apace!'
'Yet here they burn but for a space,
            Little brother!'
        (O Mother, Mary Mother,
Here for a space, between Hell and Heaven!)

'Ah! what white thing at the door has cross'd,
            Sister Helen,
Ah! what is this that sighs in the frost?'   290

'A soul that's lost as mine is lost,
            Little brother!'
        (O Mother, Mary Mother,
  Lost, lost, all lost, between Hell and Heaven!)

289.   MID-RAPTURE

Thou lovely and beloved, thou my love;
    Whose kiss seems still the first; whose summoning eyes,
    Even now, as for our love-world's new sunrise,
Shed very dawn; whose voice, attuned above
All modulation of the deep-bowered dove,
    Is like a hand laid softly on the soul;
    Whose hand is like a sweet voice to control
Those worn tired brows it hath the keeping of:—
What word can answer to thy word,—what gaze
    To thine, which now absorbs within its sphere   10
    My worshiping face, till I am mirrored there
Light-circled in a heaven of deep-drawn rays?
    What clasp, what kiss mine inmost heart can prove
    O lovely and beloved, O my love?

CHRISTINA ROSSETTI (1830–1894)

290.   A BIRTHDAY

My heart is like a singing bird
    Whose nest is in a watered shoot;
My heart is like an apple-tree
    Whose boughs are bent with thickset fruit;
My heart is like a rainbow shell
    That paddles in a halcyon sea;
My heart is gladder than all these
    Because my love is come to me.

Raise me a dais of silk and down;
    Hang it with vair and purple dyes;   10
Carve it in doves, and pomegranates,
    And peacocks with a hundred eyes;
Work it in gold and silver grapes,
    In leaves, and silver fleurs-de-lys;
Because the birthday of my life
    Is come, my love is come to me.

291.   SONG

> When I am dead, my dearest,
>   Sing no sad songs for me;
> Plant thou no roses at my head,
>   Nor shady cypress tree:
> Be the green grass above me
>   With showers and dewdrops wet:
> And if thou wilt, remember,
>   And if thou wilt, forget.
>
> I shall not see the shadows,
>   I shall not feel the rain;   10
> I shall not hear the nightingale
>   Sing on as if in pain:
> And dreaming through the twilight
>   That doth not rise nor set,
> Haply I may remember,
>   And haply may forget.

WALT WHITMAN (1819–1892)

292.   THE WORLD BELOW THE BRINE

The world below the brine,
Forests at the bottom of the sea, the branches and leaves,
Sea-lettuce, vast lichens, strange flowers and seeds, the
    thick tangle, openings, and pink turf,
Different colors, pale gray and green, purple, white, and
    gold, the play of light through the water,
Dumb swimmers there among the rocks, coral, gluten, grass,
    rushes, and the aliment of the swimmers,
Sluggish existences grazing there suspended, or slowly crawl-
    ing close to the bottom,
The sperm-whale at the surface blowing air and spray, or
    disporting with his flukes,
The leaden-eye shark, the walrus, the turtle, the hairy sea-
    leopard, and the sting-ray,
Passions there, wars, pursuits, tribes, sight in those
    ocean-depths, breathing that thick-breathing air, as
    so many do,

The change thence to the sight here, and to the subtle air
    breathed by beings like us who walk this sphere,   10
The change onward from ours to that of beings who walk
    other spheres.

293.   CAMPS OF GREEN

Not alone those camps of white, old comrades of the wars,
When as order'd forward, after a long march,
Footsore and weary, soon as the light lessens we halt for
    the night,
Some of us so fatigued carrying the gun and knapsack,
    dropping asleep in our tracks,
Others pitching the little tents, and the fires lit up
    begin to sparkle,
Outposts of pickets posted surrounding alert through the
    dark,
And a word provided for countersign, careful for safety,
Till to the call of the drummers at daybreak loudly beat-
    ing the drums,
We rise up refresh'd, the night and sleep pass'd over, and
    resume our journey,
Or proceed to battle.   10

Lo, the camps of the tents of green,
Which the days of peace keep filling, and the days of war
    keep filling,
With a mystic army, (is it too order'd forward? is it too
    only halting awhile,
Till night and sleep pass over?)

Now in those camps of green, in their tents dotting the
    world,
In the parents, children, husbands, wives, in them, in
    the old and young,
Sleeping under the sunlight, sleeping under the moonlight,
    content and silent there at last,
Behold the mighty bivouac-field and waiting-camp of all,
Of the corps and generals all, and the President over the
    corps and generals all,
And of each of us O soldiers, and of each and all in the
    ranks we fought,   20
(There without hatred we all, all meet.)

For presently O soldiers, we too camp in our place in the
    bivouac-camps of green,
But we need not provide for outposts, nor word for the
    counter-sign,
Nor drummer to beat the morning drum.

294.   RECONCILIATION

Word over all, beautiful as the sky,
Beautiful that war and all its deeds of carnage must in
    time be utterly lost,
That the hands of the sisters Death and Night incessantly
    softly wash again, and ever again, this soil'd world;
For my enemy is dead, a man divine as myself is dead,
I look where he lies white-faced and still in the coffin
    —I draw near,
Bend down and touch lightly with my lips the white face
    in the coffin.

295.   WHEN LILACS LAST IN THE DOORYARD
                    BLOOM'D

I

When lilacs last in the dooryard bloom'd,
And the great star early droop'd in the western sky in the night,
I mourn'd, and yet shall mourn with ever-returning spring.

Ever-returning spring, trinity sure to me you bring,
Lilac blooming perennial and drooping star in the west,
And thought of him I love.

II

O powerful western fallen star!
O shades of night—O moody, tearful night!
O great star disappear'd—O the black murk that hides the star!
O cruel hands that hold me powerless—O helpless soul of me!   10
O harsh surrounding cloud that will not free my soul.

III

In the dooryard fronting an old farm-house near the white-wash'd
    palings,
Stands the lilac-bush tall-growing with heart-shaped leaves of rich
    green,

With many a pointed blossom rising delicate, with the perfume
  strong I love,
With every leaf a miracle—and from this bush in the dooryard,
With delicate-color'd blossoms and heart-shaped leaves of rich green,
A sprig with its flower I break.

IV

In the swamp in secluded recesses,
A shy and hidden bird is warbling a song.
Solitary the thrush,   20
The hermit withdrawn to himself, avoiding the settlements,
Sings by himself a song.

Song of the bleeding throat,
Death's outlet song of life, (for well dear brother I know,
If thou wast not granted to sing thou would'st surely die.)

V

Over the breast of the spring, the land, amid cities,
Amid lanes and through old woods, where lately the violets peep'd
  from the ground, spotting the gray debris,
Amid the grass in the fields each side of the lanes, passing the
  endless grass,
Passing the yellow-spear'd wheat, every grain from its shroud in the
  dark-brown fields uprisen,
Passing the apple-tree blows of white and pink in the orchards,   30
Carrying a corpse to where it shall rest in the grave,
Night and day journeys a coffin.

VI

Coffin that passes through lanes and streets,
Through day and night with the great cloud darkening the land,
With the pomp of the inloop'd flags with the cities draped in black,
With the show of the States themselves as of crape-veil'd women
  standing,
With processions long and winding and the flambeaus of the night,
With the countless torches lit, with the silent sea of faces and the
  unbared heads,
With the waiting depot, the arriving coffin, and the sombre faces,
With dirges through the night, with the thousand voices rising
  strong and solemn,   40
With all the mournful voices of the dirges pour'd around the coffin,

The dim-lit churches and the shuddering organs—where amid these
    you journey,
With the tolling tolling bells' perpetual clang,
Here, coffin that slowly passes,
I give you my sprig of lilac.

VII

(Not for you, for one alone,
Blossoms and branches green to coffins all I bring,
For fresh as the morning, thus would I chant a song for you O sane
    and sacred death.

All over bouquets of roses,
O death, I cover you over with roses and early lilies,   50
But mostly and now the lilac that blooms the first,
Copious I break, I break the sprigs from the bushes,
With loaded arms I come, pouring for you,
For you and the coffins all of you O death.)

VIII

O western orb sailing tne neaven,
Now I know what you must have meant as a month since I walk'd,
As I walk'd in silence the transparent shadowy night,
As I saw you had something to tell as you bent to me night after
    night,
As you droop'd from the sky low down as if to my side, (while the
    other stars all look'd on,)
As we wander'd together the solemn night, (for something I know
    not what kept me from sleep,)   60
As the night advanced, and I saw on the rim of the west how full
    you were of woe,
As I stood on the rising ground in the breeze in the cool transparent
    night,
As I watch'd where you pass'd and was lost in the netherward black
    of the night,
As my soul in its trouble dissatisfied sank, as where you sad orb,
Concluded, dropt in the night, and was gone.

IX

Sing on there in the swamp,
O singer bashful and tender, I hear your notes, I hear your call,
I hear, I come presently, I understand you,

But a moment I linger, for the lustrous star has detain'd me,
The star my departing comrade holds and detains me.   70

X

O how shall I warble myself for the dead one there I loved?
And how shall I deck my song for the large sweet soul that has gone?
And what shall my perfume be for the grave of him I love?

Sea-winds blown from east and west,
Blown from the Eastern sea and blown from the Western sea, till there on the prairies meeting,
These and with these and the breath of my chant,
I'll perfume the grave of him I love.

XI

O what shall I hang on the chamber walls?
And what shall the pictures be that I hang on the walls,
To adorn the burial-house of him I love?   80

Pictures of growing spring and farms and homes,
With the Fourth-month eve at sundown, and the gray smoke lucid and bright,
With floods of the yellow gold of the gorgeous, indolent, sinking sun, burning, expanding the air,
With the fresh sweet herbage under foot, and the pale green leaves of the trees prolific,
In the distance the flowing glaze, the breast of the river, with a wind-dapple here and there,
With ranging hills on the banks, with many a line against the sky, and shadows,
And the city at hand with dwellings so dense, and stacks of chimneys,
And all the scenes of life and the workshops, and the workmen homeward returning.

XII

Lo, body and soul—this land,
My own Manhattan with spires, and the sparkling and hurrying tides, and the ships,   90
The varied and ample land, the South and the North in the light, Ohio's shores and flashing Missouri,
And ever the far-spreading prairies cover'd with grass and corn.

Lo, the most excellent sun so calm and haughty,
The violet and purple morn with just-felt breezes,
The gentle soft-born measureless light,
The miracle spreading bathing all, the fulfill'd noon,
The coming eve delicious, the welcome night and the stars,
Over my cities shining all, enveloping man and land.

XIII

Sing on, sing on you gray-brown bird,
Sing from the swamps, the recesses, pour your chant from the
    bushes,   100
Limitless out of the dusk, out of the cedars and pines.

Sing on dearest brother, warble your reedy song,
Loud human song, with voice of uttermost woe.

O liquid and free and tender!
O wild and loose to my soul—O wondrous singer!
You only I hear—yet the star holds me, (but will soon depart,)
Yet the lilac with mastering odor holds me.

XIV

Now while I sat in the day and look'd forth,
In the close of the day with its light and the fields of spring, and
    the farmers preparing their crops,
In the large unconscious scenery of my land with its lakes and
    forests,   110
In the heavenly aerial beauty, (after the perturb'd winds and the
    storms,)
Under the arching heavens of the afternoon swift passing, and the
    voices of children and women,
The many-moving sea-tides, and I saw the ships how they sail'd,
And the summer approaching with richness, and the fields all busy
    with labor,
And the infinite separate houses, how they all went on, each with
    its meals and minutia of daily usages,
And the streets how their throbbings throbb'd, and the cities pent—
    lo, then and there,
Falling upon them all and among them all, enveloping me with
    the rest,
Appear'd the cloud, appear'd the long black trail,
And I knew death, its thought, and the sacred knowledge of death.

Then with the knowledge of death as walking one side of me,   120
And the thought of death close-walking the other side of me,
And I in the middle as with companions, and as holding the hands
    of companions,
I fled forth to the hiding receiving night that talks not,
Down to the shores of the water, the path by the swamp in the
    dimness,
To the solemn shadowy cedars and ghostly pines so still.

And the singer so shy to the rest receiv'd me,
The gray-brown bird I know receiv'd us comrades three,
And he sang the carol of death, and a verse for him I love.

From deep secluded recesses,
From the fragrant cedars and the ghostly pines so still,   130
Came the carol of the bird.

And the charm of the carol rapt me,
As I held as if by their hands my comrades in the night,
And the voice of my spirit tallied the song of the bird.

Come lovely and soothing death,
Undulate round the world, serenely arriving, arriving,
In the day, in the night, to all, to each,
Sooner or later delicate death.

Prais'd be the fathomless universe,
For life and joy, and for objects and knowledge curious,   140
And for love, sweet love—but praise! praise! praise!
For the sure-enwinding arms of cool-enfolding death.

Dark mother always gliding near with soft feet,
Have none chanted for thee a chant of fullest welcome?
Then I chant it for thee, I glorify thee above all,
I bring thee a song that when thou must indeed come, come
*   unfalteringly.*

Approach strong deliveress,
When it is so, when thou hast taken them I joyously sing the dead,
Lost in the loving floating ocean of thee,
Laved in the flood of thy bliss O death.   150

From me to thee glad serenades,
Dances for thee I propose saluting thee, adornments and feastings
*   for thee,*

*And the sights of the open landscape and the high-spread sky are
     fitting,*
And life and the fields, and the huge and thoughtful night.

The night in silence under many a star,
*The ocean shore and the husky whispering wave whose voice I
     know,*
And the soul turning to thee O vast and well-veil'd death,
And the body gratefully nestling close to thee.

Over the tree-tops I float thee a song,
*Over the rising and sinking waves, over the myriad fields and the
     prairies wide,*   160
Over the dense-pack'd cities all and the teeming wharves and ways,
I float this carol with joy, with joy to thee O death.

XV

To the tally of my soul,
Loud and strong kept up the gray-brown bird,
With pure deliberate notes spreading filling the night.

Loud in the pines and cedars dim,
Clear in the freshness moist and the swamp-perfume,
And I with my comrades there in the night.

While my sight that was bound in my eyes unclosed,
As to long panoramas of visions.   170

And I saw askant the armies,
I saw as in noiseless dreams hundreds of battle-flags,
Borne through the smoke of the battles and pierc'd with missiles
     I saw them,
And carried hither and yon through the smoke, and torn and bloody,
And at last but a few shreds left on the staffs, (and all in silence,)
And the staffs all splinter'd and broken.

I saw battle-corpses, myriads of them,
And the white skeletons of young men, I saw them,
I saw the debris and debris of all the slain soldiers of the war,
But I saw they were not as was thought,   180
They themselves were fully at rest, they suffer'd not,
The living remain'd and suffer'd, the mother suffer'd,
And the wife and the child and the musing comrade suffer'd,
And the armies that remain'd suffer'd.

XVI

Passing the visions, passing the night,
Passing, unloosing the hold of my comrades' hands,
Passing the song of the hermit bird and the tallying song of my soul,
Victorious song, death's outlet song, yet varying ever-altering song,
As low and wailing, yet clear the notes, rising and falling, flooding
 the night,
Sadly sinking and fainting, as warning and warning, and yet again
 bursting with joy,   190
Covering the earth and filling the spread of the heaven,
As that powerful psalm in the night I heard from recesses,
Passing, I leave thee lilac with heart-shaped leaves,
I leave thee there in the door-yard, blooming, returning with spring.

I cease my song for thee,
From my gaze on thee in the west, fronting the west, communing
 with thee,
O comrade lustrous with silver face in the night.

Yet each to keep and all, retrievements out of the night,
The song, the wondrous chant of the gray-brown bird,
And the tallying chant, the echo arous'd in my soul,   200
With the lustrous and drooping star with the countenance full of
 woe,
With the holders holding my hand nearing the call of the bird,
Comrades mine and I in the midst, and their memory ever to keep,
 for the dead I loved so well,
For the sweetest, wisest soul of all my days and lands—and this for
 his dear sake,
Lilac and star and bird twined with the chant of my soul,
There in the fragrant pines and the cedars dusk and dim.

296.   CHANTING THE SQUARE DEIFIC

I

Chanting the square deific, out of the One advancing, out of the
 sides,
Out of the old and new, out of the square entirely divine,
Solid, four-sided, (all the sides needed,) from this side Jehovah am I,
Old Brahm I, and I Saturnius am;
Not Time affects me—I am Time, old, modern as any,
Unpersuadable. relentless, executing righteous judgments,

As the Earth, the Father, the brown old Kronos, with laws,
Aged beyond computation, yet ever new, ever with those mighty
laws rolling,
Relentless I forgive no man—whoever sins dies—I will have that
man's life;
Therefore let none expect mercy—have the seasons, gravitation, the
appointed days, mercy? no more have I,   10
But as the seasons and gravitation, and as all the appointed days
that forgive not,
I dispense from this side judgments inexorable without the least
remorse.

II

Consolator most mild, the promis'd one advancing,
With gentle hand extended, the mightier God am I,
Foretold by prophets and poets in their most rapt prophecies and
poems,
From this side, lo! the Lord Christ gazes—lo! Hermes I—lo! mine
is Hercules' face,
All sorrow, labor, suffering, I, tallying it, absorb in myself,
Many times have I been rejected, taunted, put in prison, and cruci-
fied, and many times shall be again,
All the world have I given up for my dear brothers' and sisters'
sake, for the soul's sake,
Wending my way through the homes of men, rich or poor, with the
kiss of affection,   20
For I am affection, I am the cheer-bringing God, with hope and all
enclosing charity,
With indulgent words as to children, with fresh and sane words,
mine only,
Young and strong I pass knowing well I am destin'd myself to an
early death;
But my charity has no death—my wisdom dies not, neither early
nor late,
And my sweet love bequeath'd here and elsewhere never dies.

III

Aloof, dissatisfied, plotting revolt,
Comrade of criminals, brother of slaves,
Crafty, despised, a drudge, ignorant,
With sudra face and worn brow, black, but in the depths of my
heart, proud as any,

Lifted now and always against whoever scorning assumes to rule
    me,   30
Morose, full of guile, full of reminiscences, brooding, with many
    wiles,
(Though it was thought I was baffled and dispel'd, and my wiles
    done, but that will never be,)
Defiant, I, Satan, still live, still utter words, in new lands duly
    appearing, (and old ones also,)
Permanent here from my side, warlike, equal with any, real as any.
Nor time nor change shall ever change me or my words.

IV

Santa Spirita, breather, life,
Beyond the light, lighter than light,
Beyond the flames of hell, joyous, leaping easily above hell,
Beyond Paradise, perfumed solely with mine own perfume,
Including all life on earth, touching, including God, including
    Saviour and Satan,   40
Ethereal, pervading all, (for without me what were all? what were
    God?)
Essence of forms, life of the real identities, permanent, positive,
    (namely the unseen,)
Life of the great round world, the sun and stars, and of man, I, the
    general soul,
Here the square finishing, the solid, I the most solid,
Breathe my breath also through these songs.

297.   TO A LOCOMOTIVE IN WINTER

Thee for my recitative,
Thee in the driving storm even as now, the snow, the winter-day
    declining,
Thee in thy panoply, thy measur'd dual throbbing and thy beat
    convulsive,
Thy black cylindric body, golden brass and silvery steel,
Thy ponderous side-bars, parallel and connecting rods, gyrating,
    shuttling at thy sides,
Thy metrical, now swelling pant and roar, now tapering in the
    distance,
Thy great protruding head-light fix'd in front,
Thy long, pale, floating vapor-pennants, tinged with delicate purple,
The dense and murky clouds out-belching from thy smoke-stack,

Thy knitted frame, thy springs and valves, the tremulous twinkle
of thy wheels, 10
Thy train of cars behind, obedient, merrily following,
Through gale or calm, now swift, now slack, yet steadily careering;
Type of the modern—emblem of motion and power—pulse of the
continent,
For once come serve the Muse and merge in verse, even as here I
see thee,
With storm and buffeting gusts of wind and falling snow,
By day thy warning ringing bell to sound its notes,
By night thy silent signal lamps to swing.

Fierce-throated beauty!
Roll through my chant with all thy lawless music, thy swinging
lamps at night,
Thy madly-whistled laughter, echoing, rumbling like an earth-
quake, rousing all, 20
Law of thyself complete, thine own track firmly holding,
(No sweetness debonair of tearful harp or glib piano thine,)
Thy trills of shrieks by rocks and hills return'd,
Launch'd o'er the prairies wide, across the lakes,
To the free skies unpent and glad and strong.

GEORGE MEREDITH (1828–1909)

298.   "HE FOUND HER BY THE OCEAN'S
MOANING VERGE"

He found her by the ocean's moaning verge,
Nor any wicked change in her discerned;
And she believed his old love had returned,
Which was her exultation, and her scourge.
She took his hand, and walked with him, and seemed
The wife he sought, though shadow-like and dry.
She had one terror, lest her heart should sigh,
And tell her loudly she no longer dreamed.
She dared not say, 'This is my breast: look in.'
But there's a strength to help the desperate weak. 10
That night he learned how silence best can speak
The awful things when Pity pleads for Sin.
About the middle of the night her call
Was heard, and he came wondering to the bed.

'Now kiss me, dear! it may be, now!' she said.
Lethe had passed those lips, and he knew all.

299.   "THUS PITEOUSLY LOVE CLOSED WHAT
                      HE BEGAT"

Thus piteously Love closed what he begat:
The union of this ever-diverse pair!
These two were rapid falcons in a snare,
Condemned to do the flitting of the bat.
Lovers beneath the singing sky of May,
They wandered once; clear as the dew on flowers:
But they fed not on the advancing hours:
Their hearts held cravings for the buried day.
Then each applied to each that fatal knife,
Deep questioning, which probes to endless dole.   10
Ah, what a dusty answer gets the soul
When hot for certainties in this our life!—
In tragic hints here see what evermore
Moves dark as yonder midnight ocean's force,
Thundering like ramping hosts of warrior horse,
To throw that faint thin line upon the shore!

WILLIAM MORRIS (1834–1896)

300.   THE HAYSTACK IN THE FLOODS

Had she come all the way for this,
To part at last without a kiss?
Yea, had she borne the dirt and rain
That her own eyes might see him slain
Beside the haystack in the floods?

Along the dripping leafless woods,
The stirrup touching either shoe,
She rode astride as troopers do;
With kirtle kilted to her knee,
To which the mud splash'd wretchedly;   10
And the wet dripp'd from every tree
Upon her head and heavy hair,
And on her eyelids broad and fair;
The tears and rain ran down her face.

By fits and starts they rode apace,
And very often was his place
Far off from her; he had to ride
Ahead, to see what might betide
When the roads cross'd; and sometimes, when
There rose a murmuring from his men,   20
Had to turn back with promises.
Ah me! she had but little ease;
And often for pure doubt and dread
She sobb'd, made giddy in the head
By the swift riding; while, for cold,
Her slender fingers scarce could hold
The wet reins: yea, and scarcely, too,
She felt the foot within her shoe
Against the stirrup: all for this,
To part at last without a kiss   30
Beside the haystack in the floods.

For when they near'd that old soak'd hay,
They saw across the only way
That Judas, Godmar, and the three
Red running lions dismally
Grinn'd from his pennon, under which,
In one straight line along the ditch,
They counted thirty heads.

                        So then,
While Robert turn'd round to his men,
She saw at once the wretched end,   40
And, stooping down, tried hard to rend
Her coif the wrong way from her head,
And hid her eyes; while Robert said:
"Nay, love, 'tis scarcely two to one;
At Poictiers where we made them run
So fast—why, sweet my love, good cheer,
The Gascon frontier is so near,
Nought after this."

                        But, "O," she said,
"My God! my God! I have to tread
The long way back without you; then   50
The court at Paris; those six men;
The gratings of the Chatelet;

The swift Seine on some rainy day
Like this, and people standing by,
And laughing, while my weak hands try
To recollect how strong men swim.
All this, or else a life with him,
For which I should be damned at last,
Would God that this next hour were past!"

He answer'd not, but cried his cry,   60
"St. George for Marny!" cheerily;
And laid his hand upon her rein.
Alas! no man of all his train
Gave back that cheery cry again;
And, while for rage his thumb beat fast
Upon his sword-hilt, some one cast
About his neck a kerchief long,
And bound him.

                    Then they went along
To Godmar; who said: "Now, Jehane,
Your lover's life is on the wane   70
So fast, that, if this very hour
You yield not as my paramour,
He will not see the rain leave off—
Nay, keep your tongue from gibe and scoff,
Sir Robert, or I slay you now."

She laid her hand upon her brow,
Then gazed upon the palm, as though
She thought her forehead bled, and—"No!"
She said, and turn'd her head away,
As there were nothing else to say,   80
And everything were settled: red
Grew Godmar's face from chin to head:
"Jehane, on yonder hill there stands
My castle, guarding well my lands:
What hinders me from taking you,
And doing that I list to do
To your fair wilful body, while
Your knight lies dead?"

                    A wicked smile
Wrinkled her face, her lips grew thin,
A long way out she thrust her chin: 90

"You know that I should strangle you
While you were sleeping; or bite through
Your throat, by God's help—ah!" she said,
"Lord Jesus, pity your poor maid!
For in such wise they hem me in,
I cannot choose but sin and sin,
Whatever happens: yet I think
They could not make me eat or drink,
And so should I just reach my rest."
"Nay, if you do not my behest,   100
O Jehane! though I love you well,"
Said Godmar, "would I fail to tell
All that I know." "Foul lies," she said.
"Eh? lies, my Jehane? by God's head,
At Paris folks would deem them true!
Do you know, Jehane, they cry for you,
'Jehane the brown! Jehane the brown!
Give us Jehane to burn or drown!'—
Eh—gag me Robert!—sweet my friend,
This were indeed a piteous end   110
For those long fingers, and long feet,
And long neck, and smooth shoulders sweet;
An end that few men would forget
That saw it—So, an hour yet:
Consider, Jehane, which to take
Of life or death!"

        So, scarce awake,
Dismounting, did she leave that place,
And totter some yards: with her face
Turn'd upward to the sky she lay,
Her head on a wet heap of hay,   120
And fell asleep: and while she slept
And did not dream, the minutes crept
Round to the twelve again; but she,
Being waked at last, sigh'd quietly,
And strangely childlike came, and said:
"I will not." Straightway Godmar's head,
As though it hung on strong wires, turn'd
Most sharply round, and his face burn'd.

For Robert—both his eyes were dry,
He could not weep, but gloomily   130

He seem'd to watch the rain; yea, too,
His lips were firm; he tried once more
To touch her lips; she reach'd out, sore
And vain desire so tortured them,
The poor grey lips, and now the hem
Of his sleeve brush'd them.

                    With a start
Up Godmar rose, thrust them apart;
From Robert's throat he loosed the bands
Of silk and mail; with empty hands
Held out, she stood and gazed, and saw,   140
The long bright blade without a flaw
Glide out from Godmar's sheath, his hand
In Robert's hair; she saw him bend
Back Robert's head; she saw him send
The thin steel down; the blow told well,
Right backward the knight Robert fell,
And moan'd as dogs do, being half dead,
Unwitting, as I deem: so then
Godmar turn'd grinning to his men,
Who ran, some five or six, and beat   150
His head to pieces at their feet.

Then Godmar turn'd again and said:
"So, Jehane, the first fitte is read!
Take note, my lady, that your way
Lies backward to the Chatelet!"
She shook her head and gazed awhile
At her cold hands with a rueful smile,
As though this thing had made her mad.

This was the parting that they had
Beside the haystack in the floods.   160

301.   "I KNOW A LITTLE GARDEN CLOSE"

I know a little garden close
Set thick with lily and red rose,
Where I would wander if I might
From dewy dawn to dewy night,
And have one with me wandering.

And though within it no birds sing,
And though no pillared house is there,
And though the apple boughs are bare
Of fruit and blossom, would to God,
Her feet upon the green grass trod,   10
And I beheld them as before.
   There comes a murmur from the shore,
And in the place two fair streams are,
Drawn from the purple hills afar,
Drawn down unto the restless sea;
The hills whose flowers ne'er fed the bee,
The shore no ship has ever seen,
Still beaten by the billows green,
Whose murmur comes unceasingly
Unto the place for which I cry.   20
   For which I cry both day and night,
For which I let slip all delight,
That maketh me both deaf and blind,
Careless to win, unskilled to find,
And quick to lose what all men seek.
   Yet tottering as I am, and weak,
Still have I left a little breath
To seek within the jaws of death
An entrance to that happy place,
To seek the unforgotten face   30
Once seen, once kissed, once reft from me
Anigh the murmuring of the sea.

A. C. SWINBURNE (1837–1909)

302.   THE GARDEN OF PROSERPINE

Here, where the world is quiet;
  Here, where all trouble seems
Dead winds' and spent waves' riot
  In doubtful dreams of dreams;
I watch the green field growing
For reaping folk and sowing,
For harvest-time and mowing,
  A sleepy world of streams.

I am tired of tears and laughter,
  And men that laugh and weep;   10
Of what may come hereafter
  For men that sow to reap:
I am weary of days and hours,
Blown buds of barren flowers,
Desires and dreams and powers
  And everything but sleep.

Here life has death for neighbour,
  And far from eye or ear
Wan waves and wet winds labour,
  Weak ships and spirits steer;   20
They drive adrift, and whither
They wot not who make thither;
But no such winds blow hither,
  And no such things grow here.

No growth of moor or coppice,
  No heather-flower or vine,
But bloomless buds of poppies,
  Green grapes of Proserpine,
Pale beds of blowing rushes
Where no leaf blooms or blushes   30
Save this whereout she crushes
  For dead men deadly wine.

Pale, without name or number,
  In fruitless fields of corn,
They bow themselves and slumber
  All night till light is born;
And like a soul belated,
In hell and heaven unmated,
By cloud and mist abated
  Comes out of darkness morn.   40

Though one were strong as seven,
  He too with death shall dwell,
Nor wake with wings in heaven,
  Nor weep for pains in hell;
Though one were fair as roses,
His beauty clouds and closes;
And well though love reposes,
  In the end it is not well.

Pale, beyond porch and portal,
  Crowned with calm leaves, she stands   50
Who gathers all things mortal
  With cold immortal hands;
Her languid lips are sweeter
Than love's who fears to greet her
To men that mix and meet her
  From many times and lands.

She waits for each and other,
  She waits for all men born;
Forgets the earth her mother,
  The life of fruits and corn;   60
And spring and seed and swallow
Take wing for her and follow
Where summer song rings hollow
  And flowers are put to scorn.

There go the loves that wither,
  The old loves with wearier wings;
And all dead years draw thither,
  And all disastrous things;
Dead dreams of days forsaken,
Blind buds that snows have shaken,   70
Wild leaves that winds have taken
  Red strays of ruined springs.

We are not sure of sorrow,
  And joy was never sure;
To-day will die to-morrow;
  Time stoops to no man's lure;
And love, grown faint and fretful,
With lips but half regretful
Sighs, and with eyes forgetful
  Weeps that no loves endure.   80

From too much love of living,
  From hope and fear set free,
We thank with brief thanksgiving
  Whatever gods may be
That no life lives for ever;
That dead men rise up never;
That even the weariest river
  Winds somewhere safe to sea.

Then star nor sun shall waken,
  Nor any change of light: 90
Nor sound of waters shaken,
  Nor any sound or sight:
Nor wintry leaves nor vernal,
Nor days nor things diurnal;
Only the sleep eternal
  In an eternal night.

303.   A FORSAKEN GARDEN

In a coign of the cliff between lowland and highland,
  At the sea-down's edge between windward and lee,
Walled round with rocks as an inland island
  The ghost of a garden fronts the sea.
A girdle of brushwood and thorn encloses
  The steep square slope of the blossomless bed
Where the weeds that grew green from the graves of its roses
  Now lie dead.

The fields fall southward, abrupt and broken,
  To the low last edge of the long lone land.   10
If a step should sound or a word be spoken,
  Would a ghost not rise at the strange guest's hand?
So long have the grey bare walks lain guestless,
  Through branches and briars if a man make way,
He shall find no life but the sea-wind's, restless
  Night and day.

The dense hard passage is blind and stifled,
  That crawls by a track none turn to climb
To the strait waste place that the years have rifled
  Of all but the thorns that are touched not of time.   20
The thorns he spares when the rose is taken;
  The rocks are left when he wastes the plain.
The wind that wanders, the weeds windshaken,
  These remain.

Not a flower to be pressed of the foot that falls not;
  As the heart of a dead man the seedplots are dry;
From the thicket of thorns whence the nightingale calls not,
  Could she call, there were never a rose to reply.
Over the meadows that blossom and wither
  Rings but the note of a sea-bird's song;   30

Only the sun and the rain come hither
    All year long.

The sun burns sere and the rain dishevels
    One gaunt bleak blossom of scentless breath.
Only the wind here hovers and revels
    In a round where life seems barren as death.
Here there was laughing of old, there was weeping,
    Haply, of lovers none ever will know,
Whose eyes went seaward a hundred sleeping
      Years ago.   40

Heart handfast in heart as they stood, "Look thither,"
    Did he whisper? "look forth from the flowers to the sea;
For the foam-flowers endure when the rose-blossoms wither,
    And men that love lightly may die—but we?"
And the same wind sang and the same waves whitened,
    And or ever the garden's last petals were shed,
In the lips that had whispered, the eyes that had lightened,
    Love was dead.

Or they loved their life through, and then went whither?
    And were one to the end—but what end who knows?   50
Love deep as the sea as a rose must wither,
    As the rose-red seaweed that mocks the rose.
Shall the dead take thought for the dead to love them?
    What love was ever as deep as a grave?
They are loveless now as the grass above them
      Or the wave.

All are at one now, roses and lovers,
    Not known of the cliffs and the fields and the sea.
Not a breath of the time that has been hovers
    In the air now soft with a summer to be.   60
Not a breath shall there sweeten the seasons hereafter
    Of the flowers or the lovers that laugh now or weep,
When as they that are free now of weeping and laughter,
    We shall sleep.

Here death may deal not again for ever;
    Here change may come not till all change end.
From the graves they have made they shall rise up never,
    Who have left nought living to ravage and rend.

Earth, stones, and thorns of the wild ground growing,
   While the sun and the rain live, these shall be: 70
Till a last wind's breath upon all these blowing
    Roll the sea.

Till the slow sea rise and the sheer cliff crumble,
   Till terrace and meadow the deep gulfs drink,
Till the strength of the waves of the high tides humble
   The fields that lessen, the rocks that shrink,
Here now in his triumph where all things falter,
   Stretched out on the spoils that his own hand spread,
As a god self-slain on his own strange altar,
    Death lies dead.   80

EDWARD LEAR (1812–1888)

304.   THE JUMBLIES

They went to sea in a sieve, they did;
   In a sieve they went to sea;
In spite of all their friends could say,
On a winter's morn, on a stormy day,
   In a sieve they went to sea.
And when the sieve turned round and round,
And everyone cried, "You'll all be drowned!"
They called aloud, "Our sieve ain't big,
But we don't care a button; we don't care a fig—
   In a sieve we'll go to sea!"   10
    Far and few, far and few,
      Are the lands where the Jumblies live.
    Their heads are green, and their hands are blue;
      And they went to sea in a sieve.

They sailed away in a sieve, they did,
   In a sieve they sailed so fast,
With only a beautiful pea-green veil
Tied with a ribbon, by way of a sail,
   To a small tobacco-pipe mast.
And everyone said who saw them go,   20
"Oh! won't they be soon upset, you know,
For the sky is dark, and the voyage is long;
And, happen what may, it's extremely wrong
   In a sieve to sail so fast."

The water it soon came in, it did;
 The water it soon came in.
So, to keep them dry, they wrapped their feet
In a pinky paper all folded neat;
 And they fastened it down with a pin.
And they passed the night in a crockery-jar; 30
And each of them said, "How wise we are!
Though the sky be dark, and the voyage be long,
Yet we never can think we were rash or wrong,
 While round in our sieve we spin."

And all night long they sailed away;
 And, when the sun went down,
They whistled and warbled a moony song
To the echoing sound of a coppery gong,
 In the shade of the mountains brown,
"O Timballoo! how happy we are 40
When we live in a sieve and a crockery-jar!
And all night long, in the moonlight pale,
We sail away with a pea-green sail
 In the shade of the mountains brown."

They sailed to the Western Sea, they did—
 To a land all covered with trees;
And they bought an owl, and a useful cart,
And a pound of rice, and a cranberry-tart,
 And a hive of silvery bees;
And they bought a pig, and some green jackdaws, 50
And a lovely monkey with lollipop paws,
And forty bottles of ring-bo-ree,
 And no end of Stilton cheese.

And in twenty years they all came back—
 In twenty years or more;
And everyone said, "How tall they've grown!
For they've been to the Lakes, and the Torrible Zone,
 And the hills of the Chankly Bore."
And they drank their health, and gave them a feast
Of dumplings made of beautiful yeast; 60
And everyone said, "If we only live,
We, too, will go to sea in a sieve,
 To the hills of the Chankly Bore."

Far and few, far and few,
  Are the lands where the Jumblies live.
Their heads are green, and their hands are blue;
  And they went to sea in a sieve.

LEWIS CARROLL (CHARLES L. DODGSON)
(1832–1898)

305.   "A-SITTING ON A GATE"

I'll tell thee everything I can:
  There's little to relate.
I saw an aged aged man,
  A-sitting on a gate.
'Who are you, aged man?' I said.
  'And how is it you live?'
And his answer trickled through my head,
  Like water through a sieve.

He said 'I look for butterflies
  That sleep among the wheat: 1 ᴸ
I make them into mutton-pies,
  And sell them in the street.
I sell them unto men,' he said,
  'Who sail on stormy seas;
And that's the way I get my bread—
  A trifle, if you please.'

But I was thinking of a plan
  To dye one's whiskers green,
And always use so large a fan
  That they could not be seen.   20
So, having no reply to give
  To what the old man said,
I cried 'Come, tell me how you live!'
  And thumped him on the head.

His accents mild took up the tale:
  He said 'I go my ways,
And when I find a mountain-rill,
  I set it in a blaze;
And thence they make a stuff they call
  Rowland's Macassar-Oil—   30

Yet twopence-halfpenny is all
 They give me for my toil.'

But I was thinking of a way
 To feed oneself on batter,
And so go on from day to day
 Getting a little fatter.
I shook him well from side to side,
 Until his face was blue:
'Come, tell me how you live,' I cried,
 'And what it is you do!' 40

He said 'I hunt for haddocks' eyes
 Among the heather bright,
And work them into waistcoat-buttons
 In the silent night.
And these I do not sell for gold
 Or coin of silvery shine,
But for a copper halfpenny,
 And that will purchase nine.

'I sometimes dig for buttered rolls,
 Or set limed twigs for crabs: 50
I sometimes search the grassy knolls
 For wheels of Hansom-cabs.
And that's the way' (he gave a wink)
 'By which I get my wealth
And very gladly will I drink
 Your Honour's noble health.'

I heard him then, for I had just
 Completed my design
To keep the Menai bridge from rust
 By boiling it in wine. 60
I thanked him much for telling me
 The way he got his wealth,
But chiefly for his wish that he
 Might drink my noble health.

And now, if e'er by chance I put
 My fingers into glue,
Or madly squeeze a right-hand foot
 Into a left-hand shoe,

Or if I drop upon my toe
  A very heavy weight,   70
I weep for it reminds me so
Of that old man I used to know—
Whose look was mild, whose speech was slow
Whose hair was whiter than the snow,
Whose face was very like a crow,
With eyes, like cinders, all aglow,
Who seemed distracted with his woe,
Who rocked his body to and fro,
And muttered mumblingly and low,
As if his mouth were full of dough,   80
Who snorted like a buffalo—
That summer evening long ago,
  A-sitting on a gate.

EMILY DICKINSON (1830–1886)

306.   "I KNOW SOME LONELY HOUSES"

I know some lonely houses off the road
A robber'd like the look of,—
Wooden barred,
And windows hanging low,
Inviting to
A portico,

Where two could creep:
One hand the tools,
The other peep
To make sure all's asleep.   10
Old-fashioned eyes,
Not easy to surprise!

How orderly the kitchen'd look by night,
With just a clock,—
But they could gag the tick,
And mice won't bark;
And so the walls don't tell,
None will.

A pair of spectacles ajar just stir—
An almanac's aware.   20
Was it the mat winked,

Or a nervous star?
The moon slides down the stair
To see who's there.

There's plunder,—where?
Tankard, or spoon,
Earring, or stone,
A watch, some ancient brooch
To match the grandmamma,
Staid sleeping there.   30

Day rattles, too,
Stealth's slow;
The sun has got as far
As the third sycamore.
Screams chanticleer,
"Who's there?"

And echoes, trains away,
Sneer—"Where?"
While the old couple, just astir,
Think that the sunrise left the door ajar!   40

307.   "HE PREACHED UPON 'BREADTH'"

He preached upon "breadth" till it argued him narrow,—
The broad are too broad to define;
And of "truth" until it proclaimed him a liar,—
The truth never flaunted a sign.

Simplicity fled from his counterfeit presence
As gold the pyrites would shun.
What confusion would cover the innocent Jesus
To meet so enabled a man!

308.   "A ROUTE OF EVANESCENCE"

A route of evanescence
With a revolving wheel;
A resonance of emerald,
A rush of cochineal;
And every blossom on the bush
Adjusts its tumbled head,—
The mail from Tunis, probably,
An easy morning's ride.

309.   "I LIKE TO SEE IT LAP THE MILES"

I like to see it lap the miles,
And lick the valleys up,
And stop to feed itself at tanks;
And then, prodigious, step

Around a pile of mountains,
And, supercilious, peer
In shanties by the sides of roads;
And then a quarry pare

To fit its sides, and crawl between,
Complaining all the while   10
In horrid, hooting stanza;
Then chase itself down hill

And neigh like Boanerges;
Then, punctual as a star,
Stop—docile and omnipotent—
At its own stable door.

310.   "IN WINTER, IN MY ROOM" *

In winter, in my room,
I came upon a worm,
Pink, lank, and warm.
But as he was a worm
And worms presume,
Not quite with him at home—
Secured him by a string
To something neighboring,
And went along.

A trifle afterward   10
A thing occurred,
I'd not believe it if I heard—
But state with creeping blood;
A snake, with mottles rare,
Surveyed my chamber floor,
In feature as the worm before,
But ringed with power.
The very string

With which I tied him, too,
When he was mean and new,   20
That string was there.

I shrank—"How fair you are!"
Propitiation's claw—
"Afraid," he hissed,
"Of me?"
"No cordiality?"
He fathomed me.
Then, to a rhythm slim
Secreted in his form,
As patterns swim,   30
Projected him.

That time I flew,
Both eyes his way,
Lest he pursue—
Nor ever ceased to run,
Till, in a distant town,
Towns on from mine—
I sat me down;
This was a dream.

311.   "THERE CAME A WIND"

There came a wind like a bugle;
It quivered through the grass,
And a green chill upon the heat
So ominous did pass
We barred the windows and the doors

As from an emerald ghost;
The doom's electric moccasin
That very instant passed.
On a strange mob of panting trees,
And fences fled away,   10

And rivers where the houses ran
The living looked that day.
The bell within the steeple wild
The flying tidings whirled.
How much can come
And much can go,
And yet abide the world!

312.   "I HEARD A FLY" *

I heard a fly buzz when I died;
  The stillness round my form
Was like the stillness in the air
  Between the heaves of storm.

The eyes beside had wrung them dry,
  And breaths were gathering sure
For that last onset, when the king
  Be witnessed in his power.

I willed my keepsakes, signed away
  What portion of me I   10
Could make assignable,—and then
  There interposed a fly,

With blue, uncertain, stumbling buzz,
  Between the light and me;
And then the windows failed, and then
  I could not see to see.

313.   "IT WAS NOT DEATH"

It was not death, for I stood up,
And all the dead lie down;
It was not night, for all the bells
Put out their tongues, for noon.

It was not frost, for on my flesh
I felt siroccos crawl,—
Nor fire, for just my marble feet
Could keep a chancel cool.

And yet it tasted like them all;
The figures I have seen   10
Set orderly, for burial,
Reminded me of mine,

As if my life were shaven
And fitted to a frame,
And could not breathe without a key;
And 'twas like midnight, some,

---

* From Poems of Emily Dickinson, Centenary Ed., 1935, by permission of Little, Brown & Co. Copyright 1914, by Martha Dickinson Bianchi.

When everything that ticked has stopped,
And space stares, all around,
Or grisly frosts, first autumn morns,
Repeal the beating ground.   20

But most like chaos,—stopless, cool,—
Without a chance or spar,
Or even a report of land
To justify despair.

314.   "BECAUSE I COULD NOT STOP FOR DEATH"

Because I could not stop for Death,
He kindly stopped for me;
The carriage held but just ourselves
And Immortality.

We slowly drove, he knew no haste,
And I had put away
My labor, and my leisure too,
For his civility.

We passed the school where children played
At wrestling in a ring;   10
We passed the fields of gazing grain,
We passed the setting sun.

We paused before a house that seemed
A swelling of the ground;
The roof was scarcely visible,
The cornice but a mound.

Since then 'tis centuries; but each
Feels shorter than the day
I first surmised the horses' heads
Were toward eternity.   20

315.   "MY LIFE HAD STOOD A LOADED GUN"*

My life had stood a loaded gun
In corners, till a day
The owner passed—identified,
And carried me away.

* From Poems of Emily Dickinson, Centenary Ed., 1935, by permission of Little,
Brown & Co. Copyright 1914, by Martha Dickinson Bianchi.

And now we roam the sov'reign woods,
And now we hunt the doe—
And every time I speak for him
The mountains straight reply.

And do I smile, such cordial light
Upon the valley glow—   10
It is as a Vesuvian face
Had let its pleasure through.

And when at night, our good day done,
I guard my master's head,
'Tis better than the eider duck's
Deep pillow to have shared.

To foe of his I'm deadly foe,
None stir the second time
On whom I lay a yellow eye
Or an emphatic thumb.   20

316.   "AFTER GREAT PAIN . . ." *

After great pain a formal feeling comes—
The nerves sit ceremonious like tombs;
The stiff Heart questions—was it He that bore?
And yesterday—or centuries before?

The feet mechanical
Go round a wooden way
Of ground or air or Ought, regardless grown,
A quartz contentment like a stone.

This is the hour of lead
Remembered if outlived,   10
As freezing persons recollect the snow—
First chill, then stupor, then the letting go.

317.   "A NARROW FELLOW . . ."

A narrow fellow in the grass
Occasionally rides;
You may have met him,—did you not?
His notice sudden is.

* From Poems of Emily Dickinson, Centenary Ed., 1935, by permission of Little,
Brown & Co. Copyright 1914, by Martha Dickinson Bianchi.

The grass divides as with a comb,
A spotted shaft is seen;
And then it closes at your feet
And opens further on.

He likes a boggy acre,
A floor too cool for corn.   10
Yet when a child, and barefoot,
I more than once, at morn,

Have passed, I thought, a whip-lash
Unbraiding in the sun,—
When, stooping to secure it,
It wrinkled, and was gone.

Several of nature's people
I know, and they know me;
I feel for them a transport
Of cordiality;   20

But never met this fellow,
Attended or alone,
Without a tighter breathing,
And zero at the bone.

BRET HARTE (1836–1902)

318.

PLAIN LANGUAGE FROM
TRUTHFUL JAMES

Which I wish to remark,
    And my language is plain,
That for ways that are dark
    And for tricks that are vain,
The heathen Chinee is peculiar,
    Which the same I would rise to explain.

Ah Sin was his name;
    And I shall not deny,
In regard to the same,
    What that name might imply;   10
But his smile it was pensive and childlike,
    As I frequent remarked to Bill Nye.

It was August the third,
    And quite soft was the skies;
Which it might be inferred
    That Ah Sin was likewise;
Yet he played it that day upon William
    And me in a way I despise.

Which we had a small game,
    And Ah Sin took a hand: 20
It was Euchre. The same
    He did not understand;
But he smiled as he sat by the table,
    With the smile that was childlike and bland.

Yet the cards they were stocked
    In a way that I grieve,
And my feelings were shocked
    At the state of Nye's sleeve,
Which was stuffed full of aces and bowers,
    And the same with intent to deceive.   30

But the hands that were played
    By that heathen Chinee,
And the points that he made,
    Were quite frightful to see,—
Till at last he put down a right bower,
    Which the same Nye had dealt unto me.

Then I looked up at Nye,
    And he gazed upon me;
And he rose with a sigh,
    And said, "Can this be?   40
We are ruined by Chinese cheap labor,"—
    And he went for that heathen Chinee.

In the scene that ensued
    I did not take a hand,
But the floor it was strewed
    Like the leaves on the strand
With the cards that Ah Sin had been hiding,
    In the game "he did not understand."

In his sleeves, which were long,
    He had twenty-four jacks,—   50

Which was coming it strong,
 Yet I state but the facts;
And we found on his nails, which were taper,
 What is frequent in tapers,—that's wax.

Which is why I remark,
 And my language is plain,
That for ways that are dark
 And for tricks that are vain,
The heathen Chinee is peculiar,—
 Which the same I am free to maintain. 60

GERARD MANLEY HOPKINS (1844–1889)

319.   GOD'S GRANDEUR

The world is charged with the grandeur of God.
 It will flame out, like shining from shook foil;
 It gathers to a greatness, like the ooze of oil
Crushed. Why do men then now not reck his rod?
Generations have trod, have trod, have trod;
 And all is seared with trade; bleared, smeared with toil;
 And wears man's smudge and shares man's smell: the soil
Is bare now, nor can foot feel, being shod.

And for all this, nature is never spent;
 There lives the dearest freshness deep down things; 10
And though the last lights off the black West went
 Oh, morning, at the brown brink eastward, springs—
Because the Holy Ghost over the bent
 World broods with warm breast and with ah! bright wings.

320.   THE WINDHOVER

TO CHRIST OUR LORD

I caught this morning morning's minion, king-
 dom of daylight's dauphin, dapple-dawn-drawn Falcon, in
   his riding
Of the rolling level underneath him steady air, and striding
High there, how he rung upon the rein of a wimpling wing
In his ecstasy! then off, off forth on swing,

As a skate's heel sweeps smooth on a bow-bend; the hurl and
    gliding
Rebuffed the big wind. My heart in hiding
Stirred for a bird,—the achieve of, the mastery of the thing!

Brute beauty and valour and act, oh, air, pride, plume, here
    Buckle! AND the fire that breaks from thee then, a billion   10
Times told lovelier, more dangerous, O my chevalier!

No wonder of it: shéer plód makes plough down sillion
Shine, and blue-bleak embers, ah my dear,
Fall, gall themselves, and gash gold-vermilion.

321.   DUNS SCOTUS'S OXFORD

Towery city and branchy between towers;
Cuckoo-echoing, bell-swarmèd, lark-charmèd, rook-racked, river-
    rounded;
The dapple-eared lily below thee; that country and town did
Once encounter in, here coped and poisèd powers;

Thou hast a base and brickish skirt there, sours
That neighbour-nature thy grey beauty is grounded
Best in; graceless growth, thou hast confounded
Rural rural keeping—folk, flocks, and flowers.

Yet ah! this air I gather and I release
He lived on; these weeds and waters, these walls are what   10
He haunted who of all men most sways my spirits to peace;

Of realty the rarest-veinèd unraveller; a not
Rivalled insight, be rival Italy or Greece;
Who fired France for Mary without spot.

322.   SPRING AND FALL:

TO A YOUNG CHILD

Márgarét, are you gríeving
Over Goldengrove unleaving?
Leáves, líke the things of man, you
With your fresh thoughts care for, can you?
Ah! ás the heart grows older
It will come to such sights colder
By and by, nor spare a sigh

Though worlds of wanwood leafmeal lie;
And yet you wíll weep and know why.
Now no matter, child, the name: 10
Sórrow's spríngs áre the same.
Nor mouth had, no nor mind, expressed
What heart heard of, ghost guessed:
It ís the blight man was born for,
It is Margaret you mourn for.

FRANCIS THOMPSON (1859–1907)

323.   THE HOUND OF HEAVEN

I fled Him, down the nights and down the days;
 I fled Him down the arches of the years;
I fled Him, down the labyrinthine ways
 Of my own mind; and in the mist of tears
I hid from Him, and under running laughter.
         Up vistaed hopes I sped;
         And shot, precipitated,
Adown Titanic glooms of chasmèd fears,
 From those strong Feet that followed, followed after.
         But with unhurrying chase,   10
         And unperturbèd pace,
 Deliberate speed, majestic instancy,
         They beat—and a Voice beat
         More instant than the Feet—
"All things betray thee, who betrayest Me."

         I pleaded, outlaw-wise,
By many a hearted casement, curtained red,
 Trellised with intertwining charities;
(For, though I knew His love Who followèd,
         Yet was I sore adread   20
Lest, having Him, I must have naught beside);
But, if one little casement parted wide,
 The gust of His approach would clash it to.
Fear wist not to evade, as Love wist to pursue.
Across the margent of the world I fled,
 And troubled the gold gateways of the stars
Smiting for shelter on their clangèd bars;

Fretted to dulcet jars
And silvern chatter the pale ports o' the moon.
I said to dawn, Be sudden; to eve, Be soon;   30
  With thy young skiey blossoms heap me over
    From this tremendous Lover!
Float thy vague veil about me, lest He see!
  I tempted all His servitors, but to find
My own betrayal in their constancy,
In faith to Him their fickleness to me,
  Their traitorous trueness, and their loyal deceit.
To all swift things for swiftness did I sue;
  Clung to the whistling mane of every wind.
    But whether they swept, smoothly fleet,   40
      The long savannahs of the blue;
        Or whether, Thunder-driven,
        They clanged his chariot 'thwart a heaven
Plashy with flying lightnings round the spurn o' their feet—
  Fear wist not to evade as Love wist to pursue.
      Still with unhurrying chase,
      And unperturbèd pace,
    Deliberate speed, majestic instancy,
      Came on the following Feet,
      And a Voice above their beat—   50
    "Naught shelters thee, who wilt not shelter Me."

I sought no more that after which I strayed
        In face of man or maid;
But still within the little children's eyes
        Seems something, something that replies;
They at least are for me, surely for me!
I turned me to them very wistfully;
But, just as their young eyes grew sudden fair`
        With dawning answers there,
Their angel plucked them from me by the hair.   60
"Come then, ye other children, Nature's—share
With me" (said I) "your delicate fellowship;
      Let me greet you lip to lip,
      Let me twine with you caresses,
        Wantoning
      With our Lady-Mother's vagrant tresses,
        Banqueting
      With her in her wind-walled palace,

Underneath her azured daïs,
Quaffing, as your taintless way is,   70
     From a chalice
Lucent-weeping out of the dayspring."
     So it was done:
I in their delicate fellowship was one—
Drew the bolt of Nature's secrecies.
     I knew all the swift importings
     On the wilful face of skies;
     I knew how the clouds arise
     Spumèd of the wild sea-snortings;
     All that's born or dies   80
     Rose and drooped with—made them shapers
Of mine own moods, or wailful or divine—
     With them joyed and was bereaven.
     I was heavy with the even,
     When she lit her glimmering tapers
     Round the day's dead sanctities.
     I laughed in the morning's eyes.
I triumphed and I sadden with all weather,
     Heaven and I wept together,
And its sweet tears were salt with mortal mine;   90
Against the red throb of its sunset-heart
     I laid my own to beat
     And share commingling heat;
But not by that, by that, was eased my human smart.
In vain my tears were wet on Heaven's gray cheek.
For ah! we know not what each other says,
     These things and I; in sound *I* speak—
Their sound is but their stir, they speak by silences.
Nature, poor stepdame, cannot slake my drouth;
     Let her, if she would owe me,   100
Drop yon blue bosom-veil of sky, and show me
     The breasts o' her tenderness:
Never did any milk of hers once bless
     My thirsting mouth.
     Nigh and nigh draws the chase,
     With unperturbèd pace,
     Deliberate speed, majestic instancy;
     And past those noisèd Feet
     A Voice comes yet more fleet—
"Lo! naught contents thee, who content'st not Me."   110

Naked I wait Thy love's uplifted stroke!
My harness piece by piece Thou hast hewn from me,
          And smitten me to my knee;
          I am defenseless utterly.
          I slept, methinks, and woke,
And, slowly gazing, find me stripped in sleep.
In the rash lustihead of my young powers,
          I shook the pillaring hours
And pulled my life upon me; grimed with smears,
I stand amid the dust o' the mounded years—   120
My mangled youth lies dead beneath the heap.
My days have crackled and gone up in smoke,
Have puffed and burst as sun-starts on a stream.
          Yea, faileth now even dream
The dreamer, and the lute the lutanist;
Even the linked fantasies, in whose blossomy twist
I swung the earth a trinket at my wrist,
Are yielding; cords of all too weak account
For earth with heavy griefs so overplussed.
          Ah! is Thy love indeed   130
A weed, albeit an amaranthine weed,
Suffering no flowers except its own to mount?
          Ah! must—
          Designer infinite!—
Ah! must Thou char the wood ere Thou canst limn with it?
My freshness spent its wavering shower i' the dust;
And now my heart is as a broken fount,
Wherein tear-drippings stagnate, spilt down ever
          From the dank thoughts that shiver
Upon the sighful branches of my mind.   140
          Such is; what is to be?
The pulp so bitter, how shall taste the rind?
I dimly guess what Time in mists confounds;
Yet ever and anon a trumpet sounds
From the hid battlements of Eternity;
Those shaken mists a space unsettle, then
Round the half-glimpsèd turrets slowly wash again.
          But not ere him who summoneth
          I first have seen, enwound
With glooming robes purpureal, cypress-crowned;   150
His name I know, and what his trumpet saith.

Whether man's heart or life it be which yields
　　Thee harvest, must Thy harvest fields
　　Be dunged with rotten death?

　　　Now of that long pursuit
　　　Comes on at hand the bruit;
　　That Voice is round me like a bursting sea:
　　　"And is thy earth so marred,
　　　Shattered in shard on shard?
　　Lo, all things fly thee, for thou fliest Me!　　　160
　　　Strange, piteous, futile thing,
Wherefore should any set thee love apart?
Seeing none but I makes much of naught" (He said),
"And human love needs human meriting:
　　　How hast thou merited—
Of all man's clotted clay the dingiest clot?
　　　Alack, thou knowest not
How little worthy of any love thou art!
Whom wilt thou find to love ignoble thee　　　170
　　　Save Me, save only Me?
All which I took from thee I did but take,
　　　Not for thy harms,
But just that thou might'st seek it in My arms.
　　　All which thy child's mistake
Fancies as lost, I have stored for thee at home:
　　　Rise, clasp My hand, and come!"

　　　Halts by me that footfall:
　　　Is my gloom, after all,
　　Shade of His Hand, outstretched caressingly?　　　180
　　　"Ah, fondest, blindest, weakest,
　　　I am He whom thou seekest!
Thou dravest love from thee, who dravest Me."

THOMAS HARDY (1840–1928)

324.　　　　　　　　　　HAP *

　　If but some vengeful god would call to me
　　From up the sky, and laugh: "Thou suffering thing,
　　Know that thy sorrow is my ecstasy,
　　That thy love's loss is my hate's profiting!"

Then would I bear it, clench myself, and die,
Steeled by the sense of ire unmerited;
Half-eased in that a Powerfuller than I
Had willed and meted me the tears I shed.

But not so. How arrives it joy lies slain,
And why unblooms the best hope ever sown?   10
—Crass Casualty obstructs the sun and rain,
And dicing Time for gladness casts a moan. . . .
These purblind Doomsters had as readily stown
Blisses about my pilgrimage as pain.

325.   DRUMMER HODGE *

    They throw in Drummer Hodge, to rest
      Uncoffined,—just as found:
    His landmark is a kopje-crest
      That breaks the veldt around;
    And foreign constellations west
      Each night above his mound.

    Young Hodge the Drummer never knew—
      Fresh from his Wessex home—
    The meaning of the broad Karoo,
      The Bush, the dusty loam,   10
    And why uprose to nightly view
      Strange stars amid the gloam.

    Yet portion of that unknown plain
      Will Hodge for ever be;
    His homely Northern breast and brain
      Grow to some Southern tree,
    And strange-eyed constellations reign
      His stars eternally.

R. L. STEVENSON (1850–1894)

326.   "I WILL MAKE YOU BROOCHES"

I will make you brooches and toys for your delight
Of bird-song at morning and star-shine at night.
I will make a palace fit for you and me
Of green days in forests and blue days at sea.

* Hardy, *Collected Poems.* Copyright 1925 by The Macmillan Company and used
with their permission.

I will make my kitchen, and you shall keep your room,
Where white flows the river and bright blows the broom,
And you shall wash your linen and keep your body white
In rainfall at morning and dewfall at night.

And this shall be for music when no one else is near,
The fine song for singing, the rare song to hear! 10
That only I remember, that only you admire,
Of the broad road that stretches and the roadside fire.

A. E. HOUSMAN (1859–1936)

327. "LOVELIEST OF TREES, THE
CHERRY NOW"

Loveliest of trees, the cherry now
Is hung with bloom along the bough,
And stands about the woodland ride,
Wearing white for Eastertide.

Now, of my threescore years and ten,
Twenty will not come again,
And take from seventy springs a score,
It only leaves me fifty more.

And since to look at things in bloom
Fifty springs are little room, 10
About the woodlands I will go
To see the cherry hung with snow.

328. "ON WENLOCK EDGE THE WOOD'S
IN TROUBLE"

On Wenlock Edge the wood's in trouble;
His forest fleece the Wrekin heaves;
The gale, it plies the saplings double,
And thick on Severn snow the leaves.

'Twould blow like this through holt and hanger
When Uricon the city stood;
'Tis the old wind in the old anger,
But then it threshed another wood.

Then, 'twas before my time, the Roman
At yonder heaving hill would stare;   10
The blood that warms an English yeoman,
The thoughts that hurt him, they were there.

There, like the wind through woods in riot,
Through him the gale of life blew high;
The tree of man was never quiet—
Then 'twas the Roman, now 'tis I.

The gale, it plies the saplings double;
It blows so hard, 'twill soon be gone.
Today the Roman and his trouble
Are ashes under Uricon.   20

329.   "WITH RUE MY HEART IS LADEN"

            With rue my heart is laden
                For golden friends I had,
            For many a rose-lipt maiden
                And many a lightfoot lad.

            By brooks too broad for leaping
                The lightfoot boys are laid;
            The rose-lipt girls are sleeping
                In fields where roses fade.

330.   "YONDER SEE THE MORNING BLINK"

            Yonder see the morning blink:
                The sun is up, and up must I,
            To wash and dress and eat and drink
            And look at things and talk and think
                And work, and God knows why.

            Oh often have I washed and dressed
                And what's to show for all my pain?
            Let me lie abed and rest:
            Ten thousand times I've done my best
                And all's to do again.   10

331.   "COULD MAN BE DRUNK FOREVER"

            Could man be drunk forever
                With liquor, love, or fights,

Lief should I rouse at morning
And lief lie down of nights.

But men at whiles are sober
And think by fits and starts,
And if they think, they fasten
Their hands upon their hearts.

ROBERT BRIDGES (1844–1930)

332.   LONDON SNOW

When men were all asleep the snow came flying,
In large white flakes falling on the city brown,
Stealthily and perpetually settling and loosely lying,
  Hushing the latest traffic of the drowsy town;
Deadening, muffling, stifling its murmurs failing;
Lazily and incessantly floating down and down;
  Silently sifting and veiling road, roof and railing;
Hiding difference, making unevenness even,
Into angles and crevices softly drifting and sailing.
  All night it fell, and when full inches seven   10
It lay in the depth of its uncompacted lightness,
The clouds blew off from a high and frosty heaven;
  And all woke earlier for the unaccustomed brightness
Of the winter dawning, the strange unheavenly glare:
The eye marvelled—marvelled at the dazzling whiteness;
  The ear hearkened to the stillness of the solemn air;
No sound of wheel rumbling nor of foot falling,
And the busy morning cries came thin and spare.
  Then boys I heard, as they went to school, calling;
They gathered up the crystal manna to freeze   20
Their tongues with tasting, their hands with snow-balling;
  Or rioted in a drift, plunging up to the knees;
Or peering up from under the white-mossed wonder,
"O look at the trees!" they cried. "O look at the trees!"
  With lessened load, a few carts creak and blunder,
Following along the white deserted way,
A country company long dispersed asunder:
  When now already the sun, in pale display
Standing by Paul's high dome, spread forth below
His sparkling beams, and awoke the stir of the day.   30

For now doors open, and war is waged with the snow;
And trains of somber men, past tale of number,
Tread long brown paths, as toward their toil they go:
  But even for them awhile no cares encumber
Their minds diverted; the daily word is unspoken,
The daily thoughts of labor and sorrow slumber
At the sight of the beauty that greets them, for the charm they have
    broken.

RUDYARD KIPLING (1865–1936)

333.   RECESSIONAL *

God of our fathers, known of old,
    Lord of our far-flung battle-line,
Beneath whose awful Hand we hold
    Dominion over palm and pine—
Lord God of Hosts, be with us yet,
Lest we forget—lest we forget!

The tumult and the shouting dies;
    The Captains and the Kings depart:
Still stands Thine ancient sacrifice,
    An humble and a contrite heart.   10
Lord God of Hosts, be with us yet,
Lest we forget—lest we forget!

Far-called, our navies melt away;
    On dune and headland sinks the fire:
Lo, all our pomp of yesterday
    Is one with Nineveh and Tyre!
Judge of the Nations, spare us yet,
Lest we forget—lest we forget!

If, drunk with sight of power, we loose
    Wild tongues that have not Thee in awe,   20
Such boastings as the Gentiles use,
    Or lesser breeds without the Law—
Lord God of Hosts, be with us yet,
Lest we forget—lest we forget!

For heathen heart that puts her trust
    In reeking tube and iron shard,
All valiant dust that builds on dust,
    And guarding, calls not Thee to guard,

For frantic boast and foolish word—
Thy mercy on Thy People, Lord! 30

334. DANNY DEEVER *

'What are the bugles blowin' for?' said Files-on-Parade.
'To turn you out, to turn you out,' the Colour-Sergeant said.
'What makes you look so white, so white?' said Files-on-Parade.
'I'm dreadin' what I've got to watch,' the Colour-Sergeant said.
  For they're hangin' Danny Deever, you can hear the Dead March
    play,
  The Regiment's in 'ollow square—they're hangin' him to-day;
  They've taken of his buttons off an' cut his stripes away,
  An' they're hangin' Danny Deever in the mornin'.

'What makes the rear-rank breathe so 'ard?' said Files-on-Parade.
'It's bitter cold, it's bitter cold,' the Colour-Sergeant said. 10
'What makes that front-rank man fall down?' said Files-on-Parade.
'A touch o' sun, a touch o' sun,' the Colour-Sergeant said.
  They are hangin' Danny Deever, they are marchin' of 'im round,
  They 'ave 'alted Danny Deever by 'is coffin on the ground;
  An' 'e'll swing in 'arf a minute for a sneakin' shootin' hound—
  O they're hangin' Danny Deever in the mornin'!

''Is cot was right-'and cot to mine,' said Files-on-Parade.
''E's sleepin' out an' far to-night,' the Colour-Sergeant said.
'I've drunk 'is beer a score o' times,' said Files-on-Parade.
''E's drinkin' bitter beer alone,' the Colour-Sergeant said. 20
  They are hangin' Danny Deever, you must mark 'im to 'is place,
  For 'e shot a comrade sleepin'—you must look 'im in the face;
  Nine 'undred of 'is county an' the Regiment's disgrace,
  While they're hangin' Danny Deever in the mornin'.

'What's that so black agin the sun?' said Files-on-Parade.
'It's Danny fightin' 'ard for life,' the Colour-Sergeant said.
'What's that that whimpers over'ead?' said Files-on-Parade.
'It's Danny's soul that's passin' now,' the Colour-Sergeant said.
  For they're done with Danny Deever, you can 'ear the quickstep
    play,
  The Regiment's in column, an' they're marchin' us away; 30
  Ho! the young recruits are shakin', an' they'll want their beer
    to-day,
  After hangin' Danny Deever in the mornin'!

* From *Departmental Ditties and Ballads and Barrack-Room Ballads* by Rudyard Kipling. Reprinted by permission of Mrs. George Bambridge and Doubleday & Company, Inc.

VI. THE MODERN PERIOD

THE MODERN PERIOD

The Victorians had cultivated many kinds of poetry—philosophical, meditative, dramatic, patriotic, hortatory, picturesque, decorative, exhibitionist, using themes derived from history, earlier literature, personal emotion and circumstance, and "nature," with techniques which utilized all kinds of stanza forms and exploited rhythmic effects and vowel music with considerable virtuosity. But the virtuosity grew increasingly narrow, becoming the mere refinement of traditional forms or the clever patterning of rhymes and rhythms (as in the later poems of Swinburne): it was rarely the technical response to a new imaginative need, but rather a careful scraping of the barrel of a poetic tradition. There were, as we have seen, a few individual innovators, chief among whom was Gerard Manley Hopkins, whose technical experiments and new approach to poetic expression *were* the results of new imaginative needs; but Hopkins was virtually unknown in his generation and had no influence in the nineteenth century. In France the Symbolist movement, headed by Verlaine and Mallarmé, had well before the end of the century developed a magical, incantatory kind of poetry, with the meaning flowering obliquely out of mood and imagery without being sustained by a recognizable intellectual sequence, and this was in many respects a revolutionary movement: a historian of French poetry has claimed that with the Symbolists "French versification cut the painter that linked it to its recognized meters, even to rhyme, and embarked on a voyage of discovery which led it progressively farther and farther from fixed forms, just as its content increasingly ceased to be an imitation of recognized and recognizable forms of nature, passed from the suggestion of mood and atmosphere to plumb the misty and inchoate deeps of the subconscious, the formless and embryonic reactions, the arbitrary associations that melt and mingle in the confused stream of human awareness. . . ." But as far as this movement affected English poetry in the nineteenth century, it was only in the direction of encouraging a more or less conventional dreamlike verse, which represented an exaggeration of what

579

after all had been an important side of Tennyson. In the twentieth century, however, the Symbolists had a more revolutionary effect, and represented one of the many currents which eventually combined to produce "modern" poetry.

The characteristic poetry of the first decade and a half of the twentieth century was limited in scope and low in temperature. The so-called Georgian poets in England (whose first cooperative volume appeared in 1912) were on the whole inclined to take one of the areas cultivated by the Victorians and produce some mild refinements or variations. Many of these poets were regionalists, celebrating the part of the English countryside they knew best; some turned to the East for glamour and mystery; many cultivated a certain coy wisdom or a self-conscious irony. On the whole it can be said that in the face of a changing world they adopted an eclectic traditionalism, limited, refined, carefully hedged round, and within these confines sang softly but confidently. Some voices were more distinctive than others: Edward Thomas had a remarkable ability to distil strange meanings out of quite ordinary sights and sounds by pointing at them in an almost trancelike way; Rupert Brooke had a note of subdued humor and irony that gave an interesting twist to his best poems: both might have developed into major figures—Thomas was well on his way to achieving major status—if they had survived the first World War to come under the influence of later movements.

The first World War might well be taken as a dividing line in any attempt to mark off a distinctively "modern" period, even though, like all such attempts, it can only be approximate, and some of T. S. Eliot's influential early poems were written between 1909 and 1913. The impact of the war and its aftermath on sensitive minds was tremendous: it increased enormously the sense that civilization had losts its norms and its central core of community belief, and made the religious doubts of Tennyson and Arnold seem genteel exercises in skepticism by comparison. It also hastened the process of revolt against all that the Victorians were now considered to represent, and encouraged the search for radically new poetic devices for expressing or evoking or illustrating this new sensibility. Already in the poetry of Wilfred Owen (perhaps the most promising of all the poets killed in the first World War) we find a new attitude seeking expression in a new technique: in Owen's case the direct impact of personal war experiences is largely responsible. By the early 1920's there had developed, at least among the younger poets most sensitive to the social, moral, and literary atmosphere of the time, a veritable revolution in poetry, equally effective in Britain and the United States, a revolution most clearly illustrated by Eliot's much discussed long poem, *The Waste Land,* but also represented by other and shorter poems that he had written by this time.

But the war only hastened a movement that had already been under way for some time and whose origins are manifold. One aspect of the movement was an attack on that exploiting of individual personality which had been not only a characteristic of romantic poetry but an element in all artistic expression since the Renaissance. T. E. Hulme (another English writer who was killed in the first World War, in 1917) began this attack before the war in a number of essays and lectures in which he drew distinctions between two kinds of attitude and two kinds of art, one kind (which he decried) being humanistic, optimistic, and (in art) "vital and realistic," while the other (which he supported) was authoritarian, accepted the dogma of original sin, and believed in a "geometrical or abstract" kind of art. "The re-emergence of geometrical art at the present day may be the precursor of the re-emergence of the final break-up of the Renaissance," he wrote in an article in *The New Age.* He proclaimed himself a classicist, an antiromantic, out "to clean the world of these sloppy dregs of the Renaissance." Or again: "I object even to the best of the romantics. I object still more to the receptive attitude. I object to the sloppiness which doesn't consider that a poem is a poem unless it is moaning or whining about something or other. . . . The thing has got so bad now that a poem which is all dry and hard would not be considered poetry at all." He predicted a revival of classicism, of "cheerful, dry, and sophisticated verse."

Hulme constructed an elaborate antithesis: on the one side were romanticism, humanism, the Renaissance, liberalism, optimism, realism, all of which were repudiated, while on the other were classicism, "the religious attitude," selected aspects of ancient, Elizabethan, and eighteenth-century poetry, discipline, belief in original sin, and geometrical abstraction. We do not need to accept Hulme's view of the connection between the different items on each side in order to understand his central position or appreciate his influence on poetic theory and practice. His belief that images should be dry and precise, that the poet should keep his personality and his emotion out of the poem and concentrate on accurate impersonal words which get "the exact curve" of things being described lay behind the imagist movement (which flourished on both sides of the Atlantic) and encouraged a whole school of poets to concentrate on the "actually realized visual objective," regardless of whether it is "a lady's shoe or the starry heavens." Instead of aiming directly at the infinitely evocative, the poet aimed at the precise and the unique, avoiding conventional poetic language and associations and avoiding equally any introduction of his own emotions. Shortly after Hulme announced his program, Eliot was proclaiming that "poetry is not a turning loose of emotion, but an escape from emotion; it is not the expression of personality, but an escape from personality." And some twenty years later John Crowe Ransom remarked that "a good poem, even if it is signed with a full and well-known name, intends as a work of art to lose the identity of the author." Between Hulme and Ransom a new kind of poetic theory and practice had run its course.

But the antiromanticism of Hulme was only one aspect of the picture. The disintegration of patterns of public belief far beyond anything contemplated by the Victorians was also an important factor in developing a "modern" poetry: for it set the poet to creating or discovering his own myths, and this in turn led to serious problems affecting the relation of the poet to his audience—part cause and part effect of the new use of myth in poetry—reacted in its turn on the poets and produced new techniques and new criteria for discovering not so much what was good and to be sought after but what was bad and to be avoided. (One interesting result of all this is that in our time, for the first time, perhaps, in literary history, we have had a substantial number of able minor poets much clearer in their minds about what they wanted to avoid than about what they wanted to achieve.) The situation can best be illustrated by looking at three specific poets—Yeats, Eliot, and W. H. Auden.

Yeats's poetic activity covered a period of almost sixty years, and during that period his mood and style changed many times, so that there are in fact many Yeatses. He more or less ran the gamut of modern poetic moods and techniques, never too young to be original, never too old to learn from his younger contemporaries. So that part of his greatness lies in his extraordinary versatility, in his refusal to mark time at any one period, and his continued change and development until his very last years. But obviously a poet does not become great simply because he changes a great deal. Yeats not only changed, but at each period in his career he produced remarkable poetry, absorbing with brilliant originality the new influences to which he was continually exposing himself—Spenser and Shelley, the pre-Raphaelites, Irish folklore and contemporary Irish life, William Blake, Walter Savage Landor, John Donne and other metaphysical poets of the seventeenth century—to mention only a few of the poets and the factors that influenced his work. Throughout his poetic career he ran eagerly from one esoteric mystical doctrine to another, ever anxious to explore the hidden aspects of man's mind and to find somewhere a system of symbols that would give power and richness to his poetic expression.

It is that search for a language of symbols that is the clue to Yeats's many changes in poetic style and vocabulary. "I am very religious," he wrote in an autobiographical essay, "and deprived by Huxley and Tyndall, whom I detested, of the simple-minded religion of my childhood, I had made a new religion, almost an infallible church of poetic tradition, of a fardel of stories, and of personages, and of emotions, inseparable from their first expression, passed on from generation to generation by poets and painters with some help from philosophers and theologians." This was Yeats's reaction to the disintegration of public belief brought about by the growing claims of science and later encouraged by new developments in psychology and sociology and by the factual evidence (notably the first World War and its aftermath) that Western civilization did not seem to be working any more. There was enough of the Christian humanist tradition left for Tennyson and, more directly, Matthew Arnold, to use in coming to some kind of personal system of beliefs and attitudes, but for Yeats that tradition was no longer available (for many reasons, both historical and personal). He developed something more esoteric and more original, eventually working out a complete mystical or pseudo-mystical system, which was at once a philosophy of history, a philosophy of human nature, and a source of poetic symbols.

In the past a poet's symbols have derived from a consciously held literary and cultural tradition which in turn was nourished by basic patterns of belief and attitude. The threat to these basic patterns of belief and attitude was already manifest in the Victorian period, and it was at first met by an attempt to separate the cultural tradition from the underlying system of beliefs: this is what Matthew Arnold tried to do in such works as *Culture and Anarchy* and in many of his critical essays. "There is not a creed which is not shaken, not an accredited dogma which is not shown to be questionable, not a received tradition which does not threaten to dissolve," Arnold wrote in 1880. "Our religion has materialized itself in the fact, in the supposed fact; it has attached its emotion to the fact, and now the fact is failing it. But for poetry the idea is everything; the rest is a world of illusion, of divine illusion. Poetry attaches its emotion to the idea; the idea *is* the fact. The strongest part of our religion to-day is its unconscious poetry." But whence is the poet to derive his symbols if he can fall back on no public system of belief? Yeats answered that question by constructing his own system, and then finding new poetic techniques which would enable him to get across to the reader the meaning of the symbols he derived from that system. His system was thus more important to himself as creator than to his readers: the system gave order and coherence to his thought, provided him with a base from which to operate, as it were: but the images which flowered out of this system were made to carry their own conviction poetically. This illustrates how the modern poet carries a double burden: he cannot simply exploit themes and images in terms of a pattern of belief already known to and shared by his readers; he must find a pattern of belief that will enable him to organize his own themes and images, and make that pattern significant to the reader while he reads. This is one reason for the obscurity of much modern poetry. The alternative to obscurity is often deadness—the presentation of a subject in terms of a tradition which is no longer really alive and which therefore cannot yield vital symbols. (This does not mean that obscurity in poetry is a good thing, but only that in certain phases of culture the genuine poet may find it hard to avoid without losing his integrity.)

Yeats, like so many other poets of the period, came under the influence of Ezra Pound in the years immediately preceding the first World War. Pound was one of the great catalytic forces in modern English and American poetry: his position was in many ways close to that of T. E. Hulme, though he was both personally and intellectually more erratic. He was all in favor of Hulme's "hard, dry" kind of poetry, and worked, in a rather dilettante manner, with Chinese, Japanese, Provençal and early Italian poetry in an effort to find models for this kind of verse. His effect on Yeats was to wean him finally from the romanticism of his youth and turn him towards a firmer and more sternly disciplined kind of poetry, with its rhythms often more conversational and its vocabulary often more colloquial than in his earlier work. This combination of a symbolism built on a personal system of thought with a shrewd and dry verse explains the special flavor of much of Yeats's middle and later poetry. Pound was having a similar effect on many other poets at the same time, with his belligerent antiromanticism, his enthusiasm for relatively unknown areas of earlier European literature, and his aggressive personality. Both he and Hulme had a decisive influence on T. S. Eliot, who was to become the central figure in a whole poetic movement.

Eliot exhibits many influences besides those of Hulme and Pound, but his sources—which include the French Symbolists and, more significantly, such French poets as Gautier, Baudelaire, and Laforgue, together with the English metaphysicals—are less important than the use he makes of them. From the beginning it was clear that Eliot regarded himself as in revolt against the tradition of nineteenth-century English poetry, now represented, in somewhat attenuated form, by the Georgians. The poems in his early volumes made this quite clear. Abandoning all traditional stanza forms, he constructed his poems out of a series of verse paragraphs each of which was molded by the thought which it expressed and contained a series of dry, allusive images which combined to suggest a certain kind of mood. The distillation of meaning through the effective juxtaposition of carefully chosen images, and without any dependence on the decorated propositional statement which most people thought of as the norm of poetic utterance, drew attention to a major difference between the medium of poetry and that of prose which had become more and more obscured in what might be called the ebb of the Tennysonian tradition. These poems of Eliot's do not have, even implicitly, a plot like Tennyson's "Sir Galahad," Rossetti's "Blessed Damozel," or Swinburne's "Forsaken Garden." They have no specific setting; there is no direct account of a situation, nor is the poet expressing his own emotions in his own person. Instead, he carves out images which, when placed beside each other in this particular way, express both a mood and an attitude.

The attitude as well as the technique was in large measure new. Eliot looked at urban Western civilization not to compare it unfavorably with the peace and beauty of the countryside, or to denounce it as a prophet preaching a new way of life, or to find in it moments of excitement or drama or excuses for moralizing or for the play of sensibility—he looked at it in order to see it and present it as a symbol of a basic failure on the part of modern man, as a picture of life without faith and without value.

This was a new kind of pessimism in either English or American poetry. In the first place, it was wholly impersonal: the poet kept himself completely out of sight in all these poems and wrote dramatically, expressing himself through the very characters whose lives he considered so barren. There was thus not a trace of romantic *Weltschmerz* in these poems of Eliot's; there was no passion, no indignation, no self-indulgence of any kind. The poet himself remained (or liked to think of himself as remaining), like the artist in James Joyce's *Portrait of the Artist as a Young Man,* "invisible, indifferent, paring his fingernails."

In his later work Eliot sounded a more positive note, attempting to express poetically the road to the proper state of spiritual health, which, as he saw it, ran (though not in a straight line) from doubts and questionings through self-abnegation and passivity to a mood of tense calmness such as we get in "Marina" and intermittently in the *Four Quartets.* By this time he had accepted a specific religious tradition and was working within its terms. Yet he still felt the necessity of creating and discovering images and symbols in terms of which he could adequately present the situations he was concerned with, and found himself unable to fall back into a traditional kind of poetry simply because he had accepted a traditional religious position. He did, however, learn to curb the excessive allusiveness of his earlier poems (in which he had piled up references to and quotations from relatively little known earlier works of English and other literatures in an attempt both to convey ironically the contrast between the present state of civilization and the past and to find a more effective poetic symbolism than the exhausted state of the nineteenth-century tradition could provide), although he never gave up his endeavor to combine wit with passion, emotion with irony, and lyrical feeling with ironic undertones, which he had learned from the metaphysicals fairly early in his career. In this endeavor he was illustrating his belief in the necessity of a "unified sensibility" —the ability to combine thought and emotion and to confront a situation with both aspects of his sensibility operative simultaneously. Eliot and many of the poets who have been influenced by him pride themselves on having re-introduced wit into serious poetry: in this they were developing the antiromanticism of T. E. Hulme, who saw the typically romantic attitude in poetry as a humorless exploitation of personal emotion, with the intellect in abeyance. Such devices as the pun and the ironic anticlimax, which had been banished from serious English poetry since the end of the seventeenth century, now became respectable again; colloquial words and rhythms alternated with esoteric if precise references and cunningly cadenced lines; and at every point the attempt was made to fit the "exact curve" of the meaning without recourse to any standard or expected poetic device.

By 1930 Eliot's influence on both British and American poetry was something that could be taken for granted. W. H. Auden, who began his career as a poet in England in the early 1930's and settled in America some ten years later, took the necessity for dryness and irony pretty much for granted, and turned, with his contemporaries, to Gerard Manley Hopkins among others for further lessons in technique. (Hopkins' poems were first published in England in 1918, and a second edition appeared in 1930.) Auden and his contemporaries were at the outset of their careers much more concerned with the economic and social evidences of the decay of a tradition than with the spiritual side, and in their poetry they tried to diagnose the trouble by a combination of Freud and Marx. But can you expose the decay of a tradition with symbols drawn from that same tradition? This was a difficult question for the early Auden, who was in doubt both of the audience he was addressing and of the terms in which to address it. Yeats had built up a personal system to supply him with a language of symbols (though that system was drawn from some fundamental and recurring phases of human thought), and Eliot had used an eccentric erudition combined with anthropological references and (in his later work) aspects of the Christian mystical tradition: the poets of the thirties, out to diagnose and then to cure the social and economic ills of their time, looked forward to a new society which was not yet in being and so could not yet provide them with poetic symbols. As a result, they often talked to each other in a language full of private references which had no meaning except to those who had shared their experiences and ideas, or else tried to create myths out of the material provided for them by Freud and Marx. Later in his career Auden, abandoning his earlier position, moved towards a more religious view of civilization and searched widely for a tradition through which he could present freshly, and without abandoning the new techniques, his new sense of the meaning of the human situation. At some point or other all modern poets have had to face the problem of finding a language of symbols that can speak cogently to a reading public in an age of dissolving public belief. To say that the poet should avoid the problem by avoiding symbols is to advocate his abandonment of poetry, for all poetry is in a sense symbolic expression.

Modern poets, like modern critics, have been much concerned with the nature and function of myth, because an age which lacks common myths is most likely to be self-conscious about them. Some have deliberately tried to create composite myths, and notable among these is the Welsh poet Dylan Thomas, whose combination of folklore, Freudian psychology, and Christianity has given him a rich and powerful poetical vocabulary which he handles with a fine lyric intensity. Thomas shows a movement away from what might be called the Eliot position. He is in his own way an intensely romantic poet: that is, his works are full of a stormy personal passion, hurled at the reader in images that arrest and shock. His imagination burns in his poems at white heat, and although his best poems are always carefully wrought and the progression of thought is often intricate and subtle, there is none of that rather self-conscious irony and dryness that is to be found among Eliot and his followers. The lesson first preached by Hulme had been well learned, and every poetaster with pretensions to modernity was being dry and witty to the point where the "little" magazines were filled with gymnastic verse quite empty of poetic power. Thomas's poetry is no less "difficult" than Eliot's, but it has a flaming lyrical quality quite foreign to Eliot's genius. Whereas Eliot's characteristic fault, in moments where inspiration failed, was to fall into arid verse chat, Thomas's fault is the opposite one of choked and congested verse in which thundering images stifle each other's voices in their vain attempts to get free.

These examples do not, of course, exhaust the characteristically modern poetic situations and achievements. There were many poets who faced these problems in their own way, and some who, by reason of their special intellectual position or personal experience, were able to by-pass the main movements of their time without merely echoing conventional patterns of verse expression. Robert Frost was one of these lone figures; and Hart Crane, in a very different way, wrestled almost with success with the problem of hewing out a modern mythology in the light of his own American experience. In England, George Barker developed a lyrical note of his own, and many other interesting poets cannot be helpfully explained in terms of the preceding discussion. But it is the poetry and not the explanation that matters, and it is to be hoped that in spite of the very limited selection of modern poetry included here (limited for reasons of space and of copyright) there are enough good modern poems presented to give the reader some idea of what has been going on in the world of poetry in our own century and—more important—to give him pleasure in the reading.

EDWIN ARLINGTON ROBINSON (1869–1935)

335.   EROS TURANNOS *

> She fears him, and will always ask
> What fated her to choose him;
> She meets in his engaging mask
> All reasons to refuse him;
> But what she meets and what she fears
> Are less than are the downward years,
> Drawn slowly to the foamless weirs
> Of age, were she to lose him.

Between a blurred sagacity
    That once had power to sound him,   10
And Love, that will not let him be
    The Judas that she found him,
Her pride assuages her almost,
As if it were alone the cost,—
He sees that he will not be lost,
    And waits and looks around him.

A sense of ocean and old trees
    Envelops and allures him;
Tradition, touching all he sees,
    Beguiles and reassures him;   20
And all her doubts of what he says
Are dimmed with what she knows of days—
Till even prejudice delays
    And fades, and she secures him.

The falling leaf inaugurates
    The reign of her confusion;
The pounding wave reverberates
    The dirge of her illusion;
And home, where passion lived and died,
Becomes a place where she can hide,   30
While all the town and harbor side
    Vibrate with her seclusion.

We tell you, tapping on our brows,
    The story as it should be,—
As if the story of a house
    Were told, or ever could be;
We'll have no kindly veil between
Her visions and those we have seen,—
As if we guessed what hers have been,
    Or what they are or would be.   40

Meanwhile we do no harm; for they
    That with a god have striven,
Not hearing much of what we say,
    Take what the god has given;
Though like waves breaking it may be,
Or like a changed familiar tree,
Or like a stairway to the sea
    Where down the blind are driven.

336.   MR. FLOOD'S PARTY *

    Old Eben Flood, climbing alone one night
    Over the hill between the town below
    And the forsaken upland hermitage
    That held as much as he should ever know
    On earth again of home, paused warily.
    The road was his with not a native near:
    And Eben, having leisure, said aloud,
    For no man else in Tilbury Town to hear:

    "Well, Mr. Flood, we have the harvest moon
    Again, and we may not have many more;   10
    The bird is on the wing, the poet says,
    And you and I have said it here before.
    Drink to the bird." He raised up to the light
    The jug that he had gone so far to fill,
    And answered huskily: "Well, Mr. Flood,
    Since you propose it, I believe I will."

    Alone, as if enduring to the end
    A valiant armor of scarred hopes outworn,
    He stood there in the middle of the road
    Like Roland's ghost winding a silent horn.   20
    Below him, in the town among the trees,
    Where friends of other days had honored him,
    A phantom salutation of the dead
    Rang thinly till old Eben's eyes were dim.

    Then, as a mother lays her sleeping child
    Down tenderly, fearing it may awake,
    He set the jug down slowly at his feet
    With trembling care, knowing that most things break;
    And only when assured that on firm earth
    It stood, as the uncertain lives of men   30
    Assuredly did not, he paced away,
    And with his hand extended paused again:

    "Well, Mr. Flood, we have not met like this
    In a long time; and many a change has come
    To both of us, I fear, since last it was
    We had a drop together. Welcome home!"
    Convivially returning with himself,

Again he raised the jug up to the light;
And with an acquiescent quaver said:
"Well, Mr. Flood, if you insist, I might.   40

"Only a very little, Mr. Flood—
For auld lang syne. No more, sir; that will do."
So, for the time, apparently it did,
And Eben evidently thought so too;
For soon amid the silver loneliness
Of night he lifted up his voice and sang,
Secure, with only two moons listening,
Until the whole harmonious landscape rang—

"For auld lang syne." The weary throat gave out,
The last word wavered, and the song was done.   50
He raised again the jug regretfully
And shook his head, and was again alone.
There was not much that was ahead of him,
And there was nothing in the town below—
Where strangers would have shut the many doors
That many friends had opened long ago.

W. B. YEATS (1865–1939)

337.   WHEN YOU ARE OLD *

When you are old and grey and full of sleep,
And nodding by the fire, take down this book,
And slowly read, and dream of the soft look
Your eyes had once, and of their shadows deep;

How many loved your moments of glad grace,
And loved your beauty with love false or true,
But one man loved the pilgrim soul in you,
And loved the sorrows of your changing face;

And bending down beside the glowing bars,
Murmur, a little sadly, how Love fled   10
And paced upon the mountains overhead
And hid his face amid a crowd of stars.

338.   THE FOLLY OF BEING COMFORTED †

One that is ever kind said yesterday:
'Your well-belovèd's hair has threads of grey,

---

* Yeats, *Poetical Works Vol. I.* Copyright 1906, 1934 by The Macmillan Company and used with their permission.

† Yeats, *Seven Woods.* Copyright 1903, 1931 by The Macmillan Company and used with their permission.

And little shadows come about her eyes;
Time can but make it easier to be wise
Though now it seems impossible, and so
All that you need is patience.'
                          Heart cries, 'No,
I have not a crumb of comfort, not a grain.
Time can but make her beauty over again:
Because of that great nobleness of hers   10
The fire that stirs about her, when she stirs,
Burns but more clearly. O she had not these ways
When all the wild summer was in her gaze.'

O heart! O heart! if she'd but turn her head,
You'd know the folly of being comforted.

339.   NO SECOND TROY *

Why should I blame her that she filled my days
With misery, or that she would of late
Have taught to ignorant men most violent ways,
Or hurled the little streets upon the great,
Had they but courage equal to desire?
What could have made her peaceful with a mind
That nobleness made simple as a fire,
With beauty like a tightened bow, a kind
That is not natural in an age like this,
Being high and solitary and most stern?   10
Why, what could she have done, being what she is?
Was there another Troy for her to burn?

340.   TO A SHADE †

If you have revisited the town, thin Shade,
Whether to look upon your monument
(I wonder if the builder has been paid)
Or happier-thoughted when the day is spent
To drink of that salt breath out of the sea
When grey gulls flit about instead of men,
And the gaunt houses put on majesty:
Let these content you and be gone again;
For they are at their old tricks yet.

                                          A man   10
Of your own passionate serving kind who had brought
In his full hands what, had they only known,
Had given their children's children loftier thought,
Sweeter emotion, working in their veins
Like gentle blood, has been driven from the place,
And insult heaped upon him for his pains,
And for his open-handedness, disgrace;
Your enemy, an old foul mouth, had set
The pack upon him.   20
                    Go, unquiet wanderer,
And gather the Glasnevin coverlet
About your head till the dust stops your ear,
The time for you to taste of that salt breath
And listen at the corners has not come;
You had enough of sorrow before death—
Away, away! You are safer in the tomb.

341.   ON A POLITICAL PRISONER *

          She that but little patience knew,
          From childhood on, had now so much
          A grey gull lost its fear and flew
          Down to her cell and there alit,
          And there endured her fingers' touch
          And from her fingers ate its bit.

          Did she in touching that lone wing
          Recall the years before her mind
          Became a bitter, an abstract thing,
          Her thought some popular enmity: 10
          Blind and leader of the blind
          Drinking the foul ditch where they lie?

          When long ago I saw her ride
          Under Ben Bulben to the meet,
          The beauty of her country-side
          With all youth's lonely wildness stirred,
          She seemed to have grown clean and sweet
          Like any rock-bred, sea-borne bird:

          Sea-borne, or balanced on the air
          When first it sprang out of the nest   20

* Yeats, *Later Poems from Michael Robartes and Dancer.* Copyright 1924 by The
Macmillan Company and used with their permission.

Upon some lofty rock to stare
Upon the cloudy canopy,
While under its storm-beaten breast
Cried out the hollows of the sea.

342.   THE SECOND COMING *

Turning and turning in the widening gyre
The falcon cannot hear the falconer;
Things fall apart; the centre cannot hold;
Mere anarchy is loosed upon the world,
The blood-dimmed tide is loosed, and everywhere
The ceremony of innocence is drowned;
The best lack all conviction, while the worst
Are full of passionate intensity.

Surely some revelation is at hand;
Surely the Second Coming is at hand.   10
The Second Coming! Hardly are those words out
When a vast image out of *Spiritus Mundi*
Troubles my sight: somewhere in sands of the desert
A shape with lion body and the head of a man,
A gaze blank and pitiless as the sun,
Is moving its slow thighs, while all about it
Reel shadows of the indignant desert birds.
The darkness drops again; but now I know
That twenty centuries of stony sleep
Were vexed to nightmare by a rocking cradle,   20
And what rough beast, its hour come round at last,
Slouches towards Bethlehem to be born?

343.   LEDA AND THE SWAN †

A sudden blow: the great wings beating still
Above the staggering girl, her thighs caressed
By the dark webs, her nape caught in his bill,
He holds her helpless breast upon his breast.

How can those terrified vague fingers push
The feathered glory from her loosening thighs?
And how can body, laid in that white rush,
But feel the strange heart beating where it lies?

* Yeats, *Later Poems from Michael Robartes and Dancer*. Copyright 1924 by The Macmillan Company and used with their permission.
† Yeats, *The Tower*. Copyright 1928 by The Macmillan Company and used with their permission.

A shudder in the loins engenders there
The broken wall, the burning roof and tower   10
And Agamemnon dead.
                              Being so caught up,
So mastered by the brute blood of the air,
Did she put on his knowledge with his power
Before the indifferent beak could let her drop?

344.   BYZANTIUM *

The unpurged images of day recede;
The Emperor's drunken soldiery are abed;
Night resonance recedes, night-walkers' song
After great cathedral gong;
A starlit or a moonlit dome disdains
All that man is,
All mere complexities,
The fury and the mire of human veins.

Before me floats an image, man or shade,
Shade more than man, more image than a shade;   10
For Hades' bobbin bound in mummy-cloth
May unwind the winding path;
A mouth that has no moisture and no breath
Breathless mouths may summon;
I hail the superhuman;
I call it death-in-life and life-in-death.

Miracle, bird or golden handiwork,
More miracle than bird or handiwork,
Planted on the star-lit golden bough,
Can like the cocks of Hades crow,   20
Or, by the moon embittered, scorn aloud
In glory of changeless metal
Common bird or petal
And all complexities of mire or blood.

At midnight on the Emperor's pavement flit
Flames that no faggot feeds, nor steel has lit,
Nor storm disturbs, flames begotten of flame,
Where blood-begotten spirits come
And all complexities of fury leave,
Dying into a dance,   30
An agony of trance,
An agony of flame that cannot singe a sleeve.

* Yeats, *Winding Stair*. Copyright 1933 by The Macmillan Company and used
with their permission.

Astraddle on the dolphin's mire and blood,
Spirit after spirit! The smithies break the flood,
The golden smithies of the Emperor!
Marbles of the dancing floor
Break bitter furies of complexity,
Those images that yet
Fresh images beget,
That dolphin-torn, that gong-tormented sea. 40

345.   LONG-LEGGED FLY *

That civilisation may not sink,
Its great battle lost,
Quiet the dog, tether the pony
To a distant post;
Our master Caesar is in the tent
Where the maps are spread,
His eyes fixed upon nothing,
A hand under his head.
Like a long-legged fly upon the stream
His mind moves upon silence. 10

That the topless towers be burnt
And men recall that face,
Move most gently if move you must
In this lonely place.
She thinks, part woman, three parts a child,
That nobody looks; her feet
Practise a tinker shuffle
Picked up on a street.
Like a long-legged fly upon the stream
Her mind moves upon silence. 20

That girls at puberty may find
The first Adam in their thought,
Shut the door of the Pope's chapel,
Keep those children out.
There on that scaffolding reclines
Michael Angelo.
With no more sound than the mice make
His hand moves to and fro.
Like a long-legged fly upon the stream
His mind moves upon silence. 30

* Yeats, *Last Poems and Plays*. Copyright 1940 by Georgie Yeats and used with the permission of The Macmillan Company, Publishers.

EDWARD THOMAS (1878–1917)

346.   ## THE GALLOWS

There was a weasel lived in the sun
With all his family,
Till a keeper shot him with his gun
And hung him up on a tree,
Where he swings in the wind and the rain,
In the sun and in the snow,
Without pleasure, without pain
On the dead oak tree bough.

There was a crow who was no sleeper,
But a thief and a murderer   10
Till a very late hour; and this keeper
Made him one of the things that were,
To hang and flap in the rain and wind,
In the sun and in the snow.
There are no more sins to be sinned
On the dead oak tree bough.

There was a magpie, too,
Had a long tongue and a long tail;
He could both talk and do—
But what did that avail?   20
He, too, flaps in the wind and rain
Alongside weasel and crow,
Without pleasure, without pain,
On the dead oak tree bough.

And many other beasts
And birds, skin, bone and feather,
Have been taken from their feasts
And hung up there together,
To swing and have endless leisure
In the sun and in the snow,   30
Without pain, without pleasure,
On the dead oak tree bough.

347.   ## TEARS

It seems I have no tears left. They should
    have fallen—

Their ghosts, if tears have ghosts, did fall—
    that day
When twenty hounds streamed by me, not yet
    combed out
But still all equals in their rage of gladness
Upon the scent, made one, like a great dragon
In Booming Meadow that bends towards the sun
And once bore hops: and on that other day
When I stepped out from the double-shadowed
    Tower
Into an April morning, stirring and sweet
And warm. Strange solitude was there and silence.   10
A mightier charm than any in the Tower
Possessed the courtyard. They were changing guard,
Soldiers in line, young English countrymen,
Fair-haired and ruddy, in white tunics. Drums
And fifes were playing 'The British Grenadiers.'
The men, the music piercing that solitude
And silence, told me truths I had not dreamed,
And have forgotten since their beauty passed.

VACHEL LINDSAY (1879–1931)

348.   DANIEL *

Darius the Mede was a king and a wonder.   *Beginning with*
His eye was proud, and his voice was thunder.   *a strain of*
He kept bad lions in a monstrous den.   *"Dixie"*
He fed up the lions on Christian men.

Daniel was the chief hired man of the land.   *With a touch of*
He stirred up the music in the palace band.   *"Alexander's*
He whitewashed the cellar. He shovelled in the coal.   *Ragtime Band."*
And Daniel kept a-praying:—"Lord save my soul."
Daniel kept a-praying:—"Lord save my soul."
Daniel kept a-praying:—"Lord save my soul."   10

Daniel was the butler, swagger and swell.
He ran up stairs. He answered the bell.
And he would let in whoever came a-calling:—
Saints so holy, scamps so appalling.
"Old man Ahab leaves his card.

* Lindsay, *Golden Whales of California.* Copyright 1920, 1948 by The Macmillan
Company and used with their permission.

Elisha and the bears are a-waiting in the yard.
Here comes Pharaoh and his snakes a-calling.
Here comes Cain and his wife a-calling.
Shadrach, Meshach and Abednego for tea.
Here comes Jonah and the whale,   20
And the Sea!
Here comes St. Peter and his fishing pole.
Here comes Judas and his silver a-calling.
Here comes old Beelzebub a-calling."
And Daniel kept a-praying:—"Lord save my soul."
Daniel kept a-praying:—"Lord save my soul."

His sweetheart and his mother were Christian and meek.
They washed and ironed for Darius every week.
One Thursday he met them at the door:—
Paid them as usual, but acted sore.   30

He said:—"Your Daniel is a dead little pigeon.
He's a good hard worker, but he talks religion."
And he showed them Daniel in the lions' cage.
Daniel standing quietly, the lions in a rage.
His good old mother cried:—
"Lord save him."
And Daniel's tender sweetheart cried:—
"Lord save him."

And she was a golden lily in the dew.   *This to be*
And she was as sweet as an apple on the tree,   *repeated three*
And she was as fine as a melon in the corn-field,   *times, very*
Gliding and lovely as a ship on the sea,   *softly and*
Gliding and lovely as a ship on the sea.   *slowly.*

    43

And she prayed to the Lord:—
"Send Gabriel. Send Gabriel."

King Darius said to the lions:—
"Bite Daniel. Bite Daniel.
Bite him. Bite him. Bite him!"

Thus roared the lions:—   *Here the audience*
"We want Daniel, Daniel, Daniel,   *roars with the*
We want Daniel, Daniel, Daniel."   *leader.*
And Daniel did not frown,   51
Daniel did not cry.

He kept on looking at the sky.
And the Lord said to Gabriel:—
"Go chain the lions down.
Go chain the lions down.
Go chain the lions down.
Go chain the lions down."

*The audience
sings with the
leader, to the
old Negro tune.*

And Gabriel chained the lions,
And Gabriel chained the lions,
And Gabriel chained the lions,
And Daniel got out of the den,
And Daniel got out of the den,
And Daniel got out of the den.
And Darius said:—"You're a Christian child,"
Darius said:—"You're a Christian child,"
Darius said:—"You're a Christian child,"
And gave him his job again,
And gave him his job again,
And gave him his job again.

60

70

ROBERT FROST (1875–   )

349

MENDING WALL

Something there is that doesn't love a wall,
That sends the frozen-ground-swell under it,
And spills the upper boulders in the sun;
And makes gaps even two can pass abreast.
The work of hunters is another thing:
I have come after them and made repair
Where they have left not one stone on a stone,
But they would have the rabbit out of hiding,
To please the yelping dogs. The gaps I mean,
No one has seen them made or heard them made,
But at spring mending-time we find them there.
I let my neighbor know beyond the hill;
And on a day we meet to walk the line
And set the wall between us once again.
We keep the wall between us as we go.
To each the boulders that have fallen to each.
And some are loaves and some so nearly balls

10

We have to use a spell to make them balance:
'Stay where you are until our backs are turned!'
We wear our fingers rough with handling them.   20
Oh, just another kind of out-door game,
One on a side. It comes to little more:
There where it is we do not need the wall:
He is all pine and I am apple orchard.
My apple trees will never get across
And eat the cones under his pines, I tell him.
He only says, 'Good fences make good neighbors.'
Spring is the mischief in me, and I wonder
If I could put a notion in his head:
'*Why* do they make good neighbors? Isn't it   30
Where there are cows? But here there are no cows.
Before I built a wall I'd ask to know
What I was walling in or walling out,
And to whom I was like to give offense.
Something there is that doesn't love a wall,
That wants it down.' I could say 'Elves' to him,
But it's not elves exactly, and I'd rather
He said it for himself. I see him there
Bringing a stone grasped firmly by the top
In each hand, like an old-stone savage armed.   40
He moves in darkness as it seems to me,
Not of woods only and the shade of trees.
He will not go behind his father's saying,
And he likes having thought of it so well
He says again, 'Good fences make good neighbors.'

350.   THE ROAD NOT TAKEN

Two roads diverged in a yellow wood,
And sorry I could not travel both
And be one traveler, long I stood
And looked down one as far as I could
To where it bent in the undergrowth;

Then took the other, as just as fair,
And having perhaps the better claim,
Because it was grassy and wanted wear;
Though as for that the passing there
Had worn them really about the same,   10

And both that morning equally lay
In leaves no step had trodden black.
Oh, I kept the first for another day!
Yet knowing how way leads on to way,
I doubted if I should ever come back.

I shall be telling this with a sigh
Somewhere ages and ages hence:
Two roads diverged in a wood, and I—
I took the one less traveled by,
And that has made all the difference.   20

351.   THE GRINDSTONE

Having a wheel and four legs of its own
Has never availed the cumbersome grindstone
To get it anywhere that I can see.
These hands have helped it go, and even race;
Not all the motion, though, they ever lent,
Not all the miles it may have thought it went,
Have got it one step from the starting place.
It stands beside the same old apple tree.
The shadow of the apple tree is thin
Upon it now, its feet are fast in snow.   10
All other farm machinery's gone in,
And some of it on no more legs and wheel
Than the grindstone can boast to stand or go.
(I'm thinking chiefly of the wheelbarrow.)
For months it hasn't known the taste of steel,
Washed down with rusty water in a tin.
But standing outdoors hungry, in the cold,
Except in towns at night, is not a sin.
And, anyway, its standing in the yard
Under a ruinous live apple tree   20
Has nothing any more to do with me,
Except that I remember how of old
One summer day, all day I drove it hard,
And someone mounted on it rode it hard,
And he and I between us ground a blade.

I gave it the preliminary spin,
And poured on water (tears it might have been),
And when it almost gaily jumped and flowed,

A Father-Time-like man got on and rode,
Armed with a scythe and spectacles that glowed.   30
He turned on will-power to increase the load
And slow me down—and I abruptly slowed,
Like coming to a sudden railroad station.
I changed from hand to hand in desperation.
I wondered what machine of ages gone
This represented an improvement on.
For all I knew it may have sharpened spears
And arrowheads itself. Much use for years
Had gradually worn it an oblate
Spheroid that kicked and struggled in its gait,   40
Appearing to return me hate for hate;
(But I forgive it now as easily
As any other boyhood enemy
Whose pride has failed to get him anywhere).
I wondered who it was the man thought ground—
The one who held the wheel back or the one
Who gave his life to keep it going round?
I wondered if he really thought it fair
For him to have the say when we were done.
Such were the bitter thoughts to which I turned.   50

Not for myself was I so much concerned.
Oh no!—although, of course, I could have found
A better way to pass the afternoon
Than grinding discord out of a grindstone,
And beating insects at their gritty tune.
Nor was I for the man so much concerned.
Once when the grindstone almost jumped its bearing
It looked as if he might be badly thrown
And wounded on his blade. So far from caring,
I laughed inside, and only cranked the faster,   60
(It ran as if it wasn't greased but glued);
I'd welcome any moderate disaster
That might be calculated to postpone
What evidently nothing could conclude.
The thing that made me more and more afraid
Was that we'd ground it sharp and hadn't known.
And now were only wasting precious blade.
And when he raised it dripping once and tried
The creepy edge of it with wary touch,

And viewed it over his glasses funny-eyed,   70
Only disinterestedly to decide
It needed a turn more, I could have cried
Wasn't there danger of a turn too much?
Mightn't we make it worse instead of better?
I was for leaving something to the whetter.
What if it wasn't all it should be? I'd
Be satisfied if he'd be satisfied.

352.   ## STOPPING BY WOODS ON A
SNOWY EVENING

Whose woods these are I think I know
His house is in the village though;
He will not see me stopping here
To watch his woods fill up with snow.

My little horse must think it queer
To stop without a farmhouse near
Between the woods and frozen lake
The darkest evening of the year.

He gives his harness bells a shake
To ask if there is some mistake.   10
The only other sound's the sweep
Of easy wind and downy flake.

The woods are lovely, dark and deep
But I have promises to keep,
And miles to go before I sleep,
And miles to go before I sleep.

353.   ## THE STRONG ARE SAYING NOTHING

The soil now gets a rumpling soft and damp,
And small regard to the future of any weed.
The final flat of the hoe's approval stamp
Is reserved for the bed of a few selected seed.

There is seldom more than a man to a harrowed piece.
Men work alone, their lots plowed far apart,
One stringing a chain of seed in an open crease,
And another stumbling after a halting cart.

To the fresh and black of the squares of early mold
The leafless bloom of a plum is fresh and white;   10
Though there's more than a doubt if the weather is not too cold
For the bees to come and serve its beauty aright.

Wind goes from farm to farm in wave on wave,
But carries no cry of what is hoped to be.
There may be little or much beyond the grave,
But the strong are saying nothing until they see.

D. H. LAWRENCE (1885–1930)

354   BAVARIAN GENTIANS

Not every man has gentians in his house
in Soft September, at slow, Sad Michaelmas.

Bavarian gentians, big and dark, only dark
darkening the day-time torch-like with the smoking
          blueness of Pluto's gloom,
ribbed and torch-like, with their blaze of darkness
          spread blue
down flattening into points, flattened under the sweep
          of white day
torch-flower of the blue-smoking darkness, Pluto's
          dark-blue daze,
black lamps from the halls of Dis, burning dark blue,
giving off darkness, blue darkness, as Demeter's pale
          lamps give off light,
lead me then, lead me the way.   10

Reach me a gentian, give me a torch
let me guide myself with the blue, forked torch of this
          flower
down the darker and darker stairs, where blue is
          darkened on blueness.
even where Persephone goes, just now, from the
          frosted September
to the sightless realm where darkness is awake upon the
          dark
and Persephone herself is but a voice
or a darkness invisible enfolded in the deeper dark

of the arms Plutonic, and pierced with the passion of
    dense gloom,
among the splendour of torches of darkness, shedding
    darkness on the lost bride and her groom.

355.   PIANO

Softly, in the dusk, a woman is singing to me;
Taking me back down the vista of years, till I see
A child sitting under the piano, in the boom of the tingling strings
And pressing the small, poised feet of a mother who smiles as she
    sings.

In spite of myself, the insidious mastery of song
Betrays me back, till the heart of me weeps to belong
To the old Sunday evenings at home, with winter outside
And hymns in the cozy parlor, the tinkling piano our guide.

So now it is vain for the singer to burst into clamor
With the great black piano appassionato. The glamour   10
Of childish days is upon me, my manhood is cast
Down in the flood of remembrance, I weep like a child for the past.

RUPERT BROOKE (1887–1915)

356.   HEAVEN

    Fish (fly-replete, in depth of June
    Dawdling away their wat'ry noon)
    Ponder deep wisdom, dark or clear,
    Each secret fishy hope or fear.
    Fish say, they have their Stream and Pond;
    But is there anything Beyond?
    This life cannot be All, they swear,
    For how unpleasant, if it were!
    One may not doubt that, somehow, good
    Shall come of Water and of Mud;   10
    And, sure, the reverent eye must see
    A Purpose in Liquidity.
    We darkly know, by Faith we cry,
    The future is not Wholly Dry.
    Mud unto Mud!—Death eddies near—
    Not here the appointed End, not here!

But somewhere, beyond Space and Time,
Is wetter water, slimier slime!
And there (they trust) there swimmeth One
Who swam ere rivers were begun,   20
Immense, of fishy form and mind,
Squamous, omnipotent and kind;
And under that Almighty Fin
The littlest fish may enter in.
Oh! never fly conceals a hook,
Fish say, in the Eternal Brook,
But more than mundane weeds are there,
And mud, celestially fair;
Fat caterpillars drift around,
And Paradisal grubs are found;   30
Unfading moths, immortal flies,
And the worm that never dies.
And in that Heaven of all their wish,
There shall be no more land, say fish.

WILFRED OWEN (1893–1918)

357.   ANTHEM FOR DOOMED YOUTH

What passing-bells for these who die as cattle?
Only the monstrous anger of the guns.
Only the stuttering rifles' rapid rattle
Can patter out their hasty orisons.
No mockeries for them; no prayers nor bells,
Nor any voice of mourning save the choirs,—
The shrill, demented choirs of wailing shells;
And bugles calling for them from sad shires.

What candles may be held to speed them all?
Not in the hands of boys, but in their eyes   10
Shall shine the holy glimmers of good-bys.
The pallor of girls' brows shall be their pall;
Their flowers the tenderness of patient minds,
And each slow dusk a drawing-down of blinds.

358.   FUTILITY

Move him into the sun—
Gently its touch awoke him once,

At home, whispering of fields unsown.
Always it woke him, even in France,
Until this morning and this snow.
If anything might rouse him now
The kind old sun will know.

Think how it wakes the seeds,—
Woke, once, the clay of a cold star.
Are limbs, so dear-achieved, are sides   10
Full-nerved—still warm—too hard to stir?
Was it for this the clay grew tall?
—Oh, what made fatuous sunbeams toil
To break earth's sleep at all?

359.   STRANGE MEETING

It seemed that out of the battle I escaped
Down some profound dull tunnel, long since scooped
Through granites which Titanic wars had groined.
Yet also there encumbered sleepers groaned,
Too fast in thought or death to be bestirred.
Then, as I probed them, one sprang up, and stared
With piteous recognition in fixed eyes,
Lifting distressful hands as if to bless.
And by his smile, I knew that sullen hall.
By his dead smile I knew we stood in Hell.   10
With a thousand pains that vision's face was grained;
Yet no blood reached there from the upper ground,
And no guns thumped, or down the flues made moan.
"Strange friend," I said, "here is no cause to mourn."
"None," said the other, "save the undone years,
The hopelessness. Whatever hope is yours
Was my life also; I went hunting wild
After the wildest beauty in the world,
Which lies not calm in eyes, or braided hair,
But mocks the steady running of the hour,   20
And if it grieves, grieves richlier than here.
For by my glee might many men have laughed,
And of my weeping something has been left,
Which must die now. I mean the truth untold,
The pity of war, the pity war distilled.
Now men will go content with what we spoiled,
Or, discontent, boil bloody, and be spilled.

They will be swift with swiftness of the tigress,
None will break ranks, though nations trek from progress.
Courage was mine, and I had mystery,   30
Wisdom was mine, and I had mastery;
To miss the march of this retreating world
Into vain citadels that are not walled.
Then when much blood had clogged their chariot-wheels
I would go up and wash them from sweet wells,
Even with truths that lie too deep for taint.
I would have poured my spirit without stint
But not through wounds; not on the cess of war.
Foreheads of men have bled where no wounds were.
I am the enemy you killed, my friend.   40
I knew you in this dark; for so you frowned
Yesterday through me as you jabbed and killed.
I parried; but my hands were loath and cold.
Let us sleep now. . . ."

ELINOR WYLIE (1885–1928)

360.   THE EAGLE AND THE MOLE *

Avoid the reeking herd,
Shun the polluted flock,
Live like that stoic bird,
The eagle of the rock.

The huddled warmth of crowds
Begets and fosters hate;
He keeps, above the clouds,
His cliff inviolate.

When flocks are folded warm,
And herds to shelter run,   10
He sails above the storm,
He stares into the sun.

If in the eagle's track
Your sinews cannot leap,
Avoid the lathered pack,
Turn from the steaming sheep.

If you would keep your soul
From spotted sight or sound,
Live like the velvet mole;
Go burrow underground.   20

And there hold intercourse
With roots of trees and stones,
With rivers at their source,
And disembodied bones.

361.   LET NO CHARITABLE HOPE *

Now let no charitable hope
Confuse my mind with images
Of eagle and of antelope:
I am in nature none of these.

I was, being human, born alone;
I am, being woman, hard beset;
I live by squeezing from a stone
The little nourishment I get.

In masks outrageous and austere
The years go by in single file;   10
But none has merited my fear,
And none has quite escaped my smile.

EZRA POUND (1885–   )

362.   ANCIENT MUSIC

Winter is icummen in,
Lhude sing Goddamm,
Raineth drop and staineth slop,
And how the wind doth ramm!
                    Sing: Goddamm.
Skiddeth bus and sloppeth us,
An ague hath my ham.
Freezeth river, turneth liver,
                    Damn you, sing: Goddamm.
Goddamm, Goddamm, 'tis why I am, Goddamm,   10
                    So 'gainst the winter's balm.
Sing goddamm, damn, sing Goddamm,
Sing goddamm, sing goddamm, DAMM.

* Reprinted from *The Collected Poems of Elinor Wylie* by Elinor Wylie, by permission of Alfred A. Knopf, Inc. Copyright, 1923, 1932 by Alfred A. Knopf, Inc.

363. THE SEAFARER

FROM THE ANGLO-SAXON

May I for my own self song's truth reckon,
Journey's jargon, how I in harsh days
Hardship endured oft.
Bitter breast-cares have I abided,
Known on my keel many a care's hold,
And dire sea-surge, and there I oft spent
Narrow nightwatch nigh the ship's head
While she tossed close to cliffs. Coldly afflicted,
My feet were by frost benumbed.
Chill its chains are; chafing sighs   10
Hew my heart round and hunger begot
Mere-weary mood. Lest man know not
That he on dry land loveliest liveth,
List how I, care-wretched, on ice-cold sea,
Weathered the winter, wretched outcast
Deprived of my kinsmen;
Hung with hard ice-flakes, where hail-scur flew,
There I heard naught save the harsh sea
And ice-cold wave, at whiles the swan cries,
Did for my games the gannet's clamour,   20
Sea-fowls' loudness was for me laughter,
The mews' singing all my mead-drink.
Storms, on the stone-cliffs beaten, fell on the stern
In icy feathers; full oft the eagle screamed
With spray on his pinion.
                              Not any protector
May make merry man faring needy.
This he little believes, who aye in winsome life
Abides 'mid burghers some heavy business,
Wealthy and wine-flushed, how I weary oft   30
Must bide above brine.
Neareth nightshade, snoweth from north,
Frost froze the land, hail fell on earth then,
Corn of the coldest. Nathless there knocketh now
The heart's thought that I on high streams
The salt-wavy tumult traverse along.
Moaneth alway my mind's lust
That I fare forth, that I afar hence
Seek out a foreign fastness.

For this there's no mood-lofty man over earth's midst, 40
Not though he be given his good, but will have in his youth greed;
Nor his deed to the daring, nor his king to the faithful
But shall have his sorrow for sea-fare
Whatever his lord will.
He hath not heart for harping, nor in ring-having
Nor winsomeness to wife, nor world's delight
Nor any whit else save the wave's slash,
Yet longing comes upon his to fare forth on the water.
Bosque taketh blossom, cometh beauty of berries,
Fields to fairness, land fares brisker, 50
All this admonisheth man eager of mood,
The heart turns to travel so that he then thinks
On flood-ways to be far departing.
Cuckoo calleth with gloomy crying,
He singeth summerward, bodeth sorrow,
The bitter heart's blood. Burgher knows not—
He the prosperous man—what some perform
Where wandering them widest draweth.
So that but now my heart burst from my breastlock,
My mood 'mid the mere-flood, 60
Over the shale's acre, would wander wide.
On earth's shelter cometh oft to me,
Eager and ready, the crying lone-flyer,
Whets for the whale-path the heart irresistibly,
O'er tracks of ocean; seeing that anyhow
My lord deems to me this dead life
On loan and on land, I believe not
That any earth-weal eternal standeth
Save there be somewhat calamitous
That, ere a man's tide go, turn it to twain. 70
Disease or oldness or sword-hate
Beats out the breath from doom-gripped body.
And for this, every earl whatever, for those speaking after—
Laud of the living, boasteth some last word,
That he will work ere he pass onward,
Frame on the fair earth 'gainst foes his malice,
Daring ado, . . .
So that all men shall honour him after
And his laud beyond them remain 'mid the English,
Aye, for ever, a lasting life's-blast, 80
Delight 'mid the doughty.

                    Days little durable,
And all arrogance of earthen riches,
There come now no kings nor Caesars
Nor gold-giving lords like those gone.
Howe'er in mirth most magnified,
Whoe'er lived in life most lordliest,
Drear all this excellence, delights undurable!
Waneth the watch, but the world holdeth.
Tomb hideth trouble. The blade is layed low.   90
Earthly glory ageth and seareth.
No man at all going the earth's gait,
But age fares against him, his face paleth,
Grey-haired he groaneth, knows gone companions,
Lordly men, are to earth o'ergiven,
Nor may he then the flesh-cover, whose life ceaseth,
Nor eat the sweet nor feel the sorry,
Nor stir hand nor think in mid heart,
And though he strew the grave with gold,
His born brother, their buried bodies   100
Be an unlikely treasure hoard.

364.   EXILE'S LETTER

To So-Kin of Rakuyo, ancient friend, Chancellor of Gen.
Now I remember that you built me a special tavern
By the south side of the bridge at Ten-Shin.
With yellow gold and white jewels, we paid for songs and laughter
And we were drunk for month on month, forgetting the kings and
        princes.
Intelligent men came drifting in from the sea and from the west
        border,
And with them, and with you especially
There was nothing at cross purpose,
And they made nothing of sea-crossing or of mountain-crossing,
If only they could be of that fellowship,   10
And we all spoke out our hearts and minds, and without regret.
And then I was sent off to South Wei,
        smothered in laurel groves,
And you to the north of Raku-hoku
Till we had nothing but thoughts and memories in common.
And then, when separation had come to its worst,
We met, and travelled into Sen-Go,

Through all the thirty-six folds of the turning and twisting waters,
Into a valley of the thousand bright flowers,
That was the first valley;
And into ten thousand valleys full of voices and pine-winds.   20
And with silver harness and reins of gold,
Out came the East of Kan foreman and his company.
And there came also the 'True man' of Shi-yo to meet me,
Playing on a jewelled mouth-organ.
In the storied houses of San-Ko they gave us more Sennin music,
Many instruments, like the sound of young phoenix broods.
The foreman of Kan Chu, drunk, danced
                    because his long sleeves wouldn't keep still
With that music playing,
And I, wrapped in brocade, went to sleep with my head on his lap,
And my spirit so high it was all over the heavens,   30
And before the end of the day we were scattered like stars, or rain.
I had to be off to So, far away over the waters,
You back to your river-bridge.

And your father, who was brave as a leopard,
Was governor in Hei Shu, and put down the barbarian rabble.
And one May he had you send for me,
                    despite the long distance.
And what with broken wheels and so on, I won't say it wasn't hard
    going,
Over roads twisted like sheep's guts.
And I was still going, late in the year,
                    in the cutting wind from the North,
And thinking how little you cared for the cost,   40
                    and you caring enough to pay it.
And what a reception:
Red jade cups, food well set on a blue jewelled table,
And I was drunk, and had no thought of returning.
And you would walk out with me to the western corner of the
    castle,
To the dynastic temple, with water about it clear as blue jade,
With boats floating, and the sound of mouth-organs and drums,
With ripples like dragon-scales, going grass-green on the water,
Pleasure lasting, with courtesans, going and coming without
    hindrance,
With the willow flakes falling like snow,
And the vermilioned girls getting drunk about sunset,   50

And the water, a hundred feet deep, reflecting green eyebrows
—Eyebrows painted green are a fine sight in young moonlight,
Gracefully painted—
And the girls singing back at each other,
Dancing in transparent brocade,
And the wind lifting the song, and interrupting it,
Tossing it up under the clouds.
            And all this comes to an end.
            And is not again to be met with.
I went up to the court for examination,   60
Tried Layu's luck, offered the Choyo song,
And got no promotion,
            And went back to the East Mountains
            White-headed.
And once again, later, we met at the South bridgehead.
And then the crowd broke up, you went north to San palace,
And if you ask how I regret that parting:
It is like the flowers falling at Spring's end
            Confused, whirled in a tangle.
What is the use of talking, and there is no end of talking,
There is no end of things in the heart.   70
I call in the boy,
Have him sit on his knees here
            To seal this,
And send it a thousand miles, thinking.

T. S. ELIOT (1888–   )

365.   GERONTION

*Thou hast nor youth nor age
But as it were an after dinner sleep
Dreaming of both.*

Here I am, an old man in a dry month,
Being read to by a boy, waiting for rain.
I was neither at the hot gates
Nor fought in the warm rain
Nor knee deep in the salt marsh, heaving a cutlass,
Bitten by flies, fought.
My house is a decayed house,
And the jew squats on the window sill, the owner,
Spawned in some estaminet of Antwerp,
Blistered in Brussels, patched and peeled in London.   10

The goat coughs at night in the field overhead;
Rocks, moss, stonecrop, iron, merds.
The woman keeps the kitchen, makes tea,
Sneezes at evening, poking the peevish gutter.
                                        I an old man,
A dull head among windy spaces.

Signs are taken for wonders. 'We would see a sign!'
The word within a word, unable to speak a word,
Swaddled with darkness. In the juvescence of the year
Came Christ the tiger   20

In depraved May, dogwood and chestnut, flowering judas,
To be eaten, to be divided, to be drunk
Among whispers; by Mr. Silvero
With caressing hands, at Limoges
Who walked all night in the next room;
By Hakagawa, bowing among the Titians;
By Madame de Tornquist, in the dark room
Shifting the candles; Fraülein von Kulp
Who turned in the hall, one hand on the door. Vacant shuttles
Weave the wind. I have no ghosts,   30
An old man in a draughty house
Under a windy knob.

After such knowledge, what forgiveness? Think now
History has many cunning passages, contrived corridors
And issues, deceives with whispering ambitions,
Guides us by vanities. Think now
She gives when our attention is distracted
And what she gives, gives with such supple confusions
That the giving famishes the craving. Gives too late
What's not believed in, or if still believed,   40
In memory only, reconsidered passion. Gives too soon
Into weak hands, what's thought can be dispensed with
Till the refusal propagates a fear. Think
Neither fear nor courage saves us. Unnatural vices
Are fathered by our heroism. Virtues
Are forced upon us by our impudent crimes.
These tears are shaken from the wrath-bearing tree.

The tiger springs in the new year. Us he devours. Think at last
We have not reached conclusion, when I
Stiffen in a rented house. Think at last   50

I have not made this show purposelessly
And it is not by any concitation
Of the backward devils.
I would meet you upon this honestly.
I that was near your heart was removed therefrom
To lose beauty in terror, terror in inquisition.
I have lost my passion: why should I need to keep it
Since what is kept must be adulterated?
I have lost my sight, smell, hearing, taste and touch:
How should I use them for your closer contact?　　　　60

These with a thousand small deliberations
Protract the profit of their chilled delirium,
Excite the membrane, when the sense has cooled,
With pungent sauces, multiply variety
In a wilderness of mirrors. What will the spider do,
Suspend its operations, will the weevil
Delay? De Bailhache, Fresca, Mrs. Cammel, whirled
Beyond the circuit of the shuddering Bear
In fractured atoms. Gull against the wind, in the windy straits
Of Belle Isle, or running on the Horn,　　　　70
White feathers in the snow, the Gulf claims,
And an old man driven by the Trades
To a sleepy corner.

　　　　　　　　　　　　Tenants of the house,
Thoughts of a dry brain in a dry season.

366.　　　　JOURNEY OF THE MAGI

'A cold coming we had of it,
Just the worst time of the year
For a journey, and such a long journey:
The ways deep and the weather sharp,
The very dead of winter.'
And the camels galled, sore-footed, refractory,
Lying down in the melting snow.
There were times we regretted
The summer palaces on slopes, the terraces,
And the silken girls bringing sherbet.　　　　10
Then the camel men cursing and grumbling
And running away, and wanting their liquor and women,
And the night-fires going out, and the lack of shelters.
And the cities hostile and the towns unfriendly

And the villages dirty and charging high prices:
A hard time we had of it.
At the end we preferred to travel all night,
Sleeping in snatches,
With the voices singing in our ears, saying
That this was all folly.   20

Then at dawn we came down to a temperate valley,
Wet, below the snow line, smelling of vegetation;
With a running stream and a water-mill beating the darkness,
And three trees on the low sky,
And an old white horse galloped away in the meadow.
Then we came to a tavern with vine-leaves over the lintel,
Six hands at an open door dicing for pieces of silver,
And feet kicking the empty wine-skins.
But there was no information, and so we continued
And arrived at evening, not a moment too soon   30
Finding the place; it was (you may say) satisfactory.

All this was a long time ago, I remember,
And I would do it again, but set down
This set down
This: were we led all that way for
Birth or Death? There was a Birth, certainly,
We had evidence and no doubt. I had seen birth and death,
But had thought they were different; this Birth was
Hard and bitter agony for us, like Death, our death.
We returned to our places, these Kingdoms,   40
But no longer at ease here, in the old dispensation,
With an alien people clutching their gods.
I should be glad of another death.

367.   MARINA

*Quis hic locus, quae
regio, quae mundi plaga?*

What seas what shores what grey rocks and what islands
What water lapping the bow
And scent of pine and the woodthrush singing through the fog
What images return
O my daughter.

Those who sharpen the tooth of the dog, meaning
Death

Those who glitter with the glory of the hummingbird, meaning
Death   10
Those who sit in the stye of contentment, meaning
Death
Those who suffer the ecstasy of the animals, meaning
Death

Are become unsubstantial, reduced by a wind,
A breath of pine, and the woodsong fog
By this grace dissolved in place

What is this face, less clear and clearer
The pulse in the arm, less strong and stronger—
Given or lent? more distant than stars and nearer than the eye   20

Whispers and small laughter between leaves and hurrying feet
Under sleep, where all the waters meet.

Bowsprit cracked with ice and paint cracked with heat.
I made this, I have forgotten
And remember.
The rigging weak and the canvas rotten
Between one June and another September.
Made this unknowing, half conscious, unknown, my own.
The garboard strake leaks, the seams need caulking.
This form, this face, this life   30
Living to live in a world of time beyond me; let me
Resign my life for this life, my speech for that unspoken,
The awakened, lips parted, the hope, the new ships.

What seas what shores what granite islands towards my timbers
And woodthrush calling through the fog
My daughter.

368.   BURNT NORTON

Τοῦ λόγου δ' ἐόντος ξυνοῦ ζώουσιν
οἱ πολλοὶ ὡς ἰδίαν ἔχοντες φρόνησιν.
I. p. 77. Fr. 2.

ὁδὸς ἄνω κάτω μία καὶ ὡυτή.
I. p. 89. Fr. 60.

Diels: *Die Fragmente der Vorsokratiker* (Herakleitos).

I

Time present and time past
Are both perhaps present in time future,

And time future contained in time past.
If all time is eternally present
All time is unredeemable.
What might have been is an abstraction
Remaining a perpetual possibility
Only in a world of speculation.
What might have been and what has been
Point to one end, which is always present.   10
Footfalls echo in the memory
Down the passage which we did not take
Towards the door we never opened
Into the rose-garden. My words echo
Thus, in your mind.
                But to what purpose
Disturbing the dust on a bowl of rose-leaves
I do not know.
             Other echoes
Inhabit the garden. Shall we follow?   20
Quick, said the bird, find them, find them,
Round the corner. Through the first gate,
Into our first world, shall we follow
The deception of the thrush? Into our first world.
There they were, dignified, invisible,
Moving without pressure, over the dead leaves,
In the autumn heat, through the vibrant air,
And the bird called, in response to
The unheard music hidden in the shrubbery,
And the unseen eyebeam crossed, for the roses   30
Had the look of flowers that are looked at.
There they were as our guests, accepted and accepting.
So we moved, and they, in a formal pattern,
Along the empty alley, into the box circle,
To look down into the drained pool.
Dry the pool, dry concrete, brown edged,
And the pool was filled with water out of sunlight,
And the lotos rose, quietly, quietly,
The surface glittered out of heart of light,
And they were behind us, reflected in the pool.   40
Then a cloud passed, and the pool was empty.
Go, said the bird, for the leaves were full of children,
Hidden excitedly, containing laughter.
Go, go, go, said the bird: human kind

Cannot bear very much reality.
Time past and time future
What might have been and what has been
Point to one end, which is always present.

II

Garlic and sapphires in the mud
Clot the bedded axle-tree.   50
The trilling wire in the blood
Sings below inveterate scars
And reconciles forgotten wars.
The dance along the artery
The circulation of the lymph
Are figured in the drift of stars
Ascend to summer in the tree
We move above the moving tree
In light upon the figured leaf
And hear upon the sodden floor   60
Below, the boarhound and the boar
Pursue their pattern as before
But reconciled among the stars.

At the still point of the turning world. Neither
    flesh nor fleshless;
Neither from nor towards; at the still point,
    there the dance is,
But neither arrest nor movement. And do not call
    it fixity.
Where past and future are gathered. Neither
    movement from nor towards,
Neither ascent nor decline. Except for the point,
    the still point,
There would be no dance, and there is only the
    dance.   70
I can only say, *there* we have been: but I cannot
    say where.
And I cannot say, how long, for that is to place
    it in time.

The inner freedom from the practical desire,
The release from action and suffering, release
    from the inner
And the outer compulsion, yet surrounded

By a grace of sense, a white light still and moving,
Erhebung without motion, concentration
Without elimination, both a new world
And the old made explicit, understood
In the completion of its partial ecstasy,   80
The resolution of its partial horror.
Yet the enchainment of past and future
Woven in the weakness of the changing body,
Protects mankind from heaven and damnation
Which flesh cannot endure.

      Time past and time future
Allow but a little consciousness.
To be conscious is not to be in time
But only in time can the moment in the rose-garden,
The moment in the arbour where the rain beat,   90
The moment in the draughty church at smokefall
Be remembered; involved with past and future.
Only through time time is conquered.

III

Here is a place of disaffection
Time before and time after
In a dim light: neither daylight
Investing form with lucid stillness
Turning shadow into transient beauty
With slow rotation suggesting permanence
Nor darkness to purify the soul   100
Emptying the sensual with deprivation
Cleansing affection from the temporal.
Neither plenitude nor vacancy. Only a flicker
Over the strained time-ridden faces
Distracted from distraction by distraction
Filled with fancies and empty of meaning
Tumid apathy with no concentration
Men and bits of paper, whirled by the cold wind
That blows before and after time,
Wind in and out of unwholesome lungs   110
Time before and time after.
Eructation of unhealthy souls
Into the faded air, the torpid
Driven on the wind that sweeps the gloomy hills
  of London.

Hampstead and Clerkenwell, Campden and Putney,
Highgate, Primrose and Ludgate, Not here
Not here the darkness, in this twittering world.

Descend lower, descend only
Into the world of perpetual solitude,
World not world, but that which is not world,   120
Internal darkness, deprivation
And destitution of all property,
Desiccation of the world of sense,
Evacuation of the world of fancy,
Inoperancy of the world of spirit;
This is the one way, and the other
Is the same, not in movement
But abstention from movement; while the world moves
In appetency, on its metalled ways
Of time past and time future.   130

IV

Time and the bell have buried the day,
The black cloud carries the sun away.
Will the sunflower turn to us, will the clematis
Stray down, bend to us; tendril and spray
Clutch and cling?
Chill
Fingers of yew be curled
Down on us? After the kingfisher's wing
Has answered light to light, and is silent, the
          light is still   140
At the still point of the turning world.

V

Words move, music moves
Only in time; but that which is only living
Can only die. Words, after speech, reach
Into the silence. Only by the form, the pattern,
Can words or music reach
The stillness, as a Chinese jar still
Moves perpetually in its stillness.
Not in the stillness of the violin, while the
          note lasts,   150
Not that only, but the co-existence,

Or say that the end precedes the beginning,
And the end and the beginning were always there
Before the beginning and after the end.
And all is always now. Words strain,
Crack and sometimes break, under the burden,
Under the tension, slip, slide, perish,
Decay with imprecision, will not stay in place,
Will not stay still. Shrieking voices
Scolding, mocking, or merely chattering,   160
Always assail them. The Word in the desert
Is most attacked by voices of temptation,
The crying shadow in the funeral dance,
The loud lament of the disconsolate chimera.

The detail of the pattern is movement,
As in the figure of the ten stairs.
Desire itself is movement
Not in itself desirable;
Love is itself unmoving,
Only the cause and end of movement,   170
Timeless, and undesiring
Except in the aspect of time
Caught in the form of limitation
Between un-being and being.
Sudden in a shaft of sunlight
Even while the dust moves
There rises the hidden laughter
Of children in the foliage
Quick now, here, now, always—
Ridiculous the waste sad time   180
Stretching before and after.

HART CRANE (1899–1932)

TO BROOKLYN BRIDGE

369.

How many dawns, chill from his rippling rest
The seagull's wings shall dip and pivot him,
Shedding white rings of tumult, building high
Over the chained bay waters Liberty—

Then, with inviolate curve, forsake our eyes
As apparitional as sails that cross

Some page of figures to be filed away;
—Till elevators drop us from our day . . .

I think of cinemas, panoramic sleights
With multitudes bent toward some flashing scene   10
Never disclosed, but hastened to again,
Foretold to other eyes on the same screen;

And Thee, across the harbor, silver-paced
As though the sun took step of thee, yet left
Some motion ever unspent in thy stride,—
Implicitly thy freedom staying thee!

Out of some subway scuttle, cell or loft
A bedlamite speeds to thy parapets,
Tilting there momently, shrill shirt ballooning,
A jest falls from the speechless caravan.   20

Down Wall, from girder into street noon leaks,
A rip-tooth of the sky's acetylene;
All afternoon the cloud-flown derricks turn . . .
Thy cables breathe the North Atlantic still.

And obscure as that heaven of the Jews,
Thy guerdon. . . Accolade thou dost bestow
Of anonymity time cannot raise:
Vibrant reprieve and pardon thou dost show.

O harp and altar, of the fury fused,
(How could mere toil align thy choiring strings!)   30
Terrific threshold of the prophet's pledge,
Prayer of pariah, and the lover's cry,—

Again the traffic lights that skim thy swift
Unfractioned idiom, immaculate sigh of stars,
Beading thy path—condense eternity:
And we have seen night lifted in thine arms.

Under thy shadow by the piers I waited;
Only in darkness is thy shadow clear.
The City's fiery parcels all undone,
Already snow submerges an iron year. . .   40

O Sleepless as the river under thee,
Vaulting the sea, the prairies' dreaming sod,

Unto us lowliest sometime sweep, descend
And of the curveship lend a myth to God.

370.   PRAISE FOR AN URN

IN MEMORIAM: ERNEST NELSON

It was a kind and northern face
That mingled in such exile guise
The everlasting eyes of Pierrot
And, of Gargantua, the laughter.

His thoughts, delivered to me
From the white coverlet and pillow,
I see now, were inheritances—
Delicate riders of the storm.

The slant moon on the slanting hill
Once moved us toward presentiments   10
Of what the dead keep, living still,
And such assessments of the soul

As, perched in the crematory lobby,
The insistent clock commented on,
Touching as well upon our praise
Of glories proper to the time.

Still, having in mind gold hair,
I cannot see that broken brow
And miss the dry sound of bees
Stretching across a lucid space.   20

Scatter these well-meant idioms
Into the smoky spring that fills
The suburbs, where they will be lost.
They are no trophies of the sun.

E. E. CUMMINGS (1894–   )

371.   "NONSUN BLOB A" *

nonsun blob a
cold to
skylessness
sticking fire

* From *One Times One*, published by Henry Holt and Company. Copyright 1944
by E. E. Cummings.

                    my are your
                    are birds our all
                    and one gone
                    away the they
                    leaf of ghosts some
                    few creep there
                    here or on
                    unearth

W. H. AUDEN (1907–   )

372. "OUR HUNTING FATHERS TOLD THE STORY" *

Our hunting fathers told the story
   Of the sadness of the creatures,
Pitied the limits and the lack
   Set in their finished features;
Saw in the lion's intolerant look,
   Behind the quarry's dying glare,
Love raging for the personal glory
   That reason's gift would add,
The liberal appetite and power,
   The rightness of a god.   10

Who nurtured in that fine tradition
   Predicted the result,
Guessed love by nature suited to
   The intricate ways of guilt?
That human ligaments could so
His southern gestures modify,
And make it his mature ambition
   To think no thought but ours,
To hunger, work illegally,
   And be anonymous?   20

373.   "O WHAT IS THAT SOUND WHICH SO THRILLS THE EAR" †

O what is that sound which so thrills the ear
   Down in the valley drumming, drumming?
Only the scarlet soldiers, dear,
   The soldiers coming.

O what is that light I see flashing so clear
  Over the distance brightly, brightly?
Only the sun on their weapons, dear,
    As they step lightly.

O what are they doing with all that gear;
  What are they doing this morning, this morning?   10
Only the usual manoeuvres, dear,
    Or perhaps a warning.

O why have they left the road down there;
  Why are they suddenly wheeling, wheeling?
Perhaps a change in the orders, dear;
    Why are you kneeling?

O haven't they stopped for the doctor's care;
  Haven't they reined their horses, their horses?
Why, they are none of them wounded, dear,
    None of these forces.   20

O is it the parson they want with white hair;
  Is it the parson, is it, is it?
No, they are passing his gateway, dear,
    Without a visit.

O it must be the farmer who lives so near;
  It must be the farmer so cunning, so cunning?
They have passed the farm already, dear,
    And now they are running.

O where are you going? stay with me here!
  Were the vows you swore me deceiving, deceiving?   30
No, I promised to love you, dear,
    But I must be leaving.

O it's broken the lock and splintered the door,
  O it's the gate where they're turning, turning;
Their feet are heavy on the floor
    And their eyes are burning.

374.   VOLTAIRE AT FERNEY *

Perfectly happy now, he looked at his estate.
An exile making watches glanced up as he passed,
And went on working; where a hospital was rising fast

* Copyright 1945 by W. H. Auden. Reprinted by permission of Random House, Inc.

A joiner touched his cap; an agent came to tell
Some of the trees he'd planted were progressing well.
The white alps glittered. It was summer. He was very great.

Far off in Paris, where his enemies
Whispered that he was wicked, in an upright chair
A blind old woman longed for death and letters. He would write   10
"Nothing is better than life." But was it? Yes, the fight
Against the false and the unfair
Was always worth it. So was gardening. Civilise.

Cajoling, scolding, scheming, cleverest of them all,
He'd led the other children in a holy war
Against the infamous grown-ups; and, like a child, been sly
And humble when there was occasion for
The two-faced answer or the plain protective lie,
But, patient like a peasant, waited for their fall.

And never doubted, like D'Alembert, he would win: 20
Only Pascal was a great enemy, the rest
Were rats already poisoned; there was much, though, to be done,
And only himself to count upon.
Dear Diderot was dull but did his best;
Rousseau, he'd always known, would blubber and give in.

Night fell and made him think of women: Lust
Was one of the great teachers; Pascal was a fool.
How Emilie had loved astronomy and bed;
Pimpette had loved him too like scandal; he was glad.   30
He'd done his share of weeping for Jerusalem: As a rule
It was the pleasure-haters who became unjust.

Yet, like a sentinel, he could not sleep. The night was full of wrong,
Earthquakes and executions. Soon he would be dead,
And still all over Europe stood the horrible nurses
Itching to boil their children. Only his verses
Perhaps could stop them: He must go on working. Overhead
The uncomplaining stars composed their lucid song.   40

375.   "LAY YOUR SLEEPING HEAD, MY LOVE" *

Lay your sleeping head, my love,
Human on my faithless arm;

Time and fevers burn away
Individual beauty from
Thoughtful children, and the grave
Proves the child ephemeral:
But in my arms till break of day
Let the living creature lie,
Mortal, guilty, but to me
The entirely beautiful. 10

Soul and body have no bounds:
To lovers as they lie upon
Her tolerant enchanted slope
In their ordinary swoon,
Grave the vision Venus sends
Of supernatural sympathy,
Universal love and hope;
While an abstract insight wakes
Among the glaciers and the rocks
The hermit's sensual ecstasy. 20

Certainty, fidelity
On the stroke of midnight pass
Like vibrations of a bell,
And fashionable madmen raise
Their pedantic boring cry:
Every farthing of the cost,
All the dreaded cards foretell,
Shall be paid, but from this night
Not a whisper, not a thought,
Not a kiss nor look be lost. 30

Beauty, midnight, vision dies:
Let the winds of dawn that blow
Softly round your dreaming head
Such a day of sweetness show
Eye and knocking heart may bless,
Find the mortal world enough;
Noons of dryness see you fed
By the involuntary powers,
Nights of insult let you pass
Watched by every human love. 40

LOUIS MacNEICE (1907–   )

376.   BAGPIPE MUSIC *

It's no go the merrygoround, it's no go the rickshaw,
All we want is a limousine and a ticket for the peepshow.
Their knickers are made of crepe-de-chine, their shoes are made of
    python,
Their halls are lined with tiger rugs and their walls with heads
    of bison.

John MacDonald found a corpse, put it under the sofa,
Waited till it came to life and hit it with a poker,
Sold its eyes for souvenirs, sold its blood for whiskey,
Kept its bones for dumb-bells to use when he was fifty.

It's no go the Yogi-Man, it's no go Blavatsky,
All we want is a bank balance and a bit of skirt in a taxi.   10

Annie MacDougall went to milk, caught her foot in the heather,
Woke to hear a dance record playing of Old Vienna.
It's no go your maidenheads, it's no go your culture,
All we want is a Dunlop tyre and the devil mend the puncture.

The Laird o' Phelps spent Hogmanay declaring he was sober,
Counted his feet to prove the fact and found he had one foot over.
Mrs. Carmichael had her fifth, looked at the job with repulsion,
Said to the midwife 'Take it away; I'm through with over-
    production.'

It's no go the gossip column, it's no go the Ceilidh,
All we want is a mother's help and a sugar-stick for the baby.   20

Willie Murray cut his thumb, couldn't count the damage,
Took the hide of an Ayrshire cow and used it for a bandage.
His brother caught three hundred cran when the seas were lavish,
Threw the bleeders back in the sea and went upon the parish.

It's no go the Herring Board, it's no go the Bible,
All we want is a packet of fags when our hands are idle.

It's no go the picture palace, it's no go the stadium,
It's no go the country cot with a pot of pink geraniums.
It's no go the Government grants, it's no go the elections,
Sit on your arse for fifty years and hang your hat on a pension.   30

It's no go my honey love, it's no go my poppet;
Work your hands from day to day, the winds will blow the profit.
The glass is falling hour by hour, the glass will fall for ever,
But if you break the bloody glass you won't hold up the weather.

377.   SUNDAY MORNING *

Down the road someone is practising scales,
The notes like little fishes vanish with a wink of tails,
Man's heart expands to tinker with his car
For this is Sunday morning, Fate's great bazaar,
Regard these means as ends, concentrate on this Now,
And you may grow to music or drive beyond Hindhead anyhow,
Take corners on two wheels until you go so fast
That you can clutch a fringe or two of the windy past,
That you can abstract this day and make it to the week of time
A small eternity, a sonnet self-contained in rhyme.   10

But listen, up the road, something gulps, the church spire
Opens its eight bells out, skulls' mouths which will not tire
To tell how there is no music or movement which secures
Escape from the weekday time. Which deadens and endures.

STEPHEN SPENDER (1909–   )

378.   AN ELEMENTARY SCHOOL CLASSROOM
              IN A SLUM †

Far far from gusty waves, these children's faces.
Like rootless weeds the torn hair round their paleness.
The tall girl with her weighed-down head. The paper-
seeming boy with rat's eyes. The stunted unlucky heir
Of twisted bones, reciting a father's gnarled disease,
His lesson from his desk. At back of the dim class,
One unnoted, sweet and young: his eyes live in a dream
Of squirrels' game, in tree room, other than this.

On sour cream walls, donations. Shakespeare's head
Cloudless at dawn, civilized dome riding all cities.   10
Belled, flowery, Tyrolese valley. Open-handed map

* Copyright 1937, 1939, 1940 by Louis MacNeice. Reprinted by permission of
Random House, Inc.
   † Copyright 1942 by Stephen Spender. Reprinted by permission of Random
House, Inc.

Awarding the world its world. And yet, for these
Children, these windows, not this world, are world,
Where all their future's painted with a fog,
A narrow street sealed in with a lead sky,
Far far from rivers, capes, and stars of words.

Surely Shakespeare is wicked, the map a bad example
With ships and sun and love tempting them to steal—
For lives that slyly turn in their cramped holes
From fog to endless night? On their slag heap, these children   20
Wear skins peeped through by bones and spectacles of steel
With mended glass, like bottle bits on stones.
All of their time and space are foggy slum
So blot their maps with slums as big as doom.

Unless, governor, teacher, inspector, visitor,
This map becomes their window and these windows
That open on their lives like crouching tombs
Break, O break open, till they break the town
And show the children to the fields and all their world
Azure on their sands, to let their tongues   30
Run naked into books, the white and green leaves open
The history theirs whose language is the sun.

DYLAN THOMAS (1914–   )

379.   "THE FORCE THAT THROUGH THE
            GREEN FUSE DRIVES THE FLOWER"

The force that through the green fuse drives the flower
Drives my green age; that blasts the roots of trees
Is my destroyer.
And I am dumb to tell the crooked rose
My youth is bent by the same wintry fever.

The force that drives the water through the rocks
Drives my red blood; that dries the mouthing streams
Turns mine to wax.
And I am dumb to mouth unto my veins
How at the mountain spring the same mouth sucks.   10

The hand that whirls the water in the pool
Stirs the quicksand; that ropes the blowing wind
Hauls my shroud sail.

And I am dumb to tell the hanging man
How of my clay is made the hangman's lime.

The lips of time leech to the fountain head;
Love drips and gathers, but the fallen blood
Shall calm her sores.
And I am dumb to tell a weather's wind
How time has ticked a heaven round the stars.   20

And I am dumb to tell the lover's tomb
How at my sheet goes the same crooked worm.

380.   IN MEMORY OF ANN JONES

After the funeral, mule praises, brays,
Windshake of sailshaped ears, muffle-toed tap
Tap happily of one peg in the thick
Grave's foot, blinds down the lids, the teeth in black,
The spittled eyes, the salt ponds in the sleeves,
Morning smack of the spade that wakes up sleep,
Shakes a desolate boy who slits his throat
In the dark of the coffin and sheds dry leaves
That breaks one bone to light with a judgment clout,
After the feast of tear-stuffed time and thistles   10
In a room with a stuffed fox and a stale fern,
I stand, for this memorial's sake, alone
In the snivelling hours with dead, humped Ann
Whose hooded, fountain heart once fell in puddles
Round the parched worlds of Wales and drowned each sun
(Though this for her is a monstrous image blindly
Magnified out of praise; her death was a still drop;
She would not have me sinking in the holy
Flood of her heart's fame; she would lie dumb and deep
And need no druid of her broken body).   20
But I, Ann's bard on a raised hearth, call all
The seas to service that her wood-tongued virtue
Babble like a bellbuoy over the hymning heads,
Bow down the walls of the ferned and foxy woods
That her love sing and swing through a brown chapel,
Bless her bent spirit with four, crossing birds.
Her flesh was meek as milk, but this skyward statue
With the wild breast and blessed and giant skull
Is carved from her in a room with a wet window
In a fiercely mourning house in a crooked year.   30

I know her scrubbed and sour humble hands
Lie with religion in their cramp, her threadbare
Whisper in a damp word, her wits drilled hollow,
Her fist of a face died clenched on a round pain;
And sculptured Ann is seventy years of stone.
These cloud-sopped, marble hands, this monumental
Argument of the hewn voice, gesture and psalm
Storm me forever over her grave until
The stuffed lung of the fox twitch and cry Love
And the strutting fern lay seeds on the black sill.   40

381.   THE MARRIAGE OF A VIRGIN

Waking alone in a multitude of loves when morning's light
Surprised in the opening of her nightlong eyes
His golden yesterday asleep upon the iris
And this day's sun leapt up the sky out of her thighs
Was miraculous virginity old as loaves and fishes
Though the moment of a miracle is unending lightning
And the shipyards of Galilee's footprints hid a navy of doves.

No longer will the vibrations of the sun desire on
Her deepsea pillow where once she married alone,
Her heart all ears and eyes, lips catching the avalanche   10
Of the golden ghost who ringed with his streams her mercury bone,
Who under the lids of her windows hoisted his golden luggage,
For a man sleeps where fire leapt down and she learns through his
     arm
That other sun, the jealous coursing of the unrivalled blood.

NOTES

NOTES

1. *"My galley chargèd with forgetfulness."* One of the most characteristic verse forms not only of Elizabethan literature in England but of Renaissance European literature as a whole was the sonnet, a form which arose in Italy in the twelfth century and which passed from Italy into France and then into England. Wyatt, facing the problem of restoring gravity and cogency of utterance to English verse after a period of linguistic change during which pronunciation had altered and metrical patterns had gone to pieces, turned to the Italian sonnet for help. Here was a highly conventional verse form, a form which demanded discipline and craftsmanship on the poet's part, a form which challenged the poet to mold his thought with wit and aptness to the precise shape of those fourteen balanced lines.

The sonnet was not simply a stanza of fourteen lines with a certain rhyme scheme: the lines were deftly balanced, the links and pauses between them creating a movement which, in most Italian sonnets, was in four parts—two of four lines each (*quatrains*) and two of three lines each (*tercets*). There were other ways of balancing the sonnet—such as Shakespeare's, who balanced it on a final couplet of rhyming lines—but the pattern most common in Italy employed two quatrains with a single pair of rhymes, *a b b a, a b b a,* the first and fourth rhyming, and the two middle lines rhyming (as in Tennyson's *In Memoriam*), followed by two tercets in any one of a variety of arrangements— *c d c, c d c;* or *c d c, d c d;* or *c d e, c d e;* or other groupings. In such a scheme the four parts of the sonnet really resolve themselves into two, the first consisting of two pairs of four lines (the *octave*) and the second of two pairs of three lines (the *sestet*).

As we shall see in examining some later sonnets, there were many other ways of patterning the fourteen lines, but the pattern just described was that most frequently used by the fourteenth-centu. y Italian poet Petrarch, whose sonnets celebrating his ideal love of Laura were immensely influential and represent the most important single influence on later love sonnets throughout Europe.

There are periods in the history of any literature when what poets need most is a formal convention, which will enable them to study the demands of the medium quite objectively, with a craftsman's eye, and prevent them from merely splashing about in language that has not been tempered to meet the precise curve of the meaning. The sonnet form met this need for English poets in the first half of the sixteenth century and later; and Wyatt's sonnets represent one of the most interesting movements towards metrical discipline to be found anywhere. Wyatt's problem was to handle the ten-syllabled iambic line with gravity in the individual line and at the same time to achieve a significant unity in the poem as a whole. The metrical tradition established by Chaucer had lost its usefulness because of the numerous shifts in accentuation which accompanied the change from Middle English to Modern English. While these changes made it possible for Wyatt to experiment freely and effectively in numerous short-line stanzas where the sustained gravity of regular metrical utterance throughout a series of long lines was not required, they seriously handicapped him in writing the heavier kind of line demanded by the sonnet. As a result, his sonnets are less good than his lighter lyrics: he is not always quite sure where the accent falls in a given word, nor is he always able to keep before the reader's ear the basic swell of the metrical design, so necessary in this kind of formal utterance.

It was not only the sonnet form that later poets got from Petrarch; the whole nature of the relation between the poet and his beloved became conventionalized in terms of the idealized "courtly love" attitude which Petrarch manifested towards Laura in his love sonnets. This notion of the lover as the humble servant of the often cruel fair, wounded by the glance of her eye, tempest-tossed in seas of despair when his love is rejected, changing in mood according to the presence or absence of his beloved—all this is derived ultimately from that strange and powerful new view of the relation between the sexes which was originally developed at the end of the eleventh century in Provence. Petrarch had moved this courtly love to a high, ideal plane on which subsequent sonneteers for the most part kept it.

Thus the Petrarchan sonnet provided for the English poet both a conventional form and conventional sentiments. (One might add that innumerable Italian and French sonneteers after Petrarch had helped to conventionalize both form and content by the time the English sonneteers began writing.) We are accustomed to regard conventionality as a fault in poetry, and the question arises: can a conventional poem be a good poem, and if so, what kind of "goodness" can it possess?

The answer, of course, depends on what we mean by convention. All art is in one sense conventional, and the communication of artistic effects would be impossible if that were not so. Language itself is a set of conventions, and if we ignored them we should be unintelligible to each other. To depersonalize an emotional experience through the conventional medium of art is to move from the autobiographical to the aesthetic. That is, in art we construct a significant pattern of expression which can contain in itself the totality of meanings originally present in the experience of the artist. To achieve this, the artist must have complete control over his medium; if he is a poet, he must be able to bend language to his will, organize its interacting levels of meaning, its rhythmic potentialities, the qualities of vowel and consonantal sounds, and any other qualities of language, until he has made his poem contain what he wants it to contain. The poet can achieve this end in varying degrees, and with greater or less dependence on conventions. But he always uses *some* conventions.

The lowest satisfactory level is that of mere craftsmanship, and until this level has been attained the poet can go no higher. Mere craftsmanship represents the ability to handle conventions as conventions and does not go further to produce that tension between the original and the conventional elements in art in which the highest artistic greatness resides. The convention represents a mold into which the poet can pour his material, and if he uses the mold carefully he can produce an interesting piece of craftsmanship. To go further and take the mold for granted, suggest it, and refer to it without actually using it, is a more difficult achievement; but it should be noted that unless the molds (or conventions) existed, this higher achievement, which plays teasingly around the conventions without altogether accepting or following them, would be impossible. Great poetry depends on good poetry for its existence—or, to put it in another way, great art builds on good craftsmanship, not only in itself but in others.

As far as Wyatt's sonnets go, then, he is merely struggling to be a good craftsman. He is doing a kind of poetic homework which, if wholly successful, would constitute good, workmanlike verse, and if not wholly successful, would be historically interesting as showing a poet in the process of exercising the language, and aesthetically interesting as illustrating something of the relation between art and craft.

Such is the interest of this sonnet. It shows Wyatt trying to find appropriate English form for the popular 156th sonnet of Petrarch ("Passa la nave mia colma d' obblio") which is itself an elaborate "conceit" in which Love is regarded as the pilot of the ship which represents the poet's soul, his thoughts are oarsmen, and his tears and sighs are rain and wind. The form is Petrarchan, except that Wyatt has arranged the tercets in *c d d, c e e* form, which is not found in Petrarch (this is Wyatt's favorite form). One cannot feel that the poet has here completely dominated his medium: the extra foot in the third line reads as though it were a mistake; the rhyming of "forgetfulness," "cruelness," "readiness," and "fearfulness" forces the accent onto an unimportant suffix in each case; and altogether we get the impression of a poet struggling with language rather than mastering it. Yet there is a strength to this sonnet, a rough-hewn vigor, as though the poet were chiseling a meaning out of flinty language through sheer determination. The pause in the poem does not really come after the octave, but after the eleventh line, which is followed by a new turn of thought and a rising emotion:

> The stars be hid that led me to this pain.

With this sentence Wyatt links his state with its cause—the stars that led him "to this pain"—providing the poem with a background, as it were, a suggestion of how the present distress came about. This is an original turn in the meaning. Petrarch had written:

> Celansi i duo miei dolci usati segni
> Hidden are my two sweet familiar stars [signs],

the stars being, of course, his lady's eyes. But Wyatt praises and blames the lady in a single breath, by at the same time identifying her eyes with stars and making them the cause of his unhappy state. After this turn in the meaning the poem ends in a climax of desolation:

> Drownèd is reason that should me comfórt;
> And I remain despairing of the port.

These two lines ring out with a certain grandeur at the close of the poem, and in doing so tend to shift the balance of the sonnet structure, for while the last six lines are arranged in *c d d, c e e* pattern, that is, in two groups of three, the final couplet seems to break off from the sestet and stand as a foundation for the whole poem. English sonnets have a tendency to ground themselves on a couplet, as we shall see in looking at Shakespeare's.

This poem is an exercise, then, but a most interesting and instructive one. It is metrically uncertain and lacks ease in the handling, but it does show a certain originality in treating conventional material, and does succeed in moving into a fine climax at the end.

2. *"Forget not yet the tried intent."* This charming song shows how much more effective Wyatt was with lighter lyric measures than with the graver sonnet form. As Saintsbury and Tillyard have pointed out, the shifts in pronunciation between Chaucer's day and Wyatt's brought new freedom and variety in these light meters, but wrought disaster to the standard five-foot iambic line of Chaucer. It was almost certainly because Wyatt was helped by the rhythm of the lute music in the lighter songs that he shows so much firmer rhythmic control there.

The poem is written to a pattern with great deftness. Each stanza is identically constructed, with three rhyming lines and a shorter refrain; each opens and closes with the same phrase, "forget not yet." The poem rises steadily to the end. Each "forget not yet" at the opening of each successive stanza contains greater force and emotion, until the fourth stanza, where the poet with a perfect piece of modulation repeats "forget not yet" with a significant difference

> Forget not yet, forget not this

and the two following "–iss" rhymes sustain the change in key, as it were. Tillyard sees in the movement to *this* "the sudden change of musical note that a priest would make in intoning," and thinks of the poem as a "love-litany" inspired by church ritual.

In the final stanza the new key is maintained: the poet is elaborating the *this,* his own constancy and faithfulness, and at the same time by beginning the stanza with "Forget not, *then"* (a logical, not a temporal, "then"), making this point sum up the whole poem.

One should note also the effect of the three rhymes in each verse, emphasizing the overtone of constancy and length of service with their repetitions of similar sounds, and so effectively broken at the end of each verse by the shorter, unrhymed refrain. The shift of the refrain in the final stanza to "Forget not this" adds a note of finality, like a satisfying concluding chord in music.

The short lines, the shorter refrain, and the threefold rhymes give a pleasing note of lightness to the poem as a whole, so that we cannot take it *wholly* seriously as an unhappy lover's plea to his cruel lady: a certain confidence and intimacy emerges from the general tone of the poem, as though the poet and the lady are smiling at each other as he sings to her; yet there is a melancholy undertone.

3. *The Lover Showeth How He Is Forsaken.* Here Wyatt is using the longer line again, but interestingly enough, the metrical uncertainties which reveal themselves when he uses "heavier" measures seem here less the result of imperfect control than of a deliberate attempt to place pauses in unusual and strangely effective places.

The poem opens with an almost fierce abruptness:

> They flee from me that sometime did me seek

(i.e., those who once sought me now avoid me). The line runs on immediately without pause, to give the impression of something tensely remembered (*naked foot* and *stalking* carry overtones of stealth and mystery). The verse (which has the rhyme scheme *a b a b b c c,* known as "rhyme royal" because it was used in the *Kingis Quair* by James I of Scotland) is balanced on a concluding couplet, but in this first stanza Wyatt takes advantage of the concluding couplet rhyme without separating the last two lines from the body of the stanza. There is a pause—marking the break between recollection of the past and awareness of the present—in the middle of the second last line, and then, in language charged with irony and indignation, the poet proceeds

> and now they range
> Busily seeking in continual change.

The last line is anything but an iambic pentameter $(\cup-/\cup-/\cup-/\cup-/\cup-)$, yet it does not do violence to the basic metrical pattern of the poem: on the contrary, the variations from the iambic norm here help to give emphasis to the opening "busily" and bring out the scornful "s's" in "busily seeking." The actual metrical scheme of this line is $-\cup\cup/-\cup/-\cup\cup/-\cup/-$, whose pattern is dactyllic or trochaic rather than iambic: but such a pattern can be effectively counterpointed to an iambic ground bass, as the reader can discover by experimenting in reading aloud.

The second stanza is in a completely different mood. Lost in an ecstasy of recollection, the poet has turned to picture a scene from the past. The transition is marked by a sturdy affirmation

> Thankèd be fortune it hath been otherwise
> Twenty times better,

and this leads into a description of a particular experience in the past done with a limpid accuracy, and a smooth flowing verse, which suggests how far the poet has moved mentally from the opening verse.

In the third and last verse he jerks himself out of his trance:

> It was no dream; I lay broad waking.

The lack of a foot here forces the reader to make a long pause after "dream," and this helps to give the impression of the distraught mood in which the poet finds himself as he tears himself away from contemplation of that vivid picture from the past. The note changes from distraction to elegy:

> But all is turned, thorough my gentleness,
> Into a strange fashion of forsaking.

Again we have, in the second of these lines, a desertion of the iambic meter, but the irregularity here only emphasizes the "strangeness" of the "forsaking" —the line, indeed, is oddly haunting, partly because of the pause forced on the reader with "stránge fáshion": we linger in a sad and bemused way until the line dies away on the elegiac "forsaking." The poet pulls himself together on a note of irony:

> And I have leave to go, of [i.e., from] her goodness;

but he does not really know what to make of the whole business, and he ends with an appeal to his audience:

> I would fain know what she hath deserved.

The text of the poem, as emended after Wyatt's death in *Tottel's Miscellany*, that collection of "songs and sonnets" by Wyatt, Surrey, and others, published in 1557, concludes thus:

> But, since that I unkindly so am served:
> How like you this, what hath she now deserved?

which is both more regular metrically and more pointed; but it is not what
Wyatt wrote. Wyatt actually wrote:

> But syns that I so kyndely am served,
> I wold fain knowe what she hath deserved,

which scans regularly if we pronounce the "e" in "kyndely" and in "knowe."
By "so kyndely" Wyatt meant "in such fashion"; both the pronunciation and
the meaning seem to have shifted by 1557. It is hardly possible, however, that
Wyatt pronounced the final "e" in "knowe": but the point illustrates the kind
of difficulties Wyatt faced.

4. *"Marvel no more."* Another example of Wyatt's mastery of the lighter
lyric. This is a tongue-in-cheek kind of poem, wild with mixed metaphors and
platitudes ("how can a mournful man rejoice?") thrust at us with a cunning
air of profundity. The thing is carried off with perfect poise: the steady trip
of the poem is just the sort of movement required for this half-serious content.
We know all along, from the very movement of the verse, that the poet is
waiting for an excuse to be cheerful, and the final stanza, saucily ringing the
changes on the words "chance" and "change," is a most apt conclusion to a
delightful poem.

5. *The Lover Complaineth.* This is the most celebrated of Wyatt's poems,
and properly so. It rises above the conventional Petrarchan complaint to the
cruel fair, to ring out with a note both lyrical and dramatic. Note how steadily
the emotion rises until it is eventually transferred from the poet to the lady.
The climax of the poem is in those two remarkable stanzas beginning

> Perchance thee lie withered and old.

This turning of the tables is achieved with great skill: the reader is drawn
right into the heart of the lady's imagined experience "plaining in vain unto
the moon," as the poet deliberately removes himself from that scene—

> Care then who list, for I have done.

The second of these two stanzas points the great moral:

> Then shalt thou know beauty but lent,

and then, with the last stanza, the poem comes to an end with a sudden hush.
Note how skilfully the refrain in the last line of each stanza is varied and how
the persistence of the same rhyme in the third and fifth line of each verse adds
to the effectiveness of the poem.
The first three lines of the second stanza mean: "My song may pierce her
heart as readily as it could be heard with no ear to hear it, or as lead could
engrave letters in marble." He means, of course, that it is impossible for his
song to touch her heart.

6. *"Prisoned in Windsor, he recounteth his pleasure there passed."* It will
be seen at once that Surrey can handle the iambic pentameter with an assurance lacking in Wyatt: nevertheless, there is a vigor in Wyatt's poetry which

we do not find in Surrey's. This poem, written in 1545, when, as a result of intrigues against him by personal enemies, he was temporarily imprisoned in Windsor Castle, gives one of the most perfect descriptions in English poetry of the ideals and activities of knightly youth. Surrey, like other sixteenth-century English courtiers, represents a sort of Indian Summer of the medieval chivalric ideal.

This is a descriptive poem, and its value lies in the cogency, dignity, and musical eloquence of the description. It is not the kind of poem where we are justified in looking for any elaborate patterns of meaning. But note the effectiveness of the slow-moving line, the clear way in which each precisely etched picture rises before the reader's eyes, and the emotional overtones given to the whole by its being presented as a prisoner's memory of lost delights. The note of personal feeling surrounds and gives depth to the pictures of his former activities. There is the moral feeling of a civilization here, too, a sense of the glory and the value of this kind of knightly behavior amid friendly rivals and the approval of fair ladies, which is achieved purely by the imagery. Friendship, love, honor, and a splendid gracefulness of action are the ideals which blossom forth from the poem, and the reader will find it worth his while to inquire as precisely as he can how this implicit affirmation of a knightly faith is in fact achieved.

Line 11. that tigers could but rue: that could even melt tigers.
    13. palm play: a kind of handball (a predecessor of tennis).
    16. thc leads above: above the flat roof tops, from which the ladies watched the game.
    30. avaled: slackened.
    46. fere: companion.

7. *Description of Spring, Wherein Each Thing Renews.* This sonnet has a very different kind of rhyme scheme from Wyatt's: it has alternate rhymes all the way down, with the final two lines a rhymed couplet. Surrey uses the same two pairs of rhymes throughout, but Shakespeare and others used different rhymes in each four of the first twelve lines before ending also with a couplet. Alternate rhymes and a closing couplet become the characteristic English form of the sonnet from now on. Note that this arrangement completely eliminates the octave-sestet division, putting the pause at the end of the twelfth line. Surrey uses this pause simply and effectively by closing his description of the delights of spring at this point, and in the concluding couplet giving, with almost epigrammatic force, the contrasting description of his sorrowful self. The poem is a graceful piece of craftsmanship and nothing more. There is no distillation of meaning to echo beyond the ostensible subject matter.

Line 1. soote: sweet.

8. *The Lover Comforteth Himself.* This little poem might be compared with some of Wyatt's shorter pieces. Consider what is achieved, in the way of effective expression, by the rhyme scheme, the reference to the siege of Troy and Agamemnon's sacrifice of his daughter (he had been told by the seer Calchis that only his daughter's death could end the calm which prevented the Greek fleet from sailing against Troy) and the whole device of contrast and recollection which moves the poem away from the poet himself in its middle section, to return to him at the end.

Line 28. draweth in ure: becomes prevalent.

9. *Amantium Irae Amoris Redintegratio Est.* (*"The quarrelling of lovers is the renewal of love."*) This strangely effective poem is written in "fourteeners," i.e., lines containing seven iambic feet and fourteen syllables: this is a very old English metrical form, to be found fairly often in the thirteenth century and quite common in the sixteenth. Split up into two lines (the first of four feet and the second of three), it becomes the "ballad measure" more familiar to modern readers. But note that the line has a wholly different movement in its original form. The actual physical arrangement of verses on a page is often important as indication of the *tempo* of the poem, the placing of pauses, the counterpointing of rhythmic pauses to pauses demanded by the meaning, etc.

The naïveté of this poem is thoroughly effective: it gives the whole piece a fresh, primitive quality. The moral is crude, the "plot" equally so, but this very crudeness, combined with the singsong rhythms and the recurring refrain (with its deliberate change of the metrical beat in the fifth and sixth foot) gives the poem the air of a genuine primitive. The flavor of the poem is quite unique: we have the impression of a man forced to make his point in this manner because his perception of the particular truth he enunciates is profoundly associated with the kind of domestic situation described in the opening lines. Consider what is added to the poem by putting so much of it into the mouth of a mother singing to her child. Wyatt, in a verse fable too long to include in this collection, achieves a similar effect by opening his story thus:

> My mother's maids when they do sew and spin,
> They sing a song made of the fieldish mouse. . . .

Do you know any modern poems using similar devices?

10. *Gascoigne's Lullaby.* Consider the part played by the rhyme and metrical schemes in achieving the effectiveness of this beautiful poem. Examine the fifth line of each stanza, noting that it comes after a pause and begins a new movement in each case. Consider also the nature of the thought progression in the poem, and of the imagery which carries it.

Line 24. eft: again.
    42. ware: goods.

11. *Epigram.* This is a verse epigram, a kind of poem whose special virtues are neatness and compactness of expression and a straightforward sort of wit. This epigram is built on the last two lines, coming to an effective climax on the final line, in which three things generally regarded as of very different degrees of desirability, are cited as equally desirable. Note how the verse builds up to this climax. An epigram is generally an exercise in pure craftsmanship, and is to be appreciated as such.

12. *"My true love hath my heart."* This poem is essentially a piece of formal ingenuity, but the directness and simplicity of the opening line (which is repeated twice) start it off in a folk mood which adds to the subsequent playing with the notion of exchange of hearts a note of ingenuousness. It is this mixture of ingenuousness and ingenuity (not uncommon in Sidney) which gives the poem its special flavor. Another, and somewhat more elaborate, version of this poem exists in sonnet form.

13. *"With how sad steps, O moon, thou climb'st the skies!"* Notice how the opening lines consist of words of one syllable each: this, with the two long vowels of "O moon" side by side in the middle of the line, slows down the pace of the line and makes the poem open softly on a note of slow plaintiveness. In the third line the tempo changes abruptly, as the poet moves from melancholy to bitterness. That "What!" at the beginning of the line brings the reader up short, and he turns his attention from the moon to the poet, who is, of course, the real subject of the poem. Consider the kind of *tone* which the questions in the last five lines provide.

This sonnet is similar in arrangement to Wyatt's (No. 1), but handles the tercets differently. Although the last two lines rhyme, the sonnet is not balanced on the final couplet: the last line rings out by itself.

14. *"Come sleep! O sleep, the certain knot of peace."* Notice how an invocation to sleep is deftly turned at the end into a love poem to Stella. Consider what effect is achieved by the series of epithets for sleep in the second, third, and fourth lines. It might be worth while, too, to examine the effect of the line

O make in me those civil wars to cease

in the very center of the poem.

Line 5. prease: press.

15. *"Stella oft sees the very face of woe."* The interest of this sonnet lies in the technical accomplishment with which the idea which is developed in the poem is adapted to the sonnet form. One might almost say that the whole poem exists for the sake of the last line, in which the final point emerges with effective aptness. There is a kind of poetry where the form *can* be separated from the content, and the value lies in the apt fitting of one to the other. Most Elizabethan sonnets have this kind of value. Would you say that this is true of the previous poem?

16. *"Leave me, O love, which reachest but to dust."* This is Sidney's famous farewell to love, written after he had already produced the sequence of love sonnets, *Astrophel and Stella* (from which the two previous poems are taken). One might call this a rhetorical sonnet: it is full of a sonorous eloquence, a deliberate gravity of utterance, which begins in the first line with its four opening strong beats—Leáve mé, Ó lóve. He finds difficulty in sustaining that sonority of tone, and in the ninth line takes breath again, as it were, with "O take fast hold," another four strong beats together. This is the "English" or Shakespearean form of the sonnet, with a heavily weighted final couplet which points the moral. The poet had begun by dismissing earthly love, and by the end of the poem he has crossed the seas of self-persuasion to anchor securely in divine love. There is a deliberate parallelism between the opening

Leave me, O love, which reachest but to dust

and the concluding

Eternal Love, maintain thy life in me,

and it is worth examining carefully how the poet moves from one statement to the other.

17. *"My mind to me a kingdom is."* This is an excellent example of a simple, didactic kind of poetry which has always been popular yet which is so rarely well done. Here the confidently tripping iambic feet marching through the stanzas with their neat rhymes—alternating at first, and coming sententiously together at the end of each verse—reinforce the note of almost debonair confidence which gives a faint swagger to the moral tone of the poem. The poem might be compared with John Pomfret's *The Choice* (No. 121), written over a hundred years later at the opening of the eighteenth century in a very different moral and social atmosphere. Pomfret's recipe for content, and his means of expressing it poetically, are significantly different from Dyer's.

Line 12. For why: because.

18. *"Love, the delight of all well-thinking minds."* Notice how each line in this ingenious poem contains a new thought, yet how artfully the lines are linked. Observe, too, how the poem turns back upon itself in the final couplet. The first four lines read like a series of philosophical propositions, but they are turned into a compliment to the poet's mistress (who is, of course, the subject of the poem) in the couplet that concludes the stanza. The second stanza can now concentrate directly on the lady, and it does so with an expansiveness (note the effectiveness of the disyllabic rhymes—"pleasure" with "measure") lacking in the first. In the third and last verse philosophy and compliment flourish together equally, moving the poem easily into the final couplet, in which the four words, "love," "delight," "virtue," and "reason," which figured in the first verse as objects of philosophic definition, now join in direct compliment to the lady.

This is in many ways a typical Renaissance poem: Greville has that mixture of eager philosophical curiosity and aesthetic sensitivity possessed by so many men of the age. He was a close friend of Sir Philip Sidney.

19. *"I with whose colors Myra drest her head."* This fine poem has a magnificent directness. The repeated "I" of the first three lines gives a fine note of indignation, and the subsequent picture of his earlier relationship with Myra, besides being "full of country customs" (as Geoffrey Bollough, Greville's editor, has pointed out) possesses a most impressive immediacy. That angry "I" begins all the stanzas except the last, where the poem moves from indignation to reflection. The thought of the last four lines is that while the cautious Myra would kiss him, a kiss leaving no imprint, she would never put her love in writing.

Line 12. follow Cupid for his loaves and fishes: he does not want to be one of five thousand competing for her favors.
 15. committed theft: i.e., stole glances.
 19. Argus: of the hundred eyes, sent by Hera to watch over Io, but sent to sleep by Hermes' playing on his flute.
 20. Greville is referring to the myth in which Vulcan finds his wife Venus making love with Mars and, surrounding the two with a net, exposes them to the laughter of the gods. The thought is: Do our present-day Vulcans keep strong men away from their loves with nets, forcing them out into the cold?
 29. as: so that. leave: stop.

20. *"Who can live in heart so glad."* This lighthearted country song, with its fast-moving octosyllabic meter, represents one of the many kinds of pastoral poetry to be found in this period. The impulse to write about shepherds and shepherdesses living and loving in an idealized rustic setting seems to be a perennial one with urban man, and at least from the time of the Sicilian Greek Theocritus (third century B.C.) a pastoral tradition had existed in European literature; by the sixteenth century it had developed many forms and conventions. Satire, political and religious argument, elegy, debate, and compliment, had all been put into pastoral dress, as though a context of country labor gave an elemental force to the presentation of the theme. The elemental nature of agricultural activity makes it an effective symbol of man at work, abstracted from any trivializing factors, and pastoral love poetry can thus at its best attain a kind of purity—a simplicity, in the best sense of the word—in presenting sex against a background (either explicit or implied) of idealized but fruitful labor. It is this which in large measure accounts for the charm and freshness of Nicholas Breton's pastoral. It might be compared in movement and feeling with Milton's *L'Allegro* (poem No. 109), which has a much deeper moral feeling and a more elaborate structure, while at the same time preserving something of the pastoral simplification of life.

21. *The Passionate Shepherd to His Love.* This is the very essence of pastoral idealism. Consider the devices—meter, rhyme scheme, line lengths, imagery—which enable Marlowe to build up the atmosphere of this poem so successfully.

22. *The Nymph's Reply to the Shepherd.* A reply to the previous poem. Note how much more slowly the lines move, and consider the effect of the disyllabic rhymes ("roses," "posies"; "forgotten," "rotten") in the fourth verse; notice, too, the repeated "r's" in the last line of that verse. Observe how the spaciousness of the opening line

If all the world and love were young

gives way to narrower and more specific images, until the poem expands again in the final verse.

23. *"Even such is Time."* This piece, which was probably although not certainly written by Ralegh (but is not the epitaph on himself it has traditionally been taken to be), has the lapidary quality we associate with the verse epitaph and moral verse epigram.

24. *To His Son.* Here we have a rather striking idea worked out in verse with neatness and dexterity.

25. *The Passionate Man's Pilgrimage.* In a manuscript version this poem is entitled "Verses made by Sir Walter Ralegh the night before he was beheaded," but it was probably written in 1603 when he was expecting execution which did not take place, however, until 1618. Note the tenseness of the verse (and how the effect is achieved), which hurries to its close, where, in the last two lines, the tension relaxes and the poem ends slowly. Note the line lengths.

26. *"It fell upon a holy eve."* The reader who cannot rejoice in this happily dancing poem is beyond salvation by critical commentaries. This comes from the eighth (August) eclogue of Spenser's *Shepherd's Calendar*.

Line 3. wont: are accustomed to. shrieve: hear confession and give absolution.

    8. spill: injure.
  14. greete: mourning.
  15. saye: fine cloth.
  23. wood: mad.
  27. roved: shot.
  35. levin: lightning.
  43. gryde: pierced.
  64. prief: proof.

27–30. These four sonnets of Spenser's (from his *Amoretti*, a sonnet sequence addressed to his future wife) are most effective examples of what can be done in this verse form. The first has a very interesting movement; lines five to twelve develop a point with deliberate repetition of phrase, and the final couplet is a logical conclusion of the sequence of thought as well as the natural conclusion of the form of the stanza. Consider the metrical variations within the individual lines, and their relation to the development of the thought. The second of these sonnets is more deliberately weighted and possesses a fine sonority. Note the effect of the repetition in the second last line (love, dear love): it forces a pause, produces two strong beats together (deár lóve), and so heightens the emotion. Consider the characteristic qualities of the other two, and note the rhyme scheme of all four. One can see what an easy mastery Spenser has over his medium, compared with Wyatt as a sonnet writer.

31. *Prothalamion.* This is a wedding song, written by Spenser in celebration of the double wedding of Lady Elizabeth and Lady Catherine Somerset, daughters of Edward Somerset, Earl of Worcester, to Henry Guilford and William Petre, in 1596. The massive and musical stanza he uses so effectively here derives from the Italian *canzone,* a stanza form which weaves together lines of differing lengths with irregularly recurring rhymes. Notice the *architectonic* quality both of the individual stanza and of the poem as a whole: each stanza is built up into a beautifully balanced structure, while the poem as a whole, which is a narrative told in simple chronological sequence, moves in stately, processional fashion from the introduction, describing the poet wandering rather gloomily by the banks of the Thames, to the final picture of the two bridegrooms coming forth to greet the brides (who are symbolically represented as white swans).

A careful *listening* to this poem will reveal how completely Spenser had mastered those heavier measures which caused Wyatt so much trouble. Here is complete domination of the language, an ability to work it into an impressive fabric, rich both pictorially and musically, a poise and a balance in the handling of lines and verses which show complete technical maturity. It is easy to see, even from this one poem, why Spenser has traditionally been regarded as the greatest nondramatic poet of his age, the greatest since Chaucer, and, with Milton, one of the topmost peaks in English nondramatic poetry.

Notice the effect of the varying line lengths, especially of the two short lines which precede the last two lines of each stanza. The effect is that of a wave curling in on itself before crashing over and spreading out. (This effect is even more vivid in the *Epithalamion*, the poem Spenser wrote in celebration of his own wedding, where the final line, which, as in the *Prothalamion*, is the refrain, has an extra foot. The *Epithalamion* is not included in this collection, but it is worth looking up and comparing with this poem.)

The poem opens with a hushed picture of early morning. The first line inverts at once the basic iambic metrical scheme of the poem to emphasize the word "calm." (Note the metrical pattern of the phrase "calm was the day" and its relation to the iambic pentameter which is the underlying rhythm of this line.) A sense of brooding expectation is distilled in the first four lines. Then, in a sudden short line, the poet turns to himself, moodily walking by the river. (Spenser was in fact at this time in London, hoping in vain for an appointment from the Queen which would save him from the necessity of returning to his virtual exile in Ireland.) Immediately the "silver streaming Thames," with all the sights and sounds surrounding it, comes into the poem to provide its dominant imagery. The Thames, with its flowery banks, has already "eased his pain" and charged his mood before he meets the nymphs in the second stanza. The gentle, purling sound of the Thames brings this first stanza to a close and is to run as rippling refrain throughout the poem.

The proper expectation having been set up in the first stanza, Spenser introduces us in the second stanza to the "nymphs" who are gathering flowers for the wedding. Here every device is used to create an atmosphere of innocent freshness and beauty. There is a deliberately old-fashioned use of English ("feateously" and "on hye" sounded old-fashioned even to Spenser's contemporaries), and the touch of conscious artifice which this provides adds that note of ceremoniousness so important to the poem.

The swans represent the two brides, and this kind of symbolism is perfectly appropriate to the poem, which has a tapestry quality, a note of almost heraldic stylization, which Spenser manages to combine (consider how!) with the fresh, autobiographical note on which he opened. We must remember, too, that the Thames was the great highway of London at this period, the very spirit and symbol of the city, while its swans were famous. This is a London poem, and the city's river is from the beginning both the poet's accompaniment and his inspiration.

The greeting of the swans by the nymphs in the fourth and fifth stanzas is done with fine ceremony, the classical references (Peneus, Tempe) strengthening the note of happy formality. The benediction pronounced on the swans by one of the nymphs has a grave stateliness unsurpassed in English poetry. Consider the effect of the placing of the pauses, the nature of the rhymes, and the variation of line length, in the first five lines alone:

> Ye gentle birds, the world's fair ornament,
> And heaven's glory, whom this happy hour
> Doth lead into your lovers' blissful bower,
> Joy may you have and gentle heart's content
> Of your love's couplement.

Note how the emphasis moves up gently until it falls emphatically on "Joy" in the fourth line, inverting the iambic pattern. This whole stanza is worth reading carefully, and reading aloud.

The gravity and formality of the poem does not exclude a personal note on which, as we have seen, the *Prothalamion* opened. It recurs in the eighth stanza when London becomes "merry London" and the poet's "most kindly nurse." The poet, as one of the well-wishers of the two couples, does not have to keep himself in the background even during the more ceremonious parts of the activity. These autobiographical touches also help to keep the poem from stiffening into a painted back-cloth. This ceremonious procession increases the grace and beauty of the living figures, gives life an aesthetic quality by imposing a *style* on it, but the figures *are* living and it *is* life we are looking at.

The poem ends with just a tinge of abruptness. It might have been better to conclude with the two bridegrooms welcoming their brides—a picture of arrested movement, a tableau on which the curtain could be rung down—instead of moving on to give a very summary account of the wedding ("Which at th' appointed tide/ Each one did make his bride"). But the refrain restores calm evenness of pace at the end.

Line　3. delay: allay.
　　13. variable: various.
　　27. feateously: neatly, delicately.
　　28. on hye: in haste.
　　38. Lee: apparently means simply "stream."
　　67. Somers-heat: a pun on the name Somerset.
　110. undersong: refrain, or accompaniment.
　121. shend: surpass.
　137. a stately place: Essex House, by the Thames, was former Leicester House, residence of the Earl of Leicester, Spenser's old patron.
　153. The reference is to Robert Devereux (French "heureux," happy) second Earl of Essex, who was then at the height of his glory, having recently engaged in a brilliantly successful attack on Cadiz.
　173. twins of Jove: Castor and Pollux, the "Gemini" (twins) of the zodiac.
　174. baldric of the heavens: belt of the heavens—i.e., the zodiac.

　　32–43. Shakespeare's sonnets are not so immensely superior to the sonnets of some of the other Elizabethans as his plays are to other Elizabethan plays, but they possess a fine cogency of utterance and a firm intellectual structure not easily paralleled. Shakespeare makes no attempt to run the same two pairs of rhymes through the octave, but has two different pairs in each quatrain. His sonnets are in fact built of three quatrains, with different alternate rhymes in each and a concluding couplet. Observe how he uses the couplet in each of these sonnets. Consider the advantages which Shakespeare's more flexible rhyme scheme gives him, and how he avails himself of them. Read No. 42 carefully and see if you can see anything in its movement and technique which distinguishes it from the others. Notice in No. 43 the rejection of the usual Petrarchan compliments, and consider what this does to the poem.

32. Line　4. date: end.
　　　　10. ow'st: ownest.
33. Line　7. art: skill.
　　　　10. haply: by chance.
34. Line　6. dateless: without fixed conclusion.
　　　　8. expense: loss.
　　　　9. grievances foregone: past griefs.
　　　　10. tell: count.

36. Line 13. Judgement: Judgement Day.
40. Line 3. Gor'd: injured.
     4. made new friends and in so doing neglected old ones.
     7. blenches: glances aside.
41. Line 4. remover: inconstant one.
     8. Although the altitude of a star is known, its influence and value
      are unknown.
42. Line 1. expense: expenditure.
     2. till action: until expressed in action.

44. *Winter*. This vivid little etching of winter—reminding one of Flemish realism in painting—comes at the end of Shakespeare's early comedy, *Love's Labour's Lost*. Note the deft contrast between the chill imagery of the world outside and the warm and homely (in both senses of the word!) interior imagery. The secret of this poem's success in creating so convincingly the very feel of an Elizabethan country winter lies largely in the selection and organization of the images. How much less effective the poem would be if Joan were not "greasy." But consider also what is achieved by the rhyme and metrical schemes and the owl-call refrain.

Line 9. keel: cool by stirring.
  11. saw: maxim.
  14. crabs: crab apples.

45. *"O mistress mine."* This song from *Twelfth Night* has that haunting mixture of happiness and melancholy—the melancholy echoing gently in the background—characteristic of many of the incidental songs in Shakespeare's plays. Consider how this effect is achieved.

46. *"Fear no more the heat o' the sun."* This dirge (song for the dead) is from *Cymbeline*. Notice the pause at the end of the fourth line of the first verse, followed by the moral, as it were; and note the imagery here—*golden, chimney-sweepers, dust*. The fourth stanza is quite different in tone and movement from the other three. Is this a defect?

47. *"When men shall find thy flower, thy glory, pass."* This is a favorite theme in European poetry. Compare its treatment here with that in Yeats's sonnet "When you are old" (No. 337), which is itself based on a well-known sonnet of the sixteenth-century French poet Ronsard.

48. *"Since there's no help, come let us kiss and part."* This is from Drayton's sonnet sequence to "Idea." Notice the significant pause after the eighth line, and the turn in the mood and meaning which follows.

49. *A Coronet for his Mistress Philosophy*. This sonnet is an interesting variation of the conventional Petrarchan subject, though of course it depends on the prevalence of that conventional subject for a large part of its effect.

50. *"His golden locks time hath to silver turned."* The poem is built on the contrast between two pairs of images and ideas—summed up in the last two lines of the first verse. Notice how this contrasting imagery is handled, and consider the kind of resolution to be found in the last verse, where the aged former knight turns beadsman. Notice also how the stanza form, with its slow-moving lines and its pair of rhymes at the end of each verse, builds up the proper movement for this kind of subject.

51. *"Adieu, farewell earth's bliss."* An impressive treatment of a familiar theme. The short but heavy lines, with the pauses coming at the end of each, provide a ritual and a penitential note, while the refrain tolls like a bell throughout the poem. Examine the effect of the abstract noun "brightness" in the third verse—indeed, the effect of that whole line, so simple and so final, is worth inquiry. Consider how a simple classical allusion (Helen's eye, Hector brave) can add depth and poignancy. Helen was, of course, ideally beautiful, and Hector ideally brave. These characters have become symbols. Could those lines have the same effect to a reader unacquainted with the parts played by Helen and Hector in Greek story and in subsequent literature? It is sometimes difficult to draw a distinction between the simple denotational meaning of a word and the meaning it derives from all sorts of implied references, historical, mythological, or literary. Historical knowledge is thus often necessary for the reader who wishes to appreciate poetry fully, in order that he may be in a position to receive the full impact of the words' meanings. What is contained in a poem is contained only for those who know how to release it: a poem in Greek looked at by someone who knew no Greek would be only a series of marks on paper.

52. *"Golden slumbers kiss your eyes."* This musical lullaby positively sings itself to the reader. A large part of its effect depends on the shift in rhyme and in some degree in rhythms after the second line of each verse. The third line begins with a dactyl (— ∪ ∪), and imparts a lilt and a rocking motion to the poem.

53. *"Call for the robin redbreast and the wren."* This "mad song" comes from Webster's strangely powerful play, *The White Devil*. Note the desolation of the line

The friendless bodies of unburied men

and the uncanny effect of the list of animals which follows.

54. *"Hark, all you ladies."* Thomas Campion, a musician as well as a poet, had a fine ear for movement and vowel music in poetry. Notice the effect of the repetition of the same second line in each verse, and observe the sudden shutting off of musical echoes in the very last line. What is achieved by this? And what is achieved by the shift in movement in the last four lines of each verse?

55. *"When thou must home to shades of underground."* Note how this grave and beautifully balanced poem moves towards its remarkable climax. The first verse begins with "when," and the second, after a slight pause, with "then," thus neatly complementing the thought. Then, after the tenth line of the second verse, there is another pause, and the poet moves forward to the final, startling statement, in which both "when" and "then" are contained—

When thou hast told these honors done to thee,
Then tell, O tell, how thou didst murder me.

This adroit placing of the "when's" and "then's" in the poem helps to provide that balance which is one of its most interesting features. And note how that final *murder me* springs out at the reader, to shock the poem to a conclusion.

56. *"Rose-cheeked Laura, come."* Campion was much concerned with problems of poetic technique and craftsmanship, and discussed them in a tract entitled *Observations in the Art of English Poesy.* In this tract he argued against the use of rhyme, maintaining that by the careful patterning of long and short syllables, as in the poetry of Greece and Rome, a more harmonious poetry could be achieved. "The world is made by symmetry and proportion, and is in that respect compared to music, and music to poetry." "Rose-cheeked Laura" is one of the many poems included in this tract as examples of effective unrhymed English poetry, and it is one of the few wholly successful examples of unrhymed lyric poetry (as distinct from blank verse) in English. The basic metrical beat is trochaic, and this enables Campion to linger on the opening syllable of a line and bring out the full quality of the vowel. "Vowel music"— the exploitation of the varying sounds of vowels chiming against each other without rhyming—is most effectively employed by Campion in this poem, and should be listened for.

57. *"Follow your saint."* A very skilful lyric: note the variations in line lengths.

58. *Inviting a Friend to Supper.* An excellent example of "occasional" poetry, that is, of poetry written for some specific social occasion, fairly low-pressured, but elegant, dexterous, and unpretentious in tone. This is a kind of poetry that the more sophisticated literary critic tends to ignore, for one cannot demonstrate any deep spiritual insight or magnificently paradoxical use of language in this skilful social verse. But this kind of relaxed poetry is an important part of literature, and should not be ignored because it does not represent the highest form of poetic expression. The reader of poetry who has not learned to enjoy this "familiar" or "occasional" verse is missing a great deal. Compare Milton's sonnet to Mr. Lawrence (No. 113) and some of Prior's poems (Nos. 123–127).

59. *On my First Son.* A finely turned, lapidary poem, showing perfect control of the emotion and no squandering of self-pity.

60. *Epitaph on S. P.* The charm and grace and quietly subdued pathos of this skilful epitaph represent a technical accomplishment of a high order.

61. *Epitaph on Elizabeth, L. H.* Another example of the carefully chiseled verse epitaph. Ben Jonson excelled in this kind of verse.

62. *Song, to Celia.* Many of Jonson's verse epigrams and epitaphs are modeled on the epigrams of the Roman poet Martial, but in this well-known song he is weaving together notions derived from a number of different passages in a collection of love letters (*Epistolae Eroticae*) by the late Greek prose writer Philostratus. Jonson was always the conscious craftsman, and did not believe that poetry welled up unbidden from sources of inspiration beyond the knowledge or control of the poet.

63. *"Queen and huntress, chaste and fair."* The "queen and huntress" is the goddess Diana, but a complimentary reference to Queen Elizabeth is also in-

tended. The poem is from Jonson's play, *Cynthia's Revels.* Note how the trochaic movement gives vigor and energy to the verse.

64. *"Still to be neat."* From Jonson's play, *Epicœne, or the Silent Woman.* Note how the middle couplet of the first stanza binds the stanza together: the pause occurs in the middle of the couplet. The same device is used in the second stanza.

65. *A Proper New Ballad.* This lively song, with its fine swinging move- ment, is a lighthearted lament for the disappearance of country superstitions as a result of the spread of Puritanism. "There never was a merry world," wrote the seventeenth-century antiquary John Selden, "since the fairies left dancing and the parson left conjuring." Over a hundred years later Bishop Hurd, comparing earlier ages of romantic imagination with his own age of rationality and decorum, concluded: "What we have gotten by this revolution, you will say, is a great deal of good sense. What we have lost, is a world of fine fabling."

Note the effect of the extra syllable in the fifth and seventh lines of each verse.

Line 57. William Chourne: the servant of Dr. Hutten, Corbet's father-in-law.

66. *The Good-Morrow.* The direct break into the poem with a passionate question is characteristic of Donne. We get the impression in the first stanza that the passion carves out the stanza form, and that, the form having been carved out, subsequent verses are molded to that form with more deliberate craftsmanship. Donne's openings have a quality difficult to parallel in English poetry.

The second stanza moves much more slowly and musically than the first, which is deliberately jerky in movement. After the opening outburst there is a pause; then, beginning with the first line of the second stanza, the poem swells out into a much more ample verse.

There is a powerful, logical mind working in Donne's poems, and by ex- pressing itself in subtle logical forms the passion, far from being diminished, is made more articulate and more individual. Consider, for example, the development of the thought in the first stanza. He begins with a rhetorical question, then, unexpectedly, answers it seriously in the affirmative: all previous love affairs were simply anticipatory dreams of the present one: they *had,* in fact, "snorted in the seven sleepers' den" before they fell in love with each other.

The second stanza builds on the thought of the first. If they had been asleep and dreaming in their previous experience, they are awake now—and he there- fore appropriately turns to his love and bids her good morning. Theirs are now at last "waking souls." As they watch each other, awake and in love, it occurs to the poet that the verb "watch" also suggests jealousy or suspicion, so he proceeds at once to develop the point that their mutual watching is not based on fear: their love has reduced the whole world to their two selves, and in watching each other they "possess one world." Notice the characteristic pushing of the thought in, "Each *hath* one [i.e., one world] and *is* one."

In the third stanza he develops the geographical imagery very effectively, then moves to a sudden climax with the philosophical statement, "Whatever dies was not mixed equally." This thought, and its development in the two final lines, derive from scholastic philosophy. The notion is that simple elements (the soul, for example,) cannot be dissolved, nor can those compounds which are made up of perfectly compatible elements. ("Corruption is not found except where contrariety is found," wrote St. Thomas Aquinas. "Generation and corruption spring from contrariety and exist in contrariety.") Thus the unity of their two loves is proof of their love's immortality.

The ordinary Petrarchan sonneteer had used time and again the notion that the lover was wounded by a glance from his lady's eye, but Donne develops this idea of mutual glancing in quite a new way, and anchors his thought in very precise, if not always simple, philosophical concepts. Consider also the significance in this poem of words such as "sea-discoverers," "maps," "hemispheres."

Line 4. The seven sleepers' den: Donne is referring to the story of the seven young men of Ephesus who took refuge in a cave during the persecution of Christians by the Emperor Diocletian; they fell asleep, and were entombed, but were found alive over two hundred years later.

13. "Let maps have shown worlds on worlds to others."

67. *Woman's Constancy.* Again we have the sudden opening question. Note the effect of the short lines (lines 4, 11, 15, and 16). The poem turns unexpectedly in line 14 and moves to a most effective conclusion.

68. *The Sun Rising.* Here again the poem opens in a great burst of energy, with a violent question couched in realistic, colloquial language. Note how the shape of the stanza (the varied line lengths, etc.) is molded by the thought and the passion. As the poem develops, everything becomes concentrated more and more on that one bed where the lovers lie: the contracting of the whole world into that single epitome of all experience is the main theme of the poem (cf. "The Good-Morrow"). Note how this idea is developed out of the opening image of the sun shining in on them. The last two lines of the second stanza concentrates the idea in an image of extreme force, and the final stanza expands its significance and draws out its implications, returning to the sun and its shining on them with a new meaning.

Line 17. i.e., The East Indies (source of spices) and The West Indies (source of gold).

69. *The Canonization.* Once again we have the abrupt and passionate opening, with the passionate thought molding the shape of the first stanza. The temperature drops somewhat (as so often in Donne) in the succeeding stanzas, where, after a pause, he begins to brood over his passion and reason about it. But it rises again to a fine climax in the last verse, which is the invocation addressed by the public to the lovers, who have become "canonized for love." The poem has a most interesting progression. The first stanza dismisses the gossips with angry contempt—let them leave him alone to love, and do whatever else they please. The second stanza carefully separates the lovers from the common world: their loving does not affect the outside world, which goes on as usual, with all its follies and disasters, in spite of this love affair. (This is first cited as a reason for the world's leaving them alone and not interfering, but by the end of the stanza it has served to bring a spotlight on the isolated lovers.) The lovers having been removed from any distracting context, the poet concentrates on their love in the next two stanzas, elaborating its nature and stressing its intensity by a variety of ingenious but wholly apt images (note, in the third stanza, the image of the tapers, the references to the eagle and the dove, the riddle of the phoenix, and the notion that "to one neutral thing both sexes fit"). ⌊The description of their love by analogies and metaphors reaches its climax in the fourth stanza, where the ˋcarefully worked-out notion of their dying by love brings the idea that instead of an elaborate funeral monument they will be commemorated in well-wrought verse, which will reveal that they have been canonized for love. It is to this idea of canonization that the whole poem has been working, and the concluding stanza effectively utilizes it by introducing an invocation to the canonized lovers, bringing the poem to a new climax of intensity.

Line   7. stamped: i.e., on coins.
      14. plaguy bill: weekly list of deaths from the plague.
      22. the eagle and the dove: i.e., each being both.
      23. phoenix: the miraculous bird which, having been consumed with fire after living five hundred years, was born anew out of the ashes.
      26. die: this verb also had the secondary meaning of achieving consummation in sexual intercourse. Donne plays with this notion obliquely here and in line 28. Note the connection of this idea with the image of the phoenix.

70. *Lovers' Infiniteness.* This poem has a much graver and more musical line than is characteristic of Donne's secular poems. But as usual it opens with an arresting statement: its effect is heightened by breaking the sentence with "Dear" at the opening of the second line. The first verse states the central idea, the second elaborates it with images and ideas largely derived from the law, and the third turns back on itself, as it were, and resolves the paradox by showing how he can accept both sides of the question at once. The thought is not difficult to follow if the poem is read carefully. The reader will get little out of Donne if he reads the poems in a vague romantic haze: he must use his mind keenly at each point, for with Donne the thought helps to light up the passion, and the intellectual ingenuities are the other side of a tense emotional movement.

71. *Song: "Sweetest love, I do not go."* This has something of the movement of a typical Elizabethan song lyric, but the development of the thought is in fact much more subtle and more thorough than in a characteristic piece from an Elizabethan songbook. Note how, after a careful development of the main idea, Donne in his final four lines achieves a magnificent note of calm serenity.

72. *A Nocturnal upon St. Lucy's Day.* St. Lucy's day (December 13) was, according to the old calendar style, the shortest day of the year. But the "Lucy" has also been held to be a reference to Lucy, Countess of Bedford: in which case the poem was written in December, 1612, when the Countess of Bedford was dangerously ill, and the poem anticipates her death. Whether we accept this or not (and it is a dubious interpretation), the poem is an elegy, and the combination of "the year's midnight" and the poet's loss produces in the poet a sense of utter desolation, whose nature he explores and describes in a variety of carefully worked out analogies. "This poem," remarks Sir Herbert Grierson, "illustrates Donne's strength and weakness, his power to produce an intense impression by the most abstract means, here an impression of the sense of nothingness which may overtake one who has lost the central motive of his life. But here and there he refines too much and weakens the effect." The reader must make up his own mind on this question of refining too much, and how far ingenuity of thought can work profitably in a poem without producing too labored and frigid an effect.

The first stanza is masterly, with its carefully wrought picture of a world deprived of all vitality, and the sudden shift at the end of the stanza to the poet himself, far more dead than the dead world, the dead world's very Epitaph. Having moved the poem to himself, he concentrates on picturing his nothingness, the complete emptiness of his being. After the somewhat rugged movement of the middle verses, the poem slows down at the end to a grave and mournful pace with a return to the original thought, now enriched by his own fully developed mood and his orientation towards the dead woman who "enjoys her long night's festival."

Line 3. flasks: powder flasks.
     12. every dead thing: i.e., he is the very sum and quintessence of pure nothingness. Cf. line 15, and the whole of stanza four.
     21. limbec: alembic, still.
     29. elixir: quintessence. "Made nothing by Love, by the death of her he loves he is made the elixir (i.e., the quintessence) not now of ordinary nothing, but of 'the first nothing,' the nothing which preceded God's first act of creation. The poem turns upon the thought of degrees in nothingness." (Grierson)
     39. Goat: Capricorn, one of the signs of the zodiac. The goat was associated with lust.

73. *Love's Deity.* Note once again the strangely powerful opening two lines. The attitude to love presented here is very far from that of the conventional Petrarchan sonneteers, whom in a sense the poet is attacking.

Line 6. vice-nature: deputy for nature.
     26. she loves before: she already has another love.

74. *The Funeral.* The haunting elegiac note is achieved in this poem by very interesting means. Consider the imagery of the opening stanza, and its rhythms. The thought is carefully worked out, and follows the curve of the emotion most effectively.

Line 9. sinewy thread: spinal cord.
     23. bravery: boldness, swagger.

75. *"Death, be not proud."* Donne's religious poems are as a rule very different in tone from his secular love poems, and have a graver movement. This "holy sonnet" has a massive quality to it not easily paralleled among the *Songs and Sonnets* (from which the preceding poems by Donne are taken). Note that Donne uses the same modification of the Petrarchan sonnet as that employed by Wyatt.

76. *"Batter my heart, three-personed God."* This powerful poem, with its fiercely sudden opening, shows the intense inner conflicts out of which Donne's

religious faith developed. It might be contrasted with the more equable religious poems of George Herbert. Note the important part played by paradox in this poem.

77. *A Hymn to God the Father.* This impressive religious lyric needs no commentary. Notice how effectively each stanza tapers down to that final line. There is, of course, a pun on "done" and "Donne" in the fifth line of each stanza: the pun in the seventeenth century was a serious poetic device in which identity or similarity of sound, combined with difference in meaning, could be made to contribute impressively to the total significance. It was not until the eighteenth century that the pun came to be regarded as a "low" figure of speech.

78. *The British Church.* The quality of Herbert's religious feeling is quite different from that of Donne. Herbert is a much more confident and contented member of the Anglican Church, that *via media* that stands midway between the Roman Catholic Church on the one side ("She on the hills") and Puritanism ("She in the valley") on the other. Contrast the calm and happy opening of this poem with Donne's "Batter my heart, three-personed God."
This poem, while it has a fine simplicity, is not in the least "soft." It has a grave precision of utterance, and concludes with a line of surprising sternness.

79. *The Church Floor.* Herbert's ideas are often as ingeniously worked out as Donne's, but he works with simpler and more concrete images. The quiet assurance suggested by the stanza form in the first four verses swells gently into a note of gratitude and benediction at the end. Notice the structure and rhyme scheme of each of the two parts of the poem, and the effect each achieves.

80. *Redemption.* The allegory here is startling in its ingenious simplicity: the little tale (which, of course, is an allegory of the Christian story of the redemption) begins on an almost casual note and moves briskly to its short conclusion.

81. *L-ve.* Nowhere has Herbert's delicate simplicity of style achieved a finer rendering of one aspect of the Christian view than in this deftly turned little poem.

82. *The Collar.* The dramatic opening here is somewhat reminiscent of Donne. But the poem as a whole has a quality quite different from Donne's. Herbert's internal struggles were less violent and more purely symbolic than Donne's. The poem works up, with subtle handling of rhythms and pauses, to a climax of rebellion, which is suddenly and effectively hushed at the conclusion. It has been suggested that the title is Herbert's spelling of "choler" (anger) and has nothing to do with "collar" in the modern sense.

Line 1. board: table.
  5. store: abundance.
  6. in suit: dancing attendance, hoping for favors or reward.
  9. cordial: restorative.
  14. bays: laurel wreath of triumph.
  29. Call in thy death's head: i.e., remove the emblems of mortality (which had hitherto restrained him from having a good time.)

83. *Virtue.* Perhaps the best known of Herbert's poems. The calm movement of the stanzas, the steady progression of the images, and the regular repetition of the refrain (varied slightly in each of the first three verses and reversed, as it were, at the conclusion) give a fine weight and balance to the poem. The metaphors and similes are handled with a precise logic. In the last verse Herbert means that "seasoned timber" is excellent fuel, and by glowing in the heart of a fire "chiefly lives" in a conflagration. But of course he is also referring to the final conflagration at the Day of Judgment—when the virtuous soul will "chiefly live."

Line 11. closes: in the musical sense, the conclusion of a musical phase or resolution of a series of chords.

15. coal: charcoal, ashes.

84. *A Song.* Crashaw's religious poetry has a note of passion, even of ecstasy, not to be found in either Donne or Herbert. This intense little poem derives much of its effect from the adaptation of the imagery of secular love poetry to describe a religious experience. Note how the stanza form contributes to the effect, with the final pair of rhymed couplets in each stanza coming to an emotional climax. There is an interesting relation between the pause after the first four lines of each stanza and that before the final two lines. The substitution of a trochee ($-$ ᴜ) for an iamb (ᴜ $-$) in the first foot of a climactic line ("Dead to myself, I live in thee") is a common technical device, and worth studying. The poem opens with a trochaic beat ("Lord, when the sense . . ."); there are also lines which open with two heavy stresses ("Ó lóve, I am thy sacrifice." "Stíll líve in me this loving strife."). Variations of this kind in such a short poem produce a fine flexibility that enables the verse to follow the curve of the emotion to its climax.

85. *The Waterfall.* The poet moves from contemplation of the waterfall to contemplation of the "sublime truths" of religion and of his own future spiritual state. Note how the transition is made. The first stanza is quite different in movement and structure from the two following: the long, slow lines cut by short, abrupt ones give the very feel of what is being described, and then as the poet's emotion rises under the influence of the religious ideas suggested by the waterfall the poem moves into a more regular beat. The march of the rhymed couplets in the second and third stanzas (they are verse paragraphs rather than stanzas) carries the reader steadily from the waterfall to the religious mood. Consider the difference between the opening of the second part ("Dear stream! dear bank"), with its spontaneous welling up of personal feeling, and the opening of the third ("O useful element and clear!"), which, though equally exclamatory, is on a different level, the poet's eyes being by now turned inward: contemplation of the waterfall has led him from simple pleasure in nature into a trancelike mood in which he turns what he sees into analogies of another kind of reality which eventually takes over the poem completely.

Lines 30–32. Cf. Genesis, I, 2: "And the Spirit of God moved upon the face of the waters." The verb translated "moved" in the King James Bible has a connotation of "hatching" or "brooding," and was so understood by several of the Church Fathers. Thomas Browne, in his *Religio Medici,* wrote: "This is that gentle heat that

brooded on the waters, and in six days hatched the world." Cf.
also Milton, *Paradise Lost*, I, 19–22:

> Thou from the first
> Wast present, and with mighty wings outspread
> Dove-like satst brooding on the vast Abyss
> And mad'st it pregnant.

86. *The World.* This remarkable poem does not quite live up to the promise
of its opening, which leaps at the reader with the calm assurance of a great
mystical utterance (we find something of the same assurance and calmness in
Blake). But it is a powerful piece, building up its mood and its argument
entirely by images, which are partly allegorical and symbolic, and partly
realistic. Notice the stanza form.

87. *"They are all gone into the world of light."* It is not often in poetry
that the sheer intensity of the poet's mental or emotional state carves out a
channel of expression for itself which, considered simply from the point of
view of technique, would not seem to be adequate. This simple verse form,
which does not appear to be handled with any special skill or subtlety as the
poet pushes on to say what he must say, nevertheless succeeds perfectly in conveying that reaching after the lost spiritual vision which is the subject of the
poem. The progression in the poem is not inevitable: in his excited state the
poet shifts from one point to another in an almost groping manner—yet at the
end he comes to rest in the perfect conclusion. The strong note of compulsion
that beats through the poem adds to its impressiveness: it is one of the great
spiritual utterances in English poetry. From the first line, with its immense
simplicity and cogency of utterance—note that it consists entirely of mono-
syllabic words—we are caught up into the poem, and we follow perforce
through the poet's experience to the concluding prayer. It is worth looking
carefully to see how Vaughan gets that compelling note into the poem.

Line   1. they: i.e., the heavenly spirits of whom he has had a vision.
   10. trample on my days: i.e., make my days appear contemptible by
     comparison.
   35. resume: take back. The poet is asking God to take back his (the
     poet's) spirit and restore it to a purely spiritual world.
   38. perspective (accent on first syllable): telescope.

88. *Wonder.* The almost mystical sense of the glory of innocent observation
here produces a poem whose deliberately naïve imagery creates a powerful impression of the freshness and the excitement of the world when first seen. This
was a favorite theme of Traherne's, whose prose meditations deal with it more
than once. The poem's bright colors and clear surfaces, its deliberate simplicity
of emotion, are not often successfully achieved in English poetry. The reader
might contrast some of Wordsworth's, whose simplicity is of a quite different
kind.

Line 49. proprieties: ownerships.

89. *The Garden.* This strangely beautiful poem works up into a distillation
of the very quintessence of "gardenness." Its effects do not, as a hasty reading
might suggest, depend mainly on the progression of the imagery, for the

imagery is itself built around a number of leading ideas, and the quality of the imagery changes only as one idea gives way to another. The poem opens with a turning away from vain human ambitions to the peace and quiet of the garden, and soon develops the notion that the garden provides a complete world in itself, with all that men seek in life being found there in ideal form —quiet, love, variety of sensual enjoyment, mental activity, spiritual activity. When the poet reaches the stanza describing the various sensual enjoyments provided by the garden, he slows down his pace, and indeed brings the poem to a stop for a while, to kindle in a very ecstasy of garden enjoyment (stanza 5). The mind then takes over, and succeeds in reducing everything "to a green thought in a green shade." The mood is by now trancelike, and so the poem moves naturally into a presentation of the spiritual possibilities of the garden, the poet's soul gliding in the boughs of trees to sit like a bird awaiting its "longer flight" to eternal bliss. The implied comparison between the heavenly and the earthly paradise leads naturally to a discussion of the Garden of Eden (a notion which had been indirectly suggested in the second stanza). The poem then ends on a note of benediction and relaxed happiness.

Line 1. amaze: perplex.
   7. close: join.
   37. curious: exquisite.
   41. from pleasure less: made less by pleasure (?). The thought seems to be that excess of pleasure has contracted the mind, and in this contracted state it can more easily resolve everything within it to greenness.

90. *Bermudas.* The singers of the song are supposed to be the early seventeenth-century settlers in Bermuda who went there to obtain religious freedom. The clear, bright imagery, the steady beat of the iambic octosyllables, and the simple optimism of the mood, give great charm to the poem.

Line 20. Ormus: Ormuz, a city on an island at the mouth of the Persian Gulf, known to seventeenth-century geographers as the gateway to the fabulous wealth of India, and therefore the very symbol of wealth and luxury. Cf. Milton, *Paradise Lost,* II, 1–2:

> High on a Throne of Royal State, which far
> Outshone the wealth of Ormus and of Ind . . .

   23. apples: pineapples.

91. *The Picture of Little T. C.* This poem has the freshness of imagery and of feeling so characteristic of Marvell. Note how he turns it to its conclusion.

92. *The Definition of Love.* An interesting "metaphysical" poem. Note the relation between the thought and the imagery, and the special effects achieved by the images from geography and geometry.

Line 24. planisphere: a projection of the globe on a plane surface.

93. *To his Coy Mistress.* This is a highly original and impressive poetic rendering of the "gather ye rosebuds while ye may" theme. The first part of the poem, in which the poet describes how he would love "had we but world enough and time," has a splendid extravagance of imagery which underlines the hypothetical nature of such a situation. In the second part he moves from this playful exercise of his imagination into a much more serious mood; the imagery becomes more personal and urgent, the tone more tense, the thought more searching, until we reach the packed ironical lines about the grave. (Note that a poet can be serious and ironical simultaneously: the ironic note in this second section of the poem emphasizes the poet's seriousness.) The third and final section, rejecting alike the hypothetical love-making of a timeless world and the haunting thought of the passing of time, concentrates on the present and narrows everything down to the present experience. There is a magnificent use of imagery throughout the poem that will repay the closest attention. Note also Marvell's use of the octosyllabic couplet: this simple-seeming verse form can be used in a great variety of ways—compare Prior, and Burns's "Tam o' Shanter."

94–102. Herrick, one of the "sons of Ben," was the disciple of Jonson who in many respects most effectively followed the master. Like Jonson, he had an ear for the Greek and Latin lyric, and his best poems have a neatness and a delicacy quite different from the richer tone and heavier texture of poems in the Petrarchan tradition. He had a lighter touch than Jonson, and he learned from Anacreon, Catullus, and Horace a franker paganism than Jonson ever professed. His nonreligious lyrics deal with "wine, women, and song," and the pleasures of the countryside, with a deliberate hedonism. His lyrics have little depth of feeling, and his love poems often have too much conscious gallantry about them. But the very limitations of his poetry constitute their chief virtue: he sustains a lighthearted tone very deftly, skirting the deeper emotions and producing a surface art of great elegance. He is often ingenious without being subtle, but at his best (in "To Daffodils" or "To Daisies" for example) his light touch in metrics and imagery achieves a work of real delicacy. He can turn a commonplace with a fine grace (as in "Gather ye rosebuds"), and can produce a lively impression of country customs and country mirth in such a poem as "The Hock-cart," where the rhymed octosyllabic couplets march along with a gay confidence and the imagery of rustic merrymaking builds up to a fine climax of hedonism. His religious poems are simple-minded and even naïve, with a childlike faith conquering a childlike fear: far removed indeed from Donne's holy sonnets.

94. Line 3. Hock-carts: the carts which brought in the last load of the harvest.
wakes: merrymakings.
96. Line 3. lawn: scarf of lawn or linen.
5. erring: wandering.
12. civility: good breeding, order.
99. Line 9. maukin: malkin, a coarse-colored cloth.
21. fill-horse: the horse that draws the cart ("fills" are the shafts of the cart).
40. fats: vats.
45. neat: cattle.
100. Lines 5–6. Sun, Dog, Triple Tun: names of London taverns.
102. Line 22. unflead: unflayed—hence uncut.

103. *The Spring*. A fresh and skilful variation of an old Petrarchan theme.

104. *A Song.* A charming and neatly turned poem in the tradition of Ben Jonson's "Drink to me only with thine eyes." Note the slow gravity with which the verse flows, and the effect of the repeated "Ask me no more" at the beginning of each stanza.

105. *Song.* This is "light" poetry at its best. Notice the effective turn (in both the thought and the mood) in the final stanza.

106. *"Out upon it! I have loved."* Another breezy little piece, done with a happy touch. This is a kind of poetry which the "cavalier poets" could handle very skilfully.

107. *To Althea, from Prison.* Notice the steady rising of the emotion, until it reaches its climax in the last four lines. The poem is built on a series of rather obvious paradoxes: it is the balancing of the thought within each smoothly moving stanza and the linking together of the whole by the mutual correspondence of the concluding lines of each verse, rather than any passionately witty working out of the central paradox, that gives the poem its appeal. Note the verse form and the effect of the pause after the first four lines of every stanza.

108. *On the Morning of Christ's Nativity.* This Christmas ode, one of the earliest of Milton's poems, consists of an introduction and hymn, both done with a combination of deliberate quaintness in imagery and "conceits" and a studied simplicity of feeling which produce a remarkable effect. Tillyard has compared the poem to a fifteenth-century Italian painting of the Nativity, with its combination of brilliant coloring and naïve juxtaposition of realistic and symbolic detail. It has indeed a remarkable pictorial quality, but it also has a significant musical quality both in the handling of the language and in the form of the whole. In structure it is like an "introduction and trio" in seventeenth-century music, with the introduction more heavily orchestrated and going at a graver tempo than the hymn which follows. There is a sense of movement in the poem, too: the poet states in the fourth verse (the last of the introduction) that he is going to bring his poem as an offering to the Infant Christ, "preventing" (i.e., going before) the Wise Men from the East who came bringing gifts, led by a star, and by the end of the poem the star has stopped over the birthplace, the journey of the Magi is over, and the gifts have been delivered.

The poem opens on a swelling note of triumph, with the normal iambic foot reversed into a trochee in

This is the month, and this the happy morn.

The seven-line stanza of the introduction is balanced effectively on the concluding long line. A sense of the Divine Order manifesting itself in this event emerges from this opening setting of the scene, especially in the last line of the third stanza, with its imagery of brightness and order:

And all the spangled host keep watch in squadrons bright.

The harmonious order of the heavens is a theme which runs right through the poem; it leads to the account of the music of the spheres (the result of the perfect harmony in the structure of the universe) and eventually the final stress on order and stability in the imagery of the very last line.

The sense of movement emerges in the fourth stanza, after which there is a shift in key and tempo, and the hymn begins. The stanza here, though also of seven lines and balanced on the final longer line, is lighter and moves faster. It is a strange and effective picture that Milton now gives us, of Nature "doffing her gaudy trim" in awe of the divine infant and "hiding her guilty front with innocent snow." These "conceits" may sound forced to modern ears, but they are part of the baroque style of the poem, and if we see them simply as too contrived or inappropriate we are not reading the poem properly. There is a species of conscious primitivism about this kind of imagery which has a charm of its own for the reader who can attune his ear to the poem's tone and style. The picture of "meek-eyed Peace" descending with dove's wings from the heavens, crowned with "olive green" and waving a "myrtle wand," is another of those brightly colored, stylized pictures in which the poem abounds.

Milton is using the old tradition that there was no war in the world at the time of the Nativity. Notice how the clanging images of battle ("spear," "shield," "chariot," "hostile blood," "trumpet," etc.) are suddenly hushed in the fifth stanza of the hymn, with an effective rustling of sibilants ("whist," "kissed," "whispering") producing a sense not only of quiet but also of arrested motion. The idea of arrested motion is developed in the next two stanzas. The stars "stand fixed in steadfast gaze" and the sun itself hesitates to rise. As the daily routine of the universe is stilled and halted in the presence of the divine event, we look down on the shepherds "simply chatting in a rustic row"—a most effective blending of realistic simplicity with symbolic grandeur. Our eye having been led from heaven to earth, our ears are accosted by the angelic music which greets the innocent shepherds below. As the music continues it suggests new visual images as well as moral ideas—images of cherubim and seraphim "in glittering ranks with wings displayed" and ideas of a heaven on earth and a total and permanent regeneration of mankind. The music of the spheres—that mystical symbol of the ultimate beauty and harmony of the universe—now rings out, and in the thirteenth verse of the hymn, which is the climactic moment of the poem, the poet, in an ecstasy of joy and hope, hails the divine music as harbinger of the golden age.

This notion of the music of the spheres (Pythagorean and Platonic in origin) was a favorite of Milton's, himself a keen musician. He seems to have believed that this heavenly music could not, as a rule, be heard by men after the Fall of Adam and Eve in Eden, but that a man who kept himself wholly pure and virtuous in his daily life might hope to be able to hear it. It is characteristic of the optimistic idealism of the young Milton that it is with the greatest reluctance that he tears himself away from contemplation of a wholly regenerate mankind developing at once as a result of the birth of the Infant Deity. In verse sixteen of the hymn he has to admit that "wisest fate says no": the golden age is not yet due—it will, in fact, have to await the second coming, and the sound of the great trumpet at the Last Judgment. The poem, one might almost say, starts out to be a triumphant celebration of the new golden age to be brought about by the birth of Christ, but history (to say nothing of theology) intervenes in the middle, and forces a more moderate conception on the poet.

From the climactic thirteenth stanza of the hymn, with its triumphant hailing of the music of the spheres, the poem gradually dies away to a close. But there is a minor rise and fall in this second half, describing Christ's victory over the pagan gods he has come to replace. Milton depicts the pagan gods as false, but not unreal (in *Paradise Lost* they are the fallen angels, deliberately deceiving mankind), and he gives us here a remarkable picture of the departure of the defeated deities. The oracle of Apollo now speaks no more, local divinities and woodland nymphs flee away weeping, pagan gods no more answer their worshippers, and the ritual of their priests and magicians is in vain. There is ample allusion here to both classical and Biblical story (it would never have occurred to Milton that he would be read by people who did not know the Bible and the Latin and Greek classics) and in his descriptions of strange pagan rites with the clashing of cymbals and "dismal dance about the furnace blue" he sounds what is almost an anthropological note, the note of Frazer's *The Golden Bough* and of travelers' accounts of weird observances among primitive peoples.

Milton has a wonderful time with names in this description of the "twilight of the gods." In listing the Egyptian gods he gives the effect of the strange horrors to be associated with their gloomy religion by lingering on the slow, musical syllables:

> Isis and Orus, and the dog Anubis, haste.

The daylight of Christianity conquers the twilight of superstition as

> The flocking shadows pale
> Troop to th' infernal jail

and there is an almost elegiac note in Milton's picture of their dismissal: after all, Milton was a classical humanist as well as a Christian, and he contemplated the departure of classical civilization with mixed feelings. This elegiac note is sounded most clearly in the twentieth stanza of the hymn, which describes the "voice of weeping" heard from springs and dales as nymphs and local gods depart. We are reminded of the Biblical description of "Rachel weeping for her children." This is enough to suggest the subdued feeling for the other side that manifests itself in this hymn to Christian victory over paganism.

Basically, however, it *is* a Christian victory or at least a victory of Christ over his pagan rivals. Christ himself is conceived not as the "suffering servant" or the man of sorrows (Milton did not like to dwell on the "Passion," on Christ crucified or suffering) but as the hero whose strength goes out from Judah's land while he is yet in the cradle, the Divine Babe who

> Can in his swaddling bands control the damned crew,

reminiscent of Hercules, who strangled snakes in his cradle.

The poem comes to a quiet close on two images—the first an image of nature, the sun rising, cushioning his head on the horizon as the pagan spirits flee before him, and the second a peaceful domestic image, of the Virgin laying her babe to rest. The star that led the Wise Men has now completed its journey and stands fixed over Bethlehem. The poem ends with a glance at the Divine Order surrounding the sleeping child:

> Bright-harnessed angels sit in order serviceable.

This image of rank, order, courtliness, and stability, gives Milton's conception of a harmonious universe, and on this note the poem ends.

Line 23. star-led wizards: the "wise men from the East" who were led by a star to the new-born child. (Matthew, 2.)

28. Cf. Isaiah, 6, 6–7: "Then flew one of the seraphim unto me, having a live coal in his hand, which he had taken with the tongs from off the altar: And he laid it upon my mouth, and said, Lo, this hath touched thy lips; and thine iniquity is taken away, and thy sin purged."

41. pollute: polluted.

59. awful: full of awe, respectful and reverent.

64. whist: hushed.

71. precious influence: referring to the astrological notion that the stars poured down an ethereal liquid which nourished life on the earth.

74. Lucifer: probably the planet Venus, the morning star.

75. orbs: the spheres in which, according to the Ptolemaic astronomy, the planets and stars were supposed to move, circling the earth, which was thought to be at the center.

89. Pan: the Greek god who was the special guardian of sheep and shepherds: this aspect of Pan led him to be associated with Christ quite early in the history of Christianity.

98. took: entranced, captivated.

100. close: see poem No. 83, note to line 11.

103. Cynthia: the moon. The reference is to the sphere in which the moon moved.

116. unexpressive: inexpressible.

119. Cf. Job 38, 6–7: "Whereupon are the foundations thereof fastened? or who laid the corner stone thereof; When the morning stars sang together, and all the sons of God shouted for joy?"

157–9. The reference is to the description of the giving of the law to Moses on Mount Sinai, in the nineteenth chapter of Exodus.

163–4. The last judgment.

186. Genius: *genius loci,* or local divinity.

191. Lars: Roman domestic gods, guardians of individual homes or families.
Lemures: spirits of the dead.

194. flamens: Roman priests.
quaint: ingenious.

197. Peor and Baalim: "Baalim" is the plural form of "Baal," the generic name of the supreme god of the ancient Canaanites. His individual manifestations took different forms and names; the shrine at Peor was known as "Baal-Peor."

199. This refers to the Philistine god, Dagon, whose image at Ashdod was "twice battered" miraculously. See I Samuel, 5, 4.

200. Ashtaroth: the Phoenician moon-goddess Ashtoreth or Astarte.

203. Hammon: an Egyptian god, with his chief shrine in Lybia.

204. Thammuz: the lover of Ashtoreth, whose death was annually mourned by the Tyrian (Phoenician) women as a symbol of summer beauty slain by the boar, winter. In Greece he became Adonis: cf. the story of Venus and Adonis.

205. Moloch: the most horrible of the ancient Palestinian gods: men used to sacrifice their children to him by burning.

212. Isis, Orus, Anubis: Egyptian gods. Orus (Horus) was a sun god.

Isis was his mother, Anubis was associated with the underworld and was shown with a jackal's head.

213. Osiris. Egyptian god, lord of the Nile: his chief shrine was at Memphis (hence "Memphian," line 214).

220. sable-stoled: black-robed.

226. Typhon: either the crocodile god of Egypt or the Greek serpent god overthrown by Zeus and Hercules.

240. youngest teemèd: most recently born.

244. bright-harnessed: attired in bright armor.

109. *L'Allegro*. *L'Allegro* and *Il Penseroso* are two companion poems, the former giving a poetic rendering of the activity of the cheerful man in an appropriate setting, the latter dealing with the thoughtful and melancholy man. Each poem creates a mood, and by a most skilful use of imagery achieves the tone and quality appropriate to the theme.

L'Allegro opens with nine violent lines quite different in mood and movement from the lines that follow. It is a crashing of chords, after which comes (following line 10) a long pause: then the smoothly tripping solo instrument takes up the main theme. The introduction dismisses melancholy with deliberately exaggerated horror: the imagery is extravagant and harsh, and the alternating long and short lines (contrasting with the even flow of the rest of the poem) emphasize this mood of mock indignation. This is the cheerful man cheerfully booting loathed melancholy out of the door. There follow the happily modulated lines in which appropriate mythological and pastoral imagery is developed in order to build up a mood of contented living.

It is a carefully stylized picture that Milton gives us, with his description of Euphrosyne, mirthful daughter of the west wind (Zephyr) and the dawn (Aurora); of a vine-covered rustic cottage, of milkmaids singing, mowers whetting their scythes, and shepherds making love under the hawthorn. The poem is full of light and movement. Its structure is chronological, beginning with "the dappled dawn" rising to the accompaniment of the lark's song, and going through a day of cheerful pastoral activities until sunset turns L'Allegro's thoughts to tournaments, pageants, poetry, and music. Milton exploits classical mythology, English folklore, and medieval romance in the course of this variegated poem, which is a study in the collocation of imagery to build up a mood, the whole presented in a cantering rhythm which adds its share to the total effect. The images are precise although generalized. The whole of the pastoral tradition, as well as the lore of the English countryside, lies behind such a simple-seeming couplet as

> And every shepherd tells his tale
> Under the hawthorn in the dale.

These stylized pictures—such as the cottage standing between two aged oaks in lines 80–81—are all the more effective for being stylized. This is a very formal art; every activity has its proper symbols (evening celebrations by the fire, for example, are accompanied by "nut-brown ale") and these symbols link the poem up at all points with a complex tradition in both art and life.

Line 2. Cerberus: the three-headed dog of the underworld.

3. Stygian: adjective from Styx, one of the rivers of the underworld.

5. uncouth: solitary, gloomy.

9. ragged: rugged.

10. Cimmerian: gloomy (the land of the Cimmerians was, according to Homer, a sunless land of cloudy gloom).

12. yclept: called.

Euphrosyne: Mirth, one of the three Graces. The first of the two genealogies for Euphrosyne which Milton gives is traditional; the second is his own.

24. buxom: lively, cheerful.

27. cranks: odd turns of speech, humorous expressions.

29. Hebe: Greek goddess of youth. Also the cupbearer to Zeus.

40. unreproved: unreprovable.

57. not unseen: contrast Il Penseroso, who *is* unseen.

60. state: formal progress.

75. pied: many colored, spotted.

80. cynosure of neighboring eyes: object to which neighboring eyes are directed.

83. The proper names here are regularly used in the pastoral poets from Theocritus on.

91. secure: in the sense of the Latin *securus,* free from care.

94. rebeck: an early form of the violin.

104. friar's lantern: will-o'-the-wisp.

120. weeds: garments.

125. Hymen: The god of marriage. Milton is thinking of the great wedding celebrations of the nobility of his day, which often included performances of masques and plays.

133. Jonson's learned sock: Ben Jonson's learned comedy. "Sock" was the low-heeled slipper worn by Greek comic actors: tragic actors wore the high-heeled "buskin."

136. Lydian. One of the three "modes" of Greek music. The other two were Dorian and Phrygian. The Lydian was the gentlest and sweetest.

139. bout: a passage in music.

145–50. Milton is referring to the story of Orpheus and Eurydice. When Orpheus' wife Eurydice died, he went down to the underworld to recover her, and by his sweet music won from Proserpine, wife of Pluto, god of the underworld, permission to take Eurydice back to earth with him, on the one condition that he should not look back at her as she followed him up to the sunlight. Just before emerging from the underworld, Orpheus looked back, and lost Eurydice.

110. *Il Penseroso.* Here the images are organized in order to present a mood of contemplation and grave intellectual activity. Note that both *L'Allegro* and *Il Penseroso* treat of kinds of happiness: Il Penseroso is not a pessimist, but a man who finds happiness in the serious, contemplative life. The coloring of this poem is much darker than that of *L'Allegro*: moonlight, dark woods, the song of the nightingale, are appropriate symbols here. The sound of the far-off curfew, the glowing embers of a dying fire half-lighting a gloomy room, the midnight lamp of the lonely student in the tower—these images are as stylized as their counterparts in *L'Allegro,* and distill a mood in the same way. Note the climax of immobility in lines 41–44, as contrasted with the

rapid movement of *L'Allegro*. The progression of images in both these poems should be noted carefully.

Line 3. bestead: help.
    4. toys: trifles.
    6. fond: foolish.
  10. pensioners: attendants.
  14. hit: suit, agree with.
  18. Memnon: An Ethiopian prince, mentioned in the *Odyssey* as famous for his beauty. Later Greek tradition gave him a sister, Himera.
  19. Ethiop queen: Cassiopeia, who boasted that her daughter was more beautiful than the sea nymphs, and as a punishment was turned into the constellation which bears her name. Milton changes the Greek myth to make Cassiopeia boast about her own beauty.
23–30. Milton invents a parentage for Melancholy as in *L'Allegro* he did for Mirth. He makes her the daughter of purity and contemplation. The goddess Vesta was the symbol of purity; Saturn was associated with melancholy and the contemplative character.
  30. Jove eventually overthrew and supplanted his father Saturn.
  35. cyprus lawn: black crepe or gauze.
  36. decent: comely, handsome.
  43. sad: serious.
  56. Philomel: Philomela, the nightingale.
  59. Cynthia: Diana, the moon-goddess.
  83. bellman: night watchman.
  87. The Bear: The constellation of the Great Bear. The sense of the line is, "May I sit up all night reading."
  88. Hermes: Hermes Trismegistus, reputed author of a whole library of mystical works, became the symbol of magical activities and profound delvings into the ultimate mysteries of things.
  93. daemons: spirits.
  95. consent: agreement, sympathy.
  98. pall: robe.
99–100. These are the main themes of Greek Tragedy. Of "Pelops' line" were Agamemnon and his children Orestes, Iphigenia, and Electra.
 102. See note to *L'Allegro,* line 133.
 104. Musaeus: a semimythological character, supposed to be one of the earliest of Greek poets.
105–8. See note to *L'Allegro,* lines 145–50.
109–15. Milton is referring to Chaucer's uncompleted *Squire's Tale.*
118–20. Milton is thinking not only of medieval and Italian romance but also of Spenser's *Faerie Queene.*
 124. Attic boy: Cephalus, a hunter beloved of Aurora (Eos, to the Greeks), goddess of dawn.
 145. consort: harmony.
 157. embowed: arched.
 170. spell: study, meditate on.

III. *On Time.* Note the carefully balanced stanza, with the lines narrowing down to

So little is our loss,
So little is thy gain,

and then, when the poet moves from time to eternity, swelling out organlike to the final, triumphant long line.

Line 3. plummet: the weight which moves the works of a clock. The lines were written "to be set on a clockcase."
      12. individual: indivisible.

112. *At a Solemn Music.* Another poem constructed out of a single skilfully balanced verse paragraph. Its movement is worth careful notice. Note the long pause after line 24.

Line 6. concent: harmony.
      27. consort: group of musicians.

113. *"Lawrence, of virtuous father virtuous son."* This is Milton in undress, as it were, writing an invitation to dinner to a friend. Note the sonnet form he employs.

Line 6. Favonius: the west wind.
      10. Attic: i.e., like the famous banquets, *Symposia,* of the ancient Athenians.
      12. Tuscan: used generally, for "Italian."
   13–14. Spare to interpose them oft: refrain from having them too often. Some critics, however, take "spare" to mean "spare the time," making the sense of the phrase: "spare time to have them often." The reader must choose between these two contradictory interpretations.

114. *Lycidas.* This great "pastoral elegy" is ostensibly a lament on the death of Milton's friend Edward King, but in fact it is a meditation on the problem of an ambitious and religious young poet faced with the prospect of being cut off before his talents have matured. The problem is, in fact, enlarged to the point where it becomes that of an ambitious and dedicated man in the precarious world. Milton draws on almost all the resources accumulated by the poetic tradition of the Western world in order to develop his theme and objectify it in terms of art. We are not commenting on or annotating this poem, because the provision of the proper critical apparatus for the full understanding and appreciation of a work of this kind—so personal and yet so conventional —is the best possible exercise for both teacher, student, and lay lover of poetry. We felt it would be advisable to leave one important and (to the modern reader) difficult poem in its virgin state, as a test and a challenge. We might, however, refer the reader to a full discussion of the poem in a work by one of the present editors—*A Study of Literature,* by David Daiches (Cornell University Press), pp. 171–95.

115. *"Go, lovely rose."* A graceful poem of compliment, in the Cavalier tradition, yet in its simple mellifluousness illustrating the lyrical ideal of the late seventeenth century.

116. *Of the last verses in the book.* An interesting and unusual use of the heroic couplet in a short lyric. Notice how the emotion rises in the third and last section. This poem, possessing neither the passionate subtlety of Donne nor Pope's smooth elegance, yet having some suggestion of both poets, is historically interesting as exhibiting a transitional style.

117. *Prologue to the Tempest.* This prologue, written by Dryden to be spoken at the performance of his and Davenant's version of Shakespeare's *Tempest,* is typical of his style in this species of poetry, of which he produced many examples. The tone is one of studied casualness, the couplets run on with a fine vigor and a conversational ease, the vocabulary is drawn from what Dryden called elsewhere "the conversation of gentlemen." The colloquial element is stronger in Dryden's prologues than in his more formal poetry, but there is some element of it in all his nonlyrical poetry—in his great satires in particular, which are too long for presentation in this anthology. Wit, elegance, ease, and a certain vitality and virility of utterance are Dryden's poetic ideals: the first three of these are to be in large measure the ideals of the succeeding age. The graceful singing quality of the Cavalier poets and the passionate argumentation of the Metaphysicals are alike absent from this kind of poetry, which is essentially a spoken verse, with a rhetorical element which can be remarkably impressive.

118. *Mac Flecknoe.* This poem is an attack on Thomas Shadwell (1640–1692), a poet and dramatist with whom Dryden had quarreled. Richard Flecknoe was an Irish priest who erroneously considered himself a poet. The poet Andrew Marvell had visited Flecknoe in Rome, and written a mocking poem about him, *Flecknoe, an English Priest at Rome.* He was dead by the time Dryden wrote Mac Flecknoe, but his name remained as a symbol of bad poetry. The theme of this poem is the choice of Shadwell by Flecknoe as his heir (Mac Flecknoe, i.e., son of Flecknoe) and successor to the kingdom of nonsense and dullness in prose and verse.

Line 29. Heywood and Shirley: Dramatists of an earlier generation, considered in Dryden's time to be crude and old-fashioned.

    33. Norwich drugget: a coarse cloth made at Norwich.

    36. Flecknoe had visited Portugal and claimed that he had received patronage from King John of Portugal.

  38–44. Evidently a reference to Shadwell's participation in a pageant on the Thames, at which the classical myth of Arion and the dolphin was presented. Shadwell was proud of his musical ability, to which he refers in the preface to his opera *Psyche* (mentioned in line 54).

    42. Epsom blankets: An allusion both to Shadwell's comedy *Epsom Wells* and to an incident in *The Virtuoso,* another of his plays, where a character is tossed in a blanket.

    53. St. André's feet: St. André was a well-known French dancing master of the time.

    57. Singleton: A musical performer and actor.

    64. Augusta: London. The reference in the following line is to the fears excited in London by the so-called "Popish Plot."

    74. Nursery: School for the training of children to be actors.

    78. Maximins: Maximin was the hero of an early play of Dryden's, *Tyrannic Love,* whose extravagantly ranting style Dryden had outgrown.

    79. Fletcher: John Fletcher, the Elizabethan playwright, best known as a member of the dramatic team of Beaumont and Fletcher.

    81. Simkin: a popular character in the farces performed by strolling players.

83. Clinches: puns.
84. Panton: A well-known punster of the day.
87. Dekker: Thomas Dekker, the Elizabethan dramatist.
91. Misers: A reference to Shadwell's comedy, *The Miser*. "Humorists" in the following line is a reference to his play *The Humorists*. Shadwell followed the "comedy of humours" (characters with one particular trait emphasized) first developed by Ben Jonson.
93. Raymond . . . Bruce: Characters in two of Shadwell's plays.
97. The two streets named here are dreary streets in London which are not, in fact, far apart—the suggestion being that Shadwell's reputation was confined to this small and shabby area.
102. Ogleby: John Ogleby, a Scottish hack writer who produced numerous translations and bad epics.
104. bilk'd stationers: booksellers who had been cheated, since they had been loaded up with copies of Shadwell's works which they were unable to sell.
105. Herringman: A prominent London bookseller and publisher.
108. Ascanius: In Virgil's Aeneid, Ascanius, Aeneas' son, is represented as the hope of his people: similarly, Shadwell is the new hope of the kingdom of dullness.
122. *Love's Kingdom:* A play by Flecknoe, a "pastoral tragicomedy."
151. gentle George: Sir George Etherege, Restoration dramatist. He was known for his courtliness and wit, and admired by Dryden. The names mentioned in lines 152–3 are characters in his plays.
163. S—dl—y: Sir Charles Sedley, Restoration poet, dramatist, and wit. The suggestion is that Sedley had assisted in writing some of Shadwell's plays: he had, in fact, written a prologue for Shadwell's *Epsom Wells*.
168. Sir Formal: Sir Formal Trifle, a character in Shadwell's play *The Virtuoso*.
170. northern dedications: dedications of his plays by Shadwell to the Duke and Duchess of Newcastle. (Newcastle is in northeastern England.)
179. Prince Nicander: a character in Shadwell's *Psyche*.
181. sold he bargains: "To sell a bargain" was a phrase meaning to lead someone to ask, in all innocence, a question to which a coarse reply was given. The reference is to the devices used by Shadwell in his plays to give an air of realism to the dialogue.
189–92. These lines are a close parody of four lines in the epilogue to Shadwell's play *The Humorists*:

> A humour is the bias of the mind,
> By which with violence 'tis one way inclined:
> It makes our actions lean on one side still,
> And in all changes that way bends the will.

Shadwell was very proud of his ability to imitate the Jonsonian comedy of humours.
195. tun of man: a "tun" is a large cask used for wine. Dryden is punning.
196. kilderkin: a small barrel.

202. A reference to the belief that there were no snakes in Ireland, and any snake brought there immediately died. Flecknoe was Irish.

207. An allusion to the practice followed by some of the "metaphysical" poets of arranging their stanzas in the form of wings and altars. Later critics attacked this sort of thing as "false wit."

212. Bruce and Longvil: Two characters in Shadwell's *The Virtuoso* who play a trick of this kind on Sir Formal Trifle.

216. An allusion to the Biblical story of Elijah's mantle falling on Elisha (I Kings 19, 19 and II Kings 2, 9).

119. *To my Dear Friend Mr. Congreve.* Another fine example of Dryden's combination of ease and strength. The conversational tone of this poem does not prevent or clash with the note of formal compliment which also emerges. Dryden, in his sixties, is welcoming the twenty-three-year-old Congreve to the ranks of dramatic writers on the production of his play *The Double Dealer*.

Line 7. Janus: the Roman god of "beginnings," among whose numerous functions was presiding over the sowing of crops and similar agricultural activities.

15. Vitruvius: Roman military engineer who wrote a celebrated book on architecture.

29–30. Etherege and Wycherley were older Restoration dramatists; Southerne, younger than these but older than Congreve, was a dramatist, manager, and actor.

35. Fabius, Scipio: Quintus Fabius Maximus, by his brilliant delaying ("Fabian") tactics, saved Rome from conquest by Hannibal. After his retirement and the Roman military disaster that followed, the young Scipio was given the command and became the most powerful man in Roman affairs. Dryden's analogy is not historically accurate because Fabius was in fact jealous of the younger man's popularity and opposed his more aggressive military strategy.

39. Giulio Romano was Raphael's pupil and his successor in the Roman school of Italian painting.

45–46. Edward II, one of the weaker of England's kings, was deposed in 1327 and succeeded by his son, Edward III, who won great military glory in France in the early part of his reign.

48. Tom the First was Thomas Shadwell, Poet Laureate and Historiographer Royal from 1688 to 1692. Tom the Second was Thomas Rymer, who was appointed Historiographer Royal on Shadwell's death. Both offices had been taken from Dryden after the "Glorious Revolution" of 1689, for Dryden, who had become a Catholic, was not *persona grata* to the Protestants, William and Mary, who were brought in to succeed the exiled Catholic king, James II. Dryden had no love for either Shadwell (whom he attacked in his satires) or Rymer, who was an extremely narrow and rigid neoclassic critic.

120. *Alexander's Feast.* This is the second of two odes Dryden wrote for St. Cecilia's Day. St. Cecilia, whose feast was on November 22, was regarded as the patron saint of music, and the day was celebrated in England at this time by musical festivities. Dryden got the essential facts in the poem from Plutarch's life of Alexander, but Timotheus and his all-powerful music seem to be Dryden's own invention. The ode is an attempt to modulate the verse expression at each point to conform to the incident and the emotion being described. The techniques employed are perhaps rather obvious, but the immense verve of the poem, with its crashing echoes and its bold repetitions, gives the effect of a magnificent brass band. The irregular stanza forms help the effect, and variations in line lengths, together with the handling of the rhymes, are well worth studying. Altogether, the ode is a remarkable *tour de force* and shows a side of Dryden that we would not guess at from reading his couplet verse. This flamboyant kind of lyricism was regarded as proper for an "ode," a form in which the late seventeenth- and early eighteenth-century poets would occasionally forget their insistence on ease, elegance, and wit and really let their hair down.

Line 2. Philip's warlike son is, of course, Alexander.
      30. Olympia: Alexander's mother. A tradition developed that Alexander was really the son of Olympia and Zeus—Zeus having visited Olympia in the form of a serpent.
      75. Darius: Darius III, the last of the old Persian dynasty, who came to the miserable end Dryden describes.
      97. Lydian: The softest and most effeminate of the Greek musical "modes."

121. *The Choice.* This poem, published in 1700, was immensely popular in the eighteenth century. It epitomizes one aspect of early eighteenth-century civilization in a verse form which is itself typical of its period. The tone of the poem is that of Horace's odes: the ideal is one of gentlemanly ease, of the golden mean, and it still carries the mild charm of the leisured dilettanti of the period. It is a completely relaxed poem, with no passionate fusion of form and content, no impressive use of the imagination, nothing, in fact, that could not be said effectively in a graceful prose essay. But the neat and simple couplets are pleasant to read, done as they are with an unambitious and minor skill. This is not "poetry" in the sense that "Lycidas" or an ode of Keats is poetry: it is a quite different use of the medium of verse. But it is a legitimate and an agreeable use, and much more satisfactory as a literary production than a passionately serious lyric which does not come off. Pomfret knew exactly what he could achieve in verse, and set his sights accordingly. The result is a charming verse essay.

122. *On a Lady with Foul Breath.* Another piece of verse by a minor poet of the late seventeenth and early eighteenth century. It has a mild wit of its own. It also serves to show that modern advertising has no monopoly on this subject.

123–127. The "occasional" verse of Matthew Prior includes some of the best examples in English of a kind of poetry equally removed from Donne's and Milton's, from Keats's and Tennyson's. Prior commented in graceful but relaxed verse on a great variety of topical matters, writing not, as Milton wrote *Paradise Lost,* "with his garland and singing robes about him," but with deliberate informality. There is no passionate fusion of form and content in this kind of poetry, but the deliberate turning of a preconceived content into witty and agreeable verse. This *vers de société* has the tone of an educated man speaking to his fellows; it can be humorous, playful, complimentary, or reflective, but it always keeps its social tone. In terms of "aesthetic distance" we might say that the poet keeps close to his readers—and he never thinks of a single reader, but rather of a fairly convivial group. At his most grave—as in "Written in Mezeray's History of France"—he can sound a deeper note with a fine simplicity, but more characteristic is a poem like "The Secretary" where in a deliberately tripping measure he describes the tenor of his daily life as Secretary to the English Ambassador at the Hague. This kind of thing is minor verse rather than great poetry, but it is good minor verse and should be read and enjoyed for what it is without any irrelevant comparisons with other kinds of poetry which handle language in a different way and have other functions.

128–129. The social tone of Gay's poetry is very like that of Prior. There is a higher degree of formality in "To a Lady on her Passion for Old China" than one might expect in this kind of verse, but it is a playful formality of utterance which (as in Prior) produces an informality of tone.

130. *A Description of a City Shower.* An effective example of a pedestrian verse used successfully to convey accurate description. The rhymed couplets here serve the purpose of adding point and neatness to the expression: the verse form plays no organic part in the total expression. This too is a kind of minor verse similar to that of Prior and Gay. Successful low-pressured verse of this kind is much more valuable as literature than pretentious splutterings towards a profounder style.

131. *Ode on Solitude.* An early poem of Pope's, a variation on an air he got from the Latin poets—rural content. It has a grave simplicity achieved in large part by the stanza form and by the slow movement of the verse.

132. *The Rape of the Lock.* This is a "mock epic"—that is, a poem written on a relatively trivial subject, but with all the devices and "epic machinery" which, as a result of a long tradition which started with Homer, had come to be regarded as appropriate for epic or heroic poetry. The effect of using such an apparatus in dealing with a lock of hair stolen from a lady's head by a young man is, of course, ironical, and Pope exploits the ironic possibilities of the mock epic with great effect. But the poem is much more than a society jest. It is a brilliant and subtle picture of man (and more especially, woman) as a social animal, a deft penetration through all the layers of convention and decoration which overlays social behavior and perverts our value judgments of human affairs and relationships to the hidden realities below:

> Oh! if to dance all night, and dress all day,
> Charmed the small-pox, or chased old-age away;
> Who would not scorn what housewife's cares produce,
> Or who would learn one earthly thing of use? . . .
> But since, alas! frail beauty must decay,
> Curled or uncurled, since locks will turn to grey;
> Since painted or not painted all shall fade,
> And she who scorns a man must die a maid;
> What then remains but well our pow'r to use,
> And keep good-humour still whate'er we lose?

For all its lightness of touch, its wit, its irony, its clever distortions of the pettinesses of society behavior by deliberately disproportionate epic descriptions and analogies, "The Rape of the Lock" is a serious poem—perhaps the most truly serious of all Pope's poems—and a more profound discussion of man than his "Essay on Man." For the "high seriousness" which Matthew Arnold claimed for the greatest poetry need not be overt seriousness: one can develop a serious point humorously and obliquely. For a poet operating within the tradition that Pope operated in, employing his social tone and having his attitude to the poetic medium, the method he chose in "The Rape of the Lock" was the most appropriate method of projecting his characteristic insights.

The occasion of the poem was the theft of a lock of Miss Arabella Fermor's hair by Lord Petre. John Caryll, a relative of Lord Petre, suggested to Pope that he might write a poem on the subject that would laugh the families of Miss Fermor and Lord Petre out of the mutual hostility that had resulted from the affair. The first version of the poem was considerably briefer than the version we have here: Pope recast it later into a more elaborate form, adding the supernatural "machinery" of the sylphs. The speech of Clarissa in Canto V, from which the passage quoted above is taken, was added later still, to make explicit a moral that was hitherto only implicit in the poem. But all the additions were a rounding out of the original conception, and the revised poem stands today as a perfect unity.

Nowhere in English literature has the heroic couplet been used with more grace and delicacy than in this poem. The reader should note how Pope handles the run of each line, which, though generally end-stopped, contains much subtle variety within the individual line. The verse appears completely effortless, yet it is the product of the most cunning craftsmanship. Pope was a master of the verse catalogue, and by simply describing a list of objects can at the same time produce a sympathetic sense of the essential quality of the civilization which valued such objects and an ironic criticism of the human frailties which they illustrate. His use of anticlimax in such lines as

> Whether the nymph shall break Diana's law,
> Or some frail China jar receive a flaw;
> Or stain her honour or her new brocade . . .

or

> Puffs, powders, patches, Bibles, billet-doux

is more than merely humorous or ironical: such a device implicitly sets beside the pretended standards that are supposed to govern civilized behavior the real, and infinitely trivial, standards which do in fact govern it. Yet there is no moralizing in these passages. The note is kept light, the wit is always more in evidence than the implicit philosophy.

There is a high surface polish throughout the poem. In addition to the more obvious devices, such as the anticlimax already discussed, and such tricks as

> Now lap-dogs give themselves the rousing shake,
> And sleepless lovers, just at twelve, awake,

there is the steady flow of beautifully turned phrases, exquisitely geared to the rhyming couplets:

> A third interprets motions, looks, and eyes;
> At every word a reputation dies.

"The Rape of the Lock" is a satire, a mock epic, and at the same time it is the most perfect rendering in English literature of the social tone of the age of Queen Anne: and it is more than that, too—it is a comment on "social tone" itself, on the trivial artificialities with which the leisured classes obscure for themselves the real facts of life, but a comment done with such wit and tact that Pope seems to be at the same time a member of the social class he is displaying and an aloof outsider ironically observing it. The poem is perhaps the fine flower of the Age of Queen Anne.

CANTO I.
Line 17. the slipper knocked the ground: to summon the servant.
　　20. The sylphs were part of the "epic machinery" introduced in the second version of the poem.
　　23. birth-night beau: a man of fashion dressed for a royal birthday ball.
　　32. The silver token refers to the silver penny found in the slipper of good housemaids (cf. "A Proper New Ballad," poem No. 65: "Yet who of late for cleanliness/ Finds sixpence in her shoe"), and the circled green is the magic ring where the fairies sport.
　　44. box: at the theater.
　　　　Ring: the course for carriages at Hyde Park.
　　56. Ombre: a card game.
　105. who thy protection claim: who claim the right of protecting thee.

CANTO II.
　　25. springes: traps.

CANTO III.
　25–100. A description, in mock-heroic terms, of a game of ombre.
　　41. garbs succint: robes gathered up with a girdle.
　106. The coffee beans are being ground in the coffee mill.
122–124. Nisus, king of Megara, had a purple lock on which his life and the safety of his kingdom depended. Scylla, daughter of Nisus, was in love with Minos, leader of the Cretan army which besieged Megara, and to show her love for Minos she cut off her father's magic lock while he was asleep. Scylla and Nisus were both changed to birds. The story is told in Ovid's *Metamorphoses*.
　147. forfex: shears.
　165. *Atalantis:* a notorious novel by Mrs. Manley, purporting to be the court memoirs of an imaginary kingdom, but actually containing, in a slightly veiled form, scandalous anecdotes about real people.

CANTO IV.
　16 ff. The Cave of Spleen (bad temper) is a parody of the journeys to the underworld found in both the *Odyssey* and the *Aeneid*.
　102. double loads of lead: ladies' curl papers used to be fastened with pliant strips of lead.
　118. sound of Bow: of the bells of St. Mary-le-Bow in Cheapside.

CANTO V.
　　53. sconce: candle with a metal reflector.
　　64. the words of a song in a popular opera of the day.
　89 ff. "In imitation of the progress of Agamemnon's scepter in Homer, *Iliad*, II." (Pope.)

129. Berenice's locks: Berenice, wife of Ptolemy III or Egypt, dedicated her hair for her husband's safe return from a military expedition, and it was eventually changed into a constellation.

137. Partridge: "John Partridge was a ridiculous star-gazer, who in his Almanacks every year never failed to predict the downfall of the Pope, and the King of France, then at war with the English." (Pope.)

133. *Elegy to the Memory of an Unfortunate Lady.* This poem shows Pope using the same verse form to achieve a very different end. This is a rhetorical, even a melodramatic, poem, whose rudimentary but half-concealed plot can be made out by any careful reader. There is a deliberate eloquence as well as a formal sententiousness here which are quite different from the wit and polish of "The Rape of the Lock." The reader might ask himself how Pope achieves this difference in effect and tone, and whether Pope is as successful in this kind of poetry as in the other.

The poet imagines himself meeting the ghost of the unfortunate lady whose unhappy destiny had led her to stab herself. He describes her ill-treatment, curses those who ill-treated her, gives an account of her death abroad and her lonely foreign grave, and ends by switching his pity from the lady to himself.

134. *Epistle to Dr. Arbuthnot.* This is a fine example of Pope's personal and satirical poetry. Note once again the combination of a conversational tone with a deliberate formality (the attack on Addison—"Atticus"—is a very formal set piece). This is *vers de société* of a somewhat different kind from Prior's: Pope is speaking to the relatively closed circle of the London literary world, and there is an intimacy which is lacking in his own "The Rape of the Lock." This intimacy makes the satire all the more biting, for it is not directed at human folly but at real or real-seeming individuals who, except for the very thin disguise of some classical or pseudo-classical names, are not in any way expanded into symbols of more than themselves. The scale of Pope's satire is larger than Dryden's, and his perspective is smaller. The "aesthetic distance" between writer and reader is short, and we are close to the persons being described. This very social kind of poetry breathes the very spirit of the literary London of its day.

This poem is in a sense Pope's *apologia* for his other satirical writings: he explains the circumstances which forced him into satire.

Line 1. good John: Pope's servant, John Searl.

13. the Mint: in the neighborhood of the Mint insolvent debtors enjoyed a traditional exemption from legal process.

21. Twit'nam: Twickenham, where Pope had his villa.

23. Arthur: Arthur Moore, an unscrupulous politician of the day, whose son fancied himself as a poet.

25. Cornus: Sir Robert Walpole, whose wife had left him shortly before this poem was written.

53. Curll: Edmund Curll, the unscrupulous bookseller and publisher, with whom Pope had quarreled.

56. virgin tragedy: "Alludes to a tragedy called the *Virgin Queen,* by Mr. R. Barford, published in 1729, who displeased Pope by daring to adopt the fine machinery of his Sylphs in an heroicomical poem called *The Assembly.*" (Explanation by one of Pope's early editors.)

62. Lintot: Bernard Lintot, who published Pope's Homer.
85. Codrus: a pretentious and incompetent poetaster, mentioned in Juvenal's third Satire.
97. Colley: Colley Cibber, a contemporary poet and dramatist, for whom Pope had an especial contempt.
98. Henley: A popular orator who used to harangue the butchers in Newport Market and Butcher Row.
99. Bavius: Baevius and Maevius were two bad poets mentioned by Virgil: they became symbolic names for incompetent poets.
100. Ambrose Philips ("Namby Pamby" as he was nicknamed) whose pastoral poetry Pope despised. (He had written an ironical article in which he pretended to find Philips's pastorals superior to his own.)
101. Sappho: Pope's name for Lady Mary Wortley Montagu, a literary lady with whom he had quarreled.
135 ff. Pope lists here, as men who encouraged or admired him, some of the most celebrated literary men of the age or of the immediately preceding age.
146. "By no means authors of the same class, though the violence of party might hurry them into the same mistakes. But if the first offended this way, it was only through an honest warmth of temper, that allowed too little to an excellent understanding. The other two, with very bad heads, had hearts still worse." (Pope)
151. Gildon: Sir Charles Gildon, who had satirized Pope.
153. Dennis: John Dennis, whom Pope had satirized in his "Essay on Criticism" (under the name of "Appius") as being unable to bear any kind of criticism that was not wholly favorable. Dennis himself was, in Pope's words, "a furious old critic by profession who wrote against [the "Essay on Criticism"] and its author, in a manner perfectly lunatic."
164. Bentley: Richard Bentley, the great classical scholar, who nevertheless made himself ridiculous by his emendations of *Paradise Lost*.
Tibbalds: Lewis Theobald, who produced an edition of Shakespeare, had attacked Pope's edition. In his edition Theobald had produced some happy emendations.
179. the bard: Ambrose Philips again.
190. Tate: Nahum Tate, an inferior poet, and Poet Laureate from 1692 till his death in 1715.
193 ff. This famous attack on Addison was written earlier and subsequently embodied in this poem. It stands out from the poem as a carefully polished individual satire.
230 ff. Bufo: said to be Charles Montagu, Earl of Halifax, an enemy of Dryden. The identification of the character is not, of course, necessary for full appreciation of this passage: the kind of behavior Pope is satirizing is clear enough.
248. "Mr. Dryden, after having lived in exigencies, had a magnificent Funeral bestowed upon him by the contribution of several persons of quality." (Pope)
260. Queensbury: The Duchess of Queensbury, patroness of the poet Gay, who died at her house.
280. The references are to contemporary political characters.
299. "Meaning the man who would have persuaded the Duke of Chandos

that Mr. P. meant him in those circumstances ridiculed in the Epistle on Taste." (Pope)

305. Sporus: John, Lord Hervey, an active and influential figure in politics and at court.

319. In *Paradise Lost* Satan, in the form of a toad, squatted by Eve's ear while she slept and whispered evil fancies. See *Paradise Lost,* Book IV, lines 800 ff.

363. Japhet in a jail: Japhet Crooke was a notorious forger.

375. Welsted's lie: "This man had the impudence to tell in print, that Mr. P. had occasioned a *Lady's death,* and to name a person he never heard of. He also publish'd that he libell'd the Duke of Chandos; with whom (it was added) that he had lived in familiarity, and received from him a present of *five hundred pounds:* the falsehood of both which is known to his Grace. Mr. P. never received any present, farther than the subscription for Homer, from him, or from *Any great Man* whatsoever." (Pope)

378. "*Budgel,* in a weekly pamphlet called the Bee, bestowed much abuse on him, in the imagination that he writ some things about the *Last Will* of Dr. *Tindal,* in the *Grub-street Journal;* a paper wherein he never had the least hand, direction, or supervisal, nor the least knowledge of its Author." (Pope)

380. two Curlls: Edmund Curll the publisher, and Lord Hervey.

380-1. "In some of Curll's and other pamphlets, Mr. Pope's father was said to be a Mechanic, a Hatter, a Farmer, nay a Bankrupt. But, what is stranger, a *Nobleman* (if such a Reflection could be thought to come from a Nobleman) had dropt an allusion to that pitiful untruth, in a paper called an *Epistle to a Doctor of Divinity.* And the following line, *Hard as thy Heart, and as thy Birth obscure,* had fallen from a like *Courtly* pen, in certain *Verses to the Imitator of Horace.* Mr. Pope's Father was of a Gentleman's Family in Oxfordshire. . . ." (Pope)

135. *Verses on the Prospect of Planting Arts and Learning in America.* An interesting poem in the eighteenth-century rhetorical tradition: note the diction and the tone of deliberate formality.

136. *The Ballad of Sally in Our Alley.* A poem reflecting a very different side of eighteenth-century poetic activity from the preceding. It is in some degree in the street-ballad tradition, and has, in addition to its swinging rhythms, a consciously assumed naïveté.

137. *An Epigram.* Notice the difference between this kind of wit and the wit of, say, John Donne.

138. *Grongar Hill.* A poem in which this minor but attractive poet describes an aspect of his native Welsh landscape. This is an unpretentious kind of descriptive poetry, with the moral idea emerging at the end naturally but not inevitably. Like so much eighteenth-century verse, pressure is low, and there seems to be no vital organic relationship between the parts or between the form and the content (which is paraphrasable quite simply). The qualities of this kind of verse are a quiet grace and elegance, a controlled simplicity.

139. *A Hymn.* This poem concludes Thomson's *Seasons,* a long work in four parts descriptive of the four seasons. The formality and sententiousness of the verse (blank verse very different from either Shakespeare's or Milton's) seem far removed from the witty polish of Pope, though the tone is not very different from that of Berkeley's poem (No. 135). This rhetorical quality is, however, by no means unknown in Pope: it represents another aspect of the civilization of which social wit was only one kind of reflection. Thomson is not talking to literary London, as Pope generally was, but enunciating from an eminence to an ideal universal audience. The "aesthetic distance" is greater with Thomson.

140–141. These two hymns are excellent examples of this species of poetry. The hymn must have certain qualities which might seem defects in other kinds of lyric—it is intended to be sung by large popular audiences, and must reflect an emotion and enunciate a principle of immediate general applicability. Subtlety or passionate wit would be quite out of place in a hymn: a very special kind of skill is required in order to give expression to a communal emotion in simple, singable verse, and to treat profound themes so as to make them amenable to popular communal utterance.

142. *Written in an Inn at Henley.* A typical "occasional" poem of the period, with its mixture of formality and informality. This minor kind of verse is extremely interesting to the historian of society and of manners, as well as being agreeable in itself.

143. *Ode Written in the Beginning of the Year 1746.* This perfectly chiseled little poem has a lapidary beauty of its own. The personifications of Spring, Fancy, etc. are wholly appropriate to this highly formal kind of utterance.

144. *Ode to Evening.* This is one of the few successful examples in English poetry of the unrhymed lyric (compare Campion's poem, No. 56). Collins' use of varied vowel sounds, as well as the rhythmic effects, should be carefully observed.

145. *Ode on a Distant Prospect of Eton College.* Gray wrote this poem at Stoke Poges, a few miles north of Windsor and Eton, which face each other on opposite sides of the Thames. Gray had gone to school at Eton.

This contemplative poem, starting off as an address to Eton College and moving through a recollection of his own youth there, through thoughts on what is in store for youth in general, to come to rest on what is really a note of self-pity, is written in a deliberately elevated style. Note the "poetic diction" ("To chase the rolling circle's speed,/or urge the flying ball"), the personifications, and the invocations and apostrophes. Gray is elevating his theme from a contemplation of Eton College to a contemplation of the fate of man, and his stylized diction is one of his ways of doing this. The note of self-pity is sounded indirectly: he does not overtly talk about himself at the end of the poem. He returns at the end to the "little victims" and concludes with a generalization which rings like a proverb (and has become one). The reader should consider both the tone and the progression of thought in this poem, before considering the appropriateness and effectiveness of the style and diction.

Line 4. Henry's holy shade: "King Henry VI, founder of the College." (Gray)

146. *Sonnet on the Death of Mr. Richard West.* Wordsworth singled out this poem for attack on the grounds of the artificiality of its diction. Is this a just criticism?

147. *Elegy Written in a Country Churchyard.* After attacking the style of most of Gray's other poems, Dr. Johnson, in his *Lives of the Poets,* had this to say of the Elegy: "In the character of his *Elegy* I rejoice to concur with the common reader; for by the common sense of readers uncorrupted with literary prejudices, after all the refinements of subtilty and the dogmatism of learning, must be finally decided all claim to poetical honours. The *Church-yard* abounds with images which find a mirrour in every mind, and with sentiments to which every bosom returns an echo." The reader might consider whether this is a valid criterion on which to judge the quality of a poem.

Note how effectively the poem opens by gradually emptying the landscape of both sights and sounds as dusk descends. Consider the qualities of this simple and slow-moving verse form. The elegiac, meditative tone is sustained throughout a variety of turns in the thought, and it would be a mistake to concentrate on an analysis of the thought and imagery and ignore this tone in any critical discussion of the poem. The poem moves with ease from a contemplation of the landscape to a consideration of "the short and simple annals of the poor" and to suggest moral ideas which arise from this consideration. The presentation of these ideas is done indirectly, often through the imagery or the choice of a verb or an adjective ("Some *mute, inglorious* Milton" is balanced by "Some Cromwell, *guiltless* . . .") But when the poet turns to address himself in line 93, and to move the poem round until it reveals his own epitaph, it is impossible not to feel that there is a break in the continuity which only the tone, and not the structure, of the poem can hope to mend. In terms of the pervasive elegiac tone and movement, the concluding epitaph is prepared for and appropriate, but not in terms of the thought progression. It is that tone of self-indulgent melancholy suggested at the very beginning by the line

> And leaves the world to darkness and to me

that prepares for the shift at the end: a man in this mood, meditating over the graves of others, is bound to end up, we cannot help feeling, by thinking of his own grave. The Elegy is thus an interesting example of a poem where the mood justifies the thought, rather than vice versa.

148. *Ode on the Death of a Favourite Cat.* Gray in lighter mood, with a deliberately ironic elevation of style.

149. *The Vanity of Human Wishes.* This poem is one of the best examples in English of what might be called the rhetorical use of verse. Here the balanced phrases, the marching couplets, the clanging rhymes, serve to give pith and emphasis to the historical descriptions and the moral generalizations. Instead of the meaning flowering out of the organic unity of the poem, as in an ode of Keats or a lyric of Marvell, it is thrust at the reader piece by piece, with the metrical and rhyme schemes providing sonority and cogency to the expression. The technique of verse is here, one might almost say, added to the previously conceived content, so as to convey it to the reader as impressively as possible. In an ode of Keats it is impossible to distinguish any preconceived content from the poetic expression in the actual poem. For Johnson, poetry was a witty and weighty expression or illustration of general truths either through accounts of particular instances or through well-balanced generalizations. The poise and balance of his verse are remarkable—note the double balance in such lines as

> Remark each anxious toil, each eager strife,

and

> Shuns fancied ills, or chases airy good,

and

> The dangers gather as the treasures rise,

and

> One shows the plunder, and one hides the thief.

This use of verse technique is not highly valued either by modern criticism or by the Romantic tradition; but it is a robust form of literature which should not be dismissed merely because it can be described by that much abused word "rhetorical" (used here, it should be said, in no sense of blame at all). Neither passionate expression of personal emotion nor a witty and ironic use of paradox can be found in Johnson's poetry: there *is* passion here, but it is the sententious passion of a man who is a moralist before he is an exhibitionist, and there *is* wit, but it is not the paradox so dear to many modern critics; it is the simple and weighty accumulation of parallels and contrasts. There is a grave eloquence in these weighty couplets with their punching rhymes which is as far removed from the lighter, more highly polished art of Pope, on the one hand, as from the lyrical passion of a Shelley on the other.

Line 49. Democritus. The so-called "laughing philosopher" who was reputed to have continually laughed at the follies of men.

    97. Parliamentary elections had to be held at least every seven years: "septennial ale" is the ale distributed by the candidates at an election in order to win votes.

  127. Villiers: George Villiers, Duke of Buckingham, King James I's "favourite," who was assassinated in 1628.

  128. Harley: Robert Harley, Earl of Oxford, Tory minister under Queen Anne, impeached for high treason in 1715.

  129. Wentworth: Thomas Wentworth, Earl of Strafford, supporter of Charles I in his struggle with Parliament, was executed in 1641. Hyde: Edward Hyde, Earl of Clarendon, Charles II's Lord Chancellor immediately after the Restoration, lost favor and was exiled in 1667.

  137. Bodley's dome: The Bodleian library, Oxford.

  138. There was a tradition that Roger Bacon's study, built on an arch over Folly Bridge, Oxford, would fall when a man greater than Bacon passed under it.

  162. Lydiat: Thomas Lydiat, 1572–1646, an Oxford scholar who, having Royalist sympathies, was allowed to die in utter poverty.

166. Laud: William Laud, Charles I's Archbishop of Canterbury, executed in 1645.
177. The rapid Greek: Alexander the Great.
180. Referring to Marlborough's campaigns in the War of the Spanish Succession.
190. Swedish Charles: Charles XII of Sweden, who, after some spectacular military successes, was defeated by the Russians in 1709 at Pultowa.
198. Frederick IV of Denmark joined with Augustus II of Poland in alliance against Charles XII. Frederick capitulated to Charles in 1700, and Augustus resigned his crown to Charles in 1704.
209–212. After his defeat at Pultowa, Charles took refuge in Turkey, trying to get assistance there against Russia. He finally got back to Sweden and was shot at the "petty fortress" of Frederikshald in the course of a campaign against Norway (line 218).
222. Bavaria's lord: Charles Albert, Elector of Bavaria, who claimed the crown of the Holy Roman Empire and thus precipitated the War of the Austrian Succession, 1740–48. Although he was chosen Emperor in 1742, he died shortly afterwards, exhausted by the struggle.
225 ff. This is the familiar story of the Persian king Xerxes who, while preparing to invade Greece, became so angry when the bridge of boats he had built over the Hellespont was destroyed in a storm that he ordered the sea to be given three hundred strokes of the lash.
239. The bold Bavarian: see note to line 222.
243. Fair Austria: Maria Theresa, who opposed Charles Albert's imperial claims and fought on the opposite side in the War of the Austrian Succession.
311. Lydia's monarch. Croesus, the fabulously wealthy king of Lydia, who was said to have been warned by the philosopher and lawgiver Solon to call no man happy until his life had been completed.
319. Vane: Anne Vane, mistress of Frederick, Prince of Wales, who eventually left her.
320. Sedley: Catherine Sedley, mistress of the Duke of York (later James II).

150. *On the Death of Mr. Robert Levet.* There is a simple gravity about this poem which is very attractive. It has not the weight and sonority of *The Vanity of Human Wishes,* but, in spite of the different verse form, it is a lighter example of what is essentially the same kind of use of verse.

Line 7. officious: full of good offices.

151. *The Deserted Village.* This picture of an idyllic country scene (the reader might compare and contrast other examples of pastoral poetry in this anthology) set against its subsequent degeneration is instinct with a deep moral feeling. Note the devices employed by Goldsmith to get this moral feeling across. Would you consider that this use of the heroic couplet is similar in kind to its use in Johnson's "Vanity of Human Wishes"? Are the devices for indicating moral feeling similar to those employed in Gray's "Elegy"?

Line 232. twelve good rules: twelve rules of conduct attributed to Charles I: they were often hung up on the wall.

game of goose: a game where the players moved their men on a board, according to the throw of the dice.

344. Altama: a river in Georgia.

418. The river Tornio is in northern Sweden: Pambamarca is a mountain in Ecuador (it was then a part of Peru).

152. *Light Shining Out of Darkness.* See note to poems No. 140 and 141.

153. *On the Receipt of My Mother's Picture Out of Norfolk.* The passionate eloquence of these lines is equally different from the sonorous poetic rhetoric of Dr. Johnson and the brilliant surface polish of Pope. The language is most elevated at the beginning and at the end—when Cowper is working himself into a mood of reminiscence by apostrophizing his mother's picture, and when he is drawing his final conclusions. The central part of the poem, dealing with childhood reminiscences, is more "familiar" in tone and diction, but it never becomes mere autobiographical chat: the passion never dies, and keeps the diction formal and even stylized. (While spontaneous passionate utterance may be incoherent and the very reverse of formal, passion as developed in a poem, which is a very different matter, demands some heightening of the diction.) The note of personal suffering, rising to a climax in lines 100–105, is suffused throughout the poem and makes its tone very different from anything by Pope or Johnson. Note how the poem runs down to a quiet close.

154. *The Castaway.* This is a remarkable distillation of a mood of despair through a symbolic incident whose suggestions are continuously developed and reinforced by the imagery and the verse form. Note the relentless beat of the rhythms which carries the poem on with a note of doomed inevitability. The effect of the final rhymed couplet in each stanza should be studied. Note, too, how deftly and effectively Cowper shifts the application to himself at the end of the poem.

155. *Holy Willie's Prayer.* Burns supplied the following "argument" to this poem:

"Holy Willie was a rather oldish bachelor elder, in the parish of Mauchline, and much and justly famed for that polemical chattering which ends in tippling orthodoxy, and for that spiritualized bawdry which refines to liquorish devotion. In a sessional process with a gentleman in Mauchline—a Mr. Gavin Hamilton—*Holy Willie* and his priest, Father Auld, after full hearing in the Presbytery of Ayr, came off but second best, owing partly to the oratorical powers of Mr. Robert Aiken, Mr. Hamilton's counsel; but chiefly to Mr. Hamilton's being one of the most irreproachable and truly respectable characters in the country. On losing his process, the muse overheard him at his devotions, as follows."

The poem is one of the most remarkable poetic satires ever written. The satire is directed against the Calvinist belief that the vast majority of men are damned as a result of Adam's sin, but that the tiny minority are "elected" —through no merit of their own, but out of God's free grace, in order to demonstrate His goodness—to a predestined salvation. The rest are all predestined to damnation.

The device of having Holy Willie condemn himself by reciting a prayer overheard by the reader is simple enough, but it enables Burns to achieve a crushing indictment of the Calvinist doctrine of election by showing the kind of hypocrisy such a belief forces on one who considers himself among the elect. For the point of the poem is not simply that Holy Willie is a hypocrite: it is that some kind of unconscious hypocrisy is made inevitable by the views he professes. If you imagine you are predestined to salvation you become both self-righteous and morally reckless: if, on the other hand, you believe that your lot is cast with the great majority of predestinately damned, then it does not matter how you behave. Either way, your character is ruined.

The poem never degenerates into farce or burlesque: the liturgical note is maintained throughout, but it becomes more monstrous as the poem progresses and the character of the speaker reveals itself until, with that final "Amen, Amen," the whole religious tradition of which Holy Willie is the spokesman dissolves itself in irony. The apparent humility moving invisibly into self-congratulation increases as the poem develops, until at the resounding conclusion we are positively staggered by the cool impertinence of the proposition he makes to the Almighty, so that when this preposterous prayer crashes to its final close with the two-fold "Amen," we are utterly overcome by this combination of self-interest and apparent piety. We even have a sort of admiration for the man who can combine the two with an air of such complete conviction. But there is certainly nothing left of his creed by the time the poem comes to an end.

Line 51. fou: drunk.
    54. steer: disturb.
    67. Gawn Hamilton: Gavin Hamilton, friend and patron of Burns, who was brought before the Kirk Session and accused of various kinds of laxity in religious observance, but who, greatly to the chagrin of Holy Willie and his like, was vindicated on appeal to the Presbytery of Ayr, largely as a result of the forensic abilities of Robert Aiken. See the two following stanzas.
    74. splore: disturbance.
    78. kail: cabbage.

156. *Address to the Deil.* This is another, and more indirect, attack by Burns on an aspect of Calvinist theology. The sinister tempter who lies in wait for man in order to seduce him from the straight and narrow path is reduced to earthy human dimensions. Burns sets the tone immediately by the names he gives the devil in the opening stanza—"Auld Hornie, Satan, Nick, or Clootie" —which represent the devil of folklore rather than of theology. The picture of Auld Nick "spairging about the burstane cootie to scaud poor wretches" is a humorous parody of the Devil's activities in innumerable sermons of the period. The Devil is just a naughty boy having his fun, and Burns wags an amused but admonitory finger at him. It is to be noted that the Biblical references in the poem (to Job, for example) are treated with a deliberate lack of reverence—but not in such a way as to imply any contempt for the Bible; rather, in order to see the Bible story as a series of documents which can be immediately related to the daily life of contemporary man. The description of Adam and Eve in the Garden of Eden presents them as very human lovers with no theological aura around them at all.

The poem has a clearly defined structure. After the invocation, in which the names he applies to the Devil set the tone for his treatment, Burns proceeds to define the Devil's activities in terms of folklore (with more than once a mischievous suggestion that accidents popularly attributed to the Devil have purely natural causes, such as the drunkenness of the victim—the same device that he uses in "Tam o' Shanter") and then in terms of his Biblical and theological activities. The third and concluding section expresses the poet's own view of the Devil, with a cheerful *insouciance* that sums up the mood of the poem. The final suggestion that even the Devil might perhaps repent and escape from "yon den" is not the mere sentimentality it might appear to be at first sight: it is a satiric thrust at the Calvinist view adroitly disguised as sentimentality. It is not, of course, a serious suggestion, but made with the lighthearted airiness that characterizes the poem as a whole. But the picture of the poet wagging his finger at the Devil in friendly admonition and suggesting that even he might be saved sets the whole theological conception of original sin in a context where it cannot survive: in such surroundings the doctrine dissolves, or one might perhaps say blows up.

Line 2. Clootie: cloven-footed.
     5. spairges: spatters.
        cootie: wooden dish.
     6. scaud: scald.
   15. lowin' heugh: blazing pit.
   18. blate nor scaur: bashful nor timid.
   22. tirling: unroofing.
   30. eldritch croon: unearthly moan.
   32. douce: respectable.
   35. boortries: elder trees.
   38. sklentin: slanting.
   41. rash-buss: tuft of rushes.
   42. sough: a sighing sound (as of wind).
   43. nieve: fist.
   45. stoor: deep.
   47. squatter'd: flapped.
   54. howkit: dug-up.
   56. kirn: churn.
   59. dawtit: petted.
       twal-pint hawkie: twelve-pint cow.
   60. as dry as the bull.
   62. crouse: merry.
   63. wark-lume: tool.
   64. cantrip: magic.
   67. thowes: thaws.
   91. snick-drawing: latch-drawing, i.e., stealthy, scheming.
   93. brogue: trick.
   95. shog: shake.
   96. 'maist: almost.
   97. bizz: ferment.
   98. with smoked clothes and shriveled wig.
   99. smoutie phiz: smutty face.
  101. man of Uz: Job.

107. scawl: scold.
110. fechtin: fighting.
111. Michael: "Vide Milton, Book VI." (Burns)
113. ding: beat.
      Lallan: Lowland.
      Erse: Gaelic.
123. aiblins: perhaps.

157. *To a Louse.* Notice how skilfully Burns works the poem to its final moral lesson. The "fine lady" of line 10 is gradually reduced to the familiar "Jenny" of line 37, and in that reduction lies in part the morality of the poem, which is made explicit in the concluding proverbial note.

Line   1. ferlie: wonder.
       3. strunt: strut.
       7. wonner: wonder.
      13. swith: be off!
          hauffet: temple.
      17. bane: toothcomb.
      20. fatt'rels: trimmings.
      26. grozet: gooseberry.
      28. smeddum: powder.
      30. droddum: breech.
      32. flainen toy: flannel cap.
      33. duddie: ragged.
      34. wyliecoat: flannel vest.
      35. Lunardi: balloon-shaped bonnet.

158. *Tam o' Shanter.* This remarkable narrative poem is based on local folk story. Notice how skilfully Burns manipulates the contrast between the warm and inviting interior of the "pub" and the harsh weather outside. The climax of this interior comes with

> Kings may be blest, but Tam was glorious,
> O'er a' the ills o' life victorious!

The lines about the transience of pleasure which follow are written in regular neoclassic English, and deliberately so, for they point, with deliberate sentensiousness, the moral which serves as the transition from the cozy interior to the threatening weather outside. Burns is careful to provide the reader with a rational explanation of Tam's vision if he wishes to have one—we can always say that Tam was drunk—but the suggestion is never openly made, and Burns himself tells the whole story with a straight face. The invocation to liquor ("John Barleycorn") comes just before the terrifying and fantastic description of what Tam saw at Kirk Alloway, as a sly reminder of what *might* be the explanation of it all. The deliberately oversimplified moral at the end of the poem is, of course, purely ironical.

Line   1. chapman billies: peddler fellows.
       2. drouthy: thirsty.
       4. gate: road.
       5. nappy: ale.
       6. fou: drunk.

8. slaps: gaps in hedges.
19. skellum: good-for-nothing.
20. blellum: chatterer.
23. melder: meal-grinding.
33. gars me greet: makes me weep.
38. unco: uncommonly, very.
40. reaming swats: foaming ale.
41. Souter: shoemaker.
42. drouthy crony: thirsty companion.
55. lades: loads.
81. skelpit: dashed.
     dub: puddle.
85. glow'ring: staring.
86. bogles: ghosts, bogies.
88. houlets: owls.
90. smoored: smothered.
93. whins: gorse bushes.
     cairn: heap of stones.
103. ilka bore: every chink.
107. tippeny: twopenny ale.
108. usquabae: whisky.
109. the swats sae reamed: the ale so frothed.
110. he car'd na deils a boddle: he cared not a farthing for devils.
116. brent: brand.
119. winnock-bunker: window seat.
121. touzie tyke: shaggy dog.
123. skirl: sound shrilly.
124. dirl: ring.
125. presses: cupboards.
127. cantraip slight: magic trick.
131. airns: irons.
133. rape: rope.
134. gab: mouth.
147. cleekit: joined hands.
148. swat and reekit: sweated and smoked.
149. coost her duddies: cast off her rags.
150. linket: tripped.   sark: shirt, shift.
151. queans: girls.
153. creeshie flannen: greasy flannel.
154. seventeen-hunder: woven in a reed of 1,700 divisions (and thererore of best quality).
157. hurdies: hips.
158. burdies: losses.
160. rigwoodie: lean and bony.
     spean: wean.
161. leaping and kicking on a staff.
164. wawlie: choice.
169. meikle: much.
     bear: barley.
171. cutty: short.
     harn: yarn.

174. vauntie: proud.
176. coft: bought.
188. tint: lost.
193. fyke: bustle.
194. herds: herdboys.
      byke: hive.
195. pussie's: the hare's.
200. eldritch skreich: unearthly yell.
201. fairin: deserts.
210. the fient a tail: the devil a tail.
213. ettle: intent.
215. ae: one.
      hale: whole.
217. claught: seized.

159. *Green Grow the Rashes.* A lively and spontaneous song, expressing complete abandonment to the mood of the moment.

Line 9. warly: worldly.
     16. tapsalteerie: topsy-turvy.
     17. douce: grave, respectable.

160. *John Anderson My Jo.* Here is a simple love song in which images of domesticity and companionship are fused together with images suggestive of the familiar theme of the passing of time. The wife is addressing the husband. Sentimentality is avoided by the absence of generalizations and the projection of the emotion through a concrete situation. It should be remembered that this is a song, meant to be sung rather than read or spoken, and songs deal with "great commonplaces" rather than with subtle individual perceptions.

Line 1. jo: sweetheart.
     4. brent: smooth.
     7. pow: head.
    11. cantie: cheerful.

161. *Ca' the Yowes.* A song written for one of the most beautiful of Scottish melodies. The imagery distils a mood of perfect pastoral peace, which prepares the way for the simple benediction of the fourth stanza, and against this atmosphere of benediction and hushed nature the concluding profession of love is made.

Line 1. yowes: ewes.
     7. a-faulding: folding sheep.

162. *Go Fetch to Me a Pint o' Wine.* Burns has managed to infuse into this song the whole atmosphere of medieval romance and martial ballad, combining a note of ceremony and even pageantry with a genuine folk feeling on the one hand and a tone of formal compliment on the other. The domiciling of different kinds of imagery in a single emotional context is superbly done. The elemental formality of the opening two lines is set suddenly against a realistic picture of a stormy embarkation at Leith, with the specification of place names ("the pier o' Leith," "Berwick-law"—a conspicuous hill overlooking the Firth of Forth) that is an effective trick of the ballads. The second stanza conjures up all the panoply of ceremonial warfare: that single line

> The glittering spears are rankèd ready

is an absolute epitome of the medieval heroic phase of Scottish history. From the panoply of war we move to its horror ("thick and bloody"), and the final turn of the poem comes when both the horror of battle and the dangers of the storm are put aside as nothing compared with "leaving thee, my bonie Mary."

This is a love poem set in an atmosphere of history—history with all its ceremony and violence—and of nature with all *its* violence; and through it all the opening gesture of drinking a health "in a silver tassie" (goblet) works as a unifying image, a grave salute to love in the midst of natural and human warfare.

163. *A Red, Red, Rose.* The mixture of swagger and tenderness which is achieved by the imagery of this poem is a perfect epitome of one aspect of the male attitude to love. This, too, is a song, and should be considered as such when it is read.

164. *Auld Lang Syne.* Here, too, is a song which seeks to achieve a community emotion. It is perhaps the greatest of all poems on the theme of remembered friendship. Its effectiveness lies in the linking of the central emotion to the idea of time and change through precise contrasts between past and present. The sublimation of nostalgia for the past in present good fellowship brings the song to a close with a formal social gesture, in the light of which everything falls into shape: past and present are held together for one tenuous moment by ritual, which is man's way of marking permanently the fleeting meanings of things.

Line 9. be your pint-stowp: pay for your pint-stoup.
     14. gowans: daisies.
     21. fiere: comrade.
     23. guid-willie waught: goodwill drink.

165. *The Village.* This is an obvious contrast to Goldsmith's "Deserted Village," but it should not be read simply as a reply to Goldsmith. Its somber realism and sense of the desolate landscape of the Suffolk coast (where Crabbe was born and grew up) produce a remarkable effect of their own. Crabbe succeeds in linking the dreariness of natural objects to his sense of futility and tragedy in human life, and his imagery should be examined carefully from this point of view. He is the great antipastoral poet, setting the truth about country life against the idyllic creations of generations of poets. Yet "The Village" is not merely a piece of naturalistic description in heroic couplets: it is shot through with a fierce moral emotion which is related through the use of imagery to the quality of the landscape. Crabbe's couplets have neither the polish of Pope's or the rhetorical force of Dr. Johnson's: underlying the almost savage gloom there is an elegiac feeling which is conveyed by the run of the verse as well as by the imagery.

Crabbe uses the pastoral tradition merely for scornful contrast: in all other respects, he is one of the most tradition-less poets in English. Using a verse form generally associated with the eighteenth century, he developed a mood and a kind of observation which have no relation to anything that had previously been done in English poetry, and which have had very little influence on subsequent poets. Criticism, which likes to arrange poets in schools, has therefore tended to neglect Crabbe. But he is an original poet of great gifts, with a remarkable sense of atmosphere, a somber wit, and real skill at realistic verse narrative.

Line 27. honest Duck: Stephen Duck, the "thresher poet." A versifier of humble origin who was patronized by Pope and others and was appointed by Queen Caroline keeper of her library at Richmond.

101 ff. The reference is to smuggling.

114. See note to Johnson's "Vanity of Human Wishes" (poem No. 149) line 97.

166. *Song: "How sweet I roamed."* Blake's early lyrics have a freshness combined with deliberate symbolic overtones, neither of which qualities are easily found in earlier eighteenth-century poetry. There is an Elizabethan quality about this and the next poem, a complete absence of the urban, social tone that we find, for example, in Prior. The simple delicacy of the imagery, the sense of a direct personal vision which makes the most commonplace image into an original symbol, give a unique charm to these poems.

167. *Song: "My silks and fine array."* The tone here is more purely Elizabethan than in the preceding poem. Notice again how conventional imagery can be used freshly and powerfully.

168. *Mad Song.* Here both imagery and verse form are less conventional, and the result is a strangely haunting distillation of a mood.

169–171. These three poems are from Blake's *Songs of Innocence,* a remarkable collection of lyrics whose general theme is enunciated in the "Introduction." It is a picture of a world of children, delighted with the beauty and innocence of all creation. Experience is bathed in love, and redeemed by love if anything should go wrong. The imagery is fresh and immediate, the rhythms flowing and musical. Confidence, wonder, simplicity are key attitudes and qualities, and the childlike nature of the feeling is appropriate to the atmosphere of innocence and what the theologians would call "prelapsarian" (before the Fall) emotions. This is a kind of poetry which turns its back on the forms and conventions of civilization to develop an individual vision through a naked confrontation of experience. Later, this approach led Blake to develop, through a study of a variety of mystical traditions, a complex personal symbolic language of his own. But at this stage of his career it led him to produce these limpid lyrics, which are so difficult to parallel in English or any other literature.

172–176. These poems are from *Songs of Experience,* a collection of lyrics which parallel those in the *Songs of Innocence* from a very different point of view. Here innocence has been lost, love has been perverted, man with his "civilization" has corrupted the pristine glory of things; nature is enigmatic and terrible, man's good instincts have been changed by the coercion of moral laws into a cold, restrictive morality:

> I went to the Garden of Love,
> And saw what I never had seen:
> A Chapel was built in the midst,
> Where I used to play on the green.
>
> And the gates of this Chapel were shut,
> And "Thou shalt not" writ over the door. . . .

A note of doom runs through these poems, dark and passionate moods are distilled by the imagery. But there are other notes here, too, and if the poems are read separately as individual poems rather than as parts of a sequence, it can be seen that Blake is doing more than protesting against what the Industrial Revolution was doing to "England's green and pleasant land" and asserting his belief in spontaneous love against legal compulsion; he was also giving expression to moods of wonder, pity, mystery, and other less definable emotions, through a variety of images which are made symbolic by their organization in the poem and by the atmosphere with which he surrounds them.

"Holy Thursday" should be contrasted with the poem of the same title in "Songs of Innocence." "The Tyger" (Blake's spelling is worth preserving, as it adds to the note of terror and mystery) is an expression of the other side of nature from that portrayed in the earlier collection. "Ah! Sunflower," with its slow movement and muted music, has its own mystery and melancholy. "The Garden of Love" is an allegory conveyed through an imagery both simple and powerful (notice the effect of the double rhyme in the second last line). "London," a poem of bitterness and terror, is his condemnation of urban civilization done with a brilliant handling of imagery which is worth careful examination.

177. *"Never seek to tell thy love."* Notice the effect of the short final line in this strangely symbolic poem.

178. *"And did those feet in ancient time."* This rousing poem—which, very appropriately, is often sung in England as a hymn—is placed at the head of Blake's long poem, *Milton*.

179. *Lines Written in Early Spring.* Here is poetry used to express a point of view about the relation between man and Nature in a manner not fundamentally different from that of the verse essays of the eighteenth century. Wordsworth's diction lacks the deliberate poetic polish of many of the earlier poets, and his verse form is one which demands a less rhetorical use of language, but this poem, like so many eighteenth-century poems, is a preconceived thought given effective expression in verse, with the metrical and rhyme schemes adding to the effectiveness and agreeableness of the communication; it is not the kind of poem in which the meaning is so closely bound up with the form of expression employed that it cannot be said to exist apart from that form.

180. *Expostulation and Reply.* This poem is perhaps more interesting to students of Wordsworth's philosophy than as a poem in its own right. Like so many of Wordsworth's poems, it represents a *point* expressed in verse: rhyme and meter have been (to use Wordsworth's own term) "superadded" in order to carry the point more effectively into the reader's mind and emotions than could be done by a prose statement.

181. *To My Sister.* Here the rhymes, rhythms, and imagery help to communicate the mood out of which the poem arose, so that the poem is not the communication of a preconceived point in verse but rather the projection of a mood by poetic means.

182. *Tintern Abbey.* This poem is a favorite one for students of Wordsworth's mind, for it tells of the stages in the development of his attitude toward Nature. But it is also remarkably successful as a poem, and a poem much richer and more complex than any of the three discussed above. The blank verse, with its shifting of pauses to follow the line of the emotion and the rise and fall of its verse-paragraphs, conveys the throb of rising feeling without any lushness or sentimentality; at each point the thought is given significance by its emotional context, until the poem finally moves into an expression of love for the poet's sister, at which point it comes to rest. The whole poem is a finely modulated expression of a state of mind and sensibility; its slow and moving utterance is sustained without any lowering of tension until the last line. This is a very different use of the medium of poetry from that in "Lines Written in Early Spring" or "Expostulation and Reply." The important part of the poem is not here the preconceived point, which was suitably expressed in meter, but the close-woven pattern of mood, thought, and sensibility which emerges cumulatively from the poetic expression.

183. *We Are Seven.* This poem is one of those highly individual verse fables through which Wordsworth expressed some of his perceptions about childhood. The studied simplicity of the style owes something to the ballads, those folk verse-narratives in which a new and growing interest developed in the latter part of the eighteenth century.

184. *The Old Cumberland Beggar.* Notice how Wordsworth uses his description of the beggar as a jumping-off place for generalizations about poverty and moral worth. Is this the same general technique as that employed in "Tintern Abbey"? What about the function of the blank verse here? Notice how Wordsworth returns to the beggar in the concluding verse paragraph, and what effect is achieved in this return.

185–188. These "Lucy" poems of Wordsworth stand apart from the body of the poet's work not only on account of their subject (scholars are still arguing over the identity of Lucy, and some hold that she is purely imaginary) but because of the strange and almost trancelike moods which they distil. Here is Wordsworth's simple ballad style put to its most effective use—to give the impression of a quietly desperate honesty in recollecting a profoundly moving experience. These poems reach very deeply into those experiences out of which Wordsworth developed his characteristic philosophy of man and Nature.

189. *Michael.* A "pastoral poem" quite different from the products of any earlier phase of the pastoral tradition. This simple story, with its relatively bare blank verse, achieves a sense of insight into an elemental experience which at least in some degree arises out of Wordsworth's fixing his eye carefully on the object and picking out details at once overwhelmingly convincing in their accurately observed realism and symbolic in their implications. The steady beat of the blank verse sustains the emotional tone and adds gravity and dignity to the story. Notice how at the crisis of the poem Wordsworth breaks into a generalization (line 449) and then brings it powerfully home by the particular description which follows—a description which culminates in a line (469) overwhelming in its stark matter-of-factness. This is one of the poems Wordsworth wrote in order "to show that men who do not wear fine clothes can feel deeply," but its poetic value goes far beyond this doctrinaire interest. Whatever Wordsworth may have thought, the significance of the tale arises out of the way it is told: the sense of a deep human reality being concentrated in this single rustic situation comes from that effective combination of grave matter-of-factness and underlying emotion, which in turn is achieved by rhythms and imagery.

190. *Resolution and Independence.* This poem might be compared with "The Old Cumberland Beggar" and "Michael." What is achieved by the rhymed stanza form? Observe the relation between generalization and particular description in the poem, and consider how successful it is. Is Lewis Carroll's parody (poem No. 305) a fair criticism?

191. *London, 1802.* The sonnet was not much practiced in England between Milton and Wordsworth (though we have already included one by Gray). Notice Wordsworth's use of the sonnet form (compare note to poem No. 1).

192. *Composed by the Seaside, near Calais.* The variation of the pauses within the line adds much to the effectiveness of this sonnet. Notice how the poem takes a new turn and gains new force with

> There! that dusky spot
> Beneath thee, that is England; there she lies.

193. *Composed upon Westminster Bridge.* This justly famous sonnet succeeds brilliantly in conveying the sense of early morning hush before the city has awakened. Wordsworth begins with an emphatic line, couched in purely general terms and end-stopped; and he follows this up with two rhyming lines (though the rhyme is imperfect and muted) which still keep us in suspense about the real subject of the poem. After a pause (which cuts across the structure of the sonnet, coming between the third and fourth lines of the first quatrain) he comes down to particulars, with a gesture of pointing conveyed by "*This* city......" The sentence which begins thus is one of those grave and beautiful utterances, conveying at once a description of what is observed and the quality of the observer's mood, which Wordsworth at his best could achieve so memorably: the mood of the poet and the early morning appearance of the silent city are now linked permanently, so that the remainder of the poem, building on this unification, can develop naturally into a statement that is at once descriptive and confessional. The contrast between the hushed stillness of the city and the bustling activity which is generally associated with urban imagery is implied but never overtly asserted. After the expressive sentence of lines 4–5, the objects reveal themselves to the observer one by one, but not before they have been described as "silent, bare." (Notice the importance of having these adjectives *before* the list of "ships, towers, domes, theatres, and temples.") Having been revealed, they are linked at once to Nature: they lie "open unto the fields and to the sky" and the fact that the city in this moment of dawn is so transfigured as to be removed completely from normal urban associations into the world of Nature is emphasized by the adjectives "bright," "glittering," and "smokeless." The sense of shimmering beauty is communicated in line 8, and developed further in the next two lines, which constitute another of those grand descriptive sentences that sum up so magnificently the impact of the scene on the poet. In lines 10–11, also, the link between the city and Nature is confirmed. We then move to the poet, who for the first time introduces explicitly his own emotions—which are at once clinched with those two words, *calm* and *deep.*

With this projection of the idea of calmness and stillness, all the previous images fall into place and the silence of the city becomes part of the poet's mood. The river is now described by the verb *glideth,* which again develops the notion of calm silence, and the poem ends on a note of controlled emotion, with the poet exclaiming at the sense of utter peace which arises from the city. That this is a state of unstable equilibrium, a rare moment of repose for a mighty organism, is suggested in the last line, where the real cause for wonder is now fully evident—the fact that a great city can be at once identified with *natural* beauty (cf. lines 9–10) and with *human* behavior ("the very houses seem asleep"). Thus Nature, the poet, and the city finally come together, and their doing so symbolizes the poet's mood.

194. *"It is a beauteous evening, calm and free."* This sonnet has been much knocked about by recent criticism, since it is a good example of a poem which, admirable in itself, is also interesting biographically—the "dear Child" addressed in line 9 is Wordsworth's illegitimate daughter, whose existence was not suspected until twentieth-century scholarship discovered it. It should not take much discussion to prove, however, that while this fact is important to students of Wordsworth's mind, and to his biographers, it is not necessary to know it in order to appreciate the poem. Notice the effective handling of religious imagery: "holy," "Nun," "adoration" in the first part of the sonnet are echoed by "solemn," "divine," and "worshipp'st" in the second part. The turn in the poem at the beginning of the octave is handled with great skill, and the rising emotion communicated by the repetition ("Dear Child! dear Girl!") carries the contemplative mood of the octave into the sestet so as to associate the earlier idea of God in nature with the later idea of God in the child. (It is worth noting that God is referred to only indirectly in the first part, by such terms as "heaven" and "mighty Being"—which is the sea reflecting the grandeur of God—while in the second part the religious imagery is more conventional and specific, culminating in the actual mention of God: the idea around which the poem is built is, of course, that an adult sees God through the contemplation of Nature, but a child sees God directly and less self-consciously.) Notice again how Wordsworth links his own mood to the point he is making, so that the point is of poetic interest in so far as it reflects and illuminates a state of mind.

195. *"The world is too much with us."* Consider once again the relation between the point communicated and the mood evoked as a result of the method of the communication.

Line 13. Proteus: the old man of the sea of Greek legend.
     15. Triton: in Greek mythology, son of Poseidon, god of the sea, who was supposed to dwell with his parents in a golden palace at the bottom of the sea.

196. *The Solitary Reaper.* Notice the sustained cadences of this poem, and the rising emotion of the first stanza. With the second stanza the emotion is kept steady, as Wordsworth throws around the situation two effective analogies which culminate in two lines which characteristically evoke the full quality of the poet's mood while at the same time enriching the account of what he hears. There is a long pause after the second stanza, while the meaning and the cadence echo in the mind, and then comes the turn in the poem, with the poet moving from the rich and strange to the homely and familiar, and in doing so linking these two aspects of experience in a way which illuminates both. The final stanza introduces the poet and his reactions explicitly, anchoring the whole poem in a remembered experience.

197. *"I wandered lonely as a cloud."* Notice how the excitement grows through the first three stanzas, until the poet returns to himself, gazing. The technique employed here—stanza form, imagery, etc.—might be compared with that of the previous poem.

198. *Composed upon an Evening of Extraordinary Splendor and Beauty.* A much later poem than any of the Wordsworth poems discussed above, with some significant differences in technique. Here, as in so many of the other poems, Wordsworth is describing an experience (visual in the first instance) and linking it with a mood and with certain moral ideas. How are these elements fused together in the poem?

199. *Mutability.* Another later poem (from *Ecclesiastical Sonnets*). Wordsworth's handling of the sonnet here might be compared with some of the previous examples. There is a significant difference in the kind of imagery employed and the manner in which it is handled.

200. *The Rime of the Ancient Mariner.* This remarkable poem has given rise to a host of critical commentaries, important among which is John Livingstone Lowes's *The Road to Xanadu: A Study in the Ways of the Imagination,* which shows how Coleridge used the many suggestions he got from travel books and other sources (not, of course, always consciously). With this kind of rich imaginative fable it is tempting to produce a verse-by-verse commentary indicating how Coleridge has taken the simple ballad form and through his uncannily brilliant handling of rhythms and imagery produced a great symbolic poem whose reverberating meanings cannot be pinned down by any single interpretation. But this is perhaps more interesting to the critic than useful for the reader: the impact of "The Ancient Mariner" is immediate and impressive on any reasonably sensitive reader of poetry, and if we need any assistance in discovering and appreciating the tone and atmosphere of the poem, it is provided by the quietly archaic prose commentary in the margin which Coleridge added in a revision.

201. *Frost at Midnight.* Notice how the poet's reverie moves from the exterior to the interior scene, thence to himself and to his child, and at the end back again to the exterior scene, to conclude with a line indicative of perfect silence and peace. The movement of the poem, sustained throughout by the rhythmic intensity of the blank verse, does not depend on free association but on a carefully controlled pattern which might be compared with that of Wordsworth's "Tintern Abbey." The relation of the normal speech rhythms to the beat of the blank verse is worth careful observation, as are the moments of heightened emotion indicated by repetitions and metrical variations (as in lines 23–24). As in so many of Wordsworth's poems, this poem of Coleridge's links observation of physical objects to the poet's mood by a most interesting use of imagery.

202. *Kubla Khan.* Here is Coleridge's own note on the origin of this poem, the result (in a sense) of an opium dream:

> "In the summer of the year 1797, the Author, then in ill health, had retired to a lonely farm-house between Porlock and Linton, on the Exmoor confines of Somerset and Devonshire. In consequence of a slight indisposition, an anodyne had been prescribed, from the effects of which he fell asleep in his chair at the moment that he was reading the following sentence, or words of the same substance, in 'Purchas's Pilgrimage': 'Here the Khan Kubla commanded a palace to be built, and a stately garden thereunto. And thus ten miles of fertile ground were inclosed with a wall.' The Author continued for about three hours in a profound sleep, at least of the external senses, during which time he has the most vivid confidence, that he could not have composed less than from two to three hundred lines; if that indeed can be called composition in which all the images rose up before him as *things,* with a parallel production of the correspondent expressions, without any sensation or consciousness of effort. On awaking he appeared to himself to have a distinct recollection of the whole, and taking his pen, ink, and paper, instantly and eagerly wrote down the lines that are here preserved. At this moment he was unfortunately called out by a person on business from Porlock, and detained by him above an hour, and on his return to his room, found, to his no small surprise and mortification, that though he still retained some vague and dim recollection of the general purport of the vision, yet, with the exception of some eight or ten scattered lines and images, all the rest had passed away like the images on the surface of a stream into which a stone has been cast, but alas! without the after restoration of the latter!"

What Coleridge actually read in Samuel Purchas's *Pilgrimage* was:

> "In Xamdu did Cubla Can build a stately Palace, encompassing sixteen miles of plaine ground with a wall, wherein are fertile Meddowes, pleasant springs, delightfull Streames, and all sorts of beasts of chace and game, and in the middest thereof a sumptuous house of pleasure, which may be removed from place to place."

Coleridge wove together an extraordinary number of recollections from different travel books, old and new, in producing this strangely visionary poem. Would you consider the poem a collection of impressive images loosely strung together by free association, or a unified poem whose tone and texture unite the images into a significant whole?

203. *Dejection: an Ode.* Here is another poem in which the development of the poet's mood is linked to the carefully chosen aspects of the external world which he sees and describes. Its subject is that loss of emotional and imaginative vitality which develops when the individual loses all sense of integral relation with the external world: in describing this situation and giving it poetic force by associating it as the poem progresses with different natural sights and sounds (and note, too, the deftly varied line lengths and the rise and fall of verse paragraphs which follow the curve of the emotion) Coleridge achieves an impressively organized work of art. Notice how the poem returns at its conclusion to a situation parallel to (but not identical with) the opening: the resolution of the poet's problem is achieved by his moving away from autobiographical lament into a note of peaceful benediction, when he invokes for the lady to whom the poem is addressed that joy which can no longer be his.

Line 120. Otway: Coleridge had originally written "Wordsworth," but in order to disguise the personal reference he changed the name somewhat inappropriately to that of the Restoration dramatist.

204. *Hester.* A simple and neatly turned epitaph which is in some respects reminiscent of the lyrics of Ben Jonson.

205. *Lochinvar.* This galloping narrative verse is perfectly suited to this ballad-like poem. Notice how Scott achieves the impression of romantic action in a heroic world.

206. *The Rover's Farewell.* This song is one of the inserted lyrics in Scott's long narrative poem, *Rokeby.* Notice the effect achieved by the short line just before the conclusion of each stanza.

207. *Proud Maisie.* Madge Wildfire's song in *The Heart of Midlothian.* There is great artistry in this little lyric. The simple and direct opening is followed by the question and answer which develop an eerie note of foreboding. The answer to the second question continues into the final stanza and swells out into a haunting prophecy of doom. There is a folk note in the poem: notice how elemental are the images suggestive of death.

208. *Rose Aylmer.* A finely controlled lapidary poem, with the expression of grief canalized at the end into an almost ritual gesture. Compare Landor's "Hester" (No. 204).

209. *"Past ruined Ilion Helen lives."* The poise and control of Landor's short poems are here excellently illustrated. This is an epigrammatic art, and represents a very special way of handling verse. Consider what is required of this kind of verse expression.

Line 1. Ilion: Troy.

210. *On his Seventy-Fifth Birthday.* Perhaps the best known of Landor's verse epigrams. Its quality needs no demonstration.

211. *Let Erin Remember the Days of Old.* Thomas Moore's poetry is extremely "soft": that is, it uses rather obvious rhythms and conventionally "poetic" associations, appealing on a somewhat superficial level to the reader's surface emotions. Literature has its "soft" classics, and some of Thomas Moore's poems are among them.

212. *Scotch Air.* Another "soft" classic. It might be compared, in mood, tone, and imagery, with Burns's "Auld Lang Syne," which, while on a similar theme, has none of Moore's softness. Consider just what it is that makes the difference.

Many of Moore's poems, like Burns's songs, were intended to be sung. A song demands a certain kind of simplicity, but simplicity is not the same as softness.

213. *Lines to Mr. Hodgson.* This high-spirited and amusing poem represents one side of Byron, an aspect of him which is very far removed from the romantic attitudinizing in which he sometimes indulged.

214. *Written after Swimming from Sestos to Abydos.* Byron is referring to the well-known story of Hero and Leander: the latter, a young man of Abydos, swam every night across the Hellespont to visit Hero, a priestess of Aphrodite, at Sestus. He was drowned one stormy night while making the trip.

215. *The Destruction of Sennacherib.* This poem might be compared in rhythms and general effect to Scott's "Young Lochinvar" (No. 205). The theme, however, is Biblical rather than heroic, and the significance of the imagery in the final stanza should be noted.

216. *Stanzas for Music.* This is a more typically "romantic" lyric than any of the previous examples of Byron's poetry. Much of the success of this poem lies in the movement and the cadence—the "feminine" endings should be noted. The association of beauty, music, water, sleep, moonlight, and summer is worth examining. It is common enough in the poetry of the period—and in much other poetry. The Elizabethans used this kind of association frequently: its function is, of course, to establish mood and tone rather than to indicate stock poetic properties. The reader might ask himself how the poet prevents such images from functioning simply as stock poetic properties.

217. *Hymn to Intellectual Beauty.* The ideal beauty which man infrequently glimpses, but which he can never apprehend directly, is a notion that Shelley got from Plato. Note how the stanza form fits the exalted mood of the poet. The poem is as much about the poet as about the idea: it is characteristic of Shelley to associate his own feelings in moments of emotional stress with some truth about the universe—compare the relation between the poet's mood and the nature imagery selected for description in the preceding poems by Wordsworth and Coleridge. Consider Shelley's use of imagery in the final stanza.

218. *Ozymandias.* The dry concentration of this poem sets it sharply apart in tone and technique from such an obviously "romantic" poem as the preceding. Note Shelley's handling of the sonnet form here.

219. *Ode to the West Wind.* Here again we have a natural phenomenon associated with the mood of the poet. The first stanzas contain purely objective description, but they are turned suddenly into a discussion of the poet himself in the fourth stanza, and in the final stanza an elaborate comparison between the wind's activity and the poet's needs draws the poem together and brings it from despondency to triumph. Note how the stanza form (which is worth careful examination) helps to sustain the mood.

Line 21. Maenad: worshipper of Bacchus, god of wine and revelry.

220. *The Cloud.* "This is the most perfect example of Shelley's using the best scientific knowledge of his day to symbolize higher truths." (Ernest Bernbaum). The poem cumulatively projects a human feeling into the activities of nature until all the natural phenomena with which the cloud is concerned take on a passionate life of their own. Notice once again the effects achieved by the stanza form, and the use of the internal rhymes.

221. *To Night.* Notice how lines 4–6 of each stanza, with their sustained cadence, add a quality of tenseness. The chiming and echoing of vowel sounds in these lines in the first stanza are particularly effective.

222. *To—* (*"Music, when soft voices die"*). Is this poem epigrammatic in the sense that Landor's are?

223. *To—* (*"One word is too often profaned"*). Here, as so often in Shelley, a self-indulged emotion is redeemed by craftsmanship, by a tight neatness of expression, from mere sentimentality.

224. *Adonais.* Shelley's lament for the death of Keats, written in the high strains of pastoral elegy. His models are the Greek pastoral poets, Bion and Moschus, the former of whom wrote a "Lament for Adonis" and the latter a "Lament for Bion." The name Adonais is a modification of Adonis, the youth beloved of Venus, who was slain by a boar, even as (Shelley believed) Keats was slain by the critics. Shelley's preface to the first edition of the poem expresses his view of the cause of Keats's death (a quite erroneous view, it might be added: Keats died of tuberculosis, and was not "snuffed out by an article"). Shelley wrote:

"The genius of the lamented person to whose memory I have dedicated these unworthy verses was not less delicate and fragile than it was beautiful; and where cankerworms abound, what wonder if its young flower was blighted in the bud? The savage criticism of his *Endymion,* which appeared in *The Quarterly Review,* produced the most violent effect on his susceptible mind; the agitation thus originated ended in the rupture of a blood-vessel in the lungs; a rapid consumption ensued, and the succeeding acknowledgments from more candid critics of the true greatness of his powers were ineffectual to heal the wound thus wantonly inflicted.

"It may be well said that these wretched men know not what they do. They scatter their insults and their slanders without heed as to whether the poisoned shaft lights on a heart made callous by many blows or one like Keats's composed of more penetrable stuff. One of their associates is, to my knowledge, a most base and unprincipled calumniator. As to *Endymion,* was it a poem, whatever might be its defeats, to be treated contemptuously by those who had celebrated, with various degrees of complacency and panegyric, *Paris,* and *Woman,* and a *Syrian Tale,* and Mrs. Lefanu, and Mr. Barrett, and Mr. Howard Payne, and a long list of the illustrious obscure? Are these the men who in their venal good nature presumed to draw a parallel between the Rev. Mr. Milman and Lord Byron? What gnat did they strain at here, after having swallowed all those camels? Against what woman taken in adultery dares the foremost of these literary prostitutes to cast his opprobrious stone? Miserable man! you, one of the meanest, have wantonly defaced one of the noblest specimens of the workmanship of God. Nor shall it be your excuse, that, murderer as you are, you have spoken daggers, but used none."

The passionate elevation of style which enables Shelley to associate his deepest personal beliefs with his expression of grief for Adonais' death is achieved by the relation of image to idea as well as by his use of the stanza form (the "Spenserian" stanza). The poem turns out to be about himself as much as about Adonais; but this is no fault. It is characteristic of the romantic poets that they see all problems and situations in relation to their own emotional needs and profoundest beliefs, so that their poems become in some sense professions of faith in which the imagery burns and flashes with the most intensely felt meaning. The richness and splendor of "Adonais" (so different from the equally rich and splendid "Lycidas" of Milton, also a pastoral elegy) derives in part at least from this unifying imagery which links Shelley's symbolic account of Keats's death to his Platonic view of the nature of reality and at last to his own relation to that reality. Shelley does not run away from his subject to indulge in self-pity: rather, he contemplates his subject with the kind of imaginative vision which eventually resolves it into a part of a larger unity of which the poet himself is also a central part. It is important to understand the place of personal emotion in such a poem as "Adonais," especially in these days when criticism is so often directed against this kind of poetry on the grounds of its emotional excess. Emotion is used in order to resolve the different elements in the poem into a unity, one might almost say as a structural device, in this case to link the poet's view of his subject to his view of reality. A poet like Shelley operated most effectively when he was able to link his specific theme to his most profound personal beliefs about the universe; this is achieved by a use of imagery so charged with personal emotion and significance that it keeps on expanding the meaning of the poem. By the time Shelley introduces himself again at the end of the poem, he, too, has become a symbol which both illustrates and unites the various overtones of meaning that have been sent echoing through the poem.

Line 12. Urania: the heavenly poetic muse, invoked by Milton in *Paradise Lost*.
30–36. The reference is to Milton.
47. Urania is widowed because of the evil days on which poetry has fallen.
55. Capital: Rome, where Keats died.
94. anadem: garland.
107. clips: embraces.
140. Phoebus (Apollo) was in love with Hyacinth, who was struck and killed by a quoit while playing quoits with the god. The hyacinth flower sprang from his blood.
141. Narcissus: the youth who fell in love with his own image, as reflected in a fountain.
160. brere: briar.
179. the intense atom: the soul.
198. the fading Splendor: Urania.

250. The reference is to Byron, who had attacked the reviewers in his *English Bards and Scotch Reviewers.*

264. The Pilgrim of Eternity: Byron.

268. Ierne: Ireland. Shelley is referring to Thomas Moore.

271 ff. The reference is to Shelley himself.

276. Actaeon-like: Actaeon had looked on Diana naked while she was bathing, and as a punishment the goddess changed him to a stag and he was hunted to death by his own dogs.

280. pardlike: leopard-like.

307 ff. The reference is to Leigh Hunt, devoted friend of Keats.

319. nameless worm: the anonymous reviewer of Keats's *Endymion* who, according to Shelley, was responsible for Keats's death.

404. Lucan: It is easy to see why Shelley names Chatterton and Sidney in this stanza, but the Latin poet Lucan seems an odd choice. Shelley is presumably thinking of him as a champion of liberty: he joined a conspiracy against Nero, and on its discovery was compelled to commit suicide.

439. slope of green: the Protestant cemetery at Rome, where Keats was buried.

444. pyramid: the pyramid of Cestius.

453 ff. A reference to William Shelley, the poet's son, who had been buried in the same cemetery in 1819.

225. *Chorus from 'Hellas.'* The concluding chorus in Shelley's verse drama, *Hellas.* There is a fine prophetic roll about the poem, achieved in part by the emphatic concluding couplet of each stanza. The classical names are the more familiar ones—references to places in ancient Greece (Hellas) or to stories from Greek mythology (Jason and the Argonauts; Orpheus and his lute; Ulysses detained by Calypso on his way home to Ithaca; the siege of Troy; Laius, king of Thebes and father of the ill-fated Oedipus, who killed him in ignorance of his identity during a quarrel on the road between Delphi and Daulis).

226. *Lines: "When the lamp is shattered."* The plangent quality of this lyric is achieved by the effective combination of imagery, stanza form, and "feminine" rhymes. Note how the imagery moves out, as it were, in the final stanza, to suggest the desolation of a barren winter landscape: the earlier imagery is mostly suggestive of indoor living (the lamp and the lute suggest an intimate indoor scene). This expansion of imagery pushes the emotion home with great force.

227. *"When I have fears that I may cease to be."* A "Shakespearean" sonnet. The resolution of the poem is a mood of trancelike contemplation.

228. *"In a drear-nighted December."* The muted elegiac tone of the effective little poem is largely achieved by the stanza form, with the sustained cadence and "feminine" rhymes of lines 5–7 of each stanza. Notice that in this expression of a personal grief at "passed joy" the poet never once mentions himself.

229. *The Eve of St. Agnes.* There was a popular superstition that on the Eve of St. Agnes (January 21) a girl could see a vision of her future husband: Keats uses this as the motivating power of this "rich and strange" narrative poem. He here distils the very essence of romantic action; but the poem is more than a fancy romantic story. Notice the remarkable use of symbolic imagery: the storm outside, the religious ritual, the architectural detail, the feasting of the noblemen, the heraldic forms and colors, the exotic list of dainties, to pick out only a few examples. Keats has taken one of the great "archetypical" incidents of folklore (a young lover stealing his bride away from a hostile environment—one might compare Scott's "Young Lochinvar") and wrought it up to the highest pitch of symbolic romance that such a narrative can bear. The atmosphere is that of the Middle Ages, but a symbolic Middle Ages in which art, ritual, superstition, revelry, and luxury form a background in which nameless evil threatens perfect love. Keats has ransacked every relevant literary source in order to enrich his imagery and create his atmosphere. Notice the contrasts in the poem—between the "bitter chill" outside and the warmth and luxury within, between "dwarfish Hildebrand" and the handsome Porphyro, between the old beldame and the beautiful Madeline, etc.— and their purpose in the poem. Note, too, the concluding stanza: the whole story is pushed into the past, where it becomes even richer and stranger.

230. *To Sleep.* Note the rhyme scheme of this sonnet.

231. *La Belle Dame Sans Merci.* The folk theme of the beautiful but evil lady is here developed into a remarkable expression of a sense of loss, mystery, and terror. Notice the skill with which Keats handles this simple stanza—the short final line adds to the impression of mystery and sometimes, as in the fourth line of the poem, the quiet beat of three emphatic syllables coming together creates an impression of utter loneliness. This poem is notable for its handling of imagery and rhythms: each develops the symbolic significance of the other, so that, for example, a phrase such as "on the cold hill's side" (line 36) takes on an uncanny intensity because of its place in the rhythm pattern of the stanza.

The meaning of the title is "the beautiful lady without pity."

232. *"Bright star, would I were steadfast as thou art."* Notice how Keats develops his description of the star continually watching the sea and how this choice of language here builds up a whole implicit picture of waves beating on silent shores while the world sleeps. Such a picture is important for the mood of the poem, even though he builds it up in order to deny the parallel. Do you consider the imagery in the last six lines of the sonnet effective?

Line 4. Eremite: hermit, religious solitary.

233. *Ode to a Nightingale.* All of Keats's great odes deal with some aspect of the relation between pleasure and pain, happiness and melancholy, imagination and reality. The rich and slow-moving verse of this ode develops a mood and a tone in which such contrasts are reconciled: the climax is the second last stanza, where the nightingale's song has resolved the contrast between past and present and distilled all history into an enchantment. The return from this mood to the categories of everyday life occurs in the final stanza, as the nightingale's song moves off into the distance.

Line 4. Lethe-wards: Lethe in classical mythology was the river in the underworld from which the shades drank and obtained forgetfulness.

16. Hippocrene: A fountain in Mount Helicon, sacred to the Muses: its waters granted poetic inspiration.

66. The reference is, of course, to the Biblical book of Ruth.

234. *Ode on a Grecian Urn.* This poem has received much critical attention in our time, and more than one acute analyst has tried out his skill on it. All we need note here, however, is that the poem deals with the relation between art and life through the poet's responses to the figures on a Grecian urn, which are developed until a poised, "tiptoe effect" (the phrase is G. Wilson Knight's) has been achieved, this effect being itself a symbol of art and its relation to life; the poem then concludes by a return to an awareness of the difference between the "cold pastoral" of timeless art and the warm life of men that is wasted by time into old age (compare the ending of the nightingale ode), stressing in conclusion the aspect of reality symbolized by the "marble men and maidens"—for them "beauty is truth, truth beauty." It should be noted that Keats is not addressing this aphorism to the world at large, as expressing his personal philosophy: it is the message of the urn, a message to be delivered by a "cold pastoral" when the poet's generation has become wasted with old age. The proposition becomes true only for those who can escape time and change —and, in a sense, life. Compare the ending of "Bright star, would I were steadfast as thou art."

Line 41. brede: embroidery (in this case, sculptural relief).

235. *Ode on Melancholy.* This ode exploits the bitter-sweet implications of the melancholy mood, and develops the paradox at the very center of all enjoyment. Notice the shifts in tempo from stanza to stanza.

236. *To Autumn.* The slow and heavy lines carry a rich imagery to develop the associations of "mellow fruitfulness"; but notice how at the end the mood shifts: with the mention of spring the theme of the changing year comes to the fore, and autumn ceases to be a series of static pictures to become instead a precursor of winter. The faint note of foreboding is suggested by the concluding images, but the quiet affection with which these sights and sounds are picked out almost obscure it. The perfect calm of the ending, as the poem comes gently to a close with a series of observations both casual and precise, is a masterly achievement.

237. *Rondeau.* The rondeau is a form derived from the French: it usually consists of thirteen and often of ten lines on two rhymes with the opening phrase repeated as a refrain. Its effective use calls for dexterity and neatness.

238. *It Is Not Beauty I Demand.* This poem has something of the limpid clarity of the best seventeenth-century Cavalier lyrics. F. T. Palgrave, the editor of the *Golden Treasury,* actually mistook it for a seventeenth-century poem and at first included it among the poems of that period.

239. *Isbrand's Song.* This song, from Beddoes' tragedy, *Death's Jest Book,* has that deliberately exotic quality which Beddoes, much influenced by the Jacobean dramatists, assiduously cultivated. It is something of a *tour de force,* a remarkable attempt to capture the picturesque wildness of fancy, the morbid passion, to be found in such a dramatist as Webster. There is, however, a sensationalism in Beddoes of a kind one does not get in his seventeenth-century models.

240. *Resurrection Song.* The macabre humor of this poem is equally characteristic of Beddoes.

241. *Song at Amala's Wedding.* Also from *Death's Jest Book.* This shows Elizabethan, rather than Jacobean, influence, though again it has the unmistakable note of a conscious nineteenth-century romanticism. Notice the rhythms and the effect of the "enclosed" rhymes in the last four lines of each stanza.

242. *Dirge for Wolfram.* Another poem from *Death's Jest Book.* Notice once again the rhythms. Both Darley and Beddoes made interesting contributions to English metrics.

243. *Song on the Water.* An exercise in the exotic. Consider the effects and the way they are achieved.

244. *Song: "Who tames the lion now?"* The note of incipient hysteria, suggested by the rhythms as well as by the imagery, is achieved here with considerable skill.

245. *Signs of Winter.* John Clare, the "Northamptonshire Peasant Poet," who spent the last twenty years of his life in a lunatic asylum, was one of those gifted men of humble origin who was never able to achieve a proper status from which to exercise his talents. He did produce some admirable poems, however, notable for their quiet intensity of observation. Notice the selection and organization of detail here: it might be compared with the concluding stanza of Keats's "Ode to Autumn."

246. *Badger.* Here again it is the organization of detail that makes the poem.

247. *I Am.* This is Clare's account of his own life in the asylum: it has a plangent simplicity that rises to its quiet climax in the final stanza.

248. *To a Waterfowl.* The incident at the end of Bryant's youth which inspired this poem explains not its excellence but, in part, its perennial appeal. Walking among the hills of western Massachusetts at sunset on a winter day of 1815, the year he entered the profession of law, he had a depressing sense of coldness and darkness of the world he now faced alone. At that moment the bird he darkly saw against the red sky gave to his mood a sort of universality; at the same time it renewed his faith and courage. Like "Thanatopsis," the poem succeeds partly because, rather than in spite, of the formal rhetoric through which he drew upon a tradition of thought and expression. The final stanza provides an exercise in judgment: is the "moral" extraneous, or is it, as Yvor Winters says, an explicit statement of the idea governing the poem, inherent but insufficiently obvious in what has gone before? Note that short lines are rhymed with long ones, and that, like Whitman, Bryant uses a final short line in each stanza to slow his thought to the pace of brooding contemplation.

249. *The Prairies.* One fact about America that impressed the Old World was the extent and magnificence of its wildernesses. But many Europeans wished to believe that geographically these were as immature as American ideas about man, and that both man and the inferior orders of nature that inhabited the West must suffer degradation. Americans, in reply, sought not only to defend the beauty of nature but to prove that it had nourished civilizations as old and "romantic," if not as advanced, as Europe's.

It is in this context of international debate that "The Prairies" must be understood. Bryant's treatment is at times sentimental, but he is detached enough to imply that the incoming white settlers of the prairies may be deprived of "the quickening breath of God" like that other "race of living things" that inhabited Athens.

Line 21. Sonora: A state in Mexico, bordering on Arizona.
42. mounds: supposed to have been made by the extinct Mound Builders.
48. Pentelicus: marble from the quarries of Pentelicus, used in building the Parthenon.
96. Oregon: the Columbia River.

250. *Romance.* The importance of this poem to Poe may be judged by the fact that he labeled it as the "Preface" to one section of verse in his 1829 edition, and as the "Introduction" to the whole of his collection of 1831. But to the latter edition of the poem he added forty-five lines of some of the worst poetry that he ever wrote, which, fortunately, he deleted from the final text. The reader will learn something about Poe's intention, and about the poetic process, by looking at the deleted lines, and other alterations, in Killis Campbell's edition of the *Poems.* Note the rhyme pattern of the poem as printed here; line 5 should rhyme with line 7. Observe the function of bird imagery throughout the poem. The last six lines should be considered in relation to Wordsworth's theory of poetry as "emotion recollected in tranquillity."

251. *The City in the Sea.* Before he settled on this final title, Poe called the poem in various editions "The Doomed City," "The City of Sin," and "The City in the Sea: a Prophecy." Although he exploits the traditional Biblical symbols of sin, his intent is not moral but aesthetic: gorgeous wickedness simply enforces his central theme of horror and death. It is worth noting that recurrent water imagery in Poe's work ordinarily connotes gloom or horror, whereas in Whitman it is associated with life and fertility. Note also that after letting the magnificent forty-first line stand in two editions, Poe changed it—for one edition only—to "On oceans not so sad-serene."

252. *The Haunted Palace.* This poem is an independent unit, but it has an added interest when it is read in its context as an utterance of the "hero" in "The Fall of the House of Usher." Poe stated, "By 'The Haunted Palace' I mean to imply a mind haunted by phantoms—a disordered brain." Is it true, as one critic says, that the shift, in the fifth stanza, from the image of the head to the subject of insanity is unmotivated and inexplicable?

Line 22. Porphyrogene: born to the purple.

253. *Mariana.* Mariana is a character in Shakespeare's *Measure for Measure* who, having been deserted by her lover Angelo, lives in dejection at a "moated grange"—i.e., a manor house protected by a moat. "There at the moated grange resides this dejected Mariana" is the actual phrase which set Tennyson's imagination going. Tennyson draws on his native Lincolnshire scenery in building up this picture of desolation. The imagery is adapted to the mood with a fine craftsmanship: consider, for example, the second last stanza in this connection. Tennyson—a poetic craftsman in search of a subject—often did his best work when endeavoring to capture the mood of an experience or the quality of a situation he had read about.

254. *The Lady of Shalott.* This is Tennyson's first poem on an Arthurian subject. The stories of Arthur and his knights, as told by Malory in the fifteenth century, haunted Tennyson's imagination: the background of enchantment, the dream quality of much of the action, the courtesy and ritual surrounding so much of the behavior of the knights and ladies, and combination of Christian ideals and pagan magic—these and other elements in Malory fascinated Tennyson, and he handled Arthurian material many times. The name "Shalott" is Tennyson's alteration of "Scalott," which in turn is a variant of "Astolat," the form of the name found in Malory.

Tennyson himself is said to have given the following summary of the poem's meaning: "The newborn love for something, for some one in the wide world from which she has been so long excluded, takes her out of the region of shadows into that of realities." Clearly, however, this is a rather unhelpful oversimplification, if not a rationalization. The force of the poem lies in its distillation of the quality of enchantment and its relation to everyday life. The background of the story is left in deliberate mystery, and the combination of concrete, even realistic, imagery with this sense of mystery is most effective. The stanza is deftly handled, and the use of nature imagery is most skilfully adapted to the mood and tone of the poem. Notice the conclusion.

Line 5. Camelot: The city in Cornwall where King Arthur kept his court.

255. *The Lotos Eaters.* The inspiration of this poem is a brief passage in the *Odyssey* describing how Odysseus (Ulysses, as the Romans called him) and his men, on their journey back to Ithaca from the siege of Troy, came to the land of the lotos-eaters:

Thence for nine days I [Odysseus is speaking] was carried by terrible winds over the teeming sea; but on the tenth day we went ashore on the land of the lotos-eaters, who eat a flowery food. There we stepped on to the land and drew water, and immediately my companions took their meal by the swift ships. But when we had eaten and drunk I sent out some of my companions to discover who they were who ate bread upon the earth: I chose two men, and sent a third with them as a herald. They went at once and mixed with the lotos-eaters; and the lotos-eaters did not plan death for my companions but gave them the lotos to taste. And whoever of them ate of the honey-sweet fruit of the lotos had no longer any desire to bring home news or to return, but they wanted to stay there among the lotos-eaters, eating the lotos and forgetting their homeward journey. I therefore brought these men forcibly back to the ships, though they wept, dragging them under the benches and binding them fast in the hollow ships. And I ordered the rest of my trusty comrades to embark on the swift ships speedily, lest anyone should eat of the lotos and forget all about his homeward journey.

Tennyson builds his rich and musical verse as an elaboration of this theme. Notice the complicated and irregular stanza forms of the choric song, and the quickening of purpose in the final stanza, where temptation is succumbed to and the possibility of remaining on the island becomes a certainty. The lines grow longer as the decision is reached and a note almost of exultation emerges. Yet the poem closes on a note of utter surrender and peace.

Line 133. amaranth: a mythical, never-fading flower.
moly: the magical herb that saved Ulysses from harm when he fell into the hands of Circe, the enchantress.
142. acanthus: a plant sacred to the gods.
169. Elysian: The Elysian fields are in Greek mythology the eternally happy land where there is neither cold, nor snow, nor rain, where the shades of the Blessed go after death.
170. asphodel: the daffodils which covered the Elysian fields.

256. *Morte D'Arthur.* This version of the death of Arthur is based on the account given in the fifth chapter of the twenty-first book of Malory. Tennyson writes it as the fragment of an epic (it opens with the conjunction "so"), using a stately and slow-moving blank verse and an imagery suggestive of a world heroic, religious, and remote. Notice what perfect control Tennyson maintains over the tempo of the poem.

"Morte D'Arthur" was later incorporated in "The Passing of Arthur," one of the *Idylls of the King,* a series of connected poems on Arthurian themes.

Line 4. Lyonnesse: a district of Cornwall (since supposed to have sunk back into the sea, beyond Land's End) which figures prominently in the Arthurian legends.
31. samite: heavy silk material.
139. the reference is to the aurora borealis ("northern lights").
140. moving isles of winter: icebergs.
232. the reference is to the Star of Bethlehem, which led the Wise Men to the infant Christ.
259. Avilion: Avalon, the Arthurian equivalent of the Elysian fields.

257. *Ulysses.* The story of Ulysses' setting out again on his travels long after his perilous voyage back from Troy to Ithaca does not come from classical sources: Tennyson found it in the twenty-sixth canto of Dante's *Inferno.* Dante meets Ulysses in hell, and Ulysses tells him of his final and fatal voyage: he sailed westward with his companions into the unknown, and just after catching sight of a distant mountain in a new land, a storm arose and destroyed the ship. Tennyson is not, however, interested in the actual adventure: he is concerned with the state of mind which prompted the aging Ulysses to undertake it. The poem was written soon after the death of Tennyson's close friend Arthur Hallam (in whose memory *In Memoriam* was written). Tennyson told his son that it "gave my feeling about the need of going forward, and braving the struggle of life, perhaps more simply than anything in *In Memoriam.*"

There is a deliberate loftiness of utterance here, an eloquence and a dignity not incompatible with simplicity, that Tennyson was not often able to sustain without striking a false note at some point. The regular rhythms of the blank verse add gravity and sonority to the tone, while at the same time variations of the pause within the line prevent stiffness and give the poem ease and flexibility. The emotion rises as the poem draws to a conclusion, and so does the note of simple and almost fatalistic confidence.

Line 10. Hyades: a group of seven stars in the constellation Taurus which rise with the sun at the season of the spring rains.
 63. Happy Isles: The Islands of the Blessed, home of heroes after death (cf. the Elysian fields, poem No. 255, line 169, note).

258. *Tithonus.* Tithonus in Greek legend was beloved of Eos, goddess of Dawn, who obtained for him from the gods the gift of immortality, but forgot to ask at the same time for the gift of perpetual youth, so that Tithonus grew ever older and more withered, though immortal.

Nowhere is Tennyson's ability to render a mood of deep plangency in language finely chiseled and cadenced better illustrated than in this poem. The opening four lines evoke the very essence of change in earthly things, against which the situation of Tithonus is set. As in "Ulysses," the reference to Greek mythology gives the poem dignity and universality without any suggestion of cliché or stereotype. This is in the best and strictest sense of the word a *classical* poem, with its poise and polish and Virgilian tone.

Line 25. the silver star: the morning star.
 29. kindly: according to their nature; natural.
 39. team: the horses that drew the dawn goddess' chariot.
 63. Ilion: Troy, whose walls were supposed to have risen to the music of Apollo's lyre.

259. *"Break, break, break."* This lyric, with its pure elegiac tone and its effective association of the indifferent sea on the one hand, and equally indifferent human sounds on the other, with the personal emotion which is at once the source and the end of the poem, puts individual grief into an environment which both controls and illustrates it. The waves breaking on cold gray stones are obviously enough symbols of "thoughts that do often lie too deep for tears," but the simple and direct quality of the poem makes this obviousness appropriate. Having introduced the sea, the poet stays with it until the end of the poem. The first verse uses the breaking of the waves on a cold and stony shore to suggest the mood of the poet. (Notice how the adjective "cold," though applied to the stones, also becomes associated with the sea and with the general setting: we think of a gray and chilly dawn on a deserted coast.) The suggestion of loneliness that emerges from the first verse is modified in the second, when we hear the shouts of the children at play and the singing of the sailor lad. But the indifference of these happy youngsters to the poet's mood really increases or at least emphasizes his loneliness, so that the tone of the poem is not changed. The "stately ships" of the third stanza also symbolize the daily activities of men proceeding as usual in total indifference to the poet's mood: the adjective "stately" suggests a dignity and even a pretentiousness in human affairs which is in sharp contrast to the poet's sense of loss—a sense now overtly introduced into the poem. The final verse rounds out the statement with a return to the pattern of the first verse; but this time the unnamed thoughts are named and the poet's mood is more clearly defined.

This poem is an example of Tennyson's ability to build up a mood through appropriate images: its significance lies less in its structure, in the organization of the images (though this is of course important enough), than in the actual relation which does exist between the elements in nature which he describes and the mood he is creating. Modern criticism as a rule dislikes the appeal to mere experience, but it is a fact that the splashing of a cold, gray sea on a stony shore has always been, at least for men who know the sea and who have lived by it, a powerful symbol of "lacrimae rerum," of the sadness at the heart of things, and that Tennyson is drawing on this in achieving his effect. We remember that when, in the *Iliad*, Achilles is mourning for his dead friend Patroclus, Homer sets the scene "in an open place where the waves plashed upon the shore." The opening two lines in Tennyson's poem make contact at once with this whole tradition in human emotion and expression, and it is this which gives the poem its elemental quality. But it must be admitted that in this kind of poem the appeal is to those readers who, in virtue of their own experience, do recognize that association of emotion with setting, and those whose experience has not included this sort of thing, will never be able to prove the poem satisfactory by mere analysis of the imagery and its organization.

Modern criticism is a little embarrassed in the presence of this kind of poem, with its controlled self-pity and its deliberate appeal to the emotional value of symbolic situations. It might be more interesting to note how the sea imagery at once *suggests* the poet's mood and shows nature's *indifference* to it. This is indeed an interesting aspect of the poem, but we can only tell that the sea imagery does suggest the poet's mood by the appeal to experience (not the appeal to the internal structure of the poem), and if we rule out that kind of appeal we have to rule out the poem. There is no reason in the world, however, why such an appeal should be ruled out: there is a whole area of English lyric poetry that depends on it.

260. *"Sweet and low."* This and the next four poems are songs from Tennyson's long poem, *The Princess.* In this musical lullaby the association of sea imagery (very different here from the bleak sea imagery of "Break, break, break") with a mood and an emotional atmosphere is most successfully achieved.

261. *"The splendour falls on castle walls."* This is one of the most remarkable of all Tennyson's lyrics. The imagery here is selected with an uncanny appropriateness in order to suggest a mood and present a situation which cannot in fact be discussed in any other terms. The first line of the first verse suggests at once the sense of medieval heroic living, which is removed into the picturesque past in the second line. The light and water images of the next two lines (the double rhyme in line 3 and the strange precision of "long" and "shakes" combine to produce a brilliant effect) modify and enrich the heroic mood, and the concluding long lines with their musical echoes and their suggestion of distance and a note of melancholy which is, however, still heroic, because it is *bugles* that are blowing. The context expands in the second stanza, where a more explicitly magical note is introduced and the physical setting is widened (note line 9 and line 11), and in the third and last stanza the speaker suddenly reveals himself and his position, and the mood achieved by the two preceding stanzas is put at the service of a specific human situation.

262. *"Tears, idle tears."* This is one of the few blank verse lyrics in English. Again, it is the distillation of a mood through imagery. Is the lack of rhyme felt as a defect?

263. *"Now sleeps the crimson petal, now the white."* The technique here is comparable to that in "Tears, idle tears."

Line 7. Danaë: The Greek princess who, though locked up by her father in a brazen tower, was visited by Zeus in a shower of gold.

264. *"Come down, O maid, from yonder mountain height."* Tennyson, according to his son, considered this poem one of his most successful "for *simple* rhythm and vowel music." This also is in blank verse, and Tennyson is trying to compensate by "vowel music" for the lack of rhyme. The effects he achieves are worth a careful examination.

265. These eight lyrics are from Tennyson's *In Memoriam,* a series of a hundred and thirty-one linked poems written on the death of his dear friend Arthur Hallam. "The sections were written at many different places," wrote Tennyson, "and as the phases of our intercourse came to my memory and suggested them. I did not write them with any view of weaving them into a whole, or for publication, until I found that I had written so many. The different moods of sorrow as in a drama are dramatically given, and my conviction that fear, doubts, and suffering will find answer and relief only through Faith in a God of Love." The poems, or at least many of them, are in fact quite independent and can be read and appreciated without reference to the general framework of *In Memoriam* as poems dealing with different phases of grief and with general problems about man and his destiny suggested to Tennyson by his loss. The poems as a whole are a very interesting record of a Victorian sensibility grappling with the problem of faith in an increasingly scientific age: one can compare (and contrast) Donne's "The new philosophy calls all in doubt."

The rhyme scheme employed throughout *In Memoriam—a b b a*—is unusual, though by no means elsewhere unknown, in English poetry. Tennyson hands this stanza form with considerable skill, using the two rhymes within the stanza to raise the emotion and then coming to rest, as it were, on the returning rhyme at the end of the fourth line.

The "dark house" in the first poem is the house in London where Hallam had lived.

266. *Crossing the Bar.* The use of imagery here might be compared with that in "Sweet and Low." Notice the effect of the short final line in the second and third stanzas: the variations in the stanza form from stanza to stanza are very adroitly done.

267. *Soliloquy of the Spanish Cloister.* This vigorous monologue in which Browning develops what Professor DeVane has called "a brilliant analysis of the passion of hate such as too close and steady propinquity might develop in an uncharitable man" is very different in temper and technique from Tennyson's *Ulysses* or *Tithonus.* Instead of Tennyson's stately and well-modulated utterance, Browning is seeking to give a vivid and violent impression of a personality caught unawares, as it were, rather than carefully posed in representative gestures. He achieves his effects by his rhythms, his vocabulary, and his use of something not very dissimilar from the "stream-of-consciousness" method of more modern poets and novelists. Notice how much more effective the colloquial rhythms are when they are set against a regular stanza form than they would be if there was no metrical and stanzaic norm with reference to which the poem's violence could be indicated. The reader might compare Browning's handling of the dramatic monologue with that of Burns in "Holy Willie's Prayer."

Line 10. *Salve tibi:* hail to thee!
    37. illustrate: honor symbolically.
    39. Arian: Arius was a fourth-century theologian who denied the Trinitarian doctrine of the equality of the Son with the Father, this denial being known as the Arian heresy.
    56. Manichee: the Manichaean heresy maintained that the forces of good and evil were equally powerful and constantly at war.

268. *My Last Duchess.* The speaker in this poem is the Duke of Ferrara: he is showing a portrait of his former wife to a representative of an unnamed count, with whom he is negotiating with a view to marrying the count's daughter. The characters are imaginary figures of the late Italian Renaissance, a period which fascinated Browning because of its psychological lushness. The combination of cruelty and aesthetic sensibility, or of religious feeling with skepticism, or any other such complicated psychological situation which Browning thought of as being particularly prevalent in Italy during this period, challenged him to project the character concerned in a dramatic monologue in which the speaker reveals himself. The vigor and liveliness of this monologue require no demonstration. Notice Browning's handling of pentameter couplets.

Lines 45–46. In response to an inquiry about the precise nature of these "commands," Browning explained: "The commands were that she should be put to death, or he might have had her shut up in a convent." But of course the abruptness and ambiguity of the phrase gives the sinister quality so important to the poem.

269. *The Pied Piper of Hamelin.* A boisterous and skilful narrative poem written for the young son of the actor William Macready. Browning's verbal and rhythmic ingenuity and his lively dramatic and narrative sense are here admirably illustrated. The story is based on an old legend.

Line 89. Cham: the ruler of the Tartar Empire in Central Asia.
    91. Nizam: the ruler of Hyderabad, an Indian state.
    123. Julius Caesar: Caesar is said to have swum to safety carrying the manuscript of his *Gallic War* after his ship was captured at the siege of Alexandria in 54 B.C.
    139. nuncheon: light lunch.
    182. stiver: A Dutch coin, worth about two cents or an English penny.
258–60. The reference is to the famous text in Matthew 19:24.

270. *The Bishop Orders his Tomb at St. Praxed's Church.* Ruskin's description of this poem in his *Modern Painters* is often quoted: "I know no other piece of modern English, prose or poetry, in which there is so much told, as in these lines, of the Renaissance spirit,—its worldliness, inconsistency, pride, hypocrisy, ignorance of itself, love of art, of luxury, and of good Latin. It is nearly all that I have said of the central Renaissance in thirty pages of the *Stones of Venice,* put into as many lines, Browning's being also the antecedent work." This is the only key necessary to the poem.

Line 1. Vanity: cf. *Ecclesiastes* 1:2.

21. the epistle-side: as one faces the altar, the epistle is on the right, the gospel on the left.

31. onion-stone: a poor quality marble that flakes easily.

41. olive-frail: a basket for holding olives.

42. *lapis luzuli:* a semiprecious, blue gem stone.

46. Frascati: a suburb of Rome, used as a resort by the wealthy.

49. the Jesu Church: Il Jesu, the church of the Jesuits at Rome.

51. Cf. Job 7:6: "My days are swifter than a weaver's shuttle, and are spent without hope."

57. Pans: the Bishop means several figures of Pan—there was only one god Pan.

58. tripod: the three-legged stool on which the priestess at Delphi sat when giving responses to those who came to inquire of the oracle of Apollo there.
    thyrsus: the staff of the followers of the Greek god Bacchus, god of wine and revelry. Notice the deliberate mixture of pagan and Christian imagery here.

62. tables: the tables of the law, which Moses brought down from Mount Sinai.

66. travertine: a kind of limestone.

68. jasper: a dark green, smooth-surfaced stone.

77. Tully: Cicero, whose full name was Marcus Tullius Cicero. Cicero's style was taken to be a model of good Latin prose.

79. Ulpian: a late Latin writer whose style was *not* a model of good Latin prose.

82. the reference is to the Sacrament of the Mass.

87. crook: crozier, the bishop's pastoral staff and symbol of his episcopal rank.

89. mortcloth: funeral pall.

95. The Bishop is confusing St. Praxed (who was a woman) with Christ: his mind is beginning to wander.

99. *elucescebat:* "he shone forth," i.e., "he was illustrious." The classical form of the verb is "eluceo" which would have the imperfect "elucebat." The Bishop is deriding the unclassical inchoative form "elucesco" with its imperfect "elucescebat."

108. vizor: mask.
     term: bust on a pedestal.

116. gritstone: sandstone, a relatively cheap and soft stone.

271. *A Toccata of Galuppi's.* Baldassare Galuppi was an eighteenth-century Venetian composer of considerable reputation. A *toccata* ("touch piece") is a light musical composition intended to illustrate the technical virtuosity of the player. In his tripping three-line stanzas, which echo the movement of the toccata, Browning is projecting the gay and empty social life of the Venice of the period which the music recalls and symbolizes. But notice how the poem is enclosed within brackets, as it were: this picture of Venetian gaiety has an underlying sadness for the poet, since it reminds him of the evanescence of human happiness and of his own mortality, and the poem opens and concludes with an expression of this mood. Behind it all we hear the ghostly tinkling of a distant clavichord.

Line 6. St. Mark's: the famous cathedral in Venice.
Doges: Every year the Venetians celebrated the symbolic wedding of Venice to the Adriatic sea: a ring was dropped into the sea by the Doge of Venice.

8. Shylock's bridge: the Rialto, a bridge over the Grand Canal. There is, of course, a reference here to the Venice of Shakespeare's *Merchant of Venice*.

18. clavichord: string instrument with a keyboard, forerunner of the piano.

35 ff. This is what the music says to the imaginary Englishman who is the speaker in the poem.

272. *A Grammarian's Funeral.* "I doubt whether all the laborious prose written, in history and criticism, on the revival of learning, will ever express better than this short poem the inexhaustible thirst of the Renaissance in its pursuit of knowledge, or the enthusiasm of the pupils of a New Scholar for his desperate strife to know in a short life the very center of the universe." (Stopford Brooke) In the verse form, the tricky rhymes, and the erratic movement of this poem, Browning is trying to communicate the essential quality of the life and character of this Renaissance scholar, whose zeal for the "New Learning" (as the revived study of Latin and Greek in the Renaissance was generally called) was typical of those indefatigable scholars who laid the foundations of modern classical scholarship.

Line 3. crofts: small farms.
thorpes: villages.

34. Apollo: Greek sun god, also god of song and music.

50. gowned: put on the scholar's gown, i.e., became a scholar.

60. i.e., he has mastered the text of the manuscript, but there is still the commentary, included in the manuscript with the text.

86. calculus: the disease called the stone, such as gallstones.

88. tussis: bronchial cough.

127. rattle: the death rattle.

129–31. The Greek particles *hoti, oun,* and *de* possess a variety of meanings: *hoti* is basically the conjunction "that," *oun* means "so" or "therefore" but is often slipped in after the first words of a sentence with no very specific meaning other than to indicate continuity: *de* is a particle which has no single translatable English meaning—it is sometimes used as the antithesis of another particle, *men,* to suggest contrast ("on the one hand" . . . "on the other hand"), and it is sometimes used by itself simply to ease the flow of narrative.

273. *Andrea del Sarto.* The painter Andrea del Sarto is addressing his wife, Lucrezia. Browning became interested in this painter (whose real name was Andrea d'Angelo di Francesca, 1486–1531) when a friend asked him to send him from Italy a photograph of Andrea's portrait of himself and his wife. Browning, unable to procure a photograph of the painting, sent instead this poem, in which we see Andrea towards the end of his life meditating on this, the last important picture he was to paint. Andrea, son of a tailor (hence "del Sarto") married a beautiful widow who served as a model for many of his best paintings, but who, according to the biographer of Andrea consulted by

Browning, had a disastrous effect on his career. Andrea was invited to paint at the court of the French king, Francis I, where he did some of his best work, but his wife Lucrezia prevailed upon him to return to Florence and to spend the money he had received from Francis (to buy paintings for him) on a house of his own in Florence. Vasari, Andrea's pupil and biographer, mentioned the "timidity of mind," the "diffidence and want of force in his nature," which prevented him, brilliant painter though he was as far as craftsmanship went, from achieving the greatest heights. Browning develops this notion, and in this dramatic monologue presents the painter towards the end of his life revealing the causes and the nature of this lack of ultimate power in his work.

The self-portrait of Andrea is revealed by oblique strokes, in the course of which much of the story of his life emerges, and the feeling of resignation before circumstances—a sort of acquiescent pragmatism—is developed ever more strongly as the poem develops and comes to its climax when Andrea cheerfully lets his wife go to her "cousin" (really, as Andrea knows, her lover). The poem shows Browning's complete mastery of the technique of the dramatic monologue—a technique in all essential respects developed by himself, as perhaps his most significant contribution to the forms of English poetry.

Line 15. Fiesole: a suburb of Florence.
 65. Legate: the Pope's representative.
 93. Morello: a peak in the Apennines, north of Florence.
 105. The Urbinate: the painter Raphael, born in Urbino.
 130. Agnolo: Michelangelo.
 149. Francis: King Francis I of France.
 178. The Roman's: i.e., Raphael's.
 210. cue-owls: small European owls that make a noise like "cue" (or Italian *ciù*).
 220. Cousin: really Lucrezia's lover, as Andrea is aware.
 241. scudi: plural of *scudo*, an Italian coin worth about a dollar.
 262. meted: measured out.
 263. Leonard: Leonardo da Vinci.

274. *"I thought once how Theocritus had sung."* The first of Mrs. Browning's *Sonnets from the Portuguese,* recording her love for Robert Browning. The sonnet is in the "Italian" (as distinct from the "English" or Shakespearean) form.

Line 1. Theocritus: the Greek writer of pastoral poetry. The reference here is to his fifteenth idyll.
 13. Death: not as farfetched a fancy as might appear, for Elizabeth Barrett was an invalid who supposed herself incurable before she met Robert Browning who roused her out of her invalidism and married her.

275. *The Latest Decalogue.* A cynically epigrammatic poem by one of the most thoughtful and troubled of the Victorian poets.

276. *The Jewish Cemetery at Newport.* This poem has often been compared with Gray's "Elegy," but it must be read as an adventure in historical imagination, which the "Elegy" is not. It is not an elegy (literally, "song of mourning"), and there is no identification, through mood, of poet and subject.

Rather, identification is inhibited by emphasis of the themes of strangeness, of alienation, of the exclusion of the Jews (like the Indians) as race or nation from the march of progress. Recognition by the reader of the idea of progress as the dominant concept of mid-nineteenth century America sets the poem in historical perspective, but the last stanza reveals some of the limitations of that idea. Yet though the implied thinking behind the poem is dated, the feeling is not.

Line 2. seaport town: Newport, Rhode Island, where there was a settlement of Portuguese Jews.

      32. Ishmaels, Hagars: see the story in Genesis 16, 21.

      34. Ghetto and Judenstrasse: sections in which the Jews were segregated in European towns and cities.

      41. Anathema maranatha: a curse. See I Corinthians 16:22.

      43. Mordecai: see the Book of Esther.

277–278. *Divina Commedia* (two sonnets). These are the first two sonnets in a set of six that Longfellow used to introduce and complete the three divisions of his translation of Dante's *Divina Commedia*. He wrote them during the "tumult" of the Civil War. They are the product of a mind saturated in the poetry of Dante and the literature of the Middle Ages, but Longfellow's erudition creates no barriers for the unlearned reader. There are no hidden effects in either the form or meaning of these sonnets.

279. *Give All to Love.* To the devotee of love poetry, this poem should seem somewhat disappointing, for in arguing that there are limits to love Emerson seems to take back, after line 30, more than he gives in preceding lines. But the poem must be read in the full context of Emerson's thought. The "gods" of the last line are to be realized, paradoxically enough, in the flight "of the alone to the alone," to cite Emerson's quotation from Plotinus. By the same token, the "half-gods" include all earthly attachments, not excepting the amatory. In Emerson's view, love, considered in the purest sense, is an absolute, but it is "impure" when restricted as to object.

Pace, as a factor in rhythm, is well illustrated by comparing the movement of this poem with that of some of Emily Dickinson's short-line lyrics.

280. *Days.* It would be easy to impute to this poem some such crass meaning as "Grasp your opportunity"; and, indeed, every reader's interpretation of it is a reflection of his own limitations or experience. Certainly, for Emerson, the poem was an expression of his sense of failure to rise to his particular kinds of opportunity. To quote F. O. Matthiessen, "Emerson's belief in the ballast of experience and his belief that experience is illusory; his trust in the fullness of the moment, and his sense that the moment eluded him, and his Puritanic scruple at the waste; his sense of being on the verge of a great discovery and of being inadequate to grasp it—all lie behind 'Days.'" Emerson thought it the best of his poems, although, testifying to "the selfless release of creation," he could not remember having composed or corrected it.

281. *The Snow-Storm.* This poem is an assertion of the doctrine of organic form. Nature, as Emerson said, finds its forms in facts. The objects which snow covers and the wind which blows it are the facts to which the marvelous snow-shapes correspond. Art makes a laborious attempt to achieve a similar correspondence between content and form, but the poet, like the architect, is hindered by the demands of "number and proportion," which, unlike nature, he must heed. Yet it is through "number and proportion" as well as through imagery that Emerson here recreates something of the sight, sound, and tempo of the snow-storm.

Line 18. Parian: a dazzling white marble much used in ancient Greece.

282. *Hamatreya.* In 1845, shortly before he wrote this poem, Emerson copied into his journal a passage from the Hindu sacred book, *The Vishnu Purana.* It spoke of the folly of princes who boast that they conquer the earth yet "behold not death, which is not far off." Contemplating the idea that "the words *I* and *mine* constitute ignorance" because they violate the concept of unity, Emerson found that his Concord neighbors, with their Yankee feeling for property, better illustrated this violation than Oriental kings. The first twenty-seven lines of the poem are unusually direct and concrete, for Emerson. The rhythm of the Earth-Song has a curious and perhaps appropriate resemblance to that of Anglo-Saxon verse.

Line 8. flags: water plants.

283. *The Scholar Gipsy.* Arnold found the story of the scholar gipsy in Joseph Glanvil's *Vanity of Dogmatizing* (1661). Arnold quoted the relevant passage as follows (it differs in being considerably condensed from the actual text of the 1661 edition of Glanvil):

> There was very lately a lad in the University of Oxford, who was by his poverty forced to leave his studies there; and at last to join himself to a company of vagabond gipsies. Among these extravagant people, by the insinuating subtilty of his carriage, he quickly got so much of their love and esteem as that they discovered to him their mystery. After he had been a pretty while well exercised in the trade, there chanced to ride by a couple of scholars, who had formerly been of his acquaintance. They quickly spied out their old friend among the gipsies; and he gave them an account of the necessity which drove him to that kind of life, and told them that the people he went with were not such impostors as they were taken for, but that they had a traditional kind of learning among them, and could do wonders by the power of imagination, their fancy binding that of others: that himself had learned much of their art, and when he had compassed the whole secret, he intended, he said, to leave their company, and give the world an account of what he had learned.

This poem is really about the poet himself and his generation: the scholar gipsy becomes a symbol in the light of which Arnold can develop his own position and state his own problems. Drawing on his knowledge of rustic scenes around Oxford for much of his imagery, Arnold produces a meditative pastoral poem whose language owes something to the Greek pastoral poet Theocritus but whose tone and emotional coloring are characteristically Arnold's. The fairly elaborate stanza form helps to keep the movement of the poem slow and develop the note of introspection. Notice how at the end of the poem the poet moves right away from himself to etch a clear picture of grave Tyrian traders coming to Spain to avoid the livelier Greeks. Arnold may have intended a specific symbolism here, and critics have speculated on what it might be: but the important point (apart from any analogy between the Tyrians and the gipsies) is that the concluding picture of the "shy traffickers" on the beach below the "cloudy cliffs" sustains the mood of quiet gravity so important to the poem, while removing any trace of melodramatic gesture (almost suggested by the phrase "our feverish contact" in line 221) and self-pity. The poem broadens out at the end into an objective calm, symbolized by this clear yet dreamlike scene on the beach.

Line   2. wattled cotes: sheepfolds made of interwoven twigs and branches.

     10. the quest: the search for the scholar gipsy.

     13. cruse: jar.

     34. parts: abilities, intellectual endowments.

     57. the Hurst: Cumner Hurst, a hill in "the Cumner country," as Arnold called the district westward across the Thames from Oxford which he knew so well and where he had so often rambled with his friend Clough. This district is also the scene of "Thyrsis." The other place names in the poem also refer to real places in the Cumner country.

     59. ingle-bench: bench by the chimney corner.

     95. lasher: pool in a river below a dam.

   129. Christ-Church hall: the dining hall of the Oxford college of Christ Church.

   147. teen: sorrow.

   149. the just-pausing Genius: the spirit of the world, to which, Arnold suggests, the individual life returns at death.

   155. peers: contemporaries.

   167. term: end.

182–83. one who suffered: Arnold is said to have explained that he was referring to Goethe, but Carlyle and Tennyson have each been suggested as more likely.

   190. anodynes: drugs which temporarily alleviate pain.

208–9. In Virgil's *Aeneid,* Aeneas abandoned Dido, though she was in love with him, and later, when Aeneas visited the underworld, the shade of Dido turned from him in scorn.

   232. Tyrian: from Tyre, one of the chief cities of Phoenicia. Before the Greeks, the Phoenicians were the principal traders in the Mediterranean.

   238. Chian wine: wine from Chios, one of the Aegean isles of line 236.

   239. tunnies: tunas, a kind of large fish.

   244. Midland waters: Mediterranean Sea.

   245. Syrtes: the Gulf of Sidra, on the north coast of Africa.

   247. western straits: the Strait of Gibraltar, leading out of the Mediterranean into the Atlantic: few ancient traders passed westward through these straits. (Cf. Tennyson's "Ulysses.")

   249. Iberians: the early inhabitants of Spain and Portugal.

284. *Thyrsis.* This "pastoral elegy" (with which it has long been the custom to compare two other great English pastoral elegies, "Lycidas" and "Adonais") was written to commemorate Arnold's friend Arthur Hugh Clough, who had died at the end of 1861. It is closely linked to "The Scholar Gipsy," though written many years after it: it has the same stanza form, the same general tone, it is set in the same Cumner country southwest of Oxford where Arnold and Clough had often walked together, and it contains actual references to "The Scholar Gipsy," a favorite poem of Clough's and one which seems to have continued some special symbolism known only to Arnold and his friend.

The influence of the Greek pastoral poets is clearly discernible, as for example in lines 81–100, which suggest Moschus' lament for Bion. Yet the poem is steeped in that same deep feeling for the English countryside that we find in "The Scholar Gipsy," and, as with the earlier poem, the theme is really Arnold himself, his doubts and problems and introspective melancholy, developed indirectly in an elegiac context and (as so often in Arnold) in association with aspects of the English landscape which are most appropriate to the contemplative mood. This linking of the physical setting to the poet's mood is a device Arnold may well have got from Wordsworth, who employed it effectively (e.g. in the sonnet "It is a beauteous evening, calm and free"): one might compare Arnold's "Dover Beach" in this respect.

Shortly after the poem's composition, Arnold wrote about it in a letter to his mother as follows: "The diction of the poem was modelled on that of Theocritus, whom I have been much reading during the two years this poem has been forming itself. . . . I meant the diction to be so artless as to be almost heedless. The images are all from actual observation. . . . The cuckoo on the wet June morning I heard in the garden at Woodford, and all those three stanzas you like are reminiscences of Woodford." In another letter written shortly afterwards Arnold called "Thyrsis" "a very quiet poem, but I think solid and sincere" and expressed the opinion that he had perhaps said too little about Clough.

The place names in "Thyrsis" all refer to places in the Cumner country.

Line   4. Sibylla's name: "Not just the name you would expect to find on a tavern sign-board. But Arnold was not inventing. The hostess of the Cross Keys in South Hinksey was, in sober fact, one Sybella Curr." (Sir Francis Wylie)

     10. Thyrsis: Arnold's pastoral name for Clough: Arnold himself is Corydon (line 80).

     35. A reference to their poetic activity.

     40. Clough resigned his fellowship at Oriel College, Oxford, in 1848, in protest against the requirement that fellows should subscribe to the Church of England's Thirty-nine Articles.

     45. silly: simple.

     48. See note to poem No. 275.

     85. unpermitted ferry: the river Styx, over which only the dead were allowed to go, on their way to the underworld.

     86. Pluto: god of the underworld. His wife was Proserpine (line 88).

     90. See note on Milton's "L'Allegro" (poem No. 109), lines 145–50.

     92. Dorian: Doric was the dialect of Greek employed by the Greek pastoral poets of Sicily; hence "Dorian" here means "Sicilian." (Cf. "Doric lay" in "Lycidas," line 189.)

    106. the Fyfield tree: cf. "the Fyfield elm" in "The Scholar Gipsy," line 83.

    135. sprent: sprinkled.

    167. Arno: Clough died in Florence, which is on the River Arno.

    175. boon: pleasant.

177. the great Mother: Nature.
182–85. "Daphnis, the ideal Sicilian shepherd of Greek pastoral poetry, was said to have followed into Phrygia his mistress Piplea, who had been carried off by robbers, and to have found her in the power of the king of Phrygia, Lityerses. Lityerses used to make strangers try a contest with him in reaping corn and put them to death if he overcame them. Hercules arrived in time to save Daphnis, took upon him the reaping contest with Lityerses, overcame him, and slew him. The Lityerses-song, connected with this tradition, was, like the Linus-song, one of the early plaintive strains of Greek popular poetry, and used to be sung by corn-reapers. Other traditions represented Daphnis as beloved by a nymph, who exacted from him an oath to love no one else. He fell in love with a princess, and was struck blind by the jealous nymph. Mercury, who was his father, raised him to Heaven, and made a fountain spring up in the place from which he ascended. At this fountain the Sicilians offered yearly sacrifices." (Arnold)

285. *Dover Beach.* The first stanza of this poem, with its effective description of a hushed moonlit night, the silence broken only by the sound of the waves breaking on the pebbly beach (Arnold is looking out from Dover across the narrow Strait of Dover to the French coast), sets the mood and tone for the melancholy speculation which develops. The reference to Sophocles in the second stanza (and note the irregular stanza forms) links the poet's interpretation of the sea's note as one of "eternal sadness" to a less personal, more universal view of human misery, and having thus expanded his context he returns to the sea and finds in it a new meaning—a symbol of the ebbing of the "sea of faith." The imagery of this stanza is brilliantly managed. In this desolation all that man has to depend on is the integrity of personal relationships, and the poem ends with an appeal for such integrity in the meaningless and blind struggles which surround him. The impact of science on religious faith and of the facts of industrial civilization on men's optimistic hopes for continual progress produced a characteristic Victorian melancholy to be found in nearly all poets of the period: but nowhere has it been more perfectly captured and expressed than in this poem of Arnold's.

286. *Rugby Chapel.* This poem was written in memory of the poet's father, Dr. Thomas Arnold, the great headmaster of Rugby. Dr. Arnold had died suddenly in 1842, and was buried in Rugby Chapel. The poem is more rhetorical than Arnold's more characteristic elegies, but this unrhymed and flexible verse has an elegiac cadence of its own, particularly noticeable in the early part of the poem. Notice again how Arnold associates an emotion with an appropriate physical scene.

287. *The Blessed Damozel.* This poem is said to have been inspired by Poe's "The Raven." "I saw," Rossetti is reported to have said, "that Poe had done the utmost it was possible to do with the grief of the lover on earth, and so I determined to reverse the conditions, and give utterance to the yearning of the loved one in heaven." Rossetti projects a tensely quiet picture in which every detail is placed where it will have greatest symbolic significance. His sense of color and of texture is that of the painter—and Rossetti was a painter before he was a poet. The influence of medieval Italian literature with its association of love imagery with religious themes is clearly discernible, yet the note is quite different from that sounded, say, in Dante's sonnets about Beatrice: for Rossetti, the combination of sensuousness and mysticism was in the service of the former at least as much as of the latter.

Line 9–10. i.e., being a virgin, and in the service of the Virgin Mary, she could appropriately wear a flower which was the symbol of virginity.

54. cf. *Job,* 38:7. ". . . when the morning stars sang together, and all the sons of God shouted for joy."

86. that living mystic tree: the tree of life (cf. *Revelation,* 22:2).

87. Dove: symbol of the Holy Spirit.

107–8. These are the names of Christian saints, chosen for musical effect in the stanza.

126. citherns and citoles: medieval stringed instruments.

288. *Sister Helen.* This powerful poem is an imitation ballad, and has the stanza form of such a ballad as "Edward." Helen is melting a waxen image of her false lover in order to cause his death—it was a common medieval superstition that one could harm a person by making and harming a waxen image of him. The story is told indirectly, with considerable skill; the horror mounts to a climax as the dialogue between brother and sister proceeds relentlessly. The refrain—much more complicated and sophisticated than in a genuine folk ballad—adds to the tension by slowing down the narrative and at the same time suggesting nameless forebodings.

289. *Mid-Rapture.* This sonnet is from Rossetti's sonnet sequence, *The House of Life,* recording his love for his wife and subsequent bereavement. The ecstatic quality of the expression is intended, and is not the result of mere exclamatory excess. The sonnet has a careful structure and a climax that deliberately echoes, on a different emotional level, the opening line.

290. *A Birthday.* A fresh and charming poem which captures the very essence of excited joy.

291. *Song: "When I am dead, my dearest."* This little poem has a contrived simplicity, which is not ineffective.

292. *The World Below the Brine.* Here a traditional concept—the chain of being (the idea that there are innumerable but progressive gradations from the lowest forms of life on up to the divine forms) is the climax of a description of deep-sea life. But the implication of continued spiritual progress in the last line is prepared for in earlier lines by physical ascension from the ocean bed, to surface, to earth level.

293. *Camps of Green.* The concepts of war, life, death, and human equality are played against each other, but are brought into harmony by the use of color imagery and military terminology. Compare this poem with "Reconciliation."

294. *Reconciliation.* The form of this poem is almost mathematical. In the first three lines the increase in the number of stresses from four to eight to twelve corresponds to the rhetorical expansion of the poet's reflection. The second three lines, each of six stresses, present the object and episode which inspired the reflection.

295. *When Lilacs Last in the Dooryard Bloom'd.* Many of Whitman's failures in verse are the result of unresolved conflicts between his impulses to teach and to express himself as a private person. In this poem the conflict is resolved. The death of Lincoln, who was for Whitman a symbol of the potentialities of democratic culture, was for the poet a profound personal experience rather than a new opportunity for propagandizing democracy. The twelve-day journey of the president's body from Washington to Springfield in the spring of the year, and the mourning of the nation, are the common ground for the feeling of the poet and his readers. But the images through which he crystallizes his emotion on this public occasion had always had for Whitman private associations: the April lilacs are like his leaves of grass—"every leaf a miracle"· —but they also fix the event in point of time; stars were for him symbols of aspiration and mystery, but here the star is both "western" and "fallen"; in his youth the bird-song had acquired associations with death. The three images recur in different contexts throughout the poem. Emotional climax is reached in the italicized "aria" in Section XIV—a celebration of "lovely and soothing death" which, far from being a stock response to the death of a beloved leader, comes from the depths of Whitman's most inward experience. Compare the jigging platitudes which he perpetrated in "O Captain! My Captain!," another poem on the death of Lincoln.

296. *Chanting the Square Deific.* Whitman was not at his best in the poetry of ideas, but here he relates his thinking to traditional symbols—Father (Section I), Son (Section II), and Holy Ghost (Section IV), plus Satan (Section III). The pattern should horrify theologians and exasperate logicians (consider that what Whitman presents is not a square but a triangle enclosed in a circle); but the poem is his most condensed statement of his doctrine of unity and inclusiveness.

297. *To a Locomotive in Winter.* The earlier romantic poets tended to deny that the symbols of industrialism had potentialities for poetry. Whitman affirmed not only their beauty but their vitality. The development of theme and the management of image in this poem are worth careful study. Observe his use of the senses of hearing and sight. (Whitman exploited more of the physical senses than any other American poet.) Compare Emily Dickinson's response to the same object in "I like to see it lap the miles."

298. *"He found her by the ocean's moaning verge."* This is the second last of Meredith's sequence of fifty sixteen-lined "sonnets" which, under the title *Modern Love,* tell of the breakup of his first marriage. The poems have a combination of a dry intellectual quality with a vivid psychological realism not easily duplicated in English poetry.

299. *"Thus piteously Love closed what he begat."* The final poem in *Modern Love.* Note how the poem turns at line 11, moving the emotional force outward, as it were, into a generalization about all human passion.

300. *The Haystack in the Floods.* The narrative is set in the fourteenth century. Sir Robert de Marny, an English knight who had fought at the battle of Poitiers, where the English, though greatly outnumbered, defeated the French, is riding through France to Gascony (a French province then under English control) with Jehane, his mistress. They are waylaid and trapped by

Godmar, "that Judas," who wants to carry off Jehane. The story is told with great vigor and a cunning eye for detail. Notice how Morris handles the octosyllabic couplet.

Line 9. kirtle: skirt.
    51. those six men: the judges who would try her as a witch. She would be subjected to "trial by ordeal" and cast into the River Seine—if she swam, she would be deemed guilty; if she drowned, she would be declared innocent!
    52. Chatelet: a prison in Paris, on the banks of the Seine.
    57. him: Godmar.
    61. "St. George for Marny": Robert's battle cry. St. George was the patron saint of England. Marny is Robert.
    153. fitte: division of a·tale.

301. *"I know a little garden close."* This is a song from Book IV of Morris's poetic romance, *The Life and Death of Jason.* It is sung by a water nymph to the handsome Theban youth Hylas, with whom she has fallen in love and whose love in turn she has won.

302. *The Garden of Proserpine.* Proserpine, in classical mythology, was abducted by Pluto, god of the underworld, and carried off there to be his queen. But on her mother's intercession she was allowed to spend six months of the year above ground. Her mother was Ceres, goddess of agriculture and of the fruits of the earth (lines 60–61). The somewhat melodramatic desire for extinction expressed in this poem, the sense of a self-indulgent weariness, might be contrasted with the melancholy of Matthew Arnold's "Dover Beach." Swinburne was a great master of rhythms, and this poem has an effective musical lilt to it.

Line 14. blown buds: buds that have already blossomed.
    27. poppies: the flowers of forgetfulness, sacred to Proserpine.
    76. the image is from falconry: the falconer brings the falcon down to earth by displaying the *lure* which, during the bird's training, has food concealed in it.
    94. diurnal: belonging to day (as opposed to night).

303. *A Forsaken Garden.* A skilful use of rhythms and imagery to project an atmosphere suggestive of a deliberately vague nostalgia.

Line 1. coign: corner.

304. *The Jumblies.* Edward Lear, best known for his crazy limericks and his nonsense verse, often has method in his madness. This poem, like several other of his longer poems, has much of the vague, magical imagery that is found in some degree in so many of the romantic and Victorian poets, and by employing this imagery to tell a palpably absurd story he laughs effectively at a whole poetic tradition. The echoing melancholy of the chorus, "Far and few, far and few . . .," for a moment almost conceals its absurdity.

305. *"A-sitting on a Gate."* Compare this poem with Wordsworth's "Resolution and Independence."

306. *"I know some lonely houses off the road."* This still life of a moonlit New England farmhouse interior is essentially feminine and occasionally coy, but it is full of small surprises in impressionistic imagery like "spectacles ajar," "an almanac's ware," and "trains away." Every detail derives from the central robber theme.

307. *"He preached upon 'breadth' till it argued him narrow."* One of the great characteristics of the Puritan tradition, of which Emily Dickinson was a beneficiary, is implicit in this poem.

308. *"A route of evanescence."* Every line of this poem, which is almost a *tour de force* of concision, contributes to the theme of motion so swift as to be almost invisible. Like the hummingbird itself, the poem is gone before it is fully comprehended, but a second reading resolves most of the difficulties.

309. *"I like to see it lap the miles."* The values of this poem become more obvious when it is compared with another poem about a railroad train, Whitman's "To a Locomotive in Winter."

310. *"In winter, in my room."* This haunting poem is a playground for amateur Freudians, but no biographical interpretation is necessary.

311. *"There came a wind like a bugle."* The extraordinary imagery of the first twelve lines of this poem invites the closest inspection. It is worth considering whether the last five lines add to or detract from the effects previously produced.

312. *"I heard a fly buzz when I died."* The text here given is the one that is usually printed. Corrected from her manuscript it should read as follows: line 2, "round my form": "in the room"; line 5, "beside": "around"; line 6, "sure": "firm"; line 8, "his power": "the room"; the third stanza,

> I willed my keepsakes, signed away
> What portion of me be
> Assignable—and then it was
> There interposed a fly.

313. *"It was not death, for I stood up."* Emily Dickinson's mastery of the poetry of personal, almost abstract, terror is here evident. The body senses, and the sense of time and space are drawn upon to communicate one of the most incommunicable of human experiences.

314. *"Because I could not stop for Death."* This exploration of the experience of death is deceptively simple. The terms of the experience are time and motion—just the opposite of what is expected of an event which obliterates both. Motion is implied in the central theme of the carriage, and in the words "horses," "drove," and "passed." "Stop," "slowly," "haste," "leisure," and "paused" are time words. In the crucial third stanza, the implication is that we have "passed" motion ("wrestling," "gazing") and time ("the setting sun") forever. Yet all this is subordinate to the affirmation of immortality, an idea which is not only explicit in the first stanza but implicit in the rest of the poem.

315. *"My life had stood a loaded gun."* Biography can be useful as an aid to the understanding of the total work and thought of a poet, but sometimes biographical speculation inhibits rather than enhances appreciation. Putting Emily Dickinson's love poetry into the traditional romantic framework of a specific frustrated love affair (as many biographers have attempted to do), limits rather than extends the imaginative appeal of that poetry. It is as futile a procedure as attempting to link her death poems with a specific escape from death.

316. *"After great pain a formal feeling comes."* Compare this poem with No. 313. Here she evokes not terror but the experience of devastating emotional shock. Except for the oblique reference to the agony of Christ, in the third line, and to the time sense, in the fourth, the experience is stated in physical terms.

317. *"A narrow fellow in the grass."* A recent editor asserts that there should be no question mark after line 3, and that in line 12 "morn" should read "noon." Emily Dickinson's "rhymes" are usually assonance or consonance. An early reviewer, in attempting to define her defects, really described her skill when he said that her rhythm "cheats the ear into a supposition of rhyme where it does not exist."

318. *Plain Language from Truthful James.* The literary values of the rhythms and the color of American dialects were recognized by prose writers at least as early as 1820, and were analyzed critically by James Russell Lowell in 1867. Not until the twentieth century, however, did poets like Frost make any considerable serious use of the potentialities of native idioms, though increasingly after Lowell's *Biglow Papers* in 1848, minor writers had exploited them for humorous and satiric verse. In "Plain Language" the "Pike" dialect (the general meaning of this term is simply "western") is not merely picturesque; it is a cutting instrument of characterization and irony. Harte's mixture of local terms with more cultivated language ("intent to deceive," "leaves on the strand") is a conscious humorous device, but it is also historically correct.

319. *God's Grandeur.* This sonnet is very different in rhythms and movement from any previous one in this anthology. Notice how flexibly Hopkins uses the line, bending it to fit the precise curve of the emphasis he wishes to achieve; notice, too, how he wrenches the regular metrical foot to stamp the full meaning on the line, as in the second half of line 6, or the sudden and immensely effective exclamation in the last line. By and large, Hopkins preserves the same number of beats in each line, but the unstressed syllables between the beats vary more than is usual in any earlier English poetry (leaving medieval poetry out of account), and he has a trick of bringing two beats together in moments of high excitement. In the spacing of the beats with reference to the emotional pattern of the poem lies its greatest skill.

320. *The Windhover.* This is about as far as can be gone in poetry to capture the very feel of the subject in rhythms and images. Notice again the placing of the emphatic beats (as in "and striding High there," where there is a pause on "high" longer than on any other word in the line). This, too, though it may not be immediately recognized as such, is a sonnet.

Line   1. minion: darling.
          dauphin: heir.

3. wimpling: rippling.
4. rung upon the rein: there is an implied comparison to a horse circling around its trainer at the end of a long rein.
7. in hiding: i.e., dedicated to Christ (to whom the poem is dedicated, and who is addressed twice in the poem—"O my chevalier!" line 11, and "ah my dear" line 13).
10. Buckle: "In its diverse meanings (1. 'clasp, fasten together,'; 2. 'bend, crumple'), this imperative verb seems to apply *directly* to the kestrel and *obliquely* to Christ. . . . Through Christ, moreover, 'Buckle' comes home again to the poet-disciple himself, for the adverb 'here' (1.9) can mean 'in this bird' and in 'my heart in hiding' (1.7), i.e., dedicated to Christ. Thus, in the sestet, the concept of disciplined physical activity (repression) merges into that of disciplined spiritual activity (sublimation)—the beauty of sacrifice." (W. H. Gardner)
11. sillion: furrow.

321. *Duns Scotus's Oxford.* Duns Scotus, the thirteenth-century Scholastic philosopher, is supposed to have taught at Oxford about 1301. Hopkins was a great admirer of Scotus. In this poem he builds up an impression of medieval Oxford, then links this to Scotus through himself ("this air I gather and I release/ He lived on") to end with a passionate tribute to him. It is a carefully controlled poem, shaping down to a single sharp point at its conclusion.

Line 4. coped: set off one against the other.
12. realty: reality.

322. *Spring and Fall: to a Young Child.* The most limpid of all Hopkins' poems. Notice Hopkins' stress marks.

Line 8. "I take wanwood to be a noun (the meaning 'bloodless' being combined with the older meaning 'dark,' 'livid'—O. E. *wann*). *Leafmeal* I take for an adverb, made 'by substitution' from *piecemeal* on the analogy of Shakespeare's *inch-meal* and *limb-meal:* hence it suggests the leaves falling one by one, then rotting to form pale, mealy fragments." (W. H. Gardner)
13. ghost: spirit.

323. *The Hound of Heaven.* A powerful picture of the human soul in its flight from divine love. The poem is not sustained throughout on the level of its sudden and vivid opening—the language sometimes drops into the conventionally poetic and the handling of the irregular stanza is unequal—but it does suggest an emotional experience carving out perforce an adequate verbal expression. This may not be how the best poetry is written, and indeed the reader has the feeling that Thompson has here got away with it by some happy appropriateness of imagination which cannot be counted on for a second performance. The conclusion suggests George Herbert.

324. *Hap.* There is a craggy simplicity about Hardy's poetry well illustrated in this sonnet.

Line 13. Doomsters: masters of fate.

325. *Drummer Hodge.* This is a lament for a soldier killed in the South African War: Drummer Hodge is a symbolic figure representing the humble private soldier who dies in distant lands in wars he did not plan and does not understand. The poem is simply built around the contrast between familiar English things and the unfamiliar names and landscape of the veldt.

Line 3. kopje: the Boer term for a small hill.
     4. veldt: the Boer term for prairie.
     9. Karoo: a plain in South Africa.

326. *"I will make you brooches."* The fresh and elemental imagery keeps this unpretentious poem justly popular. It is a sophisticated simplicity, but it comes off. Notice the effect of the long, slow line.

327–331. Housman worked within very narrow limits, but achieved something approaching technical perfection within his chosen field. A sense of the beauty of nature, the passing of youth, the inevitable fate that awaits all men, of the fact that (in Dr. Johnson's words) "life is a state in which there is much to be endured and little to be enjoyed" combined with a poignant awareness of how significant yet how transient that "little" is—these are his main themes, and he treats them with a tight cogency of expression which at its best produces a poetry with no fat on it at all. He had a tendency to surround his etchings of situations illustrating these themes with melodramatic gestures or an exhibitionist stoicism, but when he curbed this and let the situation speak for itself in carefully chiseled yet simple language and rhythms (as in the poems here chosen), he produced some memorable lyrics.

332. *London Snow.* The quiet and meticulous imagery combines with the slowly moving lines to produce the effect here. Notice, too, the effect of the "weak" endings.

333. *Recessional.* A hymn for Queen Victoria's Diamond Jubilee. It has a simple gravity of utterance appropriate for such an occasion, and in putting the other side of imperial self-congratulation, strikes a note peculiarly fitting in a "recessional" (which is technically a hymn sung at the end of a church service, as the clergy and choir leave the church in procession).

334. *Danny Deever.* "One of the most interesting exercises in the combination of heavy beat and variation of pace is found in *Danny Deever,* a poem which is technically (as well as in content) remarkable. The regular recurrence of the same end-words, which gain immensely by imperfect rhyme (*parade* and *said*), gives the feeling of marching feet and the movement of men in disciplined formation—in a unity of movement which enhances the horror of the occasion and the sickness which seizes the men as individuals; and the slightly quickened pace of the final lines marks the change in movement and in music. There is no single word or phrase which calls too much attention to itself, or which is not there for the sake of the total effect; so that when the climax comes [lines 27–8] . . . (the word *whimper* being exactly right) the atmosphere has been prepared for a complete suspension of disbelief." (T. S. Eliot)

335. *Eros Turannos.* The title means "Love, the Tyrant." The poem is a fine illustration of the poet's ability to explore a complex situation within the confines of a rigid formal pattern. The eight-line stanza is full of variety. The first and second lines consist metrically of four and three feet, but they contain only three and two rhetorical stresses. The three feminine endings in each stanza would have an inappropriately playful lilt if the triplet of the fifth, sixth, and seventh lines did not interrupt the alternation of feminine and masculine rhymes. Artificially complex as this stanza is, Robinson communicates through it a subtle human story involving four points of view concerning one situation. Emotional connotations are embodied in one central image—that of water. The achievement of this poem is the better appreciated if one compares it with a seventeenth-century poem, George Wither's "Christmas Carol," where almost the same rhythm and stanza are used for a completely different purpose.

336. *Mr. Flood's Party.* This is one of the tenderest of Robinson's poems of human failures who reveal both their weakness and their dignity. The pathos of lonely old age is evoked without a touch of sentimentality, because pity is balanced by admiration for courage, and courage is touchingly demonstrated in its context of alcoholic reinforcement.

337. *When you are old.* This is a free adaptation of a sonnet by the sixteenth-century French Poet Ronsard ("Quand vous serez bien vieille, au soir, à la chandelle"). But Yeats's version is wholly original in tone and treatment, especially in the conclusion, with its effectively surprising image. Note that this poem is not strictly a sonnet: it has three four-line stanzas, each with the "enclosed" rhyme order.

338. *The Folly of Being Comforted.* Yeats here manages to use rhymed couplets with a purely conversational movement. Notice his placing of the pauses. The final couplet—in which the poet's rationalization that his beloved is really more beautiful now that she is older, is suddenly and devastatingly shattered by the physical reality—has an almost epigrammatic quality.

339. *No Second Troy.* Here again the strength of the poem lies in its concluding "punch." There is irony and even anger in the conclusion, but it is blended with admiration. The reference to Helen of Troy (for whom Troy was sacked) indicates both the heroine's beauty and her impatient pride. This is a very different use of classical imagery from that found in eighteenth- or nineteenth-century poetry: the sharp conversational tone and the almost casual way in which the reference is brought in, free the image from any conventionality or obviousness.

340. *To a Shade.* Yeats is addressing the shade of the Irish patriot C. S. Parnell, expressing his bitterness by advising him that he is better off where he is—in the grave—than in contemporary Ireland. The stately movement of the verse, the monumental phrasing, and the undulating flow of the poem, which comes to a temporary climax at the end of each of the first two verses and then to its overwhelming final climax at the end of the third and last stanza, produce a most impressive effect. Yeats displays, too, the "metaphysical" quality of being able to take up more than one attitude at a time (in this case both an elegiac and an ironic one), as the third line shows. The emotion rises steadily to the conclusion. The contemptuously anonymous "they" in line 9 marks but the first step in the mood of the poem, which progresses from contempt to epic anger. The second stanza (referring to the Dubliners' shabby treatment of Hugh Lane, who offered to present his fine collection of modern French paintings to Dublin provided the Dublin Corporation housed them properly, which they refused to do) begins mildly and rises at the conclusion to stronger abuse than the conclusion of the first. The third stanza (or, more accurately, verse paragraph) gathers up the implications of the previous two and rises to complete the indictment of contemporary Dublin by suggesting that the Shade is safer in the tomb than among these people.

341. *On a Political Prisoner.* The balanced movement and gravity of tone do not in the least interfere with the conversational air of this poem—the ability to combine these is one of Yeats's outstanding characteristics in his middle and later periods. The poem proceeds by gradually widening the contrast between prison and freedom: at first the sea gull, symbol of freedom, is actually by the prisoner's cell, but as the poem develops the images of freedom grow more and more removed from the prison, until the poem ends with the gull in a wide and stormy seascape, symbol of all that the prisoner has lost and from which she is now farthest away.

342. *The Second Coming.* This powerful poem has often been taken as a prophecy of the destruction of civilization amid violent and cruel political movements which subsequently very nearly took place. Yeats, however, had no specific political prophecy in mind: he was employing his own mystical system (hence the reference to such a mystical work as *Spiritus Mundi*, "the spirit of the world") in order to evoke a sense of the horror of dissolution and the terror of new birth. The sense of the falling apart of the old system is brilliantly communicated by the image of the falcon turning in ever wider circles as it soars out of reach of the falconer until all communication has been lost. Following hard on this evocation of disintegration comes the image of "the blood-dimmed tide" with its suggestions of universal civil war (note the effect of the verb "loosed": it suggests that men have started something they can no longer control) and its drowning of "the ceremony of innocence," a phrase which symbolizes that combination of ritual gesture and purity of heart which for Yeats was the basis of all true civilized living. ("How but in custom and in ceremony/ Are innocence and beauty born?" he asked in another poem.) The first stanza concludes with two hard lines, almost spat out in despair and anger, which epitomize one of the perennial problems of the man of good will.

There is a long pause after the first stanza, and when the second opens, the mood has changed somewhat. We turn, with a sense of awed expectation, to read the signs of the future, and the relentless image which Yeats conjures up to symbolize the elemental violence with which a really new idea impinges on the world marches through the poem (notice the fascinated precision with which Yeats describes its movements, as in "moving its slow thighs") to emerge as a mysterious but powerful successor (and in a sense antitype) to Christianity. The "rocking cradle" of line 20 is presumably a reference to the infant Christ: the real meaning of the Christian centuries is now about to emerge, and the new birth that has been maturing in the womb of time will not be the pretty picture-post-card affair of conventional Christian sentimentality but something uncouth and unpredictable. There is a whole philosophy of history distilled in this poem. We need not trouble ourselves too much with the specific mystical notions which Yeats used in working up this poem: as

Mr. Richard Ellmann has remarked, "an awareness of [Yeats's mystical] system was more useful for writing than it is for reading the poem."

The reader should notice carefully the movement of the lines, the varying of pauses and emphases, and the total effect of ominous gravity.

343. Leda and the Swan. The subject of this poem is not unconnected with "The Second Coming." Yeats wrote: "After the individualistic, demagogic movements, founded by Hobbes and popularized by the Encyclopaedists and the French Revolution, we have a soil so exhausted that it cannot grow that crop again for centuries. Then I thought 'Nothing is now possible but some movement, or birth from above, preceded by some violent annunciation.' My fancy began to play with Leda and the Swan for metaphor, and I began this poem, but as I wrote, bird and lady took such possession of the scene that all politics went out of it."

According to Greek legend, Leda was visited by Zeus in the form of a swan, and the result was the birth of Helen of Troy and of Clytemnestra, wife and slayer of Agamemnon. Knowledge and power (line 13) were opposites which, Yeats speculates, could perhaps be reconciled momentarily in the sex act.

344. Byzantium. Byzantium had become for Yeats the symbol of art or artifice as opposed to the natural world of biological activity. In an earlier poem, "Sailing to Byzantium," he had contrasted the world of youth, sensuality, and change with the timeless world of art. Both "Byzantium" and "Sailing to Byzantium" were written in order to come to terms with his feeling of advancing age and to present a state of mind from which he could look back with satisfaction on his escape from the passions and conflicts of his earlier years. This new state of mind is also the state of mind of the artist, who captures and gives permanence to a vision which transcends what he called in another poem "all those antinomies/ Of day and night," transcends those opposing elements between which feeling and suffering man moves, by capturing "the artifice of eternity."

Yeats used in this poem many of the ideas he had worked out in his mystical prose writings, which were developed into a system in his prose work, *A Vision,* and he also used details of Byzantine civilization he derived from W. G. Holmes's *The Age of Justinian and Theodora* and O. M. Dalton's *Byzantine Art and Archaeology.* In *A Vision* he had written:

> "I think that if I could be given a month of antiquity and leave to spend it where I chose, I would spend it in Byzantium a little before Justinian opened St. Sophia and closed the Academy of Plato. . . . I think that in early Byzantium, and maybe never before or since in recorded history, religious, aesthetic and practical life were one, and that architects and artificers . . . spoke to the multitude and the few alike. The painter and the mosaic worker, the worker in gold and silver, the illuminator of Sacred Books, were almost impersonal, almost perhaps without the consciousness of individual design, absorbed in their subject matter and that the vision of a whole people."

The poem opens with the pushing back of images suggestive of the gross behavior of natural man—images associated with day, as the images of art are associated with night. On the one side is natural man and the world of nature to which he belongs, sensuality, daylight, and implication in the complexities of changing events and passions, while on the other side is the world of artifice, abstraction, bodilessness, night (with which the moon and stars are naturally enough associated), changelessness, and escape from the "complexities of mire or blood" into a state in which all opposites are resolved. Gradually the noises of ordinary daily life die away, and there emerges a trancelike picture of the still Byzantine night. With the stars or the moon illuminating the cathdral dome, "the fury and the mire of human veins" vanish into insignificance, they become "*mere* complexities" to be "scorned" by the symbols of the higher state.

The second stanza explores the significance of this newly acquired state, now symbolized by "an image, man or shade." And notice the haunting music with which Yeats emphasizes and repeats the notion:

> Shade more than man, more image than a shade.

"Hades' bobbin" that "unwinds the winding path" is the spool of man's fate unwinding, to lead him into that spiritual realm in which man transcends himself ("I hail the superhuman"), conquers the opposition between life and death, escapes from time and change—becomes artist, in fact.

In the third stanza we have symbols of the work of art—

> Miracle, bird or golden handiwork—

and the process of incantation continues as Yeats repeats a cadence found in the same position in the previous stanza—

> More miracle than bird or handiwork.

The images here are all deliberately antinatural: the bird is not a natural bird but one wrought of gold (there is a reminiscence here of Hans Andersen's story, "The Nightingale"); it is free from the confusions and changes of "common bird or petal," for, "by the moon embittered" (that is, presumably, strengthened and hardened in its scorn of mere natural things by this symbol of the world of artifice—though other interpretations are possible here, since the moon is itself a symbol of change) it has transcended the limitations of natural creatures to become "like the cocks of Hades," those symbolic birds which, standing outside time, proclaim the cycles of rebirth to mortal beings.

A strange hush falls on the poem as it proceeds into its fourth stanza—·

> At midnight on the Emperor's pavement flit
> Flames that no faggot feeds, nor steel has lit.

(Notice the alliteration). These "flames begotten of flame" are again symbols of the changeless, of the "artifice of eternity," and are implicitly contrasted with ordinary flames which consume what they burn and then die down. Here the spirits (they are "blood-begotten"—that is, they are born of flesh-and-blood man, though they are now no longer flesh and blood: this emphasizes a paradox at the heart of the poem) learn to leave behind the complexities and passions of their earlier life and move into "an agony of trance" which is compared to "flame that cannot singe a sleeve" (unlike ordinary flame, which consumes and dies).

In the final stanza the note changes into one of controlled ecstasy. Having by now completely identified himself with the midnight world of artifice, changelessness, and death, the poet can live out the remainder of his days untouched by the "complexities of mire or blood," the passions and changes of human life. He is in this world, yet he is out of it; in Ireland, yet of Byzantium; in the midst of life he is in death; he has become a spirit who sails over the flood of human life without even getting his feet wet by it:

> Astraddle on the dolphin's mire and blood,
> Spirit after spirit!

(Yeats had learned from Mrs. Arthur Strong's books, *Apotheosis* and *After Life,* of the symbolic significance of the dolphin in ancient art: it was the soul in transit from one state to another.) The dolphin, a creature both animal and mystical, mediates, as it were, between the world of mire and blood and the timeless spiritual world, just as man, himself a physical creature, can yet make contact with a nonphysical realm of unchanging entities. But notice that the "flood" of human passions is rising nevertheless, though it is broken by "the golden smithies of the Emperor"—that is, the symbolic works of artifice, wrought in "changeless metal"—and even as the poet is borne by the dolphin above the flood, and even though the "marbles of the dancing floor" (the mystical dance of the neo-Platonic philosopher Plotinus, another symbol of the timeless world) help to stem the flood and "break bitter furies of complexity," the human images break through and beget yet further images, so that the poem ends on a note of human passion—

> That dolphin-torn, that gong-tormented sea.

The symbols of abstraction and artifice that he has created for himself to preserve him from succumbing to the siren call of the human passions cannot prevent that other world from breaking in: the "gong-tormented sea," human life torn by changing emotions, seethes around his feet and speaks to him as he rides the dolphin's back. That is the paradox of art: it escapes from the changing world of natural activity, only to be haunted (and indeed nourished) by what it has escaped from.

A sketchy analysis such as the foregoing says little about the real appeal of the poem—its impressive shifts in mood and tempo, its skilful use of varying line-lengths, its sheer incantatory quality, and the mysterious beauty of such a line as the last line of all, which echoes hauntingly in the mind ever after the first rapid reading when the meaning of the poem is still highly dubious. The poem communicates a kind of experience, a mental and emotional state, long before it has been analyzed by the reader to determine its precise meaning and construction: one knows that there is something significant and impressive there before one can locate it in intellectual terms. This is not to say that the "meaning" is unimportant—the poem would not have these exciting qualities if there was not a clearly apprehended vision at the center of it—but it does mean that the total "meaning" is something very different from a mere analysis of the sequence of ideas and explanation of the references.

345. *Long-Legged Fly.* This strangely haunting poem, like so many of Yeats's later poems, communicates before its meaning is fully known. The first stanza shows Caesar planning one of his history-making campaigns: any disturbing noise now will alter the course of civilization. In the second stanza we see Helen of Troy as a child unselfconsciously practicing a part: again, the future of Troy depends on her being allowed to train herself as a woman without interruption. (The "topless towers" of line 11 are, of course, the towers of Troy, eventually to be burned for Helen's sake: the reference here is to the well-known lines in Marlowe's *Dr. Faustus*—

> Was this the face that launch'd a thousand ships,
> And burnt the topless towers of Ilium?)

In the third stanza we see Michael Angelo working silently at a masterpiece in Rome: he, too, must be undisturbed if his art is to be unspoiled so that it can communicate to future generations and give disturbing thoughts to "girls at puberty" in later ages. Great and critical works of man and woman, whether they are military campaigns, the development of a woman's charm, or a work of art, are achieved in a mood of trancelike silence, in which the doer, like one possessed, makes contact with something outside of himself. If you break in on these moments, you change the history of the world. The apparent casualness of these moments, and their inability to be detected by the onlooker, are suggested by the refrain, with its comparison of the mind of each of the three characters in their critical moment to "a long-legged fly upon the stream." The tense clarity of detail is perhaps the most remarkable thing about this poem, but notice also the rhythms—for example, the shift in accentuation in line 22.

346. *The Gallows.* "Edward Thomas cultivated a type of what might be called metaphysical observation which enabled him to infuse into a meticulous account of an event in nature a certain unexpected thought or vision which reflects a strange light around the whole poem. His imagery, when examined image by image, seems to derive simply from careful observation, yet on reading any of the poems we are aware of some unexpected meaning emerging from the imagery, though it is difficult to explain how or why. The poem 'The Gallows' is a typical example of this simplicity which results in the final emergence of a strange vision." (D. Daiches, *Poetry and the Modern World*)

347. *Tears.* This poem distils the essence of an experience with a simplicity and a directness which defy analysis. Notice the abrupt opening, and the way in which the two experiences described are linked and given meaning by the introductory statement.

348. *Daniel.* This is an imitation of communal poetry. The terms of communal poetry are these: that is composed—improvised—in the presence of an audience; that the subject matter of the poem is familiar to the audience; that the audience participates in the improvisation by joining in at points where repetition is indicated; that a strong basic rhythm invites the audience to chant or sing the words or even to dance to them. This particular poem is based on the subject matter, rhythms, and devices of Negro preaching.

349. *Mending Wall.* This is one of the best known of all Frost's poems, and well illustrates his dry conversational idiom and his sense of the elemental in human behavior.

350. *The Road Not Taken.* A simple but effective poem, saved from banality by its poise and control and the wry note, almost of self-mockery, in the background.

351. *The Grindstone.* Notice how the conversational idiom and movement are used to give a touch of irony and a kind of shrugging wisdom to the poem.

352. *Stopping by Woods on a Snowy Evening.* Another well-known poem of Frost's, illustrating another side of his talent. This is a perfectly constructed lyric, with an unusual rhyme scheme (*a a b a, b b c b, c c d c, e e e e*) which is neatly resolved by the repetition of the last line.

353. *The Strong Are Saying Nothing.* Notice how the poem works up to the "punch" of the last two lines and how the full impact of those two lines depends on the preceding imagery.

354. *Bavarian Gentians.* The lines grow longer and the rhythms looser as the images of darkness increase in number and intensity. Notice the climax.

Line 7. Pluto: god of the underworld. (The same as Dis, line 8.)
    9. Demeter: mother of Persephone; the Romans called her Ceres. Persephone or Proserpine was wife of Pluto and queen of the underworld (line 14).

355. *Piano.* Notice the use of the long line again. The poem begins with a hushed musical cadence and a very specific scene, and gradually, as the emotion rises, the images become more generalized, until the conclusion, where the terms are, in a sense, quite abstract ("remembrance," "past"). The relation in this poem between the specific, concrete image and the more general term is worth careful examination.

356. *Heaven.* A neat and ironic use of octosyllabic couplets.

357. *Anthem for Doomed Youth.* This is one of the poems Owen wrote as a result of his experience as a soldier in the First World War (in which he was killed in 1918). The controlled bitterness gives way as the sonnet proceeds to an elegiac note which rises to its slow and plangent climax in the last line.

358. *Futility.* Another of Owen's war poems. Notice how Owen uses the sun as a mediating image between man and nature, and how at the end this notion, first developed in order to give comfort, suggests its own bitter conclusion.

359. *Strange Meeting.* Notice the half-rhymes ("pararhymes"), such as "groined" with "groaned," "years" with "yours." Owen was continually experimenting with new kinds of sound effects. This particular device has had considerable influence on modern poets.

360. *The Eagle and the Mole.* The imagery of this poem is simple and needs no explication, but a careless reading frequently results in a misunderstanding of the total meaning.

361. *Let No Charitable Hope.* It is not impossible to extract nourishment from this wry and dry summation.

362. *Ancient Music.* This is a parody of a well-known medieval English lyric:

> Sumer is icumen in,
>   Lhude sing cuccu;
> Groweth sed and bloweth med
> And springth the wude nu.
>   Sing cuccu!
> Ewe bleteth after lomb,
>   Lhouth after calve cu;
> Bulluc sterteth, bucke verteth;
>   Murie sing cuccu.
>   Cuccu, cuccu,
> Wel singes thu, cuccu,
> New swik thu naver nu.
>
> Sing cuccu nu! Sing cuccu!
> Sing cuccu! Sing cuccu nu!

(lhude: loud. med: meadow. lhouth: loweth. sterteth: leapeth. verteth: harbors in the green. swik: cease.)

363. *The Seafarer.* This is a rendering of one of the finest existing Anglo-Saxon poems. The poem is a monologue by an old sailor whose thoughts move between the hardships of the seafaring life and its irresistible attractions. Pound is remarkably successful in capturing the movement and tone of the original: he keeps as far as he can to the Anglo-Saxon word order and to the kind of compound words so characteristic of Anglo-Saxon poetry. He omits the last ten lines of the poem, which introduce a conventionally religious note and may represent a later addition.

364. *Exile's Letter.* A version of a poem by the Chinese poet Li Po, whom Pound, evidently in ignorance, calls by the Japanese version of his name, Rihaku. The present editors are incompetent to judge its merits as a translation of the Chinese, and it is presented here as a poem in its own right. The meticulously precise imagery, the conversational rhythms coming to a dying fall at the end of each sustained verse paragraph, and the almost quizzical realism which precludes sentimentality in a situation where sentimentality might otherwise obtrude, are characteristic of what Pound was trying to bring into English and American poetry at this time.

365. *Gerontion.* The poem is made up of a series of symbolic images that flit through the mind of the speaker and add up to a picture of modern life as the poet sees it. What is the life of man without the organizing and vitalizing spirit, without religion, faith, a sense of value? Nothing but a dry and meaningless desert. A more traditional poet would have begun by posing the question more or less explicitly before proceeding to answer it. In Eliot the questions are always implicit, never explicit, and the poem is a symbolic answer. Dryness has always been for Eliot the basic symbol of life without faith and hope. The old man in a dry month waiting for rain is therefore a perfect symbol of modern life as Eliot saw it. The old man is "being read to by a boy"; he even gets his art at secondhand from children—perhaps it is not fantastic to see this, in one of its aspects at least, as a symbol of modern civilization getting its adolescent literature from Hollywood.

The old man broods over his empty life and thinks of heroic adventures in which such as he had no part. And, one by one, the dry and hopeless images take their place in the picture:

> The goat coughs at night in the field overhead;
> Rocks, moss, stonecrop, iron, merds.
> The woman keeps the kitchen, makes tea,
> Sneezes at evening, poking the peevish gutter.
> I an old man,
> A dull head among windy spaces.

There is, of course, no point in asking where the goat is that coughs at night, or its geographical relation to the other images; they all lie together in the speaker's mind, "thoughts of a dry brain in a dry season."

There are the two kinds of images in the poem—purely symbolic images, such as those of dryness, and images (like "the woman keeps the kitchen, makes tea") which are a literal part of the futile life which is the subject of the poem. Both kinds of images are symbolic, but symbolic in different ways. The second kind presents the part as a symbol of the whole, while the first is more abstract and occasionally more arbitrary, suggesting the general mood of futility by a variety of analogies. This simultaneous use of concrete and abstract imagery, of two different kinds of symbols, is an important part of Eliot's style in many of his better known poems. The concrete imagery provides us with implicit instructions in interpreting the abstract, while the abstract enlarges the meaning until it becomes more than a criticism of a particular way of life and develops into a tortured picture of man without belief.

Together with this simultaneous use of concrete and abstract imagery—or perhaps it would be better to say literal and nonliteral symbols, since such a nonliteral symbol as rain or dry rock can be concrete enough—Eliot uses a simple but effective kind of contrast. He will make a reference to some noble and heroic action in literature or history, in the light of which modern behavior seems more futile than ever. This kind of contrast is often made very swiftly and obliquely, and may result in obscurity for those who have not learned to follow Eliot's technique. Thus in "Gerontion," the movement from religious symbols to a picture of what F. R. Leavis has called "stale cosmopolitan depravity" serves to emphasize the fact that religion, which once dealt with the high emotions and mysteries of life, now serves only a shabby social function. Lines 17 to 25 represent a sort of symbolic history of Christianity, as Eliot sees it. It is followed immediately by a reaffirmation of futility:

> . . . Vacant shuttles
> Weave the wind. I have no ghosts,
> An old man in a draughty house
> Under a windy knob.

Disillusion, lack of faith, is a kind of cynical knowledge, a perverted wisdom; it is the opposite of innocence and the enemy of salvation:

> After such knowledge, what forgiveness?

There is no hope in the past; even what was good in history now brings forth evil (lines 34–47). After a suggestion of the Jacobean dramatists (both by verse movement and through a parody of some lines from Middleton's *Changeling*) made again for the purpose of contrast, the poem breaks into a scattering of dreamlike images, all of which suggest a common, inescapable fate and repeat the note of futility. And "Gerontion" closes with the lines already quoted:

> Thoughts of a dry brain in a dry season.

Another technical device much employed by Eliot, and to be found in this poem, is the use of an epigraph at the head of the poem. This is usually a quotation from some earlier work of literature, and its function is to help set the tone of the poem either by suggesting a contrast or by creating a mood. At the head of "Gerontion" Eliot has set three lines from Shakespeare's *Measure for Measure*. This is from the scene where the Duke, disguised as a friar, attempts to prepare the unfortunate Claudio to go to his death (though the Duke knows all the time that Claudio will in the end escape death). The meaning here is very complex. First, there is the surface meaning, referring to the state of Gerontion, not really alive but not yet dead. But when we remember the full context of the passage in *Measure for Measure,* this meaning becomes ironical. The passage is part of a mock consolation offered by a mock friar to a young man who thinks he has soon to face the executioner, while, in fact, as the mock friar very well knows, he will eventually be released unharmed. The speech, then, is a mockery of religious consolation. Again, if we extend the context of the passage to the play as a whole, we remember that this is one of Shakespeare's so-called "bitter comedies," a play whose dominant note seems to be disillusion and cynicism, in which there is not a single attractive character (not even the heroine). It is a bitter play of moral confusion in which even such few good deeds as are done are done for the wrong reasons. If we read "Gerontion"—as Eliot would have us read always— with all that is worth while in earlier literature alive in our minds, this epigraph would cast an effective light over the whole poem.

366. *Journey of the Magi.* The speaker in the poem is one of the Wise Men from the East who came to bring gifts to the infant Christ. He is looking back years afterwards on this strange experience, remembering everything about it except the journey's central significance, for he is lost in doubt and confusion. The atmosphere of the journey is developed with a skilful use of imagery. And notice the rhythms—jerky in the first section of the poem, then broadening out into a more supple movement as the travelers come down to the "temperate valley" and the mood and the imagery change. The image of the "three trees on the low sky" and the galloping white horse fix the scene with a tense precision; but the meaning of it all somehow evaporates—"it was (you may say) satisfactory." The note of confusion and weariness emerges in the final section as the dominant note of the poem.

It is interesting to put beside the opening of the poem the source from which it is derived—a sermon by the late sixteenth- and early seventeenth-century churchman and theologian, Lancelot Andrewes. This is the relevant passage (quoted by Eliot in his essay on Andrewes): "It was no summer progress. A cold coming they had of it at this time of the year, just the worst time of the year to take a journey, and specially a long journey in. The ways deep, the weather sharp, the days short, the sun farthest off, *in solstitio brumali,* 'the very dead of winter.'"

367. *Marina.* Marina is a character in Shakespeare's play, *Pericles, Prince of Tyre*, Pericles' daughter who is lost and found again, a symbol of reconciliation and redemption. The poem evokes the mood of one who has found grace, who awakes after a nightmare of doubt and danger to discover that the doubts have been resolved and the dangers avoided (the four kinds of danger that have been avoided are listed in the second stanza). There is the notion, too, of an earlier innocence recaptured ("What images return/ O my daughter") through the mediation of the symbolic Marina. The speaker in the poem is as one just recovered from illness or insanity; the epigraph, from Seneca's play *Hercules Furens*, is from Hercules' speech on recovering from madness. The symbolism of the poem is not obscure, nor is the significance of the water imagery and other images from nature. This is one of the freshest and most limpid of all Eliot's poems.

The epigraph means: "What place is this, what country, what region of the world?"

368. *Burnt Norton.* This poem was later grouped with three others, written subsequently, to form the "Four Quartets." But it was originally written as an independent poem, and was included as such in Eliot's *Collected Poems, 1909–1935.* Its subject is "an experience for which theology provides an explanation and on which religion builds a discipline, the immediate apprehension of a timeless reality, felt in time and remembered in time, the sudden revelation of 'the one end, which is always present.'" (Helen L. Gardner) The setting is an English country house, to which the title refers, and which supplies much of the imagery. As Miss Gardner has pointed out: *"Burnt Norton* is a land-locked poem: its whole feeling is enclosed. It builds up, by suggestion, the picture of a house and formal garden. Its imagery is social and civilized, weighted with human history and culture. A formal garden is an admirable symbol for man's attempt to impose a pattern on his experience and to discipline nature. The picture gradually given here is of shrubbery and alley-walk, rose-garden, low box-borders and pool, sunflowers in the borders, clematis hanging from the wall, and clipped yews. Within the house there are dried rose-leaves in a bowl, and there are references to a Chinese jar and to the music of the violin. All this is human and civilized, and the image used for reality is human too—the hidden laughter of children among the leaves of the garden."

The poem uses image and symbol to probe into the nature of a certain kind of experience, to illustrate the search for the tense moment of vision which fades almost as soon as it arrives. Man's experience is in time, with the past irrevocable, and the future unpredictable, and only the present available to provide the momentary apprehension of a reality which lies outside time. The poem explores the significance of this, its emotional pitch rising and falling, its tone hovering between flatness and intensity, in the course of its tentative search. There is a quietness about the whole, a calm flow of speculation and distillation of mood, which has its affinities with the mystical poetry of the seventeenth century; yet at the same time there is a deliberately modern, sophisticated atmosphere projected, as though to emphasize that this is modern man in search of his vision, not a generalized Man in search of Truth.

One might say that the bird which reappears several times in the poem is a symbol of what leads man to his vision, the vision itself being represented symbolically by the sound of "the hidden laughter of children in the foliage."

But this would be to take a crude view of Eliot's technique. There is no direct and specific use of symbols in the poem: the strokes are all oblique, tentative, exploratory. One might almost say that the poet is trying to find out what he means by saying it. One must learn to read this kind of poetry with an ear for these oblique meanings, these subdued overtones which arise from the nature of the image itself, and from the context of tone in which it occurs, rather than for any single idea that the image "stands for." The rose garden, the shrubbery, the drained pool (it is significant that the pool *is* drained, although the sunlight playing on the concrete makes it appear to be filled with water) are all there for what they are as well as for what they point to: they help to build up a quiet mood balanced between resignation and excitement, and we must perceive—*receive* in fact—this mood before we can begin to read the poem adequately.

It is a commonplace of genuine mystical thought that we must enter into a state of complete spiritual emptiness before we can hope to achieve that vision. We must proceed downwards towards blank nothingness—the "dark night of the soul" as St. John of the Cross called it—before we can rise up to the heights of spiritual exaltation. ("The road up and the road down are one and the same" is the translation of the quotation from Heraclitus which Eliot prefixed to this poem.) This notion is basic in "Burnt Norton," as in several other of Eliot's poems. There is always a sinking which precedes the rising, always a doubt as to whether the rising towards the momentary vision will ever take place, and always a sense of the blank moments, the "sad waste time stretching before and after."

The sense of penetrating to "the still point of the turning world"—or rather, of *endeavoring* to penetrate—is conveyed in a variety of ways throughout the poem, but nowhere more effectively than in the first ten lines of the fourth section, where the verse slows down to that one-word line, "chill," and nature images are fraught with a sense of incommunicable vision. Eliot's handling of varied line-lengths is well worth some attention.

Line 49.   Garlic and sapphires in the mud: garlic is the symbol of the poor man's food (bread and garlic), while sapphires, of course, represent something quite antithetical. The idea is that both alike pass away, and are dug up in later ages with historic remains. Eliot goes on in the following lines (51–52) to say that life passes on and covers up old scars. The life process is figured in larger, long-term units, such as "the drift of stars" (line 56).

61.   the boarhound and the boar: i.e., the old mythologies, representing the old orders. The theme of this whole passage (lines 49–63) is that time passes and eventually the differing patterns of human civilization which manifest themselves in history are reconciled in terms of a larger perspective. The relation between existence inside and outside time is one of the implicit themes of the poem.

77.   *Erhebung:* rising.

The translation of the first of the two Greek quotations at the head of the poem is: "But, while the word is common, the many live as though they have their own peculiar wisdom." The translation of the second quotation is given above, in the general note to the poem.

369. *To Brooklyn Bridge.* This is the opening poem of Crane's poem-sequence, *The Bridge.* Notice the shift from the fresh sea imagery of the first stanza to the urban office imagery of the second, with the sudden and effective projection of the reader into an office building in line 8. The poem, like the bridge, moves between these two extremes; it is an attempt to view the bridge as a redeeming symbol in modern civilization, linking its disparate elements and transcending them to create a significance that will fulfil man's need for order and value in a fragmented world.

370. *Praise for an Urn.* Allen Tate has commented on "the hard firm style" of this poem, "which is based upon a clear-cut perception of moral relations." The precise and forceful images through which the mood and meaning are communicated give the poem a fine poise and authority. The point made towards the conclusion of the poem is that remembrance of the dead man's physical reality makes the "well-meant idioms" of conventional "assessments of the soul" sound futile, to be abandoned to the suburban fatuity that bred them: "they are no trophies of the sun."

371. *"nonsun blob a"* E. E. Cummings uses language without employing those intermediate words which, though of no force themselves, round out the syntactical meaning. The result is immediacy rather than obscurity. The meaning of this poem, and the feel of the scene and the mood he is describing, come across with remarkable directness. Notice his use of prefixes ("non," "un") instead of more discursive ways of indicating a negative, and consider what is achieved by this device.

372. *"Our hunting fathers told the story."* This poem might almost be called an allegory on the present state of civilization, yet the statement is not really allegorical at all, but quite direct. Auden, in his earlier poetry (this poem comes at what could be considered the end of his early period), showed an interesting gift for laying his finger on a scene or an object or a situation which not only stood for but in a sense *was* the disease of civilization which was his favorite subject. The shift from the earlier view of the meaning of the lion's character and behavior to our modern awareness of the relation between love and guilt is the shift from a naïve to a corrupt society: and the comment is made explicit, contemporary, and detailed by the anticlimactic climax, with its provocative assortment of modern ills. Notice the use of Owen's pararhymes ("add" and "god"; "result" and "guilt").

373. *"O what is that sound which so thrills the ear."* This is a very effective use of an old ballad style, in which the traditional language of poetic premonition is combined with a modern conversational idiom that gives the poem a very special kind of force. There is no need to ask for a more explicit account of the situation than the poet gives, for what he gives about it is all that matters—all that matters to it as a situation deserving of poetic treatment. Notice the use of a short fourth line in each stanza. The dialogue form in which the poem is cast helps to provide the dramatic quality, and at the end a whole verse spoken by one speaker gives a sense of tragic climax.

374. *Voltaire at Ferney.* A presentation of Voltaire in old age, living in Switzerland and looking back on his earlier life and activities. Themes from Voltaire's life and work are woven into the poem with considerable dexterity; the quiet, reasonable tone—symbolic of Voltaire's own intellectual position—is maintained throughout. Without any explicit character drawing, the picture emerges of a humane and wise old man who had lived well and fully, watching over a Europe that was soon to burst into flames and doing what he could to avert disaster and make men behave rationally. Consider the effect of the final line.

375. *"Lay your sleeping head, my love."* A very modern version of the old "gather ye rosebuds" theme. Notice the rare combination of irony and gentleness, and the fine movement of the verse.

376. *Bagpipe Music.* A lively fling at modern civilization, written in Scotland and using appropriate imagery. Everything that was wrong with the country in the middle 1930's—unemployment, weary arguments about political panaceas, the tiredness and decadence of cultural as well as economic life, the halfhearted search for an escape from it all—is presented here through precise ironic images, each of which is both a part and a symbol of what is wrong.

Line 19. Ceilidh (pronounced kaley): A Scottish Gaelic word meaning a
   social evening spent in singing and storytelling.

377. *Sunday Morning.* Another comment on the state of British civilization in the 1930's, written with that dry yet evocative precision so characteristic of MacNeice.

378. *An Elementary School Classroom in a Slum.* This poem of Spender's might be contrasted with the preceding MacNeice poems. Spender deals with the same general subject as MacNeice—what is wrong with present civilization —and like MacNeice makes his point by seizing on particular aspects of the general situation rather than by declaiming about it: but Spender has none of MacNeice's dryness and deliberate refusal to be emotionally implicated in the problems he is presenting. Spender is essentially a lyrical poet, and irony is not his characteristic weapon. Here the poem broadens out as it proceeds, with the emotion rising and the horizon expanding, to end on a note of fine passion. Notice the deliberate use of exclamation in line 28 ("Break, O break open") to suggest the growing urgency of the emotion. The emotion, however, is in the poem rather than in the poet: that is, the poem is not an outburst provoked by emotion so much as a vehicle deliberately contrived in order to develop and present the emotion.

379. *"The force that through the green fuse drives the flower."* There is a fierceness about Thomas's use of nature imagery that is like nothing else in English poetry. The combination of echoes of myth and folklore with symbols drawn from modern psychology and anthropology provides him with a rich— sometimes an overrich—poetic vocabulary which he puts at the service of an intense personal vision. Notice the use of the recurring phrase, the effect of the short third line in each stanza, and the deliberate violence of the language. The theme of the poem is man's mysterious links with the forces of nature, forces which, while they produce growth and maturity, also inevitably produce eventual death.

380. *In Memory of Ann Jones.* This is an elegy on the death of a gnarled old working woman with "scrubbed and sour humble hands." Thomas draws on all the resources of his rich and violent imagery to give an impression of her death and burial, the quality of the experience of attending her funeral, and the significance of her life and death. He reaches out for the reality of the experience in fiercely suggestive images and compressed metaphors ("The spittled eyes, the salt ponds in the sleeves" gives the physical as well as the emotional quality of the mourning). Such a phrase as "Morning smack of the spade that wakes up sleep" well illustrates Thomas's ability to use descriptive language with a packed intensity: he often invents new compounds or uses nouns as adjectives or otherwise deliberately confounds the parts of speech in order to increase the immediacy of the impact. And "transferred epithets" (such as "tear-stuffed time") help to get into the very center of the situation being presented. Notice how, at the end of the poem, the dreary funeral experience and the memory of Ann Jones's kind of existence when alive are modulated into a new key, as though by sheer intensity of contemplation the poet can transmute the dead woman into a symbol of life and love. This is very different from the traditional close of a formal elegy, where the poet turns away from a contemplation of death to celebrate the hero's eternal life in another sphere (cf. "Lycidas" and "Adonais"), but the difference is one of technique rather than of central idea.

381. *The Marriage of a Virgin.* "The first section of the poem is a complimentary conceit based on the attribute of miraculous virginity. The conflicting images composing the conceit are drawn from pagan and Christian miracles of love. The physical desirability of the woman with whom the sun has consorted is spiritualized by the compliment. In the second section of the poem the mortal lover, who will take the place of the sun, receives his share of praise. Traditionally the epithalamium (marriage song) is a pagan song, and Thomas has emphasized this characteristic. The sun is a god. The dove, the Holy Ghost, is God, but has none of the sun's sensual attributes. The opposition is solved by an equation of miracle. [In lines 1–7] Thomas achieves a blending of sensual and metaphysical elegance reminiscent of Marvell . . . He has put the sensual reference, 'thighs,' in a central position, and has made it a central point of rhyme into which the dominant sound is struck from 'light,' 'nightlong,' 'iris,' 'sky,' 'lightning,' and 'hide.' In the pattern of spiritual reference, 'manna' has been converted into the New Testament symbol of the Sacrament which is prefigured." (John L. Sweeney)

The poem is built around the contrast between the girl before marriage, awakened by the sun as she lay in her virgin bed, and the girl after marriage who now finds a man—"that other sun"—beside her on waking. Thomas has developed new meanings out of this central situation by playing with Christian (the miracle of the loaves and the fishes) and pagan (the implicit comparison of the sun to a god) notions of the miraculous. The poem gives the impression that Thomas has made contact with deep-seated, elemental myths, and the marriage is thus put in an anthropological setting, as it were, to stand as a symbol of a ritual change in status in which the whole world of nature is involved. There is also a suggestion of the correspondence between the tides in the blood of the individual and the workings of cosmic forces—the two are both paralleled and contrasted, and it is this combined parallel and contrast that provides the conclusion of the poem:

she learns through his arm
That other sun, the jealous coursing of the unrivalled blood.

INDEX OF AUTHORS, TITLES, AND FIRST LINES

(Authors are in capitals, titles in italics)

Page

Page

Page

Page